MW00597548

GENESIS

Kabbalah Publishing is a registered DBA of
The Kabbalah Centre International, Inc.

For further information:

The Kabbalah Centre
155 E. 48th St., New York, NY 10017
1062 S. Robertson Blvd., Los Angeles, CA 90035

1.800.Kabbalah
www.kabbalah.com

First Edition
August 2008
ISBN10: 1-57189-606-6
ISBN13: 978-1-57189-606-3

Design: HL Design (Hyun Min Lee) www.hldesignco.com

THE KABBALISTIC BIBLE

GENESIS

TECHNOLOGY FOR THE SOUL™

www.kabbalah.com™

EDITED BY **YEHUDA BERG**

TABLE OF CONTENTS

INTRODUCTION

Whether you know it or not, you have just taken one of the most positive and momentous actions of your life: you have decided to open this book. There are a thousand reasons why you may have taken that action—or why you think you took it—but the real reason is much deeper, much more concealed, and infinitely more powerful. The action you've taken is an expression of your deepest desires as a human being. You may not realize that now, but when you reach the last page of the book you'll know it's true. In fact, even by the time you finish reading this Introduction, you'll see the huge opportunity that this book represents and you'll be ready to take part in it to the fullest extent.

The book you've just opened is part of a unique category. The word for this kind of book is *Chumash*, which is derived from the Hebrew word for "five." The Five Books of Moses are inscribed into the scroll of the Torah; the *Chumash* is a book version of the weekly Torah stories together with relevant commentary and interpretation. You may have seen other books of this kind, since there are many in the stores right now. Some *Chumashim* were composed hundreds of years ago, while others are very recent. With the recent upsurge of interest in spirituality, there are probably more books available in this category now than at any other time in history.

But is *Chumash* just another literary classification? Is it simply another genre that can continue indefinitely? Just as Hollywood turns out movies and music companies produce DVDs, can there be *Chumashim* forthcoming for many years to come?

The answer to this is most definitely no—because a *Chumash* is not just an object made of ink and paper. In fact, it's nothing less than a spiritual tool for transforming yourself and the world.

This is a critically important point. It takes us to the heart of kabbalistic wisdom about who we are, where we came from, and where we're going—not just physically, but in the spiritual dimension that is the seed level of our existence. Grasping this begins with a single, fundamental insight: Kabbalah teaches that the universe and our lives in it have a direction. We're not here just to fill up time and space. In short, there is an end point, and the purpose of our existence is to reach it.

What is that end point? There's a certain irony in the answer to that question, because understanding the end requires us to look at the beginning. The unity, the Oneness that existed between humanity and the Creator before the beginning of time is the goal that we're all striving to reach. Kabbalah calls that original state of Oneness the Endless World, because it existed outside all the finite boundaries that we take for granted in our everyday lives.

In the Endless World there was no pain, no suffering, no illness and, most importantly, there was immortality. Death and every other kind of chaos had no place in our lives in the Endless World—nor are they a necessary part of our lives today, despite the way things may seem. Chaos will remain with us only until we return to the Endless World through our spiritual work, through the tools and teachings of Kabbalah—and most immediately, through the power of the book you're reading right now. This is not just a metaphor. In very practical terms, the end of all suffering, the end of all pain, even the end of death itself is in your grasp.

The ultimate purpose of the *Chumash* is to bring about its own end; to terminate our very need for it!

The whole history of humanity—and, believe it or not, of your life as an individual human being—is the story of our painstaking return to the Oneness with God that was ours in the Endless World. But when will that return be complete? When will the exile be over? The truth is, on one occasion we came very, very close to achieving that objective. This occurred at the foot of Mount Sinai, when Moses received the Tablets inscribed by the Creator with the Ten Utterances—often mistakenly called the Ten Commandments. But the Utterances are much more than the list of "thou shalts" and "thou shalt nots" that we're so familiar with. In fact, even the term "Ten Utterances" is a coded message, and it refers to the ten dimensions that constitute total reality.

We live in the tenth and lowest dimension, the physical realm where darkness and despair constantly try to find their way into our lives. The hidden dimensions above us are an infinite pool of spiritual Light that can remove darkness from our own being and banish darkness from this world. They are the source of our joy, the root of our happiness and fountainhead of all wisdom. When we make contact with these hidden realms, we experience fulfillment. When we disconnect, we experience chaos.

The Tablets at Mount Sinai connected us to the full power of infinite Light swirling in these hidden realities. And they could have ignited a critical mass—a spiritual explosion in which everything would have been fundamentally rebuilt, reconfigured, reconstructed, and reconstituted. In short, they could have brought us to the Endless World—Heaven on Earth. But only Moses held the Tablets! Only Moses possessed the kabbalistic wisdom that gave access to all ten dimensions. The people as a whole excluded themselves by the sin of the golden calf, which caused Moses to shatter the Tablets. So the possibility for the ultimate transformation on Mount Sinai was lost when Moses shattered the Tablets.

But there was still hope!

What Moses achieved on Mount Sinai was fundamentally similar to what modern science has been seeking for at least a century, since the beginning of the revolution that began with Albert Einstein's theory of relativity. Throughout his life, Einstein fervently believed in the existence of an even greater theory, the so-called "theory of everything" that would unite all scientific knowledge in a single, all-inclusive explanation of the universe.

Here Einstein was simply expressing in physical terms the same quest for Oneness that Kabbalah understands to be fundamentally spiritual. Though Einstein never succeeded in his quest, he and others who came after him made great progress in that direction. Physics has shown that time, mass, and speed are all relative. If a mass attains a high enough speed, time stops.

More recently, medicine and genetics are showing that aging, illness, and death are not inherently "necessary" and can be eliminated at the most basic biological levels. Science is correct in these insights. But what science is trying to achieve physically through genetic engineering or the construction of particle accelerators, Moses achieved spiritually at Mount Sinai. The Tablets had the power to take us beyond time and space, because they connected us to the infinite realm of Light, a reality without time and space. But when the Israelites built the golden calf, and the Tablets were smashed, "the clock started ticking again."

Thus we lost the opportunity to replenish and restore the full power of the Light in one flashpoint, which Moses offered us on Mount Sinai. Now, with time back in the picture, the work of regaining the Endless World would become an ongoing endeavor within the borders of time. Enter the weekly *Chumash*—and this book in particular—whose purpose is to activate the kabbalistic technology utilized by Moses to connect the planet to the Light of the hidden dimensions.

Once this is understood, it's clear that the *Chumash* you now hold in your hands is no ordinary book. The infinite energy of the Mount Sinai Tablets is in these pages—the power to connect us to **all** ten dimensions, the power to replenish **all** the Light we had on Mount Sinai, the power to reveal **all** the infinite aspects of the Divine that manifest throughout the universe. This infinitely diverse yet fundamentally unified energy is what the kabbalists refer to as the Creator's Light.

Consider, for example, what scientists refer to as "white light"—the unfiltered radiance that exists all around us during all our waking hours. Actually, this white light contains red, yellow, blue, green, and all the others colors of the spectrum. When these colors are combined as one, the result is white light. The Light of the Creator works in a similar fashion. Each dimension of the Light is another "color," another aspect of the Creator's Energy. Together, the dimensions comprise the totality of the Creator's Light, which is pure, infinite, and all-encompassing.

Moses' Tablets were a complete connection to the Light, all instantly at once. Since the smashing of the Tablets, we must reestablish that connection within the realm of time. That's exactly what the weekly *Chumashim* have done. But there will be an end point, a completion, a final *Chumash* that ignites the critical mass which was just about to detonate at Mount Sinai. This is the true meaning of the End of Days—the revelation of kabbalistic wisdom **now**, so that we can finish the job once and for all.

In the best and most positive sense of the term, this is truly "the end of the world." Not a radioactive mushroom cloud or a rapidly spreading epidemic, but a quantum change in the soul of humanity. That's what the term "Messiah" really means. It's the Final Redemption, the supreme transformation of all humanity.

You can experience this transformation by connecting with the energy of this book. Though science tells us that the speed of light can never be attained, you can indeed reach the speed of Light—the Creator's Light—with the kabbalistic tools and teachings in these pages. Rest assured this book is not just another example of biblical scholarship. Like Einstein's $E=MC^2$ formula, the kabbalistic *Chumash* reveals a new and higher reality. What's more, the *Chumash* is also a tool for entering that reality. And now you are invited to step through that door.

BERESHEET

THE LESSON OF BERESHEET
(Genesis 1:1-6:8)

This is the first time in history that the insights of Kabbalah, traditionally hidden from all but a few, are opening up the secrets of Creation for all humanity. The fabric of reality itself is becoming radically altered, transforming the destiny of humanity, as the world takes a giant leap toward a future that is finally perfected. By opening our hearts to this truth and experiencing the yearning of our souls for their own completion, we become increasingly aware that the conclusion to the drama of human existence is in our hands. As we wash dishes, work out in the gym, travel to the office, or sit answering e-mails, it is worth bearing in mind that all this humdrum activity is simply part of a quest to complete Creation. If our lives seem impossibly menial, they are not. Indeed, they are as essential to the universe as the implosion of stars and the explosion of new galaxies.

"In the beginning, God created the heavens and the Earth..." (Genesis 1:1)

We begin to re-read the Torah (the Five Books of Moses) again right after the High Holy Days with this most resonant of all sentences opening the account of Creation at the beginning of the Bible. By imposing the cyclical lunar year on top of linear time in this fashion, the Bible reveals to us the ever-present opportunity that exists through the mercy of God for personal transformation. The prospect is every bit as awesome as the Creation itself, since it is truly the purpose of Creation. It is a reminder both of humanity's origins and of our goal. As the great cycle once more returns to its beginning, which is also the beginning of all things, we ask ourselves these vital questions: Why did God create the heavens and the Earth? Who am I? Why am I here?

The kabbalists say that the Creator is a hidden treasure and that the world was created for us to find God. If we have failed to find the Creator, it means only that we should look a little harder. As we review the past year to prepare for the future—measuring out our lives with their joys and sorrows, successes and failures—it becomes apparent that what we expect from a new year and a new beginning is far more than just more happiness and less sorrow. It is the transcendence of these two conditions, these two mighty opposites. It is to become free forever from the shuttling between happiness and misery that is for most of us the experience of our lives. Such experience has shown us that either happiness is the space between periods of sorrow or sorrow is the space between periods of happiness. They amount to the same thing. The kind of happiness that we seek instead is an unending happiness—happiness undisturbed by sorrow.

Whether we call these experiences of duality Heaven and Earth, good and evil, positive and negative, or happiness and sorrow, the fact still remains that God created these opposing states as the framework of a stage upon which the great drama of humanity would be played out. The end of this drama is the reconciliation of opposites. If things are to be different in the new year, however, it is not the things that need to change, but rather it is our awareness of them that we need to change. In other words, our own consciousness has to change.

If we are to truly comprehend the Bible's opening statement, we have to understand that before the Beginning, there was neither Heaven nor Earth. There were no mighty opposites, no duality. There was only the original Thought-Consciousness of the Creator, the Thought of Oneness. From a kabbalistic point of view, the Creator and the creation are a unity, so we cannot be as separated from the Creator as we imagine ourselves to be.

The Bible is a cosmic code, and Kabbalah—the ancient universal wisdom and technology—is the key to its understanding and our transformation. While we can barely appreciate the scope and sheer complexity of Creation, the core of Kabbalah, which is embodied in the Bible, is simplicity itself: the oneness of the Creator and the creation. Thus, to comprehend the Bible is to connect—or reconnect— with the Creator, for it is a connection that we once had but then lost. To connect with the Creator is to experience the unity that transcends opposites. Our hopes for a new year are therefore identical with the goal of life itself: to return the many to the One.

In this opening sentence of Genesis, the Bible offers us the key to overcoming the inevitable negativity of life. To be fully conscious of the Creator's Oneness is to be immune to sorrow, unmoved by defeat, and unvisited by chaos. Indeed, the sages of the *Zohar*, the chief text of Kabbalah, state on more than one occasion that if a person truly understood the meaning of this first sentence of Genesis, there would be no need to read any further.

Just as creativity is admired above all other qualities in a human being, the Creator's creativity is presented by the Bible as God's quintessential quality. The unthinkable vastness and incomparable grandeur of this Universe is ample testimony to the power of its Creator. The reading of Genesis (Beresheet) gives us an opportunity to connect to the current of our lives; to the power of Creation itself. Kabbalah teaches that the very shape and sound of the Aramaic letters in the original text—even the little crown that appears above some letters—have the ability to transform an individual, to elevate a soul, even to save a life. The words themselves contain an element of the Divine Creative Force. As with the universe itself, every component is crucial to the whole.

As the *Talmud* explains, the Creator looked at the Bible and then created the world according to what it said. Without the spiritual power of the Bible and its governing principles, the material world and its physical laws would not exist. All other laws, including those of physics, exist because of the primal Universal Law, the Bible. Gravity itself, which allows the Earth to revolve around our sun, is subject to this fundamental Universal Law. Indeed, both the Earth and the sun exist only because of it. The Torah, the Bible, is thus far more than merely a book: It is the nearest we can get to the essence of God.

To pay tremendous attention to the Bible, to open one's consciousness fully to its reality and power, is to be placed at the center of the Earth, the still point around which all else revolves.

For when we connect to the energy of Creation, we contact the Creator, the Source and the Destination of all things, the still point in a Universe of furious energy and movement. Once we perceive the direct connection of everything to this still point, we can more easily answer the 10,000 "whys."

Why is there a Creation? The answer becomes clearer when we understand that even our physical possessions—and the desire for them—are present in our lives only because of the Universal Law that is the Bible. In spite of the spiritual laws that prohibit us from taking other people's possessions, something in our nature causes us to desire things that belong to others. Why? Again, the answer becomes clear once we understand that the whole purpose of this desire—indeed, the very purpose of physical possessions—is to give us the opportunity to transcend the desire for them. For this same reason, the material world exists. All of Creation exists, therefore, in order to supplant the need for it to exist. When that need vanishes, the many return to the One, to utter stillness and unlimited peace. The seed of all this is in the Story of Creation. By connecting with the Bible's energy through this guided reading, we are fulfilling the purpose of Creation.

The sages tell us that before the world was created, each of the Aramaic letters came before God and said, "Why do You not create the world with me?"

The Creator patiently explained to each letter why this was not possible. Finally, the letter *Bet* appeared before God and said, "Master of the Universe, create the world with me. For with me, all the blessings in the Higher World and in the Lower World will come to You because I am the first letter of the Aramaic word brachah, or blessing." The Creator was persuaded by this argument and so agreed. This, we are told, is why the Bible—and thus the Creation of the world itself—begins with the letter *Bet*, for "blessing."

Rav Yehuda Ashlag, the founder of The Kabbalah Centre in 1922, wrote a commentary on the *Zohar* called The *Sulam* (The Ladder). In The *Sulam*, Rav Ashlag tells us that negativity can enter only where there is a vacuum, a space for it. Thus, since the blessing of the Creator is present everywhere, there is no opening for negative forces in either the Upper or the Lower Worlds. However, we can create an opening for negativity through the quality of our consciousness, our speech, and our actions. By disconnecting from the Light and connecting to the desires of our egos, we offer a foothold to the negativity that is ever ready to flood into our souls.

So we see that the choice is always ours. Humanity's free will is inviolable, but this greatest of all gifts is accompanied by a potential for great danger. The mind and heart are battlefields upon which our higher aspirations battle our lower ones. Whether found in the politics of nations or in the politics of the Spirit, freedom is far more difficult to endure than oppression and slavery.

By connecting with the energy of the Story of Genesis, the power of Creation itself, we are able to transcend the dualities that cause the misery of material existence, attaining what Rav Berg often refers to as the "Tree of Life Reality." In that Reality, we have a permanent connection to God. We have reached our goal, and no further spiritual work is needed. Existence there is unending bliss, partaking of the Creator's own nature. The connection is ever-present, constant, and continuous.

By cultivating an understanding of the process and power in the Genesis account of Creation, an account that also contains a connection to the Tree of Knowledge of Good and Evil, we take a very decisive step. The Bible is really telling us that a linear year spent striving toward the Light will result in a quantifiable change in the nature of that year, a difference that will appear obvious when the cyclical year comes around again. A reflection of this process is even contained within the theory of relativity, which Albert Einstein once explained to a person with no scientific knowledge as "the difference between the time the train takes to arrive at the station and the time the station takes to arrive at the train." Any movement we make toward the Light results in a movement by the Light toward us. Just as success is the reward of success, so, too, do spiritual yearnings swiftly expand into Divine connection.

We know what material success looks like, but who is able to recognize true happiness in another person? We cannot meaningfully compare one person's happiness with that of another. And our own happiness becomes elusive the moment it is questioned, giving us the hint that it is a state of being rather than any action that is under our control. In other words, happiness is being happy. So we should also re-evaluate the nature of what it means to connect with the Light. Engagement with or connection to the Light is far more about taking the steps toward inner change and transformation than it is about understanding the nature of Divinity.

Kabbalah provides the technology or spiritual science necessary to look beneath the surface of reality and glimpse the cosmic laws that are the true measure of all things. A person can sit down in front of a computer but lack some knowledge required to make the computer useful to him. If we suppose that there are many files on the machine but for some reason they are password-protected, the user must have the password to access the information in those files. Kabbalah can be thought of as the password that lets us access the supernal knowledge so critical to our own enlightenment and transformation. Like the training required to develop computer skills, advanced training is also required to be able to use the tools that Kabbalah has to offer. Part of this training consists of learning to read and understand the Bible in a much deeper and more intuitive way than we are used to doing.

Though all of us may read the Bible, not all of us understand it the same way. Just as there are many varieties of fruits from many different trees, each person understands the Story of Genesis—and therefore connects with it—in his or her own unique way. While extremes of comprehension exist, most of us dwell somewhere in the spiritual middle. We are not wicked, yet we are also far from perfect. We experience compassion and concern for the plight of others, but most of the time we are engrossed in ourselves. We truly do yearn for the Light, yet our yearning is constantly sidetracked by the physical world in which we live.

What is important, however, is not where we are or where we think we are, but that we each contain a spark of the Light of the Creator. That spark is our soul. We contain this spark because in the beginning, we were all one endless manifestation of the Light. Thus, we are not attempting to attain some impossibly lofty height, a place where no one has been before. We are attempting to regain a consciousness we know we have—but one which we somehow forgot.

For the fulfillment of Creation—the final transformation of humanity—to take place, we merely need return to the consciousness of unity, our essential Oneness through the Light and with the Light. In this, there is no hierarchy. No one is more or less important; all must attain the same awareness. Everyone is essential, just as every brick in a house is essential, even though some bricks might look bigger and stronger than others. We cannot have any consciousness of difference at all, for the slightest sense of being greater or lesser prevents the success of the entire enterprise. The democracy of spirit is absolute.

There is a story about Rav Berg that illustrates this point well. The Rav was offered the position of Chief Rabbi of a large temple in Holland. Although he agreed to the invitation, the Rav asked if he could give a talk while he was there, a talk that would be open to everyone in the community. A huge crowd turned out for the Rav's discourse. It seemed that more people attended the Rav's lecture than even attended services on the High Holy Days. The Rav talked about Kabbalah, including his characteristic sprinkling of leading-edge physics and mathematics. The people loved every word.

After the talk, the community leaders approached Rav Berg and enthusiastically told him, "We definitely want you as our rabbi, but not the rabbi of the people." They wanted him to minister only to the regular attendees and not to the general public, who might have had an interest in learning Kabbalah. When he heard this, the Rav declined the position. If he could not be a teacher for everyone, he explained, he would not be able to commit himself to the task because the world can only be transformed when we consider it in its entirety as one.

To the Creator, there is no higher or lower: God's blessing is available for all people. To connect with that blessing, however, we must work each year to transform ourselves more than we did in the previous one. Reb Nachman of Breslev wisely observed: "If a person is not better today than yesterday, why does he need tomorrow?" We need tomorrow for the very same reason that we are in the world to begin with: to reveal the Light through actively connecting with it. The spiritual essence of the Story of Beresheet entails our knowing where we came from—and thus who we are. Connecting with and comprehending this powerful story in the Bible imbues us with the strength to achieve our goal, requiring only that we change our nature. As the *Zohar* observes, the hardest thing to do is to change oneself, yet it is also the only thing that we are here to do—and, moreover, it is something that we will eventually have to do anyway. Why, then, are we putting off doing something that inevitably has to be done to allow us to escape the prison of our human condition? Each of us dreams of the key, yet when it is given to us, we forget that to open the door, we still have to turn the key in the lock.

SYNOPSIS OF BERESHEET

The Seed

To most people, the Book of Genesis is simply an account of an historical event. It is, admittedly, a momentous event—the most profound and important event in all of history. Yet it is still seen as nothing more than a story from the distant past, with scarcely any relevance to the present day. To the kabbalist, however, the biblical story of Creation invokes the power of a seed. Just as an apple seed contains the entire tree from initial root to final fruit, the seed of Creation contains the entire spiritual evolution of humankind. Thus, the Story of Beresheet holds within itself the final outcome of a perfected humanity living in eternal bliss, unified with the Light of the Creator.

Contained within the opening verses of the Story of Beresheet is the spiritual energy for an entire year. It is as if our soul is born anew. These seven traditional readings are like seedlings for the next twelve months, and in them the Bible grants us the power both to redesign and control our lives and to determine the quality of our lives, both individually and collectively. The Light therefore nourishes these seedlngs in a manner that is unique and unprecedented.

It is an awesome prospect. The Light that shines from Beresheet exterminates the root of all evil. A deathblow is dealt to the Angel of Death himself, clearing the way for our own immortality and endless fulfillment.

The Bible recounts the seven days of Creation. In truth, the process of Creation is a model for the process that we, the souls of humanity, must undergo to remove the barriers we have placed between ourselves and the Light. What all of us seek, in every aspect of our lives, is the ability to shrink this distance so that we may connect deeply with loved ones, friends, our own soul, and the Source of all fulfillment—the Light of the Creator.

The purpose of this reading is to bridge the gap and thus eradicate the distance between us and the Light. However, as in any endeavor, when we set our hearts upon a goal, there is always a process we must go through before we can realize our objective. It is this process (where we encounter obstacles, challenges, and turmoil) that creates an opening for negativity. We can immunize ourselves against this negativity by understanding thoroughly the Universal Law governing such processes of change.

FIRST READING - ABRAHAM - CHESED

1[1] In the beginning God created the heavens and the Earth.

2 The Earth was without form and empty, darkness was over the surface of the deep, and the Spirit of God hovered over the waters.

3 And God said, "Let there be light," and there was light.

4 And God saw the light that it was good, and God separated the light from the darkness.

5 God called the light "day," and the darkness God called "night." And there was evening, and there was morning—Day One.

6 And God said, "Let there be a firmament between the waters to divide water from water."

FROM THE RAV

As the *Zohar* explains, there were two Creations—two separate "versions" of Genesis. The deeper and more authentic one was the Creation of consciousness—a potential non-physical state known in Kabbalah as the 99 Percent Realm. The other Creation was the formation of the physical universe, which is known in Kabbalah as the 1 Percent Realm. The physical realm dominates the lives of most people, but it needs to be put in its proper perspective. Consciousness is the real you and me. Both science and Kabbalah agree that the physical dimension of our existence is far less significant than—and is even contingent upon—our existence as non-physical energy and awareness. The more we understand this, the better we will be able to place the material world in its proper perspective.

בְּרֵאשִׁית

Genesis 1:1 – This is the ultimate embryonic state that existed before the Sin of Adam, where everything was in an unsullied state of wholeness. This day is known as Day One, as opposed to the first day. The term "first" suggests more than one, whereas the word "one" implies oneness, wholeness, and perfect unity. Here we remove the "process" from our lives; time and space are eradicated. When we complete our Final Redemption, we will return to this state of unity and no longer require the processes that led us there. Day One corresponds to Sunday.

As we open our hearts to this text, our cells and our souls revert to a state of oneness as we dip in the pure and pristine supernal waters that cleanse us of all negativity.

The large Bet: As we have already learned, the reason the world was created with the letter *Bet*, as opposed to the letter *Alef* or any other letter, is that *Bet* begins the Aramaic word *brachah* (blessing). The inner significance of the word "blessing" includes the concept of free will and the ability to make choices. Blessing is our payback for actions of a sharing, proactive nature. When we resist our innate selfishness and ego-driven desires, and choose not to react to chaos, we attract blessings to our life.

Rav Yehuda Tzvi Brandwein stated in a letter written to Rav Berg, his pupil, that "...the only vessel for blessing is peace, and man becomes like a vessel in the hands of the Creator, as in God both sides and ends are unified." At the moment of Creation, all the blessings of the Light were concealed, hidden away inside Creation,

FIRST READING - ABRAHAM - CHESED

1 1 בראשית ברא קנ"א - ב"ן אלהים ילה, מום את השמים י"פ טל, י"פ כוזו ואת
הארץ אלהים דההין ע"ה; ר"ת אהוה: 2 והארץ אלהים דההין ע"ה היתה תהו ובהו וחשך
ש"ך ניצוצות של ז' מלכים על-פני חכמה - בינה תהום י"פ מ"ה ע"ה ורוח מלוי אלהים דיודין אלהים
ילה, מום מרחפת מת פרוז על-פני חכמה - בינה המים: 3 ויאמר אלהים ילה, מום יהי
אור רז, אין-סוף ויהי אל-אור רז, אין-סוף: 4 וירא אלהים ילה, מום את-האור רז, אין-סוף
כי-טוב והו, אום ויבדל אלהים ילה, מום בין האור רז, אין-סוף ובין החשך:
ש"ך ניצוצות של ז' מלכים: 5 ויקרא עם ה' אותיות = ב"פ קס"א אלהים ילה, מום | לאור רז, אין-סוף יום
נגד, זן, מזבח ולחשך: ש"ך ניצוצות של ז' מלכים קרא לילה מלה ויהי אל-ערב רבוע אלהים רבוע יהוה
ויהי אל-בקר יום נגד, זן, מזבח אחד אהבה, דאגה; ר"ת סוף הפסוקים צמרכד: [פ]
6 ויאמר אלהים ילה, מום יהי רקיע בתוך המים ויהי מבדיל בין מים

---

waiting for man to reveal them through his own actions. This is what the sages meant by saying that "God is a hidden treasure and the world was created in order that the Light might be found." Therefore, blessings take the form of all the joys and fulfillment we could ever wish for. Just as white light contains all the colors of the rainbow, blessings contain all varieties of delight.

The letter *Vav* begins each column of the Torah Scroll, except for six places where another Aramiac letter from a specific word is chosen to start the column. These other letters are *Bet, Yud, Hei, Shin, Mem,* and *Vav,* and they represent the six dimensions (or *Sefirot*) of the Tree of Life, which are known collectively in Kabbalah as *Zeir Anpin.* According to the *Zohar,* at the moment of Creation, six of the ten dimensions or points of the Tree of Life contracted inward to coalesce into one dimension known as *Zeir Anpin.* This left four dimensions, which comprise our three-dimensional world plus the fourth dimension of space–time.The *Zohar* explains:

The shape of the letter Vav of Yud, Hei, Vav, and Hei implies that the Upper World, which is Zeir Anpin, initiates an extension in order to shine upon the Lower World, which is Malchut. This extension is affected by means of six extremities, namely the Sefirot of Chesed, Gevurah, Tiferet, Netzach, Hod, and Yesod, which are completely interconnected. One Sefira is the image of the next, and each of the six extremities shines in a similar manner to the others. Thus, by means of the Creator's Emanations of Loving kindness (Chesed), Judgment (Gevurah), Beauty (Tiferet), Eternity (Netzach), Splendor (Hod), and Foundation (Yesod), Zeir Anpin is our channel to the Light above.

– The Zohar, Beresheet (Zohar Chadash) 120

וַיֹּאמֶר

Genesis 1:6 – Unlike Day One, which proceeds from a simple, elegant, and irreducible unity, the second day features the birth of separation. One

[7] So God made the firmament and divided the water under the firmament from the water above the firmament. And it was so.

[8] God called the firmament "heaven." And there was evening, and there was morning—Day Two.

[9] And God said, "Let the water under the heaven be gathered to one place, and let dry land appear." And it was so.

[10] God called the dry land "Earth," and the gathered waters God called "seas." And God saw that it was good.

[11] And God said, "Let the land put forth grass: seed-bearing plants and fruit-bearing trees, according to their various kinds." And it was so.

[12] The land produced grass; plants bore seed according to their kinds and trees bore fruit with seed in it according to their kinds. And God saw that it was good.

[13] And there was evening, and there was morning—Day Three.

---

becomes two, and thus the unity is broken. In its place came the mighty opposites of chaos and harmony that still rule our universe today, and the *Zohar* tells us that as a result of the unresolved duality, Hell was created on this second day.

> *In the work of Creation, there was a dispute between the left and the right. And in that dispute, which the left provoked, Gehenom (Hell) was created and Gehenom held on to the left.*
> – *The Zohar, Beresheet A 6:45*

This signifies the dangers arising from disunity and disharmony between people, and we must never underestimate this peril. It is worthy of note that this is the only day of Creation at the end of which God did not say that it was good.

To heal this wound of division, we must ignite a unifying force, a Divine Light that shines its beam down upon our world where the one has been split into the many, illuminating our path back to the Realm of One. From this Light, we receive inspiration and wisdom to be both independent and interdependent souls. We must acquire the ability to unify the parts into a whole, while at the same time retaining our individuality as we work together in unison to ensure there is no space for negative forces to enter.

The second day of Creation traditionally corresponds to Monday.

The sages consequently advise us to avoid beginning any new enterprise on this day of fragmentation because it provides an opening for negative forces to enter and infect our ventures.

וַיֹּאמֶר

Genesis 1:9 – The third day corresponds to the creation of what is known as *Central Column* energy. According to Kabbalah, there are three primal energy forces at the heart of all existence: the *Right*, *Left*, and *Central Columns*.

- The *Right Column* represents the positive (+) force of sharing, associated with the soul and the *Desire to Share*.
- The *Left Column* represents the negative (–) force of receiving, associated with the ego and the *Desire to Receive*.
- The *Central Column* corresponds to the gift of free will that allows us to resist the selfish desires born from the ego and to choose to live life according to the will of our soul. This results in the *Desire to Receive for the Sake of Sharing*.

לַמָּיִם׃ 7 וַיַּעַשׂ אֱלֹהִים ילה, מום אֶת־הָרָקִיעַ וַיַּבְדֵּל בֵּין הַמַּיִם אֲשֶׁר מִתַּחַת
לָרָקִיעַ וּבֵין הַמַּיִם אֲשֶׁר מֵעַל עלם לָרָקִיעַ וַיְהִי אל ־כֵן׃ 8 וַיִּקְרָא
עם ה' אותיות = ב"פ קס"א אֱלֹהִים ילה, מום לָרָקִיעַ שָׁמָיִם י"פ טל, י"פ כוזו וַיְהִי אל ־עֶרֶב
רבוע אלהים רבוע יהוה וַיְהִי אל ־בֹקֶר יוֹם נגד, זן, מזבח שֵׁנִי׃ [פ] 9 וַיֹּאמֶר אֱלֹהִים ילה, מום יִקָּווּ
הַמַּיִם מִתַּחַת הַשָּׁמַיִם י"פ טל, י"פ כוזו אֶל־מָקוֹם יהוה ברבוע אֶחָד אהבה, דאגה וְתֵרָאֶה
הַיַּבָּשָׁה וַיְהִי אל ־כֵן׃ 10 וַיִּקְרָא עם ה' אותיות = ב"פ קס"א אֱלֹהִים ילה, מום | לַיַּבָּשָׁה
אֶרֶץ אלהים דאלפין וּלְמִקְוֵה קנ"א, אלהים + אדני הַמַּיִם קָרָא יַמִּים נלך וַיַּרְא אֱלֹהִים
ילה, מום כִּי־טוֹב והו, אום׃ 11 וַיֹּאמֶר אֱלֹהִים ילה, מום תַּדְשֵׁא הָאָרֶץ אלהים דההין ע"ה
דֶּשֶׁא עֵשֶׂב ע"ב שמות מַזְרִיעַ זֶרַע עֵץ ע"ה קס"א פְּרִי ע"ה אלהים דאלפין עֹשֶׂה פְּרִי
ע"ה אלהים דאלפין לְמִינוֹ אֲשֶׁר זַרְעוֹ־בוֹ עַל־הָאָרֶץ אלהים דההין ע"ה וַיְהִי אל ־כֵן׃
12 וַתּוֹצֵא הָאָרֶץ אלהים דההין ע"ה דֶּשֶׁא עֵשֶׂב ע"ב שמות מַזְרִיעַ זֶרַע לְמִינֵהוּ וְעֵץ
ע"ה קס"א עֹשֶׂה־פְּרִי ע"ה אלהים דאלפין אֲשֶׁר זַרְעוֹ־בוֹ לְמִינֵהוּ וַיַּרְא אֱלֹהִים ילה, מום
כִּי־טוֹב והו, אום׃ 13 וַיְהִי אל ־עֶרֶב רבוע אלהים רבוע יהוה וַיְהִי אל ־בֹקֶר יוֹם נגד, זן, מזבח

We are not helpless entities torn by opposing forces; rather, we have the ability—our free will—to discern and thus to choose which force we would like to activate. To fall under the seductive influences of the *Left Column*, known as the Evil Inclination, requires not so much an act of will as the absence of effort, whereas to rise up to the sublime influence of the *Right Column* requires great effort. Climbing a mountain is hard, as the sages tell us, but falling down that mountain requires no work at all.

Just as darkness is not the opposite of light but the absence of light (the absence of a quality not being, strictly speaking, a quality in itself), so evil is not to be perceived as the opposite of good so much as the absence of good. Likewise, chaos is merely the absence of harmony. Reminding ourselves of this can provide us with the desire and strength required to make the effort to tear ourselves away from the grip of the Evil Inclination.

For every individual triumph over the impulses of the Evil Inclination, the collective consciousness of human kind is also elevated a notch and fortified permanently against the influences of the negative forces that dwell within the *Left Column*. Thus, we do not go into battle merely against our own negativity, but also on behalf of the whole of humanity; knowing this can strengthen our resolve to continue striving to reveal the Light, no matter what obstacles or challenges we may face.

It is said that a butterfly moving its wings in Japan can cause a tornado to form somewhere in America. Just as weather patterns are dependent on millions of tiny factors and causes, so, too, are all human actions interconnected, and for that reason, it is very difficult to find the root cause of anything that happens. The truth is that there are a thousand causes for every action and reaction, and not one of them in this great tangled ball of yarn can be disentangled from the others. It is the same case for humanity's interwoven histories and fates.

14 And God said, "Let there be lights in the firmament of the heaven to separate the day from the night, and let them serve as signs to indicate the seasons and the days and the years,

15 and let them be lights in the firmament of the heaven to give light to the Earth." And it was so.

16 God made two great lights—the greater light to rule the day and the lesser light to rule the night. God also made the stars.

17 God set them in the firmament of the heaven to give light upon the earth,

18 to rule over the day and over the night, and to divide the light from the darkness. And God saw that it was good.

19 And there was evening, and there was morning—Day Four.

20 And God said, "Let the water teem with swarms of living creatures, and let birds fly above the earth across the firmament of heaven."

On the third day of Creation, "God saw that it was good." (Genesis 1:12) Here we learn that the *Central Column*, which is our willingness to reject selfish behavior, propagates goodness both in our individual lives and in the lives of others all over the world. It thus follows that our responsibility for the quality of all life should motivate us, even when our responsibility for our own lives does not. When we make a genuine connection to this reading, goodness emanates throughout all existence.

וַיֹּאמֶר

Genesis 1:14 – The fourth day brings with it the seed of the origin of jealousy, which kabbalists identify as the root of all evil. We read in the *Zohar* that the moon and sun were once of equal importance and value in the heavens. But the moon was not satisfied with its stature, desiring to be greater than the sun, indeed to be considered sole monarch of the cosmos.

> *The moon was not at ease with the sun because it felt embarrassed before it. The moon said TO THE SUN, "Where do you feed your flock? Why do you make your flock to rest at noon?" (Song of Songs 1:7) THIS IS AS IF TO SAY: How can a tiny candle shine in the middle of the day? "Why should I be like one who cloaks himself?" (ibid.) That is: How can I remain in shame? Then it lowered itself to be head of the lower beings, as it is written: "Go your way forth by the footsteps of the flock" (ibid., 8). Thus, God said to it, "Go forth and subjugate yourself."*
>
> *– The Zohar, Beresheet A 10:113*

Consider how this scenario plays itself out every day of our lives. Incessantly, we look with a jealous eye at the physical and spiritual assets of friends and neighbors, even though we may often possess those very same treasures ourselves. It is our nature to blindly crave what others possess, yet we do it without ever thinking about the price they may have paid in life to acquire their possessions.

The thing to focus on here is the awakening of consciousness required before we can come to understand the most fundamental of all principles operating in life: Cause and Effect. This package deal means that everything comes with a price. Material possessions have the highest price combined with the longest payment plan—your

שְׁלִישִׁי: [פ] 14 וַיֹּאמֶר אֱלֹהִים ילה, מום יְהִי מְאֹרֹת בִּרְקִיעַ הַשָּׁמַיִם י״פ טל, י״פ כוזו
לְהַבְדִּיל בֵּין הַיּוֹם נגד, זן, מזבח וּבֵין הַלָּיְלָה מלה וְהָיוּ לְאֹתֹת וּלְמוֹעֲדִים וּלְיָמִים
נלך וְשָׁנִים: 15 וְהָיוּ לִמְאוֹרֹת בִּרְקִיעַ הַשָּׁמַיִם י״פ טל, י״פ כוזו לְהָאִיר עַל־הָאָרֶץ
אלהים דההין ע״ה וַיְהִי אל ־כֵן: 16 וַיַּעַשׂ אֱלֹהִים ילה, מום אֶת־שְׁנֵי הַמְּאֹרֹת הַגְּדֹלִים
להוו, מבה, יזל, אום אֶת־הַמָּאוֹר הַגָּדֹל להוו, מבה, יזל, אום לְמֶמְשֶׁלֶת הַיּוֹם נגד, זן, מזבח וְאֶת־
הַמָּאוֹר הַקָּטֹן לְמֶמְשֶׁלֶת הַלַּיְלָה מלה וְאֵת הַכּוֹכָבִים: 17 וַיִּתֵּן אֹתָם אֱלֹהִים
ילה, מום בִּרְקִיעַ הַשָּׁמָיִם י״פ טל, י״פ כוזו לְהָאִיר עַל־הָאָרֶץ אלהים דההין ע״ה: 18 וְלִמְשֹׁל
בַּיּוֹם נגד, זן, מזבח וּבַלַּיְלָה מלה וּלְהַבְדִּיל בֵּין הָאוֹר רז, אין-סוף וּבֵין הַחֹשֶׁךְ
ש״ך ניצוצות של ז׳ מלכים וַיַּרְא אֱלֹהִים ילה, מום כִּי־טוֹב והו, אום: 19 וַיְהִי אל ־עֶרֶב
רבוע אלהים רבוע יהוה וַיְהִי אל ־בֹקֶר יוֹם נגד, זן, מזבח רְבִיעִי: [פ] 20 וַיֹּאמֶר אֱלֹהִים ילה, מום

---

life. This price includes physical pain and emotional suffering. Moreover, as anyone who has acquired many material possessions will readily admit, such possessions yield the least amount of pleasure.

Spiritual treasures, on the other hand, are a bargain. Their price is merely the ego that we do not want or need anyway, and the pleasure they bring endures for eternity.

The Light emanating from this fourth day is designed to eradicate envy from our inner nature. We can uproot and exterminate the cosmic seed of jealousy, ending its tyrannical rule over human hearts. When we understand this, a deeper appreciation for our own lot in life will blossom forth, bringing in its wake the inner peace and contentment that we truly crave to fill the space within our souls.

As Rav Brandwein wrote in one of his extraordinary letters to Rav Berg: "...if they walk the straight path, they draw every good therein; but if, Heaven forbid, they do not walk the good path, they bring about the opposite. This law is inviolable."

In the *Zohar*, *Beresheet A 458*, we find that Cain killed Abel, not only because God had rejected his offering but also because he was jealous of his brother's second wife. This pivotal early event in the history of mankind, as told in the Bible, is a good example of how evil began to work its way into the world as a result of jealousy.

The kabbalists have duly advised us to try to avoid beginning new ventures on the second day (Monday)—the first real separation from the Light—and they advise the same thing for this fourth day (Wednesday) because this was the day when evil was born.

וַיֹּאמֶר

Genesis 1:20 – According to the *Zohar*, the fifth day, when God brought forth all the creatures, joins us to the true Light of the Bible. This wave of Light can thus be viewed as our umbilical cord, which links us to the Creator throughout the coming year.

To connect with this Light on a deep level enriches and strengthens our continuous association with the infinite emanation of Divine energy, bringing fortitude and clarity to our otherwise unremittingly arduous toil in this darkened material dimension. We are able to draw sustenance for our lives from the Bible, as though it were food and drink.

21 And God created the great creatures of the sea, and every creeping creature and
moving living thing with which the water teems, according to their kinds; and every
winged bird according to its kind. And God saw that it was good.

22 And God blessed them and said, "Be fruitful and multiply and fill the water in the
seas, and let the birds multiply on the earth."

23 And there was evening, and there was morning—Day Five. 24 And God said, "Let
the land produce living creatures according to their kinds: cattle, and creatures that
creep along the ground, and wild animals, each according to its kind." And it was
so.

25 God made the wild animals according to their kinds, the cattle according to their
kinds, and all the creatures that creep along the ground according to their kinds. And
God saw that it was good.

26 Then God said, "Let us make man in Our image, after Our likeness, and let them
rule over the fish of the sea and the birds of the air, over the cattle, over all the earth,
and over all the creatures that creep along the ground."

27 So God created man in His own image, in the image of God He created him; male
and female He created them.

28 God blessed them and said to them, "Be fruitful and multiply; and replenish the
earth and subdue it, and have dominion over the fish of the sea and the birds of the
air and over every living creature that creeps on the ground."

29 And God said, "Behold, I have given you every seed-bearing plant on the face of
the whole earth and every tree that has fruit with seed in it. They will be yours for food;
30 and to all the beasts of the earth and all the birds of the air and all the creatures
that creep on the ground—wherein is a living soul—I give every green plant for food."
And it was so.

Rav Isaac Luria (the Ari) wrote:

> *"Our God delights in the Bible that is compared to water as in, 'every one that thirsts, come to the water' (Isaiah 55:1)."*
>
> – *Writings of the Ari, Torah Compilations 4*

וַיֹּאמֶר

Genesis 1:24 – Man was created on the sixth day. The Light that radiates from this action empowers us with the Divine gift of free will. As we acquire the wisdom and strength required to make correct choices in life, the key choice is always ours. We can choose to take the path of materialism, which is ultimately one of pain and suffering, or we can choose to grow spiritually through the subjugation of our ego-driven desires. Though this latter path will take much longer, it will inevitably lead to the cleansing of our egocentric behavior. When we make the choice of spirituality over materialism, when we choose a spiritual action and the elevation of the soul, we help elevate all of Creation as well. We should note the actions of Moses when he pleaded for his people; in doing this, he was engaged in a righteous action that helped to

יִשְׁרְצוּ הַמַּיִם שֶׁרֶץ נֶפֶשׁ רמ״ח ‑ ד׳ הויות חַיָּה וְעוֹף ציון, יוסף, ו״פ יהוה, ה״פ אל יְעוֹפֵף עַל־
הָאָרֶץ אלהים דההין ע״ה עַל־פְּנֵי וחכמה ‑ בינה רְקִיעַ הַשָּׁמָיִם י״פ טל, י״פ כוזו: 21 וַיִּבְרָא
אֱלֹהִים ילה, מום אֶת־הַתַּנִּינִם הַגְּדֹלִים להח, מבה, יזל, אום וְאֵת כָּל ילי ־נֶפֶשׁ רמ״ח ‑ ד׳ הויות
הַחַיָּה | הָרֹמֶשֶׂת אֲשֶׁר שָׁרְצוּ הַמַּיִם לְמִינֵהֶם וְאֵת כָּל ילי ־עוֹף
ציון, יוסף, ו״פ יהוה, ה״פ אל כָּנָף ע״ה קנ״א, אלהים ‑ אדני לְמִינֵהוּ וַיַּרְא אֱלֹהִים ילה, מום כִּי־טוֹב
והו, אום: 22 וַיְבָרֶךְ עסמ״ב אֹתָם אֱלֹהִים ילה, מום לֵאמֹר פְּרוּ וּרְבוּ וּמִלְאוּ אֶת־
הַמַּיִם בַּיַּמִּים נלך וְהָעוֹף ציון, יוסף, ו״פ יהוה, ה״פ אל יִרֶב בָּאָרֶץ אלהים דאלפין: 23 וַיְהִי־ אל
עֶרֶב רבוע אלהים רבוע יהוה וַיְהִי אל ־בֹקֶר יוֹם נגד, זן, מזבח חֲמִישִׁי: [פ] 24 וַיֹּאמֶר
אֱלֹהִים ילה, מום תּוֹצֵא הָאָרֶץ אלהים דההין ע״ה נֶפֶשׁ רמ״ח ‑ ד׳ הויות חַיָּה לְמִינָהּ בְּהֵמָה
ב״ן, לכב וָרֶמֶשׂ וְחַיְתוֹ־אֶרֶץ אלהים דאלפין לְמִינָהּ וַיְהִי אל ־כֵן: 25 וַיַּעַשׂ אֱלֹהִים
ילה, מום אֶת־חַיַּת הָאָרֶץ אלהים דההין ע״ה לְמִינָהּ וְאֶת־הַבְּהֵמָה ב״ן, לכב לְמִינָהּ וְאֵת
כָּל ילי ־רֶמֶשׂ הָאֲדָמָה לְמִינֵהוּ וַיַּרְא אֱלֹהִים ילה, מום כִּי־טוֹב והו: 26 וַיֹּאמֶר
אֱלֹהִים ילה, מום נַעֲשֶׂה אָדָם מ״ה בְּצַלְמֵנוּ כִּדְמוּתֵנוּ וְיִרְדּוּ ר״י בִדְגַת הַיָּם ילי
וּבְעוֹף ציון, יוסף, ו״פ יהוה, ה״פ אל הַשָּׁמַיִם י״פ טל, י״פ כוזו וּבַבְּהֵמָה ב״ן, לכב וּבְכָל לכב ־הָאָרֶץ
אלהים דההין ע״ה וּבְכָל לכב ־הָרֶמֶשׂ הָרֹמֵשׂ עַל־הָאָרֶץ אלהים דההין ע״ה: 27 וַיִּבְרָא
אֱלֹהִים ילה, מום | אֶת־הָאָדָם מ״ה בְּצַלְמוֹ בְּצֶלֶם ע״ה קס״א אֱלֹהִים ילה, מום בָּרָא
קנ״א ‑ ב״ן אֹתוֹ זָכָר וּנְקֵבָה בָּרָא קנ״א ‑ ב״ן אֹתָם: 28 וַיְבָרֶךְ עסמ״ב אֹתָם אֱלֹהִים
ילה, מום וַיֹּאמֶר לָהֶם אֱלֹהִים ילה, מום פְּרוּ וּרְבוּ וּמִלְאוּ אֶת־הָאָרֶץ אלהים דההין ע״ה
וְכִבְשֻׁהָ וּרְדוּ י״פ אהיה בִּדְגַת הַיָּם ילי וּבְעוֹף ציון, יוסף, ו״פ יהוה, ה״פ אל הַשָּׁמַיִם י״פ טל, י״פ כוזו
וּבְכָל לכב ־חַיָּה הָרֹמֶשֶׂת עַל־הָאָרֶץ אלהים דההין ע״ה: 29 וַיֹּאמֶר אֱלֹהִים ילה, מום
הִנֵּה מ״ה יה נָתַתִּי לָכֶם אֶת־כָּל ילי ־עֵשֶׂב ע״ב שמות | זֹרֵעַ זֶרַע אֲשֶׁר עַל־פְּנֵי
וחכמה ‑ בינה כָל ילי ־הָאָרֶץ אלהים דההין ע״ה וְאֶת־כָּל ילי ־הָעֵץ ע״ה קס״א אֲשֶׁר־בּוֹ פְרִי
ע״ה אלהים דאלפין ־עֵץ ע״ה קס״א זֹרֵעַ זָרַע לָכֶם יִהְיֶה ייי לְאָכְלָה: 30 וּלְכָל יה ‑ אדני ־חַיַּת
הָאָרֶץ אלהים דההין ע״ה וּלְכָל יה ‑ אדני ־עוֹף ציון, יוסף, ו״פ יהוה, ה״פ אל הַשָּׁמַיִם י״פ טל, י״פ כוזו

31 And God saw all that He had made, and it was very good. And there was evening, and there was morning—Day Six.

2 1 And the heavens and the Earth, in their vast array, were completed.

2 And on the seventh day God had finished the work which He had made; and God rested on the seventh day from all His work, which He had made.

3 And God blessed the seventh day and made it holy, because on it He rested from all the work of creating that which He had made.

SECOND READING - ISAAC - GEVURAH

4 These are the generations of the heavens and the Earth when they were created,
when the Lord God made the Earth and the heavens, 5 no shrub of the field had yet

---

protect and elevate many others in addition to himself. In the Ari's writings, Rav Chaim Vital states:

> *My teacher also told me that I have to cause the wicked to gain more merit, even more than other people, since all the wicked in this generation are like the mixed multitudes, who are mostly from the root of Cain, in which there are good sparks mixed with a larger portion of evil. Therefore, I have to restore them because they are of my own root. Not only that, but by my actions I can restore even the wicked from the generations of the ancient, who lived in primordial times, and who are now in Gehenom (Hell); I can raise them from Gehenom and put them in bodies so they will come into this world and be corrected.*
>
> – *Writings of the Ari: The Gate of Reincarnation 38*

Genesis 2:1 – To the kabbalist, the concept of a day of rest on Shabbat is a code. The word "rest" alludes to a realm beyond time, space, or motion, a dimension of infinite stillness, irreducible wholeness, and perfect unity. This sacred realm is the very embodiment of spiritual Light. On Shabbat, therefore, our souls are meant to ascend into this sublime reality so that that we may cleanse and purify ourselves, eradicating the burden of negative energies that we have accumulated in this life and during past lives. Consequently, to the kabbalist, Shabbat, far from being a "day of rest," is, in fact, the one day out of the week requiring from us the hardest work of all. This is because no labor is more exacting or demanding than the process of identifying and uprooting the egocentric elements in our nature. Yet in spite of this hard work, Shabbat is a day of joy.

As we read about Shabbat on the Sabbath Day, and contemplate and connect to the words of Genesis, we are more easily able to arouse repentance in ourselves for wrong actions and to confess in our hearts the petty jealousies and numerous flaws of character that have hindered us on our quest for the Light. Few actions are more difficult than the true confession of error, yet it is this very difficulty that provides the force for using the admission of our past iniquities to purify our souls. This act of repentance summons to our aid the Light of all Shabbat days since the beginning

וּלְכָל יה - אדני | רוֹמֵשׂ עַל־הָאָרֶץ אלהים דההין ע״ה אֲשֶׁר־בּוֹ נֶפֶשׁ רמ״ח - ז הויות חַיָּה
אֶת־כָּל ילי ־יֶרֶק עֵשֶׂב ע״ב שמות לְאָכְלָה וַיְהִי אל ־כֵן׃ 31 וַיַּרְא אֱלֹהִים ילה, מום
אֶת־כָּל ילי ־אֲשֶׁר עָשָׂה וְהִנֵּה מ״ה יה ־טוֹב והו מְאֹד מ״ה וַיְהִי אל ־עֶרֶב
רבוע אלהים רבוע יהוה וַיְהִי אל ־בֹקֶר יוֹם נגד, זן, מזבח הַשִּׁשִּׁי׃ [פ] 2 1 וַיְכֻלּוּ ע״ב, ריבוע יהוה
הַשָּׁמַיִם י״פ טל, י״פ כוזו וְהָאָרֶץ אלהים דההין ע״ה, ר״ת והו וְכָל ילי ־צְבָאָם׃ 2 וַיְכַל אֱלֹהִים
ילה, מום בַּיּוֹם נגד, זן, מזבח הַשְּׁבִיעִי מְלַאכְתּוֹ אֲשֶׁר עָשָׂה וַיִּשְׁבֹּת בַּיּוֹם נגד, זן, מזבח
הַשְּׁבִיעִי מִכָּל ילי ־מְלַאכְתּוֹ אֲשֶׁר עָשָׂה׃ 3 וַיְבָרֶךְ עסמ״ב אֱלֹהִים ילה, מום אֶת־
יוֹם נגד, זן, מזבח הַשְּׁבִיעִי וַיְקַדֵּשׁ אֹתוֹ כִּי בוֹ שָׁבַת מִכָּל ילי ־מְלַאכְתּוֹ אֲשֶׁר־
בָּרָא קנ״א - ב״ן אֱלֹהִים ילה, מום לַעֲשׂוֹת׃ [פ]

SECOND READING - ISAAC - GEVURAH

4 אֵלֶּה תוֹלְדוֹת הַשָּׁמַיִם י״פ טל, י״פ כוזו וְהָאָרֶץ אלהים דההין ע״ה
בְּהִבָּרְאָם בְּיוֹם נגד, זן, מזבח עֲשׂוֹת יְהֹוָהאדניאהדונהי אֱלֹהִים ילה, מום, יב״ק

of time. In *The Gate of Reincarnation*, we find the Ari himself expounding on this very theme as he explains the maxim that: "any man can be like Moses if he wishes his deeds to be purer..." All that stands between us and the summit of total connection with the Light and complete fulfillment is our consciousness, the nature of which—elevated or debased—is a direct consequence of our actions in this and past lives. No matter what our past actions may have been, however, they can be atoned for and transcended, elevating us to the ultimate condition of absolute unity with the Light in the life we are now blessed to have.

אֵלֶּה

Genesis 2:4 – Genesis contains the only verses in the Bible where goodness and Light are mentioned alone—verses that tellingly precede both the Sin of Adam and the Sin of the Golden Calf. By profoundly comprehending and connecting with these verses, it is possible to atone for all the sins and iniquities committed in this and past lives, not just for ourselves but for the whole human race, thus hastening the arrival of the time of perfection in a manner that exemplifies the tender mercy that is our Creator's nature.

בְּהִבָּרְאָם

In Genesis 2:4, we find the verse: "When they were created." In Aramaic, this verse is written "BeHibaram." Here we find a small version of the Aramaic letter *Hei*. This phrase contains the same letters that spell out "BeAvraham," which means "for the sake of Abraham." To the kabbalist, this means that the world was created for the sake of Abraham. This small letter *Hei* will eventually appear in the name of Abraham (*Lech Lecha 17:5*) when the name is changed from Abram to Abraham. Here this small letter *Hei* represents the Divine spark with which Abraham's nature was imbued, telling us that our goal in life is to shrink our ego and transform ourselves from selfish, reactive individuals into people who *appeared on the Earth and no plant of the field had yet sprung up, for the Lord God had caused it to rain upon the earth and there was no man to till the ground; [6] but a mist came up from the earth and watered the whole surface of the ground.*

[7] Then the Lord God formed man from the dust of the ground and breathed into his nostrils the breath of life; and the man became a living soul.

[8] Now the Lord God had planted a garden in the east, in Eden; and there He put the man whom He had formed.

[9] And the Lord God made all kinds of trees grow out of the ground—trees that were pleasing to the eye and good for food; and the Tree of Life in the middle of the garden, and the Tree of Knowledge of Good and Evil.

Desire to Receive for the Sake of Sharing. Through this transformation, we come to personify the nature of the Patriarch Abraham, which was one of unconditional sharing. Abraham is, in effect, our seed, and just as the final fruit is contained within the seed our final perfected state of sharing is contained within Abraham. Accordingly, the small *Hei* in this verse is now implanted in our soul, igniting a spark of divinity within us. We are thus empowered with the courage to seek spiritual transformation, to share, and to resist self-serving desires—in short, to become like Abraham.

אֶרֶץ

Genesis 2:4 – There are two aspects to Creation: the metaphysical blueprint and the physical manifestation where humans make their appearance upon the stage of the material world. Genesis 2:4 unfurls the second aspect.

The Garden of Eden is created and comes into existence, and what it represents is similar to the concept of parallel universes. On one hand, there is the realm of the Tree of Life; on the other, the domain of the Tree of Knowledge of Good and Evil.

The Tree of Life corresponds to the 99 Percent Reality, which we are not able to perceive with our five senses. It is a realm of perfect order, bliss, harmony, and enlightenment. All the joy and wisdom of the world flow out from this reality to ours.

The Tree of Knowledge of Good and Evil corresponds to our 1 Percent Illusionary World, which represents only a minute fraction of true reality. It is our physical dimension, characterized by darkness, disorder, and unpredictable chaos that is a pattern designed by God for our own experiences to unfold.

Both of these worlds exist side by side. When a scientist makes a startling discovery or an artist conceives something of transcendent beauty, they have been in contact with the 99 Percent Reality. Similarly, when a parent experiences the sublime joy of a child's hug, this joy originates in and flows out from the 99 Percent Realm. Indeed, all our truly pleasurable or serene moments in life are indications of our connection to the Tree of Life. Whenever our consciousness is positive and strong, whenever we feel the potent truth and Light of the Creator in our hearts, we are connected to the realm of the Tree of Life. As ineffable as such experiences invariably are we can never doubt their reality afterwards.

Conversely, when we are in doubt or are overcome with sadness, depression, or selfish concerns, we sever our connection to the Tree of Life and end up floundering in the dimension of the Tree of Knowledge of Good and Evil. Unfortunately, this is where people dwell for most of their lives. One need only look around at the faces on any street or watch the evening news to know that this is the sad truth. It is also true, however, that the evening news reports consist almost entirely of horrible crimes and natural disasters, although these account for only a small

ארץ אלהים דאלפין ושמים י"פ טל, י"פ כוזו: 5 וכל ילי | שיח השדה שדי
טרם רפ"ח ע"ה יהיה ייי בארץ אלהים דאלפין וכל ילי -עשב ע"ב שמות השדה
שדי טרם רפ"ח ע"ה יצמח כי לא המטיר יהוה יאהדונהי אלהים ילה, מום, יב"ק
על-הארץ אלהים דההין ע"ה ואדם מ"ה אין לעבד את-האדמה: 6 ואד
יעלה מן-הארץ אלהים דההין ע"ה והשקה את-כל ילי -פני חכמה - בינה האדמה:
7 וייצר יהוה יאהדונהי אלהים ילה, מום, יב"ק את-האדם מ"ה עפר מן-
האדמה ויפח באפיו נשמת חיים בינה ע"ה ויהי אל האדם מ"ה לנפש
רמ"ח - ז' הויות חיה: 8 ויטע יהוה יאהדונהי אלהים ילה, מום, יב"ק גן-בעדן
מקדם רבוע כן וישם שם את-האדם מ"ה אשר יצר: 9 ויצמח
יהוה יאהדונהי אלהים ילה, מום, יב"ק מן-האדמה כל ילי -עץ ע"ה קס"א נחמד
למראה וטוב והו למאכל יהוה אדני ועץ ע"ה קס"א החיים בינה ע"ה בתוך הגן
ועץ ע"ה קס"א הדעת טוב והו ורע: 10 ונהר יצא מעדן להשקות את-

---

proportion of daily life on this planet. To remain positively connected to the Tree of Life means finding a way to maintain perspective on what we see and hear, and to retain our own inner harmony as a means to further spiritual progress.

To seek solutions to the countless problems of our lives in the Tree of Knowledge of Good and Evil Realm is an utterly fruitless activity, much like a panicked man who has stumbled into quicksand and begins to sink. The more he tries to scramble out, pushing at the sand with his feet, the deeper he sinks. His only possible means of escape is to reach out and grab onto something like the branch of a nearby tree. Similarly, to free ourselves from the grip of the Good and Evil Reality—our realm of duality—we must find a way to cling to the Tree of Life Reality, where we can access the supernal energy to effect positive and permanent change in our physical world.

According to Kabbalah, this is the only way to transcend the illusion of the 1 Percent Reality—the Tree of Knowledge of Good and Evil.

In this section of Genesis, a branch of Light extending from the Tree of Life shines down upon us. If we take hold of it, if we make the profound connection, we are lifted up out of this world of pain and chaos, to be placed gently in a world of Light and perfection. More importantly, as we meditate on sharing this Light with our fellow human beings, we bring about, through the mercy of the Creator, our personal Final Redemption. According to the sages, the most effective means of producing this profound revelation and connection to the Tree of Life for which we yearn is to create a desire within us—a craving, if you will—to transform ourselves. Then we must use kabbalistic tools like scanning the *Zohar* and meditating on the Ana Beko'ach and the 72 Names of God to further the process of inner transformation.

10 And a river flowed out from Eden to water the garden; from there it was parted and became four heads.

11 The name of the first is Pishon, which winds through the entire land of Havilah, where there is gold.

12 And the gold of that land is good; there is bedillium and stones of onyx.

13 The name of the second river is Gihon, which winds through the entire land of Cush.

14 The name of the third river is Tigris, which runs along the east side of Ashur. And the fourth river is the Euphrates.

15 The Lord God took the man and put him in the Garden of Eden to dress it and to keep it.

16 And the Lord God commanded the man, saying: "Of every tree of the garden
you may freely eat; 17 but of the Tree of Knowledge of Good and Evil you must not
eat, for when you eat of it you will surely die."

18 The Lord God said, "It is not good for the man to be alone. I will make him a help meet."

19 And out of the ground the Lord God formed all the beasts of the field and all the birds of the air; and brought them to the man to see what he would name them; and whatever the man called each living creature, that would be its name.

וְכֹל

Genesis 2:19 – The Bible tells us that Adam bestowed names upon all the creatures. A name is composed of letters selected from an alphabet. To the kabbalist, this means primarily that the Genesis blueprint refers in concept to DNA, the complex chain of amino acids with its double helix that is based on a genetic alphabet and amounts to the very code for life.

DNA can be described as an instruction manual for our cells. All cells begin their existence in an undifferentiated state, aware only of the need to grow. Our DNA then determines which cells will evolve to become internal organs, or bone, or brain matter, or any other tissue. When a cell loses its ability to receive instructions regarding its evolution, it reverts to the undifferentiated state where it knows only how to grow. This kind of unchecked growth is called cancer. Like any instruction manual, DNA is written in a language that makes use of an alphabet. But it was not until the 1950s when geneticists cracked the code of life itself, determining that the DNA alphabet was composed of four "letters," which they designated A, T, C, and G, which refer to four different kinds of nucleotides—adenine, thymine, cytosine, and guanine. These four nucleotides combine to create twenty amino acids, which produce the "words" and "sentences" that make up the physical genetic code of every individual of every species. We have about three billion letters in our genetic codes. The differences between individuals lie in the combination and sequencing of these four nucleotides.

הַגָּן וּמִשָּׁם יִפָּרֵד וְהָיָה יהוה, יהה לְאַרְבָּעָה רָאשִׁים ריבוע אלהים ◦ אלהים דיודין ע״ה:

11 שֵׁם יהוה שדי הָאֶחָד אהבה, דאגה פִּישׁוֹן הוּא הַסֹּבֵב אֵת כָּל ילי ־אֶרֶץ

אלהים דאלפין הַחֲוִילָה אֲשֶׁר־שָׁם הַזָּהָב והו: 12 וּזֲהַב הָאָרֶץ אלהים דההין ע״ה

הַהִוא טוֹב והו שָׁם הַבְּדֹלַח וְאֶבֶן יוד הה ואו הה הַשֹּׁהַם מהש: 13 וְשֵׁם יהוה שדי

־הַנָּהָר הַשֵּׁנִי גִּיחוֹן הוּא הַסּוֹבֵב אֵת כָּל ילי ־אֶרֶץ אלהים דאלפין כּוּשׁ

שכ״ה ע״ה: 14 וְשֵׁם יהוה שדי הַנָּהָר הַשְּׁלִישִׁי חִדֶּקֶל הוּא הַהֹלֵךְ מ״ה

קִדְמַת אַשּׁוּר אבגיתץ ע״ה, ושר ע״ה וְהַנָּהָר הָרְבִיעִי הוּא פְרָת: 15 וַיִּקַּח

חעם יְהֹוָאדני אהדונהי אֱלֹהִים ילה, מום, יב״ק אֶת־הָאָדָם מ״ה וַיַּנִּחֵהוּ בְגַן־עֵדֶן

לְעָבְדָהּ וּלְשָׁמְרָהּ: 16 וַיְצַו פוי יְהֹוָאדני אהדונהי אֱלֹהִים ילה, מום, יב״ק עַל־

הָאָדָם מ״ה לֵאמֹר מִכֹּל ילי עֵץ ע״ה קס״א ־הַגָּן אָכֹל תֹּאכֵל: 17 וּמֵעֵץ

ע״ה קס״א הַדַּעַת טוֹב והו וָרָע לֹא תֹאכַל מִמֶּנּוּ כִּי בְּיוֹם נגד, זן, מזבח

אֲכָלְךָ מִמֶּנּוּ מוֹת תָּמוּת: 18 וַיֹּאמֶר יְהֹוָאדני אהדונהי אֱלֹהִים

ילה, מום, יב״ק לֹא־טוֹב והו הֱיוֹת הָאָדָם מ״ה לְבַדּוֹ מ״ב אֶעֱשֶׂה־לּוֹ

עֵזֶר כְּנֶגְדּוֹ זן, מזבח: 19 וַיִּצֶר יְהֹוָאדני אהדונהי אֱלֹהִים ילה, מום, יב״ק

מִן־הָאֲדָמָה כָּל ילי ־חַיַּת הַשָּׂדֶה שדי וְאֵת כָּל־ ילי

עוֹף ציון, יוסף, ו״פ יהוה, ה״פ אל הַשָּׁמַיִם י״פ טל, י״פ כוזו וַיָּבֵא אֶל־הָאָדָם מ״ה

לִרְאוֹת מַה מ״ה ־יִּקְרָא־לוֹ וְכֹל ילי אֲשֶׁר יִקְרָא־לוֹ הָאָדָם מ״ה

נֶפֶשׁ רמ״ח ◦ ז׳ הויות חַיָּה הוּא שְׁמוֹ מהש ע״ה:

In the Bible, names are principally concerned with a person's spiritual genetic essence, the fundamental qualities of spirit that are variously configured to conceive and give birth to a specific entity in this dimension of existence. Thus, the names of the great patriarchs, matriarchs, and other major biblical figures can be seen to represent the DNA of their soul, or in other words, their respective spiritual attributes.

A change in a name—Avram (Abram) becoming Avra(ha)m (Abra[ha]m), for example—always signifies a changed spiritual destiny.

A person's name, therefore, has great significance in relation to his or her soul. As is commonly found in other traditions, the kabbalists advise us to name our children after the great spiritually minded figures of the past. By naming our children after these spiritual

THIRD READING - JACOB - TIFERET

[20] And the man gave names to all the cattle, the birds of the air and all the beasts of the field; but for Adam there was not found a help meet.

[21] And the Lord God caused the man to fall into a deep sleep; and while he slept, He took one of the man's ribsand closed up the place with flesh. [22] And from the rib that the Lord God had taken out of the man, He made a woman, and He brought her to the man.

[23] The man said, "This is now bone of my bones and flesh of my flesh; she shall be called 'woman,' for she was taken out of man." [24] For this reason a man shall leave his father and mother and be united to his wife, and they will become one flesh. [25] And they were both naked, the man and his wife, and they were not ashamed.

3 [1] Now the serpent was more subtle than any of the wild animals the Lord God had made. He said to the woman, "Did God really say, 'You must not eat from any tree in the garden'?"

---

giants, they are imbued with the spiritual DNA essence of that particular patriarch, matriarch, or sage. Each of these role models from the past is a spiritual chariot with a unique quality that will assist our children through their own paths of discovery, growth, and tikkun (correction).

An extremely important passage, this reading from the Bible also strengthens the connection each of us has to his or her own name, instilling us with Divine Light and awakening the power of our soul.

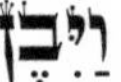

Genesis 2:22 – The Bible tells us that God created Eve from Adam, or specifically from Adam's rib. This is a passage that has roused feminist ire and been viewed as an insult to women throughout the ages. One might also term it an insult to human intelligence. Whenever a biblical passage contains such a jolt to awareness, it is always a sign to search for the deeper meaning as well as incontrovertible evidence that a correct reading of the text is possible only through Kabbalah. In fact, this passage—true to the overall theme in Genesis—indicates the beginning or seed level of all male and female relationships destined to occur in our world. The phrase "Adam and Eve" is a code, a metaphor that refers to the single, unified soul that existed before our universe came into being. This infinitely large soul is termed a Vessel, and all the souls of humankind were once contained within this single entity, in much the same manner as all the colors of a rainbow exist within a single beam of sunlight.

Another way of understanding this is to imagine tiny water droplets scattered over a surface. Each individual bead of water represents an individual human soul. When the surface is tilted, all the little drops slide together forming a single pool of water, which is the Vessel.

The Vessel is made up of two aspects or polarities: a positive (+) pole and a negative (–) pole, similar to a battery with its positive charge and negative charge. Adam corresponds to the positive charge, while Eve corresponds to the negative charge. All the female souls that have ever existed are bound up as one unified whole in Eve. Similarly, all the male souls that have ever existed are bound up as one unified whole within Adam.

THIRD READING - JACOB - TIFERET

20 וַיִּקְרָא עם ה' אותיות = ב"פ קס"א הָאָדָם מ"ה שֵׁמוֹת לְכָל יה - אדני הַבְּהֵמָה ב"ן, לכב
וּלְעוֹף ציון, יוסף, ו"פ יהוה, ה"פ אל הַשָּׁמַיִם י"פ טל, י"פ כוזו וּלְכֹל יה - אדני חַיַּת הַשָּׂדֶה שדי
וּלְאָדָם מ"ה לֹא־מָצָא עֵזֶר כְּנֶגְדּוֹ זן, מזבח: 21 וַיַּפֵּל יְהֹוָהאדניאהדונהי אֱלֹהִים
ילה, מום, יב"ק | תַּרְדֵּמָה ט"פ ע"ב עַל־הָאָדָם מ"ה וַיִּישָׁן ש"ע נהורין וַיִּקַּח וזעם אַחַת
מִצַּלְעֹתָיו וַיִּסְגֹּר בָּשָׂר תַּחְתֶּנָּה: 22 וַיִּבֶן בינה ע"ה יְהֹוָהאדניאהדונהי אֱלֹהִים
ילה, מום, יב"ק | אֶת־הַצֵּלָע אֲשֶׁר־לָקַח מִן־הָאָדָם מ"ה לְאִשָּׁה וַיְבִאֶהָ אֶל־
הָאָדָם מ"ה: 23 וַיֹּאמֶר הָאָדָם מ"ה זֹאת הַפַּעַם עֶצֶם מֵעֲצָמַי וּבָשָׂר
מִבְּשָׂרִי לְזֹאת יִקָּרֵא אִשָּׁה כִּי מֵאִישׁ ע"ה קנ"א קס"א לֻקֳחָה־זֹּאת:
24 עַל־כֵּן יַעֲזָב־אִישׁ ע"ה קנ"א קס"א אֶת־אָבִיו וְאֶת־אִמּוֹ וְדָבַק
בְּאִשְׁתּוֹ וְהָיוּ לְבָשָׂר אֶחָד אהבה, דאגה: 25 וַיִּהְיוּ שְׁנֵיהֶם עֲרוּמִּים
הָאָדָם מ"ה וְאִשְׁתּוֹ וְלֹא יִתְבֹּשָׁשׁוּ: 3 1 וְהַנָּחָשׁ רבוע אהיה - שדי הָיָה
יהה עָרוּם מִכֹּל ילי חַיַּת הַשָּׂדֶה שדי אֲשֶׁר עָשָׂה יְהֹוָהאדניאהדונהי
אֱלֹהִים ילה, מום, יב"ק וַיֹּאמֶר אֶל־הָאִשָּׁה אַף כִּי־אָמַר אֱלֹהִים ילה, מום

From this biblical passage, therefore, we learn something of vital importance: that we are all—men and women—of the same stock and source. We are all equal. No man or woman is higher or lower than another, and we are all in a state of interdependence. We are, in truth, all one. The quality of Light radiating from these verses has the power to enrich our relationships with members of the opposite sex, while also fostering a sense of unity among all human beings.

However, rather than capitulating to the view that males and females are so intrinsically different that conflict between them must always exist, it is also imperative to try to balance the male and female aspects inside each of us. The man must learn to foster within himself what are thought of as feminine traits, such as acceptance, nurturing, and intuition. The woman must learn to foster within herself what are thought of as male traits, like action and assertiveness. This is an extremely oversimplified explanation, but the point is that balance within individual human beings is of absolute importance.

וְהַנָּחָשׁ

Genesis 3:1 – Here the Bible introduces one of its most misunderstood concepts, that of the Evil Inclination or Negative Force known as Satan or the Opponent. To the kabbalist, the term "Satan" indicates both a personal attribute and a global phenomenon. As a personal attribute, Satan is essentially the unchecked human ego. As a global phenomenon, Satan represents the quality of chaos as a destabilizing force in this world.

[2] And the woman said to the serpent, "Of the fruit from the trees in the garden we may eat, [3] but of fruit from the tree that is in the middle of the garden, God did say, 'You must not eat, and you must not touch it, or you will die.' "

[4] And the serpent said to the woman, "You will not surely die [5] for God knows that when you eat of it your eyes will be opened, and you will be like God, knowing good and evil."

[6] And when the woman saw that the tree was good for food and pleasing to the eye, and that the tree was to be desired to make one wise, she took of the fruit thereof and ate it, and she also gave some to her husband, who was with her, and he ate it. [7] And the eyes of both of them were opened, and they realized they were naked; so they sewed fig leaves together and made coverings for themselves.

[8] And they heard the voice of the Lord God as He was walking in the garden in the cool of the day, and the man and his wife hid from the presence of the Lord God among the trees of the garden.

[9] But the Lord God called to the man, "Where are you?"

Moreover, besides being personally damaging, our individual egos are also the sole source of nourishment for the global Satan. In other words, Satan feeds off our personal destructive deeds by using these negative energies, which are intrinsic in our hateful actions, to create further turmoil and misery in the world. These destructive forces become in turn the source of our personal chaos. The Light revealed in this section of Genesis gives us the support and power to conquer the selfish aspect of our egos and, consequently, to deplete the global Satan of its energy and influence over humanity.

וַתֵּרֶא

Genesis 3:6 – Before the creation of the world, Adam and Eve were a single spiritual being (the Original Vessel) who incorporated all the collective souls of humanity. You and I are like the individual cells that form the body of this supernal being.

In the biblical story of Creation, we are told that after creating the other living things on Earth, God creates Adam, the first man, and his partner, Eve, the first woman. God leaves the couple in the Garden of Eden with the instruction that while they may partake of all the delights they find there, including fruit from the Tree of Life, they are forbidden to eat from the Tree of Knowledge of Good and Evil. They are told that the fruits are "unripe" and if they eat from that tree, they will surely die.

Something else is also in the Garden, however: the Serpent (Satan). Urged on by the seductive encouragement of the Serpent, Eve disobeys God by plucking a fruit from the forbidden tree and taking a bite. Then she offers the fruit to Adam, enticing him to eat it as well. He does, and with this action, their fleeting age of innocence is over.

Because mankind has become less accustomed to believing there is wisdom in ancient texts—an idea that was common as recently as a century ago—we generally dismiss the Creation story as a charming but simplistic parable, satisfying only to primitive and naive minds. Such thinking has unfortunately blinded us to the profundity concealed within this story. On a deeper level of spiritual understanding, Adam and Eve's bite of the fruit indicates a sexual connection between the original Vessel and the Serpent. In other words, the very act of succumbing to the deceitful

לֹא תֹאכְלוּ מִכֹּל ילי עֵץ ע"ה קס"א הַגָּן: 2 וַתֹּאמֶר הָאִשָּׁה אֶל-
הַנָּחָשׁ מִפְּרִי ע"ה אלהים דאלפין עֵץ ע"ה קס"א -הַגָּן נֹאכֵל: 3 וּמִפְּרִי
ע"ה אלהים דאלפין הָעֵץ ע"ה קס"א אֲשֶׁר בְּתוֹךְ-הַגָּן אָמַר אֱלֹהִים ילה, מום
לֹא תֹאכְלוּ מִמֶּנּוּ וְלֹא תִגְּעוּ בּוֹ פֶּן-תְּמֻתוּן: 4 וַיֹּאמֶר הַנָּחָשׁ
רבוע אהיה - שדי אֶל-הָאִשָּׁה לֹא-מוֹת תְּמֻתוּן: 5 כִּי יֹדֵעַ אֱלֹהִים
ילה, מום כִּי בְּיוֹם נגד, זן, מזבח אֲכָלְכֶם מִמֶּנּוּ וְנִפְקְחוּ מ"ה - קמ"ג עֵינֵיכֶם
ריבוע מ"ה וִהְיִיתֶם כֵּאלֹהִים ילה, מום יֹדְעֵי טוֹב והו וָרָע: 6 וַתֵּרֶא
הָאִשָּׁה כִּי טוֹב והו, אום הָעֵץ ע"ה קס"א לְמַאֲכָל יהוה אדני וְכִי תַאֲוָה-הוּא
לָעֵינַיִם ריבוע מ"ה וְנֶחְמָד הָעֵץ ע"ה קס"א לְהַשְׂכִּיל וַתִּקַּח מִפִּרְיוֹ וַתֹּאכַל
וַתִּתֵּן ב"פ כהת גַּם יגל -לְאִישָׁהּ עִמָּהּ וַיֹּאכַל: 7 וַתִּפָּקַחְנָה מ"ה - קמ"ג עֵינֵי
ריבוע מ"ה שְׁנֵיהֶם וַיֵּדְעוּ כִּי עֵירֻמִּם הֵם וַיִּתְפְּרוּ עֲלֵה תְאֵנָה נתה ע"ה
וַיַּעֲשׂוּ לָהֶם חֲגֹרֹת: 8 וַיִּשְׁמְעוּ אֶת-קוֹל ע"ב ס"ג ע"ה יְהֹוָהאדני יאהדונהי
אֱלֹהִים ילה, מום, יב"ק מִתְהַלֵּךְ מיה בַּגָּן לְרוּחַ מלוי אלהים דיודין הַיּוֹם נגד, זן, מזבח
וַיִּתְחַבֵּא הָאָדָם מ"ה וְאִשְׁתּוֹ מִפְּנֵי חכמה - בינה יְהֹוָהאדני יאהדונהי אֱלֹהִים
ילה, מום, יב"ק בְּתוֹךְ עֵץ ע"ה קס"א הַגָּן: 9 וַיִּקְרָא עם ה' אותיות = ב"פ קס"א
יְהֹוָהאדני יאהדונהי אֱלֹהִים ילה, מום, יב"ק אֶל-הָאָדָם מ"ה וַיֹּאמֶר לוֹ אַיֶּכָּה:

---

urging of the Serpent also connotes a sexual union between them in the sense of a merging of their consciousnesses.

Satan has two aspects: Male and Female. The Male aspect is known as (although we never pronounce this name) S-a-m-a-e-l. The Female aspect is known as (again, we do not pronounce the name) L-i-l-i-t-h. When the Vessel succumbed to the temptation of the Serpent, it means that L-i-l-i-t-h copulated with Adam and that S-a-m-a-e-l copulated with Eve. In a spiritual sense, this tells us that the originally elevated state of consciousness enjoyed by Adam and Eve was lowered and tainted by contact with the Negative Force, or Satan. In addition, this primal sexual union, or merging of two consciousnesses, caused the nature of the Vessel itself to mutate. The act of sexual connection between the Vessel and the Serpent altered the Vessel's spiritual DNA, changing its essence from the *Desire to Receive* into the *Desire to Receive for the Self Alone*. Consequently, every cell in the cosmic body of Adam and Eve (our souls) had its DNA recombined with the DNA of the Serpent. This was the birth of our "selfish gene," the ego. Thus, the dark, egocentric aspects of human nature were born from this union between the Vessel and the Serpent—a union that also gave birth to the roots of jealousy, envy, anger, greed, and all the other negative states of mind that arose from what is commonly called the Original Sin or the Sin of Adam.

10 He answered, "I heard Your voice in the garden, and I was afraid because I was naked; so I hid myself." 11 And God said, "Who told you that you were naked? Have you eaten from the tree that I commanded you not to eat from?" 12 The man said, "The woman You gave to be with me—she gave me of the tree, and I ate it." 13 Then the Lord God said to the woman, "What is this that you have done?" The woman said, "The serpent beguiled me, and I ate."

14 And the Lord God said to the serpent, "Because you have done this, cursed are you above all the cattle and all the wild animals! You will crawl on your belly and you will eat dust all the days of your life.

15 And I will put enmity between you and the woman, and between your offspring and hers; they will bruise your head, and you will strike their heel."

16 To the woman He said, "I shall greatly increase your pains in childbearing; with pain you shall give birth to children. Your desire shall be for your husband, and he will rule over you." 17 And to Adam He said, "Because you listened to your wife and ate from the tree about which I commanded you, 'You must not eat of it,' cursed is the ground because of you; through painful toil you shall eat of it all the days of your life.

Adam and Eve's fall from grace resulted in the shattering of the Vessel (the single unified soul) into countless sparks of individual souls, who then descended into this physical world in the garb of physical bodies. It became thereafter the task, first of Adam and Eve and then of all humanity, to eradicate the Negative Consciousness from their own nature, thereby reuniting all the scattered pieces of the fractured original soul into a single unified whole once more. This, in short, is the sole purpose of our lives.

By connecting with the essence of this story, we can acquire the spiritual power to eradicate Satan's influence both from our consciousness and from the world. By this means, the ego is subjugated, the soul's radiance is unfettered, selfishness is purged, and an unconditional love for all our fellow beings springs forth.

וַיֹּאמֶר

Genesis 3:10 – After Adam and Eve had eaten the forbidden fruit, God asked Adam why he had sinned. Adam's response was to blame Eve. One does not have to look far here to see a lesson concerning our own failure to take responsibility for the chaos and strife that we cause. It is our natural inclination to point the finger of blame at someone else when things go wrong in our lives. When things go very wrong, many of us point heavenward, thinking that God must be to blame. Worse still, the Creator often seems painfully indifferent to human pleas for help. In this vignette there lies an ancient truth that is central to the wisdom of Kabbalah: God does not answer our prayers; we answer them ourselves. Yet the prayers we send up, unless they are selfish prayers, are most certainly heard by the Creator, and as a result God gives us the strength and wisdom we need to manage our lives better than we did before. The *Zohar* says:

> *I heard that when Israel ask through their prayers and their pleas in their houses of prayer, then Metatron, the minister of the interior, takes all the prayers of Israel and elevates them to this firmament. And when God wants to examine the merits of Israel, He first studies this firmament, which is called Heaven, where the prayers of Israel are, and He pities them, as is written: "Then hear You (in) Heaven." The reference to Heaven is precise because there the prayers are heard.*
>
> *– The Zohar, Beresheet*
> *(Zohar Chadash 401)*

10 וַיֹּאמֶר אֶת־קֹלְךָ שָׁמַעְתִּי בַּגָּן וָאִירָא כִּי־עֵירֹם אָנֹכִי איע
וָאֵחָבֵא: 11 וַיֹּאמֶר מִי ילי הִגִּיד לְךָ כִּי עֵירֹם אָתָּה הֲמִן־הָעֵץ
ע"ה קס"א אֲשֶׁר צִוִּיתִיךָ פוי לְבִלְתִּי אֲכָל־מִמֶּנּוּ אָכָלְתָּ: 12 וַיֹּאמֶר
הָאָדָם מ"ה הָאִשָּׁה אֲשֶׁר נָתַתָּה נתה, קס"א + קנ"א + קמ"ג עִמָּדִי הִוא נָתְנָה
נתה, קס"א + קנ"א + קמ"ג לִּי מִן־הָעֵץ ע"ה קס"א וָאֹכֵל: 13 וַיֹּאמֶר יְהֹוָהאדניאהדונהי
אֱלֹהִים ילה, מום, יב"ק לָאִשָּׁה מַה מ"ה זֹּאת עָשִׂית וַתֹּאמֶר הָאִשָּׁה
הַנָּחָשׁ רבוע אהיה + שדי הִשִּׁיאַנִי וָאֹכֵל: 14 וַיֹּאמֶר יְהֹוָהאדניאהדונהי אֱלֹהִים
ילה, מום, יב"ק אֶל־הַנָּחָשׁ רבוע אהיה + שדי כִּי עָשִׂיתָ זֹּאת אָרוּר אַתָּה
מִכָּל ילי הַבְּהֵמָה ב"ן, לכב וּמִכֹּל ילי חַיַּת הַשָּׂדֶה שדי עַל־גְּחֹנְךָ תֵלֵךְ
וְעָפָר תֹּאכַל כָּל ילי יְמֵי חַיֶּיךָ: 15 וְאֵיבָה | אָשִׁית בֵּינְךָ וּבֵין
הָאִשָּׁה וּבֵין זַרְעֲךָ וּבֵין זַרְעָהּ הוּא יְשׁוּפְךָ רֹאשׁ
ריבוע אלהים + אלהים דיודין ע"ה וְאַתָּה תְּשׁוּפֶנּוּ עָקֵב ב"פ מום: [ס] 16 אֶל־
הָאִשָּׁה אָמַר הַרְבָּה אַרְבֶּה יצחק, ד"פ ב"ן עִצְּבוֹנֵךְ וְהֵרֹנֵךְ בְּעֶצֶב
תֵּלְדִי בָנִים וְאֶל־אִישֵׁךְ תְּשׁוּקָתֵךְ וְהוּא יִמְשָׁל־בָּךְ: [ס] 17 וּלְאָדָם
מ"ה אָמַר כִּי־שָׁמַעְתָּ לְקוֹל ע"ב ס"ג ע"ה אִשְׁתֶּךָ וַתֹּאכַל מִן־הָעֵץ ע"ה קס"א

The turmoil in our lives is a direct result of negative actions we have committed in this or a past life. Our prayers and the Divine Light they seek are activated only when we fully acknowledge our personal responsibility for the pain and suffering we endure. Prayers reach their goal only when we cease to see ourselves as helpless victims. When we are in denial of this truth, when our hearts are filled with self-pity, both prayer and the Bible itself are worth nothing. They become empty symbols of tradition, instead of the awesome instruments of power they truly are.

We must arouse remorse in our hearts and awaken in ourselves the consciousness of our own accountability; this will help correct our sins as the Divine Light purifies our soul and cleanses the world of its iniquities.

וּלְאָדָם

Genesis 3:17 – The Bible tells us that Adam, Eve, and the Serpent all received punishment following the Original Sin. For its part, the Serpent was condemned to slither over the earth on its belly and eat of the dust. Foreshadowing the fate of all women, Eve was sentenced to endure the pains of childbirth; before the Original Sin, the sages tell us, there was no menstruation, and child-bearing was immediate—a phenomenon of pure thought. For his role, Adam was forced to work the fields, to labor for food, to search endlessly for the Light that was once freely his for the asking.

18 It shall bring forth thorns and thistles for you and you shall eat the plants of the field.

19 By the sweat of your brow shall you eat bread until you return to the ground, since from it you were taken; for dust you are and to dust you shall return."

20 Adam named his wife Eve, because she would become the mother of all the living.

21 The Lord God made garments of skin for Adam and his wife and clothed them.

FOURTH READING - MOSES - NETZACH

22 And the Lord God said, "The man has now become like one of Us, knowing good and evil. He must not be allowed to reach out his hand and take also from the Tree of Life and eat, and live forever."

Here, once again, we have an apparently simple story that conceals deeper spiritual truths, one of which is that the concepts of punishment and reward have no basis in spirituality. If we touch a burner on the stove, whether deliberately or inadvertently, and injure ourselves, we do not claim to have been punished by the extreme heat of the hot burner. Conversely, if we use this same energy to heat our home, to cook our family food, or to heat water in which to bathe ourselves, we do not consider the heat as a reward. In fact, it is our knowledge, or our lack thereof, concerning the properties of electricity, gas, or heat combustion that actually determines its influence in our lives.

God neither punishes nor rewards humankind. And the Creator does not command, either. When Adam was originally created as the Original Vessel, he was designed by God to receive endless fulfillment and joy. He also inherited a trait, a "gene," from the Divine Force of his Creator, which was essentially the quality of being God-like. Thus, he wanted to be the "creator of his own light," for creating something is the greatest fulfillment of all. To understand fully what is going on here, we need only see ourselves as Adam, for we are each part of the Original Vessel.

But just like the light of a candle in the presence of the sun, the Light of individual souls was not apparent amid the luminous perfection of the Garden of Eden, a dimension of pure Light. After the Original Sin, Adam left this place to enter our disordered dimension of darkness, from which the Light of the Creator is concealed. But through our own labor and effort, we can now rekindle this Light and thereby share in the Divine act of Creation. In a very real sense, we become responsible for creating heaven on Earth, and in doing so, we become God-like! It is worth dwelling upon this thought until we fully comprehend it, for it is the meaning of life itself.

We have seen now that it was Adam's own decision—as the consequence of his own actions—to come to this world, not any punishment decreed by God. In other words, Adam and all humankind chose to enter a domain of darkness, where our consciousness is tainted with ego (Satan), so that we could eventually triumph over our selfish impulses by striving to bring perfection to the world.

In doing this, we are able to satisfy our deepest need, our most profound yearning, which is the desire to be both the Cause and creator of our own fulfillment. The Serpent (Satan) does not

אֲשֶׁר צִוִּיתִיךָ פוי לֵאמֹר לֹא תֹאכַל מִמֶּנּוּ אֲרוּרָה הָאֲדָמָה
בַּעֲבוּרֶךָ בְּעִצָּבוֹן תֹּאכְלֶנָּה כֹּל ילי יְמֵי חַיֶּיךָ׃ 18 וְקוֹץ וְדַרְדַּר
תַּצְמִיחַ לָךְ וְאָכַלְתָּ אֶת-עֵשֶׂב ע"ב שמות הַשָּׂדֶה שדי׃ 19 בְּזֵעַת
אַפֶּיךָ תֹּאכַל לֶחֶם ג"פ יהוה עַד שׁוּבְךָ אֶל-הָאֲדָמָה כִּי מִמֶּנָּה
לֻקָּחְתָּ כִּי-עָפָר אַתָּה וְאֶל-עָפָר תָּשׁוּב׃ 20 וַיִּקְרָא עם ה' אותיות = ב"פ קס"א
הָאָדָם מ"ה שֵׁם שדי יהוה אִשְׁתּוֹ חַוָּה וא"ו ה"א כִּי הִוא הָיְתָה אֵם יוהך
כָּל ילי -חָי חיים, בינה ע"ה׃ 21 וַיַּעַשׂ יְהֹוָאדהֹנָהי יאהדונהי אֱלֹהִים ילה, מום, יב"ק
לְאָדָם מ"ה וּלְאִשְׁתּוֹ כָּתְנוֹת עוֹר וַיַּלְבִּשֵׁם׃ [פ]

FOURTH READING - MOSES - NETZACH

22 וַיֹּאמֶר | יְהֹוָאדהֹנָהי יאהדונהי אֱלֹהִים ילה, מום, יב"ק הֵן הָאָדָם מ"ה הָיָה יהה
כְּאַחַד אהבה, דאגה מִמֶּנּוּ לָדַעַת טוֹב והו וָרָע וְעַתָּה | פֶּן-יִשְׁלַח יָדוֹ
וְלָקַח גַּם מֵעֵץ ע"ה קס"א הַחַיִּים בינה ע"ה וְאָכַל וָחַי לְעֹלָם ריבוע ס"ג + י' אותיות׃

have this opportunity; it can never evolve from its primitive state and appreciate the ineffable joy associated with being a creator. The limitations of our ego only become apparent after some time has passed—after it has become clear that its desires can never bring lasting fulfillment.

The underlying lesson in this section concerns the much-underestimated value of appreciation. When paradise is handed to us freely, without our having the slightest notion that it is something that ought to be earned or any knowledge of the darkness surrounding it, we can never truly comprehend, let alone appreciate, the treasure of the Light that we already possess.

Our spiritual work, therefore, involves learning to appreciate the abundance of what we have as well as strive to create order out of chaos through the conquest of our self-centered nature born of ego. This ultimate objective of life is something that can be realized in the here-and-now by reading this Bible verse, combined with our awareness of the deep truths contained in these penetrating insights of Kabbalah.

וַיֹּאמֶר

Genesis 3:22 – After committing the Original Sin, Adam was expelled from the Garden of Eden. But an even deeper analysis is needed here because, in truth, Adam did not possess the quality of free will during the act of sinning. Kabbalah teaches that the Original Sin is, in fact, a coded reference to a stage of development, a particular phase in the grand process of Creation. In its cryptic metaphorical manner, the Bible is thus telling us that there was no real act of disobedience or misdeed. Adam and Eve did not actually do anything wrong. Instead, the story concerns humanity's evolution to a higher level of consciousness where the gift of free will was bestowed. At our own request, we humans would

23 So the Lord God banished him from the Garden of Eden to work the ground from which he had been taken.

24 So He drove the man out, and He placed on the east side of the Garden of Eden cherubim and a flaming sword flashing back and forth to guard the way to the Tree of Life.

4 1 And Adam knew his wife Eve, and she conceived and gave birth to Cain. She said,
"I have brought forth a man with the help of God." 2 And again she gave birth to his
brother Abel. And Abel was a keeper of sheep, and Cain tilled the soil.

3 In the course of time Cain brought some of the fruits of the soil as an offering to God.

4 And Abel brought the first born of his flock and the fat portions thereof. And God
looked with respect on Abel and his offering, 5 but on Cain and his offering He did not
look with respect. So Cain was very angry, and his face was downcast.

6 Then God said to Cain, "Why are you angry? Why is your face downcast? 7 If you do
well, will it not be lifted up? But if you do not do well, sin is crouching at the door; it
desires to have you, but you must master it."

8 And Cain spoke to his brother Abel, and it came to pass while they were in the field that Cain attacked his brother Abel and killed him.

---

now become accountable for the amount of Light we receive in life. This insistence on taking responsibility for our own consciousness is, in fact, the inner meaning behind Eve and Adam's actions and the expulsion from Eden.

The expulsion also has another meaning and an additional relevance to our lives. People on a spiritual path can all too often sink into complacency while studying repositories of wisdom like Kabbalah. Such study is a noble occupation, to be sure, yet real inner growth can occur only through experiencing the world's harsh realities. Each day of our lives for a certain period of time, we must leave our Garden of comfort and complacency—even our spiritual study sessions—and throw ourselves into the chaotic drama of life. For it is only there that we can transform our reactive nature and learn to transcend our ego's primal impulses, thus learning to love our friends and foes unconditionally. This is the place where true spiritual greatness is attained; this is the ultimate objective of life on Earth.

יָדַע

Genesis 4:1 – We are told here that Adam "knew" Eve, and then Eve gave birth to Cain. The *Zohar* asks why the Bible uses the word "knew" to imply a sexual connection between man and woman, thus drawing our attention once again to the persistence of biblical metaphor.

The point here is that the pleasure derived from sex, as is the case with all the joys of life, originates in the 99 Percent Realm of spiritual Light. We are able to access this Light whenever there is a union or connection between the Lower World and the Upper Worlds. Thus, the Bible is telling us that "knowledge," which is the noun derived from the verb "knew," forms our connection to the Upper Worlds. Once we have acquired the knowledge of Kabbalah, revealing the Bible's true meaning, we can connect to or unite with the Upper World of endless Light.

23 וַיְשַׁלְּחֵהוּ יְהֹוָאדניאהדונהי אֱלֹהִים ילה, מום, יב״ק מִגַּן־עֵדֶן לַעֲבֹד אֶת־
הָאֲדָמָה אֲשֶׁר לֻקַּח מִשָּׁם׃ 24 וַיְגָרֶשׁ אֶת־הָאָדָם מ״ה וַיַּשְׁכֵּן
מִקֶּדֶם רבוע ב״ן לְגַן־עֵדֶן אֶת־הַכְּרֻבִים וְאֵת לַהַט רבוע אהיה הַחֶרֶב
רבוע ס״ג רבוע אהיה הַמִּתְהַפֶּכֶת לִשְׁמֹר אֶת־דֶּרֶךְ ב״פ יב״ק עֵץ ע״ה קס״א הַחַיִּים
בינה ע״ה׃ [ס] 1 4 וְהָאָדָם מ״ה יָדַע ב״פ מ״ב אֶת־חַוָּה וא״ו ה״א אִשְׁתּוֹ וַתַּהַר
וַתֵּלֶד אֶת־קַיִן ע״ה קס״א וַתֹּאמֶר קָנִיתִי אִישׁ ע״ה קנ״א קס״א אֶת־
יְהֹוָאדניאהדונהי׃ 2 וַתֹּסֶף לָלֶדֶת אֶת־אָחִיו אֶת־הָבֶל מלוי ס״ג וַיְהִי אל
־הֶבֶל מלוי ס״ג רֹעֵה צֹאן מלוי אהיה דיודין ע״ה וְקַיִן ע״ה קס״א הָיָה יהה עֹבֵד
אֲדָמָה׃ 3 וַיְהִי מִקֵּץ מנק יָמִים נלך וַיָּבֵא קַיִן ע״ה קס״א מִפְּרִי ע״ה אלהים דאלפין
הָאֲדָמָה מִנְחָה ע״ה ב״פ ב״ן לַיהֹוָאדניאהדונהי׃ 4 וְהֶבֶל מלוי ס״ג הֵבִיא גַם
יגל ־הוּא מִבְּכֹרוֹת צֹאנוֹ וּמֵחֶלְבֵהֶן וַיִּשַׁע יְהֹוָאדניאהדונהי אֶל־הֶבֶל
מלוי ס״ג וְאֶל־מִנְחָתוֹ׃ 5 וְאֶל־קַיִן ע״ה קס״א וְאֶל־מִנְחָתוֹ לֹא שָׁעָה וַיִּחַר
לְקַיִן ע״ה קס״א מְאֹד מ״ה וַיִּפְּלוּ פָּנָיו׃ 6 וַיֹּאמֶר יְהֹוָאדניאהדונהי אֶל־קָיִן
ע״ה קס״א לָמָּה חָרָה לָךְ וְלָמָּה נָפְלוּ פָנֶיךָ ס״ג - מ״ה - ב״ן׃ 7 הֲלוֹא אִם
יוהך ־תֵּיטִיב שְׂאֵת וְאִם יוהך לֹא תֵיטִיב לַפֶּתַח חַטָּאת רֹבֵץ
וְאֵלֶיךָ תְּשׁוּקָתוֹ וְאַתָּה תִּמְשָׁל־בּוֹ׃ 8 וַיֹּאמֶר קַיִן ע״ה קס״א

The point of all these insights is that knowledge provides the key to spiritual transformation. Knowledge is the door through which we pass to gain access to Divine Light.

Merely by being in possession of the secrets of this knowledge, we activate and "switch on" the greatest power generator in the universe: the Bible. The Light of the parchment of the Torah Scroll shines more brightly than a galaxy of stars. The *Zohar* refers to Rav Shimon bar Yochai and sometimes to other great kabbalists as "the Light of the Bible," thus lending weight to the idea that knowledge—supernal spiritual knowledge—is really the power behind the Light.

וְהֶבֶל

Genesis 4:4 – The Bible tells us that Abel "also brought" a sacrifice before God. As the sages have explained, the word "also" indicates that Abel's consciousness was not focused exclusively upon the sacrifice. This vacillation is what created the opening for negativity to enter his life, resulting in his own death at the hand of his brother, Cain.

In whatever we do, whether it is of a spiritual nature or not, it is vital that we devote 100

9 And God said to Cain, "Where is your brother Abel?" And he said, "I don't know, am I my brother's keeper?"

*10 And He said, "What have you done? The voice of your brother's blood cries out to
me from the ground. 11 And now you are cursed from the ground, which opened its
mouth to receive your brother's blood from your hand. 12 When you till the ground, it
will no longer yield its crops for you. You will be a restless wanderer on the Earth."*

*13 Cain said to God, "My punishment is more than I can bear. 14 Behold, today You
have driven me from the land, and Your presence will be hidden from me; I shall be
a fugitive and wanderer on the earth, and whoever shall find me shall slay me."*

15 And God said to him, "If anyone slays Cain, he will suffer vengeance sevenfold." Then God put a mark on Cain lest anyone who finds him shall slay him.

---

percent of our energy, desire, and certainty to the task. Whatever percentage we do not give complerely—or give up in the case of our ego—no matter how small the amount, will create the opening and space that Satan is waiting for so that he can enter and wreak havoc in our lives. The stronger the Light to be revealed the greater the Force of Darkness that tries to prevent it. When we sacrifice our ego, we must let it go completely; there can be no half measures. This section of the Bible concerning Cain and Abel empowers us with the courage to surrender completely having absolute certainty and trust that cutting loose our negative traits from our nature will not mean a loss of identity but rather the gaining of our true Self. This is the real meaning of a "sacrifice."

Rav Ashlag writes:

> *And it is always so: If they walk the straight path, they draw every good therein, but if, Heaven forbid, they do not walk the good path, they bring about the opposite. Yet sometimes [to draw goodness], one needs to attract a miracle, which is outside nature. The only way one attracts miracles is through rearranging nature from the way God designed it to be, and that can only be achieved through self-sacrifice.*

This kind of sacrifice should not be thought of as a bargaining chip, however; when we change our nature, the Laws of Nature give way to us. When we overcome our nature, we overcome all nature.

וַיַּהַרְגֵהוּ

Genesis 4:8 – In the *Zohar*, we find some astounding insights about the story of Cain and Abel that concern such arcane matters as the host of demons who dwell among us, the sexual seduction that takes place both when we are awake and during our sleep, and even the root cause of premature death in children. Demonic angels can be thought of as negative energy forces of intelligence that originate from the time of Cain. We are told:

> *Rav Yitzchak said that after Cain killed Abel, Adam separated from his wife. Two female spirits used to come and mate with him, and by them he fathered spirits and demons that now roam around the world.*
> – *The Zohar, Beresheet B 62:346*

Impervious to our five senses, these negative forces are nonetheless as influential as the unseen force of gravity and as real as the invisible currents in the air. They are behind the ailments that afflict our children and the negative, selfish, and unrestrained sexual impulses that fester within us.

Rav Shimon, the author of the *Zohar*, states:

> *Woe to the sons of man, for they are not aware and do not take heed or search for knowledge. They are all blindfolded and do not know how full the world is with*

אֶל־הֶבֶל מלוי ס״ג אָחִיו וַיְהִי אל בִּהְיוֹתָם בַּשָּׂדֶה וַיָּקָם קַיִן ע״ה קס״א
אֶל־הֶבֶל מלוי ס״ג אָחִיו וַיַּהַרְגֵהוּ׃ 9 וַיֹּאמֶר יְהֹוָאדניאהדונהי אֶל־קַיִן ע״ה קס״א
אֵי הֶבֶל מלוי ס״ג אָחִיךָ וַיֹּאמֶר לֹא יָדַעְתִּי הֲשֹׁמֵר אָחִי אָנֹכִי איע׃
10 וַיֹּאמֶר מֶה מ״ה עָשִׂיתָ קוֹל ע״ב ס״ג ע״ה דְּמֵי אָחִיךָ צֹעֲקִים אֵלַי
מִן־הָאֲדָמָה׃ 11 וְעַתָּה אָרוּר אָתָּה מִן־הָאֲדָמָה אֲשֶׁר פָּצְתָה
אֶת־פִּיהָ לָקַחַת אֶת־דְּמֵי אָחִיךָ מִיָּדֶךָ׃ 12 כִּי תַעֲבֹד אֶת־
הָאֲדָמָה לֹא־תֹסֵף תֵּת־כֹּחָהּ לָךְ נָע וָנָד תִּהְיֶה בָאָרֶץ אלהים דאלפין׃
13 וַיֹּאמֶר קַיִן ע״ה קס״א אֶל־יְהֹוָאדניאהדונהי גָּדוֹל להח, מבה, יזל, אום עֲוֺנִי
מִנְּשֹׂא׃ 14 הֵן גֵּרַשְׁתָּ אֹתִי הַיּוֹם נגד, זן, מזבח מֵעַל עלם פְּנֵי חכמה + בינה
הָאֲדָמָה וּמִפָּנֶיךָ ס״ג + מ״ה + ב״ן אֶסָּתֵר ב״פ מצר וְהָיִיתִי נָע וָנָד בָּאָרֶץ
אלהים דאלפין וְהָיָה יהוה, יהה כָל ילי ־מֹצְאִי יַהַרְגֵנִי׃ 15 וַיֹּאמֶר לוֹ
יְהֹוָאדניאהדונהי לָכֵן כָּל ילי ־הֹרֵג קַיִן ע״ה קס״א שִׁבְעָתַיִם יֻקָּם ר״ת יתרו, קין, מצרי

---

strange and invisible creatures and things. If permission were to be given to the eye to see, people would wonder greatly as to how it is possible to survive in this world.
– The Zohar, Beresheet B 62:356

Through the story of Cain and Abel, both the Bible and the *Zohar* empower us with the Divine Light necessary to eliminate all the demons and every other evil element from existence. This battle and victory occurs now—in the eternal present—not at some vague time in the future. Children are healed, diseases are eradicated, and we are able to repair the damage from humankind's sexual errors that have caused misery throughout history.

יֻקָּם

Genesis 4:15 – Here the Bible uses the Aramaic word: *yukam* (be raised). The word *YuKaM* is an acronym for Yitro (Jethro), Korach, and Mitzri, all of whom, the *Zohar* explains, were reincarnations of Cain. The *Yud* in *YuKaM* stands for Yitro (Jethro), who became the father-in-law of Moses. The *Zohar* goes on to reveal that Moses himself was the reincarnation of Cain's brother, Abel, and that Abel was known as "flesh," as stated in Genesis 6:13. The word "flesh," we are told, is also a secret code for Moses.

Thus, Jethro and Moses (Cain and Abel) were able to resolve age-old karmic obligations when Jethro gave Moses his daughter's hand in marriage. In their original incarnation, Jethro (Cain) took Moses's (Abel's) life, so as restitution in their later incarnation, Jethro provided Moses with a wife.

The *Kof* of *YuKaM* refers to Korach, who rose up to challenge Moses's leadership in a later story. Korach failed in his bid to overthrow Moses and was swallowed up by the earth. The *Mem* refers to an Egyptian (Mitzri), whom Moses killed.

16 And Cain went out from the presence of God and lived in the land of Nod, east of Eden. 17 And Cain knew his wife, and she conceived and gave birth to Enoch. And he built a city, and he named it after his son Enoch. 18 To Enoch was born Irad, and to Irad was born Mehujael, and to Mehujael was born Methushael, and to Methushael was born Lamech.

FIFTH READING - AARON - HOD

19 Lamech married two women, one named Adah and the other named Zillah. 20 Adah gave birth to Jabal; he was the father of those who live in tents and raise cattle. 21 His brother's name was Jubal; he was the father of all who play the harp and flute. 22 Zillah also bore a son, Tubal-Cain, who forged all kinds of tools out of bronze and iron. Tubal-Cain's sister was Na'amah. 23 Lamech said to his wives, "Adah and Zillah, listen to me; wives of Lamech, hear my words. I have slain a man for wounding me, a young man for hurting me. 24 If Cain is avenged sevenfold, then truly Lamech seventy-seven times."

According to the *Zohar*, Moses used two of the 72 Names of God to slay the Egyptian:

- *Kaf, Hei, Tav* - כהת
- *Yud, Kaf, Shin* - יכש

Cain's three incarnations allowed him to correct his error, complete his act of repentance, and make amends with his brother, Abel.

The two Names of God mentioned above help us achieve the impetus necessary to eradicate the fallen Cain within each of us. In this single action, we can correct all our sins from this and past lives. Furthermore, the spiritual Light emanating from these Aramaic letters is sufficient to set right the iniquities of all the generations descended from Cain—and to do this in a manner befitting of God's infinite mercy, rather than in a quality of harsh judgment. Our access to this path of mercy is a direct consequence of the Divine insights of the *Zohar* and the Torah Scroll from which we read.

אות

Genesis 4:15 – Cain knew that he himself would likely be murdered by the people of his generation in retribution for his killing of Abel. He understood the Universal Law of Cause and Effect, and thus knew that the energy emanating from him would infect anyone in his presence with the dark vibrations of his crime. It is important to note that Cain then made an attempt to repent profoundly for what he had done.

According to the *Zohar*, God inscribed the Aramaic letter *Vav* onto the forehead of Cain. The letter *Vav* connects to the *Sefira* of *Yesod*, which signifies the Covenant between God and the Israelites. Because Cain sincerely repented his murder of his brother, the letter *Vav*, in fact, protected him from the hostility he engendered through his reprehensible crime.

The lesson for us here is straightforward enough: If Cain could repent of so evil a deed as murder, then surely all of us can repent of our much more minor errors—assuming, of course, that we have elected to transform our ways forever. Adam states in the *Zohar*:

> *The strength of repentance is so great and powerful...*
> *– The Zohar, Beresheet B 62:345*

In meditating upon the Aramaic letter *Vav* during a reading of this section and by fostering an

וַיָּשֶׂם יְהֹוָהאדניאהדונהי לְקַיִן ע"ה קס"א אוֹת לְבִלְתִּי הַכּוֹת־אֹתוֹ
כָּל ילי ־מֹצְאוֹ׃ 16 וַיֵּצֵא קַיִן ע"ה קס"א מִלִּפְנֵי יְהֹוָהאדניאהדונהי וַיֵּשֶׁב
בְּאֶרֶץ אלהים דאלפין ־נוֹד קִדְמַת־עֵדֶן׃ 17 וַיֵּדַע ב"פ מ"ב קַיִן ע"ה קס"א אֶת־
אִשְׁתּוֹ וַתַּהַר וַתֵּלֶד אֶת־חֲנוֹךְ וַיְהִי אל בֹּנֶה עִיר סוזופר, ערי, סנדלפון
וַיִּקְרָא עם ה' אותיות = ב"פ קס"א שֵׁם יהוה שדי הָעִיר סוזופר, ערי, סנדלפון כְּשֵׁם יהוה שדי
בְּנוֹ חֲנוֹךְ׃ 18 וַיִּוָּלֵד לַחֲנוֹךְ אֶת־עִירָד וְעִירָד יָלַד אֶת־מְחוּיָאֵל
וּמְחִיָּיאֵל יָלַד אֶת־מְתוּשָׁאֵל וּמְתוּשָׁאֵל יָלַד אֶת־לָמֶךְ׃

FIFTH READING - AARON - HOD

19 וַיִּקַּח ועם ־לוֹ לֶמֶךְ שְׁתֵּי נָשִׁים שֵׁם יהוה שדי הָאַחַת עָדָה וְשֵׁם
יהוה שדי הַשֵּׁנִית צִלָּה׃ 20 וַתֵּלֶד עָדָה אֶת־יָבָל הוּא הָיָה יהה אֲבִי
יֹשֵׁב אֹהֶל לאה, אלד ע"ה וּמִקְנֶה׃ 21 וְשֵׁם יהוה שדי אָחִיו יוּבָל הוּא הָיָה
יהה אֲבִי כָּל ילי ־תֹּפֵשׂ כִּנּוֹר וְעוּגָב׃ 22 וְצִלָּה גַם יגל ־הִוא יָלְדָה
אֶת־תּוּבַל קַיִן ע"ה קס"א לֹטֵשׁ כָּל ילי ־חֹרֵשׁ נְחֹשֶׁת וּבַרְזֶל
ר"ת בלהה רחל זלפה לאה וַאֲחוֹת תּוּבַל־קַיִן ע"ה קס"א נַעֲמָה רבוע ס"ג׃ 23 וַיֹּאמֶר
לֶמֶךְ לְנָשָׁיו עָדָה וְצִלָּה שְׁמַעַן קוֹלִי נְשֵׁי לֶמֶךְ הַאְזֵנָּה יוד הי ואו הה
אִמְרָתִי כִּי אִישׁ ע"ה קנ"א קס"א הָרַגְתִּי לְפִצְעִי וְיֶלֶד לְחַבֻּרָתִי׃ 24 כִּי
שִׁבְעָתַיִם יֻקַּם ר"ת יתרו, קין, מצרי ־קָיִן ע"ה קס"א וְלֶמֶךְ שִׁבְעִים וְשִׁבְעָה׃

---

authentic sense of great remorse deep within our heart for all our errors, it is possible for us to receive protection from any decrees of judgment made against us. The energy emanating from this remorse also helps destroy the negative angel (whose name must not be pronounced) S-a-m-a-e-l, and correct the root causes of all sin.

הָרַגְתִּי

Genesis 4:23 – Lemech, a blind man, accidentally killed Cain, who was his great, great grandfather. Because of his blindness, Lemech could not see

[25] Adam knew his wife again, and she gave birth to a son and named him Seth. She said, "God has granted me another child instead of Abel, whom Cain slew." [26] And to Seth also a son was born, and he named him Enosh. Then men began to call on the name of the Lord.

SIXTH READING - JOSEPH - YESOD

5 [1] This is the Book of the Generations of Adam. In the day that God made man, He made him in the likeness of God. [2] He created them male and female and blessed

---

the letter *Vav* on Cain's forehead. This accidental killing of Cain demonstrates the importance of our state of consciousness as well as our awareness of the spiritual laws, both of which determine whether or not we plant positive or negative seeds in life. Ignorance of the law, as they say, is no excuse. Whether we touch a frayed wire purposely or inadvertently, we still receive a painful shock. If our consciousness is negative, if we are "blind" to the spiritual laws that govern our reality, our good intentions will still lead us into chaos and darkness.

The irrefutable truth of the great Cosmic Law of Cause and Effect is etched into our hearts and minds during this reading, as is the necessity of recognizing our accountability for all our deeds.

אָז

Genesis 4:26 – Although it is not explicitly mentioned in the Bible, this reading speaks of the destruction of a third of the world's population in what is known as Dor (the generation) of the prophet Enoch. The *Book of Enoch*, known to kabbalists throughout the ages, did not surface publicly until the 19th century. So disturbing were its contents to the Church that an attempt was made to ban the book. However, a few copies were discovered in Ethiopia and brought to Scotland, where the *Book of Enoch* was translated into English in 1821.

The sages teach us that the people of Enoch's time tried to use certain magical techniques, attempting to make a cosmic detour to connect to the Divine energy so that they could avoid having to take responsibility for their actions. This type of magic not only subverts the most portentous of all universal laws—the Universal Law of Cause and Effect—but it is also the underlying secret behind the story of the Golden Calf, which will be explored later on in the Book of Exodus.

We must allow the desire to be held accountable for our actions to stir within us, granting us the desire and will to repent, and in so doing, to control our own destiny.

זֶה

Genesis 5:1 – The *Book of Adam* is the original book of Kabbalah, and it contains all the secrets of our universe as well as all the more sublime mysteries of the Supernal Worlds above it. The *Book of Adam* is like the DNA code of the cosmos, making it beyond all doubt the most powerful book in existence. The *Zohar*, as well as all kabbalistic wisdom, is encoded in the pages of its cryptic text.

Concerning the *Book of Adam*, the *Zohar* states the following:

> *[God says:] "This is the Book of the generations of Adam," and there literally is such a book. We have already explained that when Adam was in the Garden of Eden, God sent a book down to him with*

25 וַיֵּדַע ב״פ מ״ב אָדָם מ״ה עוֹד אֶת־אִשְׁתּוֹ וַתֵּלֶד בֵּן וַתִּקְרָא אֶת־שְׁמוֹ
מהש ע״ה שֵׁת כִּי שָׁת־לִי אֱלֹהִים ילה, מום זֶרַע אַחֵר תַּחַת הֶבֶל מלוי ס״ג
כִּי הֲרָגוֹ קָיִן: ע״ה קס״א 26 וּלְשֵׁת גַּם יגל ־הוּא יֻלַּד־בֵּן וַיִּקְרָא
עם ה׳ אותיות = ב״פ קס״א אֶת־שְׁמוֹ מהש ע״ה אֱנוֹשׁ אָז הוּחַל לִקְרֹא בְּשֵׁם
יהוה שדי, ר״ת הבל יְהֹוָהאדניאהדונהי: [ס]

SIXTH READING - JOSEPH - YESOD

5 1 זֶה סֵפֶר תּוֹלְדֹת אָדָם מ״ה בְּיוֹם נגד, זן, מזבח בְּרֹא קנ״א - ב״ן אֱלֹהִים
ילה, מום אָדָם מ״ה בִּדְמוּת אֱלֹהִים ילה, מום עָשָׂה אֹתוֹ: 2 זָכָר וּנְקֵבָה

Raziel, the holy angel who is in charge of the supernal sacred secrets.
– The *Zohar*, Beresheet B 63:361

Much like Einstein's formula $E=mc^2$, whose five simple characters conceal all the mathematical equations that define time, space, matter, and energy, so the *Book of Adam* is a concise formula that conceals all the spiritual equations that define absolute reality. This book also holds the glorious Light of Creation, the endless joy and boundless bliss embodied by the Garden of Eden. In effect, it represents our world in its perfected form, in its destined state of greatness. When Adam sinned, however, the book flew away from him, and he was understandably filled with anguish.

The *Zohar* says:

Adam used to beat upon his head and weep. He went into the waters of the River Gichon up to his neck because he repented and mortified himself until his body became wrinkled and porous and his radiance changed.
– The Zohar, Beresheet B 63:364

Yet after Adam's sorrowful repentance, the *Zohar* tells us that God signaled to the Angel Raphael to return the book to Adam, who left it to his son Seth. Our own repentance can rekindle the Light that shines from the *Book of Adam*, and a deep meditation upon its letters awakens the dormant spiritual greatness within us. It sets into motion our Final Redemption with an abundance of mercy, thus commencing the Age of Messiah (Mashiach), a time characterized by unlimited tender-heartedness along with deep respect for our fellow man and our physical environment. With the potent energy of repentance, we create the Garden of Eden within us and around us. The *Book of Adam*, the *Zohar* tells us, helped Enoch (Chanoch) become a heavenly angel known as M-e-t-a-t-r-o-n (whose name we do not pronounce), who signifies eternal youth and immortality. Thus, through the *Book of Adam*, through Enoch and the angel M-e-t-a-t-r-o-n, we bring immortality to all of humanity, and heaven on Earth becomes our new reality.

מ״יץ	עו״י	מבש״
יצ״ד	וו״ה	ג״רג
הי״י	זד״ו	ד״צב
ונ״ק	שו״ה	לק״ה

*them. And He called their name Adam. 3 When Adam had lived 130 years, he had a
son in his own likeness, in his own image; and he named him Seth.*

4 And after Seth was born, Adam lived 800 years and had other sons and daughters.

5 And the days that Adam lived were 930 years, and then he died.

6 And Seth lived 105 years, and he bore Enosh.

7 And after he became the father of Enosh, Seth lived 807 years and had other sons and daughters.

8 And the days that Seth lived were 912 years, and then he died.

9 When Enosh had lived 90 years, he bore Kenan.

*10 And after he became the father of Kenan, Enoch lived 815 years and had other
sons and daughters. 11 And the days that Enosh lived were 905 years, and then he
died.*

12 When Kenan had lived 70 years, he bore Mahalalel.

13 And after he became the father of Mahalalel, Kenan lived 840 years and had other sons and daughters.

14 And the days Kenan lived were 910 years, and then he died.

15 When Mahalalel had lived 65 years, he bore Jared.

16 And after he became the father of Jared, Mahalalel lived 830 years and had other sons and daughters.

17 And the days that Mahalalel lived were 895 years, and then he died.

וַיְּוֹזִי

Genesis 5:3 – We learn here that there were ten generations from Adam to Noah. The "ten generations" is a code alluding to the Tree of Life or Ten Sefirot, the Ten Luminous Emanations or dimensions that comprise all of reality. The Light of the Creator must flow through all of these ten dimensions on its way down to our world.

This is the reason that ten men are required for a prayer service, each soul connecting to one of the dimensions to ensure a full and utter revelation of the Light. These verses of Scripture establish our connection to the Ten Sefirot so that we may be attuned to all the dimensions, securing for ourselves and for the world at large a total manifestation of Divine energy and Light.

תְּשַׁע

Genesis 5:5 – We are told that Adam, his children, and his grandchildren lived for

בְּרָאָם וַיְבָרֶךְ עסמ"ב אֹתָם וַיִּקְרָא עם ה' אותיות = ב"פ קס"א אֶת־שְׁמָם אָדָם
מ"ה בְּיוֹם נגד, זן, מזבח הִבָּרְאָם: 3 וַיְחִי אָדָם מ"ה שְׁלֹשִׁים וּמְאַת שָׁנָה
וַיּוֹלֶד בִּדְמוּתוֹ כְּצַלְמוֹ וַיִּקְרָא עם ה' אותיות = ב"פ קס"א אֶת־שְׁמוֹ מהש ע"ה
שֵׁת: 4 וַיִּהְיוּ יְמֵי־אָדָם מ"ה אַחֲרֵי הוֹלִידוֹ אֶת־שֵׁת שְׁמֹנֶה מֵאֹת
שָׁנָה וַיּוֹלֶד בָּנִים וּבָנוֹת: 5 וַיִּהְיוּ כָּל יל"י ־יְמֵי אָדָם מ"ה אֲשֶׁר־חַי
תְּשַׁע מֵאוֹת שָׁנָה וּשְׁלֹשִׁים שָׁנָה וַיָּמֹת: [ס] 6 וַיְחִי־שֵׁת חָמֵשׁ
שָׁנִים וּמְאַת שָׁנָה וַיּוֹלֶד אֶת־אֱנוֹשׁ: 7 וַיְחִי־שֵׁת אַחֲרֵי הוֹלִידוֹ
אֶת־אֱנוֹשׁ שֶׁבַע אלהים דיודין - ע"ב שָׁנִים וּשְׁמֹנֶה מֵאוֹת שָׁנָה וַיּוֹלֶד
בָּנִים וּבָנוֹת: 8 וַיִּהְיוּ מלוי ס"ג כָּל יל"י ־יְמֵי־שֵׁת שְׁתֵּים עֶשְׂרֵה שָׁנָה
וּתְשַׁע מֵאוֹת שָׁנָה וַיָּמֹת: [ס] 9 וַיְחִי אֱנוֹשׁ תִּשְׁעִים שָׁנָה וַיּוֹלֶד
אֶת־קֵינָן: 10 וַיְחִי אֱנוֹשׁ אַחֲרֵי הוֹלִידוֹ אֶת־קֵינָן חֲמֵשׁ עֶשְׂרֵה
שָׁנָה וּשְׁמֹנֶה מֵאוֹת שָׁנָה וַיּוֹלֶד בָּנִים וּבָנוֹת: 11 וַיִּהְיוּ מלוי ס"ג כָּל
יל"י ־יְמֵי אֱנוֹשׁ חָמֵשׁ שָׁנִים וּתְשַׁע מֵאוֹת שָׁנָה וַיָּמֹת: [ס] 12 וַיְחִי
קֵינָן שִׁבְעִים שָׁנָה וַיּוֹלֶד אֶת־מַהֲלַלְאֵל: 13 וַיְחִי קֵינָן אַחֲרֵי
הוֹלִידוֹ אֶת־מַהֲלַלְאֵל אַרְבָּעִים שָׁנָה וּשְׁמֹנֶה מֵאוֹת שָׁנָה וַיּוֹלֶד
בָּנִים וּבָנוֹת: 14 וַיִּהְיוּ מלוי ס"ג כָּל יל"י ־יְמֵי קֵינָן עֶשֶׂר שָׁנִים וּתְשַׁע
מֵאוֹת שָׁנָה וַיָּמֹת: [ס] 15 וַיְחִי מַהֲלַלְאֵל חָמֵשׁ שָׁנִים וְשִׁשִּׁים
שָׁנָה וַיּוֹלֶד אֶת־יָרֶד: 16 וַיְחִי מַהֲלַלְאֵל אַחֲרֵי הוֹלִידוֹ אֶת־יֶרֶד
שְׁלֹשִׁים שָׁנָה וּשְׁמֹנֶה מֵאוֹת שָׁנָה וַיּוֹלֶד בָּנִים וּבָנוֹת: 17 וַיִּהְיוּ
מלוי ס"ג כָּל יל"י ־יְמֵי מַהֲלַלְאֵל חָמֵשׁ וְתִשְׁעִים שָׁנָה וּשְׁמֹנֶה מֵאוֹת
שָׁנָה וַיָּמֹת: [ס] 18 וַיְחִי־יֶרֶד שְׁתַּיִם וְשִׁשִּׁים שָׁנָה וּמְאַת שָׁנָה

---

many centuries, some as long as 900 years. This section of the Genesis story is designed to kindle the Light of life, longevity, and even immortality so that it radiates in our souls. The Angel of Death receives a fatal blow the moment we meditate with the purpose of sharing this Light with all of humanity.

18 When Jared had lived 162 years, he bore Enoch.

*19 And after he became the father of Enoch, Jared lived 800 years and had other sons
and daughters. 20 And the days that Jared lived were 962 years, and then he died.*

*21 When Enoch had lived 65 years, he bore Methuselah. 22 And after he became the
father of Methuselah, Enoch walked with God 300 years and had other sons and
daughters.*

*23 And the days that Enoch lived were 365 years. 24 Enoch walked with God; then he
was no more, because God took him away.*

SEVENTH READING - DAVID - MALCHUT

*25 And Methuselah lived 187 years, and he bore Lamech. 26 And after he became the
father of Lamech, Methuselah lived 782 years and had other sons and daughters.*

27 And the days Methuselah lived were 969 years, and then he died.

*28 When Lamech had lived 182 years, he had a son. 29 He named him Noah and said,
"He will comfort us in the labor and painful toil of our hands caused by the ground
the Lord has cursed." 30 After Noah was born, Lamech lived 595 years and had other
sons and daughters. 31 All the days Lamech lived were 777 years, and then he
died.*

וְאֵינֶנּוּ

Genesis 5:24 – The biblical Enoch was the first person in history to become an actual angel, even attaining the lofty position of king of all the angels. The sages tell us that angels are above the constraints of time and space, and thus are able to perceive the future consequences of all their deeds. For this reason, they never knowingly commit wrongful acts.

What we are really being told here is that, in truth, we all have the power to become like angels—to foresee the repercussions associated with our actions, to avoid mistakes and evade pitfalls, and to pave the way to experience true miracles. This power of elevated consciousness is bestowed upon us through the vocalization and vibration of the Aramaic letters making up this section of the Bible.

מְתוּשֶׁלַח

Genesis 5:25 – Enoch's son, Methuselah, lived longer than any person in the history of the world: 969 years. It will come as no surprise to learn that he was a truly righteous person who exemplified the concept of mind over matter. Put simply, Methuselah received the wisdom of Kabbalah from his father, and he used it to attain control over the physical world. This is evidenced by his long life and by the fact that the Great Deluge or Flood did not occur until seven days after his death.

Here the Bible's words grant us the power of mind over matter so that we can ignite the Light of healing along with its ultimate benefit: the immortality of mankind.

וַיּוֹלֶד אֶת־חֲנוֹךְ׃ 19 וַיְחִי־יֶרֶד אַחֲרֵי הוֹלִידוֹ אֶת־חֲנוֹךְ
שְׁמֹנֶה מֵאוֹת שָׁנָה וַיּוֹלֶד בָּנִים וּבָנוֹת׃ 20 וַיִּהְיוּ מלוי ס״ג כָּל־
ילי יְמֵי־יֶרֶד שְׁתַּיִם וְשִׁשִּׁים שָׁנָה וּתְשַׁע מֵאוֹת שָׁנָה וַיָּמֹת׃ [ס]
21 וַיְחִי חֲנוֹךְ חָמֵשׁ וְשִׁשִּׁים שָׁנָה וַיּוֹלֶד אֶת־מְתוּשָׁלַח׃
22 וַיִּתְהַלֵּךְ מיה חֲנוֹךְ אֶת־הָאֱלֹהִים ילה, מום אַחֲרֵי הוֹלִידוֹ אֶת־
מְתוּשֶׁלַח שְׁלֹשׁ מֵאוֹת שָׁנָה וַיּוֹלֶד בָּנִים וּבָנוֹת׃ 23 וַיְהִי כָּל־ ילי
יְמֵי חֲנוֹךְ חָמֵשׁ וְשִׁשִּׁים שָׁנָה וּשְׁלֹשׁ מֵאוֹת שָׁנָה׃
24 וַיִּתְהַלֵּךְ מיה חֲנוֹךְ אֶת־הָאֱלֹהִים ילה, מום וְאֵינֶנּוּ כִּי־לָקַח אֹתוֹ
אֱלֹהִים ילה, מום׃ [ס]

SEVENTH READING - DAVID - MALCHUT

25 וַיְחִי מְתוּשֶׁלַח שֶׁבַע אלהים דיודין + ע״ב וּשְׁמֹנִים שָׁנָה וּמְאַת
שָׁנָה וַיּוֹלֶד אֶת־לָמֶךְ׃ 26 וַיְחִי מְתוּשֶׁלַח אַחֲרֵי הוֹלִידוֹ
אֶת־לֶמֶךְ שְׁתַּיִם וּשְׁמוֹנִים שָׁנָה וּשְׁבַע מֵאוֹת שָׁנָה וַיּוֹלֶד בָּנִים
וּבָנוֹת׃ 27 וַיִּהְיוּ מלוי ס״ג כָּל ילי ־יְמֵי מְתוּשֶׁלַח תֵּשַׁע וְשִׁשִּׁים
שָׁנָה וּתְשַׁע מֵאוֹת שָׁנָה וַיָּמֹת׃ [ס] 28 וַיְחִי־לֶמֶךְ שְׁתַּיִם
וּשְׁמֹנִים שָׁנָה וּמְאַת שָׁנָה וַיּוֹלֶד בֵּן׃ 29 וַיִּקְרָא עם ה' אותיות = ב״פ קס״א
אֶת־שְׁמוֹ מהש ע״ה נֹחַ מוחי לֵאמֹר זֶה יְנַחֲמֵנוּ מִמַּעֲשֵׂנוּ
וּמֵעִצְּבוֹן יָדֵינוּ מִן־הָאֲדָמָה אֲשֶׁר אֵרְרָהּ יְהֺוָהאדניאהדונהי׃
30 וַיְחִי־לֶמֶךְ אַחֲרֵי הוֹלִידוֹ אֶת־נֹחַ מוחי חָמֵשׁ וְתִשְׁעִים
שָׁנָה וַחֲמֵשׁ מֵאֹת שָׁנָה וַיּוֹלֶד בָּנִים וּבָנוֹת׃ 31 וַיְהִי אל כָּל ילי ־
יְמֵי־לֶמֶךְ שֶׁבַע אלהים דיודין + ע״ב וְשִׁבְעִים שָׁנָה וּשְׁבַע מֵאוֹת
שָׁנָה וַיָּמֹת׃ [ס]

32 And Noah was 500 years old, and Noah became the father of Shem, Ham, and
Japheth.

6 1 And it came to pass, when men began to increase in number on the face of the
earth and daughters were born to them, 2 the sons of God saw that the daughters of
men were fair, and they took them for wives all of them they chose. 3 Then the Lord
said, "My Spirit will not always strive with man, for he is also flesh; yet his days shall
be a hundred and twenty years." 4 There were Nephilim (giants) on the earth in those
days—and also afterward—when the sons of God went to the daughters of men and
had children by them. They were the mighty men of old, men of renown.

MAFTIR

5 And God saw how great man's wickedness on the earth had become, and that every
inclination of the thoughts of his heart was only evil continually. 6 And the Lord
repented that He had made man on the earth, and His heart was filled with grief.

וַיְהִי־נֹחַ

Genesis 5:32 – In Genesis, we read about the passage of the generations from Adam to Noah, which actually alludes to mankind's gradual separation from the realm of Endless Light and our subsequent journey to this physical world.

The last three generations leading up to Noah connect us with the three lowest *Sefirot*, or spiritual dimensions, known as *Hod*, *Yesod*, and *Malchut*, the physical realm of existence. As we draw closer to the physical domain, spiritual work becomes more difficult.

According to Kabbalah, meditating high on a mountaintop is not the path or method for achieving spiritual greatness. Instead, such spiritual elevation is to be found in the turmoil of physical existence through our efforts at transforming chaos into order, pain into pleasure, and strife into serenity. Thus, we must welcome the obstacles of life, realizing that they contain the seeds of our spiritual glory and lasting joy. This is the underlying purpose of our descent from the higher spiritual dimensions into the lower material world, although it may seem to most of us as if this material world is the only dimension that exists.

וַיִּרְאוּ

Genesis 6:2 – It is commonly said that only human beings possess the free will to choose between negative and positive behavior. However, the Bible tells us that negative angels have been known to engage in illicit sexual relations with women of this world. This shows that the angels do have free will, even though according to biblical teachings, they are not supposed to eat, drink, or partake of any activity in this mundane level of existence. They are still, however, above the limitations of time and space because they are close to the Light of the Creator, which exists in a realm without time. Eternity does not mean a very long time; instead, it is something disconnected from time altogether. For this reason, angels can observe the "future" repercussions of their deeds, so they find it relatively easy to behave according to spiritual

32 וַֽיְהִי אל ־נֹחַ מוזי בֶּן־חֲמֵשׁ מֵאוֹת שָׁנָה וַיּוֹלֶד נֹחַ מוזי אֶת־שֵׁם
יהוה שדי אֶת־חָם וְאֶת־יָפֶת׃ 6 1 וַיְהִי אל כִּי־הֵחֵל להח הָאָדָם מ״ה לָרֹב
עַל־פְּנֵי חכמה - בינה הָאֲדָמָה וּבָנוֹת יֻלְּדוּ לָהֶם׃ 2 וַיִּרְאוּ בְנֵי־
הָאֱלֹהִים ילה, מום אֶת־בְּנוֹת הָאָדָם מ״ה כִּי טֹבֹת הֵנָּה וַיִּקְחוּ ווּעם לָהֶם
נָשִׁים מִכֹּל ילי אֲשֶׁר בָּחָרוּ׃ 3 וַיֹּאמֶר יְהֹוָה יאהדונהי לֹא־יָדוֹן רוּחִי
בָאָדָם מ״ה לְעֹלָם ריבוע ס״ג - י׳ אותיות בְּשַׁגַּם מהש הוּא בָשָׂר וְהָיוּ יָמָיו
מֵאָה מלוי ע״ב וְעֶשְׂרִים שָׁנָה׃ 4 הַנְּפִלִים הָיוּ בָאָרֶץ אלהים דאלפין בַּיָּמִים
הָהֵם נלך וְגַם יגל אַחֲרֵי־כֵן אֲשֶׁר יָבֹאוּ בְּנֵי הָאֱלֹהִים ילה, מום אֶל־
בְּנוֹת הָאָדָם מ״ה וְיָלְדוּ לָהֶם הֵמָּה הַגִּבֹּרִים אֲשֶׁר מֵעוֹלָם אַנְשֵׁי
הַשֵּׁם יהוה שדי׃ [פ]

MAFTIR

5 וַיַּרְא יְהֹוָה יאהדונהי כִּי רַבָּה רָעַת הָאָדָם מ״ה בָּאָרֶץ אלהים דאלפין
וְכָל ילי ־יֵצֶר מַחְשְׁבֹת לִבּוֹ רַק רַע כָּל ילי ־הַיּוֹם נגד, זן, מזבח׃ 6 וַיִּנָּחֶם
יְהֹוָה יאהדונהי כִּי־עָשָׂה אֶת־הָאָדָם מ״ה בָּאָרֶץ אלהים דאלפין וַיִּתְעַצֵּב

---

laws. This is a form of free will, but not on the same extraordinary level as our free will.

וַיַּרְא

Genesis 6:5 – In truth, God does not punish, destroy, or reward people. The sages tell us that man is by nature a reactive creature. We learn through imitation, and most of our actions are in response to the situations we face. Our unique purpose in this world is to nullify this reactive trait and transform ourselves into proactive, spiritual beings, able to rise above our own nature and in turn acquire control over Mother Nature. The root of our reactive impulses is the human ego. We must understand this truth and strive to eradicate egocentric qualities from our being. This is what constitutes spiritual work, and it is the purpose of our existence. Ignorance of this truth and failure to effect this transformation causes continued destruction, chaos, and turmoil in our lives and in the world.

The Light of these sacred words awakens us to the meaning of our existence, instilling a deep sense of personal responsibility for our selfish and intolerant ways. Moreover, awareness of these kabbalistic insights while reading this section cleanses negative characteristics from our inner nature, and in turn, this cleansing prevents acts of devastation from occurring in the world.

[7] And the Lord said, "I will destroy mankind, whom I have created, from the face of the earth—both man and beast, and creatures that creep along the ground, and birds of the air—for it repents Me that I have made them."

[8] But Noah found grace in the eyes of the Lord.

HAFTARAH OF BERESHEET

The Haftarah of Beresheet, taken from the Book of Isaiah, talks about the process of Creation and the awesome Light and beneficence of the Creator. Our free will dictates which type of life we will lead: We can choose one of peace, mercy, and prosperity, or we can choose one full of chaos, pain, and suffering. The energy we receive from this reading is the energy that came to Moses, and it is

Isaiah 42:5-21

42 [5]This is what God the Lord says—He who created the heavens and stretched them out, who spread out the Earth and all that comes out of it, who gives breath to its people, and life to those who walk on it:

[6] "I, the Lord, have called you in righteousness; I will take hold of your hand. I will keep you and will make you to be a covenant for the people and a light for the
nations, [7] to open eyes that are blind, to free captives from prison and to release from
the dungeon those who sit in darkness.

[8] I am the Lord; that is my name! I will not give my glory to another or my praise to idols.

[9] See, the former things have taken place, and new things I declare; before they spring into being I announce them to you."

[10] Sing to the Lord a new song, His praise from the ends of the Earth, you who go down to the sea, and all that is in it, you islands, and all who live in them.

[11] Let the desert and its towns raise their voices; let the settlements where Kedar lives rejoice. Let the people of Sela sing for joy; let them shout from the mountaintops.

אֶל־לִבּוֹ׃ 7 וַיֹּאמֶר יְהֹוָה יאהדונהי אֶמְחֶה אֶת־הָאָדָם מ״ה אֲשֶׁר־
בָּרָאתִי מֵעַל פְּנֵי חכמה - בינה הָאֲדָמָה מֵאָדָם מ״ה עַד־בְּהֵמָה
ב״ן, לכב עַד־רֶמֶשׂ וְעַד־עוֹף ציון, יוסף, ו״פ יהוה, ה״פ אל הַשָּׁמָיִם י״פ טל, י״פ כוזו כִּי
נִחַמְתִּי כִּי עֲשִׂיתִם׃ 8 וְנֹחַ מוזי מָצָא ריבוע מ״ה ע״ה חֵן מוזי בְּעֵינֵי ריבוע מ״ה
יְהֹוָה יאהדונהי׃ [פ] [פ] [פ]

HAFTARAH OF BERESHEET

of an extremely high level. This powerful Light can only come to us through the filter of a righteous person rather than in a concentrated form directly from the Source because we are not yet strong enough or pure enough to handle the intense quality of the Light of the Creator.

ישעיהו פרק 42

42 5 כֹּה־אָמַר הָאֵל לאה, אלד ע״ה | יְהֹוָה יאהדונהי בּוֹרֵא הַשָּׁמַיִם
י״פ טל, י״פ כוזו וְנוֹטֵיהֶם רֹקַע הָאָרֶץ אלהים דההין ע״ה וְצֶאֱצָאֶיהָ נֹתֵן
אבגיתץ, ושר, אהבת חנם נְשָׁמָה לָעָם עלם עָלֶיהָ פהל וְרוּחַ מלוי אלהים דיודין
לַהֹלְכִים מיה בָּהּ׃ 6 אֲנִי אני יְהֹוָה יאהדונהי קְרָאתִיךָ בְצֶדֶק וְאַחְזֵק
פהל בְּיָדֶךָ בוכו וְאֶצָּרְךָ וְאֶתֶּנְךָ לִבְרִית עָם לְאוֹר רז, אין-סוף גּוֹיִם׃
7 לִפְקֹחַ מ״ה - קמ״ג עֵינַיִם ריבוע מ״ה עִוְרוֹת לְהוֹצִיא מִמַּסְגֵּר אַסִּיר
מִבֵּית ב״פ ראה כֶּלֶא יֹשְׁבֵי חֹשֶׁךְ ש״ך ניצוצות של ז׳ מלכים׃ 8 אֲנִי אני
יְהֹוָה יאהדונהי הוּא שְׁמִי וּכְבוֹדִי לְאַחֵר לֹא־אֶתֵּן וּתְהִלָּתִי
לַפְּסִילִים׃ 9 הָרִאשֹׁנוֹת הִנֵּה מ״ה יה ־בָאוּ וַחֲדָשׁוֹת אֲנִי אני מַגִּיד
בְּטֶרֶם רמ״ח ע״ה תִּצְמַחְנָה אַשְׁמִיעַ אֶתְכֶם׃ [פ] 10 שִׁירוּ לַיהֹוָה יאהדונהי
שִׁיר חָדָשׁ י״ב הוויות תְּהִלָּתוֹ מִקְצֵה ג״פ אדני הָאָרֶץ אלהים דההין ע״ה יוֹרְדֵי
הַיָּם ילי וּמְלֹאוֹ אִיִּים וְיֹשְׁבֵיהֶם׃ 11 יִשְׂאוּ מִדְבָּר וְעָרָיו חֲצֵרִים

12 Let them give glory to the Lord and proclaim His praise in the islands.

*13 The Lord will march out like a mighty man, like a warrior He will stir up his zeal;
with a shout He will raise the battle cry and will triumph over His enemies.*

*14 "For a long time I have kept silent, I have been quiet and held Myself back. But
now, like a woman in childbirth, I cry out, I gasp and pant.*

*15 I will lay waste the mountains and hills and dry up all their vegetation; I will turn
rivers into islands and dry up the pools.*

*16 I will lead the blind by ways they have not known, along unfamiliar paths I will
guide them; I will turn the darkness into light before them and make the rough places
smooth. These are the things I will do; I will not forsake them.*

*17 But those who trust in idols, who say to images, 'You are our gods,' will be turned
back in utter shame.*

*18 Hear, you that are deaf; look, you that are blind, and see! 19 Who is blind but My
servant, and deaf like the messenger I send? Who is blind like the one committed to
Me, blind like the servant of the Lord?*

*20 You have seen many things, but have paid no attention; your ears are open, but
you hear nothing."*

*21 It pleased the Lord for the sake of His righteousness to make His law great and
glorious.*

תֵּשֵׁב קֵדָר יָרֹנּוּ יֹשְׁבֵי סֶלַע מֵרֹאשׁ ריבוע אלהים - אלהים דיודין ע"ה הָרִים
יִצְוָחוּ: 12 יָשִׂימוּ לַיהֹוָה יאהדונהי כָּבוֹד ל"ב וּתְהִלָּתוֹ בָּאִיִּים יַגִּידוּ
ייז: 13 יְהֹוָה יאהדונהי כַּגִּבּוֹר יֵצֵא כְּאִישׁ ע"ה קנ"א קס"א מִלְחָמוֹת יָעִיר
קִנְאָה ציון, יוסף, ו"פ יהוה, ה"פ אל יָרִיעַ אַף־יַצְרִיחַ עַל־אֹיְבָיו יִתְגַּבָּר: [ס]
14 הֶחֱשֵׁיתִי מֵעוֹלָם אַחֲרִישׁ אֶתְאַפָּק כַּיּוֹלֵדָה אֶפְעֶה אֶשֹּׁם
וְאֶשְׁאַף יָחַד: 15 אַחֲרִיב הָרִים וּגְבָעוֹת וְכָל ילי ־עֶשְׂבָּם אוֹבִישׁ
וְשַׂמְתִּי נְהָרוֹת לָאִיִּים וַאֲגַמִּים אוֹבִישׁ: 16 וְהוֹלַכְתִּי עִוְרִים
בְּדֶרֶךְ ב"פ יב"ק לֹא יָדָעוּ בִּנְתִיבוֹת לֹא־יָדְעוּ אַדְרִיכֵם אָשִׂים
מַחְשָׁךְ לִפְנֵיהֶם לָאוֹר רז, אין-סוף וּמַעֲקַשִּׁים לְמִישׁוֹר אֵלֶּה הַדְּבָרִים
ראה עֲשִׂיתִם וְלֹא עֲזַבְתִּים: 17 נָסֹגוּ אָחוֹר יֵבֹשׁוּ בֹשֶׁת הַבֹּטְחִים
בַּפָּסֶל הָאֹמְרִים לְמַסֵּכָה אַתֶּם אֱלֹהֵינוּ ילה: [פ] 18 הַחֵרְשִׁים שְׁמָעוּ
וְהַעִוְרִים הַבִּיטוּ לִרְאוֹת: 19 מִי ילי עִוֵּר כִּי אִם יוהך ־עַבְדִּי וְחֵרֵשׁ
כְּמַלְאָכִי אֶשְׁלָח מִי ילי עִוֵּר כִּמְשֻׁלָּם וְעִוֵּר כְּעֶבֶד יְהֹוָה יאהדונהי:
20 רָאוֹת (כתיב: ראית) רַבּוֹת וְלֹא תִשְׁמֹר פָּקוֹחַ מ"ה - קמ"ג אָזְנַיִם
יוד הי ואו הה וְלֹא יִשְׁמָע: 21 יְהֹוָה יאהדונהי חָפֵץ לְמַעַן צִדְקוֹ יַגְדִּיל
תּוֹרָה ר"ת צ"ת וְיַאְדִּיר ר"ת אבג"יתצ, ושר, אהבת חנם:

NOAH

THE LESSON OF NOAH
(Genesis 6:9–11:32)

The secret of the Flood

The Story of Noah concerns one of the most horrific episodes in the whole Bible. Only a thousand years after creating the world, the Creator brings a flood that destroys virtually the entire human race. What does this teach us? What does this tell us about the nature of God? What can we learn from the fact that a general cleansing was necessary, even though the world had been in existence for only a short time?

We first need to remind ourselves that negative forces are lying in wait for us from the moment we emerge from the womb. This is true not only for individual human beings, but also for humanity as a whole. It is said that when children are born, their hands are clenched like fists, as if to say, "I am coming only to take. Give me." But such an intention isn't limited to the very young. Most of the world is governed by a selfish *Desire to Receive*. Although there hasn't been another great flood since Noah's time, it is not because we have become such righteous people; in fact, the two Temples were destroyed as a result of pure mindless hatred of one person for another. The only reason that we have been spared another flood is because of the Creator's promise to us to never again destroy the world. Instead, we have the rainbow, which is the Creator's message that although the world may deserve destruction, God's mercy has given us yet another opportunity to become better human beings.

There is only one period of time in history when the rainbow did not appear, and that was while Rav Shimon bar Yochai was in the world. In other words, throughout all of time, from Creation until the transformation of the world—the Final Redemption—the only period that the world did not require to be cleansed was during the lifetime of Rav Shimon.

In the same way that Noah had the Ark to save him from death during the Great Flood, we now have the *Zohar* to save us from spiritual death every day of our lives. It is only through the *Zohar*'s spiritual power that we can be saved from any danger that threatens us, whether it is an environmental catastrophe, war, terrorism, disease, or epidemic. How the *Zohar* protects us is entirely up to us and the way we create our own personal connection with it. To maintain a strong personal link to the *Zohar*, we need to read and scan sections of it every single day. These readings can last from one minute to more than an hour. Scanning or reading the *Zohar* is the only way we can be saved from another "Flood"—whatever its form—in our time. The *Zohar* says:

> *Awareness and inner motivation to bring about the total removal of evil and chaos from this Earth is imbued to the reader through these passages. They awaken a desire to transform our own negative nature, and to share the Light of the Zohar. According to all kabbalists, the Zohar is the most effective of all instruments for removing the Evil Inclination born into the hearts of mankind. When a critical mass of people embraces its wisdom, we will permanently eradicate all of humanity's pain and suffering.*
>
> *– The Zohar, Noah 13, Introduction*

Rav Chiya said that the world was in a state of poverty from the time that Adam transgressed the command of the Holy One, blessed be He, until the time when Noah came forward and offered his sacrifice, thereby settling the world. Rav Yosi said that the world was not settled and the land was not pure from the pollution of the Serpent until Israel stood at Mount Sinai and held onto the Tree of Life. Only then did the world settle properly.

– The Zohar, Noah 13:88

The Bible tells us that Noah was a righteous man in his generation. What does this mean? According to one interpretation, there were so many wicked people during Noah's time that it is remarkable that a man of his righteousness could even exist in such an environment. Noah's connection with the Light of the Creator was so strong, however, that no evil person could sway him to the Other Side. Had he lived in the time of Abraham when there were larger numbers of righteous people, Noah would have been an even greater figure of righteousness.

There is, however, another way of seeing this, which takes the opposite position: Only in a generation of wicked people was Noah righteous. He was not fundamentally different from his fellow men, who were by all accounts a surly, ill-intentioned lot; he was just a little better, and so he was considered a righteous person within his very negative generation. Had he lived in the time of Abraham, on the other hand, he would probably have been just an average person, not especially virtuous at all.

We are told that Noah remained outside the Ark until he was about to drown; only when he had no alternative did he enter. Commentators have debated Noah's apparent lack of trust that the flood would actually come. But one important explanation from the Ohev Yisrael (Rav Avraham Yehoshua Heshel of Apta, also known as the Opta Rebbe) says that Noah was afraid to believe too strongly in the coming catastrophe because he knew that certainty has the power to make things happen. Certainty creates and draws reality. When Rashi wrote that Noah was of small trust, he meant that Noah trusted God but was afraid to have that complete certainty which would actually create the flood. So Noah didn't go into the Ark until he was forced to do so by the waters. He waited until the last second so that his own certainty would not be the cause of the flood.

The biblical passage concerning Noah's righteousness has been debated for centuries without any clear conclusion. The important thing is that we have to view people individually—as they are within the context of themselves—and not in relation to others. Are we righteous or are we not? Are we connected to the Light of the Creator or are we not?

Noah's story has many valuable lessons. On the subject of personal comfort, we learn that whoever looks for a merely comfortable life will never achieve it, yet those who challenge themselves will gain true joy and fulfillment both in this world and in the next. A commentary in a later section of the Bible, the Story of Vayeshev, best explains this. It says: "And Jacob sat." It means that Jacob wanted to live out his remaining years in comfort, to be able to study all day without interruption. Jacob had gone through so much anguish with his brother, Esau, and with his father-in-law, Laban, that he wanted a little comfort in his twilight years. Was this too much to ask? Why would Jacob's modest wish be considered a bad thing?

The answer, as King Solomon wrote, is that everything under the sky has a time, and the time for comfort is not while we are in this world. It is not to be found here, where we spend every waking moment locked in battle with the *Desire to Receive for the Self Alone*. Our lives are one long test. We can never say to ourselves, "I am comfortable. I do not have to fight any more." Instead, we must constantly strive not to let our consciousness falter because of these tests and any failures we may experience as a consequence. We ought to cleave fast to the notion that the only true comfort is in the Light we receive and in the fulfillment that we achieve as a result of facing our challenges and working through our difficulties. True comfort is not something we should go looking for outside of ourselves and our relationship with God.

If we believe that our tests in life are over and think: "I have reached the place I am supposed to reach. I have peaked. I have finished my *tikkun* (correction) of errors," we will most assuredly learn differently. In this world, thinking we have done enough is never a real option. As long as we are still in the physical realm, chances are that we have much more left to do.

Many people begin studying at The Kabbalah Centre but then suddenly stop, perhaps telling themselves, "I now know more than when I came here and maybe that's enough." But it is not enough. There are countless things we have to do to achieve our true goal, and someone who just looks for personal comfort and rest is losing the battle with his personal process of perfection, his *tikkun*. Transcending our innate laziness is one of the first items on any spiritual wishlist. Paradoxically, when we really strive to change and grow—not seeking out simply what's comfortable—the result of our effort is lasting fulfillment, happiness, health, financial support, success, and protection.

SYNOPSIS OF NOAH

Appreciation and the Covenant

The story of Noah follows directly after the story of Creation, yet already the negative actions of mankind had destroyed nearly all that was beautiful in the world God made. Because of our nature, humanity is seduced by immediate gratification of the ego, and thus we appreciate our spiritual treasures only when they are taken from us. In this story, we receive the ability to awaken a genuine appreciation for all the good things in our lives so that we do not have to lose them in order to cherish their value and importance.

Also significant is the Covenant between Noah and God. This Covenant relates to sexual misdeeds and the wanton spilling of a man's seed for selfish, indulgent pleasure rather than for sharing and for the creation of life.

By connecting with this section, we cleanse the world of sexual sins, destroying the negative forces and beings created through the wasting of a man's sperm. The *Zohar* says:

> *When a man and a woman desire each other and join as one, the sperm from the man produces a child in whom both of their images are combined, for God created the child in an image that included both parents. This is why a person should sanctify himself at the time of sexual intercourse so that this image may be as perfect as it should be!*
>
> *– The Zohar, Lech Lecha 31:329*

Thus, we imbue our own sexual relationships with divinity, abolish all of our selfish desires, and unleash the will of our souls, ultimately meriting for ourselves a place in the World to Come.

In kabbalistic terms, the World to Come is not something in the future; it refers to the spiritual realm of *Binah*. *Binah* is a boundless array of Light from which we draw the beneficence of the Creator. Iniquity and darkness cannot prevail in the presence of the Light of *Binah*, and our connection to *Binah* helps banish all negative forces, thus preventing their corruption and destruction of our world.

FIRST READING - ABRAHAM - CHESED

9 These are the generations of Noah. Noah was a righteous man, and perfect
in his generation, and Noah walked with God. 10 Noah had three sons:
Shem, Ham, and Japheth.

11 The earth was also corrupt before God and the earth was full of violence. 12 God
looked upon the earth and saw it was corrupt, for all flesh had corrupted their ways
upon the earth. 13 And God said to Noah, "The end of all flesh is come before Me for
the earth is filled with violence because of them. And behold I will destroy them with
the earth.

FROM THE RAV

The Torah says the Ark survived the Flood, but how could that be possible? Even if the Ark had been as large and secure as an ocean liner, it could not have survived a flood of such magnitude. To explain this, the kabbalists make a point of mentioning the number of verses we have in the Story of Noah: 153, making it one of the longest stories in the Bible. They further state that the numerical equivalent of the name Betzalel is also 153, and Betzalel was the individual who constructed the Holy Tabernacle in the wilderness.

With this in mind, was the Tabernacle holy because God said to build a place where He could dwell on Earth? The answer is no: God doesn't dwell in any specific place. The presence of God fills the entire universe, with or without the Tabernacle of the Temple. We should not understand the Tabernacle or the Temple as physical structures in which God will dwell. Rather, the Tabernacle, the Temple, and the Ark that Noah built are all physical manifestations that provided a way for mankind to connect to the non-physical Light of the Creator. Noah's Ark was a material object designed to provide a means of connection to the Light, despite the fact that the entire world was eliminated. In this way, the Ark brought safety to all those who were within it—not only through their physical preservation, but also by preserving their connection to the Light.

נֹחַ

Genesis 6:9 – In Aramaic, the name Noach (Noah) means "to be comfortable." We cannot make spiritual progress when we remain within our comfort zone, when we look for the easy way out, gratifying our ego instead of yielding to the longings of our souls.

In this verse, we receive the courage and determination to tread the spiritual path that is often uncomfortable but that inevitably leads us to enduring fulfillment.

The sages teach us that Noah had the regrettable distinction of having this flood, which destroyed the people of the world, named after him because he failed to feel the pain of his fellow beings who were destined to die in the rising waters. Although Noah knew intellectually that his prayers and tears would not alter the fate of humanity because there were so few righteous souls in his generation, nevertheless, if he had truly felt the pain of others and the pain of the world, he should have cried out in protest.

Spiritual growth entails feeling the pain of others. If we genuinely experienced the anguish of those around us, we could never inflict harm upon them. In the same way, if we really knew whom we were hurting when we harm others, we would never do it, for the harm we cause is only to ourselves. Connection to this verse opens our hearts to the suffering of humanity,

FIRST READING - ABRAHAM - CHESED

9 אֵלֶּה תּוֹלְדֹת נֹחַ מוזי נֹחַ מוזי אִישׁ ע״ה קנ״א קס״א צַדִּיק תָּמִים הָיָה
יהה בְּדֹרֹתָיו אֶת־הָאֱלֹהִים ילה, מום הִתְהַלֶּךְ מיה ־נֹחַ מוזי: 10 וַיּוֹלֶד נֹחַ
מוזי שְׁלֹשָׁה בָנִים אֶת־שֵׁם יהוה שדי אֶת־חָם וְאֶת־יָפֶת: 11 וַתִּשָּׁחֵת
הָאָרֶץ אלהים דההין ע״ה לִפְנֵי הָאֱלֹהִים ילה, מום וַתִּמָּלֵא הָאָרֶץ אלהים דההין ע״ה
חָמָס: 12 וַיַּרְא אֱלֹהִים ילה, מום אֶת־הָאָרֶץ אלהים דההין ע״ה וְהִנֵּה נִשְׁחָתָה
כִּי־הִשְׁחִית כָּל ילי ־בָּשָׂר אֶת־דַּרְכּוֹ עַל־הָאָרֶץ אלהים דההין ע״ה: [ס]
13 וַיֹּאמֶר אֱלֹהִים ילה, מום לְנֹחַ מוזי קֵץ מנק כָּל ילי ־בָּשָׂר בָּא לְפָנַי
כִּי־מָלְאָה הָאָרֶץ אלהים דההין ע״ה חָמָס מִפְּנֵיהֶם וְהִנְנִי מַשְׁחִיתָם אֶת־

---

whether nearby or far away, and enlightens us to the senselessness of hurting another human being.

בְּדֹרֹתָיו

Genesis 6:9 – Noah did not attain the same spiritual heights as Moses or Abraham because he dwelt in a generation of negative, corrupt people. The sages teach us that our environment is an integral factor in determining our level of spiritual growth. When we surround ourselves with negative people, we are eventually thrown off balance and we fall. Jealousy and speaking evil of others are among the many ways we defile our souls and the world. According to the sages, airborne diseases and other maladies are born from these negative relationships, formed from the very words we use to speak ill of others. For these reasons, if for no other, it is in our own interest to surround ourselves with spiritual people in a loving, positive environment.

Through meditation upon the name of Noah, we imbue our environment with Light and positive vibrations, helping to bring an end to airborne diseases and human suffering.

כִּי־הִשְׁחִית

Genesis 6:12 – Sexual immorality was a major source of negativity during Noah's time. In addition, the *Zohar* explains that this verse also pertains to the wicked people who forced different living creatures to mix and mate with other species, resulting in the alteration of the Divinely-sanctioned genetic code in each breed of creature and thus increasing the amount of chaos rather than order in the world.

Rav Chiya said, "For 300 years before the Great Flood, Noah warned them to change their ways, but they did not listen to him until the time when the Holy One, blessed be He, had finished waiting for them to repent. THIS IS AS WRITTEN: 'YET HIS DAYS SHALL BE 120 YEARS.' Then they were lost from the world. Come and behold. It is written: 'And it came to pass, when men began to multiply on the face of the Earth, and daughters were born to them.' (Genesis 6:1) And they went naked in front of all. And then, what is written? 'And the sons of Elohim saw the daughters of men.' (Genesis 6:2) This was the main cause THAT BROUGHT

[14] *Make your self an ark of gopher wood; make rooms in it and coat it with pitch inside and out.* [15] *And this is how you are to fashion it: The length of the ark shall be 300 cubits, the breadth of it 50 cubits, and the height of it 30 cubits.*

[16] *A roof you will make to the ark and in a cubit you will finish it above. And a door you will set in the side of the ark; with lower, middle, and upper decks you will make it.*

[17] *And behold I am going to bring a flood of waters upon the earth from under the heavens, to destroy all flesh wherein there is the breath of life, and every thing that is in the earth shall die.*

[18] *But I will establish My covenant with you, and you will enter the ark—you and your sons and your wife and your sons' wives with you.*

THEM to continue sinning until it finally caused them to be destroyed. And because of that they followed the Evil Inclination, held fast to its trunk and roots, rejected the Holy faith among themselves, and became defiled. So it is written: 'The end of all flesh has come before me,' (Genesis 6:13) to teach that they were enticed."

– The Zohar, Noah 11:74

Rav Yehuda asked, "Why did the Holy One, blessed be He, bring his Judgment on the world—NAMELY, THE GENERATION OF THE FLOOD—punishing them with water and not with fire or something else?" Rav Shimon replied that there is a secret behind this. As they corrupted their ways (sexually), the upper waters and the lower waters were unable to join as the male and the female ought. Anyone who corrupts his ways also corrupts the male and female waters. THIS MEANS THAT HE CAUSES A DEFECT IN THE MALE AND FEMALE WATERS, PREVENTING THEM FROM BEING CONNECTED WITH EACH OTHER. So they were punished by water, just as they had sinned.

– The Zohar, Noah 9:58

We find the same phenomenon occurring again in our times. Sexual indulgence is rampant, and we have lost any sense of the spiritual purpose behind the intimate relations between a husband and wife.

Furthermore, as medical science attempts to find solutions to disease, the practices of cloning, animal-to-human transplants, and genetic engineering are altering the essential make-up of both human and animal. According to the *Zohar*, the cure for all ailments is found in the spiritual domain, not through any physical intervention. Modern medicine can only treat symptoms, whereas a cure exists only through finding the actual cause of an illness.

Now, just as in the time of Noah's Flood, the planet's natural environment is fighting back against humanity's excesses—with water still the point where the battle lines are drawn. Pollution, bacteria and viruses, and toxic waste are destroying our drinking water, our air, our agricultural land, and our own immune systems. This section of Noah helps heal these afflictions on a spiritual seed level because the actions of a few righteous individuals can outweigh all the negative deeds of the wicked, no matter how numerous they are. Once more, we purify our souls as well as the entire planet, and a flood of Light, not a flood of water, engulfs us. These rays of Light are pleasurable to us as well as warm and cleansing for the soul. Yet to the truly wicked—the soulless beings who propagate only evil—these sparks of Light are the very fires of Hell.

Both pleasure and pain can purify, and thus the entire world is now prepared for its Final Redemption.

הָאָרֶץ אלהים דההין ע״ה: 14 עֲשֵׂה לְךָ תֵּבַת עֲצֵי־גֹפֶר קִנִּים תַּעֲשֶׂה
אֶת־הַתֵּבָה וְכָפַרְתָּ אֹתָהּ מִבַּיִת ב״פ ראה וּמִחוּץ בַּכֹּפֶר: 15 וְזֶה
אֲשֶׁר תַּעֲשֶׂה אֹתָהּ שְׁלֹשׁ מֵאוֹת אַמָּה דמב אֹרֶךְ הַתֵּבָה חֲמִשִּׁים
אַמָּה דמב רָחְבָּהּ וּשְׁלֹשִׁים אַמָּה דמב קוֹמָתָהּ: 16 צֹהַר אלהים דההין |
תַּעֲשֶׂה לַתֵּבָה וְאֶל־אַמָּה דמב תְּכַלֶּנָּה מִלְמַעְלָה וּפֶתַח הַתֵּבָה
בְּצִדָּהּ תָּשִׂים תַּחְתִּיִּם שְׁנִיִּם וּשְׁלִשִׁים תַּעֲשֶׂהָ: 17 וַאֲנִי אני, ב״פ אהיה + יהוה
הִנְנִי מֵבִיא אֶת־הַמַּבּוּל מַיִם עַל־הָאָרֶץ אלהים דההין ע״ה לְשַׁחֵת כָּל
ילי ־בָּשָׂר אֲשֶׁר־בּוֹ רוּחַ מלוי אלהים דיודין חַיִּים בינה ע״ה מִתַּחַת הַשָּׁמָיִם
י״פ טל, י״פ כוזו כֹּל ילי אֲשֶׁר־בָּאָרֶץ אלהים דאלפין יִגְוָע: 18 וַהֲקִמֹתִי אֶת־
בְּרִיתִי אִתָּךְ וּבָאתָ אֶל־הַתֵּבָה אַתָּה וּבָנֶיךָ וְאִשְׁתְּךָ וּנְשֵׁי־

עֲשֵׂה

Genesis 6:14 – According to Kabbalah, the story of Noah and the Ark is a code:

- Noah is a metaphor for the Upper World dimension (*Sefira*) known as *Yesod*, which is the source and fountainhead for all spiritual Light flowing into our lives.
- The Ark refers to a Lower World realm known as *Malchut*, which is our physical existence.
- The wicked men of Noah's generation represent the egocentric traits that taint our own souls; these comprise the dark side of human nature.

When the Upper and Lower Worlds are linked, an action metaphorically described as Noah entering the Ark, the Light flows into our world, bringing protection, untold joy, and serenity. When these two realms are disconnected, the Light is cut off, leaving our dimension floundering in a chaotic sea of darkness—the birthplace of destruction and suffering.

From the day the world was created, Noah was destined to be joined in union with and to enter the Ark. Until they were joined as one, the world had not reached a fully stable condition. As soon as this occurred, it is written: "From these was the whole Earth overspread." (Genesis 9:19) What is meant by "overspread"? These words are analagous to the verse: "And from thence the river parted," (Genesis 2:10) MEANING THAT SPREADING OUT IS SIMILAR TO THE SUPERNAL ARK, WHICH IS THE SECRET OF THE GARDEN. For from that point in the text onward, we find the separation and diffusion of progeny into all quarters of the world.

– The Zohar, Noah 1:11

Our own sins, which are born of our ego, cause a disconnection between the Upper and Lower Worlds. As we have seen, this is the root cause behind any disaster that befalls mankind. For in truth, God does not penalize, nor does the Creator decree judgments upon humanity. Our own actions either unite us with the source of all Light or else sever our connection to the Realms of Infinite Bliss. We have the free will to choose our own course of action, just as we have the intelligence to choose to look deeper into things through the lens of Kabbalah.

19 And of every living thing of flesh, you are to bring two into the ark to keep them alive with you; they will be male and female.

20 Of birds of every kind, of cattle of every kind, and of every creeping creature of the earth of its kind, two of every sort will come to you to be kept alive.

21 And take every kind of food that is to be eaten, gather it and store it away as food for you and for them."

22 Thus did Noah accordingly all that God had commanded him, so he did.

SECOND READING - ISAAC - GEVURAH

7 1 And the Lord then said to Noah, "Come into the ark, you and your house, because I have found you righteous before Me in this generation.

2 Take with you in sevens of every kind of clean animal, a male and its female, and in twos of every kind of unclean animal, a male and its female.

3 Of every kind of bird also take in sevens, male and the female, to keep their seed alive upon the face of the earth.

A serious study of this section, combined with a kabbalistic understanding of its codes and metaphors, helps to correct the errors of humanity throughout time by linking the Upper and Lower Worlds. Just as Noah entered the Ark, the Light now enters *Malchut* (our world) to amend our iniquities, perfect our souls, and forever protect us against judgment. In the same way that the wicked people of Noah's generation were destroyed by the Flood, our negative traits meet their destruction as a flood of Light cleanses us forever of narcissism and self-indulgence.

וּמִכָּל

Genesis 6:19 – The Creator saved every animal on Earth, which indicates God's design for the interconnectedness and holiness of all life-forms. When a species is lost from this world, the natural balance, complexity, and sanctity of the world is diminished because that creature's Light is gone forever. Our planet and all of its wonderful creatures are healed through our reading of this text.

וְאַתָּה

Genesis 6:21 – The Creator instructed Noah to gather enough food to feed all the people and all the animals in the Ark throughout the whole period of the flood. The lesson here concerns caring: When we care with all of our hearts and souls for others, miracles take place and the end results of our endeavors are always positive.

Reading this verse, we awaken genuine concern and care in our hearts for our fellow human beings, an action that in turn assures the healing of our land and the rehabilitation of our water, thereby enabling a plentiful supply of food for all of God's children in the future. The same holds true for spiritual nourishment, as endless Light

בניך אתך: 19 ומכל ילי החי מכל ילי בשר שנים מכל ילי
תביא אל־התבה להחית אתך זכר ונקבה יהיו אל: 20 מהעוף
ציון, יוסף, ו״פ יהוה, ה״פ אל למינהו ומן־הבהמה ב״ן, לכב למינה מכל ילי רמש
האדמה למינהו שנים מכל ילי יבאו אליך אני להחיות: 21 ואתה
קח־לך מכל ילי מאכל יהוה אדני אשר יאכל ואספת אליך אני
והיה יהוה, יהה לך ולהם לאכלה: 22 ויעש נח מוזי ככל ילי אשר צוה
פוי אתו אלהים ילה, מום כן עשה:

SECOND READING - ISAAC - GEVURAH

7 1 ויאמר יהוהאדניאהדונהי לנח מוזי בא־אתה וכל ילי ביתך ב״פ ראה
אל־התבה כי־אתך ראיתי צדיק לפני בדור הזה והו: 2 מכל
ילי | הבהמה ב״ן, לכב הטהורה י״פ אכא תקח־לך שבעה שבעה איש
ע״ה קנ״א קס״א ואשתו ומן־הבהמה ב״ן, לכב אשר לא טהרה י״פ אכא הוא
שנים איש ע״ה קנ״א קס״א ואשתו: 3 גם מעוף ציון, יוסף, ו״פ יהוה, ה״פ אל

---

now pours down upon us to nourish our souls forever.

ויאמר

Genesis 7:1 – The great Kabbalist Rav Shimon bar Yochai revealed that the Ark is a metaphor for the protection and well-being afforded by God to mankind during times of severe judgment. The sages have furthermore explained that during our own time, this Ark will once again appear in the world. According to Rav Shimon, this Ark is the holy *Zohar* itself.

> *"But the wise shall understand." (Daniel 12:10) These are the scholars of Kabbalah. It says about them: "...and they who are wise shall shine like the brightness of the firmaments" (ibid. 3). This refers to those who place their effort in the splendor called the Zohar, that is like Noah's Ark, to which are gathered two from a city, seven from a kingdom and, occasionally, one from a city and two from a family... This is the light of this book OF ZOHAR, and all is due to you.*
>
> *– The Zohar, Beha'alot'cha 16:88*

The response of Satan to such news is to try to prevent the broad dissemination of the sacred *Zohar*. The prime objective of Satan is to flood the world with reckless behavior and turmoil so that mankind drowns in a sea of chaos. The *Zohar*'s wisdom is our protection, our Ark. The *Zohar* safeguards us from harsh judgment—providing we possess a desire to change our ways.

4 Seven days from now, I will cause it to rain upon the earth for forty days and forty nights, and every living thing that I have made I will destroy from off the face of the earth." 5 And Noah did accordingly all that the Lord commanded him.

6 And Noah was six hundred years old when the flood of waters was upon the earth.

7 And Noah and his sons and his wife and his sons' wives entered the ark because of the waters of the flood.

8 Of clean beasts and unclean beasts, and of birds and of all creatures that creep upon the earth, 9 there went in two and two towards Noah and into the ark, the male and the female, as God had commanded Noah.

Unlike Noah, we must learn to cry out in pain for others who have not yet found the Ark or its connection to the Light. We must feel the anguish of the world, using all of our powers to share the *Zohar*'s wisdom with our fellow human beings.

Judgments are not usually such calamitous global events as the flooding of the Earth. Satan is far more subtle than that, and as a result, our rivers, lakes, and groundwater have become contaminated, destroying agricultural land and drinking water, and poisoning us with the toxins we ingest through the consumption of fruit, vegetables, and liquids.

The *Zohar*'s Light combines with this section of the Bible to protect us from these unseen dangers. Through reading the verses that speak of the Ark, we reverse the judgments that have been decreed upon the world and we purify the water on our planet, including that which comprises such a large percentage of the human body.

וְהַמַּבּוּל

Genesis 7:6 – Before the Flood, water possessed an intrinsic capacity to wash away both the physical dirt of the body and the spiritual negativity of the soul. Water was a natural healing agent. This was the main reason that people during the generations before Noah lived for hundreds of years. But the Flood brought about a dramatic change in the molecular and spiritual structure of water. Water lost some of the power to heal and nourish that it had possessed before the Deluge, so while H_2O is still the lifeblood of the planet, it can no longer fully regenerate both our cells and our souls.

This specific Bible reading can restore the water of our planet to its original, antediluvian state, infusing it with the Divine Force of healing and helping us to achieve the ultimate objective—eternal life. It is interesting to note that the molecular weight of water is 18, the same numerical value as the Aramaic word *chai*, which means "life."

בִּשְׁנַת

Genesis 7:11 – The Flood occurred during the astrological month of Scorpio, long known to be one of the most negative months of the year. Abraham the Patriarch, writing in his kabbalistic treatise called *the Book of Formation* (*Sefer Yetzirah*), named this month *Mar Cheshvan* (bitter Scorpio). The *Zohar* reveals, however, that we live in a reality of perfect balance. Hence, wherever we encounter the greatest preponderance of darkness, we will also find potential for the greatest amount of spiritual Light.

As we reflect upon these lessons, a tremendous amount of Light shines down upon us, illuminating the entire world and transforming the darkness in our world. On a personal level, each of us must look inward to identify his darkest traits, allowing this Divine Light to banish

הַשָּׁמַיִם י"פ טל, י"פ כוזו שִׁבְעָה שִׁבְעָה זָכָר וּנְקֵבָה לְחַיּוֹת זֶרַע עַל־
פְּנֵי חכמה - בינה כָל ילי ־הָאָרֶץ אלהים דההין ע"ה: 4 כִּי לְיָמִים נלך עוֹד
שִׁבְעָה אָנֹכִי איע מַמְטִיר עַל־הָאָרֶץ אלהים דההין ע"ה אַרְבָּעִים יוֹם
נגד, זן, מזבח וְאַרְבָּעִים לָיְלָה מלה וּמָחִיתִי אֶת־כָּל ילי ־הַיְקוּם קס"א
אֲשֶׁר עָשִׂיתִי מֵעַל עלם פְּנֵי חכמה - בינה הָאֲדָמָה: 5 וַיַּעַשׂ נֹחַ מוזי
כְּכֹל ילי אֲשֶׁר־צִוָּהוּ פוי יְהֹוָהאדניאהדונהי: 6 וְנֹחַ מוזי בֶּן־שֵׁשׁ מֵאוֹת
שָׁנָה וְהַמַּבּוּל הָיָה יהה מַיִם עַל־הָאָרֶץ אלהים דההין ע"ה: 7 וַיָּבֹא נֹחַ מוזי
וּבָנָיו וְאִשְׁתּוֹ וּנְשֵׁי־בָנָיו אִתּוֹ אֶל־הַתֵּבָה מִפְּנֵי מֵי ילי הַמַּבּוּל:
8 מִן־הַבְּהֵמָה ב"ן, לכב הַטְּהוֹרָה י"פ אכא וּמִן־הַבְּהֵמָה ב"ן, לכב אֲשֶׁר
אֵינֶנָּה טְהֹרָה י"פ אכא וּמִן־הָעוֹף ציון, יוסף, ו"פ יהוה, ה"פ אל וְכֹל ילי אֲשֶׁר־
רֹמֵשׂ עַל־הָאֲדָמָה: 9 שְׁנַיִם שְׁנַיִם בָּאוּ אֶל־נֹחַ מוזי אֶל־הַתֵּבָה
זָכָר וּנְקֵבָה כַּאֲשֶׁר צִוָּה פוי אֱלֹהִים ילה, מום אֶת־נֹחַ מוזי: 10 וַיְהִי אל
לְשִׁבְעַת הַיָּמִים נלך וּמֵי ילי הַמַּבּוּל הָיוּ עַל־הָאָרֶץ אלהים דההין ע"ה:
11 בִּשְׁנַת שֵׁשׁ־מֵאוֹת שָׁנָה לְחַיֵּי־נֹחַ מוזי בַּחֹדֶשׁ י"ב הוויות הַשֵּׁנִי
בְּשִׁבְעָה־עָשָׂר יוֹם נגד, זן, מזבח לַחֹדֶשׁ י"ב הוויות בַּיּוֹם נגד, זן, מזבח הַזֶּה והו
נִבְקְעוּ כָּל ילי ־מַעְיְנֹת תְּהוֹם י"פ מ"ה ע"ה רַבָּה וַאֲרֻבֹּת הַשָּׁמַיִם י"פ טל, י"פ כוזו
נִפְתָּחוּ: 12 וַיְהִי הַגֶּשֶׁם י"פ אל - ל"ב נתיבות החכמה ע"ה עַל־הָאָרֶץ אלהים דההין ע"ה

---

forever all negative and uncaring aspects from our being.

After that punishment, the world was able to exist and function correctly. Noah entered the Ark and brought into it all the species of living creatures of the world. So, of course, Noah was a tree that begot fruit, MEANING THAT HE WAS YESOD WHO IS CALLED RIGHTEOUS. And then all the species of the world emerged from the Ark just as it happened Above—MEANING JUST AS YESOD AND MALCHUT ABOVE. When the tree that begets fruit is joined with the Fruit Tree, then all the species of Above—big and small animals and all their varieties—come forward, each with other members of its species, as it is written: "both small and great beasts." (Psalms 104:25) So was the case with Noah and the Ark: They all emerged from the Ark, and the world exists just as it does above. This is why Noah is called the Man of the Earth and "a just man."

– The Zohar, Noah 11:72 -73

10 And it came to pass after seven days; the waters of the flood were upon the earth.

11 In the six-hundredth year of Noah's life, on the seventeenth day of the second month—on that day all the fountains (springs) of the great deep burst forth, and the floodgates of the heavens were opened.

12 And rain fell upon the earth forty days and forty nights.

13 On that same day Noah and Shem, and Ham and Japheth, the sons of Noah and Noah's wife and the three wives of his sons with them, entered the ark.

14 They and every beast according to its kind, all the cattle according to their kinds, every creature that creeps upon the ground according to its kind and every fowl according to its kind, every bird of every sort.

15 They went towards Noah into the ark, two and two of all flesh wherein there is the breath of life.

16 And they went in, male and female of all flesh, as God had commanded Noah; and the Lord shut him in.

THIRD READING - JACOB - TIFERET

17 And the flood was forty days upon the earth, and as the waters increased they lifted the ark high above the earth.

18 The waters prevailed and increased greatly upon the earth, and the ark floated upon the face of the waters.

19 And the waters prevailed exceedingly upon the earth, and all the high hills that were under the entire heaven were covered.

20 Fifteen cubits upward did the waters prevail; and the mountains were covered.

21 And all flesh that moved upon the earth died—birds, cattle, beasts, all the creatures
that creep over the earth, and every man, 22 all in whose nostrils was the breath of
life, all that was on dry land died.

23 Every living thing on the face of the earth was destroyed; both man and cattle, and the creeping things, and the birds of the heaven were wiped from the earth; only Noah remained alive, and those that were with him in the ark.

24 And the waters prevailed upon the earth for a hundred and fifty days.

אַרְבָּעִים יוֹם נגד, זן, מזבח וְאַרְבָּעִים לָיְלָה מלה: 13 בְּעֶצֶם הַיּוֹם
הַזֶּה והו בָּא נֹחַ מוזי וְשֵׁם יהוה שדי ־וְחָם וָיֶפֶת בְּנֵי־נֹחַ מוזי נגד, זן, מזבח
וְאֵשֶׁת נֹחַ מוזי וּשְׁלֹשֶׁת נְשֵׁי־בָנָיו אִתָּם אֶל־הַתֵּבָה: 14 הֵמָּה
וְכָל יל׳ ־הַחַיָּה לְמִינָהּ וְכָל יל׳ ־הַבְּהֵמָה ב״ן, לכב לְמִינָהּ וְכָל יל׳ ־הָרֶמֶשׂ
הָרֹמֵשׂ עַל־הָאָרֶץ אלהים דההין ע״ה לְמִינֵהוּ וְכָל יל׳ ־הָעוֹף ציון, יוסף, ו״פ יהוה, ה״פ אל
לְמִינֵהוּ כֹּל יל׳ צִפּוֹר כָּל יל׳ ־כָּנָף ע״ה קנ״א, אלהים + אדני: 15 וַיָּבֹאוּ
אֶל־נֹחַ מוזי אֶל־הַתֵּבָה שְׁנַיִם שְׁנַיִם מִכָּל יל׳ ־הַבָּשָׂר אֲשֶׁר־בּוֹ
רוּחַ מלוי אלהים דיודין חַיִּים בינה ע״ה: 16 וְהַבָּאִים זָכָר וּנְקֵבָה
מִכָּל יל׳ ־בָּשָׂר בָּאוּ כַּאֲשֶׁר צִוָּה פוי אֹתוֹ אֱלֹהִים ילה, מום וַיִּסְגֹּר
יְהֹוָ‍אדניאהדונהי בַּעֲדוֹ:

THIRD READING - JACOB - TIFERET

17 וַיְהִי הַמַּבּוּל אַרְבָּעִים יוֹם נגד, זן, מזבח עַל־הָאָרֶץ אלהים דההין ע״ה וַיִּרְבּוּ
הַמַּיִם וַיִּשְׂאוּ אֶת־הַתֵּבָה וַתָּרָם מֵעַל עלם הָאָרֶץ אלהים דההין ע״ה: 18 וַיִּגְבְּרוּ
הַמַּיִם וַיִּרְבּוּ מְאֹד מ״ה עַל־הָאָרֶץ אלהים דההין ע״ה וַתֵּלֶךְ הַתֵּבָה עַל־פְּנֵי
הַמָּיִם חכמה + בינה: 19 וְהַמַּיִם גָּבְרוּ מְאֹד מ״ה מְאֹד מ״ה עַל־הָאָרֶץ אלהים דההין ע״ה
וַיְכֻסּוּ כָּל יל׳ ־הֶהָרִים י׳ הויות הַגְּבֹהִים אֲשֶׁר־תַּחַת כָּל יל׳ ־הַשָּׁמָיִם
י״פ טל, י״פ כוזו: 20 חֲמֵשׁ עֶשְׂרֵה אַמָּה דמב מִלְמַעְלָה גָּבְרוּ הַמָּיִם וַיְכֻסּוּ
הֶהָרִים י׳ הויות: 21 וַיִּגְוַע כָּל יל׳ ־בָּשָׂר | הָרֹמֵשׂ עַל־הָאָרֶץ
אלהים דההין ע״ה בָּעוֹף ציון, יוסף, ו״פ יהוה, ה״פ אל וּבַבְּהֵמָה ב״ן, לכב וּבַחַיָּה וּבְכָל
לכב ־הַשֶּׁרֶץ הַשֹּׁרֵץ עַל־הָאָרֶץ אלהים דההין ע״ה וְכֹל יל׳ הָאָדָם מ״ה:
22 כֹּל יל׳ אֲשֶׁר נִשְׁמַת־רוּחַ מלוי אלהים דיודין חַיִּים בינה ע״ה בְּאַפָּיו מִכֹּל
יל׳ אֲשֶׁר בֶּחָרָבָה מֵתוּ: 23 וַיִּמַח אֶת־כָּל יל׳ ־הַיְקוּם קס״א | אֲשֶׁר |

*8 1 And God remembered Noah and every living thing, and all the cattle that were with
him in the ark, and God made a wind to pass over the earth, and the waters assuaged.
2 The fountains also of the deep and the windows of heaven were stopped, and the
rain from heaven was restrained.*

*3 And the waters receded steadily from off the earth. At the end of the hundred and
fifty days, the waters were abated. 4 And on the seventeenth day of the seventh
month, the ark came to rest on the mountains of Ararat. 5 And the waters decreased
continually until the tenth month, and on the first day of the tenth month the tops of
the mountains became visible. 6 And it came to pass at the end of forty days that
Noah opened the window he had made in the ark, 7 and he sent out a raven, which
went forth flying back and forth until the water had dried up from off the earth.*

*8 Then he sent out a dove to see if the water had dried up from the surface of the
earth.*

*9 But the dove could find no rest for the sole of her foot because there was water over
all the surface of the earth; so she returned to Noah in the ark. He reached out his
hand and took the dove and brought it back to him in the ark.*

10 And he stayed yet another seven days and again sent out the dove from the ark.

וַיִּזְכֹּר

Genesis 8:1 – The Great Flood ended in the month of Scorpio. Dates and periods in the Bible are never given arbitrarily. Every date represents a window of opportunity, an opening to the Upper Worlds through which a particular spiritual influence flows into our world. This explains the critical importance we attach to the dates in our lives. Planting seeds at the correct time is, after all, the way to grow the sweetest fruits. The negative angel, Satan, who appears in our world as our ego, constantly compels us through our own impatience to choose the wrong dates, thus either planting a seed too early or else procrastinating too long and altogether missing the time of planting and the resultant fruits.

These emotional urges of impatience are so strong within us that we must use every tool at our disposal to keep them under control. Beginning a marriage, launching a new business venture, or selecting a date to move into a new home are just a few of the activities that are substantially affected by the cosmic timetable. The Kabbalistic Calendar and the insights of the Bible tell us the appropriate periods for engaging in or refraining from various activities of daily life.

אֶת-חַלּוֹן

Genesis 8:6 – When the floodwaters subsided, Noah opened a window before he left the Ark. The message here is simple: When a man is attempting to free himself from difficult circumstances, he must first open a window in his soul, by creating an opening in his heart that has been blocked by his ego. Often, this entails a willingness to ask for help, either from another person or from the Light of the Creator, the criteria being whichever causes the most pain to our ego. The spiritual influences in this section help to diminish our ego in a merciful fashion, creating an opening within the soul of humanity itself. A global window is thereby opened to Heaven, allowing the Light of the Creator to radiate throughout existence, heralding our Final Redemption.

עַל־פְּנֵי חכמה - בינה הָאֲדָמָה מֵאָדָם מ"ה עַד־בְּהֵמָה ב"ן, לכב עַד־רֶמֶשׂ
וְעַד־עוֹף ציון, יוסף, ו"פ יהוה, ה"פ אל הַשָּׁמַיִם י"פ טל, י"פ כוזו וַיִּמָּחוּ מִן־הָאָרֶץ
אלהים דההין ע"ה וַיִּשָּׁאֶר אַךְ אהיה ־נֹחַ מהש וַאֲשֶׁר אִתּוֹ בַּתֵּבָה: 24 וַיִּגְבְּרוּ
הַמַּיִם עַל־הָאָרֶץ אלהים דההין ע"ה חֲמִשִּׁים וּמְאַת יוֹם נגד, זן, מזבח:
8 1 וַיִּזְכֹּר ע"ב - קס"א, יהי אור ע"ה אֱלֹהִים ילה, מום אֶת־נֹחַ מהש וְאֵת כָּל ילי ־הַחַיָּה
וְאֶת־כָּל ילי ־הַבְּהֵמָה ב"ן, לכב אֲשֶׁר אִתּוֹ בַּתֵּבָה וַיַּעֲבֵר אֱלֹהִים
ילה, מום רוּחַ מלוי אלהים דיודין עַל־הָאָרֶץ אלהים דההין ע"ה וַיָּשֹׁכּוּ הַמָּיִם:
2 וַיִּסָּכְרוּ מַעְיְנֹת תְּהוֹם י"פ מ"ה ע"ה וַאֲרֻבֹּת הַשָּׁמָיִם י"פ טל, י"פ כוזו וַיִּכָּלֵא
הַגֶּשֶׁם י"פ אל - ל"ב נתיבות החכמה ע"ה מִן־הַשָּׁמָיִם י"פ טל, י"פ כוזו: 3 וַיָּשֻׁבוּ הַמַּיִם
מֵעַל עלם הָאָרֶץ אלהים דההין ע"ה הָלוֹךְ וָשׁוֹב וַיַּחְסְרוּ הַמַּיִם מִקְצֵה
ג"פ אדני חֲמִשִּׁים וּמְאַת יוֹם נגד, זן, מזבח: 4 וַתָּנַח הַתֵּבָה בַּחֹדֶשׁ י"ב הוויות
הַשְּׁבִיעִי בְּשִׁבְעָה־עָשָׂר יוֹם נגד, זן, מזבח לַחֹדֶשׁ י"ב הוויות עַל הָרֵי
אֲרָרָט: 5 וְהַמַּיִם הָיוּ הָלוֹךְ וְחָסוֹר עַד הַחֹדֶשׁ י"ב הוויות הָעֲשִׂירִי
בָּעֲשִׂירִי בְּאֶחָד אהבה, דאגה לַחֹדֶשׁ י"ב הוויות נִרְאוּ רָאשֵׁי
ריבוע אלהים - אלהים דיודין ע"ה הֶהָרִים י' הוויות: 6 וַיְהִי מִקֵּץ מנק אַרְבָּעִים
יוֹם נגד, זן, מזבח וַיִּפְתַּח נֹחַ מהש אֶת־חַלּוֹן מנד הַתֵּבָה אֲשֶׁר עָשָׂה:
7 וַיְשַׁלַּח אֶת־הָעֹרֵב וַיֵּצֵא יָצוֹא וָשׁוֹב עַד־יְבֹשֶׁת הַמַּיִם מֵעַל עלם
הָאָרֶץ אלהים דההין ע"ה: 8 וַיְשַׁלַּח אֶת־הַיּוֹנָה יהוה מ"ה מֵאִתּוֹ לִרְאוֹת
הֲקַלּוּ הַמַּיִם מֵעַל עלם פְּנֵי חכמה - בינה הָאֲדָמָה: 9 וְלֹא־מָצְאָה הַיּוֹנָה
יהוה מ"ה מָנוֹחַ לְכַף־רַגְלָהּ וַתָּשָׁב אֵלָיו אֶל־הַתֵּבָה כִּי־מַיִם

The *Zohar* says:

> *"Open to me..." (Song of Songs 5:2) MEANS OPEN TO ME an opening as thin as a needle, and I shall open to you the Celestial Gates.*
> *– The Zohar, Emor 24:129*

וַיְשַׁלַּח

Genesis 8:7 – Noah sent forth a raven and a dove to see if it was safe to leave the Ark. The raven flew away and nested somewhere, but the dove returned with a leaf from an olive tree. The raven signifies our selfish nature and the dove is

*11 And the dove returned to him in the evening, and lo, there was a freshly plucked
olive leaf in its beak. So Noah knew that the waters had receded from off the earth.*

*12 And he waited yet another seven days and sent the dove out again, but this time it
did not return to him.*

*13 By the first day of the first month of Noah's six hundredth and first year, the waters
had dried up from off the face of the earth; and Noah removed the covering from the
ark and saw that the face of the ground was dry. 14 And in the second month, on the
twenty-seventh day of the month, the earth was completely dry.*

FOURTH READING - MOSES - NETZACH

*15 And God spoke to Noah saying, 16 "Go forth from the ark, you and your wife and
your sons and your son's wives with you;*

*17 Bring out every kind of living thing that is of all flesh that is with you—the birds, the
cattle, and all the creatures that creep along the ground—so that they may breed*

---

all about loyalty. From the dove, Noah got the sign he needed to know that the water had receded enough for all the creatures to disembark. This action speaks to the importance of looking for signs in our life, be they birds or other "messengers" that can provide us with guidance. To perceive these signs, however, we must be open to them and never disregard any event, no matter how small or insignificant it might appear to be. God uses every anomaly in our lives to get our attention so that we will hear the Divine message that has been sent to us.

One of the most significant signs we can all witness today through this revelation from the Bible and the *Zohar* is that by owning the concept that God sends us signs, we take part in helping to remove and put an end to all the world's chaos, pain, and suffering.

צֵא

Genesis 8:16 – Noah's emergence from the Ark symbolizes the necessity for us to abandon the comforts and trappings of our material, self-indulgent existence to embrace the spiritual work that we must accomplish in our lifetime.

Spirituality, according to Kabbalah, is not primarily about trekking up a mountain to commune with God and nature, or about meditating alongside a clear stream as birds sing of the world's beauty. This may make for a poetic scene, but it has little to do with the true purpose of our lives; neither does divorcing ourselves from the physical world, secluding ourselves away in a cabin to contemplate the majesty of nature or furthering our wholly intellectual pursuits. These retreats are not in themselves sufficient to achieve spiritual growth and transformation, though they may at times be a vital component of that achievement.

We have entered the world of chaos, hardship, turmoil, and labor so that we can confront and root out the triggers that ignite those primal reactions that force us to remain reactive beings. Each trigger gives us an opportunity to transform reactive behaviors, allowing us to further our goal and become the cause of our own fulfillment. Through transforming our inner nature, we create Heaven on Earth and become like God. There is an old proverb that says:

עַל־פְּנֵי חכמה - בינה כָל ילי -הָאָרֶץ אלהים דההין ע"ה וַיִּשְׁלַח יָדוֹ וַיִּקָּחֶהָ
חעם וַיָּבֵא אֹתָהּ אֵלָיו אֶל־הַתֵּבָה: 10 וַיָּחֶל עוֹד שִׁבְעַת יָמִים נלך
אֲחֵרִים וַיֹּסֶף ציון, קנאה, ר"פ יהוה, ה"פ אל שַׁלַּח אֶת־הַיּוֹנָה יהוה מ"ה מִן־
הַתֵּבָה: 11 וַתָּבֹא אֵלָיו הַיּוֹנָה יהוה מ"ה לְעֵת עֶרֶב רבוע אלהים רבוע יהוה
וְהִנֵּה עֲלֵה־זַיִת אלהים אל מצפ"ץ טָרָף רפ"ח ע"ה בְּפִיהָ וַיֵּדַע נֹחַ מחי כִּי־
קַלּוּ הַמַּיִם מֵעַל עלם הָאָרֶץ אלהים דההין ע"ה: 12 וַיִּיָּחֶל עוֹד שִׁבְעַת
יָמִים נלך אֲחֵרִים וַיְשַׁלַּח אֶת־הַיּוֹנָה יהוה מ"ה וְלֹא־יָסְפָה שׁוּב־אֵלָיו
עוֹד: 13 וַיְהִי אל בְּאַחַת וְשֵׁשׁ־מֵאוֹת שָׁנָה בָּרִאשׁוֹן בְּאֶחָד
אהבה, דאגה לַחֹדֶשׁ י"ב הוויות חָרְבוּ ר"ו, גבורה הַמַּיִם מֵעַל עלם הָאָרֶץ
אלהים דההין ע"ה וַיָּסַר נֹחַ מחי אֶת־מִכְסֵה הַתֵּבָה וַיַּרְא וְהִנֵּה חָרְבוּ
ר"ו, גבורה פְּנֵי חכמה - בינה הָאֲדָמָה: 14 וּבַחֹדֶשׁ י"ב הוויות הַשֵּׁנִי בְּשִׁבְעָה
וְעֶשְׂרִים יוֹם נגד, זן, מזבח לַחֹדֶשׁ י"ב הוויות יָבְשָׁה הָאָרֶץ אלהים דההין ע"ה: [ס]

FOURTH READING - MOSES - NETZACH

15 וַיְדַבֵּר ראה אֱלֹהִים ילה, מום אֶל־נֹחַ מחי לֵאמֹר: 16 צֵא מִן־הַתֵּבָה
אַתָּה וְאִשְׁתְּךָ וּבָנֶיךָ וּנְשֵׁי־בָנֶיךָ אִתָּךְ: 17 כָּל ילי -הַחַיָּה אֲשֶׁר־

"Smooth seas do not make skillful sailors." When Adam was expelled from the Garden of Eden, he stepped into the world where the hardships encountered would be necessary to transform his soul once again into a shining light. As each one of us is descended from this first family, we therefore have the same means of working towards our own self-fulfillment.

Our negative characteristics and traits can actually give us the opportunity to effect a true transformation of character. Our wonderful and endearing qualities serve no practical purpose when it comes to awakening new levels of fulfillment and Light in our lives, as they are already in a proactive state. Thus, it is our negative characteristics that should be welcomed as tools of enlightenment. We came into this world to create positive change within ourselves as well as in the world around us, and positive change will always encounter resistance, conflict, and obstacles during that process. We must embrace all of these difficult situations, for from them we learn to transcend them. Understanding this lesson will imbue us with the courage and fortitude to accomplish our personal spiritual mission, which is to achieve transformation.

abundantly on the earth and be fruitful and multiply on the earth." 18 *And Noah came*
out, together with his sons and his wife and his sons' wives, 19 *every beast, every*
creeping thing and every bird—everything that moves on the earth—came out of the
ark, one kind after another. 20 *And Noah built an altar to the Lord and took of every*
clean beast and every clean bird and offered burnt offerings on it. 21 *And the Lord*
smelled a sweet savor and the Lord said in his heart: "I will not again curse the ground
for man's sake, for the inclination of his heart is evil from his youth: never again will I
smite every living thing, as I have done. 22 *While the earth remains, seedtime and*
harvest, and cold and heat, summer and winter, and day and night shall not
cease."

9 1 *And God blessed Noah and his sons, saying to them, "Be fruitful and multiply and*
replenish the earth. 2 *And the fear and dread of you will fall upon every beast of the*
earth and every bird of the air, upon every creature that creeps along the ground, and
upon all the fish of the sea; they are given into your hands.

3 *Every moving thing that lives will be meat for you. Just as I gave you the green herbs,*
I now give you everything. 4 *But flesh with the life thereof, which is the blood thereof,*
you shall not eat. 5 *And surely your blood of your lives will I require, at the hand of*
every beast will I require it, and at the hand of man; at the hand of every man's
brother will I require the life of man.

6 *Whosoever sheds the blood of man, by man shall his blood be shed; for in the image*

Genesis 8:20 – Upon leaving the Ark with his family, Noah offered sacrifices to thank the Creator for delivering them from the floodwaters. According to the ancient kabbalists, the concept of sacrifice refers to the sacrificing of our own negative attributes. Offering thanks concerns the awakening of appreciation—not for the sake of the Creator, who has absolutely no need for thanks or appreciation, but for our own sake. Appreciation is an actual spiritual force, a quantity of energy that protects all we hold dear. Offering thanks is thus a tool for us to safeguard the joys and treasures that we already possess.

> *After the Great Flood, the metaphysical lines of communication between the Upper and Lower Worlds were destroyed, and the flow of Light into our world was cut off. In order to reestablish a link, Noah rebuilt the metaphysical cables that run throughout the worlds. This concept is the mystery behind the altar that Noah built.*
> *– The Zohar, Noah 3, Introduction.*

וַיְבָרֶךְ

Genesis 9:1 – God bestowed a blessing upon Noah and his sons by telling them to "be fruitful and multiply, and replenish the Earth."

Bearing children and teaching them spiritual values is the most potent way to bring Light into our own lives and to the entire planet. Each new soul that enters our world to walk the spiritual path is akin to another lighted candle in a darkened room. Each new light diminishes the darkness, eventually banishing it completely. Thus, the phrase "replenish the Earth" actually refers to the replenishment of the Light that was hidden at the time of Creation. As we receive blessings to help us bring children into the world, we can also meditate to share these

אִתְּךָ מִכָּל ילי ־בָּשָׂר בָּעוֹף ציון, יוסף, ו"פ יהוה, ה"פ אל וּבַבְּהֵמָה ב"ן, לכב
וּבְכָל לכב ־הָרֶמֶשׂ הָרֹמֵשׂ עַל־הָאָרֶץ אלהים דההין ע"ה הַיְצֵא (כתיב: הוצא)
אִתָּךְ וְשָׁרְצוּ בָאָרֶץ וּפָרוּ וְרָבוּ עַל־הָאָרֶץ אלהים דההין ע"ה׃ 18 וַיֵּצֵא־
נֹחַ מוזי וּבָנָיו וְאִשְׁתּוֹ וּנְשֵׁי־בָנָיו אִתּוֹ׃ 19 כָּל ילי ־הַחַיָּה כָּל ילי ־הָרֶמֶשׂ
וְכָל ילי ־הָעוֹף ציון, יוסף, ו"פ יהוה, ה"פ אל כֹּל ילי רוֹמֵשׂ עַל־הָאָרֶץ אלהים דההין ע"ה
לְמִשְׁפְּחֹתֵיהֶם יָצְאוּ מִן־הַתֵּבָה׃ 20 וַיִּבֶן נֹחַ מוזי מִזְבֵּחַ זן, נגד
לַיהֹוָה יאהדונהי וַיִּקַּח חעם מִכֹּל ילי ׀ הַבְּהֵמָה ב"ן, לכב הַטְּהֹרָה י"פ אכא
וּמִכֹּל ילי הָעוֹף ציון, יוסף, ו"פ יהוה, ה"פ אל הַטָּהֹר י"פ אכא וַיַּעַל עֹלֹת
בַּמִּזְבֵּחַ זן, נגד׃ 21 וַיָּרַח יְהֹוָה יאהדונהי אֶת־רֵיחַ אבגיתצ, ושר, אהבת חנם
הַנִּיחֹחַ וַיֹּאמֶר יְהֹוָה יאהדונהי אֶל־לִבּוֹ לֹא־אֹסִף לְקַלֵּל עוֹד אֶת־
הָאֲדָמָה בַּעֲבוּר הָאָדָם מ"ה כִּי יֵצֶר לֵב הָאָדָם מ"ה רַע מִנְּעֻרָיו
וְלֹא־אֹסִף עוֹד לְהַכּוֹת אֶת־כָּל ילי ־חַי חיים, בינה ע"ה כַּאֲשֶׁר עָשִׂיתִי׃
22 עֹד כָּל ילי ־יְמֵי הָאָרֶץ אלהים דההין ע"ה זֶרַע וְקָצִיר וְקֹר וָחֹם וְקַיִץ
וָחֹרֶף וְיוֹם נגד, זן, מזבח וָלַיְלָה מלה לֹא יִשְׁבֹּתוּ׃ 9 1 וַיְבָרֶךְ עסמ"ב
אֱלֹהִים ילה, מום אֶת־נֹחַ מוזי וְאֶת־בָּנָיו וַיֹּאמֶר לָהֶם פְּרוּ וּרְבוּ וּמִלְאוּ
אֶת־הָאָרֶץ אלהים דההין ע"ה׃ 2 וּמוֹרַאֲכֶם וְחִתְּכֶם יִהְיֶה ייי עַל כָּל
ילי, עמם ־חַיַּת הָאָרֶץ אלהים דההין ע"ה וְעַל כָּל ילי, עמם ־עוֹף ציון, יוסף, ו"פ יהוה, ה"פ אל
הַשָּׁמָיִם י"פ טל, י"פ כוזו בְּכֹל לכב אֲשֶׁר תִּרְמֹשׂ הָאֲדָמָה וּבְכָל לכב ־דְּגֵי
הַיָּם ילי בְּיֶדְכֶם נִתָּנוּ׃ 3 כָּל ילי ־רֶמֶשׂ אֲשֶׁר הוּא־חַי לָכֶם יִהְיֶה
ייי לְאָכְלָה כְּיֶרֶק עֵשֶׂב ע"ב שמות נָתַתִּי לָכֶם אֶת־כֹּל ילי׃
4 אַךְ אהיה ־בָּשָׂר בְּנַפְשׁוֹ דָמוֹ לֹא תֹאכֵלוּ׃ 5 וְאַךְ אהיה אֶת־דִּמְכֶם

---

blessings with others who are themselves seeking to create a family.

Besides our own children, those people with whom we share the wisdom of Kabbalah are also considered to be our children—our spiritual children. Thus, the concept of being fruitful and multiplying also refers to the ever-widening dissemination of this spiritual wisdom. God's blessing to Noah is bestowed upon us here and now so that we may become beacons of Light for all the people we encounter.

of God made He man. [7] And you be fruitful and multiply; bring forth abundantly in the earth and multiply upon it."

FIFTH READING - AARON - HOD

[8] And God spoke to Noah and to his sons with him saying: [9] "Behold, I establish My covenant with you and with your seed after you; [10] and with every living creature that is with you—the birds, the cattle, and all the wild beasts of the earth with you, from all that go out of the ark to every beast on earth.

[11] And I will establish My covenant with you: Never again will all flesh be cut off by the waters of a flood; never again will there be a flood to destroy the earth.

[12] And God said, "This is the sign of a covenant which I make between Me and you and every living creature that is with you, for perpetual generations: [13] I do set my bow in the cloud, and it will be a sign of a covenant between Me and the earth.

[14] And it shall come to pass when I bring a cloud over the earth, that the bow shall be

---

שֹׁפֵךְ

Genesis 9:6 – God warned Noah about the ramifications of bloodshed and murder. In a deeper sense, murder does not refer exclusively to cold-blooded killing. We commit murder when we publicly or privately disgrace or humiliate others, causing the blood to rush to their faces in embarrassment. The kabbalists tell us that we can either kill someone physically or kill them emotionally and spiritually. We can assassinate a person's body and we can also assassinate a person's character. We can destroy someone's relationships and we can also ruin their livelihood. Although we may perceive people to be strong, they are actually very fragile; thus we must be ever-conscious of the ways that we may be harming those around us.

As we read this passage and reflect on past incidents when we shamed another person or committed the sin of spiritual murder, we help to correct our iniquities and remove hatred from the collective heart of humanity.

אֶת־בְּרִיתִי

Genesis 9:9 – The Creator made a Covenant with mankind never to destroy the world again, no matter how great its iniquities. More important than the details of this Divine contract is the notion that we require the Light of the Creator in our lives if we are to truly achieve both personal and global transformation. Our ego (Satan) creates the intellectually driven illusion that we live in a Godless world and that we alone are the architects and masterminds of our good fortune. We must never cease to remind ourselves of how false and hollow this illusion always is, no matter how it pervades the mindset of our times.

וַהֲקִמֹתִי

Genesis 9:11 – After the floodwaters subsided, God promised Noah that the world would never be cursed with another flood. However, where water once healed the body and soul of man and

לְנַפְשֹׁתֵיכֶם אֶדְרֹשׁ מִיַּד כָּל ילי ־חַיָּה אֶדְרְשֶׁנּוּ וּמִיַּד הָאָדָם מ״ה
מִיַּד אִישׁ ע״ה קנ״א קס״א אָחִיו אֶדְרֹשׁ אֶת־נֶפֶשׁ רמ״ח - ז׳ הויות הָאָדָם מ״ה׃
6 שֹׁפֵךְ דַּם רבוע אהיה הָאָדָם מ״ה בָּאָדָם מ״ה דָּמוֹ יִשָּׁפֵךְ כִּי בְּצֶלֶם
ע״ה קס״א אֱלֹהִים ילה, מום עָשָׂה אֶת־הָאָדָם מ״ה׃ 7 וְאַתֶּם פְּרוּ וּרְבוּ
שִׁרְצוּ בָאָרֶץ אלהים דאלפין וּרְבוּ־בָהּ׃ [ס]

FIFTH READING - AARON - HOD

8 וַיֹּאמֶר אֱלֹהִים ילה, מום אֶל־נֹחַ מזוי וְאֶל־בָּנָיו אִתּוֹ לֵאמֹר׃ 9 וַאֲנִי
אני, ב״פ אהיה - יהוה הִנְנִי מֵקִים אֶת־בְּרִיתִי אִתְּכֶם וְאֶת־זַרְעֲכֶם
אַחֲרֵיכֶם׃ 10 וְאֵת כָּל ילי ־נֶפֶשׁ רמ״ח - ז׳ הויות הַחַיָּה אֲשֶׁר אִתְּכֶם
בָּעוֹף ציון, יוסף, ו״פ יהוה, ה״פ אל בַּבְּהֵמָה ב״ן, לכב וּבְכָל לכב ־חַיַּת הָאָרֶץ
אלהים דההין ע״ה אִתְּכֶם מִכֹּל ילי יֹצְאֵי הַתֵּבָה לְכֹל יה - אדני חַיַּת הָאָרֶץ
אלהים דההין ע״ה׃ 11 וַהֲקִמֹתִי אֶת־בְּרִיתִי אִתְּכֶם וְלֹא־יִכָּרֵת כָּל ילי ־בָּשָׂר
עוֹד מִמֵּי ילי הַמַּבּוּל וְלֹא־יִהְיֶה ייי עוֹד מַבּוּל לְשַׁחֵת הָאָרֶץ
אלהים דההין ע״ה׃ 12 וַיֹּאמֶר אֱלֹהִים ילה, מום זֹאת אוֹת־הַבְּרִית אֲשֶׁר־
אֲנִי אני נֹתֵן אבגיתץ, ושר, אהבת חנם בֵּינִי וּבֵינֵיכֶם וּבֵין כָּל ילי ־נֶפֶשׁ רמ״ח - ז׳ הויות
חַיָּה אֲשֶׁר אִתְּכֶם לְדֹרֹת עוֹלָם׃ 13 אֶת־קַשְׁתִּי נָתַתִּי בֶּעָנָן

---

ensured long life, the water of our planet after the Flood lost its intrinsic Divine power.

Our spiritual work, in part, entails restoring the water of both our planet and the water of our physical bodies to its primal state, and reflecting upon these verses accomplishes this very thing. Each pair of eyes that reads this section and each set of ears that listens to a reading initiates the rehabilitation of Earth's waters so that they may once again possess the power to heal, rejuvenate, and regenerate the cells of the body and the souls of human beings.

אֶת־קַשְׁתִּי

Genesis 9:13 – The rainbow is a code referring to the seven *Sefirot*, or Supernal Dimensions, that directly influence our physical dimension.

seen in the cloud; 15 and I will remember My covenant which is between Me and you and every living creature of all flesh, and the waters shall no more become a flood to destroy all flesh. 16 And the bow shall be in the cloud; and I will look upon it and remember the everlasting covenant between God and every living creature of all flesh that is upon the earth." 17 And God said to Noah, "This is the sign of the covenant I have established between Me and all flesh that is upon the earth."

SIXTH READING - JOSEPH - YESOD

18 And the sons of Noah that went out of the ark were Shem, and Ham, and Japheth; and Ham is the father of Canaan. 19 These were the three sons of Noah, and from them the whole world was overspread. 20 And Noah began to be a husbandman and planted a vineyard. 21 And he drank of the wine, and became drunk and he was uncovered inside his tent.

The Tree of Life (the *Ten Sefirot*) is structured as follows:

The upper three realms (*Keter*, *Chochmah*, and *Binah*) are closest to the Light of the Creator and do not exert any direct influence over our world. The lower seven (*Chesed*, *Gevurah*, *Tiferet*, *Netzach*, *Hod*, *Yesod*, and *Malchut*), however, have a direct impact upon our lives. For this reason, there are seven colors in a rainbow, seven chakras (energy centers from the base of the spine to the crown of the head), seven musical notes in a scale, seven major continents, seven seas, seven days in the week, and so on.

Just as a single band of white sunlight contains all seven colors of the rainbow, the Light of the Creator that we receive in this world contains the full seven *Sefirot*. In other words, our world represents the refraction of this single shaft of Light into all the variety—the "colors"—that comprise Creation.

> *"And Elohim said to Noah... 'This is the sign of the Covenant which I make between me and you... I have set My rainbow in the cloud.'" (Genesis 9:8, 12–13) The Zohar explains that the rainbow is a sign indicating that a great destruction was forthcoming, but it has been prevented by the hand of God. Reading this section infuses us with the same Light of protection expressed by the sign of the rainbow.*
>
> *– The Zohar, Noah 34:261*

The rainbow spoken of in this section now connects us with the full measure of Divine Light so that we may use it to restore the waters to their pre-Flood composition, thereby empowering the water of our planet to heal and to restore immortality in all of humanity.

וַיֵּשְׁתְּ

Genesis 9:21 – The intoxication of Noah is a notoriously difficult section of the Bible and cannot be read without kabbalistic explanation if it is to yield any meaning for us at all. The *Zohar* explains that both Noah and Adam sinned under the influence of wine. Kabbalah teaches that wine is a powerful tool—an antenna for drawing in Light—just as the grape is a potent conduit of spiritual energy. Wine is therefore used in blessings as a tool to draw God's Light into our physical world. When, in the absence of a blessing, we do not prepare a large enough

וְהָיְתָה לְאוֹת בְּרִית בֵּינִי וּבֵין הָאָרֶץ אלהים דההין ע"ה׃ 14 וְהָיָה יהוה, יהה
בְּעַנְנִי עָנָן עַל־הָאָרֶץ אלהים דההין ע"ה וְנִרְאֲתָה הַקֶּשֶׁת בֶּעָנָן׃
15 וְזָכַרְתִּי אֶת־בְּרִיתִי אֲשֶׁר בֵּינִי וּבֵינֵיכֶם וּבֵין כָּל ילי ־נֶפֶשׁ
רמ"ח - ז' הויות חַיָּה בְּכָל לכב ־בָּשָׂר וְלֹא־יִהְיֶה ייי עוֹד הַמַּיִם לְמַבּוּל
לְשַׁחֵת כָּל ילי ־בָּשָׂר׃ 16 וְהָיְתָה הַקֶּשֶׁת בֶּעָנָן וּרְאִיתִיהָ לִזְכֹּר
ע"ב - קס"א, יהי אור ע"ה בְּרִית עוֹלָם בֵּין אֱלֹהִים ילה, מום וּבֵין כָּל ילי ־נֶפֶשׁ
רמ"ח - ז' הויות חַיָּה בְּכָל לכב ־בָּשָׂר אֲשֶׁר עַל־הָאָרֶץ אלהים דההין ע"ה׃
17 וַיֹּאמֶר אֱלֹהִים ילה, מום אֶל־נֹחַ מזוי זֹאת אוֹת־הַבְּרִית אֲשֶׁר
הֲקִמֹתִי בֵּינִי וּבֵין כָּל ילי ־בָּשָׂר אֲשֶׁר עַל־הָאָרֶץ אלהים דההין ע"ה׃ [פ]

SIXTH READING - JOSEPH - YESOD

18 וַיִּהְיוּ בְנֵי־נֹחַ מזוי הַיֹּצְאִים מִן־הַתֵּבָה שֵׁם יהוה שדי וְחָם וָיָפֶת
וְחָם הוּא אֲבִי כְנָעַן׃ 19 שְׁלֹשָׁה אֵלֶּה בְּנֵי־נֹחַ מזוי וּמֵאֵלֶּה נָפְצָה
כָל ילי ־הָאָרֶץ אלהים דההין ע"ה׃ 20 וַיָּחֶל נֹחַ מזוי אִישׁ ע"ה קנ"א קס"א הָאֲדָמָה
וַיִּטַּע כָּרֶם י' הויות׃ 21 וַיֵּשְׁתְּ מִן־הַיַּיִן מיכ, י"פ האא וַיִּשְׁכָּר וַיִּתְגַּל בְּתוֹךְ

Vessel to hold this energy, or if we consume wine for reasons not related to spirituality, the ensuing torrent of Light causes an uncontrollable arousal of the dark side of our nature. This is the mystery behind wine's ability to induce intoxication with its concomitant vagaries of behavior from joy to raging despair. And yet how, you may ask, did the most spiritual person on the planet during his time—Noah—suddenly fall into a state of drunkenness?

After experiencing the worst of trying times—watching the world drowned and destroyed around him—Noah believed that his spiritual work was finally over; he thought the pain had ended and the suffering had subsided for good. However, experiencing hardship without an understanding of its root causes can turn into needless suffering if the lesson is not acknowledged by the sufferer. In such cases, pain will not purify, suffering will not sanctify, and catastrophe will not cleanse.

We learn from this section that we must probe deeply to identify the cause behind our afflictions. To put an end to our own pain, we need to become accountable for our own actions and their consequences; we need to let go of our victim mindset. Moreover, we should delve deeply within ourselves to uproot those flaws in our own past behavior that have brought about our current misfortunes. The embracing of these very insights is the first step in understanding that we alone are responsible for our own and

[22] *And Ham, the father of Canaan, saw his father's nakedness and told his two brothers outside.* [23] *And Shem and Japheth took a garment and laid it across their shoulders; then they walked in backward and covered their father's nakedness; and their faces were turned away, and they did not see their father's nakedness.*

[24] *And Noah awoke from his wine and knew what his youngest son had done to him,*
[25] *and he said, "Cursed be Canaan; a servant of servants shall he be to his brothers."*

---

the world's afflictions. Through this understanding, we correct the sins of the past generations so that all the suffering throughout history acquires a spiritual value and has a purifying effect on the world.

The *Zohar* offers us a still deeper understanding of Noah's drunkenness. Noah received the wisdom of Kabbalah from God and used it to build the Ark to protect the creatures of the world. His entering into the Ark is thus a symbol for our world connecting to the Upper Realm known as *Yesod*, the source of all our Light and Divine energy.

After the waters subsided, Noah used Kabbalah to ascend into even higher spiritual realms in an attempt to examine the Sin of Adam and Eve. He did this for two reasons: He wanted to avoid repeating that sin himself, and he wanted to determine how to make reparations for it in the world.

> *Noah had come to reexamine Adam's sin so that he could refrain from repeating it and could make reparations in the world. But he was unable to do this because, after squeezing the grapes so that he could examine them, he got drunk, was uncovered, and had no strength to get up. "This is why THE VERSE SAYS, "... and was uncovered," MEANING THAT he "uncovered" a Gap in the World, which had been covered until that time.*
> *– The Zohar, Noah 38:308*

This higher spiritual realm that Noah entered is the inner meaning of both the fermented grapes that caused him to become drunk and the vineyard they were taken from.

• The vineyard is a metaphor for a higher spiritual dimension.

• The grapes pertain to the intoxicating energy that swirls in that supernal realm.

The spiritual energy radiating in this higher dimension was far too potent for Noah to handle. He had not yet purged all his own negative desires, so his connection to this higher realm was premature and the energy proved to be dangerous.

The effect is similar to what happens when a person ingests a potent narcotic, such as crack cocaine, intending it as a one-time-only experiment. The energy, however, is too intense and overwhelming, causing an immediate addiction due to the body's vulnerability to the drug. The lesson that emerges from this insight concerns our own good intentions and can best be expressed by the old adage: "The road to Hell is paved with good intentions."

We repeatedly and with the best intentions seek out enjoyment from life, but the pleasure we receive in the process often awakens selfish desires. This occurs because there is an aspect of the human ego that partakes of the joys we earn. This gratification strengthens the dark side of our nature, which in turn tightens its hold over us. We become intoxicated, drunk with self-indulgence, addicted ultimately to the incessant cravings of our ego. Pleasure has become poison.

We need to strive to learn how best to receive pleasure and fulfillment solely for the purpose of sharing it with others. We have to be watchful so that no trace of selfishness exists within us when we set and achieve our goals in life. The erasure of selfishness is a lifelong task and the basis of all spiritual work. This section of the Bible thus effectively detoxifies us, making us spiritually sober, so we can connect safely to the highest levels of spiritual Light for the purpose of sharing

אָהֳלֹה׃ 22 וַיַּרְא חָם אֲבִי כְנַעַן אֵת עֶרְוַת אָבִיו וַיַּגֵּד לִשְׁנֵי־
אֶחָיו בַּחוּץ׃ 23 וַיִּקַּח חעם שֵׁם יהוה שדי וָיֶפֶת אֶת־הַשִּׂמְלָה וַיָּשִׂימוּ
עַל־שְׁכֶם שְׁנֵיהֶם וַיֵּלְכוּ כלי אֲחֹרַנִּית וַיְכַסּוּ אֵת עֶרְוַת אֲבִיהֶם
וּפְנֵיהֶם אֲחֹרַנִּית וְעֶרְוַת אֲבִיהֶם לֹא רָאוּ׃ 24 וַיִּיקֶץ נֹחַ מחי

---

that Light with others. This immediately inaugurates the Age of Messiah, ushering in the Final Redemption of all humanity.

עֶרְוַת

Genesis 9:22 – While the Bible does not say this explicitly, Kabbalah tells us that Noah's son, Ham, raped his father while Noah was intoxicated. The lesson of this difficult section concerns the power of Satan. If there is even the slightest opening in our lives—which is signified here by Noah's drunken state, but which could equally be our ego out of control—we become vulnerable to whatever negative forces are lurking around us.

Even our closest friends and family members can be the cause of our misfortune if we allow even the smallest conflicts or problems to fester or inflame our ego. We must make every effort to block all openings where negativity can enter into our relationships, and we must completely shut down our own inclination for evil, thereby placing all our relationships upon a spiritual foundation.

On a deeper level of understanding, the rape of Noah is connected with the sexual relations that took place between Adam and the negative angel (we do not pronounce this name) L-i-l-i-t, and between Eve and the negative angel (we do not pronounce this name) S-a-m-a-e-l. In other words, Adam and Eve listened to and followed the instructions of the Serpent to eat from the Tree of Knowledge of Good and Evil. This is equivalent to us listening to our own egos telling us to eat the fruit of overindulgence.

The sexual connection between Adam and Eve and the Serpent can also be understood as the Vessel, or the collective souls of humanity, prematurely connecting to a higher level of energy before the Vessel's selfish reactive consciousness had been fully purged of its negative nature.

This relates to the power of patience, of waiting, of restricting our need to have it all now. We require the patience to subdue our self-absorbed desires before we can have the slightest chance of experiencing any form of joy. When we set out to procure physical or spiritual pleasure for selfish reasons, without any regard toward the other people in our life, we have effectively been seduced and raped by our own ego, the negative force called Satan.

> *...And we have learned that Ham, father of Canaan, was given a place to rule. And he castrated NOAH, thereby removing the secret of the Covenant, which had made him a righteous man. As we have learned that he removed the Covenant (the male organ) from him, MEANING THAT HE REMOVED THE MOCHIN OF BEGETTING, WHICH IS GIVEN ONLY BY THE POWER OF THE HOLY COVENANT. THIS REMOVAL IS CONSIDERED CASTRATION.*
>
> *– The Zohar, Noah 38:310*

The rape of Noah is thus akin to the Serpent, our ego, raping our own souls. The illuminating verses that contain this story kindle a Light that seals up any openings through which negative influences can attempt to seduce and violate us, thus eliminating the covetousness in our nature. The negative angels mentioned previously (whose names we do not pronounce) are thus banished from our existence, and ancient wounds are healed as we achieve a renewed state of purity.

26 And he said, "Blessed be the Lord, the God of Shem; and Canaan shall be his servant. 27 God shall enlarge Japheth; and he shall live in the tents of Shem, and Canaan shall be his servant." 28 And Noah lived 350 years after the flood. 29 All the days of Noah were 950 years, and he died.

10 1 Now these are the generations of the sons of Noah: Shem, Ham, and Japheth, who themselves had sons after the flood. 2 The sons of Japheth: Gomer, and Magog, and Madai, and Javan, and Tubal, and Meshech, and Tiras. 3 And the sons of Gomer: Ashkenaz, and Riphath, and Togarmah. 4 And the sons of Javan: Elishah, and Tarshish, the Kitites, and the Rodanites, 5 by these were the Gentiles spread out into their lands, each with their own language, by their families within their nations.

6 And the sons of Ham: Cush, Mizra'im, and Put, and Canaan. 7 And the sons of Cush: Seba, Havilah, and Sabtah, and Ra'amah and Sabteca, and the sons of Ra'amah: Sheba and Dedan. 8 And Cush was the father of Nimrod, who grew to be a mighty one on the earth. 9 He was a mighty hunter before the Lord; wherefore it is said, "Even as Nimrod, the mighty hunter before the Lord."

10 And the beginning of his kingdom was Babylon, and Erech, and Akkad, and Calneh, in the land of Shinar, 11 Out of that land went forth Asshur, who built Nineveh, and the city Rehoboth, and Calah, 12 and Resen, which is between Nineveh and Calah; that is the great city.

וְאֵלֶּה

Genesis 10:1 – Tremendous population growth occurred during the generations of the sons of Noah. As the population expanded, separation and division took place between individuals, nations, and portions of the land.

This section conceals a lesson about the perils of disunity, which is the root cause of all chaos, whether it manifests itself as poor health, difficult relationships, ruined finances, or global turmoil. It is about the seed and birth of disunity, which in turn has created disunity in the cells of our body, among family members, in our communities, and in our world.

Connecting with this reading helps banish the barriers that have created separation and conflict among people throughout history. A great Light of unity shines down upon us, healing and uniting our disparate elements into one true global village. This healing extends down into the very cells of our body, bringing about health and well-being everywhere.

וּבְנֵי חָם

Genesis 10:6 – The majority of the world's population, including the people of Egypt and China, is descended from the sons of Ham. The interconnectedness of all humanity is highly relevant to us. As we meditate to infuse all the nations of the world with Light, we crush the seeds of intolerance and propagate lasting peace throughout all of existence, instantly fulfilling the injunction to "love your neighbor as yourself."

מִיֵּינוֹ וַיֵּדַע אֵת אֲשֶׁר־עָשָׂה לוֹ בְּנוֹ הַקָּטָן: 25 וַיֹּאמֶר אָרוּר
כְּנָעַן עֶבֶד עֲבָדִים יִהְיֶה ייי לְאֶחָיו: 26 וַיֹּאמֶר בָּרוּךְ יהוה ע"ב רבוע מ"ה
יְהוָהאדנייאהדונהי אֱלֹהֵי דמב, ילה שֵׁם יהוה שדי וִיהִי כְנַעַן עֶבֶד לָמוֹ:
27 יַפְתְּ אֱלֹהִים ילה, מום לְיֶפֶת וְיִשְׁכֹּן בְּאָהֳלֵי־שֵׁם יהוה שדי וִיהִי אל
כְנַעַן עֶבֶד לָמוֹ: 28 וַיְחִי־נֹחַ מחי אַחַר הַמַּבּוּל שְׁלֹשׁ מֵאוֹת שָׁנָה
וַחֲמִשִּׁים שָׁנָה: 29 וַיְהִי אל כָּל ילי ־יְמֵי־נֹחַ מחי תְּשַׁע מֵאוֹת שָׁנָה
וַחֲמִשִּׁים שָׁנָה וַיָּמֹת: [פ] 10 1 וְאֵלֶּה מ"ב תּוֹלְדֹת בְּנֵי־נֹחַ מחי שֵׁם
יהוה שדי חָם וָיָפֶת וַיִּוָּלְדוּ לָהֶם בָּנִים אַחַר הַמַּבּוּל: 2 בְּנֵי יֶפֶת
גֹּמֶר וּמָגוֹג וּמָדַי וְיָוָן וְתֻבָל וּמֶשֶׁךְ וְתִירָס: 3 וּבְנֵי גֹּמֶר אַשְׁכְּנַז
וְרִיפַת וְתֹגַרְמָה: 4 וּבְנֵי יָוָן אֱלִישָׁה וְתַרְשִׁישׁ כִּתִּים וְדֹדָנִים:
5 מֵאֵלֶּה נִפְרְדוּ אִיֵּי הַגּוֹיִם בְּאַרְצֹתָם אִישׁ ע"ה קנ"א קס"א לִלְשֹׁנוֹ
לְמִשְׁפְּחֹתָם בְּגוֹיֵהֶם: 6 וּבְנֵי חָם כּוּשׁ שכ"ה ע"ה וּמִצְרַיִם מצר וּפוּט
וּכְנָעַן: 7 וּבְנֵי כוּשׁ שכ"ה ע"ה סְבָא וַחֲוִילָה וְסַבְתָּה וְרַעְמָה
וְסַבְתְּכָא וּבְנֵי רַעְמָה שְׁבָא וּדְדָן: 8 וְכוּשׁ שכ"ה ע"ה יָלַד אֶת־
נִמְרֹד קנ"א קמ"ג הוּא הֵחֵל להח לִהְיוֹת גִּבֹּר בָּאָרֶץ: 9 הוּא־הָיָה יהה
גִבֹּר־צַיִד ב"פ כ"ן לִפְנֵי יְהוָה עַל־כֵּן יֵאָמַר כְּנִמְרֹד קנ"א קמ"ג גִּבּוֹר
צַיִד ב"פ כ"ן לִפְנֵי יְהוָהאדנייאהדונהי: 10 וַתְּהִי רֵאשִׁית מַמְלַכְתּוֹ בָּבֶל
וְאֶרֶךְ וְאַכַּד וְכַלְנֵה בְּאֶרֶץ שִׁנְעָר: 11 מִן־הָאָרֶץ אלהים דההין ע"ה
הַהִוא יָצָא אַשּׁוּר אבגיתצ ע"ה, ושר ע"ה, אהבת חנם וַיִּבֶן אֶת־נִינְוֵה וְאֶת־
רְחֹבֹת עִיר סוזזפר, ערי, סנדלפו"ן וְאֶת־כָּלַח: 12 וְאֶת־רֶסֶן בֵּין נִינְוֵה
וּבֵין כָּלַח הִוא הָעִיר סוזזפר, ערי, סנדלפו"ן הַגְּדֹלָה להח, מבה, יזל, הום:
13 וּמִצְרַיִם מצר יָלַד אֶת־לוּדִים וְאֶת־עֲנָמִים וְאֶת־לְהָבִים

13 And Mizra'im became the father of the Ludites, Anamites, Lehabites, Naphtuhites,
14 and Pathrusites, Casluhites (from whom the Philistines came), and Caphtorites.

15 And Canaan was the father of Sidon, his firstborn, and the Hittites,
16 Jebusites, Amorites, Girgashites,
17 Hivites, Arkites, Sinites,
18 Arvadites, Zemarites, and Hamathites; the families of the the Canaanite spread abroad.

19 And the border of the Canaanites was from Sidon, toward Gerar, up to Gaza, and then toward Sodom, Gomorrah, and Admah, and Zebo'im, even as far as Lasha.

20 These are the sons of Ham by their families and by their languages, in their countries and in their nations.

21 Unto Shem, the father of all the children of Eber and whose older brother was Japheth, even to him children were born.

22 The children of Shem: Elam, and Ashur, and Arphaxad, and Lud, and Aram.

23 And the children of Aram: Uz, and Hul, and Gether, and Mash.

24 And Arphaxad was the father of Shelah, and Shelah was the father of Eber.

25 And two sons were born to Eber: One was named Peleg, because in his days the earth was divided; his brother's name was Joktan.

26 And Joktan was the father of Almodad, and Sheleph, and Hazar-Maveth, and
Jerah, 27 And Hadoram, and Uzal, and Diklah,
28 and Obal, and Abimael, and Sheba,
29 and Ophir, and Havilah and Jobab: all these were the sons of Joktan.

30 And their dwelling was from Mesha toward Sephar, a mount of the east.

31 These are the sons of Shem by their families and their languages, in their lands and in their nations.

32 These are the families of the sons of Noah, after their generations, in their nations; and by these were the nations divided over the earth after the flood.

וְאֶת־נַפְתֻּחִים׃ 14 וְאֶת־פַּתְרֻסִים וְאֶת־כַּסְלֻחִים אֲשֶׁר
יָצְאוּ מִשָּׁם פְּלִשְׁתִּים וְאֶת־כַּפְתֹּרִים׃ [ס] 15 וּכְנַעַן יָלַד
אֶת־צִידֹן בְּכֹרוֹ וְאֶת־חֵת׃ 16 וְאֶת־הַיְבוּסִי וְאֶת־הָאֱמֹרִי וְאֵת
הַגִּרְגָּשִׁי׃ 17 וְאֶת־הַחִוִּי וְאֶת־הַעַרְקִי וְאֶת־הַסִּינִי׃
18 וְאֶת־הָאַרְוָדִי וְאֶת־הַצְּמָרִי וְאֶת־הַחֲמָתִי וְאַחַר נָפֹצוּ
מִשְׁפְּחוֹת הַכְּנַעֲנִי׃ 19 וַיְהִי גְּבוּל הַכְּנַעֲנִי מִצִּידֹן בֹּאֲכָה גְרָרָה
עַד־עַזָּה בֹּאֲכָה סְדֹמָה וַעֲמֹרָה וְאַדְמָה וּצְבֹיִם עַד־לָשַׁע׃
20 אֵלֶּה בְנֵי־חָם לְמִשְׁפְּחֹתָם לִלְשֹׁנֹתָם בְּאַרְצֹתָם בְּגוֹיֵהֶם׃ [ס]
21 וּלְשֵׁם יהוה שדי יֻלַּד גַּם יג״ל ־הוּא אֲבִי כָּל ילי ־בְּנֵי־עֵבֶר
רבוע יהוה רבוע אלהים אֲחִי יֶפֶת הַגָּדוֹל להח, מבה, יזל, אום׃ 22 בְּנֵי שֵׁם יהוה שדי
עֵילָם וְאַשּׁוּר אבגיתצ ע״ה, ושר ע״ה, אהבת חנם וְאַרְפַּכְשַׁד וְלוּד וַאֲרָם׃
23 וּבְנֵי אֲרָם עוּץ וְחוּל וְגֶתֶר וָמַשׁ׃ 24 וְאַרְפַּכְשַׁד יָלַד
אֶת־שָׁלַח וְשֶׁלַח יָלַד אֶת־עֵבֶר רבוע יהוה רבוע אלהים׃ 25 וּלְעֵבֶר
רבוע יהוה רבוע אלהים יֻלַּד שְׁנֵי בָנִים שֵׁם יהוה שדי הָאֶחָד אהבה, דאגה פֶּלֶג יהוה אלהים ע״ה
כִּי בְיָמָיו נִפְלְגָה הָאָרֶץ אלהים דההין ע״ה וְשֵׁם יהוה שדי אָחִיו יָקְטָן׃
26 וְיָקְטָן יָלַד אֶת־אַלְמוֹדָד וְאֶת־שָׁלֶף וְאֶת־חֲצַרְמָוֶת וְאֶת־
יָרַח׃ 27 וְאֶת־הֲדוֹרָם וְאֶת־אוּזָל וְאֶת־דִּקְלָה׃ 28 וְאֶת־עוֹבָל
וְאֶת־אֲבִימָאֵל וְאֶת־שְׁבָא׃ 29 וְאֶת־אוֹפִר וְאֶת־חֲוִילָה וְאֶת־
יוֹבָב כָּל ילי ־אֵלֶּה בְּנֵי יָקְטָן׃ 30 וַיְהִי מוֹשָׁבָם מִמֵּשָׁא בֹּאֲכָה
סְפָרָה הַר רבוע אלהים - ה׳ הַקֶּדֶם רבוע ב״ן׃ 31 אֵלֶּה בְנֵי־שֵׁם יהוה שדי
לְמִשְׁפְּחֹתָם לִלְשֹׁנֹתָם בְּאַרְצֹתָם לְגוֹיֵהֶם׃ 32 אֵלֶּה מִשְׁפְּחֹת
בְּנֵי־נֹחַ מחי לְתוֹלְדֹתָם בְּגוֹיֵהֶם וּמֵאֵלֶּה נִפְרְדוּ הַגּוֹיִם בָּאָרֶץ
אלהים דאלפין אַחַר הַמַּבּוּל׃ [פ]

SEVENTH READING - DAVID - MALCHUT

*11[1] And the whole world had one language and one speech. [2] And it came to pass,
as they journeyed from the east that they found a plain in the land of Shinar and they
settled there. [3] And they said to each other, "Come, let's make bricks and bake them
thoroughly." They had brick instead of stone, and slime for mortar. [4] And they said,
"Come, let us build a city, and a tower that reaches to heaven, and let us make
ourselves a name lest we are scattered upon the face of the whole earth." [5] And the
Lord came down to see the city and the tower that the children of men were
building.*

שָׂפָה אֶחָת

Genesis 11:1 – Here we are told by the Bible that the whole Earth was of "one language" and that the people of this generation used brick and bitumen to build "a city and a tower" that reached up to Heaven. According to the *Zohar*, there are two parallel worlds in existence: the pure and the impure, the holy and the evil. Just as there are *Ten Sefirot* within the holy and pure side, there are also *Ten Sefirot* on the side of the evil, Impure World.

> *Come and behold: "And they said, 'Come, let us build ourselves a city and a tower whose top may reach to Heaven.'" The word "come" is an invitation. The words: "...let us build ourselves a city and a tower whose top may reach to Heaven" WERE UNACCOMPANIED BY ACTIONS. THE UTTERANCE OF THE WORDS ALONE CAUSED THE BUILDING OF THE CITY AND TOWER IN THE UPPER WORLDS. The people took bad advice, following the stupidity and vanity of their hearts, and going against the Holy One, blessed be He. Rav Aba then said that they followed the stupidity of their hearts, but they used the Chochmah of the klipah to leave the Upper Dominion OF HOLINESS and enter the dominion OF THE KLIPOT, exchanging His glory, blessed be He, with that of a strange El. In this, there is a secret of supreme wisdom.*
>
> *– The Zohar, Noah 42:342–3*

The city and the tower that reached to Heaven actually refer to the *Ten Sefirot* of the Impure World. The city correlates to the *Sefira* of *Chochmah* on the Dark Side, and the tower correlates to the *Sefira* of *Binah*.

The bricks used to build that "city and tower" were the letters of the Aramaic alphabet, which is also the "one language" of the Earth spoken of by the Bible and the *Zohar*. The verse: "Let us make ourselves a name" is another reference to the wondrous power of the Aramaic letters.

In the *Zohar*, we learn that the people of that generation were spiritually adept but wicked, drawn to the dark influences of the Other Side. They discovered the secret wisdom of Kabbalah that was left behind by Noah, and they used it to gain control over the world.

> *All was according to the secret of wisdom. They planned to strengthen the power of the Other Side in the world and worship it because they knew that all evil judgment descends from there to the worlds. In so doing, they hoped to drive away the level of Holiness.*
>
> *– The Zohar, Noah 42:348*

Through the power of the Aramaic letters and through the people's unbroken unity, those negative souls ascended into the highest spiritual worlds—*Chochmah* and *Binah* of the Dark Side—to use this negative energy for evil purposes. They intended to challenge God, no less, and to seek world domination. And unity, being the most powerful force in existence, made it impossible for even God to stop them. The people who built the tower were the very image of the overweening

SEVENTH READING - DAVID - MALCHUT

11 1 וַיְהִי אל כָל ילי ־הָאָרֶץ אלהים דההין ע״ה שָׂפָה ע״ה אלהים פשוט ויודין אֶחָת
וּדְבָרִים ראה אֲחָדִים אהבה, דאגה: 2 וַיְהִי אל בְּנָסְעָם מִקֶּדֶם רבוע ב״ן
וַיִּמְצְאוּ בִקְעָה בְּאֶרֶץ אלהים דאלפין שִׁנְעָר וַיֵּשְׁבוּ שָׁם: 3 וַיֹּאמְרוּ
אִישׁ ע״ה קנ״א קס״א אֶל־רֵעֵהוּ הָבָה נִלְבְּנָה לְבֵנִים וְנִשְׂרְפָה לִשְׂרֵפָה
וַתְּהִי לָהֶם הַלְּבֵנָה לְאָבֶן יוד הה ואו הה וְהַחֵמָר הָיָה יהה לָהֶם לַחֹמֶר:
4 וַיֹּאמְרוּ הָבָה | נִבְנֶה־לָּנוּ אלהים, מום עִיר םןץףך, ערי, סנדלפו״ן וּמִגְדָּל עז
וְרֹאשׁוֹ ריבוע אלהים - אלהים דיודין ע״ה בַשָּׁמַיִם י״פ טל, י״פ כוזו וְנַעֲשֶׂה־לָּנוּ אלהים, מום
שֵׁם יהוה שדי פֶּן־נָפוּץ עַל־פְּנֵי חכמה - בינה כָל ילי ־הָאָרֶץ אלהים דההין ע״ה:
5 וַיֵּרֶד ר״י יְהוָהאדניאהדונהי לִרְאֹת אֶת־הָעִיר םןץףך, ערי, סנדלפו״ן וְאֶת־

arrogance in man that is as much evident today as it was in the past. Thus, the *Zohar* states:

> *And if they, because they were of one heart and one desire, all spoke the Holy Language, as it is written: "Nothing that they have planned to do will be withheld from them...."*
>
> – *The Zohar, Noah 44:386*

We learn that unified evil will always be able to defeat and conquer the side of good if disunity exists among the good people. The only way to defeat unified evil is through total unity on the side of the good. Consequently, God was forced to create disunity to break up this rebellious people. This is why the Creator confused their language, creating 70 other tongues and thereby severing their lines of communication.

Over the generations and right up to this very day, the true power and real purpose of Aramaic has been lost to humanity. However, the great Kabbalist Rav Yehuda Ashlag wrote that in our time evil people will no longer seek out Kabbalah, for they will have been entirely seduced by the material world and all of its illusionary riches. Only the good among humanity will embrace this wisdom, and thus the kabbalistic secrets of the Aramaic letters can now once again be revealed to the world.

The information that all these wonderful forces are now available for our use is, in fact, the underlying purpose of this book. An awesome spiritual power has been placed in our hands. Through meditation, we can now demolish the "city" and tear down the "tower" of negative forces, forever freeing ourselves from its evil influence. As the *Zohar* states so emphatically:

> *Like the Holy Side, the Other Side has no power to rule in the world without a city and a tower.*
>
> – *The Zohar, Noah 42:351*

Through Kabbalah and the Bible, we bring the Age of Messiah upon us immediately in a merciful, compassionate manner, rather than in a manner imbued with the quality of harsh judgment. As the *Zohar* says:

> *For us, and for all those who occupy themselves with the spiritual work and are of one heart and one desire.... Nothing that we want to do will be withheld from us.*
>
> – *The Zohar, Noah 44:386*

6 And the Lord said, "Behold the people are one and they all have one language that they have begun to do, and now nothing will restrain them from what they plan to do.
7 Come, let Us go down and confuse their language so that they will not understand one another's speech." 8 So the Lord scattered them abroad from there over the face of all the earth, and they stopped building the city.

9 That is why it was called Babel—because there the Lord confused the language of the whole world, and from there the Lord scattered them abroad over the face of all the earth. 10 These are the generations of Shem. Shem was 100 years old, and he became the father of Arphaxad, two years after the flood. 11 And after Shem became the father of Arphaxad, he lived 500 years and had other sons and daughters. 12 And Arphaxad lived 35 years, and he became the father of Shelah. 13 And Arphaxad lived 403 years after he became the father of Shelah, and had other sons and daughters.
14 And Shelah lived 30 years, and he became the father of Eber. 15 And Shelah lived

---

אֵלֶּה

Genesis 11:10 – There were ten generations from Noah to Abraham, we are told, which is the same number of generations as there were between Adam and Noah. Kabbalah reveals that this indicates the cyclical structure of our universe. Moreover, according to the kabbalists, reality is composed of ten dimensions, which are referred to as the *Ten Sefirot*, meaning "Ten Emanations" of Light. These ten dimensions were formed when the infinite Divine Force of energy, which the sages call the Light, contracted itself. This contraction created a miniscule point of darkness into which our universe was born.

Sixteenth century Kabbalist Rav Isaac Luria (the Ari, which is Hebrew for "lion") revealed that six of the ten dimensions compacted, enfolding themselves into one super-dimension known as *Zeir Anpin*. Now, centuries after the ancients revealed that reality exists in ten dimensions and that six of those dimensions are folded into one, modern physicists have arrived at the same tentative conclusions in their superstring theory.

In his book *Hyperspace*, Dr. Michio Kaku, a theoretical physicist and a leading proponent of superstring theory, writes:

> *The Universe is a symphony of vibrating strings. And when strings move in ten-dimensional space-time, they warp the space-time surrounding them in precisely the way predicted by general relativity. Physicists retrieve our more familiar four-dimensional Universe by assuming that, during the Big Bang, six of the ten dimensions curled up (or "compactified") into a tiny ball, while the remaining four expanded explosively giving us the universe we see.*

Those six dimensions that lie just beyond our perception are the source and fountainhead of all the knowledge and fulfillment that appear in our world. This is the realm that Plato wrote about, the timeless world of Ideas or Forms that exists beyond the physical world of the five senses.

Sir Isaac Newton, discoverer of gravity and a keen student of Kabbalah (his heavily annotated copy of the *Zohar* is now in King's College Library, Cambridge), wrote:

> *Plato, traveling to Egypt when the Jews were numerous in that country, learnt there his metaphysical opinions about the superior beings and formal causes of all things, which he calls Ideas and which the Kabbalists call Sefirot....*
> *– MS. Yahuda, 15.7, p. 137v*

Connection with this multi-dimensional realm known as *Zeir Anpin* is the key to genuine control

הַמִּגְדָּל עץ אֲשֶׁר בָּנוּ בְּנֵי הָאָדָם מ״ה: 6 וַיֹּאמֶר יְהֹוָה אהדונהי הֵן
עַם אֶחָד אהבה, דאגה וְשָׂפָה שכינה אַחַת לְכֻלָּם וְזֶה הַחִלָּם לַעֲשׂוֹת
וְעַתָּה לֹא־יִבָּצֵר מֵהֶם כֹּל ילי אֲשֶׁר יָזְמוּ לַעֲשׂוֹת: 7 הָבָה נֵרְדָה
וְנָבְלָה שָׁם שְׂפָתָם אֲשֶׁר לֹא יִשְׁמְעוּ אִישׁ ע״ה קנ״א קס״א שְׂפַת רֵעֵהוּ:
8 וַיָּפֶץ יְהֹוָה אהדונהי אֹתָם מִשָּׁם עַל־פְּנֵי חכמה - בינה כָל ילי ־הָאָרֶץ
אלהים דההין ע״ה וַיַּחְדְּלוּ לִבְנֹת הָעִיר פוזפר, ערי, סנדלפון: 9 עַל־כֵּן קָרָא
שְׁמָהּ בָּבֶל כִּי־שָׁם בָּלַל יְהֹוָה אהדונהי שְׂפַת כָּל ילי ־הָאָרֶץ
אלהים דההין ע״ה וּמִשָּׁם הֱפִיצָם יְהֹוָה אהדונהי עַל־פְּנֵי חכמה - בינה
כָּל ילי ־הָאָרֶץ אלהים דההין ע״ה: [פ] 10 אֵלֶּה תּוֹלְדֹת שֵׁם יהוה שדי
שדי בֶּן־מְאַת שָׁנָה וַיּוֹלֶד אֶת־אַרְפַּכְשָׁד שְׁנָתַיִם אַחַר הַמַּבּוּל:
11 וַיְחִי־שֵׁם יהוה שדי אַחֲרֵי הוֹלִידוֹ אֶת־אַרְפַּכְשָׁד חֲמֵשׁ מֵאוֹת
שָׁנָה וַיּוֹלֶד בָּנִים וּבָנוֹת: [ס] 12 וְאַרְפַּכְשַׁד חַי חָמֵשׁ וּשְׁלֹשִׁים
שָׁנָה וַיּוֹלֶד אֶת־שָׁלַח: 13 וַיְחִי אַרְפַּכְשַׁד אַחֲרֵי הוֹלִידוֹ אֶת־
שֶׁלַח שָׁלֹשׁ שָׁנִים וְאַרְבַּע מֵאוֹת שָׁנָה וַיּוֹלֶד בָּנִים וּבָנוֹת: [ס] 14 וְשֶׁלַח
חַי שְׁלֹשִׁים שָׁנָה וַיּוֹלֶד אֶת־עֵבֶר רבוע יהוה רבוע אלהים: 15 וַיְחִי־שֶׁלַח

---

and fulfillment in life, but it is not easy to make such a connection. Thus, we have the Bible and other kabbalistic tools like the *Zohar* to help us bridge the physical and spiritual realms.

Whenever the Bible alludes to the *Ten Sefirot* in a coded fashion, such as the "ten generations," it is an indication that through the text, we are making contact with these Supernal Spheres. Light then flows into our world, creating order out of chaos, helping us correct our past errors, and hastening our Final Redemption.

וַיְחִי־שֵׁם

Genesis 11:11 – During the ten generations leading up to Noah, we are told, the average lifespan of humans was approximately 300 years. During the generations leading to Abraham, the average lifespan fell to approximately 100 years.

As we journey further away from the time of Adam and the Garden of Eden, where immortality was the norm, death becomes a stronger and stronger force in the world.

By using tools like the *Zohar*, the 72 Names of God, and the Bible, we can return to the Garden of Eden and recapture the Light of Immortality.

And we can also use those verses in the Bible that speak of all the generations as an antidote to death, thereby reversing the aging process and hastening the arrival of immortality on Earth in our lifetime.

403 years after he became the father of Eber, and had other sons and daughters.

16 *And Eber lived 34 years, and he became the father of Peleg.*

17 *And Eber lived 430 years after he became the father of Peleg, and had other sons and daughters.*

18 *And Peleg lived 30 years, and he became the father of Reu.*

19 *And Peleg lived 209 years after he became the father of Reu, and had other sons and daughters.*

20 *And Reu lived 32 years, and he became the father of Serug.*

21 *And Reu lived 207 years after he became the father of Serug, and had other sons and daughters.*

22 *And Serug lived 30 years, and he became the father of Nahor.*

23 *And Serug lived 200 years after he became the father of Nahor, and had other sons and daughters.*

24 *And Nahor lived 29 years, and he became the father of Terah.*

25 *And Nahor lived 119 years after he became the father of Terah, and had other sons and daughters.*

26 *And Terah lived 70 years, and he became the father of Abram, Nahor, and Haran.*

27 *Now these are the generations of Terah. Terah became the father of Abram, Nahor, and Haran. And Haran became the father of Lot.*

28 *And Haran died before his father in the land of his birth, in Ur of the Chaldees.*

אַבְרָם

Genesis 11:26 – In a story told in the *Midrash* (commentaries on the Bible), Abram (Abraham before his name was changed) was thrown into an oven by Nimrod, yet he was not burned and he escaped unharmed.

The sages tell us that Abram employed the instrument of the 72 Names of God, which granted him the power of mind over matter to achieve this miracle of protection. Through the name of Abram/Abraham and also with the quality of Light contained within the text of this section, we can tune ourselves into the 72 Names of God and attain a state of mind over matter.

Thus, when the going gets tough in our personal lives and we find ourselves tossed into the "fire" of challenging events, we can triumph over the physical world of chaos.

אַחֲרֵי הוֹלִידוֹ אֶת־עֵבֶר רבוע יהוה רבוע אלהים שָׁלֹשׁ שָׁנִים וְאַרְבַּע
מֵאוֹת שָׁנָה וַיּוֹלֶד בָּנִים וּבָנוֹת׃ [ס] 16 וַיְחִי־עֵבֶר רבוע יהוה רבוע אלהים
אַרְבַּע וּשְׁלֹשִׁים שָׁנָה וַיּוֹלֶד אֶת־פָּלֶג יהוה אלהים ע״ה׃ 17 וַיְחִי־עֵבֶר
רבוע יהוה רבוע אלהים אַחֲרֵי הוֹלִידוֹ אֶת־פֶּלֶג יהוה אלהים ע״ה שְׁלֹשִׁים שָׁנָה
וְאַרְבַּע מֵאוֹת שָׁנָה וַיּוֹלֶד בָּנִים וּבָנוֹת׃ [ס] 18 וַיְחִי־פֶלֶג יהוה אלהים ע״ה
שְׁלֹשִׁים שָׁנָה וַיּוֹלֶד אֶת־רְעוּ׃ 19 וַיְחִי־פֶלֶג יהוה אלהים ע״ה אַחֲרֵי
הוֹלִידוֹ אֶת־רְעוּ תֵּשַׁע שָׁנִים וּמָאתַיִם שָׁנָה וַיּוֹלֶד בָּנִים
וּבָנוֹת׃ [ס] 20 וַיְחִי רְעוּ שְׁתַּיִם וּשְׁלֹשִׁים שָׁנָה וַיּוֹלֶד אֶת־שְׂרוּג׃
21 וַיְחִי רְעוּ אַחֲרֵי הוֹלִידוֹ אֶת־שְׂרוּג שֶׁבַע אלהים דיודין - ע״ב שָׁנִים
וּמָאתַיִם שָׁנָה וַיּוֹלֶד בָּנִים וּבָנוֹת׃ [ס] 22 וַיְחִי שְׂרוּג שְׁלֹשִׁים שָׁנָה
וַיּוֹלֶד אֶת־נָחוֹר׃ 23 וַיְחִי שְׂרוּג אַחֲרֵי הוֹלִידוֹ אֶת־נָחוֹר מָאתַיִם
שָׁנָה וַיּוֹלֶד בָּנִים וּבָנוֹת׃ [ס] 24 וַיְחִי נָחוֹר תֵּשַׁע וְעֶשְׂרִים שָׁנָה
וַיּוֹלֶד אֶת־תָּרַח׃ 25 וַיְחִי נָחוֹר אַחֲרֵי הוֹלִידוֹ אֶת־תֶּרַח תְּשַׁע־
עֶשְׂרֵה שָׁנָה וּמְאַת שָׁנָה וַיּוֹלֶד בָּנִים וּבָנוֹת׃ [ס] 26 וַיְחִי־תֶרַח
שִׁבְעִים שָׁנָה וַיּוֹלֶד אֶת־אַבְרָם אֶת־נָחוֹר וְאֶת־הָרָן ע״ב רבוע ע״ב׃
27 וְאֵלֶּה תּוֹלְדֹת תֶּרַח תֶּרַח הוֹלִיד אֶת־אַבְרָם אֶת־נָחוֹר וְאֶת־
הָרָן ע״ב רבוע ע״ב וְהָרָן ע״ב רבוע ע״ב הוֹלִיד אֶת־לוֹט מ״ה׃ 28 וַיָּמָת הָרָן
ע״ב רבוע ע״ב עַל־פְּנֵי חכמה - בינה תֶּרַח אָבִיו בְּאֶרֶץ אלהים דאלפין מוֹלַדְתּוֹ
בְּאוּר כַּשְׂדִּים׃

Everything begins, however, with a total trust and certainty in the Light of the Creator as well as a desire to resist one's habitual reactive tendencies. If we have just these two qualities secure in our hearts, there is no limit to what we can do—from bringing about a miraculous change in human nature to unleashing the awesome secrets of Mother Nature.

Through an understanding of this section in Genesis, everyone can attain the power of mind over matter, and with it, absolute control over the physical world.

MAFTIR

29 And Abram and Nahor both married. The name of Abram's wife was Sarai, and the name of Nahor's wife was Milcah; the daughter of Haran, the father of Milcah and the father of Iscah.

30 But Sarai was barren; she had no child.

31 And Terah took his son Abram, and his grandson Lot, son of Haran, and Sarai, his daughter-in-law, his son Abram's wife, and together they left Ur of the Chaldeans to go to the land of Canaan. But when they came to Haran, they settled there.

32 And Terah lived 205 years, and Terah died in Haran.

HAFTARAH OF NOAH

This reading in the Book of Isaiah refers to Noah's Flood. When the cities of Sodom and Gomorrah were slated for destruction, we are told that Abraham prayed for them, and yet Noah did not pray for the people who would most certainly perish in the flood. Noah was a righteous man by the standards of his time, but he clearly lacked any sense of compassion, which would be one of the key requirements

Isaiah 54:1–54:10

54 1 "Sing, O barren woman, you who never bore a child; burst into song, shout for joy, you who were never in labor; because more are the children of the desolate woman than of her who has a husband," says the Lord.

2 "Enlarge the place of your tent, stretch your tent curtains wide, do not hold back; lengthen your cords, strengthen your stakes.

3 For you will spread out to the right and to the left; your descendants will dispossess nations and settle in their desolate cities.

4 Do not be afraid; you will not suffer shame. Do not fear disgrace; you will not be humiliated. You will forget the shame of your youth and remember no more the
reproach of your widowhood. 5 For your Maker is your Husband—the Lord Almighty
is His Name—the Holy One of Israel is your Redeemer; He is called the God of all the

MAFTIR

29 וַיִּקַּח חעם אַבְרָם וְנָחוֹר לָהֶם נָשִׁים שֵׁם יהוה שדי אֵשֶׁת־אַבְרָם
שָׂרָי וְשֵׁם יהוה שדי אֵשֶׁת־נָחוֹר מִלְכָּה ע״ה אל אדני בַּת־הָרָן ע״ב רבוע ע״ב
אֲבִי־מִלְכָּה ע״ה אל אדני וַאֲבִי יִסְכָּה׃ 30 וַתְּהִי שָׂרַי עֲקָרָה אֵין לָהּ
וָלָד׃ 31 וַיִּקַּח חעם תֶּרַח אֶת־אַבְרָם בְּנוֹ וְאֶת־לוֹט מ״ה בֶּן־הָרָן ר״ת הבל
בֶּן־בְּנוֹ וְאֵת שָׂרַי כַּלָּתוֹ אֵשֶׁת אַבְרָם בְּנוֹ וַיֵּצְאוּ אִתָּם מֵאוּר
כַּשְׂדִּים לָלֶכֶת אַרְצָה אלהים דההין ע״ה כְּנַעַן וַיָּבֹאוּ עַד־חָרָן ג״פ אלהים
וַיֵּשְׁבוּ שָׁם׃ 32 וַיִּהְיוּ מלוי ס״ג יְמֵי־תֶרַח חָמֵשׁ שָׁנִים וּמָאתַיִם שָׁנָה
וַיָּמָת תֶּרַח בְּחָרָן ג״פ אלהים׃ [פ] [פ] [פ] [פ] [פ]

HAFTARAH OF NOAH

for a righteous man today. He was, all the same, entirely obedient to God, which is what made him unique. Here Isaiah is telling us that while Noah did not cause the Flood, he made no attempt to prevent it, either.

ישעיהו פרק 54

54 1 רָנִּי עֲקָרָה לֹא יָלָדָה פִּצְחִי רִנָּה וְצַהֲלִי לֹא־חָלָה להח כִּי־
רַבִּים בְּנֵי־שׁוֹמֵמָה מִבְּנֵי בְעוּלָה אָמַר יְהוָה אדני אהדונהי׃ 2 הַרְחִיבִי ׀
מְקוֹם יהוה ברבוע, ו״פ אל אָהֳלֵךְ וִירִיעוֹת מִשְׁכְּנוֹתַיִךְ יַטּוּ אַל־תַּחְשֹׂכִי
הַאֲרִיכִי מֵיתָרַיִךְ וִיתֵדֹתַיִךְ חַזֵּקִי פהל׃ 3 כִּי־יָמִין וּשְׂמֹאול
תִּפְרֹצִי וְזַרְעֵךְ גּוֹיִם יִירָשׁ וְעָרִים נְשַׁמּוֹת יוֹשִׁיבוּ׃ 4 אַל־תִּירְאִי
כִּי־לֹא תֵבוֹשִׁי וְאַל־תִּכָּלְמִי כִּי לֹא תַחְפִּירִי כִּי בֹשֶׁת עֲלוּמַיִךְ
תִּשְׁכָּחִי וְחֶרְפַּת אַלְמְנוּתַיִךְ לֹא תִזְכְּרִי־עוֹד׃ 5 כִּי בֹעֲלַיִךְ

Earth. 6 The Lord will call you back as if you were a wife deserted and distressed in
spirit—a wife who married young, only to be rejected," says your God.

7 "For a brief moment I abandoned you, but with deep compassion I will bring you
back.

8 In a surge of anger I hid my face from you for a moment, but with everlasting
kindness I will have compassion on you," says the Lord your Redeemer.

9 "To Me this is like the days of Noah, when I swore that the waters of Noah would
never again cover the Earth. So now I have sworn not to be angry with you, never to
rebuke you again.

10 Though the mountains are shaken and the hills be removed, yet My unfailing love
for you will not be shaken nor My covenant of peace be removed," says the Lord, who
has compassion on you.

עֹשַׂיִךְ יְהֹוָהאדניאהדונהי צְבָאוֹת פני שכינה שְׁמוֹ מהש ע״ה וְגֹאֲלֵךְ קְדוֹשׁ
יִשְׂרָאֵל אֱלֹהֵי דמב, ילה כָל ילי ־הָאָרֶץ אלהים דההין ע״ה יִקָּרֵא׃ 6 כִּי־
כְאִשָּׁה עֲזוּבָה וַעֲצוּבַת רוּחַ מלוי אלהים דיודין קְרָאָךְ יְהֹוָהאדניאהדונהי
וְאֵשֶׁת נְעוּרִים כִּי תִמָּאֵס אָמַר אֱלֹהָיִךְ ילה׃ 7 בְּרֶגַע ג״פ אלהים ־ ט״ו אותיות
קָטֹן עֲזַבְתִּיךְ וּבְרַחֲמִים אלהים דיודין, מצפצ, י״פ ייי גְּדֹלִים להח, מבה, יזל, אום
אֲקַבְּצֵךְ׃ 8 בְּשֶׁצֶף קֶצֶף הִסְתַּרְתִּי פָנַי חכמה ־ בינה רֶגַע ג״פ אלהים ־ ט״ו אותיות
מִמֵּךְ וּבְחֶסֶד ע״ב, ריבוע יהוה עוֹלָם רִחַמְתִּיךְ אָמַר גֹּאֲלֵךְ
יְהֹוָהאדניאהדונהי׃ [ס] 9 כִּי־מֵי ילי נֹחַ מוזי זֹאת לִי אֲשֶׁר נִשְׁבַּעְתִּי
מֵעֲבֹר מֵי ילי ־נֹחַ מוזי עוֹד עַל־הָאָרֶץ אלהים דההין ע״ה כֵּן נִשְׁבַּעְתִּי
מִקְּצֹף עָלַיִךְ ה׳ הויות וּמִגְּעָר־בָּךְ׃ 10 כִּי הֶהָרִים י׳ הויות יָמוּשׁוּ
וְהַגְּבָעוֹת תְּמוּטֶינָה וְחַסְדִּי ע״ב, ריבוע יהוה מֵאִתֵּךְ לֹא־יָמוּשׁ וּבְרִית
שְׁלוֹמִי לֹא תָמוּט אָמַר מְרַחֲמֵךְ יְהֹוָהאדניאהדונהי׃ [ס]

LECH LECHA

THE LESSON OF LECH LECHA (Genesis 12:1–17:27)

The Story of Abraham

"Leave your country, leave your people, leave your father's household, and go to a land that I will show you." (*Genesis 12:1*)

God tells Abram, "Go out from your homeland. Leave the place you were born. Leave your father's house." As the sages have explained, here the Creator was instructing Abram to begin both a physical as well as an internal journey.

Let us deconstruct this story. It is human nature to stay with the things we are used to, to keep doing what we have always done, to imitate what our friends and family are doing. This does not just include going to the same restaurant or ballgame that everyone else is going to; it also involves adhering to what is spiritually in vogue—including whether or not it is in vogue to be spiritual at all. If it is the in thing to be spiritual, a surprising number of people will say to themselves, "Okay, let's be spiritual." Their real goal, of course, is to conform, and thus to be accepted. All of the above activities and attitudes can be summed up in one phrase: our comfort zone.

It is one of the hardest tasks in spiritual work to do what most people do not do—but it is one of the most rewarding. That is why the Creator refers to the "going out" of Abram in so many different ways and why the physical act of leaving his homeland was only one element of the patriarch's test.

Abram understood all this, we are told. He knew with absolute certainty that he had to embark on an inner change, and he freely chose to do so, electing to be totally with the Light. Abram completely abandoned the *Desire to Receive for the Self Alone.* And whoever freely chooses to go against his own ego-driven desires merits the Creator's presence all the time.

> *Abraham succeeded in his desire to get closer to God. It is written: "You love righteousness and hate wickedness." (Psalms 45:8) Because Abraham did this, he therefore drew nearer to righteousness. Therefore, it is written: "Abraham, my beloved." (Isaiah 41:8) Why "my beloved"? Because it has been said about him: "You love righteousness." This is the love for God whom Abraham loved more than anyone else of his generation did, as they were far from righteous.*
>
> *– The Zohar, Lech Lecha 1:3*

Thus, because of Abram's choice, the Creator told him, "Whoever blesses you is blessed. Whoever curses you is cursed. And with you, everyone will be blessed." (Genesis 12:3) When any of us sincerely chooses to embark upon a spiritual journey, we bring blessings to the whole world. It is important to remember that this message always concerns us now, and is not just another form of intellectual entertainment requiring little participation. This wisdom only becomes manifest and retained when we reinforce it through actions that we undertake based on the lessons we are given. In the end, if we just read these words without making a sincere attempt to apply them in our daily lives, we will accomplish nothing either for ourselves or for others.

Abram is, therefore, a symbol of the conquering of the *Desire to Receive for the Self Alone.* At the precise moment a person truly decides to give up satisfying his ego's desires, the Light of the Creator connects to him. Thus, the very instant that Abram made the decision to leave his comfort zone, he became holy. What God is really asking of us, the text implies, is not that we become righteous in one day—which is impossible—but that we make up our minds to abandon the world of the ego forever. Sincere desire is all that is needed, but this is no minor matter, and it takes some time before most of us can be certain that our sincerity and dedication are constant enough for the task.

Breaking away from the life we are familiar with is very difficult, but overcoming this difficulty of breaking away is exactly why we gain so much. Whenever a person stops himself from speaking with malice or from showing anger, for example, he receives so much Divine Light that not even angels can measure the amount.

One of the key lessons in the story of Abram is learning that the world is blessed only as a result of the effort that humans make to abandon their ego-based desires forever. The saintly Vilna Gaon, Rav Eliyahu of Vilna (1720–1797), wrote: "Conquering these desires is the most important work we have in this world."

To sum up, we do not have to become righteous in a moment; we just have to make the decision to want to become righteous—and in the very second that we decide this, we also open our hearts to receive the support of the Light in all its abundance.

The great Reb Zusha, Rav Meshulam Zusha of Anipoli (1718–1800) expands this point further. From him, we learn that:

- "Leave your land" refers to our personal garbage;
- "Leave your birthplace" refers to the negativity that came through our mother: This is the bagage of the soul, the lessons that we did not take care of the last time we were incarnated;
- "Your father's house" refers to the negativity that came through our father from our previous life.

Thus, we are being told directly that only when we have left these negative elements behind us are we able to go to the land where all the Light comes from—although this is not a physical journey, but rather a spiritual path to enlightenment. The Creator is revealing the secret of how to attain connection with the Creator and manifest the Light that is there for us.

> *Nothing is aroused Above before it is first aroused Below, so that what is aroused Above rests upon it. The secret is that the black flame OF THE CANDLE, WHICH IS THE SECRET OF THE NUKVA, does not hold onto the white flame OF THE CANDLE, WHICH IS THE SECRET OF*

ZEIR ANPIN, before it is aroused. As soon as it is aroused first, the white flame immediately rests upon it. THIS IS SO BECAUSE THE LOWER ONE HAS TO BE AROUSED FIRST.
– The Zohar, Lech Lecha 4:19

According to Rav Tzvi Elimelech Obdinov, known as the Nes Aschar, another important teaching from this story in the Bible is that life is not just a matter of finding ways to make money or to have fun. We must be aware that every moment we have and every circumstance in which we find ourselves is an opportunity given to us by the Creator to discover what it is that we truly need. The real opportunity lies not in what we do or do not do, but in the potential connection to the Light that is waiting there for us.

In other words, whatever affliction comes our way, we will find that it is always something we deserve. There are even reasons for having a headache. The beauty of Kabbalah is that it teaches us that pain has a purpose. Pain and the trials of life open us up to become bigger and better, and ultimately, they force us to connect to our God-like nature.

None of us are perfect; we all go through those moments when we feel nothing and are blind to the bigger picture. Fortunately, as the sages teach us, we are only living through a temporary concealment. It's up to each of us to beg the Light to show itself and to reveal the reason for our pain. Everything is weighed on the cosmic scale, and the consequences of every deed are—measure for measure—precise and correct.

So it is not enough just to perform good deeds because sometimes the motivation behind the good action is ego-driven. A person appears to be selfless and giving, yet when we look into their motives, we find that they only behave this way to gain power and control over others, or even that they just do it so that others will think well of them. Such people frequently believe their own deceptions, too, not realizing that motive is the key. When there is a judgment in their lives, they even tell themselves: "I did so much good, so why is the Creator not accepting that good? How could God do this to me?"

It is important that we understand that it is not for us to decide what type of judgment we ought to receive. Our purpose is to grow and learn so that when we make mistakes, we will learn from them and learn not to repeat them instead of beating ourselves up over them. We have to be aware that the Creator sees the whole picture of every life, even if we cannot see it ourselves. Only when we truly understand that we don't see everything, will we see more.

A story from the time of the Ari is useful to assist our understanding here.

One Friday afternoon, a thought came to the town's baker: He wanted to make a sacrifice to the Creator. So he baked the most fragrant, delicious bread he had ever baked in his life and then took it with him to his place of worship. He was not exactly sure what to do with his offering, so he went to the Ark and opened it, saying, "God, please accept this sacrifice. I want to be closer to you." Then he put the bread inside the Ark, closed it, and left.

Five minutes later, a beggar came into the synagogue. He had begged for food his whole life, so he went to the Ark and began to cry, pleading, "Please, God, help me." Then he opened the Ark and found inside two loaves of bread, which to him were clearly a gift from God. The beggar beamed with joy, both for the bread itself and for this miracle that the Creator obviously deemed him worthy enough to receive.

Next morning, the baker returned to the temple to see if God had accepted his sacrifice. Amazingly, the bread was gone, and the baker was the happiest person alive. He went to his wife, hugged and kissed her, and started dancing around without letting her know why he was so happy.

A week later, he looked up at the sky and said to himself, "You know, maybe God will accept another sacrifice." So he brought more bread to the Ark, and lo and behold, the same thing happened. The beggar took the loaves, and the baker beamed with happiness. This went on, week after week, year after year, until fourteen years had passed.

One Friday afternoon, the rabbi fell asleep in his office in the temple, only to be woken by the sound of someone at the Ark mumbling about a sacrifice of some sort. Very quietly, he got up and peeked into the sanctuary where he saw the baker put bread into the Ark and leave. A few minutes later, the rabbi saw the beggar enter and start pleading, "God, please give me some food." He watched as the beggar took the loaves out of the Ark, seeing the man's face fill with joy as he ran away.

The rabbi thought, "I have to fix this." The following day, he called both the baker and the beggar into his office. He said, "I do not know what the two of you think is going on here. You," he looked at the baker, "say you are giving God a sacrifice, while you," he looked at the beggar, "say God is giving you food. But no such thing is happening. One of you puts the bread in, and the other one takes it out. God is not involved in this transaction at all." At that very second, Rav Isaac Luria happened to walk in and immediately said to the rabbi, "Prepare yourself to die. You are going to leave this world before the end of the day."

The rabbi was astonished and terrified, "Why me? What did I do?" he asked.

The Ari said, "Of course, God is involved. Do you not think it is a miracle that for fourteen years, the baker always arrived just before the beggar? Not even once did they come in the wrong order in all that time. This is because the Creator was so happy to see this exchange take place that the Angel of Death himself could not enter your temple. You see, God has many ways of receiving a sacrificial offering. One way is by giving it to the needy. The happiness of the Creator is all that kept you alive for these fourteen years. You were supposed to leave this world on the very Friday when this beautiful exchange began, and you would indeed have died then were it not for God's happiness, just as this beggar would also have died if he had not received the bread."

The lesson here is to see that God works through our own actions. When we make a sacrifice of any kind, the Creator accepts it through the hand of another human being. It is in our interactions with each other that God's presence is most vibrantly felt.

SYNOPSIS OF LECH LECHA

Israel: A State of Mind, a State of Spirituality

The name of this story is Lech Lecha which means "you go out." The basic teaching behind this story concerns transcendence, where we are helped to go out and escape the bonds of our ego, break free of self-interest, and in the process emancipate ourselves from our illusionary comfort zones. True spiritual Light is only found outside the box we have grown used to living in—physically, emotionally, and spiritually.

Abram was told to migrate to Israel, the Promised Land. Israel is a code word, symbolizing a higher level of spiritual existence. According to the *Zohar*, this higher level of spirituality corresponds to the *Sefira* of *Chesed*, which radiates the energy of mercy. This, in fact, was Abram's destiny: to be the channel or conduit for bringing mercy into the physical world and to sweeten the judgments meted out on account of our negative actions.

To achieve this, Abram (not yet named Abraham) had to leave his country, his birthplace, and his father's house; all of which are codes to help us understand his lower state of consciousness. In effect, this was the way for Abram to rid himself of the negative forces or shells (*klipot*) still attached to him so that he could raise his consciousness to a higher level of spirituality.

Each of us has the same mission and destiny as Abram had. We have all been ordered to set out for the Promised Land, Israel, which is a state of mind, a level of spirituality, and a deeper connection to the Light of the Creator. Figuratively speaking, to journey to Israel means to move away from being reactive, materialistic, and selfish and become someone who is deeply proactive, spiritual, and wholly loving.

Through the merit of Abram, we are able to achieve this kind of evolutionary growth in a gentle and merciful manner, as opposed to one of torment, anguish, and agony. Going out of our country, our birthplace, and the house of our father means that we must let go of our ego, our old ways of thinking, our comfort zones, and our fruitless habitual behavioral patterns if we are to connect to the Light and find eternal fulfillment.

The sacred words that tell this story help us remove the *klipot* (shells) and blockages from our consciousness so that we can attain the state of Israel (*Chesed*, the energy of mercy) within our souls. The Light flowing through these letters also softens our intransigence in situations where our stubbornness and ego prevent us from embracing spiritual change.

FIRST READING - ABRAHAM - CHESED

*12 [1] Now the Lord had said to Abram, "Leave your country, leave your people,
leave your father's household, and go to a land that I will show you. [2] And
I will make you a great nation and I will bless you; I will make your name
great, and you will be a blessing. [3] And I will bless those who bless you, and curse*

FROM THE RAV

Abram was told to go from the land of his birth. But what is meant by "the land of your birth?" From the moment of our birth, our DNA controls exactly how we speak, how we look, how we grow—everything there is to know about us is already present at birth. If we do not alter that DNA, nothing will change. We come into the world with a great deal of baggage built into our DNA, and it must be transformed. It is our genetic makeup that condemns us to chaos in our lives.

Until we begin to change from being comfortable with chaos, until we begin to assume a consciousness of control, nothing will change. The proof is that for 3400 years, nothing has changed. The same chaos plagues us from generation to generation. The dates and the locations are a little different, but we all fall into the same behavior patterns year after year, century after century. The meaning of the Story of Lech Lecha is not that our goal should be to change the whole world, but that each of us should take the responsibility for changing ourselves. The *Zohar*, too, asks for this, telling us that removing chaos is our responsibility.

The Story of Lech Lecha says: "Not just Abraham will be blessed, but the whole world." Remember, the Bible gives us truths that are absolute. There is no disclaimer. There is no "margin for error" of any kind. We are given an opportunity to see, to listen, to learn, and to act—and when we take advantage of that oportunity, we will get a positive result. It's an absolute certainty.

וַיֹּאמֶר

Genesis 12:1 – The *Zohar* tells us that Abram became wise in the ways of the supernal worlds. He studied the *Ten Sefirot* (Tree of Life) and explored both the spiritual and physical realms of reality. He mastered the wisdom of the stars, the planets, and the signs of the zodiac. The *Zohar*, however, also states that "get you out" means that the Creator told Abram he should not limit himself to the physical aspect of astrology and horoscopes, for human beings have the ability to rise above planetary influences and become the captains of their own fate.

> *. . . Abraham knew and checked all the governors and rulers of the world that had dominion over the entire civilized world. And he was examining all those who govern and rule over the directions of the world's inhabited land, all those that have dominion over the stars and the constellations. He learned how they exercise their power over one another. In considering all the inhabited places in the world, he did well. But when he reached that place, THE POINT OF MALCHUT, he saw the force of the depths. And he could not withstand it. As soon as the Holy One, blessed be He, noticed his awakening and his passion, He immediately revealed Himself to Abraham and said, "Get you out" in order to learn about and perfect yourself.*
>
> *– The Zohar, Lech Lecha5:27–28*

Kabbalistic astrology is a genuine knowledge of the planets and stars. It is not meant to limit our horizons, but rather to be a guide to show us where our spiritual potential lies as well as how to overcome our blockages to achieve our

FIRST READING - ABRAHAM - CHESED

12 1 וַיֹּאמֶר יְהֹוָה יאהדונהי אֶל־אַבְרָם לֶךְ־לְךָ מֵאַרְצְךָ וּמִמּוֹלַדְתְּךָ
וּמִבֵּית ב״פ ראה אָבִיךָ אֶל־הָאָרֶץ אלהים דההין ע״ה אֲשֶׁר אַרְאֶךָּ׃
2 וְאֶעֶשְׂךָ לְגוֹי מלוי מ״ה גָּדוֹל להח, מבה, יזל, אום וַאֲבָרֶכְךָ וַאֲגַדְּלָה שְׁמֶךָ
וֶהְיֵה יהוה, יהה בְּרָכָה׃ 3 וַאֲבָרְכָה מְבָרְכֶיךָ וּמְקַלֶּלְךָ אָאֹר

---

purpose here in this lifetime. In this way, we can rise above the plane of the planets and their negative influences.

The story of Abram's migration to Israel is also a metaphor concealing an even deeper concept: the journey of the soul as it leaves the Upper World, which is our "Father's house," and begins its stay in the Earthly realm, where it is given the garment of a human body to wear on its quest to achieve spiritual transformation.

Spiritual transformation, in essence, concerns the nullification of the ego and the subjugation of the body's reactive, impulsive nature. When these tendencies are in check, we can unleash the will and power of our soul to inspire proactive behavior, a respect for human dignity, and an unconditional love for others.

The soul is a part of God, a spark of our supernal Father. Hence, our soul is our true father and the governor of our body. Such is the lesson and the truth to be found in the name of Abram. *Abba* is Aramaic for "father," while *ram* is Aramaic for "supernal." Therefore, God speaking to Abram is a code for God speaking to our Divine supernal soul. This is how Abram's task becomes our task. The phrase "Get you out..." is now seen to refer also to liberating our soul from its prison inside the bonds of our physical body.

לֶךְ־לְךָ

Genesis 12:1 – The sages tell us that before the soul leaves the Upper Worlds, it stands before the Creator and pledges to pursue the spiritual path and achieve transformation. However, the perpetual pull of the material world is so powerful that we can forget our true purpose in life and succumb to the seductive illusions of physical existence. Power, fame, prestige, monetary wealth, and self-indulgence are powerful enticements that increasingly lead our greedy ego astray as we grow to adulthood. We need the Light of this section to reawaken our desire to remain true to our soul's original commitment—its pledge to pursue the spiritual path.

> *When the soul is ready to descend to this world, God makes it swear to perform the precepts of Torah and do His bidding. And He gives each soul 100 keys of blessings for each and every day so that it may complete the supernal grades, which reach the numerical value of "Lech Lecha" (lit. "Get you out"), WHICH EQUALS 100. All of them are given TO THE SOUL so that it may cultivate the Garden, WHICH IS THE NUKVA, to till it and to keep it. "Your country" is the Garden of Eden.*
> *– The Zohar, Lech Lecha 3:14*

The act of connecting with this section of the Bible is in itself a step along the path toward spiritual transformation, so at the very moment you read this, you are gaining support in achieving your life's purpose. This transformation will manifest more effectively as you share this Light with others through loving behavior and selfless deeds in the days to come.

*whoever curses you; and all families of the earth will be blessed through you." 4 So
Abram departed, as the Lord had spoken to him; and Lot went with him. And Abram
was seventy-five years old when he departed from Haran.*

*5 And Abram took his wife Sarai, and Lot, his brother's son, and all their possessions
that they had accumulated, and the souls they had acquired in Haran, and they set
out for the land of Canaan, and into the Land of Canaan they came.*

*6 And Abram passed through the land to the place of Sichem in the plain of Moreh.
And the Canaanites were in the land. 7 And the Lord appeared to Abram and said,
"To your seed I will give this land." And there he built an altar to the Lord, who had
appeared to him.*

*8 And from there he went to the mountain east of Bethel and pitched his tent, having
Bethel on the west and Hai on the east. And there he built an altar to the Lord and
called on the name of the Lord.*

9 Then Abram journeyed and continued toward the south.

*10 And there was a famine in the land, and Abram went down to Egypt to live there
because the famine was dire in the land.*

וְאַבְרָם

Genesis 12:4 – Each of us is required to begin his or her task of spiritual transformation at the age of 13. This is the time when the power of free will and the upper levels of our soul are first activated. We start to comprehend the concept of Cause and Effect and in essence are no longer fully protected by the spiritual umbrella of our parents. We become the captain of our own ship and now need to accept the consequences of our choices and actions. The *Zohar* says:

> *The soul will not start fulfilling the mission it was commanded to perform until it has completed thirteen years in this world. This is because from the twelfth year onward, the soul is aroused to fulfill its task.*
>
> *– The Zohar, Lech Lecha 8:42*

We are told in the Bible that Abram was 75 years old when he left the country of Charan, which symbolizes both the negative physical world and the ego. The *Zohar* says that Abram's age when he left his home is a code that alludes to each of us: 7 + 5 = 12. During our first 12 years of life, we live within the domain of negativity without the ability to transform. At the age of 13, we acquire the power to operate outside the realm of the desires of the body, just as Abram went out of Charan.

Genesis 12:6 – At this point in time, the city of Shechem was not a significant or sacred landmark of any kind. But the righteous sage Joseph would eventually be buried there, transforming the place into a known spiritual landmark since Joseph's presence serves as a reservoir of spiritual Light that mankind uses to this very day.

In the eyes of the kabbalist, however, Shechem is not a holy site because it is Joseph's resting place, but rather that Joseph came to be buried there because it always was a holy site. The

וְנִבְרְכוּ יהוה ע"ב ריבוע מ"ה בְךָ כֹּל ילי מִשְׁפְּחֹת הָאֲדָמָה: 4 וַיֵּלֶךְ כלי
אַבְרָם כַּאֲשֶׁר דִּבֶּר ראה אֵלָיו יְהֹוָה אהדונהי וַיֵּלֶךְ כלי אִתּוֹ לוֹט מ"ה
וְאַבְרָם בֶּן־חָמֵשׁ שָׁנִים וְשִׁבְעִים שָׁנָה בְּצֵאתוֹ מֵחָרָן ג"פ אלהים:
5 וַיִּקַּח חעם אַבְרָם אֶת־שָׂרַי אִשְׁתּוֹ וְאֶת־לוֹט מ"ה בֶּן־אָחִיו וְאֶת־
כָּל ילי ־רְכוּשָׁם אֲשֶׁר רָכָשׁוּ וְאֶת־הַנֶּפֶשׁ רמ"ח + ז' הויות אֲשֶׁר־עָשׂוּ
בְחָרָן ג"פ אלהים וַיֵּצְאוּ לָלֶכֶת אַרְצָה אלהים דההין ע"ה כְּנַעַן וַיָּבֹאוּ אַרְצָה
אלהים דההין ע"ה כְּנָעַן: 6 וַיַּעֲבֹר רפ"ח, ע"ב + רי"ו אַבְרָם בָּאָרֶץ אלהים דאלפין
עַד מְקוֹם יהוה ברבוע, ר"פ אל שְׁכֶם עַד אֵלוֹן מוֹרֶה וְהַכְּנַעֲנִי אָז בָּאָרֶץ
אלהים דאלפין: 7 וַיֵּרָא יְהֹוָה אהדונהי אֶל־אַבְרָם וַיֹּאמֶר לְזַרְעֲךָ אֶתֵּן
אֶת־הָאָרֶץ אלהים דההין ע"ה הַזֹּאת וַיִּבֶן חיים שָׁם מִזְבֵּחַ זן, נגד לַיהֹוָה אהדונהי
הַנִּרְאֶה אֵלָיו: 8 וַיַּעְתֵּק מִשָּׁם הָהָרָה מִקֶּדֶם רבוע ב"ן לְבֵית ב"פ ראה ־אֵל
ייא"י וַיֵּט אָהֳלֹה בֵּית ב"פ ראה ־אֵל ייא"י מִיָּם ילי וְהָעַי מִקֶּדֶם רבוע ב"ן וַיִּבֶן
בינה ע"ה ־שָׁם מִזְבֵּחַ זן, נגד לַיהֹוָה אהדונהי וַיִּקְרָא עם ה' אותיות = ב"פ קס"א
בְּשֵׁם שדי יהוה יְהֹוָה אהדונהי: 9 וַיִּסַּע אַבְרָם הָלוֹךְ וְנָסוֹעַ הַנֶּגְבָּה: [פ]
10 וַיְהִי רָעָב רבוע אלהים רבוע יהוה בָּאָרֶץ וַיֵּרֶד רי"י אַבְרָם

same kabbalistic tenet holds true for the city of Jerusalem as well. Jerusalem is the principal energy center of the world and the spiritual storehouse of all humanity—this is why the Temple had to be built there. Jerusalem is not holy because of the Temple's presence, but rather the Temple was situated in Jerusalem because the very land itself is sacred and Divine.

The *Zohar* tells us that Joseph represents the source of sustenance for our entire world. He corresponds to the Sefira of Yesod, the chief portal through which all Light and energy flow down into our world. Thus, in this section, we can summon forth the power of Joseph and Shechem to eradicate poverty and purge the darkness from human civilization, drawing down spiritual and physical sustenance for ourselves and, in the process, for all of humankind.

וַיְהִי רָעָב

Genesis 12:10 – Any form of plague, whether of hunger or disease, occurs because of the collective negative actions of a group of people. Each of us can be a carrier of plague, spiritually speaking, if we speak evil of friends or foes, or if we consort with those whose actions are egocentric, or who display intolerance, or who bear hatred in their hearts for others. The Light radiated here in this verse can expel hatred and intolerance from our own hearts so that we can protect ourselves from disease and from being

[11] And it came to pass, as he was about to enter Egypt, he said to his wife Sarai, "Behold now, I know what a fair woman you are. [12] Therefore it will come to pass that when the Egyptians see you, they will say, 'This is his wife.' And they will kill me but will let you live. [13] Say, I pray you, that you are my sister, so that I will be treated well for your sake and my soul will be spared because of you."

SECOND READING - ISAAC - GEVURAH

[14] And it came to pass that when Abram came to Egypt, the Egyptians saw that she was a very fair woman. [15] And the princes of Pharaoh saw her, and they praised her to Pharaoh, and the woman was taken into Pharaoh's house. [16] And he treated Abram well for her sake, and he acquired sheep and oxen, and asses, and menservants and maidservants, and she-asses, and camels.

[17] And the Lord inflicted plagues on Pharaoh and his house because of Sarai, Abram's wife.

[18] And Pharaoh called for Abram and said, "What is this that you have done to me? Why didn't you tell me she was your wife?

---

carriers of plagues. This Light abolishes plague and disease from the planet, inspiring Divine joy in the hearts of all humanity.

מִצְרָיְמָה

Genesis 12:10 – The *Zohar* reveals that "Egypt" is a code word for the depths of man's own negativity, where the sparks of Divine Light have fallen. The civilization of Egypt at the time of Abram had long fallen into decadence, its people given over to pride, egotism, and forbidden magical practices. Many great spiritual leaders throughout history have descended into these negative regions to retrieve and elevate the sparks of Light that are trapped within the dark recesses of our being.

It goes against the grain of human nature, however, to look inward and reflect upon our own immoral attributes. Our five senses and our ego are more or less constantly attuned to the external world that surrounds us. Through reading about the kind of introspection and self-examination that Abram performed, we are given access to a timeless repository of Divine energy, made available to us in the vibrations that stream from reading this section.

The Light we now receive shines deep into our inner self, expelling the hardhearted, selfish qualities from the core of our being. The energy generated here can raise all the supernal sparks that have fallen into physical matter so that the "Egypt" within us and all around us is at last conquered, allowing Divine Light and freedom to radiate throughout the cosmos.

אִמְרִי-נָא

Genesis 12:13 – The *Zohar* teaches us that because it is forbidden to lie, Abram was not lying when he referred to his wife, Sarai (later to become Sarah), as his sister. Abram and Sarai are soul mates. Thus, Sarai represents the *Shechina*, the feminine side of the Divine Presence illuminating this world, and Abram represents the male Divinity. According to the *Zohar*, the *Shechina* is

מִצְרַיְמָה מצר לָגוּר שָׁם כִּי־כָבֵד הָרָעָב רבוע אלהים רבוע יהוה בָּאָרֶץ
אלהים דאלפין׃ 11 וַיְהִי כַּאֲשֶׁר הִקְרִיב לָבוֹא מִצְרָיְמָה מצר וַיֹּאמֶר אֶל־
שָׂרַי אִשְׁתּוֹ הִנֵּה מ״ה יה ־נָא יָדַעְתִּי כִּי אִשָּׁה יְפַת־מַרְאֶה אָתְּ׃
12 וְהָיָה יהוה, יהה כִּי־יִרְאוּ אֹתָךְ הַמִּצְרִים מצר וְאָמְרוּ אִשְׁתּוֹ זֹאת
וְהָרְגוּ אֹתִי וְאֹתָךְ יְחַיּוּ׃ 13 אִמְרִי־נָא אֲחֹתִי אָתְּ לְמַעַן יִיטַב־לִי
בַעֲבוּרֵךְ וְחָיְתָה נַפְשִׁי בִּגְלָלֵךְ׃

SECOND READING - ISAAC - GEVURAH

14 וַיְהִי כְּבוֹא אַבְרָם מִצְרָיְמָה מצר וַיִּרְאוּ הַמִּצְרִים מצר אֶת־
הָאִשָּׁה כִּי־יָפָה ע״ה אל אדני הִוא מְאֹד מ״ה׃ 15 וַיִּרְאוּ אֹתָהּ שָׂרֵי פַרְעֹה
וַיְהַלְלוּ ללה אֹתָהּ אֶל־פַּרְעֹה וַתֻּקַּח הָאִשָּׁה בֵּית ב״פ ראה פַּרְעֹה׃
16 וּלְאַבְרָם הֵיטִיב בַּעֲבוּרָהּ וַיְהִי אל ־לוֹ צֹאן מלוי אהיה דיודין ע״ה ־וּבָקָר
וַחֲמֹרִים וַעֲבָדִים וּשְׁפָחֹת וַאֲתֹנֹת וּגְמַלִּים׃ 17 וַיְנַגַּע יְהֹוָהאדניאהדונהי |
אֶת־פַּרְעֹה נְגָעִים גְּדֹלִים להח, מבה, יזל, אום וְאֶת־בֵּיתוֹ ב״פ ראה
עַל־דְּבַר ראה שָׂרַי אֵשֶׁת אַבְרָם׃ 18 וַיִּקְרָא עם ה׳ אותיות = ב״פ קס״א

considered to be a sister to each of us. On the surface, therefore, Sarai is the wife of Abram, but kabbalistically, she is also his sister, hence the sister of all mankind. We are thus shown that on a deep spiritual level, Abram's words were true. The sages of Kabbalah teach us never to take the Bible at face value because any contradiction, paradox, or seemingly unspiritual event appearing in the Bible always conceals within itself a deeper truth and lesson for life. Understanding these deeper truths and lessons is, of course, the purpose of the *Zohar* and of all kabbalistic wisdom.

Rav Yehuda Ashlag taught that even the smallest white lie prevents us from evolving spiritually. We must be truthful to others, but more importantly—and far harder to achieve—we must be painfully truthful to ourselves. The courage to speak and to hear the truth is summoned up by the very words that are spoken in a reading of this section.

וַיְנַגַּע

Genesis 12:17 – Abram went down into Egypt. Spiritually, the purpose of his journey was to plant the seed for the eventual redemption of the Israelites from Egypt, which would take place many centuries later in the time of Moses. During

19 Why did you say, 'She is my sister,' so that I may have taken her to be my wife? Now, therefore, here is your wife. Take her and go on your way."

20 And Pharaoh commanded his men concerning Abram, and they sent him away, and his wife, and everything that he had.

13:1 And Abram went up out of Egypt, with his wife and everything that he had, and Lot went with him into the south.

2 And Abram was very wealthy in cattle, in silver, and in gold.

*3 And he went on his journeys from the south until he came to Bethel, to the place
where his tent had been at the beginning, between Bethel and Hai; 4 and to the place
where he had first built the altar. And there Abram called on the name of the Lord.*

THIRD READING - JACOB - TIFERET

5 And Lot, who went with Abram, also had flocks, and herds, and tents.

6 And the land was not able to bear them that they might dwell together, for their substance was great, so that they could not dwell together.

---

this visit, Sarai, Abram's wife, was abducted by the Pharoah of Egypt. Abram and Sarai subsequently gained influence over the Pharoah and won Sarai's freedom using the tools and technology of the Bible and Kabbalah.

> *Come and behold: The Shechina did not leave Sarai at all during that night. When Pharaoh approached her, an angel came and hit him. And whenever Sarai said, "Hit," he hit. All the while Abram was begging his Master through his prayers, not to allow anyone to harm her. Therefore it is written: "...but the righteous are bold (trusting) as a lion." (Proverbs 28:1) This was a trial through which God tested Abram, but Abram had no doubts about the Holy One, blessed be He. "And Pharaoh commanded his men concerning him; and they sent him away...." (Genesis 12:20) Come and behold: The Holy One, blessed be He, is the protector of the righteous, Who shields them from being ruled by other people. So the Holy One, blessed be He, protected Abram, so no one could harm him or his wife.*
>
> *– The Zohar, Lech Lecha 14:122-3*

This event held cosmic significance for future generations. The act of gaining control over the king of Egypt—and thus over the negative cosmic forces he represented—created a precedent that would be recalled five generations later when the Israelites were freed from bondage in Egypt. Moreover, the plagues that occur in this section are the actual seeds of the Ten Plagues that will occur later in the Book of Exodus.

This shows how we achieve our own spiritual growth only by standing on the shoulders of the spiritual giants of the past. The Light that shines in our world today was lit by the hands of past generations. Similarly, our actions of the present moment not only assist us, but also serve and support future generations.

פַּרְעֹה לְאַבְרָם וַיֹּאמֶר מַה מ"ה ־זֹּאת עָשִׂיתָ לִּי לָמָּה לֹא־הִגַּדְתָּ
לִּי כִּי אִשְׁתְּךָ הִוא׃ 19 לָמָה אָמַרְתָּ אֲחֹתִי הִוא וָאֶקַּח אֹתָהּ לִי
לְאִשָּׁה וְעַתָּה הִנֵּה אִשְׁתְּךָ קַח וָלֵךְ׃ 20 וַיְצַו עָלָיו פַּרְעֹה אֲנָשִׁים
וַיְשַׁלְּחוּ אֹתוֹ וְאֶת־אִשְׁתּוֹ וְאֶת־כָּל יל"י ־אֲשֶׁר־לוֹ׃ 13 1 וַיַּעַל
אַבְרָם מִמִּצְרַיִם מצר הוּא וְאִשְׁתּוֹ וְכָל יל"י ־אֲשֶׁר־לוֹ וְלוֹט מ"ה עִמּוֹ
הַנֶּגְבָּה׃ 2 וְאַבְרָם כָּבֵד מְאֹד בַּמִּקְנֶה בַּכֶּסֶף וּבַזָּהָב׃ 3 וַיֵּלֶךְ כל"י
לְמַסָּעָיו מִנֶּגֶב וְעַד־בֵּית ב"פ ראה ־אֵל יי"א עַד־הַמָּקוֹם יהוה ברבוע, ר"פ אל
אֲשֶׁר־הָיָה יהה שָׁם אָהֳלֹה בַּתְּחִלָּה בֵּין בֵּית ב"פ ראה ־אֵל יי"א וּבֵין
הָעָי׃ 4 אֶל־מְקוֹם יהוה ברבוע, ר"פ אל הַמִּזְבֵּחַ זן, נגד אֲשֶׁר־עָשָׂה שָׁם
בָּרִאשֹׁנָה וַיִּקְרָא עם ה' אותיות = ב"פ קס"א שָׁם אַבְרָם בְּשֵׁם שדי יהוה
יְהֹוָהאדניאהדונהי׃

THIRD READING - JACOB - TIFERET

5 וְגַם־לְלוֹט מ"ה הַהֹלֵךְ מיה אֶת־אַבְרָם הָיָה יהה צֹאן מלוי אהיה דיודין ע"ה
־וּבָקָר וְאֹהָלִים׃ 6 וְלֹא־נָשָׂא אֹתָם הָאָרֶץ אלהים דההין ע"ה לָשֶׁבֶת

The entire chain of human existence is forever interconnected, each link requiring all the others. Relying upon the spiritual merit and work of Abraham, Moses, and Rav Shimon bar Yochai, we are able to achieve what no other generation has achieved: the Final Redemption and freedom from Egypt and its Pharaoh. We can now escape the darkness of our world and the self-destructiveness of our ego.

וַיַּעַל

Genesis 13:1 – After leaving Egypt, Abram returned to Israel. The meaning of this is that whenever we reveal Light in a place, we should always return there to maintain our connection. If a person experiences a miracle in a particular locale, the person should revisit that place to tap into the source of this miraculous energy and keep it alive in his life.

Through reading about Abram's actions, therefore, we revisit Israel—which signifies the great spiritual elevation that Abram had attained—and in doing so, we reconnect to this Light to elevate our souls and achieve a miraculously peaceful transformation of the world.

[7] And there was strife between Abram's herdsmen and the herdsmen of Lot. And the Canaanites and Perizzites also dwelled in the land. [8] And Abram said to Lot, "Let there be no strife between you and me, I pray you, or between my herdsmen and your herdsmen, for we are brethren.

[9] Is not the whole land before you? Separate yourself from me, I pray you. If you will take the left hand, then I will go to the right; or if you depart to the right hand, then I will go to the left."

[10] And Lot lifted up his eyes and saw the whole plain of Jordan and that it was well watered, before the Lord destroyed Sodom and Gomorrah, even like the garden of the Lord, like the land of Egypt, as you come to Zo'ar.

[11] So Lot chose for himself the whole plain of Jordan and Lot journeyed east. And they separated themselves, the one from the other.

[12] Abram lived in the land of Canaan, while Lot lived in the cities of the plain and pitched his tent towards Sodom. [13] But the men of Sodom were wicked and were

---

הִפָּרֶד

Genesis 13:9 – The Bible says that strife arose between the herdsmen of Abram's cattle and the herdsmen of his nephew Lot's cattle. The *Zohar* reveals that this conflict is a code for Lot's desire to return to idol worship.

> *As soon as Abram realized that Lot had reverted TO IDOLATRY, he spoke to him. And Abram said to Lot, "Separate yourself, I pray you, from me" (Genesis 13:8-9), which is to say, You are not worthy of associating with me.*
> *– The Zohar, Lech Lecha 20:176*

Whenever we allow an external object or situation to control our behavior, our thoughts, or our emotions, we are committing the sin of idol-worship. Many people, for example, worship the idol of money. They are disciples of their businesses. Others are ruled by the appearances of those around them, obsessed by images of elegance and beauty, kneeling at the altars of fashion, praying to cultural icons for the self-image they feel they must convey to others. The moment we allow the external world to control our hearts and minds, we become idol-worshippers.

When Abram discovered that his nephew was once more engaged in idol-worship, he knew immediately that he had to separate himself completely from Lot. Significantly enough, Lot then chose to go to the city of Sodom (of Sodom and Gomorrah), while Abram chose the land of Israel.

At its core, this story pertains to the influence that our immediate environment exerts upon us. Anyone concerned with treading the path to Light must associate with people who are sincere in their desire for spiritual growth. Although our own intentions may be pure, the influences that surround us inevitably affect our consciousness and behavior, so having negative people in our life will eventually exert a negative influence on our life. As the *Zohar* says:

> *Whoever accompanies a wicked person shall eventually follow in his steps.*
> *– The Zohar, Lech Lecha 20:176*

The second lesson to be learned here is that like attracts like. Abram, being pure and positive, naturally moved to Israel. Lot, who possessed

יַחְדָּו כִּי־הָיָה יהה רְכוּשָׁם רָב וְלֹא יָכְלוּ לָשֶׁבֶת יַחְדָּו׃ 7 וַיְהִי אל
־רִיב בֵּין רֹעֵי מִקְנֵה־אַבְרָם וּבֵין רֹעֵי מִקְנֵה־לוֹט מ״ה וְהַכְּנַעֲנִי
וְהַפְּרִזִּי אָז יֹשֵׁב בָּאָרֶץ אלהים דאלפין׃ 8 וַיֹּאמֶר אַבְרָם אֶל־לוֹט מ״ה
אַל־נָא תְהִי מְרִיבָה בֵּינִי וּבֵינֶךָ וּבֵין רֹעַי וּבֵין רֹעֶיךָ כִּי־אֲנָשִׁים
אַחִים אֲנָחְנוּ׃ 9 הֲלֹא כָל ילי ־הָאָרֶץ אלהים דההין ע״ה לְפָנֶיךָ ס״ג - מ״ה - ב״ן
הִפָּרֶד נָא מֵעָלָי אִם יוהך ־הַשְּׂמֹאל וְאֵימִנָה וְאִם יוהך ־הַיָּמִין
וְאַשְׂמְאִילָה׃ 10 וַיִּשָּׂא־לוֹט מ״ה אֶת־עֵינָיו ריבוע מ״ה וַיַּרְא אֶת־כָּל ילי
־כִּכַּר הַיַּרְדֵּן י״פ יהוה וד׳ אותיות כִּי כֻלָּהּ מַשְׁקֶה לִפְנֵי | שַׁחֵת
יְהֹוָה יאהדונהי אֶת־סְדֹם ב״פ ב״ן וְאֶת־עֲמֹרָה כְּגַן־יְהֹוָה יאהדונהי כְּאֶרֶץ
אלהים דאלפין מִצְרַיִם מצר בֹּאֲכָה צֹעַר׃ 11 וַיִּבְחַר־לוֹ לוֹט מ״ה אֵת כָּל
ילי ־כִּכַּר הַיַּרְדֵּן י״פ יהוה וד׳ אותיות וַיִּסַּע לוֹט מ״ה מִקֶּדֶם רבוע ב״ן וַיִּפָּרְדוּ
אִישׁ ע״ה קנ״א קס״א מֵעַל עלם אָחִיו׃ 12 אַבְרָם יָשַׁב בְּאֶרֶץ אלהים דאלפין
־כְּנָעַן וְלוֹט מ״ה יָשַׁב בְּעָרֵי הַכִּכָּר וַיֶּאֱהַל עַד־סְדֹם ב״פ ב״ן׃

---

deeply negative traits, automatically gravitated toward Sodom and Gomorrah. If we behave in a positive manner toward others and resist our selfish tendencies, we will naturally attract the Light of the Creator into our lives. Instead of receiving short-term pleasure followed by misery and chaos, we will attract long-term fulfillment.

Through the verses that relate this story, we gain the power to separate ourselves from our own negative desires. We are then able to separate from our rash impulses and self-indulgent urges born of ego, just as Abram parted company with Lot.

Through the agency of our meditation on Abram's separation from Lot, Divine power and Light extends to the entire world immediately.

The *Zohar* also reveals that "Lot" is a code for the Serpent, or Satan, who cursed our world with death and destruction. This secret is found within the name Lot, which means "curse" in Aramaic. Hence, this reading separates the Serpent—Satan and death itself—from the physical world, banishing its influence from our lives forever.

All this happens if THE SOUL deserved to amend the body in this world and overcome the power of that cursed being, NAMELY THE EVIL INCLINATION THAT IS CALLED LOT, until it is separated from it. As it is written: "And there was strife between the herdsmen of Abram's cattle (WHICH IS THE SOUL) and the herdsmen of Lot's cattle (WHICH IS THE EVIL INCLINATION)." (Genesis 13:7). Because in this world on each and every day, those camps and rulers from the side of the soul are in strife with the camps and rulers from the side of the body, and they fight with each other—while all the parts of the body are trapped in agony between them, between the soul and the Serpent, between those forces that fight each other every day.

– The Zohar, Lech Lecha 11:85

sinning greatly against the Lord. 14 And the Lord said to Abram after Lot had separated from him, "Lift up your eyes from where you are and look north and south, east and west. 15 All the land that you see I will give to you and to your seed forever.

16 And I will make your seed like the dust of the earth, so that if a man could count the dust, then your seed could be counted.

17 Arise, walk through the length and breadth of the land, for I will give it to you."

18 Then Abram removed his tent and went and dwelt in the plain of Mamre, which is in Hebron, and he built there an altar to the Lord.

FOURTH READING - MOSES - NETZACH

14 1 And it came to pass in the days of Amraphel, king of Shinar, Arioch, king of Ellasar, Chedorlo'amer, king of Elam, and Tidal, king of nations; 2 that they went to war against Bera, king of Sodom, and with Birsha, king of Gomorrah, Shinab, king of Admah, Shemeber, king of Zeboi'im, and the king of Bela, which is Zo'ar.

3 All these latter kings joined forces in the Valley of Siddim, which is the Salt Sea.

4 Twelve years they served Chedorla'omer, and in the thirteenth year they rebelled.

5 And in the fourteenth year, Chedorla'omer and the kings allied with him smote the Rephaites in Ashteroth-Karna'im, the Zuzites in Ham, the Emites in Shaveh Kiri'atha'im, 6 and the Horites in their mount Seir, to Elparan which is by the wilderness.

וַיְהִי

Genesis 14:1 – War broke out in what is now the Middle East, with five nations attempting to destroy four other nations. During the reading of this section, we must meditate on bringing peace to the Middle East today. Ironically, most wars in history and all wars in the Middle East were caused by religion. The eminent Kabbalist Rav Yehuda Brandwein has pointed out that religion has been used to create separation, division, and conflict, rather than the unity and tolerance that is intended for all of God's children. He also wrote that The Kabbalah Centre was established to promote unity and tolerance among all people.

Kabbalah's aim is not to preach, convert, or convince, but rather to arouse respect for each person's path to the Light by fostering tolerance, human dignity, and understanding among people. Most importantly, Kabbalah reveals the similarities between faiths rather than emphasizing their differences. How can it be possible for there to be peace in the world if there is no peace between the children of God? Until we accord every human being the dignity and respect they deserve, there will be nothing but discord and strife on Earth. Thus, our meditation here is designed to engender amity, respect, and understanding between people of all faiths.

13 וְאַנְשֵׁי סְדֹם ב"פ ב"ן רָעִים וְחַטָּאִים לַיהֹוָהאדנייאהדונהי מְאֹד מ"ה:
14 וַיהֹוָהאדנייאהדונהי אָמַר אֶל־אַבְרָם אַחֲרֵי הִפָּרֶד־לוֹט מ"ה מֵעִמּוֹ
שָׂא נָא עֵינֶיךָ ע"ה קס"א וּרְאֵה ראה מִן־הַמָּקוֹם יהוה ברבוע, ו"פ אל אֲשֶׁר־
אַתָּה שָׁם צָפֹנָה ע"ה עסמ"ב וָנֶגְבָּה וָקֵדְמָה וָיָמָּה: 15 כִּי אֶת־כָּל ילי
־הָאָרֶץ אלהים דההין ע"ה אֲשֶׁר־אַתָּה רֹאֶה ראה לְךָ אֶתְּנֶנָּה וּלְזַרְעֲךָ
עַד־עוֹלָם: 16 וְשַׂמְתִּי אֶת־זַרְעֲךָ כַּעֲפַר הָאָרֶץ אלהים דההין ע"ה אֲשֶׁר |
אִם יוהך ־יוּכַל אִישׁ ע"ה קנ"א קס"א לִמְנוֹת אֶת־עֲפַר הָאָרֶץ אלהים דההין ע"ה
גַּם יגל ־זַרְעֲךָ יִמָּנֶה: 17 קוּם הִתְהַלֵּךְ מ"ה בָּאָרֶץ אלהים דאלפין לְאָרְכָּהּ
וּלְרָחְבָּהּ כִּי לְךָ אֶתְּנֶנָּה: 18 וַיֶּאֱהַל אַבְרָם וַיָּבֹא וַיֵּשֶׁב בְּאֵלֹנֵי
מַמְרֵא סנז"ף ע"ה אֲשֶׁר בְּחֶבְרוֹן וַיִּבֶן בינה ע"ה ־שָׁם מִזְבֵּחַ זן, נגד
לַיהֹוָהאדנייאהדונהי: [פ]

FOURTH READING - MOSES - NETZACH

14 1 וַיְהִי בִּימֵי אַמְרָפֶל מֶלֶךְ־שִׁנְעָר אַרְיוֹךְ אהיה רי"ו מֶלֶךְ אֶלָּסָר
אלהים דאלפין כְּדָרְלָעֹמֶר ב"פ יב"ק - שדי יהוה מֶלֶךְ עֵילָם וְתִדְעָל מֶלֶךְ
גּוֹיִם: 2 עָשׂוּ מִלְחָמָה אֶת־בֶּרַע רבוע אלהים רבוע יהוה מֶלֶךְ סְדֹם ב"פ ב"ן
וְאֶת־בִּרְשַׁע רבוע אלהים ע"ב אלהים דיודין מֶלֶךְ עֲמֹרָה שִׁנְאָב | מֶלֶךְ אַדְמָה
וְשֶׁמְאֵבֶר יהוה שדי קנ"א ב"ן מֶלֶךְ צְבוֹיִם (כתיב: צביים) וּמֶלֶךְ בֶּלַע הִיא־
צֹעַר: 3 כָּל ילי ־אֵלֶּה חָבְרוּ אֶל־עֵמֶק הַשִּׂדִּים הוּא יָם ילי הַמֶּלַח
ג"פ יהוה: 4 שְׁתֵּים עֶשְׂרֵה שָׁנָה עָבְדוּ אֶת־כְּדָרְלָעֹמֶר ב"פ יב"ק - שדי יהוה
וּשְׁלֹשׁ־עֶשְׂרֵה שָׁנָה מָרָדוּ: 5 וּבְאַרְבַּע עֶשְׂרֵה שָׁנָה בָּא
כְדָרְלָעֹמֶר ב"פ יב"ק - שדי יהוה וְהַמְּלָכִים אֲשֶׁר אִתּוֹ וַיַּכּוּ אֶת־רְפָאִים
בְּעַשְׁתְּרֹת קַרְנַיִם וְאֶת־הַזּוּזִים בְּהָם וְאֵת הָאֵימִים בְּשָׁוֵה

[7] And they returned and came to Enmishpat, which is Kadesh, and they smote the whole country of the Amalekites, and also the Amorites who were living in Hazazontamar.

[8] And the king of Sodom, and the king of Gomorrah, and the king of Admah, and the king of Zeboi'im and the king of Bela (Zo'ar) joined each other to battle with them in
the Valley of Siddim; [9] against Chedorla'omer, king of Elam, and with Tidal, king of
nations, and Amraphel, king of Shinar, and Arioch, king of Ellasar—four kings against five.

[10] And the Valley of Siddim was full of slime pits, and the kings of Sodom and Gomorrah fled and fell there, and those that survived fled to the mountain.

[11] And they (the four kings) took all the goods of Sodom and Gomorrah and all their victuals, and went on their way.

[12] They also took Lot, Abram's brother's son who dwelt in Sodom, and his goods and departed.

[13] And one who had escaped came and told Abram, the Hebrew; for he dwelt in the plain of Mamre the Amorite, brother of Eshcol and brother of Aner; and they were allied with Abram.

וַיָּבֹא

Genesis 14:13 – A series of small skirmishes eventually culminated in a battle during the time that Abram lived in Mamre. The battle was between a coalition of five kings and another opposing coalition of four kings, and it took place in the Valley of Siddim, which contained a salt sea. The five kings were defeated by the forces of the four kings, and in the process, the triumphant kings captured Lot. One of Lot's men escaped to tell Abram about his master's capture. Abram quickly assembled 318 armed servants to fight the army of the four kings, and against all odds, he and his men defeated the four kings and rescued his nephew, Lot.

Obviously, a small band of men cannot overpower the great armies of four nations. The secret to this victory is found in the number 318, the numerical value of the Aramaic word *siach*, which means "speech." Kabbalist Rav Berg tells us that *siach* refers to the speech of the angels. These angels may be conceived of as packets of energy, and are, in fact, the 72 Names of God, which consist of 72 three-letter sequences of Aramaic letters. These sequences are those same angelic forces that give us the power of mind over matter, and it was these names that Abram employed to conquer the four nations.

In spiritual terms, the four nations denote our own dark tendencies and self-destructive traits: our ego, or Evil Inclination. Through the 72 Names of God, we can attain the power of mind over matter, performing miracles of human nature, such as eliminating our negative qualities. These miracles, in turn, summon forth miracles of Mother Nature.

The *Zohar* offers another insight into the capture of Lot, explaining that Lot was similar in appearance to Abram. When the kings captured Lot, they believed mistakenly that they had apprehended Abram—a feat that was, in fact, the real purpose behind the war. These kings wanted to slay Abram because his sanctity had enlightened the people, leading them away from the futile and misguided practice of idol-worship, which happened to be the source of the kings' revenues and power.

קריתים: 6 ואת-החרי בהררם שעיר עד איל פארן אשר
על-המדבר: 7 וישבו ויבאו אל-עין ריבוע מ"ה משפט ע"ה ה"פ אלהים
הוא קדש ויכו את-כל ילי -שדה העמלקי וגם יג"ל את-האמרי
הישב בחצצן תמר ב"פ ש"ך: 8 ויצא מלך-סדם ב"פ ב"ן ומלך עמרה
ומלך אדמה ומלך צבוים (כתיב: צביים) ומלך בלע הוא-צער
ויערכו אתם מלחמה בעמק השדים: 9 את כדרלעמר
ב"פ יב"ק - שדי יהוה מלך עילם ותדעל מלך גוים ואמרפל מלך
שנער ואריוך אהיה רי"ו מלך אלסר אלהים דאלפין ארבעה מלכים
את-החמשה: 10 ועמק השדים בארת בארת חמר וינסו מלך-
סדם ב"פ ב"ן ועמרה ויפלו-שמה מהש והנשארים הרה נסו:
11 ויקחו חעם את-כל ילי -רכש סדם ב"פ ב"ן ועמרה ואת-כל ילי -אכלם
וילכו כלי: 12 ויקחו חעם את-לוט מ"ה ואת-רכשו בן-אחי ר"ת רבא
אברם וילכו כלי והוא ישב בסדם ב"פ ב"ן: 13 ויבא הפליט ויגד
לאברם העברי והוא שכן באלני ממרא סוזפך ע"ה האמרי

When all those kings joined to make war against Abram, they consulted one another about how to destroy him. But as soon as they took control of Lot, Abram's nephew, they immediately left. As it is written: "And they took Lot, Abram's brother's son, and his possessions and departed." (Genesis 14:12) Why did they do this? It was because Lot looked very much like Abram. As a result, they "departed," AS THEY BELIEVED THEY HAD CAPTURED ABRAM, which was the purpose of the war.

– The Zohar, Lech Lecha 24:234

From this section, we learn that people like Abram, who dare to initiate positive change and to help others in their spiritual awakening, always encounter opposition from the dark forces who seek to propagate chaos and ignorance for their own personal gain.

Throughout human history, any major advance in civilization was initially met with opposition, defiance, and scorn from those who did not realize how they could benefit from an improvement in the human condition. This represents a spiritual principle that holds true in our personal lives. As opportunities for spiritual advancement present themselves to us, we will encounter obstacles and opposition from our ego and from negative people around us. This Bible passage thus contains an energy that overthrows the dark forces attempting to impede our spiritual progress.

14 And when Abram heard that his brethren was taken captive, he armed his trained servants, born in his own house, 318 of them, and pursued them to Dan.

15 And he divided himself and his servants from them during the night, and smote them, and he chased them to Hobah, which is on the left hand of Damascus.

16 He brought back all the goods and also brought back his brethren Lot and his goods, together with the women and the people.

17 And the king of Sodom went out to meet him when he returned from defeating Chedorla'omer and the kings that were with him, at the Valley of Shaveh, which is the King's Valley.

18 And Melchizedek, king of Salem, brought out bread and wine. He was the priest of the most high God,

19 and he blessed him, saying, "Blessed be Abram of the most high God, Creator of heaven and earth.

20 And blessed be the most high God, who delivered your enemies into your hand." And he gave him tithes of everything.

FIFTH READING - AARON - HOD

וַיִּתֶּן־לוֹ

Genesis 14:20 – After the war, Malkitzedek, king of Salem, offered Abram the spoils of war, but Abram refused to accept and instead tithed it all away.

According to Kabbalah, money possesses Light and energy that can influence our lives in unseen ways. We should thus be very careful to deal only with money that is derived through honest labor conducted for positive goals. Money gained illicitly possesses no Light. It might constitute a temporary financial or material gain, but eventually, it will usher darkness and negativity into the lives of those possessing it.

The *Zohar* also reveals a secret concerning the power that is generated through the tithing of income. Because we live in a physical world, the negative force of Satan is allowed nourishment while carrying out the task of testing us and tempting us into sin via our ego. Thus, all the financial sustenance we earn is tainted by this dark presence. By tithing our money and by sharing it, we thwart Satan's influence in our life and sever ourselves from him.

Regarding the amount of a tithe, the *Zohar* says:

> *It is one out of ten, and ten out of a hundred....*
> *– The Zohar, Lech Lecha 25:257*

אֲחִי אֶשְׁכֹּל וַאֲחִי עָנֵר ש״ך וְהֵם בַּעֲלֵי בְרִית־אַבְרָם׃ 14 וַיִּשְׁמַע
אַבְרָם כִּי נִשְׁבָּה אָחִיו וַיָּרֶק אֶת־חֲנִיכָיו יְלִידֵי בֵיתוֹ ב״פ ראה
שְׁמֹנָה עָשָׂר וּשְׁלֹשׁ מֵאוֹת וַיִּרְדֹּף עַד־דָּן׃ 15 וַיֵּחָלֵק עֲלֵיהֶם ׀
לַיְלָה מלה הוּא וַעֲבָדָיו וַיַּכֵּם וַיִּרְדְּפֵם עַד־חוֹבָה אֲשֶׁר מִשְּׂמֹאל
לְדַמָּשֶׂק׃ 16 וַיָּשֶׁב אֵת כָּל ילי ־הָרְכֻשׁ וְגַם יג״ל אֶת־לוֹט מ״ה אָחִיו
וּרְכֻשׁוֹ הֵשִׁיב וְגַם אֶת־הַנָּשִׁים וְאֶת־הָעָם׃ 17 וַיֵּצֵא מֶלֶךְ־סְדֹם
ב״פ ב״ן לִקְרָאתוֹ אַחֲרֵי שׁוּבוֹ מֵהַכּוֹת אֶת־כְּדָרְלָעֹמֶר ב״פ יב״ק ÷ שדי יהוה
וְאֶת־הַמְּלָכִים אֲשֶׁר אִתּוֹ אֶל־עֵמֶק שָׁוֵה הוּא עֵמֶק הַמֶּלֶךְ׃
18 וּמַלְכִּי־צֶדֶק מֶלֶךְ שָׁלֵם הוֹצִיא ר״ת משה לֶחֶם ג״פ יהוה וָיָיִן מיכ, י״פ ההא
וְהוּא כֹהֵן מלה לְאֵל ייא״י עֶלְיוֹן רבוע ס״ג׃ 19 וַיְבָרְכֵהוּ וַיֹּאמַר בָּרוּךְ
יהוה ע״ב רבוע מ״ה אַבְרָם לְאֵל ייא״י עֶלְיוֹן רבוע ס״ג קֹנֵה שָׁמַיִם י״פ טל, י״פ כוזו
וָאָרֶץ אלהים דאלפין׃ 20 וּבָרוּךְ יהוה ע״ב רבוע מ״ה אֵל ייא״י עֶלְיוֹן רבוע ס״ג
אֲשֶׁר־מִגֵּן ר״ת מיכאל, גבריאל, נוריאל צָרֶיךָ בְּיָדֶךָ וַיִּתֶּן י״פ מלוי ע״ב ־לוֹ
מַעֲשֵׂר ירת מִכֹּל ילי׃

It is made abundantly clear here that when we tithe ten percent of our earnings we disconnect our means of livelihood from the influence of Satan. By giving away ten percent, we create an opening to receive even greater sustenance in return. Conversely, we might save ourselves ten percent in the short term by not tithing, but we have also given Satan open access into our lives, where he will assuredly cause ten times more chaos, whether it is in the realms of finance, health, relationships, or our emotional well-being.

Moreover, the sages teach that whatever the amount of our annual income, no matter how large or how small it may be, the Divine Light has always increased it for us by an extra ten per cent to allow us to tithe without hardship. Because the process of sharing income is an important tool in preventing Satan from entering our lives, tithing is not considered charity but rather protection from the Satan. It is only the next ten percent of one's income, the portion we may choose to give over and above the original tithe, which is considered to be a genuine act of charity. The first tithe is mere self-preservation.

By tithing away all the spoils from the war, Abram received in return eternal spiritual blessings, which ensured his immortality. For this reason, because of Abram's selfless actions and merit, we who are his descendants can now summon the Light of Immortality into our world, cutting off the dark influence of the Angel of Death forever.

[21] And the king of Sodom said to Abram, "Give me the people and keep the goods for yourself."

[22] And Abram said to the king of Sodom, "I have lifted up my hand to the Lord, the most high God, Creator of heaven and earth, [23] that I will take nothing from a thread to a shoe-latchet, and that I will not take anything belonging to you, lest you should say, 'I made Abram rich.' [24] Only that which the young men have eaten, and the portion of the men that went with me, Aner, Eshcol, and Mamre, let them take their share.

15[1] After these things, the word of the Lord came to Abram in a vision saying, "Fear not, Abram. I am your shield, and your exceeding great reward."

[2] And Abram said, "Lord God, what can You give me, since I remain childless and the steward of my house is Eliezer of Damascus?" [3] And Abram said, "Behold to me You have given no seed; and so a servant born in my house is my heir."

[4] And behold, the word of the Lord came to him saying, "This man will not be your heir, but he that will come from your own body will be your heir."

[5] And He took him outside and said, "Look now toward heaven and tell the stars, if you can count them." And He said to him, "So shall your seed be." [6] And he believed the Lord, and he counted it to him as righteousness.

וַיּוֹצֵא

Genesis 15:5 – Abram cried out to God, lamenting his inability to have children because he had seen in the stars that he was not destined to father a child. The Creator explained that all people have certain judgments hanging over them as a consequence of deeds committed in this or past lives, and that these decrees of judgment are visible by means of astrology, the computation of planetary and stellar influences.

However, God also told Abram that it was up to him to rise above the planetary influences by transforming his inner nature and utilizing the power of Light of the Creator. The secret is revealed in the *Zohar*:

> *God said to him, "Do not look to this—THE WISDOM OF THE STARS—but rather to the secret of My Name, WHICH IS THE NUKVA. You shall father a son!"*
> *– The Zohar, Lech Lecha 30:322*

When a man changes his internal nature, the physical world mirrors his action. The power of mind over matter is thus activated and judgments are nullified. It is vital to realize that the positions of the planets do not mandate an irrevocable destiny for anyone; instead, they represent a potential reality, should we not transform. Humankind can rise above planetary influences; indeed, it is everyone's duty to rise above them. By granting Abram this wisdom, God actually severed him from the influences of the astrological configurations of his birth chart.

Each of us has the power to change anything—and indeed everything—in our lives. Judgments invoked against us as a consequence of our past actions can be removed, but only if we remove

FIFTH READING - AARON - HOD

21 וַיֹּאמֶר מֶלֶךְ־סְדֹם ב״פ ב״ן אֶל־אַבְרָם תֶּן־לִי הַנֶּפֶשׁ רמ״ח + ז׳ הויות
וְהָרְכֻשׁ קַח־לָךְ: 22 וַיֹּאמֶר אַבְרָם אֶל־מֶלֶךְ סְדֹם ב״פ ב״ן הֲרִמֹתִי
יָדִי אֶל־יְהֹוָהאדניאהדונהי אֵל ייא״י עֶלְיוֹן רבוע ס״ג קֹנֵה שָׁמַיִם י״פ טל, י״פ כוזו
וָאָרֶץ אלהים דאלפין: 23 אִם יוהך ־מִחוּט וְעַד שְׂרוֹךְ־נַעַל ע״ה קנ״א וְאִם
יוהך ־אֶקַּח מִכָּל ילי ־אֲשֶׁר־לָךְ וְלֹא תֹאמַר אֲנִי אני הֶעֱשַׁרְתִּי אֶת־
אַבְרָם: 24 בִּלְעָדַי רַק אֲשֶׁר אָכְלוּ הַנְּעָרִים וְחֵלֶק הָאֲנָשִׁים
אֲשֶׁר הָלְכוּ מיה אִתִּי עָנֵר ש״ך אֶשְׁכֹּל וּמַמְרֵא סוזזף ע״ה הֵם יִקְחוּ וזעם
חֶלְקָם: [ס] 15 1 אַחַר | הַדְּבָרִים ראה הָאֵלֶּה הָיָה יהה דְבַר ראה ־יְהֹוָהאדניאהדונהי
אֶל־אַבְרָם בַּמַּחֲזֶה לֵאמֹר אַל־תִּירָא אַבְרָם אָנֹכִי איע מָגֵן
ר״ת מיכאל, גבריאל, נוריאל לָךְ שְׂכָרְךָ הַרְבֵּה מְאֹד מ״ה; ר״ת משה: 2 וַיֹּאמֶר
אַבְרָם אֲדֹנָי ללה יֱהֹוִהאדניאהדונהי מַה מ״ה ־תִּתֶּן ב״פ כהת ־לִי וְאָנֹכִי איע
הוֹלֵךְ מיה עֲרִירִי וּבֶן־מֶשֶׁק בֵּיתִי ב״פ ראה הוּא דַּמֶּשֶׂק אֱלִיעֶזֶר:
3 וַיֹּאמֶר אַבְרָם הֵן לִי לֹא נָתַתָּה זָרַע וְהִנֵּה בֶן־בֵּיתִי ב״פ ראה
יוֹרֵשׁ אֹתִי: 4 וְהִנֵּה מ״ה יה דְבַר ראה ־יְהֹוָהאדניאהדונהי אֵלָיו לֵאמֹר לֹא
יִירָשְׁךָ זֶה כִּי־אִם יוהך אֲשֶׁר יֵצֵא מִמֵּעֶיךָ הוּא יִירָשֶׁךָ: 5 וַיּוֹצֵא
אֹתוֹ הַחוּצָה וַיֹּאמֶר הַבֶּט־נָא הַשָּׁמַיְמָה וּסְפֹר הַכּוֹכָבִים אִם
יוהך ־תּוּכַל לִסְפֹּר אֹתָם וַיֹּאמֶר לוֹ כֹּה הי״ יִהְיֶה יי״ זַרְעֶךָ: 6 וְהֶאֱמִן
בַּיהֹוָהאדניאהדונהי וַיַּחְשְׁבֶהָ לּוֹ צְדָקָה ע״ה ריבוע אלהים:

---

the negative trait that was the original cause of our misguided action.

Through the great power intrinsic in these verses, the entire world can overcome the planetary influences shaping our communal future. As we admit to and reflect upon our own negative traits, we are able immediately to shift the direction of our lives as well as the course of the collective destiny of mankind. In so doing, we usher in a future that embodies the tender mercies of a Messianic Age, where humanity is fully redeemed, both individually and on a global level.

SIXTH READING - JOSEPH - YESOD

[7] And He also said to him, "I am the Lord, who brought you out of Ur of the Chaldeans to give you this land to inherit it." [8] And he said, "Lord God, whereby will I inherit it?" [9] And He said to him, "Bring Me a heifer of three years old, and a she-goat of three years old, and a ram of three years old, and a dove and a young pigeon." [10] And he brought all these to Him, and he divided them in two and arranged the halves opposite each other; but the birds he did not divide.

[11] And when the fowls came down on the carcasses, Abram drove them away. [12] And when the sun was going down, a deep sleep fell upon Abram, and a dreadful darkness came over him. [13] And He said to Abram, "Know for certain that your seed will be strangers in a land that is not their own, and they will serve them and they will be mistreated four hundred years.

[14] And also that nation that they will serve, will I judge, and afterward they will come out with great substance. [15] And you will go to your fathers in peace and you will be buried at a good old age.

[16] But in the fourth generation your descendants will come back here, for the iniquity of the Amorites is not yet full." [17] And it came to pass that when the sun went down, and it was dark, a smoking furnace and a burning lamp appeared and passed between the pieces.

[18] On that same day the Lord made a covenant with Abram and said, "To your seed I give this land, from the river of Egypt to the great river, the Euphrates: [19] the Kenites, and the Kenizzites, and the Kadmonites, [20] and the Hittites, and the Perizzites, and the Rephaites,

---

וַיֹּאמַר

Genesis 15:9 – After God took Abram out of Ur, city of the Chaldeans, the first bond between the Creator and humanity was forged.

We are all a part of God. Spiritually, each of us is a Divine spark of Light, but humans did not have a physical connection to God until the first bond mentioned above was forged. The effect of it was to infuse humanity with the power to be God-like on a physical level. But there is a prerequisite for activating this inherited Divine trait: We must emulate Abram, who embodies the ideals both of unconditional caring for others and of imparting Light to one's fellow man. The failure to live in this manner is what disconnects us from the Creator and from the God-like quality embedded within the soul.

Therefore, these particular Bible verses contain vibrations that can strengthen our personal bond to the Light of the Creator and awaken in us the *Desire to Share.*

SIXTH READING - JOSEPH - YESOD

7 וַיֹּאמֶר אֵלָיו אֲנִי אני יְהֹוָהאדניאהדונהי אֲשֶׁר הוֹצֵאתִיךָ מֵאוּר
כַּשְׂדִּים לָתֶת לְךָ אֶת־הָאָרֶץ אלהים דההין ע״ה הַזֹּאת לְרִשְׁתָּהּ׃
8 וַיֹּאמַר אֲדֹנָי ללה יֱהֹוִהאדניאהדונהי בַּמָּה אֵדַע כִּי אִירָשֶׁנָּה׃ 9 וַיֹּאמֶר
אֵלָיו קְחָה לִי עֶגְלָה מְשֻׁלֶּשֶׁת וְעֵז מְשֻׁלֶּשֶׁת וְאַיִל מְשֻׁלָּשׁ וְתֹר
וְגוֹזָל׃ 10 וַיִּקַּח חעם ־לוֹ אֶת־כָּל ילי ־אֵלֶּה וַיְבַתֵּר אֹתָם בַּתָּוֶךְ וַיִּתֵּן
אִישׁ ע״ה קנ״א קס״א ־בִּתְרוֹ לִקְרַאת רֵעֵהוּ וְאֶת־הַצִּפֹּר לֹא בָתָר׃
11 וַיֵּרֶד רי״י הָעַיִט עַל־הַפְּגָרִים וַיַּשֵּׁב אֹתָם אַבְרָם׃ 12 וַיְהִי
הַשֶּׁמֶשׁ ב״פ ש״ך לָבוֹא וְתַרְדֵּמָה ט״פ ע״ב נָפְלָה עַל־אַבְרָם וְהִנֵּה אֵימָה
חֲשֵׁכָה גְדֹלָה להח, מבה, יזל, אום נֹפֶלֶת עָלָיו׃ 13 וַיֹּאמֶר לְאַבְרָם יָדֹעַ
תֵּדַע כִּי־גֵר ב״ן - קנ״א | יִהְיֶה ייי זַרְעֲךָ בְּאֶרֶץ אלהים דאלפין לֹא לָהֶם
וַעֲבָדוּם וְעִנּוּ אֹתָם אַרְבַּע מֵאוֹת שָׁנָה׃ 14 וְגַם אֶת־הַגּוֹי מלוי מ״ה
אֲשֶׁר יַעֲבֹדוּ דָּן אָנֹכִי איע וְאַחֲרֵי־כֵן יֵצְאוּ בִּרְכֻשׁ
גָּדוֹל להח, מבה, יזל, אום׃ 15 וְאַתָּה תָּבוֹא אֶל־אֲבֹתֶיךָ בְּשָׁלוֹם
תִּקָּבֵר בְּשֵׂיבָה טוֹבָה אכא׃ 16 וְדוֹר רי״ו, גבורה רְבִיעִי יָשׁוּבוּ
הֵנָּה יהוה מ״ה כִּי לֹא־שָׁלֵם ש״ע עֲוֹן ג״פ מ״ב הָאֱמֹרִי עַד־הֵנָּה יהוה מ״ה׃
17 וַיְהִי הַשֶּׁמֶשׁ ב״פ ש״ך בָּאָה וַעֲלָטָה הָיָה יהה וְהִנֵּה יהוה מ״ה תַנּוּר
עָשָׁן וְלַפִּיד אֵשׁ אלהים דיודין ע״ה אֲשֶׁר עָבַר בֵּין הַגְּזָרִים הָאֵלֶּה׃
18 בַּיּוֹם נגד, זן, מזבח הַהוּא כָּרַת יְהֹוָהאדניאהדונהי אֶת־אַבְרָם בְּרִית
לֵאמֹר לְזַרְעֲךָ נָתַתִּי אֶת־הָאָרֶץ אלהים דההין ע״ה הַזֹּאת מִנְּהַר מִצְרַיִם
מצר עַד־הַנָּהָר הַגָּדֹל להח, מבה, יזל, אום נְהַר־פְּרָת׃ 19 אֶת־הַקֵּינִי וְאֶת־
הַקְּנִזִּי וְאֵת הַקַּדְמֹנִי׃ 20 וְאֶת־הַחִתִּי וְאֶת־הַפְּרִזִּי וְאֶת־הָרְפָאִים׃
21 וְאֶת־הָאֱמֹרִי וְאֶת־הַכְּנַעֲנִי וְאֶת־הַגִּרְגָּשִׁי וְאֶת־הַיְבוּסִי׃ [ס]

[21] and the Amorites, and the Canaanites, and the Girgashites and the Jebusites."

16[1] Now Sarai, Abram's wife, had borne him no children. But she had an Egyptian maidservant named Hagar; [2] And Sarai said to Abram, "The Lord has kept me from having children. Go, sleep with my maidservant; perhaps I can build a family through her." Abram agreed to what Sarai said.

[3] So after Abram had been living in Canaan ten years, Sarai his wife took her Egyptian maidservant Hagar and gave her to her husband to be his wife.

[4] He slept with Hagar, and she conceived. When she knew she was pregnant, she began to despise her mistress.

[5] Then Sarai said to Abram, "You are responsible for the wrong I am suffering. I put my servant in your arms, and now that she knows she is pregnant, she despises me. May the Lord judge between you and me."

[6] "Your servant is in your hands," Abram said. "Do with her whatever you think best." Then Sarai mistreated Hagar; so she fled from her.

[7] The angel of the Lord found Hagar near a spring in the desert; it was the spring that is beside the road to Shur.

[8] And he said, "Hagar, servant of Sarai, where have you come from, and where are you going?" "I'm running away from my mistress, Sarai," she answered.

[9] Then the angel of the Lord told her, "Go back to your mistress and submit to her."

[10] The angel added, "I will so increase your descendants that they will be too numerous to count."

[11] The angel of the Lord also said to her: "You are now with child and you will have a son. You shall name him Ishmael, for the Lord has heard of your misery.

Genesis 16:1 – Abram's wife, Sarai, was unable to bear children, so Sarai told Abram to father a child with their Egyptian maidservant, Hagar. Abram agreed, and through this union, Ishmael, the seed and father of all the Arab nations, was born. Ishmael and Abram's future son, Isaac, the father of the Israelites are united in Abraham, their common father. One of the very few places in the world where you could once find Israelites and Muslims praying side by side is at the tomb of Abraham in Hebron.

The Light emanating from this story therefore helps to engender unconditional love and respect for human dignity, not just between Israelites and Muslims but in all of humanity. Through this teaching, intolerance can be banished from the hearts of humans, and racial or religious barriers can dissolve completely.

16 1 וְשָׂרַי אֵשֶׁת אַבְרָם לֹא יָלְדָה לוֹ וְלָהּ שִׁפְחָה ג' מלויי אהיה
מִצְרִית מצר וּשְׁמָהּ הָגָר ר"פ ב"ן׃ 2 וַתֹּאמֶר שָׂרַי אֶל־אַבְרָם הִנֵּה מ"ה יה ־נָא
עֲצָרַנִי יְהֹוָהיאהדונהי מִלֶּדֶת בֹּא־נָא אֶל־שִׁפְחָתִי אוּלַי אום אִבָּנֶה
מִמֶּנָּה וַיִּשְׁמַע אַבְרָם לְקוֹל ע"ב ס"ג ע"ה שָׂרָי׃ 3 וַתִּקַּח שָׂרַי אֵשֶׁת־
אַבְרָם אֶת־הָגָר ר"פ ב"ן הַמִּצְרִית מצר שִׁפְחָתָהּ מִקֵּץ מנק עֶשֶׂר שָׁנִים
לְשֶׁבֶת אַבְרָם בְּאֶרֶץ אלהים דאלפין כְּנָעַן וַתִּתֵּן ב"פ כהת אֹתָהּ לְאַבְרָם
אִישָׁהּ לוֹ לְאִשָּׁה׃ 4 וַיָּבֹא אֶל־הָגָר ר"פ ב"ן וַתַּהַר וַתֵּרֶא כִּי הָרָתָה
וַתֵּקַל גְּבִרְתָּהּ בְּעֵינֶיהָ ריבוע מ"ה׃ 5 וַתֹּאמֶר שָׂרַי אֶל־אַבְרָם חֲמָסִי
עָלֶיךָ ה' הויות אָנֹכִי איע נָתַתִּי שִׁפְחָתִי בְּחֵיקֶךָ וַתֵּרֶא כִּי הָרָתָה
וָאֵקַל בְּעֵינֶיהָ ריבוע מ"ה יִשְׁפֹּט יְהֹוָהיאהדונהי בֵּינִי וּבֵינֶיךָ׃ 6 וַיֹּאמֶר
אַבְרָם אֶל־שָׂרַי הִנֵּה שִׁפְחָתֵךְ בְּיָדֵךְ עֲשִׂי־לָהּ הַטּוֹב והו בְּעֵינָיִךְ
ע"ה קס"א וַתְּעַנֶּהָ שָׂרַי וַתִּבְרַח מִפָּנֶיהָ׃ 7 וַיִּמְצָאָהּ מַלְאַךְ
יְהֹוָהיאהדונהי עַל־עֵין ריבוע מ"ה הַמַּיִם בַּמִּדְבָּר רמ"ח, אברהם עַל־הָעַיִן
ריבוע מ"ה, נמם בְּדֶרֶךְ ב"פ יב"ק שׁוּר אבג"יתצ, ושר, אהבת חנם׃ 8 וַיֹּאמַר הָגָר ר"פ ב"ן
שִׁפְחַת שָׂרַי אֵי־מִזֶּה בָאת וְאָנָה תֵלֵכִי וַתֹּאמֶר מִפְּנֵי שָׂרַי
גְּבִרְתִּי אָנֹכִי איע בֹּרַחַת׃ 9 וַיֹּאמֶר לָהּ מַלְאַךְ יְהֹוָהיאהדונהי שׁוּבִי

וּבֵינֶיךָ

Genesis 16:5 – Whenever a dot appears above an Aramaic word in the Bible, as it does here over the word *uveineicha*, meaning "between you," it signifies an additional emanation of a particular spiritual force into our life. Here, for example, we receive protection from the Evil Eye, which is the negative force generated by jealous glances and resentful looks that we receive from those who harbor envy or ill will toward us. Kabbalists generally attribute most common ailments and misfortunes to the effects of the Evil Eye. This, of course, works both ways. When we inflict our own Evil Eye on others, we create an opening and space inside ourselves that attracts negativity, making us in turn more vulnerable to jealous glances and resentful looks. The act of envying or wishing harm to others is thus a vicious circle, bringing equal damage to both the envier and the envied.

The dot above the word *uveineicha*, then, signifies a force that helps eradicate the envy and ill-will that we harbor toward other people, generating in turn a field of protection around us to shield us from the effects of any Evil Eye that might be directed at us by others.

12 He will be a wild donkey of a man; his hand will be against everyone and everyone's hand against him, and he will live in hostility toward all his brothers."

13 She gave this name to the Lord who spoke to her: "You are the God who sees me," for she said, "I have now seen the One who sees me."

14 This is why the well was called Beer Lahai Roi; it is still there, between Kadesh and Bered.

15 So Hagar bore Abram a son, and Abram gave the name Ishmael to the son she had
borne. 16 Abram was eighty-six years old when Hagar bore him Ishmael.

17:1 When Abram was ninety-nine years old, the Lord appeared to Abram and said to him, "I am God Almighty; walk before Me and be you perfect.

2 And I will make My covenant between Me and you and will multiply you exceedingly."

3 And Abram fell on his face, and God talked with him saying, 4 "As for Me, this is My
covenant with you: You will be a father of many nations.

אַבְרָהָם

Genesis 17:5 – While he was still under the influence of the stars, Abraham was called Abram. After his spiritual transformation, when he was no longer ruled by fate, the Aramaic letter *Hei* was added to his name, changing it from Abram to Abraham.

According to the sages, a person's Aramaic name is the spiritual genetic code of his or her soul, and the kabbalistic concept of altering a person's name alphabetically can be compared to the science of genetic engineering, in which the genetic code of a person is altered to reduce a genetic predisposition to various diseases and ailments. Interestingly, all DNA is structured and consequently classified alphabetically, and our genetic code is written out using four chemical letters: A, T, C, and G, the initial letters of the nucleotides that make up the strand of DNA.

Therefore, just as our traits can be changed if our DNA is altered, Abram's traits were changed when his spiritual DNA was altered. When his name was changed to Abraham, his entire being was transformed.

The spiritual influences emanating from this passage of the Bible thus imbue us with the power to alter our spiritual DNA, thereby changing our destiny. By transforming the negative aspects of our nature, we rise above cosmic influences, remove judgments that may be hanging over us, and evolve to higher levels of spirituality.

Since each of the Aramaic letters also represents a number, we should look at the numerical value of Abraham's new name, which is 248, corresponding precisely to the number of bones and bone segments in the human body. Our connection to the name "Abraham" thus sets up a healing vibration, generated by the Light and by mercy from Abraham, to resonate throughout our body, restoring our natural health.

According to Kabbalah, the concept of an Aramaic name is critically important, since it allows traits and qualities associated with that particular name to be transferred to a person's soul. This is the reason we are advised to name our children after the great figures of the Bible—to imbue them with the noble traits of their namesakes.

אֶל־גְּבִרְתֵּךְ וְהִתְעַנִּי תַּחַת יָדֶיהָ: 10 וַיֹּאמֶר לָהּ מַלְאַךְ
יְהֹוָה יאהדונהי הַרְבָּה אַרְבֶּה יצחק, ד"פ ב"ן אֶת־זַרְעֵךְ וְלֹא יִסָּפֵר מֵרֹב:
11 וַיֹּאמֶר לָהּ מַלְאַךְ יְהֹוָה יאהדונהי הִנָּךְ הָרָה וְיֹלַדְתְּ ס"ת כהת בֵּן
וְקָרָאת שְׁמוֹ מהש ע"ה יִשְׁמָעֵאל כִּי־שָׁמַע יְהֹוָה יאהדונהי אֶל־עָנְיֵךְ:
12 וְהוּא יִהְיֶה ייי פֶּרֶא אָדָם מ"ה יָדוֹ בַכֹּל לכב וְיַד כֹּל ילי בּוֹ וְעַל־
פְּנֵי חכמה + בינה כָל ילי ־אֶחָיו יִשְׁכֹּן: 13 וַתִּקְרָא שֵׁם יהוה שדי ־יְהֹוָה יאהדונהי
הַדֹּבֵר ראה אֵלֶיהָ אַתָּה אֵל ייא"י רֳאִי כִּי אָמְרָה הֲגַם הֲלֹם רָאִיתִי
אַחֲרֵי רֹאִי: 14 עַל־כֵּן קָרָא לַבְּאֵר קנ"א + ב"ן בְּאֵר קנ"א + ב"ן לַחַי רֹאִי
הִנֵּה בֵין־קָדֵשׁ וּבֵין בָּרֶד: 15 וַתֵּלֶד הָגָר ד"פ ב"ן לְאַבְרָם בֵּן וַיִּקְרָא
עם ה' אותיות = ב"פ קס"א אַבְרָם שֶׁם יהוה שדי ־בְּנוֹ אֲשֶׁר־יָלְדָה הָגָר ד"פ ב"ן
יִשְׁמָעֵאל: 16 וְאַבְרָם בֶּן־שְׁמֹנִים שָׁנָה וְשֵׁשׁ שָׁנִים בְּלֶדֶת־הָגָר
ד"פ ב"ן אֶת־יִשְׁמָעֵאל לְאַבְרָם: [ס] 17 1 וַיְהִי אַבְרָם בֶּן־תִּשְׁעִים
שָׁנָה וְתֵשַׁע שָׁנִים וַיֵּרָא יְהֹוָה יאהדונהי אֶל־אַבְרָם וַיֹּאמֶר אֵלָיו
אֲנִי אני ־אֵל שַׁדַּי מהש הִתְהַלֵּךְ מיה לְפָנַי וֶהְיֵה יהוה, יהה תָמִים:
2 וְאֶתְּנָה בְרִיתִי בֵּינִי וּבֵינֶךָ וְאַרְבֶּה יצחק, ד"פ ב"ן אוֹתְךָ בִּמְאֹד
מְאֹד מ"ה: 3 וַיִּפֹּל אַבְרָם עַל־פָּנָיו וַיְדַבֵּר ראה אִתּוֹ אֱלֹהִים
ילה, מום לֵאמֹר: 4 אֲנִי אני הִנֵּה מ"ה יה בְרִיתִי אִתָּךְ וְהָיִיתָ לְאַב
הֲמוֹן גּוֹיִם: 5 וְלֹא־יִקָּרֵא עוֹד אֶת־שִׁמְךָ אַבְרָם וְהָיָה
יהוה, יהה שִׁמְךָ אַבְרָהָם ו"פ אל, רמ"ח כִּי אַב־הֲמוֹן גּוֹיִם נְתַתִּיךָ:

The reverse is also true. If a child is named after a relative who experienced hardship in life—whether health-related, financial, or marital—the spiritual traits and karmic debts of this relative are frequently passed on to that child. In such cases, we are advised to change the child's name to connect him with the people in the Bible who are chariots for positive, powerful energy. If a child has been named after a relative who had a biblical name but who also experienced great misfortune, it is still possible to change the DNA of the name currently borne by the child. For example, if the child was named after his unfortunate grandfather David, it is possible to redirect the name from the grandfather back to King David. The name remains the same, but through meditation and other spiritual tools, the DNA of the name is switched to that of King David.

[5] No longer will you be called Abram; your name will be Abraham, for I have made you a father of many nations.

[6] I will make you exceedingly fruitful; and I will make nations of you, and kings will come out of you.

SEVENTH READING - DAVID - MALCHUT

[7] And I will establish My covenant between Me and you and your seed after you for the generations to come, as an everlasting covenant to be your God to you and to your seed after you. [8] And I will give to you and to your seed after you the land in which you are a stranger, all the land of Canaan, for an everlasting possession; and I will be their God."

[9] And God said to Abraham, "You must keep My covenant, you and your seed after you for the generations to come. [10] This is My covenant you shall keep, between Me and you and your seed after you: Every male child among you shall be circumcised.

[11] And you will circumcise the flesh of your foreskin and it will be the sign of the covenant between Me and you.

[12] And he that is eight days old shall be circumcised among you, every man child in your generations, he that is born in the house, or bought with money of any stranger that is not of thy seed.

[13] He that is born in your house, and he that is bought with your money, must be circumcised: and My covenant shall be in your flesh for an everlasting covenant.

[14] And the uncircumcised male child, whose flesh of his foreskin is not circumcised, that soul will be cut off from his people; he has broken My covenant."

[15] And God said to Abraham, "As for Sarai, your wife, you are no longer to call her Sarai; her name will be Sarah.

וּנְמַלְתֶּם

Genesis 17:11 – The male sexual organ corresponds to the spiritual world of *Yesod*, which is located directly above our world of *Malchut*. *Yesod* is a vast reservoir into which the eight Upper Worlds above *Yesod* pour their individual spiritual forces.

Yesod is the portal and the funnel through which all this positive spiritual energy flows into our own dimension. This great Light is responsible for the miracle of procreation and for the pleasure of sexuality derived from the act of intercourse. But as one might expect, countless negative forces hover around *Yesod*, attempting to ensnare the great Light that flows out from there.

The situation is precisely mirrored by conditions in our world, where negative forces attach themselves to the male sexual organ (which is the physical embodiment of *Yesod*) from the moment a male child enters the world. The

6 וְהִפְרֵתִי אֹתְךָ בִּמְאֹד מ״ה מְאֹד מ״ה וּנְתַתִּיךָ לְגוֹיִם וּמְלָכִים
מִמְּךָ יֵצֵאוּ׃

SEVENTH READING - DAVID - MALCHUT

7 וַהֲקִמֹתִי אֶת־בְּרִיתִי בֵּינִי וּבֵינֶךָ וּבֵין זַרְעֲךָ אַחֲרֶיךָ לְדֹרֹתָם
לִבְרִית עוֹלָם לִהְיוֹת לְךָ לֵאלֹהִים ילה, מום וּלְזַרְעֲךָ אַחֲרֶיךָ׃
8 וְנָתַתִּי לְךָ וּלְזַרְעֲךָ אַחֲרֶיךָ אֵת | אֶרֶץ אלהים דאלפין מְגֻרֶיךָ אֵת כָּל
ילי ־אֶרֶץ אלהים דאלפין כְּנַעַן לַאֲחֻזַּת עוֹלָם וְהָיִיתִי לָהֶם לֵאלֹהִים
ילה, מום׃ 9 וַיֹּאמֶר אֱלֹהִים ילה, מום אֶל־אַבְרָהָם ח״פ אל, רמ״ח וְאַתָּה אֶת־
בְּרִיתִי תִשְׁמֹר אַתָּה וְזַרְעֲךָ אַחֲרֶיךָ לְדֹרֹתָם׃ 10 זֹאת בְּרִיתִי
אֲשֶׁר תִּשְׁמְרוּ בֵּינִי וּבֵינֵיכֶם וּבֵין זַרְעֲךָ אַחֲרֶיךָ הִמּוֹל לָכֶם כָּל
ילי ־זָכָר׃ 11 וּנְמַלְתֶּם אֵת בְּשַׂר עָרְלַתְכֶם וְהָיָה יהוה, יהה לְאוֹת
בְּרִית בֵּינִי וּבֵינֵיכֶם׃ 12 וּבֶן־שְׁמֹנַת יָמִים נלך יִמּוֹל לָכֶם כָּל ילי ־זָכָר
לְדֹרֹתֵיכֶם יְלִיד בָּיִת ב״פ ראה וּמִקְנַת־כֶּסֶף מִכֹּל ילי בֶּן־נֵכָר אֲשֶׁר
לֹא מִזַּרְעֲךָ הוּא׃ 13 הִמּוֹל | יִמּוֹל יְלִיד בֵּיתְךָ ב״פ ראה וּמִקְנַת
כַּסְפֶּךָ וְהָיְתָה בְרִיתִי בִּבְשַׂרְכֶם לִבְרִית עוֹלָם׃ 14 וְעָרֵל | זָכָר
אֲשֶׁר לֹא־יִמּוֹל אֶת־בְּשַׂר עָרְלָתוֹ וְנִכְרְתָה הַנֶּפֶשׁ רמ״ח - ז׳ הויות
הַהִוא מֵעַמֶּיהָ אֶת־בְּרִיתִי הֵפַר׃ [ס] 15 וַיֹּאמֶר אֱלֹהִים ילה, מום אֶל־

---

purpose of circumcision is to remove these spiritually harmful forces from the baby.

Performed properly with kabbalistic meditation, circumcision removes all of this negativity, and in addition, strengthens the immune system, reducing the risk of many diseases, including cancer. This act also benefits the world at large. With regard to circumcision (which is also known as the Sign of the Covenant) the *Zohar* says:

Whoever retains this Sign shall not go down to Gehenom (Hell) as long as he preserves it properly....
– The Zohar, Lech Lecha 36:385

In studying this biblical passage, we purify the realm of *Yesod*, both Above and Below, just as we strengthen the Covenant and help to prevent our souls from experiencing any form of hell.

16 And I will bless her and will give you a son by her. I will bless her and she will be a mother of nations; kings of peoples will come from her."

17 Then Abraham fell on his face; and laughed and said in his heart, "Will a child be born to a man that is a hundred years old? And will Sarah bear a child at the age of ninety?" 18 And Abraham said to God, "If only Ishmael might live before You!"

19 Then God said, "Yes, but your wife Sarah will bear you a son, and you will call him Isaac. And I will establish My covenant with him as an everlasting covenant and with his seed after him.

20 And as for Ishmael, I have heard you: Behold I have blessed him; and I will make him fruitful and will multiply him exceedingly. Twelve princes will he give birth to and I will make him into a great nation.

21 But My covenant I will establish with Isaac, whom Sarah will bear to you by this time next year." 22 And He left off talking with him, and God went up from Abraham.

23 And Abraham took Ishmael, his son, and all those born in his house and all that were bought with his money, every male among the men of Abraham's house, and circumcised the flesh of their foreskin on that same day, as God had said to him.

שָׂרָה

Genesis 17:15 – Since Sarai was unable to bear children, her name was changed from Sarai to Sarah by replacing the Aramaic letter *Yud* with the letter *Hei* at the end of her name. This indicated a spiritual genetic change that also transformed her entire being, enabling her to give birth to a child.

Many women in our own time have difficulty bearing children, yet few realize that a mere change of name can assist in removing the spiritual and physical obstacles at the root of their problem. A woman's name affects not only her own soul, but also the souls of her children. This is the reason that a woman should choose a name from the Bible, thereby ensuring that both she and her children can benefit from the most positive attributes and noble traits available. The *Zohar* says:

> *This follows a similar thought expressed by Rav Chiya that, as God has done in Heaven, so has He done on Earth. Just as there are holy names in Heaven, so are there holy names here on Earth.*
> *– The Zohar, Shemot 8:53*

The meditation for this section is thus intended to share Light with women who are having difficulty becoming pregnant or bearing children, and the power emanating from it helps destroy all the blockages or ailments that prevent healthy conception and child-birth.

וַיֹּאמֶר

Genesis 17:19 – Abraham was 99 years old and Sarah, his wife, was 89 when the Creator informed Abraham that the couple would become parents of a male child in one year. The reason that God revealed this information far in advance of the birth was to plant a seed of certainty within the consciousness of both Abraham and Sarah. If such absolute certainty had not been deeply embedded in their minds, the birth could never have taken place.

אַבְרָהָם וו"פ אל, רמ"ח שָׂרַי אִשְׁתְּךָ לֹא-תִקְרָא אֶת-שְׁמָהּ שָׂרָי כִּי
שָׂרָה אלהים דיודין ורבוע אלהים - ה' שְׁמָהּ: 16 וּבֵרַכְתִּי אֹתָהּ וְגַם נָתַתִּי
מִמֶּנָּה לְךָ בֵּן וּבֵרַכְתִּיהָ וְהָיְתָה לְגוֹיִם מַלְכֵי עַמִּים ע"ה קס"א מִמֶּנָּה
יִהְיוּ אל: 17 וַיִּפֹּל אַבְרָהָם וו"פ אל, רמ"ח עַל-פָּנָיו וַיִּצְחָק ד"פ ב"ן וַיֹּאמֶר
בְּלִבּוֹ הַלְּבֶן מֵאָה דמב, מלוי ע"ב -שָׁנָה יִוָּלֵד וְאִם יוהך -שָׂרָה
אלהים דיודין ורבוע אלהים - ה' הֲבַת-תִּשְׁעִים שָׁנָה תֵּלֵד: 18 וַיֹּאמֶר אַבְרָהָם
וו"פ אל, רמ"ח אֶל-הָאֱלֹהִים ילה, מום לוּ יִשְׁמָעֵאל יִחְיֶה לְפָנֶיךָ ס"ג - מ"ה - ב"ן:
19 וַיֹּאמֶר אֱלֹהִים ילה, מום אֲבָל שָׂרָה אלהים דיודין ורבוע אלהים - ה' אִשְׁתְּךָ
יֹלֶדֶת לְךָ בֵּן וְקָרָאתָ אֶת-שְׁמוֹ מה"ש ע"ה יִצְחָק ד"פ ב"ן וַהֲקִמֹתִי אֶת-
בְּרִיתִי אִתּוֹ לִבְרִית עוֹלָם לְזַרְעוֹ אַחֲרָיו: 20 וּלְיִשְׁמָעֵאל
שְׁמַעְתִּיךָ הִנֵּה | בֵּרַכְתִּי אֹתוֹ וְהִפְרֵיתִי אֹתוֹ וְהִרְבֵּיתִי אֹתוֹ
בִּמְאֹד מ"ה מְאֹד מ"ה שְׁנֵים-עָשָׂר נְשִׂיאִם יוֹלִיד וּנְתַתִּיו לְגוֹי
גָּדוֹל להח, מבה, יזל, אום: 21 וְאֶת-בְּרִיתִי אָקִים אֶת-יִצְחָק ד"פ ב"ן אֲשֶׁר
תֵּלֵד לְךָ שָׂרָה אלהים דיודין ורבוע אלהים - ה' לַמּוֹעֵד הַזֶּה והו בַּשָּׁנָה
הָאַחֶרֶת: 22 וַיְכַל לְדַבֵּר ראה אִתּוֹ וַיַּעַל אֱלֹהִים ילה, מום מֵעַל עלם
אַבְרָהָם וו"פ אל, רמ"ח: 23 וַיִּקַּח חעם אַבְרָהָם וו"פ אל, רמ"ח אֶת-יִשְׁמָעֵאל
בְּנוֹ וְאֵת כָּל ילי -יְלִידֵי בֵיתוֹ ב"פ ראה וְאֵת כָּל ילי -מִקְנַת כַּסְפּוֹ כָּל
ילי -זָכָר בְּאַנְשֵׁי בֵּית ב"פ ראה אַבְרָהָם וו"פ אל, רמ"ח וַיָּמָל אֶת-בְּשַׂר
עָרְלָתָם בְּעֶצֶם הַיּוֹם נגד, זן, מזבח הַזֶּה והו כַּאֲשֶׁר דִּבֶּר ראה אִתּוֹ
אֱלֹהִים ילה, מום:

The Bible here reveals a lesson concerning the power of mind over matter, demonstrating the tenet that consciousness is 99 Percent of reality, while the physical world represents a scant 1 Percent.

Our own consciousness is fortified and elevated by the contents of this section, helping all of humanity to finally achieve the miracle of mind over matter, thereby attaining absolute control over physical existence.

MAFTIR

24 And Abraham was ninety-nine years old when he was circumcised in the flesh of his foreskin.

25 And his son Ishmael was thirteen years old when he was circumcised in the flesh of his foreskin.

26 On that same day, Abraham and his son Ishmael were both circumcised.

27 And all the men of his house, born in the house and bought with money of the stranger, were circumcised with him.

HAFTARAH OF LECH LECHA

Isaiah describes the war between Abram and the kings, and how Abram engineered their defeat. This teaches us that the Creator is always with us in our battles, and if we think we can gain victory by

Isaiah 40:27-41:16

40 27 Why do you say, Jacob, and complain, Israel, "My way is hidden from the Lord; my cause is disregarded by my God?"

28 Do you not know? Have you not heard? The Lord is the everlasting God, the Creator of the ends of the Earth. He will not grow tired or weary, and His understanding no one can fathom.

29 He gives strength to the weary and increases the power of the weak.

30 Even youths grow tired and weary, and young men stumble and fall; 31 but those who hope in the Lord will renew their strength. They will soar on wings like eagles; they will run and not grow weary, they will walk and not be faint.

41 1 "Be silent before Me, you islands! Let the nations renew their strength! Let them come forward and speak; let us meet together at the place of judgment.

MAFTIR

24 וְאַבְרָהָם ו"פ אל, רמ"ח בֶּן־תִּשְׁעִים וָתֵשַׁע שָׁנָה בְּהִמֹּלוֹ בְּשַׂר
עָרְלָתוֹ׃ 25 וְיִשְׁמָעֵאל בְּנוֹ בֶּן־שְׁלֹשׁ עֶשְׂרֵה שָׁנָה בְּהִמֹּלוֹ אֵת
בְּשַׂר עָרְלָתוֹ׃ 26 בְּעֶצֶם הַיּוֹם נגד, זן, מזבח הַזֶּה והו נִמּוֹל אַבְרָהָם
ו"פ אל, רמ"ח וְיִשְׁמָעֵאל בְּנוֹ׃ 27 וְכָל ילי ־אַנְשֵׁי בֵיתוֹ ב"פ ראה יְלִיד בָּיִת
ב"פ ראה וּמִקְנַת־כֶּסֶף מֵאֵת בֶּן־נֵכָר נִמֹּלוּ אִתּוֹ׃ [פ] [פ] [פ]

HAFTARAH OF LECH LECHA

ourselves, we will most certainly lose. Like Abram, therefore, we must learn to surrender to our need for the help and power of the Creator.

ישעיהו פרק 40–41

40 27 לָמָּה תֹאמַר יַעֲקֹב יאהדונהי - אידהנויה וּתְדַבֵּר ראה יִשְׂרָאֵל
נִסְתְּרָה ב"פ מצר דַרְכִּי ב"פ יב"ק מֵיְהֹוָה אדני יאהדונהי וּמֵאֱלֹהַי דמב, ילה מִשְׁפָּטִי
יַעֲבוֹר רפ"ח, ע"ב - רי"ו׃ 28 הֲלוֹא יָדַעְתָּ אִם יוהך ־לֹא שָׁמַעְתָּ אֱלֹהֵי
דמב, ילה עוֹלָם | יְהֹוָה אדני יאהדונהי בּוֹרֵא קְצוֹת הָאָרֶץ אלהים דההין ע"ה לֹא
יִיעַף וְלֹא יִיגָע אֵין חֵקֶר לִתְבוּנָתוֹ׃ 29 נֹתֵן אבגיתצ, ושר, אהבת חנם לַיָּעֵף
כֹּחַ ר"ת נלך וּלְאֵין אוֹנִים עָצְמָה יַרְבֶּה׃ 30 וְיִעֲפוּ נְעָרִים וְיִגָעוּ
וּבַחוּרִים כָּשׁוֹל יִכָּשֵׁלוּ׃ 31 וְקוֹיֵ יְהֹוָה אדני יאהדונהי יַחֲלִיפוּ כֹחַ יַעֲלוּ
אֵבֶר ב"ן קנ"א כַּנְּשָׁרִים יָרוּצוּ וְלֹא יִיגָעוּ יֵלְכוּ כלי וְלֹא יִיעָפוּ׃ [ס]
41 1 הַחֲרִישׁוּ אֵלַי אִיִּים וּלְאֻמִּים יַחֲלִיפוּ כֹחַ יִגְּשׁוּ אָז יְדַבֵּרוּ ראה

2 *Who has stirred up one from the east, calling him in righteousness to His service?*
He hands nations over to him and subdues kings before him. He turns them to dust
with his sword, to windblown chaff with his bow. 3 *He pursues them and moves on*
unscathed, by a path his feet have not traveled before.

4 *Who has done this and carried it through, calling forth the generations from the beginning? I, the Lord—with the first of them and with the last—I am He."*

5 *The islands have seen it and fear; the ends of the Earth tremble. They approach and*
come forward; 6 *each helps the other and says to his brother, "Be strong!"*

7 *The craftsman encourages the goldsmith, and he who smoothes with the hammer spurs on him who strikes the anvil. He says of the welding, "It is good." He nails down the idol so it will not topple.*

8 *"But you, Israel, are My servant, Jacob, whom I have chosen, you descendants of*
Abraham My friend, 9 *I took you from the ends of the Earth, from its farthest corners*
I called you. I said, 'You are My servant,' I have chosen you and have not rejected
you.

10 *So do not fear, for I am with you; do not be dismayed, for I am your God. I will strengthen you and help you; I will uphold you with My righteous right hand.*

11 *All who rage against you will surely be ashamed and disgraced; those who oppose you will be as nothing and perish.*

12 *Though you search for your enemies, you will not find them. Those who wage war against you will be as nothing at all.*

13 *For I am the Lord, your God, who takes hold of your right hand and says to you, do not fear; I will help you.*

14 *Do not be afraid, you worm Jacob, you men of Israel, for I, Myself will help you," declares the Lord, your Redeemer, the Holy One of Israel.*

15 *"See I will make you into a threshing sledge, new and sharp, with many teeth. You will thresh the mountains and crush them, and reduce the hills to chaff.*

16 *You will winnow them, the wind will pick them up, and a gale will blow them away. But you will rejoice in the Lord and glory in the Holy One of Israel."*

יַחְדָּו לַמִּשְׁפָּט ע״ה ה״פ אלהים נִקְרָבָה׃ 2 מִי ילי הֵעִיר מִמִּזְרָח צֶדֶק
יִקְרָאֵהוּ לְרַגְלוֹ יִתֵּן לְפָנָיו גּוֹיִם וּמְלָכִים יַרְדְּ יִתֵּן כֶּעָפָר
חַרְבּוֹ רי״ו, גבורה כְּקַשׁ נִדָּף קַשְׁתּוֹ׃ 3 יִרְדְּפֵם יַעֲבוֹר רפ״ח, ע״ב - רי״ו
שָׁלוֹם אֹרַח בְּרַגְלָיו לֹא יָבוֹא׃ 4 מִי ילי ־פָעַל וְעָשָׂה קֹרֵא הַדֹּרוֹת
מֵרֹאשׁ ריבוע אלהים - אלהים דיודין ע״ה אֲנִי אני יְהֹוָה יאהדונהי רִאשׁוֹן וְאֶת־
אַחֲרֹנִים אֲנִי אני ־הוּא׃ 5 רָאוּ אִיִּים וְיִירָאוּ קְצוֹת הָאָרֶץ אלהים דההין ע״ה
יֶחֱרָדוּ קָרְבוּ וַיֶּאֱתָיוּן׃ 6 אִישׁ ע״ה קנ״א קס״א אֶת־רֵעֵהוּ יַעְזֹרוּ וּלְאָחִיו
יֹאמַר חֲזָק פהל׃ 7 וַיְחַזֵּק פהל חָרָשׁ אֶת־צֹרֵף מַחֲלִיק פַּטִּישׁ אֶת־
הוֹלֶם פָּעַם אֹמֵר לַדֶּבֶק טוֹב והו הוּא וַיְחַזְּקֵהוּ פהל בְמַסְמְרִים לֹא
יִמּוֹט׃ {ס} 8 וְאַתָּה יִשְׂרָאֵל עַבְדִּי יַעֲקֹב יאהדונהי - אידהנויה אֲשֶׁר
בְּחַרְתִּיךָ זֶרַע אַבְרָהָם ח״פ אל, רמ״ח אֹהֲבִי׃ 9 אֲשֶׁר הֶחֱזַקְתִּיךָ פהל
מִקְצוֹת הָאָרֶץ אלהים דההין ע״ה וּמֵאֲצִילֶיהָ קְרָאתִיךָ וָאֹמַר לְךָ עַבְדִּי־
אַתָּה בְּחַרְתִּיךָ וְלֹא מְאַסְתִּיךָ׃ 10 אַל־תִּירָא כִּי עִמְּךָ נמם ־אָנִי אני
אַל־תִּשְׁתָּע כִּי־אֲנִי אני אֱלֹהֶיךָ ילה אִמַּצְתִּיךָ אַף־עֲזַרְתִּיךָ אַף־
תְּמַכְתִּיךָ בִּימִין צִדְקִי׃ 11 הֵן יֵבֹשׁוּ וְיִכָּלְמוּ כֹּל ילי הַנֶּחֱרִים בָּךְ
יִהְיוּ אל כְאַיִן וְיֹאבְדוּ אַנְשֵׁי רִיבֶךָ׃ 12 תְּבַקְשֵׁם וְלֹא תִמְצָאֵם
אַנְשֵׁי מַצֻּתֶךָ יִהְיוּ אל כְאַיִן וּכְאֶפֶס אַנְשֵׁי מִלְחַמְתֶּךָ׃ 13 כִּי אֲנִי
אני יְהֹוָה יאהדונהי מ״ה - מ״ב אֱלֹהֶיךָ ילה מַחֲזִיק יְמִינֶךָ נמם, ה׳ הויות הָאֹמֵר
לְךָ אַל־תִּירָא אֲנִי אני עֲזַרְתִּיךָ׃ {ס} 14 אַל־תִּירְאִי תּוֹלַעַת יַעֲקֹב
יאהדונהי - אידהנויה מְתֵי יִשְׂרָאֵל אֲנִי אני עֲזַרְתִּיךְ נְאֻם־יְהֹוָה יאהדונהי
וְגֹאֲלֵךְ קְדוֹשׁ יִשְׂרָאֵל׃ 15 הִנֵּה שַׂמְתִּיךְ לְמוֹרַג חָרוּץ חָדָשׁ
י״ב הויות בַּעַל פִּיפִיּוֹת תָּדוּשׁ הָרִים וְתָדֹק וּגְבָעוֹת כַּמֹּץ תָּשִׂים׃
16 תִּזְרֵם וְרוּחַ מלוי אלהים דיודין תִּשָּׂאֵם וּסְעָרָה תָּפִיץ אוֹתָם וְאַתָּה
תָּגִיל בַּיהֹוָה יאהדונהי בִּקְדוֹשׁ יִשְׂרָאֵל תִּתְהַלָּל ללה׃ {ס}

VAYERA

THE LESSON OF VAYERA
(Genesis 18:1–22:24)

Regarding the Welcoming in of Guests

This section begins on the third day after Abraham's circumcision. Even for an infant, this is said to be the most painful day, and Abraham was hardly an infant. He was 99 years old, so we can assume the pain was far greater. Yet the Creator knew that even in the midst of his pain, Abraham would still be generous and hospitable, always ready to welcome any travelers on the road as his honored guests. We learn from this that by sharing—even when we are in our greatest pain—we draw the Light of healing and mercy of the Creator to ourselves.

It is always hot in the desert, but the Creator made this particular day even hotter than usual. The great sage Rashi described it thus: "God took the sun out of its pocket." Secular scholars have long puzzled over the meaning of this strange phrase, wondering what the sun's "pocket" could be. In fact, it refers to the ozone layer that surrounds the Earth, protecting us from the sun's ultraviolet radiation. In hearing and making a connection to this section, therefore, we can gain protection from deadly holes in the ozone layer and from the skin cancers that are caused by the sun's unfiltered rays today.

Scientists have pointed out that the destruction of the ozone layer could potentially damage all plants, animals, and water, rendering the planet unable to support human life. Our connections with the *Zohar*, with Rav Shimon bar Yochai, and with this Torah reading have the power to protect us from such a disaster.

The Bible next tells us that in spite of his pain and the unbearable heat, Abraham stayed outside, sitting at the entrance of his tent. Because of his generous nature, Abraham was not troubled by either physical pain or the soaring temperature. Instead, he was distraught that he had no guests to welcome. So the Creator sent him three angels.

It is good to pause here and think about the high spiritual level and the connection with the Light of the Creator that Abraham had reached, and about what made him so different from us.

Most of the time, fortunately, we are not in physical pain, nor is the outside temperature 120 degrees in the shade. Yet unlike Abraham, we are too busy or too preoccupied to be concerned with anyone but ourselves. Thus, the initial lesson to be learned from Abraham is to think about caring for others, regardless of our own level of discomfort. When we make this kind of effort, each according to our ability, Abraham will help us. Abraham represents the force of *Chesed,* or mercy, in the universe. By caring for others, we in effect draw the force of mercy into our lives. If we follow Abraham's path even a short way every day, the Light of the Creator will be there for us. This is the same spiritual principle that we have been shown ever since the first verses of Genesis: Each step that we make toward the Light brings the Light two steps closer to us.

The *Gemara* (tractate) reveals other lessons from this story of Abraham. We learn, for example, that welcoming guests is of greater importance than welcoming the Face of the Creator. When the Creator came to Abraham in the form of the three angels, Abraham, still in pain from his circumcision, nevertheless rose to welcome his guests. It is also worth remembering that, through Divine inspiration, he obeyed all of the biblical precepts (mitzvot) long before the Bible was handed down to humankind. Furthermore, the imperative of welcoming guests, which is indicative of a higher level of consciousness than the act of welcoming the Face of the Creator, originates with this story of Abraham. We might next ask ourselves how Abraham knew this was the right thing to do.

In the biblical commentary of Rav Zusha of Anipoli, it is explained that Abraham blessed all 248 parts of his body and all 365 ligaments, with the intention that they should always serve the will of God and never perform any task counter to God's desire. When the angels came to visit Abraham at the opening of his tent, Abraham understood that the welcoming of guests was a hugely important issue simply because of the way his body responded. His muscles gave him the strength to rise and his feet had the power to run. Consecrated as it was to do only what God willed, Abraham's body would not have allowed him to move if it had been the wrong thing to do.

By reading this explanation, we can be certain that the act of welcoming guests is a spiritually higher one than welcoming the Face of the Creator. In everything he did, Abraham's life was directly connected to God. Every breath he took, every step he walked, was exactly what the Creator wanted him to do at that moment. Abraham's hands and feet sometimes led him to perform actions of which he understood nothing, yet he was always certain that this was what the Creator wanted him to do.

We are not, of course, required to attain the spiritual level of Abraham. Indeed, almost everything we do is predicated by our own selfish desires rather than any connection with the Creator. We are, however, expected to reach the level where our individual spiritual potential is totally fulfilled. Rav Zusha put it most succinctly: "I am not afraid if they will ask me in Heaven why I was not like Abraham because I will answer that I did not have Godly powers like Abraham. But I am afraid that they will ask me why I was not like Zusha. Why was I not on the spiritual level that Zusha was supposed to reach?" Every person, therefore, is expected to transform and elevate himself spiritually according to his own level and character, which means that we should aspire to be at least as much as we can be.

There is a story told about Rav Elimelech of Lizhensk (1717–1786) and Rav Zusha that illustrates wonderfully the process through which we can start to elevate our consciousness so as to reach a level where our body will be connected to the Light of the Creator and we can reach our spiritual potential:

> *One day, Rav Zusha was arguing with his brother, Rav Elimelech. Rav Zusha said that the most important thing for a person to know is how lowly he is, and from this will come an understanding of the greatness of the Creator. Rav Elimelech said the opposite: A person should look first at the greatness of the Creator, and only by seeing this will he understand*

how lowly he really is. Their teacher, Rav Dov Ber, the Maggid of Mezrich, was asked to decide who was correct. The Maggid said they were both right in his eyes and that both these lessons lead a person to think of himself as humble before the Creator. This consciousness will elevate the person spiritually.

The Maggid's (Rav Dov Ber, 1704–1772) final statement makes it clear that the only way to ensure that all our actions mesh with the will of God is to assay our own smallness. By grasping how much we do not understand, by realizing how much more grandeur there is in the universe and inside the human mind than we think there is, the closer we are getting to the Creator. No mind can comprehend God, but our minds can comprehend our own lack of comprehension, and it is in the resulting sense of awe that we are drawn closer to God.

This section also connects us with the power inherent in the dots over the three letters, *Alef, Yud,* and *Vav* in the sentence: "And he said to him (Heb. *elav*, consisting of the letters *Alef, Lamed, Yud, Vav*), where (Heb. *ayeh*, consisting of the letters *Alef, Yud, Hei*) is Sarah?" There is a connection between *Alef, Yud, Vav* and *Alef, Yud, Hei*, or between the Upper Worlds (*Alef, Yud, Vav*) and our world of *Malchut* (*Alef, Yud, Hei*). Our world can become like the Upper Worlds only if we make ourselves smaller. Meditating on the dots in this sentence helps us to reduce our *Desire to Receive for the Self Alone* into the size of a miniscule dot.

As the pre-eminent Kabbalist Rav Berg frequently teaches, if we want to shorten the process of transformation, we can do so only by connecting the two worlds, the Upper and the Lower. And the best way to achieve this is by making ourselves smaller—not physically, of course, but by shrinking our *Desire to Receive for the Self Alone*. The three dots contained in the Aramaic of this section help us to do just this, while at the same time connecting us to the three angels who came to Abraham.

There are many ways to further the process of shrinking our own sense of self-importance. For example, we should never think that our own opinions are the only ones that have value; we must learn to listen to others and be open to their thoughts. Nor should we assume that we know what the Creator wants from us because God may want something else entirely. Perhaps there is a business opportunity that can bring us more money and success than our current line of work; on the other hand, we might need to experience difficult financial times to learn an important lesson that we can take with us through the rest of our lives. Whatever the task at hand, our crucial and overriding purpose should be to shrink our sense of self-importance, for it is this sense of self-importance that prevents us from entering the Realms of Light.

In the *Zohar (Emor 24:129)*, we read: "Open for me an opening the size of an eye of a needle, and I shall open to you the Celestial Gates." To enter through this opening, we need only deflate our ego, which is merely an illusion of our real self, a cloud-like vapor that blocks the sun and feeds off the steamy heat of our selfish desires. Once we realize that these desires can never be satisfied, only eradicated, we can cut off the ego's lifeline and begin destroying it permanently.

Rabban Gamliel used to say:

> *Desire only that which has already been given.*
> *Want only that which you already have.*
> *As a river empties into the ocean,*
> *empty yourself into Reality.*
> *When you are emptied into Reality,*
> *you are filled with compassion,*
> *desiring only justice.*
> *When you desire only justice,*
> *the will of Reality becomes your will.*
> *When you are filled with compassion,*
> *there is no self to oppose another*
> *and no other to stand against oneself.*
> *– Pirkei Avot 2:4*
> *(Pirkei Avot is translated as Ethics of the Fathers. It contains spiritual direction and connection from rabbinic scholars over many generations.)*

It is not by coincidence that we also read about the Binding of Isaac in this section of the Bible. The story is one of enormous significance. Clearly, God did not need Abraham to bring him a sacrifice, nor did the Creator need to see if Abraham loved his Maker. The Creator is omniscient and thus already knows our thoughts and feelings, which is the reason we must question why this was even considered to be a test for Abraham at all. Furthermore, when examining this episode, we should not forget that a large portion of the responsibility belonged to Isaac. At the time of the binding, he was 37 years old and certainly had the ability to choose whether or not to act as a sacrifice.

Kabbalists explain that in this incident, Abraham created an opening of Light for everyone. If there are any judgments against us, we can overcome them as a result of the spiritual structure that Abraham's Binding of Isaac created in the universe. The way we can connect to this is by binding our own ego and by continuing to make it and our own self-importance smaller and smaller.

Finally, this reading is the only section in the Bible where dots appear in two different places. The second occasion is on the word *uvkumah* (when she rose). When Lot was living with his two daughters in a cave after escaping from Sodom, it is written that they made him drunk and then raped him. This is one of many puzzling sections in the Bible, not merely the rape of a man by a woman but the rape of a father by his daughters. It highlights the indispensability of Kabbalah to any reading of the Scriptures because, as is often the case, its explanation requires some knowledge of the complete story.

The sages teach that King David was descended from Ruth the Moabite, who was descended from the son who was born as a result of the rape of Lot by one of his daughters. By means of the dots over the word *uvkumah*, therefore, the Bible is teaching us that even the worst situation can have the Light of the Creator in it. There is literally no person so corrupt that he cannot connect to the Light. King David himself was a descendant of that unholy union between Lot and his daughter, and King David was and is the channel for the energy of *Malchut* for the whole world. Furthermore, we also know that the Messiah, the embodiment of the final transformation of humanity, will come from the descendants of Ruth and David. The message here could not be clearer: Every person in this world as well as every situation they are in reveals the Light of the Creator if we will only look for it. The wisdom of the patriarchs puts it this way:

Everything that God,
the source and substance of all,
creates in this world
flows naturally from the essence
of God's Divine Nature.

Creation is not a choice
but a necessity.
It is God's Nature
to unfold time and space.

Creation is the extension of God.
Creation is God encountered in time and space.
Creation is the infinite in the garb of the finite.

To attend to Creation is to attend to God.
To attend to the moment is to attend to eternity.
To attend to the part is to attend to the whole.
To attend to Reality is to live constructively.
– Pirkei Avot 6:2

SYNOPSIS OF VAYERA

This section is deeply layered with meaning, offering us numerous lessons and spiritual Light for our lives. A single verse may be deciphered and studied for years, yet it will still not have yielded up all its spiritual treasures. Therefore, it is most important that a student never think he has "read" the Bible.

Let us now examine the third and most painful day following Abraham's circumcision. Abraham waited outside his home with a single intent: to invite opportunities into his life that would allow him to perform acts of unconditional sharing. Instead of convalescing, he sacrificed his desire for comfort. This action merited him the visitation of three "men." The *Zohar* says:

> *And even though he was in pain because of the circumcision, he ran forth to greet them so that he would not miss anything and would not behave differently than before his circumcision—as he always accepted and welcomed new guests.*
>
> *– The Zohar, Vayera 7:95*

As mentioned previously, the three men were actually angels sent to Abraham by the Creator to allow him to express his Desire to Share. These angels bestowed various blessings upon Abraham. It is these angelic blessings that help us create life and prevent the loss of life in our own times. We learn that performing acts of charity and going outside of our comfort zone have the power to reverse any sentence of death decreed against us and our loved ones. Because of Abraham's charitable actions, Light and Divine power shine down upon us now, helping to protect us and all of humankind. As the *Zohar* states:

> *When harsh Judgment hangs over the world, God remembers the charitable deeds that men performed. As it is written: "...but charity (righteousness) delivers a person from death."*
>
> *– The Zohar, Vayera 12:169*

While discussing this section, the rabbis in the *Zohar* explain that there are times when the collective misdeeds of human beings reach such epic proportions that the Angel of Death is allowed to unleash a torrent of chaos so devastating that even the innocent and righteous are swallowed up in the process:

> *When the Angel of Destruction is granted permission to destroy, the righteous are in as much danger as the wicked.*
>
> *– The Zohar, Vayera 26:369*

However, the reverse is also true, which is why the *Zohar* devotes sacred space upon its pages to explain this matter. When the *Zohar*'s Light is brought to bear—as it is now—even the unworthy are saved. They are purified by the efforts we make each day through the enormous power of this Holy Book and of the selfless actions of Abraham the Patriarch.

FIRST READING - ABRAHAM - CHESED

18 1 *The Lord appeared to Abraham in the plains of Mamre, and he sat in the tent door in the heat of the day.*

FROM THE RAV

The story of the Binding of Isaac is not about human sacrifice. It's about Abraham being transformed by certainty. But it would never have happened if he had not believed completely and totally in the positive nature of the Light.

The *Zohar* discusses this at great length. To be brief, the discussion concludes that if we do not believe we have the power and the consciousness to overcome a problem, the problem will never be overcome. But when we have certainty, then transformation takes place, and we go from an environment in which the difficulty appears insurmountable into an environment where this difficulty is the easiest thing in the world to overcome.

Until we have certainty about the power of mind over matter, such power can never exist. But once we have certainty, there is a technology and other tools of connection by which we can succeed in controlling our environment.

Because we do not necessarily behave like Abraham, we have the opportunity again here in the Story of Vayera to get this energy of healing, rebirth, and removal of chaos. But something is stopping us from realizing this, and that something is our envy and our ego, which destroy everything around us. Abraham never had an evil eye. He knew the laws of this universe. The less we behave like victims, the more Light we can receive in our lives. That is the way Abraham lived, and this is the way we will merit what is truly ours. The Binding of Isaac gives us the opportunity of binding our *Desire to Receive for the Self Alone* with sharing, giving us mastery over the energy of death by unifying the energy of the Right and the Left columns, which is the formula for removing all chaos.

מַמְרֵא

Genesis 18:1 – When Abraham was visited by the three angels, he was sitting at the entrance to his tent where it was pitched on the plains of Mamre. The *Zohar* reveals a secret about Mamre, telling us that Mamre actually refers to Jacob. In a later Bible story, Jacob, the future grandson of Abraham, is born to Isaac. By ignoring Cause and Effect in any normal timeframe, the *Zohar* frequently operates in a spiritual realm beyond the concepts of time and space, where past, present, and future are regarded as one.

The *Zohar* says:

> *This is Yaakov (Jacob) WHO IS CALLED MAMRE.*
> *– The Zohar, Vayera 2:26*

With regard to Jacob, the *Zohar* further states:

> *God established a covenant with Jacob alone, more than THE COVENANT HE ESTABLISHED with all his fathers.*
> *– The Zohar, Vayera 2:22*

The *Zohar* also makes a striking statement here regarding the illumination from both spiritual Light and the simple light of the sun. It says that all three Columns of spiritual force must be present to generate the actual radiance of spiritual Light, explaining that these three Columns correspond to Abraham (*Right Column*), Isaac (*Left Column*), and Jacob (*Central Column*). The *Zohar* then ascribes additional importance

FIRST READING - ABRAHAM - CHESED

18 1 וַיֵּרָא אֵלָיו יְהֹוָה יאהדונהי בְּאֵלֹנֵי מַמְרֵא סוזרך ע"ה וְהוּא יֹשֵׁב

---

to Jacob, without whom Light cannot illuminate, saying:

> *ABRAHAM AND ISAAC ARE NOT ABLE TO SHINE WITHOUT HIM.*
> – *The Zohar, Vayera 2:22*

This spiritual truth can be seen in our mundane world in the following way:

- The sun, which emanates a constant stream of rays, corresponds to Abraham. This is the *Right Column* (+) of sharing. These rays of sunlight do not shine in the vacuum of space because there is no daylight above Earth's atmosphere in spite of the presence of the light photons in this black void. Sunlight remains invisible and thus unobservable.

- The Earth, or any physical object for that matter, corresponds to the receiver, the recipient that catches the sun's rays. This is Isaac, the *Left Column* (–) of receiving. Although the Earth may be designated as the recipient of the sunlight, there is still no illumination during this stage of receiving.

- The Earth, however, reflects the sunlight entering the atmosphere. At the point of reflection, an immediate radiance occurs. This concept of resistance correlates to Jacob, the Central Column of resistance. It is this act of reflection and resistance that causes the rays of the sun to illuminate our world as shining light.

Thus, without reflection and resistance, sunlight remains invisible to the naked eye and darkness prevails. For this reason, Abraham and Isaac require the reflective powers of Jacob to express the Divine energy that they embody, thus allowing it to illuminate—in its entire splendor—our material plane of existence.

An ordinary light bulb operates on the same principle. The bulb possesses both a positive and a negative pole—Abraham and Isaac, or the *Right* and *Left Column* forces, respectively. However, the bulb requires a third or *Central Column* force of resistance to produce illumination. This is the function of the filament, which resists the electrical current flowing between the negative and positive poles in the bulb. The moment there is resistance—Jacob, the *Central Column*—the filament begins to incandesce, illuminating the room. In an atom, these three columns correlate to the proton (*Right Column*), electron (*Left Column*), and neutron (*Central Column*).

This particular model also has applications within the human being:

- The soul correlates to Abraham and the desire to share.

- The ego correlates to Isaac and the selfish desires.

- The free will to resist the selfish impulses of the ego and to allow the will of our souls to guide our life correlates to Jacob.

Only through free will—defined as the determination to resist our ego, or Evil Inclination—can we ever ignite spiritual Light in our life. If we allow our ego to control our behavior and govern our life, then just as the light photons emitted by the sun are present but unseen in the vacuum of space, the Light of the Creator, though ever-present, will remain hidden from us.

So by virtue of Jacob (*Mamre*), this section of the Bible can empower us with the courage to exercise our free will every day and to triumph over our ego-driven desires, thus banishing intolerance, greed, impatience, jealousy, and anxiety from our heart.

2 And he lifted up his eyes and saw three men standing nearby. And when he saw them, he ran from the entrance of his tent to meet them and bowed himself to the ground.

3 And said, "My Lord, if I have found favor in your eyes, do not pass, I pray you, from your servant.

Now we will explore the numerical value and spiritual significance of the word Mamre. There are five letters of the Aramaic alphabet that change shape (take on a different form) when they appear at the end of a word rather than somewhere inside the word. They are: *Kaf* כ-ך (20), *Mem* מ-ם (40), *Nun* נ-ן (50), *Pei* פ-ף (80) and *Tzadi* צ-ץ (90); these are known as the "five final letters." When the numerical values of all of these letters are added together, 20 + 40 + 50 + 80 + 90 + 1 (for the oneness of the Creator), the result is 281, which is also the numerical value of Mamre.

These five final letters further correlate to the time of the Final Redemption, known as the time of the Messiah, and to the concept of the Resurrection of the Dead. From a kabbalistic point of view, the time of the Messiah is a time when the consciousness of humanity will be permanently connected to the Upper Worlds, where there will be only infinite fulfillment and where pain, suffering, and death will not exist. It is through this single word *Mamre* that we can assist in bringing about in our own time both the arrival of the Messiah and the advent of the Resurrection of the Dead. The Resurrection of the Dead includes resurrecting any area of our lives that has undergone any kind of "death," whether this is the death of a business, a relationship, a marriage, or even our inner peace and happiness.

פֶּתַח-הָאֹהֶל

Genesis 18:1 – The Bible says that Abraham was "sitting at the door of the tent in the heat of the day." The *Zohar* explains that the door of the tent is a code signifying a doorway to the Upper Worlds, which Abraham was able to access by virtue of his circumcision, because the circumcision was the Covenant with the Creator.

> *In explaining the words, "appeared to him," Rav Abba said that before Abraham was circumcised, he was blocked FROM RECEIVING THE SUPERNAL LIGHTS. As soon as he was circumcised, everything appeared, INCLUDING ALL THE LIGHTS, AS HIS COVER WAS REMOVED. And the Shechina rested upon him in full perfection, as should properly be. Come and behold. IT IS WRITTEN: "...and he sat in the tent door." "He" refers to the Upper World, TO BINAH, that rests upon the Lower World, WHICH IS THE NUKVA.*
>
> -- *The Zohar, Vayera 1:13*

We are then told that when Abraham looked up, he saw three men standing near him. These three men represent *Chesed*, *Gevurah*, and *Tiferet*, the three spiritual realms of the Upper World of the Tree of Life. These realms would eventually express themselves in our physical dimension as the Patriarchs Abraham, Isaac, and Jacob.

The phrase "in the heat of the day" correlates to the realm of *Chesed*, whose particular wavelength of spiritual Light is embodied by the concept of mercy. In the middle of a summer's day, the heat is greatest because this is the time when the light from the sun is being cast upon Earth at its highest angle. *Chesed*, therefore, casts the most direct Light upon our hearts, filling them with the illumination of love and mercy. *Chesed* is the realm to which Abraham connected; therefore, we are being told that Abraham is the vehicle by which mercy enters into our world.

The spiritual force known as "mercy" sweetens any judgment that is pronounced upon us as a result of our unkind and intolerant actions. Mercy in kabbalistic terms is also defined as time because mercy offers us extra time to genuinely repent and change our ways, replacing bad actions with good, so that we may repeal any

פֶּתַח-הָאֹהֶל לאה, אלד ע״ה כְּחֹם הַיּוֹם נגד, זן, מזבח: 2 וַיִּשָּׂא עֵינָיו ריבוע מ״ה
וַיַּרְא וְהִנֵּה מ״ה יה שְׁלֹשָׁה אֲנָשִׁים נִצָּבִים עָלָיו וַיַּרְא וַיָּרָץ לִקְרָאתָם
מִפֶּתַח הָאֹהֶל לאה, אלד ע״ה וַיִּשְׁתַּחוּ אָרְצָה אלהים דההין ע״ה : 3 וַיֹּאמַר

---

decrees pending against us by way of the inevitable Universal Law of Cause and Effect.

When we rise above physical and emotional pain and direct our consciousness toward helping others, as Abraham did, we connect ourselves with the Upper Worlds where untold blessings are aroused, which in turn irradiates our own dimension with Light and mercy.

As we listen to the reading of this section, boundless blessings are ignited throughout the universe. These verses themselves instill within us the courage and strength to transcend all forms of physical discomfort, inspiring us to share and to care unconditionally for others, especially during the times when we are most self-involved. And because mercy is in such abundance here during this reading, we can devote our awareness to our self-transformation, which will assist in neutralizing the karmic judgments that hang over the world.

כְּחֹם

Genesis 18:1 – According to the *Zohar*, the phrase "heat of the day" also refers to a particular ray of Light radiating from the Supernal Realm known as *Chochmah*. When it falls upon the wicked, this Light brings judgment, but when the righteous perceive it, it heals and regenerates them. The *Zohar* further says that the phrase "heat of the day" refers to the end of time—our time, the time when the greatest revelation of Light occurs:

> *This is the Day of Judgment that burns like a furnace in order to separate the soul from the body.*
>
> *– The Zohar, Vayera 2:30*

Thus, if we have transformed our selfish nature to a sharing one, this Light will elevate us into realms of bliss. But if we are imprisoned by our own choosing in the web of our own selfishness, our path to the Light will be one of enormous difficulty, torment, and suffering.

Each and every one of us possesses both selfish and sharing traits. The Divine radiance of spiritual Light that emanates from this particular section of the Bible gently vanquishes our darkest traits, while ensuring a Final Redemption that is free of judgment and overflowing with mercy.

שְׁלֹשָׁה

Genesis 18:2 – Abraham made sure there were four entrances to his tent so that visitors could enter from every direction. He also honed his psychic faculties, opening himself up to the spiritual world with its potential for encounters with angelic forces. In fact, all of us pass by and meet angels every day, no matter where we are. But for the most part, we are so blocked and blinkered both spiritually and emotionally that we simply do not notice the subtle glories and refined radiance of these holy beings.

The key to seeing the real reality within the 1 Percent Illusionary World of mutability and death lies in removing the veils of adulthood, which taint our vision, and regaining the eyes of childhood.

Sometimes, a young child can actually be a channel for an angel. Serendipitous events or unique circumstances that seemingly appear out of nowhere often signify that an angel is sending us a message.

The more we are open to listening to messages from the world and the people around us, the more the angels will tell us. But if we are closed to messages, opinions, and viewpoints of friends and foes alike, we in turn close ourselves off to the angels and their profound wisdom.

4 Let a little water, I pray you, be fetched, and wash your feet and rest yourselves under this tree.

5 And I will fetch a morsel of bread and comfort your hearts; after that you will pass on, for you have come to your servant." And they said, "So do as you have said." 6
And Abraham hastened into the tent to Sarah and said, "Quick, make ready three measures of fine meal, knead it, and make cakes on the hearth."

7 And Abraham ran to the herd and fetched a good and tender calf and gave it to a young man, and he hurried to prepare it.

וְרַחֲצוּ רַגְלֵיכֶם

Genesis 18:4 – The *Zohar* teaches us that water, like Abraham, corresponds to the purifying Light of Mercy of the Creator, while feet correspond to the *Sefira* of *Malchut*, our material plane of existence. Therefore, the act of Abraham washing the feet of the angels—his three mysterious visitors—alludes to the power of Abraham's Light to purify and heal our world, now and always. Abraham and Sarah taught the people of their generation the spiritual importance of immersion in water to cleanse both body and soul of impurities:

> *This is how [Abraham] purified people from all sins, including sins from the Impure Side and the sin of idol-worship. And just as he purified the men, so did [Sarah] purify the women. Therefore, all those who came to him were completely purified.*
>
> – *The Zohar, Vayera 7:108*

Hence, in this section, we personally receive cleansing and purification by the Light of the Creator that is awakened from the vast compassion and care embodied by Abraham and Sarah, whose love for humanity is as ageless and constant as the shining sun.

וְהִשָּׁעֲנוּ

Genesis 18:4 – Abraham invited the three men to sit under a tree while he fetched them food. According to the *Zohar*, this tree of Abraham possessed special properties:

> *Whoever was pure was accepted by the tree. But whoever was impure was not accepted. Abraham then knew IF A PERSON WAS UNCLEAN, in which case he purified him with water.*
>
> – *The Zohar, Vayera 7:111*

If the person who sat under the tree was a positive human being, the tree would stretch out its branches to offer cool shade and protection from the harmful rays of the sun. But if the person was negative, the tree would withdraw its branches, denying shelter to the guest.

Abraham, therefore, knew who was pure and connected to the true Light of the Creator, and who was impure and connected to idolatry and selfish aims. Idolatry does not simply refer to man-made statues and anthropomorphic icons that are worshipped as if they were gods. In kabbalistic terms, an idol is defined as any material possession or external situation that enslaves our emotions and guides our behavior. Our negative tendencies lead us to become devotees of wealth and disciples of decadent pleasure. We are, indeed, obsessed with and deluged by images—both cultural icons and the self-image we feel we must project to others.

If any of these idols influences the degree of contentment and joy we have in life, then we have surrendered control. We have severed our connection to our soul and to its God-given ability to generate happiness from within our own self. For happiness has no tie to things; it is a well that gushes from its source without reason or cost. Yet many today have lost it, and they cannot again find that source of joy. This is why Abraham would offer an impure person the opportunity to wash and cleanse.

אֲדֹנָי אִם יוהך ־נָא מָצָאתִי חֵן מוחי בְּעֵינֶיךָ ע"ה קס"א אַל־נָא תַעֲבֹר
מֵעַל עלם עַבְדֶּךָ פוי: 4 יֻקַּח חעם ־נָא מְעַט־מַיִם וְרַחֲצוּ רַגְלֵיכֶם
וְהִשָּׁעֲנוּ תַּחַת הָעֵץ ע"ה קס"א: 5 וְאֶקְחָה פַת־לֶחֶם ג"פ יהוה וְסַעֲדוּ
לִבְּכֶם אַחַר תַּעֲבֹרוּ כִּי־עַל־כֵּן עֲבַרְתֶּם עַל־עַבְדְּכֶם וַיֹּאמְרוּ
כֵּן תַּעֲשֶׂה כַּאֲשֶׁר דִּבַּרְתָּ ראה: 6 וַיְמַהֵר אַבְרָהָם ח"פ אל, רמ"ח הָאֹהֱלָה
אֶל־שָׂרָה אלהים דיודין ורבוע אלהים - ה' וַיֹּאמֶר מַהֲרִי שְׁלֹשׁ סְאִים קֶמַח
סֹלֶת לוּשִׁי וַעֲשִׂי עֻגוֹת: 7 וְאֶל־הַבָּקָר רָץ אַבְרָהָם ח"פ אל, רמ"ח
וַיִּקַּח חעם בֶּן־בָּקָר רַךְ וָטוֹב והו וַיִּתֵּן אֶל־הַנַּעַר ש"ך וַיְמַהֵר לַעֲשׂוֹת

We often associate with the wrong people in life, in part because we are frequently misled by physical appearances. The reading of this section helps to raise our consciousness so that we, like Abraham, can discern between the negative and positive people we encounter in our lives.

We are further told that the tree of Abraham also alludes both to the Tree of Life and to the Tree of Knowledge of Good and Evil. The Tree of Life Reality is a flawless reality, a realm of perfect order, bliss, and infinite wisdom. This realm, which is the source of all human happiness, is imperceptible to our five senses. There are times, however, when we glimpse its reality through intuition, dreams, or visions.

> *Even when [Abraham] invited the angels, he told them to rest "yourselves under the tree" (Genesis 18:4) in order to test them. This was the way he examined every person. The secret is that he said this for the sake of God, who is THE SECRET OF the Tree of Life for everyone. This is why he TOLD THEM: "...and rest yourselves under the tree," WHICH IS GOD, and not under idol-worship.*
> *– The Zohar, Vayera 7:113*

The Tree of Knowledge of Good and Evil Reality refers to our physical dimension of death and disorder. This is the world we perceive and experience through our five senses. When we behave with intolerance, insensitivity, and blatant disregard for the welfare of others, we find ourselves consigned, unprotected, to a realm of reality equivalent to our lowered state of consciousness—the domain of the Tree of Knowledge of Good and Evil, whose leaves provide no shade from negative forces. It is then only a matter of time before turmoil boils over into our life, affecting everything: our prosperity, our relationships, even our physical health and emotional well-being.

As we hear the reading of this biblical passage, we place ourselves in the Tree of Life Reality, where a protective aura of soft Light envelopes our physical form, banishing darkness and death, and creating in their place perfection, joy, and universal immortality.

וְאֶל־הַבָּקָר

Genesis 18:7— Abraham went to get bread, meat, and other food for the three men who had come to visit him. Abraham's unconditional caring is seen by his willingness to retrieve the food himself. Even though he was still suffering pain from his circumcision, he did not assign this task to someone else. He took responsibility for feeding his guests, personally making sure that the job was completed.

Often, we fail to follow through on our own spiritual goals as well as our daily mundane responsibilities. We pass off work to other people, perhaps because we're complacent in our lofty

8 And he took butter, and milk, and the calf which he had prepared and set these before them. And he stood by them under the tree and they did eat. 9 And they asked him, "Where is your wife Sarah?" And he said, "There, in the tent." 10 And he said, "I will certainly return to you about this time next year, and Sarah your wife will have a son." And Sarah was listening at the entrance to the tent, which was behind him.

---

role as the conceiver of an idea or planner of a project. Or we just get by every day, doing as little as possible, when we ought to be forging ahead in pursuit of our goals in life, doing as much as possible to achieve them. It is important to overcome this tendency because all too often, it is the small, tedious, mundane tasks that arouse the greatest blessings and Light.

Genesis 18:9 – In ten specific locations in the Bible, a dot or a set of dots is inscribed onto the parchment above a specific word or phrase. Although tiny, these dots are potent forces of energy, each signifying the presence in the text both of an additional energy and a unique lesson.

In Genesis 18:9, we find three dots over the word *elav* (to him), which appears in the phrase "and they said to him." The letters with dots are *Alef*, *Yud*, and *Vav*, and the dots indicate that three angels came to visit Abraham: Michael, Raphael, and Gabriel. The *Zohar* also reveals that the angels are the same three men who stood near the patriarch outside his tent:

> *The verse "And lo, three men" refers to the three angels—messengers who clothe themselves with air and come down to this world in a human image.*
> – *The Zohar, Vayera 5:52*

The *Zohar* then goes on to explain the function of these angels:

> *And each OF THE THREE ANGELS served a different purpose. Raphael, who governs the power to heal, helped Abraham recover from the circumcision. Another, Michael, who came to inform Sarah that she would bear a son, rules over the Right Side; all the abundance and the blessings of the Right Side are handed over to him. And Gabriel, who came to overturn Sodom, rules over the Left Side and is responsible for all Judgments in the world, AS JUDGMENTS COME from the Left Side. The execution is done by the Angel of Death, THE KING'S CHIEF BAKER, who executes THE SENTENCES THAT ARE PASSED UNDER GABRIEL'S RULE.*
> – *The Zohar, Vayera 5:54–55*

Abraham was sterile and Sarah had already long before passed through menopause, so bearing a child at the couple's advanced age was unimaginable. The angel Michael, who correlates to the *Sefira* of *Chesed*, which embodies mercy and sharing, blessed Abraham and Sarah so that they could have a child within one year.

It is through the vibration embodied by the angel Michael that we achieve control over the material world, including our physical bodies. The level of mind over matter increases with each act of sharing that we perform, especially those acts that are difficult to do.

Gabriel corresponds to the *Sefira* of *Gevurah*, which is judgment. Gabriel's role is to channel this energy of judgment into our dimension to destroy the corrupt, negative powers of the world epitomized by the cities of Sodom and Gomorrah.

In our personal lives, we must learn to employ the power of judgment with spiritual discretion tempered by mercy. Thus, a judgment invoked righteously is akin to disciplining a child who misbehaves; it is rooted in love and concern for the welfare of the child, not in frustration or from reactive anger.

The Light emanating through Gabriel destroys our inner Sodom and Gomorrah, the negative impulses that tempt us to gratify our own ego at the expense of others. This wave of Light softens

אֹתוֹ: 8 וַיִּקַּח חעם חֶמְאָה וְחָלָב וּבֶן־הַבָּקָר אֲשֶׁר עָשָׂה וַיִּתֵּן
לִפְנֵיהֶם וְהוּא־עֹמֵד עֲלֵיהֶם תַּחַת הָעֵץ קס״א ע״ה וַיֹּאכֵלוּ: 9 וַיֹּאמְרוּ
אֵלָיו אַיֵּה שָׂרָה אלהים דיודין ורבוע אלהים - ה׳ אִשְׁתֶּךָ וַיֹּאמֶר הִנֵּה בָאֹהֶל
לאה, אלד ע״ה: 10 וַיֹּאמֶר שׁוֹב אָשׁוּב אֵלֶיךָ אני כָּעֵת חַיָּה וְהִנֵּה מ״ה יה ־בֵן
לְשָׂרָה אלהים דיודין ורבוע אלהים - ה׳ אִשְׁתֶּךָ וְשָׂרָה אלהים דיודין ורבוע אלהים - ה׳
שֹׁמַעַת פֶּתַח הָאֹהֶל לאה, אלד ע״ה וְהוּא אַחֲרָיו: 11 וְאַבְרָהָם ח״פ אל, רמ״ח
וְשָׂרָה אלהים דיודין ורבוע אלהים - ה׳ זְקֵנִים בָּאִים בַּיָּמִים נלך וְחָדַל

---

our heart so that we never judge people with excessive severity.

Raphael is the conduit through which healing enters the world. Raphael signifies the energy of balance, which is encompassed by the Sefira of Tiferet. Raphael healed the wounds of Abraham's circumcision and later also saved Abraham's nephew, Lot, when Sodom and Gomorrah were destroyed.

When we lack spiritual balance and are inclined toward the illusions of physical pleasure and material wealth, an opening is created for physical illness to enter the body's system. Through Raphael's energy, therefore, a yearning for spirituality blossoms within us and in the world. Human civilization, dangerously steeped in materialism, needs this energy to correct its ways and become more balanced. To meditate collectively on the inner truth of this reading is thus immensely beneficial to the planet.

וַיֹּאמֶר

Genesis 18:10 – The angels, through Michael's blessings, told Abraham that Sarah would give birth to a son within the year. Abraham's unconditional generosity and sharing was the key factor in facilitating this miracle of mind over matter that resulted in the birth of Isaac.

People frequently offer charity or perform acts of kindness with a hidden agenda of some sort, although the ulterior motive may be held unconsciously. Such acts do not, of course, arouse any blessings. True sharing occurs only when there are no expectations, as revealed in the *Zohar*:

> *It was very polite and proper that they (the angels) said nothing to Abraham before he invited them to eat. That way, it did not seem that he had invited them to eat just because of the good news they brought him. Therefore, only after the verse stated "and they ate" did they tell him the good news.*
>
> *– The Zohar, Vayera 7:102*

Here we learn that we must perform unconditional acts of kindness and generosity before we can expect any blessings to be returned to us or any miracles to take place. If there is expectation of any kind—let alone if we are actually calculating the blessings and miracles we can expect—our actions are nullified, and nothing will come from them. When we let go of our agenda and expectations and give unconditionally with a pure heart, we receive everything. This is the Divine paradox of true spirituality.

A miracle is essentially a mirror reflecting a profound spiritual change within human nature. Because our natural inclination is to engage in self-indulgence at the expense of others, when a person dedicates his or her life to sharing with others, the Creator causes great wonders to be revealed in the form of miracles.

11 Now Abraham and Sarah were old and well stricken in age, and Sarah was past the age of childbearing. 12 Therefore, Sarah laughed to herself as she thought, "After I am waxed old will I have pleasure, my lord being old also?"

13 And the Lord said to Abraham, "Why did Sarah laugh and say, 'Will I surely have a child, now that I am old?'

14 Is anything too hard for the Lord? I will return to you at the appointed time next year and Sarah will have a son."

SECOND READING - ISAAC - GEVURAH

15 Then Sarah denied this for she was afraid, saying, "I did not laugh." And He said, "Yes, you did laugh."

16 And the men rose to leave, they looked down toward Sodom, and Abraham went with them to see them on their way.

וַתִּצְחַק

Genesis 18:12 – A literal reading of this specific section seems to indicate that Sarah doubted the wonders of God and the possibility of giving birth at her advanced age. It even appears as if she was laughing at God; her response verges on cynicism and arrogance. But a deeper analysis of the verse reveals kabbalistic secrets that have a dramatic impact on both us and the whole world from the moment we become aware of them.

Sarah's first child would be named Isaac. The Aramaic word for Isaac, Yitzchak, means "he will laugh." Therefore, the phrase "Sarah laughed within herself" kabbalistically alludes to the "laugh" as being the implanting of the spiritual seed of Isaac within Sarah at that very moment. This is far more than clever word-play, for it reveals an inner knowledge of the events described. When women who are having difficulty conceiving connect with this section, the miracle of childbirth can be bestowed upon them.

Sarah's apparent cynicism represents our cynicism with regard to the truth of the Creator and the ability of humans to achieve control over matter with the mind alone. The prerequisite for each and every miracle of nature is absolute certainty and trust, but our ego (Satan) constantly implants doubts and cynical thoughts in our minds. Spiritual work entails transcending these artificial uncertainties, inculcating a sense of wonder appropriate to the extraordinary grandeur and order of the Universe and its Creator.

The *Zohar* also points out that the name "Isaac" tells us that this laughter refers to the joy and delight we will experience in the Age of Messiah, a time when all people and things will exist in perfect harmony. Thus, these words of the Bible implant the seed of the Messiah in the world, setting in motion a process that will ultimately lead to endless laughter and joy in our lives.

הֲיִפָּלֵא

Genesis 18:14 – In response to Sarah's laughter and her doubts that she would ever bear a son, God said to Abraham, "Is anything too hard for the Lord? At the appointed time, I will return to you at this time next year, and Sarah will have a son." The *Zohar* explains that this verse conceals

לִהְיוֹת לְשָׂרָה אלהים דיודין ורבוע אלהים - ה׳ אֹרַח כַּנָּשִׁים׃ 12 וַתִּצְחַק
שָׂרָה אלהים דיודין ורבוע אלהים - ה׳ בְּקִרְבָּהּ לֵאמֹר אַחֲרֵי בְלֹתִי הָיְתָה־
לִּי עֶדְנָה וַאדֹנִי זָקֵן׃ 13 וַיֹּאמֶר יְהֹוָהאדניאהדונהי אֶל־אַבְרָהָם
ו״פ אל, רמ״ח לָמָּה זֶּה צָחֲקָה שָׂרָה אלהים דיודין ורבוע אלהים - ה׳ לֵאמֹר הַאַף
אֻמְנָם אֵלֵד וַאֲנִי אני זָקַנְתִּי׃ 14 הֲיִפָּלֵא מֵיְהֹוָהאדניאהדונהי דָּבָר ראה
לַמּוֹעֵד אָשׁוּב אֵלֶיךָ כָּעֵת חַיָּה וּלְשָׂרָה אלהים דיודין ורבוע אלהים - ה׳ בֵן׃

SECOND READING - ISAAC - GEVURAH

15 וַתְּכַחֵשׁ שָׂרָה אלהים דיודין ורבוע אלהים - ה׳ | לֵאמֹר לֹא צָחַקְתִּי כִּי |
יָרֵאָה רי״ו, גבורה וַיֹּאמֶר | לֹא כִּי צָחָקְתְּ׃ 16 וַיָּקֻמוּ מִשָּׁם הָאֲנָשִׁים

---

secrets concerning the Resurrection of the Dead and the Age of Messiah:

> *What is meant by "the time appointed?" This is the time that is known to Me for the Resurrection of the Dead.*
> *– The Zohar, Vayera 7:135*

The *Zohar* continues in another verse:

> *I will return to you that same body which is sacred renewed as before, because you are like the holy angels. And that day shall be merry before Me and I shall rejoice in them…*
> *– The Zohar, Vayera 7:137*

This passage invokes the power of the Resurrection of the Dead—the dawning of an age of immortality, boundless joy, and laughter—so that it will appear in our own day. Reinforcing this mystery, the *Zohar* offers a remarkable insight:

> *When the body exists in this world, it has not yet reached perfection. After it becomes righteous, walks the paths of honesty, and dies in its righteousness, then it is called "Sarah" (lit. "provided what is necessary"), as it has been perfected. When it reaches the Resurrection of the Dead, it is still called Sarah so that nobody will say that God has revived a different body. And afterward it becomes alive and rejoices with the Shechina; and the Creator has wiped all distress from the world, as it is written: "He will swallow up death forever, and the Lord God will wipe away tears from off all faces;" (Isaiah 25:8) then it shall be called Yitzchak [Isaac] (lit. "he will laugh"), because of the laughter and happiness of the righteous in the future.*
> *– The Zohar, Vayera 29:401*

Here the *Zohar* is telling us that the word "Sarah" is a metaphor for mankind after it has completed its work of spiritual transformation and man's ego is dead and buried. Her son, Isaac, is a metaphor pertaining to the dawn of the Resurrection of the Dead, the rebirth of spiritual man in a world that features endless joy and laughter. Our ego is laid to rest and our soul (our true Self) is reborn through the Light revealed in this section.

17 And the Lord said, "Shall I hide from Abraham what I am about to do?

18 Seeing that Abraham will surely become a great and mighty nation and all nations on earth will be blessed through him.

19 For I know him, that he will command his children and his household after him and they will keep the way of the Lord by doing what is right and just, that the Lord will bring about for Abraham what He has spoken to him."

20 And the Lord said, "Because the cry of Sodom and Gomorrah is great and their sin
so grievous, 21 I will go down now and see if what they have done is as bad as the
outcry that has come to me. And if not, I will know."

22 And the men turned their faces away and went toward Sodom, but Abraham remained standing before the Lord.

23 And Abraham drew near and said: "Will You destroy the righteous with the wicked?

24 What if there are fifty righteous people in the city? Will You really destroy it and not spare the place for the sake of the fifty righteous people in it?

25 Far be it from You to do such a thing—to slay the righteous with the wicked; and treating the righteous as if they are wicked. Far be it from You: Will not the Judge of all the earth do right?"

26 And the Lord said, "If I find fifty righteous people in the city of Sodom, I will spare the whole place for their sake."

27 And Abraham answered: "See now that I have taken upon me to speak to the Lord,
though I am nothing but dust and ashes, 28 what if the number of the righteous is five
less than fifty? Will You destroy the whole city because of five people?" And He said,
"If I find forty-five there, I will not destroy it."

וַיֹּאמֶר

Genesis 18:20 – It may surprise us to find that Abraham pleaded to God for the salvation of Sodom and Gomorrah, the most negative centers of corruption and evil in the world. But Abraham understood that regardless of how wicked or mean-spirited a person is, each individual in the world possesses a spark of God's Light, and thus each is a child of Creation.

Abraham found it within himself to plead for the lives of the most negative people on Earth. If we were to have the same positive inclinations toward others as he did, imagine how much more tolerant and sensitive we would be toward our own friends, family, acquaintances, and foes, especially when we found ourselves casualties of their negative behavior. One of the great goals of our lives is to learn to act with tolerance and forbearance toward all, neither preferring those who are closest to us, nor rejecting those whom we do not like or do not know.

וַיַּשְׁקִפוּ עַל־פְּנֵי חכמה • בינה סְדֹם ב״פ כ״ן וְאַבְרָהָם ח״פ אל, רמ״ח הֹלֵךְ מיה
עִמָּם לְשַׁלְּחָם׃ 17 וַיהֹוָה יאהדונהי אָמָר הַמְכַסֶּה אֲנִי אני מֵאַבְרָהָם
ח״פ אל, רמ״ח אֲשֶׁר אֲנִי אני עֹשֶׂה׃ 18 וְאַבְרָהָם ח״פ אל, רמ״ח הָיוֹ יִהְיֶה ייי
לְגוֹי גָּדוֹל להח, מבה, יזל, הום וְעָצוּם וְנִבְרְכוּ יהוה ע״ב ריבוע מ״ה ־בוֹ כֹּל ילי
גּוֹיֵי הָאָרֶץ אלהים דההין ע״ה׃ 19 כִּי יְדַעְתִּיו לְמַעַן אֲשֶׁר יְצַוֶּה פוי אֶת־
בָּנָיו וְאֶת־בֵּיתוֹ ב״פ ראה אַחֲרָיו וְשָׁמְרוּ דֶּרֶךְ ב״פ יב״ק יְהֹוָה יאהדונהי
לַעֲשׂוֹת צְדָקָה ע״ה ריבוע אלהים וּמִשְׁפָּט ע״ה ה״פ אלהים לְמַעַן הָבִיא
יְהֹוָה יאהדונהי עַל־אַבְרָהָם ח״פ אל, רמ״ח אֵת אֲשֶׁר־דִּבֶּר ראה עָלָיו׃
20 וַיֹּאמֶר יְהֹוָה יאהדונהי זַעֲקַת סְדֹם ב״פ כ״ן וַעֲמֹרָה כִּי־רָבָּה
וְחַטָּאתָם כִּי כָבְדָה מְאֹד מ״ה׃ 21 אֵרְדָה־נָּא וְאֶרְאֶה הַכְּצַעֲקָתָהּ
הַבָּאָה אֵלַי עָשׂוּ | כָּלָה וְאִם יוהך ־לֹא אֵדָעָה׃ 22 וַיִּפְנוּ מִשָּׁם
הָאֲנָשִׁים וַיֵּלְכוּ סְדֹמָה וְאַבְרָהָם ח״פ אל, רמ״ח עוֹדֶנּוּ עֹמֵד לִפְנֵי
יְהֹוָה יאהדונהי׃ 23 וַיִּגַּשׁ אַבְרָהָם ח״פ אל, רמ״ח וַיֹּאמַר הַאַף תִּסְפֶּה
צַדִּיק עִם־רָשָׁע׃ 24 אוּלַי אום יֵשׁ חֲמִשִּׁים צַדִּיקִם בְּתוֹךְ הָעִיר
סוזזרך, ערי, סנדלפון הַאַף תִּסְפֶּה וְלֹא־תִשָּׂא לַמָּקוֹם יהוה ברבוע, ו״פ אל לְמַעַן
חֲמִשִּׁים הַצַּדִּיקִם אֲשֶׁר בְּקִרְבָּהּ׃ 25 חָלִלָה לְּךָ מֵעֲשֹׂת |
כַּדָּבָר ראה הַזֶּה והו לְהָמִית צַדִּיק עִם־רָשָׁע וְהָיָה יהוה, יהה
כַצַּדִּיק כָּרָשָׁע חָלִלָה לָּךְ הֲשֹׁפֵט כָּל ילי ־הָאָרֶץ אלהים דההין ע״ה לֹא
יַעֲשֶׂה מִשְׁפָּט ע״ה ה״פ אלהים׃ 26 וַיֹּאמֶר יְהֹוָה יאהדונהי אִם יוהך ־אֶמְצָא
בִסְדֹם ב״פ כ״ן חֲמִשִּׁים צַדִּיקִם בְּתוֹךְ הָעִיר סוזזרך, ערי, סנדלפון
וְנָשָׂאתִי לְכָל יה • אדני ־הַמָּקוֹם יהוה ברבוע, ו״פ אל בַּעֲבוּרָם׃ 27 וַיַּעַן
אַבְרָהָם ח״פ אל, רמ״ח וַיֹּאמַר הִנֵּה מ״ה יה ־נָא הוֹאַלְתִּי לְדַבֵּר ראה
אֶל־אֲדֹנָי ללה וְאָנֹכִי איע עָפָר וָאֵפֶר מנצפ״ך ע״ה׃ 28 אוּלַי אום יַחְסְרוּן
חֲמִשִּׁים הַצַּדִּיקִם חֲמִשָּׁה הֲתַשְׁחִית בַּחֲמִשָּׁה אֶת־כָּל ילי

29 And he spoke to Him yet again and said, "What if only forty are found there?" And
He said, "I will not do it, for the sake of forty." 30 And he said to Him, "O let not the
Lord be angry, and I will speak. What if only thirty can be found there?" And He
answered, "I will not do it if I find thirty there."

31 And he said, "See now that I have taken upon me to speak to the Lord, what if only
twenty can be found there?" And He said, "I will not destroy it, for the sake of twenty."
32 And he said, "Let not the Lord be angry, and I will speak yet just this once: What if
only ten can be found there?" And He answered, "I will not destroy it, for the sake of
ten." 33 And the Lord went his way once He finished speaking with Abraham, and
Abraham returned to his place.

THIRD READING - JACOB - TIFERET

19 1 And two angels came to Sodom in the evening, and Lot sat on the gate of Sodom:
And Lot, seeing them, rose to meet them and bowed down with his face towards the
ground. 2 And he said, "See now, my lords, turn aside, I pray you, to your servant's
house and tarry all night. And wash your feet and then go on your way early in the
morning." And they said, "No, we will spend the night in the street."

וַיָּבֹאוּ

Genesis 19:1 – Sodom and Gomorrah are representative of the lowest level of human nature, where evil becomes the norm and man's darkest, most barbaric traits reign supreme. To any civilized sensibilities, the values and mores of the cities of Sodom and Gomorrah were inverted, a world turned upside down. As an illustration of this total perversity, we are told that people who performed acts of kindness were immediately slain. Abraham's nephew, Lot, had a daughter who was caught giving bread to a beggar. She was covered with honey by the townspeople and left bound on a rooftop where she was stung to death by bees. As another example, guards would even stand at the gates of the city to prevent hospitable people from taking others into their homes for the night.

In addition, sexual perversion was rampant. Bestiality, rape, incest, and molestation were all accepted forms of behavior and were prevalent throughout both cities.

וַיֹּאמֶר

Genesis 19:2 – We can find salvation through sharing. As mentioned previously, two angels came to Earth at the time of the destruction of Sodom and Gomorrah. Gabriel came to destroy Sodom and Gomorrah, and Raphael came to save Lot. When Lot observed them entering the city, he ran over to invite them into his home, even though death was the prescribed punishment for hospitable behavior.

The Zohar explains that Abraham had appeared to Lot in a vision, telling him to warmly welcome those visitors or else he would die. So this act of sharing, of welcoming the visitors into his home, is what saved Lot's life. We should note that Lot's ability to receive the vision and to interpret the message was of pivotal importance for his survival. These are abilities that we, too, must foster in ourselves. Early evidence that this ability is developing is shown when we learn to trust and follow our highest instincts.

־הָעִיר סנזפח, ערי, סנדלפון וַיֹּאמֶר לֹא אַשְׁחִית אִם יוהך ־אֶמְצָא שָׁם
אַרְבָּעִים וַחֲמִשָּׁה׃ 29 וַיֹּסֶף ציון, קנאה, ו"פ יהוה, ה"פ אל עוֹד לְדַבֵּר ראה
אֵלָיו וַיֹּאמַר אוּלַי אום יִמָּצְאוּן שָׁם אַרְבָּעִים וַיֹּאמֶר לֹא אֶעֱשֶׂה
בַּעֲבוּר הָאַרְבָּעִים׃ 30 וַיֹּאמֶר אַל־נָא יִחַר לַאדֹנָי ללה וַאֲדַבֵּרָה
ראה אוּלַי אום יִמָּצְאוּן שָׁם שְׁלֹשִׁים וַיֹּאמֶר לֹא אֶעֱשֶׂה אִם
יוהך ־אֶמְצָא שָׁם שְׁלֹשִׁים׃ 31 וַיֹּאמֶר הִנֵּה מ"ה יה ־נָא הוֹאַלְתִּי
לְדַבֵּר ראה אֶל־אֲדֹנָי ללה אוּלַי אום יִמָּצְאוּן שָׁם עֶשְׂרִים וַיֹּאמֶר
לֹא אַשְׁחִית בַּעֲבוּר הָעֶשְׂרִים׃ 32 וַיֹּאמֶר אַל־נָא יִחַר לַאדֹנָי
ללה וַאֲדַבְּרָה ראה אַךְ אהיה ־הַפַּעַם אוּלַי אום יִמָּצְאוּן שָׁם עֲשָׂרָה
וַיֹּאמֶר לֹא אַשְׁחִית בַּעֲבוּר הָעֲשָׂרָה׃ 33 וַיֵּלֶךְ כלי יְהֹוָהאדניאהדונהי
כַּאֲשֶׁר כִּלָּה לְדַבֵּר ראה אֶל־אַבְרָהָם ח"פ אל, רמ"ח וְאַבְרָהָם ח"פ אל, רמ"ח
שָׁב לִמְקֹמוֹ׃

THIRD READING - JACOB - TIFERET

19 1 וַיָּבֹאוּ שְׁנֵי הַמַּלְאָכִים סְדֹמָה בָּעֶרֶב רבוע אלהים רבוע יהוה וְלוֹט
מ"ה יֹשֵׁב בְּשַׁעַר־סְדֹם ב"פ כ"ן וַיַּרְא־לוֹט מ"ה וַיָּקָם לִקְרָאתָם
וַיִּשְׁתַּחוּ אַפַּיִם אָרְצָה אלהים דההין ע"ה׃ 2 וַיֹּאמֶר הִנֶּה יהוה מ"ה נָּא־

Before any judgments are executed in this physical world, each of us is given an opportunity to sweeten or annul the judgment through an act of sharing or charity. These opportunities are sent to us by the Creator, but we seldom recognize them. This is because we are consumed by self-interest, which blocks our innate ability to receive information from the Upper Worlds. Consequently, pain and turmoil (harsh judgment) inevitably ensue.

The Light radiating through this story elevates our consciousness so that we can identify those moments for sharing in our life. Instead of passing such opportunities by and simultaneously rationalizing our selfish behavior, we are deeply inspired to perform charitable deeds and acts of kindness with the knowledge that we are altering our personal destiny in a way that is profoundly positive.

In addition, the Light of this passage repeals all guilty verdicts that have been declared against humanity for our past intolerant and negative deeds. We must awaken our deepest gratitude for this gift to our forefather Abraham.

[3] And he pressed upon them greatly; that they did go with him and entered his house. And he made them a feast and baked unleavened bread, and they ate.

[4] But before they had gone to bed, the men of the city of Sodom surrounded the house—both young and old—all the people from every quarter.

[5] And they called to Lot and said to him, "Where are the men who came to you tonight? Bring them out to us so that we may know them."

[6] And Lot went outside to meet them and shut the door behind him, [7] and said, "I pray you, brothers, do not do this wicked thing.

[8] See now, I have two daughters who have not known man. Let me, I pray you, bring them out to you, and you can do to them what is good in your eyes, but to these men do nothing, for they have come under the shadow of my roof."

[9] And they said, "Stand back." And they said, "This one fellow came here to sojourn, and now he wants to be a judge. Now we will treat you worse than them." They kept pressing against the man Lot, and moved near to break the door.

[10] But the men inside reached out and pulled Lot back into the house and shut the door. [11] And they smote the men who were at the door of the house, both great and small, with blindness so that they wearied themselves to find the door.

[12] And the men said to Lot, "Do you have anyone else here—sons-in-law, sons or daughters, or anyone else in the city who belongs to you? Get them out of this place,

[13] for we are going to destroy this place because the outcry of them is waxen great before the face of the Lord and the Lord has sent us to destroy it."

[14] And Lot went out and spoke to his sons-in-law, who married his daughters, and said, "Hurry and get out of this place, because the Lord is about to destroy this city!" But his sons-in-law thought he was joking.

וַיִּשְׁלְחוּ

Genesis 19:10 – Protection. When the angels were in Lot's house, the citizens of Sodom surrounded the house, demanding that Lot expel his visitors. Lot stood at the door and pleaded with the men of the city, but to no avail, and they started to move toward him.

Suddenly, the angels dragged Lot back into the house and created so brilliant a shield that the men of Sodom were blinded. This story reveals how our connection with Light, our opening to the brilliance of spiritual wisdom, makes us invisible to those who obey the dark forces of disruption, chaos, and evil.

The story also speaks to the importance of spiritual protection when people find themselves in a perilous and hostile environment as a result of associating with negative people.

אֲדֹנַי סוּרוּ נָא אֶל־בֵּית ב״פ ראה עַבְדְּכֶם וְלִינוּ וְרַחֲצוּ רַגְלֵיכֶם
וְהִשְׁכַּמְתֶּם וַהֲלַכְתֶּם מ״ה לְדַרְכְּכֶם וַיֹּאמְרוּ לֹּא כִּי בָרְחוֹב
נָלִין: 3 וַיִּפְצַר־בָּם מ״ב מְאֹד וַיָּסֻרוּ אֵלָיו וַיָּבֹאוּ אֶל־בֵּיתוֹ ב״פ ראה
וַיַּעַשׂ לָהֶם מִשְׁתֶּה וּמַצּוֹת אָפָה וַיֹּאכֵלוּ: 4 טֶרֶם רמ״ח ע״ה יִשְׁכָּבוּ
וְאַנְשֵׁי הָעִיר סוזוחך, ערי, סנדלפו״ן אַנְשֵׁי סְדֹם ב״פ ב״ן נָסַבּוּ עַל־הַבַּיִת
ב״פ ראה מִנַּעַר ש״ך וְעַד־זָקֵן כָּל ילי ־הָעָם מִקָּצֶה ג״פ אדני: 5 וַיִּקְרְאוּ
אֶל־לוֹט מ״ה וַיֹּאמְרוּ לוֹ אַיֵּה הָאֲנָשִׁים אֲשֶׁר־בָּאוּ אֵלֶיךָ אני
הַלָּיְלָה מלה הוֹצִיאֵם אֵלֵינוּ וְנֵדְעָה אֹתָם: 6 וַיֵּצֵא אֲלֵהֶם לוֹט מ״ה
הַפֶּתְחָה וְהַדֶּלֶת סָגַר אַחֲרָיו: 7 וַיֹּאמַר אַל־נָא אַחַי תָּרֵעוּ:
8 הִנֵּה מ״ה יה ־נָא לִי שְׁתֵּי בָנוֹת אֲשֶׁר לֹא־יָדְעוּ אִישׁ ע״ה קנ״א קס״א
אוֹצִיאָה־נָּא אֶתְהֶן אֲלֵיכֶם וַעֲשׂוּ לָהֶן כַּטּוֹב והו בְּעֵינֵיכֶם ריבוע מ״ה
רַק לָאֲנָשִׁים הָאֵל לאה (אלד ע״ה) אַל־תַּעֲשׂוּ דָבָר ראה כִּי־עַל־כֵּן
בָּאוּ בְּצֵל קֹרָתִי: 9 וַיֹּאמְרוּ | גֶּשׁ־הָלְאָה וַיֹּאמְרוּ הָאֶחָד אהבה, דאגה
בָא־לָגוּר וַיִּשְׁפֹּט שָׁפוֹט עַתָּה נָרַע לְךָ מֵהֶם וַיִּפְצְרוּ בָאִישׁ
ע״ה קנ״א קס״א בְּלוֹט מ״ה מְאֹד מ״ה וַיִּגְּשׁוּ לִשְׁבֹּר הַדָּלֶת: 10 וַיִּשְׁלְחוּ
הָאֲנָשִׁים אֶת־יָדָם וַיָּבִיאוּ אֶת־לוֹט מ״ה אֲלֵיהֶם הַבָּיְתָה ב״פ ראה
וְאֶת־הַדֶּלֶת סָגָרוּ: 11 וְאֶת־הָאֲנָשִׁים אֲשֶׁר־פֶּתַח הַבַּיִת ב״פ ראה
הִכּוּ בַּסַּנְוֵרִים מִקָּטֹן וְעַד־גָּדוֹל להח, מבה, יזל, אום וַיִּלְאוּ לִמְצֹא
הַפָּתַח: 12 וַיֹּאמְרוּ הָאֲנָשִׁים אֶל־לוֹט מ״ה עֹד מִי ילי ־לְךָ פֹה
מילה, ע״ה אלהים, מום חָתָן וּבָנֶיךָ וּבְנֹתֶיךָ וְכֹל ילי אֲשֶׁר־לְךָ בָּעִיר
סוזוחך, ערי, סנדלפו״ן הוֹצֵא מִן־הַמָּקוֹם יהוה ברבוע, ו״פ אל: 13 כִּי־מַשְׁחִתִים
אֲנַחְנוּ אֶת־הַמָּקוֹם יהוה ברבוע, ו״פ אל הַזֶּה והו כִּי־גָדְלָה צַעֲקָתָם אֶת־
פְּנֵי חכמה + בינה יְהֹוָה יאהדונהי וַיְשַׁלְּחֵנוּ יְהֹוָה יאהדונהי לְשַׁחֲתָהּ:
14 וַיֵּצֵא לוֹט מ״ה וַיְדַבֵּר ראה | אֶל־חֲתָנָיו | לֹקְחֵי בְנֹתָיו וַיֹּאמֶר

15 And when the morning dawned, the angels urged Lot, saying, "Arise! Take your wife and your two daughters who are here, or you will be consumed in the iniquity of the city."

16 And while he lingered, the men grasped his hand and the hands of his wife and of his two daughters and led them safely out of the city, for the Lord was merciful to them.

17 And it came to pass when they had brought them out, that He said, "Flee for your life, do not look back, and don't stop anywhere in the plain, escape to the mountains
or you will be swept away!" 18 And Lot said to them, "No, my lords, please!

19 See now, your servant has found favor in your eyes, and you have shown great kindness to me in saving my life. But I can't flee to the mountains, lest some evil take me and I die.

20 Look, here is a town near enough to run to, and it is small. Let me flee to it—it is very small, isn't it, and my soul will live."

וּכְמוֹ

Genesis 19:15 – **Letting Go.** The angels instructed Lot to gather his family together and leave Sodom at once before they unleashed a torrent of destruction upon the city. But Lot hesitated. A part of him—his ego, the Satan within—still felt a dark attraction to the city and its nefarious inhabitants.

To save himself, Lot still needed to exert a spiritual effort to willingly break all ties to his home and to overcome the unclean yearnings that he still harbored. He needed to let go and to break free of the dark, seductive energy that constantly pulled at him from Sodom.

Lot's sons-in-law thought him a fool and chose to remain behind. The angels were then forced to seize Lot by the hand and lead him, his wife, and his daughters out of the city. Because Lot had put himself in danger to act with charity toward the angels, Heaven guided him forcefully on the right path. When we go out of our nature and perform acts of sharing that are difficult for us, we awaken God's beneficence toward us. We receive Divine assistance in spite of ourselves, making it even easier for us to take the next step on our journey toward the Light and safety.
The angels warned Lot's family not to look back as they were leaving, lest they be destroyed. Nevertheless, Lot's wife did look back and was destroyed; she was turned into a pillar of salt.

Rav Shlomo Yitzchaki (Rashi, 1040–1105), author of extensive commentaries on the Torah, the Tanach, and the Talmud, states that the fate of Lot's wife—and the reason she was turned into a pillar of salt—was because she had refused Lot when he asked her to serve some salt to their guests. Rashi also suggests that she had visited her neighbors on the pretext of borrowing salt but really to gossip about her husband's activities so that he could be caught by the authorities. These interpretations see the wife's destruction as a consequence of her own uncharitable and duplicitous acts.

"Not looking back" is a metaphor for the concept of letting go. To grow spiritually, we must take the following steps:

- Letting go of the past and relinquishing our destructive and reckless traits,

- Committing ourselves to the spiritual path and to each new level that we attain,

קוּמוּ צְּאוּ מִן־הַמָּקוֹם יהוה ברבוע, ו״פ אל הַזֶּה והו כִּי־מַשְׁחִית
יְהֹוָ(אדני)ה יאהדונהי אֶת־הָעִיר סוזחף, ערי, סנדלפון וַיְהִי כִמְצַחֵק בְּעֵינֵי ריבוע מ״ה
חֲתָנָיו׃ 15 וּכְמוֹ הַשַּׁחַר עָלָה וַיָּאִיצוּ הַמַּלְאָכִים בְּלוֹט מ״ה לֵאמֹר
קוּם קַח אֶת־אִשְׁתְּךָ וְאֶת־שְׁתֵּי בְנֹתֶיךָ הַנִּמְצָאֹת פֶּן־תִּסָּפֶה
בַּעֲוֹן ג״פ מ״ב הָעִיר סוזחף, ערי, סנדלפון׃ 16 וַיִּתְמַהְמָהּ | וַיַּחֲזִיקוּ הָאֲנָשִׁים
בְּיָדוֹ וּבְיַד־אִשְׁתּוֹ וּבְיַד שְׁתֵּי בְנֹתָיו בְּחֶמְלַת יְהֹוָ(אדני)ה יאהדונהי עָלָיו
וַיֹּצִאֻהוּ וַיַּנִּחֻהוּ מִחוּץ לָעִיר סוזחף, ערי, סנדלפון׃ 17 וַיְהִי אל כְהוֹצִיאָם
אֹתָם הַחוּצָה וַיֹּאמֶר הִמָּלֵט עַל־נַפְשֶׁךָ אַל־תַּבִּיט אַחֲרֶיךָ וְאַל־
תַּעֲמֹד בְּכָל לכב ־הַכִּכָּר הָהָרָה הִמָּלֵט פֶּן־תִּסָּפֶה׃ 18 וַיֹּאמֶר
לוֹט מ״ה אֲלֵהֶם אַל־נָא אֲדֹנָי׃ 19 הִנֵּה מ״ה יה ־נָא מָצָא עַבְדְּךָ פוי
חֵן מוחי בְּעֵינֶיךָ ע״ה קס״א וַתַּגְדֵּל חַסְדְּךָ ע״ב, ריבוע יהוה אֲשֶׁר עָשִׂיתָ
עִמָּדִי לְהַחֲיוֹת אֶת־נַפְשִׁי וְאָנֹכִי איע לֹא אוּכַל לְהִמָּלֵט הָהָרָה
פֶּן־תִּדְבָּקַנִי הָרָעָה רהע וָמַתִּי׃ 20 הִנֵּה מ״ה יה ־נָא הָעִיר סוזחף, ערי, סנדלפון
הַזֹּאת קְרֹבָה לָנוּס שָׁמָּה מהש וְהִוא מִצְעָר אִמָּלְטָה נָּא שָׁמָּה
מהש הֲלֹא מִצְעָר הִוא וּתְחִי נַפְשִׁי׃

---

while resisting the desire to look back at our previously materialistic lifestyles, and

- Resisting the longing for the energy that once gratified our ego when we were in a lower, more primal state of being.

Just as a recovering alcoholic must always resist a drink, we must view ourselves as recovering egoholics who must unceasingly defy the temptations and trappings of our illusionary material world, lest we succumb and revert to our old ways.

This is not an easy task, as negative energy and the materialistic path are enticing and bewitching, exerting an enigmatic and powerful attraction on us.

And yet we must remember that if we do slip off the path, the angels will always assist us to continue on our upward journey, provided we have sincerely committed ourselves to our spiritual transformation and have thus attached ourselves to their Divine energy.

This passage is a gift to us, allowing us to draw upon the merit of Abraham and the influence of the angels to sever our ties to the sinful, self-indulgent elements of our selfish ways. When we grasp the hands of the angels, we are lifted out of the confusion of this Earthly existence.

We forever recognize the senselessness of trading away eternal spiritual assets for the artificial, fleeting pleasures we derive by catering to our untamed impulses.

FOURTH READING - MOSES - NETZACH

21 And He said to him, "Very well, I will grant this request too; I will not overthrow the city you speak of.

22 But flee there quickly, because I cannot do anything until you reach it." That is why the city was called Zo'ar.

23 By the time Lot reached Zo'ar, the sun had risen over the land.

24 Then the Lord rained down brimstone and fire on Sodom and Gomorrah—from the Lord out of heaven.

25 And he overthrew those cities and the entire plain, including all the inhabitants of the cities and that which grew upon the ground.

ויעל

Genesis 19:30 – **Forgetfulness.** The Bible says Lot and his two daughters sought refuge in a place called Tzo'ar after leaving Sodom. However, they soon left that city because Lot was afraid to stay there, and they took up residence in a cave on the mountain.

Rashi wrote that Lot was worried that the fire and brimstone meant for the two wicked cities would actually land on Tzo'ar as well, and he suspected that Tzo'ar itself would eventually become full of evil.

The *Zohar* says the Aramiac word Tzo'ar is connected to the Aramaic word *tsa'ar*, which means "agony." This is the agony of Hell, referring both to hell after death and to Hell on Earth, which is the pain and torment we suffer in this world as a result of our intolerant deeds and materialistic attachments. Lot entered "Hell" and experienced its agony as a result of the sins characteristic of idol-worshippers that had been committed in Sodom, and this is why he feared Tzo'ar.

Rashi's commentary on this verse says that even Tzo'ar was spared destruction only as long as Lot was living there. We can infer that when Lot—the "good" man—chose to leave, then Hell (Tzo'ar) itself was destroyed.

Afterward, up on the mountain in a cave, two incestuous acts took place between Lot and his daughters. Both of Lot's daughters seduced him while he was in a state of drunkenness. Although Lot feared the repercussions of sinful behavior, he was unaware of what his daughters had done to him, as shown by this verse in the *Zohar*:

> *It is written: "And they made their father drink wine." (Genesis 19:33) The way of the wicked is to go astray by drinking wine, to indulge the Evil Inclination with pleasures and arouse it until it rejoices in drunkenness and lies in its bed. Immediately then, "the first-born went in and lay with her father;" she joins him and begins to imagine all kinds of bad thoughts. The Evil Inclination joins her and clings to her, and ceases to be aware of her or of what it does to her "when she lay down" in this world or "when she arose" to the World to Come. "when she lay down..." in the World to Come, she will account for her deeds and be judged for them. And "when she arose" for the Day of Judgment, it is written: "And many of them that sleep in the dust of the earth shall awake." (Daniel 12:2) Here the Evil Inclination has no perception at all, so it*

FOURTH READING - MOSES - NETZACH

21 וַיֹּאמֶר אֵלָיו הִנֵּה מ״ה יה נָשָׂאתִי פָנֶיךָ ס״ג - מ״ה - ב״ן גַּם לַדָּבָר ראה
הַזֶּה והו לְבִלְתִּי הָפְכִּי אֶת־הָעִיר בוזוך, ערי, סנדלפון אֲשֶׁר דִּבַּרְתָּ ראה:
22 מַהֵר הִמָּלֵט שָׁמָּה מהש כִּי לֹא אוּכַל לַעֲשׂוֹת דָּבָר ראה עַד־
בֹּאֲךָ שָׁמָּה מהש עַל־כֵּן קָרָא שֵׁם יהוה שדי ־הָעִיר בוזוך, ערי, סנדלפון
צוֹעַר: 23 הַשֶּׁמֶשׁ ב״פ ש״ך יָצָא עַל־הָאָרֶץ אלהים דההין ע״ה וְלוֹט מ״ה בָּא
צֹעֲרָה: 24 וַיהֹוָה אהדונהי הִמְטִיר עַל־סְדֹם ב״פ ב״ן וְעַל־עֲמֹרָה
גָּפְרִית וָאֵשׁ מֵאֵת יְהֹוָה אהדונהי מִן־הַשָּׁמָיִם י״פ טל, י״פ כוזו: 25 וַיַּהֲפֹךְ
אֶת־הֶעָרִים הָאֵל לאה (אלד ע״ה) וְאֵת כָּל ילי ־הַכִּכָּר וְאֵת כָּל ילי ־יֹשְׁבֵי
הֶעָרִים וְצֶמַח יהוה - אהיה - יהוה - אדני הָאֲדָמָה: 26 וַתַּבֵּט אִשְׁתּוֹ
מֵאַחֲרָיו וַתְּהִי נְצִיב מֶלַח ג״פ יהוה: 27 וַיַּשְׁכֵּם אַבְרָהָם ח״פ אל, רמ״ח
בַּבֹּקֶר אֶל־הַמָּקוֹם יהוה ברבוע, ר״פ אל אֲשֶׁר־עָמַד שָׁם אֶת־פְּנֵי חכמה - בינה
יְהֹוָה אהדונהי: 28 וַיַּשְׁקֵף עַל־פְּנֵי חכמה - בינה סְדֹם ב״פ ב״ן וַעֲמֹרָה וְעַל־
כָּל ילי, עמם ־פְּנֵי חכמה - בינה אֶרֶץ אלהים דאלפין הַכִּכָּר וַיַּרְא וְהִנֵּה יהוה מ״ה
עָלָה קִיטֹר הָאָרֶץ אלהים דההין ע״ה כְּקִיטֹר הַכִּבְשָׁן: 29 וַיְהִי בְּשַׁחֵת
אֱלֹהִים ילה, מום אֶת־עָרֵי הַכִּכָּר וַיִּזְכֹּר ע״ב - קס״א, יהי אור ע״ה אֱלֹהִים
ילה, מום אֶת־אַבְרָהָם ח״פ אל, רמ״ח וַיְשַׁלַּח אֶת־לוֹט מ״ה מִתּוֹךְ הַהֲפֵכָה
בַּהֲפֹךְ אֶת־הֶעָרִים אֲשֶׁר־יָשַׁב בָּהֵן לוֹט מ״ה: 30 וַיַּעַל לוֹט מ״ה

---

clings to her, and she clings to it. Later, she arouses the other. Thus, after the great thought is attached to the Evil Inclination, the other one comes and clings to it."
– The Zohar, Vayera 23:324

Here we have a marvelous metaphor that tells us a great deal about human nature. The daughters of Lot represent the Evil Inclination and the egocentric behavior it incites. Lot's fear is our fear, namely, our recognition and admission of our negative traits during the times when we are experiencing anguish. When we are distressed, we promise to change. While we are enmeshed in the consequences of our misdeeds, we vow to alter our lifestyles and amend our conduct. But as soon as our suffering ceases and good times

[26] But his wife looked back, and she became a pillar of salt.

[27] And Abraham got up early in the morning and returned to the place where he had stood before the Lord.

[28] And he looked toward Sodom and Gomorrah, and toward all the land of the plain, and he saw smoke rising from the country, like smoke from a furnace.

[29] And it came to pass when God destroyed the cities of the plain that God remembered Abraham, and he sent Lot out of the midst of the overthrow, when He overthrew the cities in which Lot had dwelt.

[30] And Lot and his two daughters left Zo'ar and dwelt in the mountains, for he was afraid to stay in Zo'ar. He and his two daughters dwelt in a cave.

[31] And the firstborn daughter said to the younger, "Our father is old, and there is no man on earth to come lie with us, as is the manner all over the earth.

[32] Come, let us make our father drink wine and we will lie with him, that we may preserve the seed of our father."

---

return, we forget those moments of clarity and truth. We are again seduced—whether knowingly or unknowingly—by the trappings of the material world and deceived by the illusionary aspects of physicality, as shown by the following verses from the *Zohar*:

> *Rav Yitzchak said, "If [Lot] was afraid, why then does the Evil Inclination come to misguide people? Because this is truly the way of the wicked. When a man sees evil, his fear lasts only a moment; he then immediately returns to his wicked ways and fears nothing. Similarly, when the Evil Inclination sees the wicked being punished, it is afraid. But as soon as it leaves, it fears nothing."*
>
> *– The Zohar, Vayera 23:322*

The Bible verses relating to these kabbalistic truths liberate us from the seductive charms of our Evil Inclination. Memory is restored and clarity returns so that we forever remain true to our promise to transform and to spiritually elevate our souls.

וַתֹּאמֶר

Genesis 19:31 – While Lot and his two daughters were seeking refuge in Tzo'ar, the cities of Sodom and Gomorrah were annihilated by fire and brimstone. Fearing to stay in Tzo'ar, they then left, choosing to dwell in a cave up on the mountain.

While in the cave, Lot's two daughters feared that the end of civilization had come after they

מִצּוֹעַר וַיֵּשֶׁב בָּהָר אור, רז וּשְׁתֵּי בְנֹתָיו עִמּוֹ כִּי יָרֵא לָשֶׁבֶת
בְּצוֹעַר וַיֵּשֶׁב בַּמְּעָרָה הוּא וּשְׁתֵּי בְנֹתָיו: 31 וַתֹּאמֶר הַבְּכִירָה
אֶל-הַצְּעִירָה אָבִינוּ זָקֵן וְאִישׁ ע"ה קנ"א קס"א אֵין בָּאָרֶץ אלהים דאלפין
לָבוֹא עָלֵינוּ כְּדֶרֶךְ ב"פ יב"ק כָּל ילי -הָאָרֶץ אלהים דההין ע"ה: 32 לְכָה
נַשְׁקֶה אֶת-אָבִינוּ יַיִן מיכ, י"פ האא וְנִשְׁכְּבָה עִמּוֹ וּנְחַיֶּה מֵאָבִינוּ זָרַע:

---

witnessed the complete destruction of Sodom and Gomorrah. The older daughter suggested they intoxicate their father with wine and seduce him so that they would bear children and continue the human race.

Both daughters then had sexual relations with their father while he was inebriated and virtually unconscious.

Both daughters eventually gave birth to male children: the elder daughter to a boy named Moab; the younger, to a son called Amon.

The *Zohar* reveals that the child born to the older daughter, Moab, is the seed and forefather of the Messiah through Ruth and King David.

> *King David was attached to both AMON AND MOAB because Ruth issued from Moab, and King David [issued] from her. David was enthroned by the crown of Amon which was a testimony to the seed of David, as it is written: "And he brought forth the king's son, and put the crown upon him, and gave him the testimony." (II Kings 11:12) This crown came from Milcom, which is the grade of the children of Amon, as it is written: "And he took their king's (Heb. malcam) crown." (II Samuel 12:30)*
>
> *– The Zohar, Vayera 24:336*

In an attempt to unravel the mystery of a Messiah descending from an incestuous relationship, the *Zohar* offers the following insight. It tells us that the world and a man's soul are like a lump of clay spinning on a potter's stone wheel. As long as the wheel is in motion, the craftsman is able to remodel the shape of the clay into any form he chooses. Although there are many possible shapes for the pot he is making, the potter could make any of them from the same lump of clay.

We begin life as a shapeless piece of clay. Our world constantly revolves so that our souls may evolve on the wheel of life. As we shape and refashion our lives, we attempt to transform our nature completely from extreme negativity and darkness to the supremely positive Light.

The spinning of our world and the evolution of our souls over many lifetimes occur so that we can become the craftsmen of Creation. This is how we become co-creators of the Light in our lives—the cause of our own fulfillment—instead of having paradise given to us like an unearned handout from the Creator.

It is heartening to realize that the most negative situations invariably hold the greatest promise for positive growth, for ours is a world of exquisite balance. Therefore, the ultimate darkness is inherently transformable into the brightest of Light.

The Age of Messiah will occur when we generate the greatest possible spiritual Light in this world. Therefore, the Messiah must emerge from the lowest, darkest realm, which is signified by the incestuous relationship of Lot and his daughters.

Each of us is born with the power to transform our nature completely and to achieve a personal state of Messiah within. Instead of experiencing guilt or shame—or even worse, apathy—as a consequence of our negative actions, we should be inspired by the opportunity to reshape our soul into the greatest Vessel for the Light.

33 And they made their father drink wine that night, and the firstborn went in and lay with her father, and he was not aware of when she lay down or when she got up.

34 And it came to pass on the next day the firstborn said to the younger, "See, last night I lay with my father. Let us make him drink wine again tonight, and you go in and lie with him so we can preserve the seed of our father."

35 And they made their father to drink wine that night also, and the younger daughter went and lay with him and he was not aware of when she lay down or when she got
up. 36 Thus both of Lot's daughters were with child by their father.

37 And the firstborn had a son, and she named him Moab; he is the father of the Moabites unto this day.

38 The younger daughter also had a son, and she named him Ben-Ami; he is the father of the Ammonites unto this day.

וּבְקוּמָהּ

Genesis 19:33 – As stated previously, there is a dot over the letter *Vav* in the word *uvkumah* (when she arose). *Uvkumah* describes how both of Lot's daughters arose after having sexual relations with their father, unbeknownst to him. However, the word is spelled differently when it applies to the older daughter. There, the word is written with a Vav and a dot above it. About the dot, the *Zohar* states:

> *This indicates that there was help from Above in performing that action, which was ultimately to result in the birth of the Messiah…*
>
> *– The Zohar, Vayera 23:310*

Thus we see that it was Divine Providence that ensured that the Messiah would descend from the child of Lot's elder daughter.

As we meditate upon this dot above the *Vav* in the word *uvkumah*, we personally enlist help from the higher energies to ensure that our most negative traits are immediately transformed into positive attributes.

What's more, we can meditate to impart this sacred energy to the whole world, helping to transform the darkest elements of human civilization into luminous Light.

Finally, the dot over the Vav connects us to the Upper World where we use the effulgent Light—shining with radiant splendor—to initiate the arrival of the Messiah, both our internal personal Messiah and the global Messiah.

33 וַתַּשְׁקֶיןָ אֶת־אֲבִיהֶן יַיִן מיכ, י"פ האא בַּלַּיְלָה מלה הוּא וַתָּבֹא
הַבְּכִירָה וַתִּשְׁכַּב אֶת־אָבִיהָ וְלֹא־יָדַע בְּשִׁכְבָהּ וּבְקוּמָהּ׃
34 וַיְהִי אל מִמָּחֳרָת וַתֹּאמֶר הַבְּכִירָה אֶל־הַצְּעִירָה הֵן־שָׁכַבְתִּי
אֶמֶשׁ אֶת־אָבִי נַשְׁקֶנּוּ יַיִן מיכ, י"פ האא גַּם יגל ־הַלַּיְלָה מלה וּבֹאִי
שִׁכְבִי עִמּוֹ וּנְחַיֶּה מֵאָבִינוּ זָרַע׃ 35 וַתַּשְׁקֶיןָ גַּם יגל
בַּלַּיְלָה מלה הַהוּא אֶת־אֲבִיהֶן יָיִן מיכ, י"פ האא וַתָּקָם הַצְּעִירָה
וַתִּשְׁכַּב עִמּוֹ וְלֹא־יָדַע בְּשִׁכְבָהּ וּבְקֻמָהּ׃ 36 וַתַּהֲרֶיןָ שְׁתֵּי
בְנוֹת־לוֹט מ"ה מֵאֲבִיהֶן׃ 37 וַתֵּלֶד הַבְּכִירָה בֵּן וַתִּקְרָא שְׁמוֹ מהש ע"ה
מוֹאָב הוּא אֲבִי־מוֹאָב יוד הא ואו הה עַד־הַיּוֹם נגד, זן, מזבח׃
38 וְהַצְּעִירָה גַם יגל ־הִוא יָלְדָה בֵּן וַתִּקְרָא שְׁמוֹ מהש ע"ה
בֶּן־עַמִּי ב"פ אלהים הוּא אֲבִי בְנֵי־עַמּוֹן רבוע ס"ג עַד־הַיּוֹם נגד, זן, מזבח׃ [ס]

וַתַּהֲרֶיןָ

Genesis 19:36 – **Deconstructing incest.** According to the *Zohar*, the incestuous relationship between Lot and his daughters is also a metaphor for the machinations of our own Evil Inclination and for the wickedness that men do. The *Zohar* says that during sleep, the lowest level of our soul ignites evil desires and negative thoughts. These profane thoughts are then conceived and born into our heart. This process is the secret meaning behind Lot's daughters' act of sleeping with their father, and it refers specifically to the actual moment of conception.

The mention of sleep, Kabbalah says, is a reference to people who are unenlightened (i.e., asleep in life) and who live a shallow existence, lacking any awareness of spirituality. They live robotically, routinely, governed by their ego, and controlled solely by their materialistic desires. This way of life provides fertile ground for the seeds of evil thoughts.

After the lowest level of our soul generates negative desires and thoughts so that they are conceived and born in the heart, it arouses and stimulates the power of the body until an evil thought in our heart becomes completely attached to it. This is the hidden secret behind the physical birth of Lot's daughters' children, as stated by the biblical verse:

> *Thus both of Lot's daughters were with child by their father.*
> *– Genesis 19:36*

This story of incest is actually a description of how evil takes hold in the human heart, seizes control of the body, and then impels us to behave with insensitivity, intolerance, and cruelty in varied measures, large and small. It is important to understand the hidden meaning of this passage so that its power can uproot the evil desires that lurk within the heart of mankind. The lowest level of our soul is thereby subdued, and all humanity is awakened, elevated, and imbued with a higher level of soul.

Evil is not defined solely as wicked behavior that takes the form of murder, torture, or other bloodthirsty acts. Evil also includes intolerance between friends and the envy that we feel over another person's possessions. And "murder," by extension, also includes character assassination through gossip. Make no mistake: Insensitive acts, large and small, take their toll on humanity.

20[1] And Abraham journeyed from there toward the south country and for a while stayed in Gerar before dwelling between Kadesh and Shur.

[2] And Abraham said of his wife Sarah, "She is my sister." Then Abimelech, king of Gerar, sent and took Sarah.

[3] But God came to Abimelech in a dream one night and said to him, "Behold you are a dead man, for the woman you have taken; she is a man's wife."

[4] But Abimelech had not gone near her, so he said, "Lord, will you slay an innocent nation?

[5] Did he not say to me, 'She is my sister,' and she even said, 'He is my brother.' In the integrity of my heart and innocence of my hand have I done this."

[6] And God said to him in the dream, "Yes, I know you did this with integrity in your heart, and so I have kept you from sinning against me. That is why I did not let you touch her.

[7] Now return the man's wife, for he is a prophet, and he will pray for you and you will live. But if you do not return her, you may be sure that you and all that is yours will die."

[8] Therefore Abimelech rose early in the morning and summoned all his servants, and when he told them all that had happened, they were very much afraid.

[9] Then Abimelech called Abraham and said, "What have you done to us? How have I offended you that you have brought such great sin upon me and my kingdom? You have done things to me that should not be done."

[10] And Abimelech asked Abraham, "What was your reason for doing this?"

[11] Abraham replied, "Because I thought that there surely is no fear of God in this
place, and they will kill me because of my wife. [12] Besides, she is indeed my sister,
she is the daughter of my father but not the daughter of my mother; and she became
my wife. [13] And it came to pass, when God caused me to wander from my father's
household, that I said to her, 'This is how you can show your love to me: Everywhere we go, say of me, 'He is my brother.' "

בִּגְרָר

Genesis 20:1 – Sarah and Abraham traveled to the city of Gerar, where Abraham, to prevent himself from being killed, told everyone that Sarah was his sister. "Sister" is a code word that refers to the feminine Divine Presence known as the *Shechina*, while the city of Gerar is a code for negativity and darkness. The word *gerar* means "to drag away," and we can take this to mean that Abraham went to a place where he might be dragged or pulled away from his continuing connection with God. The inner meaning of this episode is offered in the following explanation:

Before Abraham went down to the darkness and negativity, he first attached himself to the Creator via the *Shechina*. The spiritual principle concealed in this story can be revealed by an analogy. If a person lowers himself into a deep,

20 1 וַיִּסַּע מִשָּׁם אַבְרָהָם ו"פ אל, רמ"ח אַרְצָה אלהים דההין ע"ה הַנֶּגֶב
וַיֵּשֶׁב בֵּין־קָדֵשׁ וּבֵין שׁוּר אבגיתצ, ושר, אהבת חנם וַיָּגָר בִּגְרָר׃ 2 וַיֹּאמֶר
אַבְרָהָם ו"פ אל, רמ"ח אֶל־שָׂרָה אלהים דיודין ורבוע אלהים - ה' אִשְׁתּוֹ אֲחֹתִי הִוא
וַיִּשְׁלַח אֲבִימֶלֶךְ מֶלֶךְ גְּרָר וַיִּקַּח ועם אֶת־שָׂרָה אלהים דיודין ורבוע אלהים - ה'׃
3 וַיָּבֹא אֱלֹהִים ילה, מום אֶל־אֲבִימֶלֶךְ בַּחֲלוֹם הַלָּיְלָה מלה וַיֹּאמֶר לוֹ
הִנְּךָ מֵת י"פ רבוע אהיה עַל־הָאִשָּׁה אֲשֶׁר־לָקַחְתָּ וְהִוא בְּעֻלַת בָּעַל׃
4 וַאֲבִימֶלֶךְ לֹא קָרַב אֵלֶיהָ וַיֹּאמַר אֲדֹנָי ללה הֲגוֹי גַּם־צַדִּיק
תַּהֲרֹג׃ 5 הֲלֹא הוּא אָמַר־לִי אֲחֹתִי הִוא וְהִיא־גַם יגל ־הוּא אָמְרָה
אָחִי הוּא בְּתָם י"פ רבוע אהיה ־לְבָבִי בוכו וּבְנִקְיֹן כַּפַּי עָשִׂיתִי זֹאת׃
6 וַיֹּאמֶר אֵלָיו הָאֱלֹהִים ילה, מום בַּחֲלֹם ג"פ יהוה גַּם אָנֹכִי איע יָדַעְתִּי
כִּי בְתָם־לְבָבְךָ בוכו עָשִׂיתָ זֹּאת וָאֶחְשֹׂךְ גַּם יגל ־אָנֹכִי איע אוֹתְךָ
מֵחֲטוֹ־לִי עַל־כֵּן לֹא־נְתַתִּיךָ לִנְגֹּעַ אֵלֶיהָ׃ 7 וְעַתָּה הָשֵׁב אֵשֶׁת־
הָאִישׁ ז"פ אדם כִּי־נָבִיא הוּא וְיִתְפַּלֵּל בַּעַדְךָ וֶחְיֵה וְאִם יוהך ־אֵינְךָ
מֵשִׁיב דַּע כִּי־מוֹת תָּמוּת אַתָּה וְכָל ילי ־אֲשֶׁר־לָךְ׃ 8 וַיַּשְׁכֵּם
אֲבִימֶלֶךְ בַּבֹּקֶר וַיִּקְרָא עם ה' אותיות = ב"פ קס"א לְכָל יה - אדני ־עֲבָדָיו
וַיְדַבֵּר ראה אֶת־כָּל ילי ־הַדְּבָרִים ראה הָאֵלֶּה בְּאָזְנֵיהֶם יוד הי ואו הה
וַיִּירְאוּ הָאֲנָשִׁים מְאֹד מ"ה׃ 9 וַיִּקְרָא עם ה' אותיות = ב"פ קס"א אֲבִימֶלֶךְ
לְאַבְרָהָם ו"פ אל, רמ"ח וַיֹּאמֶר לוֹ מֶה מ"ה ־עָשִׂיתָ לָּנוּ אלהים, מום

---

dark pit filled with deadly snakes to retrieve a great treasure, he first secures himself to a strong rope to ensure a safe retreat. The rope becomes his lifeline as he enters the dangerous environment. Likewise, Abraham attached himself to the force called the *Shechina* (Sarah) before entering the pit of negativity (the city of Gerar) so that he could maintain a lifeline to his Creator.

There are times in life when we are lured into negative situations. Without supernal assistance, we fall prey to the traps and temptations set up by the forces of negativity. In addition, we are affected by the negative influences of the stars and planets.

By attaching ourselves to the Shechina, however, we build a secure lifeline to the Creator to help us during those challenging moments in life when we stumble and fall into negativity. Thus, we are enabled to nullify all negative cosmic forces and become the masters of our own destiny.

14 And Abimelech brought sheep and oxen and menservants and women servants and gave them to Abraham, and he returned Sarah his wife to him.

15 And Abimelech said, "See, my land is before you; live wherever you like."

16 And to Sarah he said, "See, I have given your brother a thousand pieces of silver. This is to cover the offense against you before all who are with you; you are completely reproved."

17 So Abraham prayed to God, and God healed Abimelech, his wife, and his
maidservants so that they could bear children. 18 For the Lord had closed up every
womb in Abimelech's household because of Abraham's wife Sarah.

פָּקַד

Genesis 21:1 – The word "Sarah" represents the human being in a state of righteousness, when the ego is dead and the body is at rest within the grave. The verse where the Creator visits Sarah refers to the Light of the Creator arriving in this world at the End of Days (our present day) to commence the Resurrection of the Dead and the Dawn of Immortality. The *Zohar* quotes the words of the Creator:

> *"I will open your graves, and cause you to come up out of your graves, and bring you into the land of Israel," (Ezekiel 37:12) which is followed by: "And I shall put My spirit in you, and you shall live...."*
> – *The Zohar, Vayera 29:391*

The *Zohar* explains that the Creator will then make the body of man as beautiful as Adam's was when he entered the Garden of Eden:

> *Then all creatures shall know of the soul that entered them—that it is the soul of Life, the soul of Delight, which has received all pleasures and delights for the body from Above.*
> – *The Zohar, Vayera 29:393*

The End of Days will see the dawning of an abundance of spiritual energy, unprecedented in human history. Who among us will safely harness this energy to radiate Light, and who will experience instead a short-circuit that will cause the burning rays to harm them? Our fates will be largely determined by one criterion: The amount of human dignity that we accorded to our fellowman.

Whereas in the past, the consequences of our intolerant behavior were delayed for years or even lifetimes, the End of Days will see the timespan or distance between Cause and Effect contract so that the repercussions of our actions, either positive or negative, will be felt immediately—judgment and mercy will coincide.

There is a *Midrash* (biblical commentary) that Jacob wanted to reveal to his sons when the End of Days (i.e., the end of the Exile) would come, but the Creator prevented him, saying that it was His decision to conceal the matter. Some thought should be given to the concept of the End of Days. When we realize that this does not designate a point in time but rather that point outside time where the Light of the Creator always exists, we also come to realize that it is incumbent upon us to open ourselves to the idea of the End of Days now.

The reading of this single biblical verse (Genesis 21:1) initiates the Resurrection of the Dead now, with a welling forth of loving kindness and mercy. Furthermore, using the sword of Light to slay the ego, we can be spiritually resurrected and even avoid the experience of physical death and burial.

Genesis 21:2 – **Fertility.** The words that speak of the birth of Isaac (Yitzchak) radiate a force of fertility that helps all those who are unable to

וּמֶה מ״ה ־חָטָאתִי לָךְ כִּי־הֵבֵאתָ עָלַי וְעַל־מַמְלַכְתִּי חֲטָאָה
גְדֹלָה להח, מבה, יזל, אום מַעֲשִׂים אֲשֶׁר לֹא־יֵעָשׂוּ עָשִׂיתָ עִמָּדִי׃
10 וַיֹּאמֶר אֲבִימֶלֶךְ אֶל־אַבְרָהָם ו״פ אל, רמ״ח מָה מ״ה רָאִיתָ כִּי עָשִׂיתָ
אֶת־הַדָּבָר ראה הַזֶּה והו׃ 11 וַיֹּאמֶר אַבְרָהָם ו״פ אל, רמ״ח כִּי אָמַרְתִּי
י״פ אדני ע״ה רַק אֵין־יִרְאַת אֱלֹהִים ילה, מום בַּמָּקוֹם יהוה ברבוע, ו״פ אל הַזֶּה
והו וַהֲרָגוּנִי עַל־דְּבַר ראה אִשְׁתִּי׃ 12 וְגַם יגל ־אָמְנָה אֲחֹתִי בַת־אָבִי
הִוא אַךְ אהיה לֹא בַת־אִמִּי וַתְּהִי־לִי לְאִשָּׁה׃ 13 וַיְהִי אל כַּאֲשֶׁר
הִתְעוּ אֹתִי אֱלֹהִים ילה, מום מִבֵּית ב״פ ראה אָבִי וָאֹמַר לָהּ זֶה חַסְדֵּךְ
ע״ב, ריבוע יהוה אֲשֶׁר תַּעֲשִׂי עִמָּדִי אֶל כָּל ילי ־הַמָּקוֹם יהוה ברבוע, ו״פ אל
אֲשֶׁר נָבוֹא שָׁמָּה מהש אִמְרִי־לִי אָחִי הוּא׃ 14 וַיִּקַּח חעם אֲבִימֶלֶךְ
צֹאן מלוי אהיה דיודין ע״ה וּבָקָר וַעֲבָדִים וּשְׁפָחֹת וַיִּתֵּן לְאַבְרָהָם ו״פ אל, רמ״ח
וַיָּשֶׁב לוֹ אֵת שָׂרָה אלהים דיודין ורבוע אלהים - ה׳ אִשְׁתּוֹ׃ 15 וַיֹּאמֶר
אֲבִימֶלֶךְ הִנֵּה מ״ה יה אַרְצִי לְפָנֶיךָ ס״ג - מ״ה - ב״ן בַּטּוֹב והו בְּעֵינֶיךָ
ע״ה קס״א שֵׁב׃ 16 וּלְשָׂרָה אלהים דיודין ורבוע אלהים - ה׳ אָמַר הִנֵּה נָתַתִּי אֶלֶף
אלף למד - שין דלת יוד ע״ה כֶּסֶף לְאָחִיךְ הִנֵּה מ״ה יה הוּא־לָךְ כְּסוּת עֵינַיִם
ריבוע מ״ה לְכֹל יה - אדני אֲשֶׁר אִתָּךְ וְאֵת כֹּל ילי וְנֹכָחַת׃ 17 וַיִּתְפַּלֵּל
אַבְרָהָם ו״פ אל, רמ״ח אֶל־הָאֱלֹהִים ילה, מום וַיִּרְפָּא אֱלֹהִים ילה, מום אֶת־
אֲבִימֶלֶךְ וְאֶת־אִשְׁתּוֹ וְאַמְהֹתָיו וַיֵּלֵדוּ׃ 18 כִּי־עָצֹר עָצַר
יְהֹוָהאדניאהדונהי בְּעַד כָּל ילי ־רֶחֶם רמ״ח לְבֵית ב״פ ראה אֲבִימֶלֶךְ עַל־
דְּבַר ראה שָׂרָה אלהים דיודין ורבוע אלהים - ה׳ אֵשֶׁת אַבְרָהָם ו״פ אל, רמ״ח׃ [ס]
21 1 וַיהֹוָהאדניאהדונהי פָּקַד אֶת־שָׂרָה אלהים דיודין ורבוע אלהים - ה׳ כַּאֲשֶׁר
אָמָר וַיַּעַשׂ יְהֹוָהאדניאהדונהי לְשָׂרָה אלהים דיודין ורבוע אלהים - ה׳ כַּאֲשֶׁר דִּבֵּר
ראה׃ 2 וַתַּהַר וַתֵּלֶד שָׂרָה אלהים דיודין ורבוע אלהים - ה׳ לְאַבְרָהָם ו״פ אל, רמ״ח
בֵּן לִזְקֻנָיו לַמּוֹעֵד אֲשֶׁר־דִּבֶּר ראה אֹתוֹ אֱלֹהִים ילה, מום׃

21[1] And the Lord visited Sarah as He had said, and the Lord did for Sarah what He had promised. [2] For Sarah conceived and bore a son to Abraham in his old age, at the very time God had promised him.

[3] And Abraham gave the name Isaac to the son Sarah bore him. [4] And Abraham circumcised his son Isaac when he was eight days old, as God commanded him.

FIFTH READING - AARON - HOD

[5] And Abraham was a hundred years old when his son Isaac was born to him.

[6] And Sarah said, "God has brought me laughter, and everyone who hears will laugh with me."

[7] And she said, "Who would have said to Abraham that Sarah would nurse children, for I have borne him a son in his old age?"

[8] And the child grew and was weaned, and Abraham made a great feast on the day that Isaac was weaned.

---

conceive children. Through our caring and meditation, we can transfer this energy to people who are trying to have children, helping them remedy the root cause of their infertility.

Laughter. The name "Isaac" refers to the concept and emotion of laughter. To one degree or another, we all need to express our true emotions in life—to laugh or to cry or to vent frustration. We often allow emotions like anger, resentment, and grief to build up inside, preventing us from living joyfully, proactively, and peacefully. The vibration of Isaac in this reading helps us release our pent-up emotions in a proactive fashion—through laughter—so that we can experience true joy and happiness.

The Death of Death. On a deeper level of understanding, the *Zohar* explains that the name "Sarah" is code for a person who has attained a state of righteousness and spiritual completeness, and who has therefore actually slain his or her Evil Inclination. This state of existence is achieved prior to the Resurrection of the Dead and the Dawn of Immortality.

The name "Isaac" is a metaphor for a man in his immortal state following the Resurrection, after God has banished death forever. In this ultimate, eternal phase of existence, all of us will dwell in pure joy and will be united with the Light of the Creator.

This secret is revealed by the following verse of the *Zohar*:

> *"He will swallow up death forever; and the Lord God will wipe away tears from off all faces." (Isaiah 25:8) Then it [the immortal body, named Sarah] shall be called Isaac (lit. "he will laugh") because of the laughter and happiness of the righteous in the future.*
>
> *– The Zohar, Vayera 29:401*

As we listen to the Bible verses that tell of Isaac's birth, the demise of the Angel of Death is caused in the Upper Worlds and endless laughter echoes throughout eternity, giving sublime pleasure.

The Angel of Death's influence extends beyond the destruction of the physical body. This energy force is also responsible for the demise of someone's happiness, the dissolution of their marriage, or the ruin of their livelihood. Thus, we should read this verse so that any area of life in danger of coming to an end will be revitalized and resurrected.

3 וַיִּקְרָא עם ה' אותיות = ב"פ קס"א אַבְרָהָם ח"פ אל, רמ"ח אֶת־שֶׁם יהוה שדי ־בְּנוֹ
הַנּוֹלַד־לוֹ ר"ת הבל אֲשֶׁר־יָלְדָה־לּוֹ שָׂרָה אלהים דיודין ורבוע אלהים - ה' יִצְחָק
ד"פ ב"ן: 4 וַיָּמָל אַבְרָהָם ח"פ אל, רמ"ח אֶת־יִצְחָק ד"פ ב"ן בְּנוֹ בֶּן־שְׁמֹנַת
יָמִים נלך כַּאֲשֶׁר צִוָּה פוי אֹתוֹ אֱלֹהִים ילה, מום:

FIFTH READING - AARON - HOD

5 וְאַבְרָהָם ח"פ אל, רמ"ח בֶּן־מְאַת שָׁנָה בְּהִוָּלֶד לוֹ אֵת יִצְחָק ד"פ ב"ן
בְּנוֹ: 6 וַתֹּאמֶר שָׂרָה אלהים דיודין ורבוע אלהים - ה' צְחֹק עָשָׂה לִי אֱלֹהִים
ילה, מום כָּל ילי ־הַשֹּׁמֵעַ יִצְחַק ד"פ ב"ן ־לִי: 7 וַתֹּאמֶר מִי ילי מִלֵּל
לְאַבְרָהָם ח"פ אל, רמ"ח הֵינִיקָה בָנִים שָׂרָה אלהים דיודין ורבוע אלהים - ה' כִּי־
יָלַדְתִּי בֵן לִזְקֻנָיו: 8 וַיִּגְדַּל יזל הַיֶּלֶד וַיִּגָּמַל וַיַּעַשׂ אַבְרָהָם ח"פ אל, רמ"ח
מִשְׁתֶּה גָדוֹל להח, מבה, יזל, אום בְּיוֹם נגד, זן, מזבח הִגָּמֵל ג"פ יהוה אֶת־יִצְחָק
ד"פ ב"ן: 9 וַתֵּרֶא שָׂרָה אלהים דיודין ורבוע אלהים - ה' אֶת־בֶּן־הָגָר ד"פ ב"ן
הַמִּצְרִית מצר אֲשֶׁר־יָלְדָה לְאַבְרָהָם ח"פ אל, רמ"ח מְצַחֵק: 10 וַתֹּאמֶר
לְאַבְרָהָם ח"פ אל, רמ"ח גָּרֵשׁ הָאָמָה דמב, מלוי ע"ב ע"ה הַזֹּאת וְאֶת־בְּנָהּ כִּי
לֹא יִירַשׁ בֶּן־הָאָמָה דמב, מלוי ע"ב ע"ה הַזֹּאת עִם־בְּנִי עִם־יִצְחָק ד"פ ב"ן:

וַתֵּרֶא

Genesis 21:9 – **Traits of evil.** The characters Hagar and Ishmael represent our own immoral attributes. The banishment of Hagar and Ishmael corresponds to the expulsion of our own selfish desires from our innermost being.

The first step in self-transformation is to recognize and admit to our self-indulgent impulses. This acknowledgment, according to Rav Yehuda Ashlag, is 90 percent of the battle. The Light of the Creator that shines in this week's reading is then free to enter and illuminate the darkest recesses of our soul. This passage arouses self-awareness, thus banishing our Evil Inclination and negative attributes from our character.

וַתֹּאמֶר

Genesis 21:10 – Abraham fathered two sons: Ishmael, whose mother was an Egyptian woman named Hagar, and Isaac, whose mother was Sarah. Sarah was, of course, Abraham's wife, while Hagar was one of Abraham's concubines.

9 And Sarah saw the son that Hagar the Egyptian had borne to Abraham was mocking.
10 And she said to Abraham, "Cast out this bondwoman and her son, for the son of this bondwoman will not be heir with my son, with Isaac." 11 And the thing distressed Abraham greatly because it concerned his son.

12 And God said to Abraham, "Do not be so distressed about the boy and your bondwoman. Listen to whatever Sarah tells you, because it is through Isaac that your seed will be called. 13 And also of the son of the bondwoman will I make a nation, because he is your seed."

14 And Abraham rose early the next morning and took bread and a bottle of water and gave them to Hagar, putting them on her shoulders and then sent her away with the boy. And she wandered in the wilderness of Beersheba.

15 And when the water in the bottle was gone, she put the boy under one of the bushes.

16 And she went a good way off and sat down, about a bowshot away, for she said, "Let me not see the death of the child. And she sat over against him and lifted her voice and wept.

Ishmael is the seed and progenitor of Islam and the entire Arab world. Isaac is the seed from which emerged the Israelite nation.

The Bible tells us that Sarah instructed Abraham to banish Hagar and Ishmael from their home. One might ask how Abraham and Sarah, the personifications of mercy and kindness, could behave with such cruelty.

The *Zohar* sheds some Light concerning this:

> *Now Sarah was not jealous or envious of [Hagar] or her son. If she were, God would not have supported her with the words: "...listen to whatever Sarah tells you." (Genesis 21:12) In fact, it was only because she saw [Ishmael] indulging in idolatrous practices and his mother teaching him the laws of idol-worshipping that she said, "...for the son of this bondwoman shall not be heir." [Sarah was saying:] I know that he shall never inherit a portion of the Faith, and he shall have no share with my son, not in this world and not in the World to Come. And this is why the Creator supported her.*
>
> *– The Zohar, Vayera 33:467*

וַיַּשְׁכֵּם

Genesis 21:14 – **The Separation of Isaac and Ishmael.** "Isaac" is code for the *Left Column* force known as the *Desire to Receive for the Self Alone*. This is the negative anode (–) of energy found in electricity. In human terms, this is our ego.

"Ishmael" is code for the *Right Column* force known as the *Desire to Share*, which is the positive anode (+) of energy. This alludes to the material pleasures of life that indulge our ego.

In a battery, if the positive and negative poles are connected directly via a wire, the battery short-circuits and is drained of all its power. The positive and negative poles must be separated and must remain separated to prevent such a short-circuit.

Through Sarah's action of banishing Hagar and Ishmael, she separated Isaac and Ishmael, showing us that we must separate ourselves from the pleasures that gratify the ego. The Bible is telling us that if we, the children of Israel, do not separate ourselves from short-term selfish indulgences and pleasures, then there will be continued separation between Israelites and Arabs, which is itself a code for the separation,

11 וַיֵּרַע הַדָּבָר ראה מְאֹד בְּעֵינֵי ריבוע מ״ה אַבְרָהָם ח״פ אל, רמ״ח עַל
אוֹדֹת בְּנוֹ: 12 וַיֹּאמֶר אֱלֹהִים ילה, מום אֶל־אַבְרָהָם ח״פ אל, רמ״ח אַל־
יֵרַע בְּעֵינֶיךָ ע״ה קס״א עַל־הַנַּעַר ש״ך וְעַל־אֲמָתֶךָ כֹּל ילי אֲשֶׁר תֹּאמַר
אֵלֶיךָ שָׂרָה אלהים דיודין ורבוע אלהים - ה׳ שְׁמַע בְּקֹלָהּ כִּי בְיִצְחָק ד״פ ב״ן
יִקָּרֵא לְךָ זָרַע: 13 וְגַם אֶת־בֶּן־הָאָמָה דמב, מלוי ע״ב ע״ה לְגוֹי אֲשִׂימֶנּוּ
כִּי זַרְעֲךָ הוּא: 14 וַיַּשְׁכֵּם אַבְרָהָם ח״פ אל, רמ״ח | בַּבֹּקֶר וַיִּקַּח חעם ־לֶחֶם
ג״פ יהוה וְחֵמַת מַיִם וַיִּתֵּן אֶל־הָגָר ד״פ ב״ן שָׂם עַל־שִׁכְמָהּ וְאֶת־הַיֶּלֶד
וַיְשַׁלְּחֶהָ וַתֵּלֶךְ וַתֵּתַע בְּמִדְבַּר רמ״ח, אברהם בְּאֵר קנ״א - ב״ן שָׁבַע
אלהים דיודין - ע״ב: 15 וַיִּכְלוּ ע״ב, ריבוע יהוה הַמַּיִם מִן־הַחֵמֶת וַתַּשְׁלֵךְ אֶת־
הַיֶּלֶד תַּחַת אַחַד אהבה, דאגה הַשִּׂיחִם: 16 וַתֵּלֶךְ וַתֵּשֶׁב לָהּ מִנֶּגֶד
זן, מזבח הַרְחֵק כִּמְטַחֲוֵי קֶשֶׁת כִּי אָמְרָה אַל־אֶרְאֶה בְּמוֹת
הַיָּלֶד וַתֵּשֶׁב מִנֶּגֶד זן, מזבח וַתִּשָּׂא אֶת־קֹלָהּ וַתֵּבְךְּ: 17 וַיִּשְׁמַע

in the big picture, between all the nations of the world. To bring about world unity, we must live our lives according to the will of our soul, rather than the influence of our ego.

When we create this separation, we create energy for the world, and the world will be infused with love and Light. When Sarah separated Isaac and Ishmael, she was actually separating these two energy forces and desires. Such is the deeper spiritual significance behind this story. Regarding the name of Ishmael, the *Zohar* says:

> *...because his name should not be mentioned in the presence of Isaac...*
> *– The Zohar, Vayera 33:463*

The point here is profoundly simple. The Light of our soul cannot exist with the ego. The ego must be separated and removed to allow our soul to shine and thus to guide us in life.

The *Desire to Receive for the Self Alone*, which is also known as reactive behavior, is the root cause of all personal and collective chaos. If we activate only this desire, we will cause a dangerous short-circuit between nations. It is our responsibility to activate our *Desire to Receive for the Sake of Sharing*.

וַתֵּלֶךְ

Genesis 21:16 – Abraham sent Hagar and Ishmael away into the desert, giving them some bread and water for their journey. In the desert, Hagar backed away from the child until she could no longer see him because she could not bear to watch him die of thirst. However, God called out to Hagar and told her not to worry, that Ishmael would survive and be the seed of a great nation. God then opened her eyes, revealing to her a well of water.

Sometimes, people have what they need right before their eyes, but they cannot see it. That's because things of spiritual value, symbolized here by the well of water, cannot be perceived with the physical senses. This passage points out to us how limiting our five senses are and how we need to stop judging things based solely on what we see.

*17 And God heard the voice of the lad, and the angel of God called to Hagar from
heaven and said to her, "What is the matter, Hagar? Do not be afraid; God has heard
the lad crying as he lies there.*

*18 Arise, lift the lad up and take him by the hand, for I will make him a great nation."
19 And God opened her eyes and she saw a well of water, and she went and filled the
bottle with water and gave the lad to drink. 20 And God was with the lad, and he grew
and dwelt in the wilderness and became an archer. 21 While he was living in the
Desert of Paran, his mother got a wife for him from Egypt.*

SIXTH READING - JOSEPH - YESOD

*22 And it came to pass at that time that Abimelech and Phichol, the chief captain of
his host, spoke to Abraham, saying, "God is with you in all that you do. 23 Now swear
to me here before God that you will not deal falsely with me or with my son or with my
son's son; but according to the kindness that I have shown you, you will do to me and
to the land where you have sojourned." 24 And Abraham said, "I will swear." 25 And
Abraham reproved Abimelech about a well of water that Abimelech's servants had
violently taken away. 26 And Abimelech said, "I don't know who has done this. You*

Genesis 21:22 – The treaty between Abraham and Abimelech is the first peace treaty to appear in the Bible, and as such, it is the seed and source of all peace treaties between nations. Conflict and war between nations begins with friction and disunity between individuals. A nation at war is merely the ultimate consequence of the spiritual darkness born of strife and intolerance between the individuals who comprise that nation. When brothers find reason to disrespect one another, or when friends find ways to fault each other, then nations will surely devise reasons to engage in bloody battle.

The obvious corollary is that peace begins with the individual seen in the mirror. Peace is kept when that person extends friendship and shows tolerance to his neighbor.

This Bible reading can help prevent wars between nations by summoning forth tolerance and compassion for others, thus helping to end conflicts between individuals. When two people make the effort to find the good in one another, to overlook their differences for the sake of peace, then nations shall surely discover ways to achieve a lasting peace as well.

וְהוֹכִחַ

Genesis 21:25 – Abraham and Abimelech had a disagreement over a well belonging to Abraham that Abimelech's servants had seized. The significance of this disagreement is the effort made by Abraham to inject spiritual forces of healing into the water. Here Abimelech symbolizes the contamination of Earth's water, while Abraham symbolizes the rehabilitation of our oceans, lakes, rivers, and groundwater.

The sages tell us that Abraham's shepherds quarreled with Abimelech's shepherds over the ownership of the well:

> *Abraham's shepherds finally said, "The well belongs to the one for whom the*

אֱלֹהִים ילה, מום אֶת־קוֹל ע"ב ס"ג ע"ה הַנַּעַר ש"ך וַיִּקְרָא עם ה' אותיות = ב"פ קס"א
מַלְאַךְ אֱלֹהִים ילה, מום | אֶל־הָגָר ד"פ ב"ן מִן־הַשָּׁמַיִם י"פ טל, י"פ כוזו וַיֹּאמֶר
לָהּ מַה מ"ה ־לָּךְ הָגָר ד"פ ב"ן אַל־תִּירְאִי כִּי־שָׁמַע אֱלֹהִים ילה, מום אֶל־קוֹל
ע"ב ס"ג ע"ה הַנַּעַר ש"ך בַּאֲשֶׁר הוּא־שָׁם׃ 18 קוּמִי שְׂאִי אֶת־הַנַּעַר ש"ך וְהַחֲזִיקִי
אֶת־יָדֵךְ בּוֹ בוכו כִּי־לְגוֹי גָּדוֹל להח, מבה, יזל, אום אֲשִׂימֶנּוּ׃ 19 וַיִּפְקַח
מ"ה + קמ"ג אֱלֹהִים ילה, מום אֶת־עֵינֶיהָ ריבוע מ"ה וַתֵּרֶא בְּאֵר קנ"א + ב"ן מָיִם
וַתֵּלֶךְ וַתְּמַלֵּא אֶת־הַחֵמֶת מַיִם וַתַּשְׁקְ אֶת־הַנָּעַר ש"ך׃ 20 וַיְהִי
אל אֱלֹהִים ילה, מום אֶת־הַנַּעַר ש"ך וַיִּגְדָּל יזל וַיֵּשֶׁב בַּמִּדְבָּר רמ"ח, אברהם וַיְהִי
אל רֹבֶה קַשָּׁת׃ 21 וַיֵּשֶׁב בְּמִדְבַּר רמ"ח, אברהם פָּארָן וַתִּקַּח רבוע אהיה דאלפין
־לוֹ אִמּוֹ אִשָּׁה מֵאֶרֶץ אלהים דאלפין מִצְרָיִם מצר׃ [פ]

SIXTH READING - JOSEPH - YESOD

22 וַיְהִי אל בָּעֵת הַהִוא וַיֹּאמֶר אֲבִימֶלֶךְ וּפִיכֹל שַׂר אלהים דיודין ורבוע אלהים
־צְבָאוֹ אֶל־אַבְרָהָם וו"פ אל, רמ"ח לֵאמֹר אֱלֹהִים ילה, מום עִמְּךָ נמם בְּכֹל
לכב אֲשֶׁר־אַתָּה עֹשֶׂה׃ 23 וְעַתָּה הִשָּׁבְעָה לִּי בֵאלֹהִים ילה, מום
הֵנָּה מ"ה יה אִם יוהך ־תִּשְׁקֹר לִי וּלְנִינִי וּלְנֶכְדִּי כַּחֶסֶד ע"ב, ריבוע יהוה
אֲשֶׁר־עָשִׂיתִי עִמְּךָ נמם תַּעֲשֶׂה עִמָּדִי וְעִם־הָאָרֶץ אלהים דההין ע"ה
אֲשֶׁר־גַּרְתָּה בָּהּ׃ 24 וַיֹּאמֶר אַבְרָהָם וו"פ אל, רמ"ח אָנֹכִי איע אִשָּׁבֵעַ׃
25 וְהוֹכִחַ אַבְרָהָם וו"פ אל, רמ"ח אֶת־אֲבִימֶלֶךְ עַל־אֹדוֹת בְּאֵר קנ"א + ב"ן

---

water rises to water his sheep." When the water saw the sheep of the Patriarch Abraham, it immediately rose.

– Beresheet Rabba 54:5 (A third-century commentary, forming part of the Talmud, on the first book of the Bible, Genesis.)

In our present day, we see this struggle to defend the sanctity of our environment in the fight, for example, to protect water from chemical and nuclear contamination. The verses of Scripture that relate this story will help to purify the waters of our planet.

did not tell me, and I heard about it only today." [27] *And Abraham took sheep and oxen and gave them to Abimelech, and both of them made a covenant (treaty).*

[28] *And Abraham set seven ewe lambs from the flock by themselves.* [29] *And Abimelech asked Abraham, "What is the meaning of these seven ewe lambs you have set by themselves?"*

[30] *And he replied, "Accept these seven lambs from my hand as a witness that I dug this well."*

[31] *So he called that place Beersheba, because there they both swore an oath.*

[32] *After the treaty had been made at Beersheba, Abimelech and Phicol, the chief captain of his host, returned to the land of the Philistines.*

[33] *And Abraham planted a grove in Beersheba, and there he called upon the name of the Lord, the Eternal God.*

[34] *And Abraham stayed in the land of the Philistines for many days.*

SEVENTH READING - DAVID - MALCHUT

22[1] *And it came to pass after these things that God tested Abraham. He said to him, "Abraham!" And he replied, "Here I am."*

[2] *And God said, "Take your son, your only son, Isaac, whom you love, and go to the land of Moriah and offer him there for a burnt offering upon one of the mountains that I will tell you."*

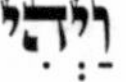

Genesis 22:1 – According to Rashi, Abraham underwent ten tests in his lifetime to allow him to evolve and strengthen himself spiritually. The ninth of these was when he expelled Ishmael, and the tenth test occurred when God instructed him to sacrifice his son, Isaac, upon an altar.

The magnitude of this last test was unprecedented. Abraham had to wait until the age of 100 to finally have a child with Sarah, and then the Creator asked him to sacrifice his only legitimate son.

This story prompts us to examine how much of what we love we are willing to sacrifice for our connection to the Light of the Creator. Paradoxically, the more we resist sacrifice and the more we avoid the tests of life, the more we will lose in the long run. But the more willingly we give and the more we embrace life's tests with certainty, the more we stand to gain.

The Light shining through the letters of this verse ignites conviction in our hearts and absolute certainty in our consciousness, allowing the truth of the Creator to be everlastingly revealed to the world.

הַמַּיִם אֲשֶׁר גָּזְלוּ עַבְדֵי אֲבִימֶלֶךְ׃ 26 וַיֹּאמֶר אֲבִימֶלֶךְ לֹא
יָדַעְתִּי מִי ילי עָשָׂה אֶת־הַדָּבָר ראה הַזֶּה והו וְגַם יגל ־אַתָּה לֹא־
הִגַּדְתָּ לִּי וְגַם אָנֹכִי איע לֹא שָׁמַעְתִּי בִּלְתִּי הַיּוֹם נגד, זן, מזבח׃ 27 וַיִּקַּח
וזעם אַבְרָהָם וז"פ אל, רמ"ח צֹאן וּבָקָר וַיִּתֵּן לַאֲבִימֶלֶךְ וַיִּכְרְתוּ שְׁנֵיהֶם
בְּרִית׃ 28 וַיַּצֵּב אַבְרָהָם וז"פ אל, רמ"ח אֶת־שֶׁבַע אלהים דיודין - ע"ב כִּבְשֹׂת
הַצֹּאן מלוי אהיה דיודין ע"ה לְבַדְּהֶן׃ 29 וַיֹּאמֶר אֲבִימֶלֶךְ אֶל־אַבְרָהָם
וז"פ אל, רמ"ח מָה מ"ה הֵנָּה מ"ה יה שֶׁבַע אלהים דיודין - ע"ב כְּבָשֹׂת הָאֵלֶּה
אֲשֶׁר הִצַּבְתָּ לְבַדָּנָה׃ 30 וַיֹּאמֶר כִּי אֶת־שֶׁבַע אלהים דיודין - ע"ב
כְּבָשֹׂת תִּקַּח מִיָּדִי בַּעֲבוּר תִּהְיֶה־לִּי לְעֵדָה כִּי חָפַרְתִּי אֶת־
הַבְּאֵר קנ"א - ב"ן הַזֹּאת׃ 31 עַל־כֵּן קָרָא לַמָּקוֹם יהוה ברבוע, ו"פ אל הַהוּא
בְּאֵר קנ"א - ב"ן שָׁבַע אלהים דיודין - ע"ב כִּי שָׁם נִשְׁבְּעוּ שְׁנֵיהֶם׃ 32 וַיִּכְרְתוּ
בְרִית בִּבְאֵר קנ"א - ב"ן שָׁבַע אלהים דיודין - ע"ב וַיָּקָם אֲבִימֶלֶךְ וּפִיכֹל
שַׂר אלהים דיודין ורבוע אלהים ־צְבָאוֹ וַיָּשֻׁבוּ אֶל־אֶרֶץ אלהים דאלפין פְּלִשְׁתִּים
י"פ אלהים׃ 33 וַיִּטַּע אֵשֶׁל בִּבְאֵר קנ"א - ב"ן שָׁבַע אלהים דיודין - ע"ב וַיִּקְרָא
עם ה' אותיות = ב"פ קס"א ־שָׁם בְּשֵׁם יהוה שדי יְהֹוָהאדניאהדונהי אֵל ייא"י עוֹלָם׃
34 וַיָּגָר אַבְרָהָם וז"פ אל, רמ"ח בְּאֶרֶץ אלהים דאלפין פְּלִשְׁתִּים י"פ אלהים יָמִים
נלך רַבִּים׃ [פ]

SEVENTH READING - DAVID - MALCHUT

22 1 וַיְהִי אל אַחַר הַדְּבָרִים ראה הָאֵלֶּה וְהָאֱלֹהִים ילה, מום נִסָּה אֶת
־אַבְרָהָם וז"פ אל, רמ"ח וַיֹּאמֶר אֵלָיו אַבְרָהָם וז"פ אל, רמ"ח וַיֹּאמֶר הִנֵּנִי׃
2 וַיֹּאמֶר קַח־נָא אֶת־בִּנְךָ אֶת־יְחִידְךָ אֲשֶׁר־אָהַבְתָּ אֶת־יִצְחָק
ד"פ ב"ן וְלֶךְ־לְךָ אֶל־אֶרֶץ אלהים דאלפין הַמֹּרִיָּה וְהַעֲלֵהוּ שָׁם לְעֹלָה עַל

[3] And Abraham rose early in the morning, and saddled his donkey and took two of his servants with him and his son Isaac, and cut the wood for the burnt offering; and rose up and went to the place of which God had told him. [4] Then on the third day Abraham lifted up his eyes and saw the place in the distance. [5] And Abraham said to his servants, "Stay here with the donkey while I and the boy go over there and worship, and then we will come back to you."

[6] And Abraham took the wood for the burnt offering and placed it on his son Isaac, and he himself carried the fire and the knife, and they went on together. [7] And Isaac spoke to his father Abraham and said, "My father?" And he replied, "Yes, my son?"

וַיַּשְׁכֵּם

Genesis 22:3 – We are told that Abraham rose early in the morning on the day he was supposed to sacrifice Isaac. Although an unimaginably painful test awaited him, Abraham proactively embraced the challenge.

Our nature is to engage eagerly in negative practices that gratify the narcissistic aspects of our personality. Yet often, we are slow to undertake the difficult spiritual tasks that we must perform to transform ourselves. In truth, while such procrastination may provide a tiny measure of comfort and relief in the immediate moment, we bear increased pain over the long term.

By virtue of the power of the *Zohar*, this final test of Abraham—the one that required such unswerving trust and obedience—can be construed as our own final test. Abraham's success is bestowed upon us, along with his fearlessness and unwavering trust in the Creator. As he walked with Isaac to the place of sacrifice, Abraham was granted a crystal clear vision of his future grandson, Jacob, the predestined son of Isaac. Abraham perceived the important role that Jacob would play in the world; nonetheless, despite this compelling vision, he remained true to his commitment to sacrifice his son. Abraham surrendered total control, placing all his trust in the Creator's words.

וַיַּעֲקֹד

Genesis 22:9 – Abraham took his son, Isaac, up the mountain, where he constructed an altar and bound Isaac on top of it. Abraham raised his arm and was just about to lower the knife to kill his son when an angel suddenly arrived to stop him. The angel made it clear to Abraham that the demanded sacrifice was just a test of faith.

Immediately, Abraham found a ram whose horns were caught in a thicket, and he sacrificed the animal in place of Isaac. The *Zohar* offers penetrating insights into this story:

> *So all his life, [Abraham] did not reach perfection until now, until water mixed with fire—RIGHT MIXED WITH LEFT—and fire with water—LEFT WITH RIGHT. This is why: "The Creator tested Abraham" and not Isaac—because God invited Abraham to be included with Judgment ACCORDING TO THE SECRET OF THE LEFT. So when he performed THE ACT OF BINDING ISAAC, the fire entered the water, THAT IS, JUDGMENT ENTERED MERCY, and they were perfected by each other. This is what the act of Judgment accomplished: It included one within the other. This is also the reason why the Evil Inclination came and accused Abraham of not being properly perfected until he performed the act of Judgment by BINDING Isaac. THE PLACE of the Evil Inclination is "after" (beyond) these "things..."*
>
> *– The Zohar, Vayera 35:491*

Sweetening Judgment with Mercy. The *Zohar* explains that Abraham represents the concept of mercy, whereas Isaac signifies the force of judgment. In our own lives, we need to sweeten and temper our judgmental behavior with kind-hearted mercy; we must also learn to awaken spiritual judgment with our *Desire to Share*. Striking a delicate balance between these

אַחַד אהבה, דאגה הֶהָרִים י׳ הויות אֲשֶׁר אֹמַר אֵלֶיךָ אני: 3 וַיַּשְׁכֵּם
אַבְרָהָם ו״פ אל, רמ״ח בַּבֹּקֶר וַיַּחֲבֹשׁ אֶת־חֲמֹרוֹ וַיִּקַּח ו״עם אֶת־שְׁנֵי
נְעָרָיו אִתּוֹ וְאֵת יִצְחָק ד״פ ב״ן בְּנוֹ וַיְבַקַּע עֲצֵי עֹלָה וַיָּקָם וַיֵּלֶךְ כלי
אֶל־הַמָּקוֹם יהוה ברבוע, ו״פ אל אֲשֶׁר־אָמַר־לוֹ הָאֱלֹהִים ילה, מום: 4 בַּיּוֹם
נגד, זן, מזבח הַשְּׁלִישִׁי וַיִּשָּׂא אַבְרָהָם ו״פ אל, רמ״ח אֶת־עֵינָיו ריבוע מ״ה וַיַּרְא
אֶת־הַמָּקוֹם יהוה ברבוע, ו״פ אל מֵרָחֹק שדי: 5 וַיֹּאמֶר אַבְרָהָם ו״פ אל, רמ״ח
אֶל־נְעָרָיו שְׁבוּ־לָכֶם פֹּה מילה (להכניע הקליפות בסוד החמור), ע״ה אלהים, מום עִם
־הַחֲמוֹר וַאֲנִי אני וְהַנַּעַר ש״ך נֵלְכָה עַד־כֹּה הי׳ וְנִשְׁתַּחֲוֶה וְנָשׁוּבָה
אֲלֵיכֶם: 6 וַיִּקַּח ו״עם אַבְרָהָם ו״פ אל, רמ״ח אֶת־עֲצֵי הָעֹלָה וַיָּשֶׂם עַל־
יִצְחָק ד״פ ב״ן בְּנוֹ וַיִּקַּח ו״עם בְּיָדוֹ אֶת־הָאֵשׁ שאה וְאֶת־הַמַּאֲכֶלֶת
וַיֵּלְכוּ שְׁנֵיהֶם יַחְדָּו: 7 וַיֹּאמֶר יִצְחָק ד״פ ב״ן אֶל־אַבְרָהָם ו״פ אל, רמ״ח
אָבִיו וַיֹּאמֶר אָבִי וַיֹּאמֶר הִנֶּנִּי בְנִי וַיֹּאמֶר הִנֵּה הָאֵשׁ שאה וְהָעֵצִים
וְאַיֵּה הַשֶּׂה לְעֹלָה: 8 וַיֹּאמֶר אַבְרָהָם ו״פ אל, רמ״ח אֱלֹהִים ילה, מום
יִרְאֶה רי״ו, גבורה ־לּוֹ הַשֶּׂה לְעֹלָה בְּנִי ר״ת הבל וַיֵּלְכוּ ס״ת ההיו שְׁנֵיהֶם
יַחְדָּו: 9 וַיָּבֹאוּ אֶל־הַמָּקוֹם יהוה ברבוע, ו״פ אל אֲשֶׁר אָמַר־לוֹ הָאֱלֹהִים
ילה, מום וַיִּבֶן שָׁם אַבְרָהָם ו״פ אל, רמ״ח אֶת־הַמִּזְבֵּחַ זן, נגד וַיַּעֲרֹךְ
אֶת־הָעֵצִים וַיַּעֲקֹד אֶת־יִצְחָק ד״פ ב״ן בְּנוֹ וַיָּשֶׂם אֹתוֹ עַל־

attributes of judgment and mercy can be lifelong spiritual work. Thankfully, the act of listening to this reading imbues our souls with the quality of mercy so that we are transformed into balanced and loving people.

Without Abraham's Light or these insights from the *Zohar*, this objective would be much more difficult to attain. There is something in our nature that repeatedly provokes us to indulge in negative behavior, even though it goes against our very will. Likewise, we seem compelled to forsake positive actions despite our best intentions to follow through. This uniquely human idiosyncrasy demonstrates the ongoing conflict between our body's *Desire to Receive* and the soul's *Desire to Share*. Our Evil Inclination is the culprit that influences our choice to succumb to the whims of the body.

"Isaac" is a code referring to *Left Column* energy—our reactive, self-centered *Desire to Receive*—and our physical body. "Abraham" is a code corresponding to the *Right Column*—our positive *Desire to Share*—and our soul. This story is a code, therefore, for man's spiritual work, which is to bind or restrict his selfish, reactive desires and unleash the power of his soul.

And he said, "See, the fire and wood are here, but where is the lamb for the burnt offering?" [8] *And Abraham answered, "God Himself will provide the lamb for the burnt offering, my son." So they went on together.* [9] *And they reached the place God had told him about, and Abraham built an altar there and laid the wood on it, and he bound Isaac, his son, and laid him on the altar, on top of the wood.*

[10] *And Abraham reached out his hand and took the knife to slay his son.*

[11] *And the angel of the Lord called out to him from heaven, "Abraham! Abraham!" And he replied, "Here I am."*

[12] *And he said, "Do not lay a hand on the boy, do not do anything to him, for now I know that you fear God, because you have not withheld from Me your son, your only son."*

[13] *And Abraham lifted up his eyes and looked, and there in a thicket behind him he saw a ram caught by its horns. And Abraham went and took the ram and sacrificed it as a burnt offering instead of his son.*

Rav Brandwein wrote about this in a letter to Rav Berg:

> *The only way one attracts miracles, to rearrange nature from what God arranged it to be, is through self-sacrifice. For in man, the force and Desire to Receive is innate for his own existence and swallows and rules over everything. If he overcomes himself, to sacrifice himself for the sake of the honor of God, then this force rises and tears all the veils, and no power among the higher and lower beings is able to stop him or prevent anything he asks for, and his prayer will be answered in full. Added to this is the interpretation of the holy Baal Shem Tov of the verse, "God is your shade." Just as the shadow imitates every movement of man, so God does with man. If a man is willing to sacrifice himself for the sanctity of God, then God annuls all the ways of nature that He set, and turns toward that self-sacrificing man.*

In place of Isaac, a ram caught in the thicket was sacrificed to God. This sacrificial ram is a code for the actual eradication of our wicked and prideful traits—the sacrificing of our Evil Inclination. Thus, we learn that a man must constantly utilize the power of his soul (Abraham) to bind his own ego (the binding of Isaac upon the altar) and then to eliminate all his selfish and self-destructive traits from his nature (the slaughtering of the ram). This entails sacrificing short-term material pleasures for eternal spiritual joy.

Once again, through Abraham's Light, which serves as a timeless repository of energy for us to draw upon, we empower our soul and completely subjugate our selfish impulses. As our wicked traits are slaughtered through our meditation during the reading of this section, wickedness in the world is slain in equal measure, for each of us is a microcosm of the world. All the sinful acts of behavior and wicked deeds depicted throughout this Bible reading are thereby bound and sacrificed forevermore.

Another insight we can gain from the sacrifice that Abraham was asked to make is this: We become attached to what we love, but more than that, we become attached to the fruits of our work. We are taught to be goal-oriented, to work toward an outcome that we can visualize. If we

הַמִּזְבֵּחַ זן, נגד מִמַּעַל עלם לָעֵצִים: 10 וַיִּשְׁלַח אַבְרָהָם וז"פ אל, רמ"ח אֶת־
יָדוֹ וַיִּקַּח חעם אֶת־הַמַּאֲכֶלֶת לִשְׁחֹט אֶת־בְּנוֹ: 11 וַיִּקְרָא
עם ה' אותיות = ב"פ קס"א אֵלָיו מַלְאַךְ יְהֹוָהאדניאהדונהי מִן־הַשָּׁמַיִם י"פ טל, י"פ כוזו
וַיֹּאמֶר אַבְרָהָם וז"פ אל, רמ"ח | אַבְרָהָם וז"פ אל, רמ"ח וַיֹּאמֶר הִנֵּנִי:
12 וַיֹּאמֶר אַל־תִּשְׁלַח יָדְךָ בוכו אֶל־הַנַּעַר ש"ך וְאַל־תַּעַשׂ לוֹ
מְאוּמָה כִּי | עַתָּה יָדַעְתִּי כִּי־יְרֵא אֱלֹהִים ילה, מום אַתָּה וְלֹא
חָשַׂכְתָּ אֶת־בִּנְךָ אֶת־יְחִידְךָ מִמֶּנִּי: 13 וַיִּשָּׂא אַבְרָהָם וז"פ אל, רמ"ח
אֶת־עֵינָיו ריבוע מ"ה וַיַּרְא וְהִנֵּה מ"ה יה ־אַיִל אַחַר נֶאֱחַז בַּסְּבַךְ בְּקַרְנָיו
כשאומר נאחז בסבך בקרניו יכוין לתיבות שאחר סב"ך הם ע"ג"ל, והשטן בעבור קיטרוג העגל היה מרחיק האיל,
כדי שישחט יצחק ; ומיכאל [(= ננא = הנה איל) אחר נאחז בקרניו (= שס"ח סממני הקטרת)] הכניע את השטן
וַיֵּלֶךְ כלי אַבְרָהָם וז"פ אל, רמ"ח וַיִּקַּח חעם אֶת־הָאַיִל וַיַּעֲלֵהוּ לְעֹלָה תַּחַת

---

meet with a setback, we forget the lessons we learned from the process of the work itself and become obsessed with the result that we hoped for but failed to achieve. The Creator requires us to work to reveal Light, and yet to let the Creator be the arbiter of what comes to fruition and what does not. Thus, just as Abraham was asked to release his attachment to the fruit of his loins, we are asked to release our attachment to the fruits of our work. Our work should always be done with the consciousness of having a goal, but also with the understanding that the journey to reaching that goal is where the most Light will be revealed. In other words, the outcome of our effort will be a result of how much Light we reveal along the way.

וַיִּשְׁלַח

Genesis 22:10 – To ignite the Light of the Creator in our lives and to pass the tests and challenges that we are presented with, we must be prepared to take physical action, indicated here by the raising of Abraham's arm to slaughter his son. Good intentions are never enough. We must follow through on our commitments to share more with others and to complete our spiritual mission.

Abraham's body was so in tune with the Light of the Creator that he knew deep in his heart that God would not let him slaughter his son—yet he was fully prepared to make the sacrifice, if necessary. When we are prepared to go all the way, we too, resonate with the Light; thus, we are certain and confident in each action that we take, knowing deep down that a positive outcome is assured.

About the sacrifice of Isaac, the great Rav Yehuda Tzvi Brandwein wrote in a letter:

> *It is written: 'And Abraham said, My son, God will provide himself a lamb for a burnt offering: so they went both of them together.' There is an allusion here that as long as there is unity and self-sacrifice, we are successful, as they explained the words, '... they went both of them together,' as with one purpose and one intention.*

14 And Abraham called that place Adonai-jireh, as it is said to this day, "On the mountain of the Lord it will be seen."

15 And the angel of the Lord called to Abraham from heaven a second time,

16 and said, "By Myself I have sworn," said the Lord, "that because you have done
this thing and have not withheld your son, your only son, 17 that in blessing I will bless
you and I will multiply your seed as numerous as the stars of the heaven and as the
sand on the seashore. And your seed will possess the gates of his enemies, 18 and
through your seed will all nations on earth be blessed, because you have obeyed My
voice."

19 So Abraham returned to his servants, and they rose and went together to Beersheba. And Abraham dwelt in Beersheba.

MAFTIR

20 And it came to pass after these things that it was told Abraham saying, "See, Milcah is also a mother; she has borne children to your brother Nahor:

21 Huz, the firstborn, and Buz, his brother, and Kemuel, the father of Aram, 22 And
Chesed, and Hazo, and Pildash, and Jidlaph and Bethuel."

23 And Bethuel became the father of Rebecca. Milcah bore these eight sons to Abraham's brother Nahor.

24 And his concubine, whose name was Reumah, also had Tebah, and Gaham, and Tahash, and Maachah.

אֶת־רִבְקָה

Genesis 22:23– When Abraham returned home after the Binding of Isaac, Sarah had passed away. However, there must always be a beacon of Light in our world, so after Sarah left this world, Rebecca was born to Bethuel. This succession holds spiritual significance for our own life: When we do not seize the opportunity to share and perform positive actions in any given moment, someone else will take our place. Accordingly, we must become enlightened and aware of opportunities for good deeds and actions, which bring about spiritual growth.

בְּנוֹ: 14 וַיִּקְרָא עם ה' אותיות = ב"פ קס"א אַבְרָהָם ח"פ אל, רמ"ח שֵׁם־ יהוה שדי
הַמָּקוֹם יהוה ברבוע, ו"פ אל הַהוּא יְהֹוָהאדניאהדונהי | יִרְאֶה רי"ו, גבורה אֲשֶׁר יֵאָמֵר
הַיּוֹם נגד, זן, מזבח בְּהַר אור, רז יְהֹוָהאדניאהדונהי יֵרָאֶה רי"ו, גבורה: 15 וַיִּקְרָא
עם ה' אותיות = ב"פ קס"א מַלְאַךְ יְהֹוָהאדניאהדונהי אֶל־אַבְרָהָם ח"פ אל, רמ"ח שֵׁנִית
מִן־הַשָּׁמָיִם י"פ טל, י"פ כוזו: 16 וַיֹּאמֶר בִּי נִשְׁבַּעְתִּי נְאֻם־יְהֹוָהאדניאהדונהי כִּי
יַעַן אֲשֶׁר עָשִׂיתָ אֶת־הַדָּבָר ראה הַזֶּה והו וְלֹא חָשַׂכְתָּ אֶת־בִּנְךָ אֶת־
יְחִידֶךָ: 17 כִּי־בָרֵךְ אֲבָרֶכְךָ וְהַרְבָּה אַרְבֶּה יצחק, ד"פ ב"ן אֶת־זַרְעֲךָ
כְּכוֹכְבֵי הַשָּׁמַיִם י"פ טל, י"פ כוזו וְכַחוֹל רבוע אהיה אֲשֶׁר עַל־שְׂפַת הַיָּם ילי
וְיִרַשׁ זַרְעֲךָ אֵת שַׁעַר אֹיְבָיו: 18 וְהִתְבָּרְכוּ יהוה ע"ב ריבוע מ"ה בְזַרְעֲךָ כֹּל
ילי גּוֹיֵי הָאָרֶץ אלהים דההין ע"ה עֵקֶב ב"פ מום אֲשֶׁר שָׁמַעְתָּ בְּקֹלִי: 19 וַיָּשָׁב
אַבְרָהָם ח"פ אל, רמ"ח אֶל־נְעָרָיו וַיָּקֻמוּ וַיֵּלְכוּ יַחְדָּו אֶל־בְּאֵר קנ"א - ב"ן
שָׁבַע אלהים דיודין - ע"ב וַיֵּשֶׁב אַבְרָהָם ח"פ אל, רמ"ח בִּבְאֵר קנ"א - ב"ן
שָׁבַע אלהים דיודין - ע"ב: [פ]

MAFTIR

20 וַיְהִי אל אַחֲרֵי הַדְּבָרִים ראה הָאֵלֶּה וַיֻּגַּד לְאַבְרָהָם ח"פ אל, רמ"ח לֵאמֹר
הִנֵּה מ"ה יה יָלְדָה מִלְכָּה ע"ה אל אדני גַם יגל ־הִוא בָּנִים לְנָחוֹר ר"ת הבל
אָחִיךָ: 21 אֶת־עוּץ בְּכֹרוֹ וְאֶת־בּוּז אָחִיו וְאֶת־קְמוּאֵל אֲבִי אֲרָם:
22 וְאֶת־כֶּשֶׂד וְאֶת־חֲזוֹ וְאֶת־פִּלְדָּשׁ וְאֶת־יִדְלָף וְאֵת בְּתוּאֵל:
23 וּבְתוּאֵל יָלַד אֶת־רִבְקָה שְׁמֹנָה אֵלֶּה יָלְדָה מִלְכָּה ע"ה אל אדני
לְנָחוֹר אֲחִי אַבְרָהָם ח"פ אל, רמ"ח: 24 וּפִילַגְשׁוֹ וּשְׁמָהּ רְאוּמָה וַתֵּלֶד גַּם
יגל ־הוּא אֶת־טֶבַח וְאֶת־גַּחַם וְאֶת־תַּחַשׁ וְאֶת־מַעֲכָה: [פ] [פ] [פ]

HAFTARAH OF VAYERA

This is the story of Elisha. Just as Abraham was promised that his son would be born after a year had passed, Elisha also promised a Shunnamite woman a son. After a year had passed, the birth took place, but only a few years later, the child died. His mother sought out Elisha and pleaded with him to come with her and resurrect her son, which he did. The sages tell us that Elisha wrought his miracles through

II Kings 4:1–23

4[1] The wife of a man from the company of the prophets cried out to Elisha, "Your servant my husband is dead, and you know that he revered the Lord. But now his creditor is coming to take my two boys as his slaves."

2 Elisha replied to her, "How can I help you? Tell me, what do you have in your house?" "Your servant has nothing there at all," she said, "except a little oil."

3 Elisha said, "Go around and ask all your neighbors for empty jars. Don't ask for just a few.

4 Then go inside and shut the door behind you and your sons. Pour oil into all the jars, and as each is filled, put it to one side."

5 She left him and afterward shut the door behind her and her sons. They brought the jars to her and she kept pouring.

6 When all the jars were full, she said to her son, "Bring me another one." But he replied, "There is not a jar left." Then the oil stopped flowing.

7 She went and told the man of God, and he said, "Go, sell the oil and pay your debts. You and your sons can live on what is left."

8 One day Elisha went to Shunem. And a well-to-do woman was there, who urged him to stay for a meal. So whenever he came by, he stopped there to eat.

9 She said to her husband, "I know that this man who often comes our way is a holy man of God.

HAFTARAH OF VAYERA

prayer. (Megillah 27a) Through this event and through the birth of Isaac to Sarah and Abraham, we are reminded of the great powers of meditation and prayer, of mind over matter, and of the Resurrection of the Dead.

מלכים 2 פרק 4

4 1 ואשה אחת מנשי בני-הנביאים צעקה אל-אלישע לאמר
עבדך פוי אישי מת י"פ רבוע אהיה ואתה ידעת כי עבדך פוי היה יהה ירא
את-יהוהאדניאהדונהי והנשה בא לקחת את-שני ילדי לו לעבדים:
2 ויאמר אליה אלישע מה מ"ה אעשה-לך הגידי לי מה מ"ה -יש-
לך (כתיב: לכי) בבית ב"פ ראה ותאמר אין לשפחתך כל ילי בבית ב"פ ראה
כי אם יוהך -אסוך שמן י"פ טל, י"פ כוז"ו, ביט: 3 ויאמר לכי כלי שאלי-לך
כלים כלי מן-החוץ מאת כל ילי -שכניך (כתיב: שכניכי) כלים כלי רקים
אל-תמעיטי: 4 ובאת וסגרת הדלת בעדך ובעד-בניך ויצקת על
כל ילי, עמם -הכלים כלי האלה והמלא תסיעי: 5 ותלך מאתו ותסגר
הדלת בעדה ובעד בניה הם מגישים אליה והיא מוצקת
(כתיב: מיצקת): 6 ויהי אל | כמלאת הכלים כלי ותאמר אל-בנה הגישה
אלי עוד כלי כלי ויאמר אליה אין עוד כלי כלי ויעמד השמן י"פ טל,
י"פ כוז"ו, ביט: 7 ותבא ותגד לאיש ע"ה קנ"א קס"א האלהים ילה, מום ויאמר לכי
כלי מכרי את-השמן י"פ טל, י"פ כוז"ו, ביט ושלמי את-נשיך (כתיב: נשיכי)
ואת ובניך (כתיב: בניכי) תחיי בנותר: [פ] 8 ויהי אל היום נגד, זן, מזבח
ויעבר רפ"ח, ע"ב - רי"ו אלישע אל-שונם ושם אשה גדולה להוח, מבה, יזל, אום
ותחזק פהל -בו לאכל-לחם ג"פ יהוה ויהי אל מדי עברו יסר שמה מהש

[10] Let's make a small room on the roof and put in it a bed and a table, a chair and a lamp for him. Then he can stay there whenever he comes to us."

[11] One day when Elisha came, he went up to his room and lay down there.

[12] He said to his servant Gehazi, "Call the Shunammite." So he called her, and she stood before him.

[13] Elisha said to him, "Tell her, 'You have gone to all this trouble for us. Now what can be done for you? Can we speak on your behalf to the king or the commander of the army?'" "She replied, "I have a home among my own people."

[14] "What can be done for her?" Elisha asked. Gehazi said, "Well, she has no son and her husband is old."

[15] Then Elisha said, "Call her." So he called her, and she stood in the doorway.

[16] "About this time next year," Elisha said, "you will hold a son in your arms." "No, my Lord," she objected. "Don't mislead your servant, man of God!"

[17] But the woman became pregnant, and the next year about that same time she gave birth to a son, just as Elisha had told her.

[18] The child grew, and one day he went out to his father, who was with the reapers.

[19] "My head! My head!" he said to his father. His father told a servant, "Carry him to his mother."

[20] After the servant had lifted him up and carried him to his mother, the boy sat on her lap until noon, and then he died.

[21] She went up and laid him on the bed of the man of God, then shut the door and went out.

[22] She called her husband and said, "Please send me one of the servants and a donkey so I can go to the man of God quickly and return."

[23] "Why go to him today?" he asked. "It's not the New Moon or the Sabbath." "It's all right," she said.

לֶאֱכָל־לָחֶם ג״פ יהוה׃ 9 וַתֹּאמֶר אֶל־אִישָׁהּ הִנֵּה מ״ה יה ־נָא יָדַעְתִּי כִּי
אִישׁ ע״ה קנ״א קס״א אֱלֹהִים ילה, מום קָדוֹשׁ הוּא עֹבֵר עָלֵינוּ רבוע ס״ג תָּמִיד
נתה, קס״א + קנ״א + קמ״ג׃ 10 נַעֲשֶׂה־נָּא עֲלִיַּת־קִיר קְטַנָּה וְנָשִׂים לוֹ שָׁם מִטָּה
וְשֻׁלְחָן וְכִסֵּא וּמְנוֹרָה וְהָיָה יהוה, יהה בְּבֹאוֹ אֵלֵינוּ יָסוּר שָׁמָּה מהש׃
11 וַיְהִי אל הַיּוֹם נגד, זן, מזבח וַיָּבֹא שָׁמָּה מהש וַיָּסַר אֶל־הָעֲלִיָּה וַיִּשְׁכַּב־
שָׁמָּה מהש׃ 12 וַיֹּאמֶר אֶל־גֵּיחֲזִי נַעֲרוֹ קְרָא לַשּׁוּנַמִּית הַזֹּאת וַיִּקְרָא
עם ה׳ אותיות = ב״פ קס״א ־לָהּ וַתַּעֲמֹד לְפָנָיו׃ 13 וַיֹּאמֶר לוֹ אֱמָר־נָא אֵלֶיהָ
הִנֵּה חָרַדְתְּ | אֵלֵינוּ אֶת־כָּל ילי ־הַחֲרָדָה הַזֹּאת מֶה מ״ה לַעֲשׂוֹת לָךְ
הֲיֵשׁ לְדַבֶּר ראה ־לָךְ אֶל־הַמֶּלֶךְ אוֹ אֶל־שַׂר אלהים דיודין ורבוע אלהים הַצָּבָא
וַתֹּאמֶר בְּתוֹךְ עַמִּי אָנֹכִי איע יֹשָׁבֶת׃ 14 וַיֹּאמֶר וּמֶה מ״ה לַעֲשׂוֹת לָהּ
וַיֹּאמֶר גֵּיחֲזִי אֲבָל בֵּן אֵין־לָהּ וְאִישָׁהּ זָקֵן׃ 15 וַיֹּאמֶר קְרָא־לָהּ
וַיִּקְרָא עם ה׳ אותיות = ב״פ קס״א ־לָהּ וַתַּעֲמֹד בַּפָּתַח׃ 16 וַיֹּאמֶר לַמּוֹעֵד הַזֶּה
והו כָּעֵת חַיָּה אַתְּ (כתיב: אתי) חֹבֶקֶת בֵּן וַתֹּאמֶר אַל־אֲדֹנִי אִישׁ ע״ה קנ״א קס״א
הָאֱלֹהִים ילה, מום אַל־תְּכַזֵּב בְּשִׁפְחָתֶךָ׃ 17 וַתַּהַר הָאִשָּׁה וַתֵּלֶד בֵּן
לַמּוֹעֵד הַזֶּה והו כָּעֵת חַיָּה אֲשֶׁר־דִּבֶּר ראה אֵלֶיהָ אֱלִישָׁע׃ 18 וַיִּגְדַּל
יזל הַיָּלֶד וַיְהִי אל הַיּוֹם נגד, זן, מזבח וַיֵּצֵא אֶל־אָבִיו אֶל־הַקֹּצְרִים׃ 19 וַיֹּאמֶר
אֶל־אָבִיו רֹאשִׁי ריבוע אלהים + אלהים דיודין ע״ה | רֹאשִׁי ריבוע אלהים + אלהים דיודין ע״ה
וַיֹּאמֶר אֶל־הַנַּעַר ש״ך שָׂאֵהוּ אֶל־אִמּוֹ׃ 20 וַיִּשָּׂאֵהוּ וַיְבִיאֵהוּ אֶל־אִמּוֹ
וַיֵּשֶׁב עַל־בִּרְכֶּיהָ עַד־הַצָּהֳרַיִם וַיָּמֹת׃ 21 וַתַּעַל וַתַּשְׁכִּבֵהוּ עַל־
מִטַּת אִישׁ ע״ה קנ״א קס״א הָאֱלֹהִים ילה, מום וַתִּסְגֹּר בַּעֲדוֹ וַתֵּצֵא׃ 22 וַתִּקְרָא
אֶל־אִישָׁהּ וַתֹּאמֶר שִׁלְחָה נָא לִי אֶחָד אהבה, דאגה מִן־הַנְּעָרִים וְאַחַת
הָאֲתֹנוֹת וְאָרוּצָה עַד־אִישׁ ע״ה קנ״א קס״א הָאֱלֹהִים ילה, מום וְאָשׁוּבָה׃
23 וַיֹּאמֶר מַדּוּעַ אַתְּ (כתיב: אתי) הֹלֶכֶת מיה (כתיב: הלכתי) אֵלָיו הַיּוֹם
נגד, זן, מזבח לֹא־חֹדֶשׁ י״ב הוויות וְלֹא שַׁבָּת וַתֹּאמֶר שָׁלוֹם׃

CHAYEI SARAH

LESSON OF CHAYEI SARAH
(Genesis 23:1–25:18)

The Lives of Sarah

There are three sizes of letters in the Bible. In the introduction to the *Zohar*, in the *Sulam* commentary, it is written: "And God made large letters that allude to *Binah* and smaller letters that allude to *Malchut*." Elsewhere, the *Zohar* explains that the regular-sized letters come from the spiritual dimension of *Zeir Anpin*, thus showing us that there is a deep meaning behind the different kinds of letters we have in the Bible.

> *Sarah died in Kiryat-Arba, which is Hebron in the land of Canaan; and Abraham came to eulogize Sarah and to weep for her.*
> *– Genesis 23:2*

In this verse, we find a small letter Kaf in the word *velivkotah*, which means "to weep for her" or "to bewail her."

It is said that when Sarah died, Abraham wept only a little, and this was because Sarah was old. But why should this have kept him from weeping? He loved Sarah more than any other man in the world could love his wife. Abraham and Sarah were soul mates, they were chariots, they were prophets—and it is even written that Sarah was a better prophet than Abraham.

In the *Midrash*, it says that:

> *She was so great that the Creator had spoken to her directly (Genesis 18:15), while to the other prophetesses, God spoke only through a messenger. She was so righteous of stature that even the angels had been subject to her command.*

What's more, the *Midrash* also says that Isaac was not at Sarah's funeral, and the explanation is that he was studying the Bible. But is this really enough of an explanation? Should studying God's word be used as an excuse for missing your own mother's funeral?

How does this relate to the presence of the small letter Kaf, and what power can we receive from this letter? There is a very important teaching here, which is related to the act of weeping.

The story of Rav Shimon bar Yochai's departure from this world, as written in the *Zohar*, will shed some light in this matter:

> *"All the same day [that Rav Shimon passed away], the fire did not stop burning in the house, and no one could reach him because of the light and the fire that was around him. All that day, I [Rav Aba] lay fallen on the earth. After the fire disappeared, I saw the holy Light, the holy of holies that had left this world, wrapped up and lying on his right side, and his face was full of laughter."*
> *– The Zohar, Ha'azinu, the Idra Zutra:197*

After the death of the great teacher, Rav Shimon's son, Rav Elazar, took his father's hands and kissed them, saying, "Father, Father, there were three and now again there is only one." This means there had been three great men in the land: Rav Elazar himself; his father, Rav Shimon; and his Elder, Rav Pinchas ben Yair. Now Rav Elazar was the only one left in the world. This is a very powerful, very emotional statement, yet it is important to realize that Rav Elazar did not weep.

When Rav Shimon left this world, his son was, of course, in pain over the loss of his father. But it was more important to Rav Elazar that from now on, the world would be without the Light that Rav Shimon had revealed. Rav Shimon's students wept, but not because of the loss of any physical connection with their rabbi; rather, it was because of the Light that they had now lost. There was yet another cause for their tremendous pain: The whole world had been full of the Light of the Creator, and now this would be lacking. In the time of Rav Shimon, "...the sign of the rainbow was not seen because Rav Shimon was the sign of the world." This is in a song that the Ben Ish Chai (Rav Yosef Chaim, 1832–1909) wrote about Rav Shimon.

Why do we weep when something happens that hurts us? Specifically, why do we cry at the death of a person who has been close to us? Is it just because of the physical absence we experience? Kabbalah teaches that the physical transition from life to death is not where our emphasis of lack should be focused. Death is not something final, according to Kabbalah, but rather the closing of one door and the opening of another. Kabbalah's teachings about reincarnation are a vital source for a higher understanding about the nature of death. Rav Shimon's disciples understood these teachings on a very deep level and were thus able to overcome their purely human grief. The deaths of all righteous souls are really a cause for rejoicing on their behalf, and if their disciples have absolutely no desires for themselves, they are able to feel gladness about the liberation of their holy teachers.

At the time of Rav Shimon's death, the tremendous Light that surrounded him and the house he lay in was an indisputable sign of the Greater Realms that awaited him as well as a subtle revelation of the joint illusions of life and death. The following account from the *Zohar* shows the enormous Light that is revealed when a righteous soul leaves the world:

> *[Rav Shimon speaks his last words:] "... that Chesed enters the holy of holies, as is written: '...for there God has commanded the blessing, even life forever more.'"*
>
> *Rav Abba said, "The holy luminary [referring to Rav Shimon] had barely finished uttering the word 'life,' when his words ceased. I was writing and was about to write more, yet heard nothing. I did not raise my head because the Light was great and I could not look. I then trembled and heard a voice calling and saying, 'For length of days, and long life...' (Proverbs 3:2), AND THEN I heard another voice, 'He asked life of You....' (Psalms 21:5)*
>
> *"All that day, the fire did not cease from the house and no one reached [Rav Shimon], for they could not because of the Light and fire that encircled him. I was prostrated all that day on the ground, crying loudly. After the fire was gone, I saw that the holy luminary, the holy of holies, was gone from the world, wrapped around and lying on his right side with a smiling face."*
>
> *– The Zohar, Ha'azinu 47-48:195-197*
>
> *Furthermore, they said, "Every time that the righteous depart this world, there is likewise annulled from this world all the harsh decrees, and the death of the righteous brings forgiveness for the sins of the generation."*
>
> *– The Zohar, Acharei Mot 1:9*

In fact, we must remember that nothing physical really makes a difference in this world because truth comes only from the spiritual realm. The small *Kaf* teaches us that we should not cry about unimportant matters in the physical world—about something we have lost, for example, whether it is a physical object like money or a quality like celebrity, status, or fame. The strength we receive from the *Kaf* (in the word *velivkotah*) is the ability to separate what is important from what is not. What is enough cause for weeping then? Should it not be because someone who was close to us has left the world physically? According to Kabbalah, the reason we should weep is for the loss of the Light that we were illuminated by when that person was here on Earth with us.

When Rav Brandwein, Rav Berg's teacher and master, left this world, Rav Berg wept for a long time and felt the absence of the Light of the Creator in his life. After some time, however, he understood that now Rav Brandwein was helping him from the World of Truth more than he could ever have helped in this world. We must remember that everything is an emanation from the Light; therefore, we should never become too involved with what takes place in the physical realm. If we let ourselves become too involved, it's as if we're saying that we do not agree with what has happened, meaning that we do not agree with the Light!

Kabbalist Michael Berg tells a story about the difference between spiritual and physical payments:

> *A great sage once held a beautiful wedding for his daughter in an expensive hotel. After the wedding, he went to the hotel owner and asked him how much the wedding cost. The owner said, "I cannot take money from you. You are my teacher." The sage insisted and the owner still refused. This went on for quite a while until finally the teacher said, "I am paying you! Because in this world we always have to pay a price and money is the cheapest payment there is!"*

When we cry over the challenges and obstacles we are having in the physical world, such as debt, health problems, or conflicts with other people, or if we ask, "Why is the Light doing this to me?" we have not learnt our lesson through them and we will cause the same payments to become due again. The only type of crying that is justified in this world is the weeping for the absence of revealed Light. It is written that except for the Gate of Tears, all the Gates to the Upper World have been locked since the destruction of the Temple.

> *". . . and the doors are shut in the street" (Ecclesiastes 12:4): These are the gates, UP HIGHER, that were all closed except the Gate of Tears that was not locked.*
>
> *– The Zohar, Shir HaShirim 6:54*

This sentence refers to the tears that are shed as a result of the Light of the Creator not being revealed. The small *Kaf* gives us the power to understand exactly why we are facing what we are facing, as well as giving us the power to receive everything with Light.

In the *Zohar,* the sages frequently cry because they do not understand the explanation of their beloved teacher, Rav Shimon. For them, the inability to reach the Light of understanding is the greatest sorrow of their lives.

Obviously, the death of Sarah caused Abraham pain, but Abraham did not weep since he knew it was for the best. We also read that Isaac was studying the Bible during his mother's funeral; this was because her death meant that the Light of the Creator would no longer be revealed to the world, so he was working on revealing that Light himself.

SYNOPSIS OF CHAYEI SARAH

Let us look at why this section is called "The Lives of Sarah" and why we turn our attention to Sarah's life only after she has already passed on. We need to understand that according to Kabbalah, life and death can exist on many levels. Someone may be physically alive but impart no energy to us; in that sense, it is as if they were dead to us. In the same way, a person who has left this world can be very much alive in our hearts and minds. When we remember someone who has passed away, we keep that person alive; if we forget, then that person is indeed dead to us. The meaning of life and death should not be limited to the physical dimension.

FIRST READING - ABRAHAM - CHESED

23 [1] *And Sarah was a hundred and twenty and seven years old. These were the
years of the life of Sarah. [2] And Sarah died at Kiriath Arba, that is Hebron in
the land of Canaan, and Abraham went to mourn for Sarah and to weep for
her.*

*[3] And Abraham rose from beside his dead, and spoke to the sons of Heth, saying, [4]
"I am an alien and a stranger among you; give me possession of a burial site here so
I may bury my dead out of sight."*

*[5] And the children of Heth answered Abraham, saying to him, [6] "Hear us, my lord,
you are a mighty prince among us; bury your dead in the choicest of our tombs. None
of us will refuse you his tomb for burying your dead."*

*[7] And Abraham rose and bowed himself down before the people of the land, to the
children of Heth.*

FROM THE RAV

The Story of Chayei Sarah is about the life of Sarah, although only the first verse in this story makes any mention of Sarah herself.

The deeper secret concerns how Sarah's age is mentioned. The Torah does not say Sarah lived 127 years, but rather "100 year, 20 year, and 7 years." The obvious question is why the 100 and the 20 are referred to in the singular while the 7 is expressed in the plural using the word "*shanim*?"

The *Zohar* says that Sarah represents the totality of unity, like the seed that contains within itself all of the elements of the subsequent tree: the branches, the roots, the fruits, and the leaves. These all emerge separately from the seed, indicated by the "7 years" (*sheva shanim*). Kabbalistically seven also refers to Malchut—the dimension of this physical world—our world of differentiation and fragmentation that is governed by time, space, and motion.

Because Sarah embodies the idea of unity, the "100 year" indicates the kabbalistic concept of 100 different spiritual dimensions—the *Ten Sefirot* each multiplied by its own individual 10 spiritual levels (also called *Sefirot*). Each one of the *Ten Sefirot* is also further comprised of another *Ten Sefirot* (10x10), introducing the concept of unity and completeness. And the "20 year," although a lower level of connection—that of 10+10, which is the *Ten Sefirot of Direct Light* plus the *Ten Sefirot of Returning Light*—is still within the realm of no separation. Only in this physical world do chaos and separation emerge, bringing with them the limitations of time, space, and motion.

The number of years that Sarah lived teaches us that this physical world is not the real reality, but rather an illusionary reality that we can transform into a world of unity. It also shows us that the life of Sarah embodied both unity and diversity, so diversity does not necessarily have to ultimately result in separation or even conflict.

FIRST READING - ABRAHAM - CHESED

23 1 וַיִּהְיוּ מלוי ס"ג חַיֵּי שָׂרָה אלהים דיודין ורבוע אלהים - ה' מֵאָה שָׁנָה וְעֶשְׂרִים
שָׁנָה וְשֶׁבַע אלהים דיודין - ע"ב שָׁנִים שְׁנֵי חַיֵּי שָׂרָה אלהים דיודין ורבוע אלהים - ה':
2 וַתָּמָת שָׂרָה אלהים דיודין ורבוע אלהים - ה' בְּקִרְיַת אַרְבַּע הִוא חֶבְרוֹן
בְּאֶרֶץ אלהים דאלפין כְּנָעַן וַיָּבֹא אַבְרָהָם ח"פ אל, רמ"ח לִסְפֹּד לְשָׂרָה
אלהים דיודין ורבוע אלהים - ה' וְלִבְכֹּתָהּ: 3 וַיָּקָם אַבְרָהָם ח"פ אל, רמ"ח מֵעַל עלם
פְּנֵי חכמה - בינה מֵתוֹ וַיְדַבֵּר ראה אֶל-בְּנֵי-חֵת לֵאמֹר: 4 גֵּר קנ"א - ב"ן -
וְתוֹשָׁב אָנֹכִי איע עִמָּכֶם תְּנוּ לִי אֲחֻזַּת-קֶבֶר עִמָּכֶם וְאֶקְבְּרָה
מֵתִי מִלְּפָנָי: 5 וַיַּעֲנוּ בְנֵי-חֵת אֶת-אַבְרָהָם ח"פ אל, רמ"ח לֵאמֹר לוֹ:
6 שְׁמָעֵנוּ | אֲדֹנִי נְשִׂיא אֱלֹהִים ילה, מום אַתָּה בְּתוֹכֵנוּ בְּמִבְחַר
קְבָרֵינוּ קְבֹר אֶת-מֵתֶךָ אִישׁ ע"ה קנ"א קס"א מִמֶּנּוּ אֶת-קִבְרוֹ לֹא-
יִכְלֶה מִמְּךָ מִקְּבֹר מֵתֶךָ: 7 וַיָּקָם אַבְרָהָם ח"פ אל, רמ"ח וַיִּשְׁתַּחוּ
לְעַם עלם -הָאָרֶץ אלהים דההין ע"ה לִבְנֵי-חֵת: 8 וַיְדַבֵּר ראה אִתָּם לֵאמֹר

חַיֵּי שָׂרָה

Genesis 23:1 – Sarah lived 127 years, eventually reincarnating as Queen Esther. Every year of Sarah's life was filled with Light, which gave her the merit in her later incarnation as Esther to rule over 127 nations. This example shows us how our actions in past lives can influence the present and future.

וְלִבְכֹּתָהּ

Genesis 23:2 – The small letter *Kaf* appears in *velivkotah*, which means "to cry over her." Often when we mourn a loss, we are feeling pain and sorrow over the physical manifestation of the loss, rather than over what has happened on the spiritual level. The small letters in the Bible represent Malchut, the level of our physical existence; these letters give us the power to transcend our present physical reality so that we can connect to and receive clarity from the Light.

וַיְדַבֵּר

Genesis 23:8– When Abraham was looking for a place to bury Sarah, he saw a small animal in the field; he followed it into a cave, where he saw Adam. Adam revealed to Abraham that this place was where he and Eve were buried, and where Abraham and Sarah should be buried, too. The *Zohar* says that while Adam was searching for a place where he and Eve could be buried, he was guided to the cave by a small Light that entered it from the Garden of Eden. In our own lives, we can strive to ensure that the places where we live are positive places that bring us blessings.

8 And he communed with them, saying, "If you are willing to let me bury my dead out of sight, hear me and intercede with Ephron, son of Zohar, on my behalf, 9 so he will give me the cave of Machpelah, which belongs to him and is at the end of his field, for the full price as a burial site among you."

10 And Ephron dwelt among the children of Heth, and Ephron the Hittite answered Abraham in the presence of all the Hittites who had come to the gate of his city, saying, 11 "No, my lord, hear me; I give you the field, and I give you the cave that is in it. I give it to you in the presence of my people. Bury your dead."

12 And Abraham bowed himself down before the people of the land.

13 And he said to Ephron in the presence of the people of the land, saying, "But if you will give it, I pray you hear me, I will give you money for the field. Accept it from me so I can bury my dead there."

14 And Ephron answered Abraham, saying, 15 "Listen to me, my lord; the land is worth four hundred shekels of silver, but what is that between me and you? Bury your dead."

16 And Abraham agreed to Ephron's terms and weighed out for him the price he had named in the presence of the Hittites: four hundred shekels of silver, current with the merchant.

SECOND READING - ISAAC - GEVURAH

17 And the field of Ephron in Machpelah, which was before Mamre—both the field and the cave in it, and all the trees that were in the field, that were within the borders of the field—were deeded 18 to Abraham as his property in the presence of all the Hittites who had come to the gate of his city.

19 And after this Abraham buried his wife Sarah in the cave in the field of Machpelah before Mamre, which is at Hebron in the land of Canaan.

20 And the field and the cave in it were deeded to Abraham by the sons of Heth as a burial site.

אִם יוהך ־יֵשׁ אֶת־נַפְשְׁכֶם לִקְבֹּר אֶת־מֵתִי מִלְּפָנַי שְׁמָעוּנִי וּפִגְעוּ־
לִי בְּעֶפְרוֹן בֶּן־צֹחַר׃ 9 וְיִתֶּן י"פ מלוי ע"ב ־לִי אֶת־מְעָרַת הַמַּכְפֵּלָה
אֲשֶׁר־לוֹ אֲשֶׁר בִּקְצֵה ג"פ אדני שָׂדֵהוּ בְּכֶסֶף מָלֵא יִתְּנֶנָּה לִּי
בְּתוֹכְכֶם לַאֲחֻזַּת־קָבֶר׃ 10 וְעֶפְרוֹן יֹשֵׁב בְּתוֹךְ בְּנֵי־חֵת וַיַּעַן
עֶפְרוֹן הַחִתִּי אֶת־אַבְרָהָם וו"פ אל, רמ"ח בְּאָזְנֵי יוד הי ואו הה בְנֵי־חֵת לְכֹל
יה ־ אדני בָּאֵי שַׁעַר־עִירוֹ סוזפך, ערי, סנדלפון לֵאמֹר׃ 11 לֹא־אֲדֹנִי שְׁמָעֵנִי
הַשָּׂדֶה שדי נָתַתִּי לָךְ וְהַמְּעָרָה ש"ך אֲשֶׁר־בּוֹ לְךָ נְתַתִּיהָ לְעֵינֵי
ריבוע מ"ה בְנֵי־עַמִּי נְתַתִּיהָ לָּךְ קְבֹר מֵתֶךָ׃ 12 וַיִּשְׁתַּחוּ אַבְרָהָם
וו"פ אל, רמ"ח לִפְנֵי עַם הָאָרֶץ אלהים דההין ע"ה׃ 13 וַיְדַבֵּר ראה אֶל־עֶפְרוֹן
בְּאָזְנֵי יוד הי ואו הה עַם־הָאָרֶץ אלהים דההין ע"ה לֵאמֹר אַךְ אהיה אִם יוהך ־אַתָּה
לוּ שְׁמָעֵנִי נָתַתִּי כֶּסֶף הַשָּׂדֶה שדי קַח מִמֶּנִּי וְאֶקְבְּרָה אֶת־מֵתִי
שָׁמָּה מהש׃ 14 וַיַּעַן עֶפְרוֹן אֶת־אַבְרָהָם וו"פ אל, רמ"ח לֵאמֹר לוֹ׃
15 אֲדֹנִי שְׁמָעֵנִי אֶרֶץ אלהים דאלפין אַרְבַּע מֵאֹת שֶׁקֶל־כֶּסֶף בֵּינִי
וּבֵינְךָ מַה מ"ה ־הִוא וְאֶת־מֵתְךָ קְבֹר׃ 16 וַיִּשְׁמַע אַבְרָהָם וו"פ אל, רמ"ח
אֶל־עֶפְרוֹן וַיִּשְׁקֹל אַבְרָהָם וו"פ אל, רמ"ח לְעֶפְרֹן אֶת־הַכֶּסֶף אֲשֶׁר
דִּבֶּר ראה בְּאָזְנֵי יוד הי ואו הה בְנֵי־חֵת אַרְבַּע מֵאוֹת שֶׁקֶל כֶּסֶף עֹבֵר
רבוע אלהים ־ ע"ב לַסֹּחֵר׃

SECOND READING - ISAAC - GEVURAH

17 וַיָּקָם | שְׂדֵה עֶפְרוֹן אֲשֶׁר בַּמַּכְפֵּלָה אֲשֶׁר לִפְנֵי מַמְרֵא סוזפך
ע"ה הַשָּׂדֶה שדי וְהַמְּעָרָה ש"ך אֲשֶׁר־בּוֹ וְכָל ילי ־הָעֵץ ע"ה קס"א אֲשֶׁר
בַּשָּׂדֶה אֲשֶׁר בְּכָל לכב ־גְּבֻלוֹ סָבִיב׃ 18 לְאַבְרָהָם וו"פ אל, רמ"ח לְמִקְנָה
לְעֵינֵי ריבוע מ"ה בְנֵי־חֵת בְּכֹל לכב בָּאֵי שַׁעַר־עִירוֹ סוזפך, ערי, סנדלפון׃

24[1] And Abraham was old and well advanced in age, and the Lord had blessed Abraham in every way.

[2] And Abraham said to the chief servant in his household, the one in charge of all that he had, "Put, I pray you, your hand under my thigh.

[3] And I will make you swear by the Lord, the God of heaven and the God of earth, that you will not take a wife for my son from the daughters of the Canaanites, among whom I am living.

[4] But you will go to my country and my own kind and take a wife for my son Isaac."

[5] And the servant asked him, "What if the woman is unwilling to come back with me to this land? Shall I then take your son back to the land from which you came?"

[6] And Abraham said, "Beware that you do not take my son back there again.

[7] The Lord God of heaven, Who brought me out of my father's house and from the land of my kind and Who spoke to me and promised me on oath, saying, 'To your seed I will give this land,' He will send His angel before you so that you can get a wife for my son from there.

[8] And if the woman is unwilling to come back with you, then you will be released from this oath of mine. Only do not take my son back there."

[9] And the servant put his hand under the thigh of Abraham, his master, and swore an oath to him concerning this matter.

וְאַבְרָהָם

Genesis 24:1 – Every day of Abraham's life was important because in each of those days, he was a channel for the Light. We are fortunate if we occasionally have such a moment when we manifest Light as he did, so we must always be ready for such opportunities.

וְלָקַחְתָּ

Genesis 24:4 – Abraham instructed his servant Eliezer to travel to the place where Abraham's family lived and to return with Rebecca (Rivka), whom Abraham had foreseen would be Isaac's soul mate.

Eliezer had intended that his own daughter marry Isaac. When he was chosen for this mission, he could have taken the opportunity to sabotage the trip, but he put aside his personal agenda and accomplished his task successfully.

It is only when we let go of our personal agendas that we find success and fulfillment in what we do. When our actions are undertaken for selfish interests, we cannot succeed.

19 וְאַחֲרֵי־כֵן קָבַר אַבְרָהָם ח״פ אל, רמ״ח אֶת־שָׂרָה אלהים דיודין ורבוע אלהים
- ה׳ אִשְׁתּוֹ אֶל־מְעָרַת שְׂדֵה הַמַּכְפֵּלָה עַל־פְּנֵי חכמה - בינה מַמְרֵא
סוזוף ע״ה הִוא חֶבְרוֹן בְּאֶרֶץ אלהים דאלפין כְּנָעַן׃ 20 וַיָּקָם הַשָּׂדֶה שד״י
וְהַמְּעָרָה ע״ך אֲשֶׁר־בּוֹ לְאַבְרָהָם ח״פ אל, רמ״ח לַאֲחֻזַּת־קָבֶר מֵאֵת
בְּנֵי־חֵת׃ [ס] 24 1 וְאַבְרָהָם ח״פ אל, רמ״ח זָקֵן בָּא בַּיָּמִים נלך
וַיהוָה אהדונהי בֵּרַךְ אֶת־אַבְרָהָם ח״פ אל, רמ״ח בַּכֹּל לכב׃ 2 וַיֹּאמֶר
אַבְרָהָם ח״פ אל, רמ״ח אֶל־עַבְדּוֹ זְקַן בֵּיתוֹ ב״פ ראה הַמֹּשֵׁל בְּכָל לכב -אֲשֶׁר־לוֹ
שִׂים־נָא יָדְךָ בוכו תַּחַת יְרֵכִי׃ 3 וְאַשְׁבִּיעֲךָ בַּיהוָה אהדונהי אֱלֹהֵי
דמב, ילה הַשָּׁמַיִם י״פ טל, י״פ כוזו וֵאלֹהֵי לכב, דמב, ילה הָאָרֶץ אלהים דההין ע״ה; ר״ת אהוה
אֲשֶׁר לֹא־תִקַּח אִשָּׁה לִבְנִי מִבְּנוֹת הַכְּנַעֲנִי אֲשֶׁר אָנֹכִי איע יוֹשֵׁב
בְּקִרְבּוֹ׃ 4 כִּי אֶל־אַרְצִי וְאֶל־מוֹלַדְתִּי תֵּלֵךְ וְלָקַחְתָּ אִשָּׁה לִבְנִי
לְיִצְחָק ד״פ ב״ן׃ 5 וַיֹּאמֶר אֵלָיו הָעֶבֶד אוּלַי אום לֹא־תֹאבֶה הָאִשָּׁה
לָלֶכֶת אַחֲרַי אֶל־הָאָרֶץ אלהים דההין ע״ה הַזֹּאת הֶהָשֵׁב אָשִׁיב אֶת־
בִּנְךָ אֶל־הָאָרֶץ אלהים דההין ע״ה אֲשֶׁר־יָצָאתָ מִשָּׁם׃ 6 וַיֹּאמֶר אֵלָיו
אַבְרָהָם ח״פ אל, רמ״ח הִשָּׁמֶר לְךָ פֶּן־תָּשִׁיב אֶת־בְּנִי שָׁמָּה מהש׃
7 יְהוָה אהדונהי | אֱלֹהֵי דמב, ילה הַשָּׁמַיִם י״פ טל, י״פ כוזו אֲשֶׁר לְקָחַנִי
מִבֵּית ב״פ ראה אָבִי וּמֵאֶרֶץ אלהים דאלפין מוֹלַדְתִּי וַאֲשֶׁר דִּבֶּר ראה -לִי
וַאֲשֶׁר נִשְׁבַּע־לִי לֵאמֹר לְזַרְעֲךָ אֶתֵּן אֶת־הָאָרֶץ אלהים דההין ע״ה
הַזֹּאת הוּא יִשְׁלַח מַלְאָכוֹ לְפָנֶיךָ ס״ג - מ״ה - ב״ן וְלָקַחְתָּ אִשָּׁה לִבְנִי
מִשָּׁם׃ 8 וְאִם יוהך -לֹא תֹאבֶה הָאִשָּׁה לָלֶכֶת אַחֲרֶיךָ וְנִקִּיתָ
מִשְּׁבֻעָתִי זֹאת רַק אֶת־בְּנִי לֹא תָשֵׁב שָׁמָּה מהש׃ 9 וַיָּשֶׂם הָעֶבֶד
אֶת־יָדוֹ תַּחַת יֶרֶךְ אַבְרָהָם ח״פ אל, רמ״ח אֲדֹנָיו וַיִּשָּׁבַע לוֹ עַל־
הַדָּבָר ראה הַזֶּה והו׃

THIRD READING - JACOB - TIFERET

*[10] And the servant took ten camels of the camels of his master and departed, taking
with him all kinds of good things from his master. And he arose and went to
Mesopotamia and to the city of Nahor. [11] He had the camels kneel down near the well
outside the city at the time of the evening, the time the women go out to draw water.
[12] And he said, "O Lord, God of my master Abraham, I pray You, send me good speed
this day, and show kindness to my master Abraham. [13] See, I stand here by the well
of water, and the daughters of the men of the city come out to draw water. [14] And let
it come to pass that the girl to whom I shall say, 'Let down your pitcher, I pray you,
that I may drink,' and she will say, 'Drink, and I will give your camels drink also,' let
her be the one You have chosen for Your servant Isaac, and thereby I will know that
You have shown kindness to my master." [15] And it came to pass, before he had done
speaking, that Rebecca came out, who was the daughter of Bethuel, son of Milca,
the wife of Nahor, Abraham's brother, with her pitcher on her shoulder. [16] And the girl
was very fair to look at, a virgin; no man had ever known her. And she went down to
the well, and filled her pitcher and came up. [17] And the servant ran to meet her and
said, "Let me, I pray you, drink a little water from your pitcher." [18] And she said,*

וַיֹּאמַר

Genesis 24:12 – Arriving in Abraham's hometown, Eliezer prayed to God for success in his mission and for a sign by which to recognize Isaac's soul mate. He met with Rebecca near a well, which shows us how water has symbolic power to help us in our relationships and even to unite us with our soul mate. We should note that Jacob's first meeting with Rachel was also by a well, as was the meeting between Moses and Tzipora. In the Writings of Rav Isaac Luria (the Ari), we read:

> *A well is called "rechovot" when a union is effected for producing souls because then the souls of the righteous rise as Female Waters, and Yesod is called a well of flowing water.*

וַיְהִי

Genesis 24:15 – Eliezer found Rebecca without even knowing her name or that she was a member of Abraham's family. He was able to do this through the power of his certainty that God would reveal Isaac's soul mate at the right moment.

> *Come and behold: When the servant reached Charan and found Rebecca "at the time of evening," (Genesis 24:11) it was time for the afternoon prayer. At the exact time when Isaac said his afternoon prayer, the servant reached Rebecca. Rebecca came to him again at that time when he prayed Mincha. THIS IS IN ACCORDANCE WITH THE VERSE: "AND ISAAC WENT OUT TO MEDITATE IN THE FIELD AT THE EVENING TIME." (ibid. 63)*
>
> *– The Zohar,*
> *Chayei Sarah 23:226*

When we have certainty and make an effort for the sake of sharing and revealing Light—that is, when we do our part—the Light will support us and help us complete our task. Indeed, the sages have told us that God sent help to Eliezer in the form of two angels: one to bring Rebecca out to him and one to accompany him. *(Beresheet Rabba 59:9)*

THIRD READING - JACOB - TIFERET

10 וַיִּקַּח ו"עם הָעֶבֶד עֲשָׂרָה גְמַלִּים מִגְּמַלֵּי אֲדֹנָיו וַיֵּלֶךְ כלי וְכָל
-טוּב והו אֲדֹנָיו בְּיָדוֹ וַיָּקָם וַיֵּלֶךְ כלי אֶל-אֲרַם נַהֲרַיִם אֶל-
עִיר מנצפך, ערי, סנדלפו"ן נָחוֹר: 11 וַיַּבְרֵךְ הַגְּמַלִּים מִחוּץ לָעִיר
מנצפך, ערי, סנדלפו"ן אֶל-בְּאֵר קנ"א - ב"ן הַמָּיִם לְעֵת עֶרֶב רבוע אלהים רבוע יהוה
לְעֵת צֵאת הַשֹּׁאֲבֹת: 12 וַיֹּאמַר | יְהֹוָהאדניאהדונהי אֱלֹהֵי דמב, ילה
אֲדֹנִי אַבְרָהָם ח"פ אל, רמ"ח הַקְרֵה-נָא לְפָנַי הַיּוֹם נגד, זן, מזבח וַעֲשֵׂה-
חֶסֶד ע"ב, ריבוע יהוה עִם אֲדֹנִי אַבְרָהָם ח"פ אל, רמ"ח: 13 הִנֵּה אָנֹכִי איע
נִצָּב עַל-עֵין ריבוע מ"ה הַמָּיִם וּבְנוֹת אַנְשֵׁי הָעִיר מנצפך, ערי, סנדלפו"ן
יֹצְאֹת לִשְׁאֹב מָיִם: 14 וְהָיָה יהוה,יהה הַנַּעֲרָ אֲשֶׁר אֹמַר אֵלֶיהָ
הַטִּי-נָא כַדֵּךְ וְאֶשְׁתֶּה וְאָמְרָה שְׁתֵה וְגַם יגל -גְּמַלֶּיךָ אַשְׁקֶה
אֹתָהּ הֹכַחְתָּ לְעַבְדְּךָ פוי לְיִצְחָק ד"פ ב"ן וּבָהּ אֵדַע כִּי-עָשִׂיתָ
חֶסֶד ע"ב, ריבוע יהוה עִם-אֲדֹנִי: 15 וַיְהִי אל -הוּא טֶרֶם כִּלָּה לְדַבֵּר
ראה וְהִנֵּה מ"ה יה רִבְקָה יֹצֵאת אֲשֶׁר יֻלְּדָה לִבְתוּאֵל בֶּן-מִלְכָּה
ע"ה אל אדני אֵשֶׁת נָחוֹר אֲחִי אַבְרָהָם ח"פ אל, רמ"ח וְכַדָּהּ עַל-שִׁכְמָהּ:
16 וְהַנַּעֲרָ טֹבַת מַרְאֶה מְאֹד מ"ה בְּתוּלָה וְאִישׁ ע"ה קנ"א קס"א לֹא
יְדָעָהּ וַתֵּרֶד הָעַיְנָה ריבוע מ"ה וַתְּמַלֵּא כַדָּהּ וַתָּעַל: 17 וַיָּרָץ
הָעֶבֶד לִקְרָאתָהּ וַיֹּאמֶר הַגְמִיאִינִי נָא מְעַט-מַיִם מִכַּדֵּךְ:
18 וַתֹּאמֶר שְׁתֵה אֲדֹנִי וַתְּמַהֵר וַתֹּרֶד כַּדָּהּ עַל-יָדָהּ וַתַּשְׁקֵהוּ:
19 וַתְּכַל לְהַשְׁקֹתוֹ וַתֹּאמֶר גַּם יגל לִגְמַלֶּיךָ אֶשְׁאָב עַד אִם יוהך
-כִּלּוּ לִשְׁתֹּת: 20 וַתְּמַהֵר וַתְּעַר כַּדָּהּ אֶל-הַשֹּׁקֶת וַתָּרָץ עוֹד
אֶל-הַבְּאֵר קנ"א - ב"ן לִשְׁאֹב וַתִּשְׁאַב לְכָל יה - אדני -גְּמַלָּיו:
21 וְהָאִישׁ ע"ה קנ"א קס"א מִשְׁתָּאֵה לָהּ מַחֲרִישׁ לָדַעַת הַהִצְלִיחַ

"Drink, my lord," and she quickly lowered the pitcher to her hand and gave him to
drink. 19 *And when she had finished giving him a drink, she said, "I will draw water*
for your camels too, until they have finished drinking." 20 *And she hurried and emptied*
her pitcher into the trough, and ran again to the well to draw water, and drew enough
for all his camels. 21 *And the man, without saying a word, watched her closely to see*
whether the Lord had made his journey successful or not.

22 *And it came to pass, as the camels had finished drinking, that the man took out a*
gold earring weighing half a shekel and two bracelets for her hands weighing ten
shekels of gold. 23 *And said, "Whose daughter are you? Tell me, I pray you, is there*
room in your father's house for us to lodge in?" 24 *And she said him, "I am the*
daughter of Bethuel, the son that Milcah born to Nahor." 25 *She said more to him,*
"We have both straw and fodder enough, and room to lodge in." 26 *And the man*
bowed down his head and worshiped the Lord.

FOURTH READING - MOSES - NETZACH

27 *And he said, "Blessed be the Lord, God of my master Abraham, who has left*
destitute my master of His mercy and truth: As for me, the Lord has led me to the
house of my master's brethren." 28 *And the girl ran and told her mother's house about*
these things. 29 *And Rebecca had a brother and his name was Laban, and Laban ran*
out to the man at the well.

30 *And it came to pass, when he saw the earring and bracelets in his sister's hands,*
and when he heard the words of Rebecca saying, "Thus spoke the man to me," that
he came to the man and found him standing by the camels near the well. 31 *And he*
said, "Come in, you who are blessed by the Lord. Why are you standing out here? I
have prepared the house and a place for the camels."

Genesis 24:29 – Laban, Rebecca's brother, was a very negative force and wanted to prevent Rebecca from marrying Isaac. Although his name means "white," Laban was very dark in appearance. The *Zohar* says that he was actually an expert on sorcery.

> *Rav Abba said, "Everyone was aware that Laban was the best at sorcery and wizardry, and he could use sorcery to do away with anyone he wished."*
> *– The Zohar, Vayishlach 2:23*

Laban, therefore, represents the dark forces that must be overcome before soul mates can be joined. From this incident of Laban trying to prevent the marriage of Rebecca and Isaac, we learn that if the start of a relationship is simple and easy, there is less likelihood of revealing Light. However, when there are obstacles at the beginning of a relationship, the potential to reveal Light is much greater.

יְהֹוָה אדני יאהדונהי דַּרְכּוֹ אִם יוהך ־לֹא: 22 וַיְהִי כַּאֲשֶׁר כִּלּוּ הַגְּמַלִּים
לִשְׁתּוֹת וַיִּקַּח חעם הָאִישׁ ז"פ אדם נֶזֶם זָהָב בֶּקַע מִשְׁקָלוֹ וּשְׁנֵי
צְמִידִים עַל־יָדֶיהָ עֲשָׂרָה זָהָב מִשְׁקָלָם: 23 וַיֹּאמֶר בַּת־מִי
ילי אַתְּ הַגִּידִי נָא לִי הֲיֵשׁ בֵּית ב"פ ראה ־אָבִיךְ מָקוֹם יהוה ברבוע, ו"פ אל
לָנוּ אלהים, מום לָלִין: 24 וַתֹּאמֶר אֵלָיו בַּת־בְּתוּאֵל אָנֹכִי איע בֶּן־מִלְכָּה
ע"ה אל אדני אֲשֶׁר יָלְדָה לְנָחוֹר: 25 וַתֹּאמֶר אֵלָיו גַּם יגל ־תֶּבֶן גַּם יגל
־מִסְפּוֹא רַב עִמָּנוּ ריבוע ס"ג גַּם יגל ־מָקוֹם לָלוּן: 26 וַיִּקֹּד הָאִישׁ
ז"פ אדם וַיִּשְׁתַּחוּ לַיהֹוָה אדני יאהדונהי:

FOURTH READING - MOSES - NETZACH

27 וַיֹּאמֶר בָּרוּךְ יהוה ע"ב רבוע מ"ה יְהֹוָה אדני יאהדונהי אֱלֹהֵי דמב, ילה אֲדֹנִי
אַבְרָהָם ח"פ אל, רמ"ח אֲשֶׁר לֹא־עָזַב חַסְדּוֹ ג"פ יהוה וַאֲמִתּוֹ מֵעִם אֲדֹנִי
אָנֹכִי איע בַּדֶּרֶךְ ב"פ יב"ק נָחַנִי יְהֹוָה אדני יאהדונהי בֵּית ב"פ ראה אֲחֵי אֲדֹנִי:
28 וַתָּרָץ הַנַּעֲרָ וַתַּגֵּד לְבֵית ב"פ ראה אִמָּהּ כַּדְּבָרִים ראה הָאֵלֶּה:
29 וּלְרִבְקָה אָח וּשְׁמוֹ מהש ע"ה לָבָן וַיָּרָץ לָבָן אֶל־הָאִישׁ ז"פ אדם
הַחוּצָה אֶל־הָעָיִן ריבוע מ"ה, נמם: 30 וַיְהִי אל | כִּרְאֹת אֶת־הַנֶּזֶם וְאֶת־
הַצְּמִדִים עַל־יְדֵי אֲחֹתוֹ וּכְשָׁמְעוֹ אֶת־דִּבְרֵי ראה רִבְקָה
אֲחֹתוֹ לֵאמֹר כֹּה היי ־דִבֶּר ראה אֵלַי הָאִישׁ ז"פ אדם וַיָּבֹא אֶל־הָאִישׁ
ז"פ אדם וְהִנֵּה עֹמֵד עַל־הַגְּמַלִּים עַל־הָעָיִן ריבוע מ"ה, נמם: 31 וַיֹּאמֶר
בּוֹא בְּרוּךְ יהוה ע"ב רבוע מ"ה יְהֹוָה אדני יאהדונהי לָמָּה תַעֲמֹד בַּחוּץ
וְאָנֹכִי איע פִּנִּיתִי הַבַּיִת ב"פ ראה וּמָקוֹם יהוה ברבוע, ו"פ אל לַגְּמַלִּים:
32 וַיָּבֹא הָאִישׁ ז"פ אדם הַבַּיְתָה ב"פ ראה וַיְפַתַּח הַגְּמַלִּים וַיִּתֵּן תֶּבֶן
וּמִסְפּוֹא לַגְּמַלִּים וּמַיִם לִרְחֹץ רַגְלָיו וְרַגְלֵי הָאֲנָשִׁים אֲשֶׁר אִתּוֹ:

32 And the man went into the house, and he unloaded his camels, and gave straw and
fodder to the camels, and water to wash his feet and the feet of the men that were
with him. 33 And food was set before him to eat, but he said, "I will not eat until I have
told you why I am here." And he said, "Speak on."

34 And he said, "I am Abraham's servant. 35 And the Lord has blessed my master
greatly, and he has become wealthy. And he has given him flocks and herds, and
silver and gold, menservants and maidservants, and camels and donkeys.

36 And Sarah, my master's wife, bore a son to my master in her old age, and he has
given him all that he has.

37 And my master made me swear an oath, and said, 'You must not get a wife for my
son from the daughters of the Canaanites, in whose land I live, 38 but go to my father's
house and to my own kind, and take a wife for my son.'

39 Then I said to my master, 'What if the woman will not come back with me?' 40 And
he replied, 'The Lord, before whom I walk, will send his angel with you and make your
journey a success, and you will take a wife for my son from my kind and of my father's
house.

41 Then, when you go to my kind, you will be released from this oath even if they
refuse to give her to you—you will be released from my oath.' 42 And I came this day
to the well, and said, 'O Lord, God of my master Abraham, if You grant success to the
journey on which I have come; 43 see, when I stand by the well of water, if the virgin
comes out to draw water and I say to her, 'Give me, I pray you, a little water from your
pitcher to drink,' 44 and she says to me, 'Drink, and I will also draw water for your
camels," let her be the one the Lord has chosen for my master's son.'

45 And before I was done speaking in my heart, Rebecca came out, with her pitcher
on her shoulder, and she went down to the well and drew water, and I said to her, 'Let
me drink, I pray you.'

46 And she quickly lowered her pitcher from her shoulder and said, 'Drink, and I will
give your camels drink also.' So I drank, and she made the camels drink also.

עֶבֶד

Genesis 24:34 – When the servant, Eliezer, spoke to Rebecca's family, he did not reveal how he had found her. Instead, he focused on the details of her name and on the fact that Abraham had told him to go to Abraham's family. The servant knew the importance of speaking to Rebecca's family at a level that was appropriate to them and that they could understand. We ourselves can receive only those messages that we are open to receiving and that correspond to our current state of spiritual development. We should continually push ourselves to grow spiritually so that we are able to accept the messages that come to us and to take the action they require.

33 וַיּוּשַׂם (כתיב: ויישם) לְפָנָיו לֶאֱכֹל וַיֹּאמֶר לֹא אֹכַל עַד אִם יוהך
דִּבַּרְתִּי ראה דְּבָרָי וַיֹּאמֶר דַּבֵּר ראה: 34 וַיֹּאמַר עֶבֶד אַבְרָהָם
ו״פ אל, רמ״ח אָנֹכִי איע: 35 וַיהֹוָה אהדונהי בֵּרַךְ אֶת־אֲדֹנִי מְאֹד מ״ה
וַיִּגְדָּל יזל וַיִּתֶּן י״פ מלוי ע״ב לוֹ צֹאן מלוי אהיה דיודין ע״ה וּבָקָר וְכֶסֶף וְזָהָב
וַעֲבָדִם וּשְׁפָחֹת וּגְמַלִּים וַחֲמֹרִים: 36 וַתֵּלֶד שָׂרָה אלהים דיודין ורבוע אלהים - ה׳
אֵשֶׁת אֲדֹנִי בֵן לַאדֹנִי אַחֲרֵי זִקְנָתָהּ וַיִּתֶּן י״פ מלוי ע״ב לוֹ אֶת־כָּל יכלי
אֲשֶׁר־לוֹ: 37 וַיַּשְׁבִּעֵנִי אֲדֹנִי לֵאמֹר לֹא־תִקַּח אִשָּׁה לִבְנִי
מִבְּנוֹת הַכְּנַעֲנִי אֲשֶׁר אָנֹכִי איע יֹשֵׁב בְּאַרְצוֹ: 38 אִם יוהך לֹא אֶל־
בֵּית ב״פ ראה אָבִי תֵּלֵךְ וְאֶל־מִשְׁפַּחְתִּי וְלָקַחְתָּ אִשָּׁה לִבְנִי:
39 וָאֹמַר אֶל־אֲדֹנִי אֻלַי לֹא־תֵלֵךְ הָאִשָּׁה אַחֲרָי: 40 וַיֹּאמֶר אֵלָי
יְהֹוָה אהדונהי אֲשֶׁר־הִתְהַלַּכְתִּי לְפָנָיו יִשְׁלַח מַלְאָכוֹ אִתָּךְ וְהִצְלִיחַ
דַּרְכֶּךָ ב״פ יב״ק וְלָקַחְתָּ אִשָּׁה לִבְנִי מִמִּשְׁפַּחְתִּי וּמִבֵּית ב״פ ראה אָבִי:
41 אָז תִּנָּקֶה מֵאָלָתִי כִּי תָבוֹא אֶל־מִשְׁפַּחְתִּי וְאִם יוהך לֹא יִתְּנוּ
לָךְ וְהָיִיתָ נָקִי ע״ה קס״א מֵאָלָתִי: 42 וָאָבֹא הַיּוֹם נגד, זן, מזבח אֶל־הָעָיִן
ריבוע מ״ה, נמם וָאֹמַר יְהֹוָה אהדונהי אֱלֹהֵי דמב, ילה אֲדֹנִי אַבְרָהָם ו״פ אל, רמ״ח
אִם יוהך יֶשְׁךָ־נָּא מַצְלִיחַ דַּרְכִּי ב״פ יב״ק אֲשֶׁר אָנֹכִי איע הֹלֵךְ מיה
עָלֶיהָ פהל: 43 הִנֵּה מ״ה יה אָנֹכִי איע נִצָּב עַל־עֵין ריבוע מ״ה הַמָּיִם וְהָיָה
יהוה, יהה הָעַלְמָה הַיֹּצֵאת לִשְׁאֹב וְאָמַרְתִּי אֵלֶיהָ הַשְׁקִינִי־נָא
מְעַט־מַיִם מִכַּדֵּךְ: 44 וְאָמְרָה אֵלַי גַּם יגל אַתָּה שְׁתֵה וְגַם יגל
לִגְמַלֶּיךָ אֶשְׁאָב הִוא הָאִשָּׁה אֲשֶׁר־הֹכִיחַ יְהֹוָה אהדונהי לְבֶן־
אֲדֹנִי: 45 אֲנִי אני טֶרֶם רמ״ח ע״ה אֲכַלֶּה לְדַבֵּר ראה אֶל־לִבִּי וְהִנֵּה
מ״ה יה רִבְקָה יֹצֵאת וְכַדָּהּ עַל־שִׁכְמָהּ וַתֵּרֶד הָעַיְנָה וַתִּשְׁאָב
וָאֹמַר אֵלֶיהָ הַשְׁקִינִי נָא: 46 וַתְּמַהֵר וַתּוֹרֶד כַּדָּהּ מֵעָלֶיהָ
פהל וַתֹּאמֶר שְׁתֵה וְגַם יגל גְּמַלֶּיךָ אַשְׁקֶה וָאֵשְׁתְּ וְגַם יגל

47 And I asked her and said, 'Whose daughter are you?' And she said, 'The daughter of Bethuel, son of Nahor, whom Milcah bore to him.' And I put the earring upon her face and the bracelets on her arms, 48 and I bowed down my head and worshiped the Lord and blessed the Lord, the God of my master Abraham, who had led me on the right road to take my master's brother's daughter for his son.

49 And now if you will deal kindly and truly with my master, tell me; and if not, tell me, so that I may turn to the right hand or to the left."

50 Then Laban and Bethuel answered and said, "This comes from the Lord; we cannot speak to you bad or good.

51 See, Rebecca is before you; take her and go, and let her become the wife of your master's son, as the Lord has spoken."

52 And it came to pass that when Abraham's servant heard their words, he worshipped the Lord, bowing himself to the earth.

FIFTH READING - AARON - HOD

53 And the servant brought out jewels of silver and jewels of gold, and raiment and gave them to Rebecca; he also gave to her brother and to her mother precious things.

54 And they ate and drank, he and the men who were with him, and spent the night there. And they rose up in the morning, and he said, "Send me on my way to my master."

וַיָּלִינוּ

Genesis 24:54 – Eliezer spent the night at the home of Rebecca. Various sources say that Rebecca's father, Bethuel, and Laban schemed to poison the servant to prevent him from taking Rebecca away. But an angel switched the food, and it was Rebecca's father who was poisoned instead. We see from this that all our actions have repercussions. Here the negative act of Rebecca's father elicited an immediate and fatal reaction. Often, there is a separation in time and/or space between an action and its consequences, but we should always be aware that, sooner or later, every Cause has its inevitable Effect.

וַתֹּאמֶר

Genesis 24:58 – Rebecca's family asked her if she wanted to stay with them or go with Abraham's servant. Knowing that she was in a negative environment, Rebecca said that she wanted to go. We are told that the dowry her family gave her consisted only of words, yet following her highest instincts, Rebecca left everything behind to seek a better, more positive life for herself. *(Beresheet Rabba 60:13)*

הַגְּמַלִּים הִשְׁקָתָה׃ 47 וָאֶשְׁאַל אֹתָהּ וָאֹמַר בַּת־מִי ילי אַתְּ
וַתֹּאמֶר בַּת־בְּתוּאֵל בֶּן־נָחוֹר אֲשֶׁר יָלְדָה־לּוֹ מִלְכָּה ע״ה אל אדני
וָאָשִׂם הַנֶּזֶם עַל־אַפָּהּ וְהַצְּמִידִים עַל־יָדֶיהָ׃ 48 וָאֶקֹּד וָאֶשְׁתַּחֲוֶה
י״פ ע״ב לַיהֹוָה יאהדונהי וָאֲבָרֵךְ אֶת־יְהֹוָה יאהדונהי אֱלֹהֵי דמב, ילה אֲדֹנִי
אַבְרָהָם ח״פ אל, רמ״ח אֲשֶׁר הִנְחַנִי בְּדֶרֶךְ ב״פ יב״ק אֱמֶת אהיה פעמים אהיה, ז״פ ס״ג
לָקַחַת אֶת־בַּת־אֲחִי אֲדֹנִי לִבְנוֹ׃ 49 וְעַתָּה אִם יוהך ־יֶשְׁכֶם עֹשִׂים
חֶסֶד ע״ב, ריבוע יהוה וֶאֱמֶת אהיה פעמים אהיה, ז״פ ס״ג אֶת־אֲדֹנִי הַגִּידוּ לִי וְאִם
יוהך ־לֹא הַגִּידוּ לִי וְאֶפְנֶה עַל־יָמִין אוֹ עַל־שְׂמֹאל׃ 50 וַיַּעַן לָבָן
וּבְתוּאֵל וַיֹּאמְרוּ מֵיְהֹוָה יאהדונהי יָצָא הַדָּבָר ראה לֹא נוּכַל דַּבֵּר ראה
אֵלֶיךָ רַע אוֹ־טוֹב והו׃ 51 הִנֵּה מ״ה יה ־רִבְקָה לְפָנֶיךָ ס״ג - מ״ה - ב״ן קַח
וָלֵךְ וּתְהִי אִשָּׁה לְבֶן־אֲדֹנֶיךָ כַּאֲשֶׁר דִּבֶּר ראה יְהֹוָה יאהדונהי׃
52 וַיְהִי אל כַּאֲשֶׁר שָׁמַע עֶבֶד אַבְרָהָם ח״פ אל, רמ״ח אֶת־דִּבְרֵיהֶם ראה
וַיִּשְׁתַּחוּ אַרְצָה אלהים דההין ע״ה לַיהֹוָה יאהדונהי׃

FIFTH READING - AARON - HOD

53 וַיּוֹצֵא הָעֶבֶד כְּלֵי־כֶסֶף וּכְלֵי זָהָב וּבְגָדִים וַיִּתֵּן לְרִבְקָה
וּמִגְדָּנֹת נָתַן לְאָחִיהָ וּלְאִמָּהּ׃ 54 וַיֹּאכְלוּ וַיִּשְׁתּוּ הוּא וְהָאֲנָשִׁים
אֲשֶׁר־עִמּוֹ וַיָּלִינוּ וַיָּקוּמוּ בַבֹּקֶר וַיֹּאמֶר שַׁלְּחֻנִי לַאדֹנִי׃ 55 וַיֹּאמֶר
אָחִיהָ וְאִמָּהּ תֵּשֵׁב הַנַּעֲרָ אִתָּנוּ יָמִים נלך אוֹ עָשׂוֹר אַחַר תֵּלֵךְ׃
56 וַיֹּאמֶר אֲלֵהֶם אַל־תְּאַחֲרוּ אֹתִי וַיהֹוָה יאהדונהי הִצְלִיחַ דַּרְכִּי
ב״פ יב״ק שַׁלְּחוּנִי וְאֵלְכָה לַאדֹנִי׃ 57 וַיֹּאמְרוּ נִקְרָא לַנַּעֲרָ וְנִשְׁאֲלָה
אֶת־פִּיהָ׃ 58 וַיִּקְרְאוּ לְרִבְקָה וַיֹּאמְרוּ אֵלֶיהָ הֲתֵלְכִי עִם־הָאִישׁ
ז״פ אדם הַזֶּה והו וַתֹּאמֶר אֵלֵךְ׃ 59 וַיְשַׁלְּחוּ אֶת־רִבְקָה אֲחֹתָם

55 And her brother and her mother replied, "Let the girl remain with us a few days, at least ten; after that she will go."

56 And he said to them, "Do not hinder me, seeing the Lord has granted success to my journey; send me on my way so I may go to my master."

57 And they said, "We will call the girl and ask her about it."

58 And they called Rebecca and asked her, "Will you go with this man?" And she said, "I will go."

59 And they sent their sister Rebecca on her way, along with her nurse and Abraham's servant and his men.

60 And they blessed Rebecca and said to her, "You are our sister, may you be the mother of thousands of millions; may your seed possess the gates of their enemies."

61 And Rebecca rose and her maids and they mounted the camels and went back with the man. And the servant took Rebecca and went on his way.

62 And Isaac came from the well Lahairoi, for he was living in the south country.

63 And Isaac went out to meditate in the field at dusk, and he lifted up his eyes and saw the camels approaching.

64 And Rebecca lifted up her eyes, and when she saw Isaac, she dismounted the camel.

65 And she asked the servant, "Who is that man in the field coming to meet us?" And the servant said, "It is my master." So she took her veil and covered herself.

66 And the servant told Isaac all the things he had done. 67 And Isaac brought her into the tent of his mother Sarah, and took Rebecca and she became his wife and he loved her; and Isaac was comforted after his mother's death.

וַיֵּצֵא

Genesis 24:63 – We read that Isaac went out toward evening to pray in the fields. Immediately before sunset is the most negative time of the day, when the negative forces are more numerous and powerful and when there are more negative angels giving assistance to anyone with destructive intentions. There are connections we can make to help us through this transitional time when the light is disappearing.

וַיְבִאֶהָ

Genesis 24:67 – Isaac brought Rebecca into his mother's tent, and from the moment she entered, the tent was filled with Light. When Sarah died, the Light in the tent had gone out, but when Rebecca was joined with Isaac, the Light reappeared. This showed Isaac that his union with Rebecca would be a channel of Light for the whole world.

וְאֶת־מֵנִקְתָּהּ וְאֶת־עֶבֶד אַבְרָהָם ו"פ אל, רמ"ח וְאֶת־אֲנָשָׁיו׃ 60 וַיְבָרְכוּ
יהוה ע"ב ריבוע מ"ה אֶת־רִבְקָה וַיֹּאמְרוּ לָהּ אֲחֹתֵנוּ אַתְּ הֲיִי הי לְאַלְפֵי
רְבָבָה וְיִירַשׁ זַרְעֵךְ אֵת שַׁעַר שֹׂנְאָיו׃ 61 וַתָּקָם רִבְקָה וְנַעֲרֹתֶיהָ
וַתִּרְכַּבְנָה עַל־הַגְּמַלִּים וַתֵּלַכְנָה אַחֲרֵי הָאִישׁ ז"פ אדם וַיִּקַּח חע"ם
הָעֶבֶד אֶת־רִבְקָה וַיֵּלַךְ כלי׃ 62 וְיִצְחָק ד"פ ב"ן בָּא מִבּוֹא בְּאֵר
קנ"א - ב"ן לַחַי רֹאִי וְהוּא יוֹשֵׁב בְּאֶרֶץ אלהים דאלפין הַנֶּגֶב׃ 63 וַיֵּצֵא
יִצְחָק ד"פ ב"ן לָשׂוּחַ בַּשָּׂדֶה לִפְנוֹת עָרֶב רבוע אלהים רבוע יהוה וַיִּשָּׂא עֵינָיו
ריבוע מ"ה וַיַּרְא וְהִנֵּה גְמַלִּים בָּאִים׃ 64 וַתִּשָּׂא רִבְקָה אֶת־עֵינֶיהָ
ריבוע מ"ה וַתֵּרֶא אֶת־יִצְחָק ד"פ ב"ן וַתִּפֹּל מֵעַל עלם הַגָּמָל ג"פ יהוה׃
65 וַתֹּאמֶר אֶל־הָעֶבֶד מִי ילי ־הָאִישׁ ז"פ אדם הַלָּזֶה הַהֹלֵךְ מיה בַּשָּׂדֶה
לִקְרָאתֵנוּ וַיֹּאמֶר הָעֶבֶד הוּא אֲדֹנִי וַתִּקַּח הַצָּעִיף וַתִּתְכָּס׃
66 וַיְסַפֵּר הָעֶבֶד לְיִצְחָק ד"פ ב"ן אֵת כָּל ילי ־הַדְּבָרִים ראה אֲשֶׁר
עָשָׂה׃ 67 וַיְבִאֶהָ יִצְחָק ד"פ ב"ן הָאֹהֱלָה שָׂרָה אלהים דיודין ורבוע אלהים - ה'
אִמּוֹ וַיִּקַּח חע"ם אֶת־רִבְקָה וַתְּהִי־לוֹ לְאִשָּׁה וַיֶּאֱהָבֶהָ וַיִּנָּחֵם יִצְחָק
ד"פ ב"ן אַחֲרֵי אִמּוֹ׃ [פ]

"And Isaac brought her into his mother Sarah's tent." (Genesis 24:67) Rav Yosi said that this is a difficult verse. It is literally written: "...to the tent, Sarah, his mother," but it should have been written "Sarah's tent." What is the meaning of "to the tent"? He says that the Shechina returned, THAT IS CALLED TENT. THEREFORE IT SAYS HA'OHELAH (TO THE TENT), WHICH IS THE SHECHINA, for the Shechina never left Sarah as long as she was in the world. And the candle burned in the tent all the days of the week, from Shabbat eve to Shabbat eve. After she died, the candle was extinguished. Since Rebecca came, the Shechina returned and the candle burned again.

– The Zohar, Chayei Sarah 25:248

Rashi tells us that Scripture narrates Rebecca's ancestry to show that although she was the daughter and sister of wicked men and came from a wicked city, she did not learn wickedness herself.

SIXTH READING - JOSEPH - YESOD

25 1 Then again Abraham took a wife, whose name was Keturah.

2 And she bore him Zimran, and Jokshan, and Medan, and Midian, and Ishbak, and Shuah.

3 And Jokshan begat Sheba and Dedan; and the sons of Dedan were the Asshurites, the Letushites, and the Leummites.

4 And the sons of Midian were Ephah, and Epher, and Hanoch, and Abida, and
Eldaah. All these were the children of Keturah.
5 And Abraham gave all that he had
to Isaac.

6 But to the sons of the concubines which Abraham had, Abraham gave gifts and sent them away from his son Isaac, while he lived eastward, to the land of the east.

7 And these are the days of the years of Abraham's life which he lived, a hundred and seventy-five years.

8 Then Abraham breathed his last breath and died at a good old age, an old man and full of years; and he was gathered to his people.

9 And his sons Isaac and Ishmael buried him in the cave of Machpelah, in the field
of Ephron, the son of Zohar the Hittite, which is near Mamre;
10 the field which
Abraham had purchased from the sons of Heth. There Abraham was buried with his
wife Sarah.

11 And it came to pass after the death of Abraham that God blessed his son Isaac, and Isaac lived by the well Lahairoi.

וַיֹּסֶף

Genesis 25:1 – Abraham married Keturah and had children by her, but Keturah was actually Hagar, who had changed her name. The children of this union would travel to the East to spread the teachings of Kabbalah.

It is written: "And Solomon's wisdom excelled the wisdom of all the children of the east country." (I Kings 5:10) These are the sons of the concubines of Abraham.

– The Zohar, Chayei Sarah 27:264

Abraham's intention was to share the Light with all the nations of the world and to bring them assistance through knowledge of Kabbalah.

SIXTH READING - JOSEPH - YESOD

25 1 ויסף ציון, קנאה, ו"פ יהוה, ה"פ אל אברהם ח"פ אל, רמ"ח ויקח חעם אשה
ושמה קטורה: 2 ותלד לו את־זמרן ואת־יקשן ואת־מדן ואת־
מדין ואת־ישבק ואת־שוח: 3 ויקשן ילד את־שבא ואת־דדן
ובני דדן היו אשורם ולטושם ולאמים: 4 ובני מדין עיפה
ועפר וחנך ואבידע ואלדעה כל ילי ־אלה בני קטורה: 5 ויתן
אברהם ח"פ אל, רמ"ח את־כל ילי ־אשר־לו ליצחק ד"פ ב"ן: 6 ולבני
הפילגשים אשר לאברהם ח"פ אל, רמ"ח נתן אברהם ח"פ אל, רמ"ח מתנת
וישלחם מעל עלם יצחק ד"פ ב"ן בנו בעודנו חי קדמה אל־ארץ
אלהים דאלפין קדם רבוע ב"ן: 7 ואלה מ"ב ימי שני־חיי אברהם ח"פ אל, רמ"ח
אשר־חי מאת שנה ושבעים שנה וחמש שנים: 8 ויגוע וימת
אברהם ח"פ אל, רמ"ח בשיבה טובה אכא זקן ושבע אלהים דיודין ־ ע"ב
ויאסף אל־עמיו: 9 ויקברו אתו יצחק ד"פ ב"ן וישמעאל בניו
אל־מערת המכפלה אל־שדה עפרן בן־צחר החתי אשר על־
פני חכמה ־ בינה ממרא סוזחך ע"ה: 10 השדה שדי אשר־קנה אברהם
ח"פ אל, רמ"ח מאת בני־חת שמה מהש קבר אברהם ח"פ אל, רמ"ח ושרה
אלהים דיודין ורבוע אלהים ־ ה' אשתו: 11 ויהי אל אחרי מות אברהם
ח"פ אל, רמ"ח ויברך עסמ"ב אלהים ילה, מום את־יצחק ד"פ ב"ן בנו וישב
יצחק ד"פ ב"ן עם־באר קנ"א ־ ב"ן לחי ראי: [פ]

ואלה

Genesis 25:7 – Because he had accomplished tremendous spiritual work, Abraham died at an advanced age. Every day, we ourselves should diligently perform our spiritual work while we still have time on Earth to do so.

SEVENTH READING - DAVID - MALCHUT

12 Now these are the generations of Abraham's son Ishmael, whom Sarah's maidservant, Hagar the Egyptian, bore to Abraham.

13 And these are the names of the sons of Ishmael, by their names, according to their generations: Nebaioth, the firstborn of Ishmael, and Kedar, and Adbeel, and Mibsam,
14 and Mishma, and Dumah, and Massa, 15 Hadad, and Tema, Jetur, Naphish, and
Kedemah.

MAFTIR

16 These are the sons of Ishmael, and these are their names, by their towns and by their castles; twelve princes according to their nations.

17 And these are the years of the life of Ishmael, a hundred and thirty-seven years, and he breathed his last breath and died, and he was gathered to his people.

18 And they dwelled from Havilah to Shur, near the border of Egypt, as you go towards Assyria. And he died in the presence of all his brethren.

Genesis 25:12 – Reading about the 12 sons of Ishmael helps us to rise above the influences of the planets and other astrological forces. From kabbalistic astrology, we understand that the stars and planets influence our lives but cannot compel us in any way. We have free will, meaning that we can choose to allow the stars and planets to influence us or we can choose to rise above their influence.

SEVENTH READING - DAVID - MALCHUT

12 וְאֵלֶּה תֹּלְדֹת יִשְׁמָעֵאל בֶּן־אַבְרָהָם ו״פ אל, רמ״ח אֲשֶׁר יָלְדָה הָגָר
ד״פ בין הַמִּצְרִית מצר שִׁפְחַת שָׂרָה אלהים דיודין ורבוע אלהים - ה׳ לְאַבְרָהָם
ו״פ אל, רמ״ח: 13 וְאֵלֶּה מ״ב שְׁמוֹת בְּנֵי יִשְׁמָעֵאל בִּשְׁמֹתָם לְתוֹלְדֹתָם
בְּכֹר יִשְׁמָעֵאל נְבָיֹת וְקֵדָר וְאַדְבְּאֵל וּמִבְשָׂם: 14 וּמִשְׁמָע
וְדוּמָה וּמַשָּׂא: 15 חֲדַד וְתֵימָא יְטוּר נָפִישׁ וָקֵדְמָה:

MAFTIR

16 אֵלֶּה הֵם בְּנֵי יִשְׁמָעֵאל וְאֵלֶּה שְׁמֹתָם בְּחַצְרֵיהֶם וּבְטִירֹתָם
שְׁנֵים־עָשָׂר נְשִׂיאִם לְאֻמֹּתָם: 17 וְאֵלֶּה שְׁנֵי חַיֵּי יִשְׁמָעֵאל מְאַת
שָׁנָה וּשְׁלֹשִׁים שָׁנָה וְשֶׁבַע אלהים דיודין - ע״ב שָׁנִים וַיִּגְוַע וַיָּמָת וַיֵּאָסֶף
אֶל־עַמָּיו: 18 וַיִּשְׁכְּנוּ מֵחֲוִילָה עַד־שׁוּר אבגיתצ, ושר, אהבת חנם אֲשֶׁר
עַל־פְּנֵי חכמה - בינה מִצְרַיִם מצר בֹּאֲכָה אַשּׁוּרָה עַל־פְּנֵי חכמה - בינה כָל
ילי ־אֶחָיו נָפָל: [פ] [פ] [פ]

וְאֵלֶּה

Genesis 25:17 – Although he had been very negative all his life, Ishmael repented before his death and became a righteous person. No matter how negative some people are, no matter how much everyone believes these people are lost—no matter how much these people even believe it themselves—Ishmael shows us that change is possible, even at the very last moment.

HAFTARAH OF CHAYEI SARAH

The biblical lesson of Chayei Sarah deals with Abraham's last days, and the Haftorah in I Kings shows the correspondence with the last days of King David. For most people, reaching a certain age means they are simply waiting to die, but even on the last day of their lives, Abraham and King David asked

I Kings 1:1-31

1[1] When King David was old and well advanced in years, he could not keep warm even when they put covers over him.

[2] So his servants said to him, "Let us look for a young virgin to attend the king and take care of him. She can lie beside him so that our Lord the king may keep warm."

[3] Then they searched throughout Israel for a beautiful girl and found Abishag, a Shunammite, and brought her to the king.

[4] The girl was very beautiful; she took care of the king and waited on him, but the king had no intimate relations with her.

[5] Now Adonijah, whose mother was Haggith, put himself forward and said, "I will be king." So he got chariots and horses ready, with fifty men to run ahead of him.

[6] (His father had never interfered with him by asking, "Why do you behave as you do?" He was also very handsome and was born next after Absalom.)

[7] Adonijah conferred with Joab son of Zeruiah and with Abiathar the priest, and they gave him their support.

[8] But Zadok the priest, Benaiah son of Jehoiada, Nathan the prophet, Shimei and Rei and David's special guard did not join Adonijah.

[9] Adonijah then sacrificed sheep, cattle and fattened calves at the Stone of Zoheleth near En Rogel. He invited all his brothers, the king's sons, and all the men of Judah

HAFTARAH OF CHAYEI SARAH

themselves: “What Light can I reveal today?” They were never merely waiting to take their rest. Instead, they were always seeking higher spirituality and more opportunities for sharing.

מלכים 1 פרק 1

1 1 וְהַמֶּלֶךְ דָּוִד זָקֵן בָּא בַּיָּמִים נלך וַיְכַסֻּהוּ בַּבְּגָדִים וְלֹא
יִחַם לוֹ: 2 וַיֹּאמְרוּ לוֹ עֲבָדָיו יְבַקְשׁוּ לַאדֹנִי הַמֶּלֶךְ נַעֲרָה
שכ״ה בְתוּלָה וְעָמְדָה לִפְנֵי הַמֶּלֶךְ וּתְהִי־לוֹ סֹכֶנֶת וְשָׁכְבָה
בְחֵיקֶךָ וְחַם לַאדֹנִי הַמֶּלֶךְ: 3 וַיְבַקְשׁוּ נַעֲרָה שכ״ה יָפָה ע״ה אל אדני
בְּכֹל לכב גְּבוּל יִשְׂרָאֵל וַיִּמְצְאוּ אֶת־אֲבִישַׁג הַשּׁוּנַמִּית וַיָּבִאוּ
אֹתָהּ לַמֶּלֶךְ: 4 וְהַנַּעֲרָה שכ״ה יָפָה ע״ה אל אדני עַד־מְאֹד מ״ה וַתְּהִי
לַמֶּלֶךְ סֹכֶנֶת וַתְּשָׁרְתֵהוּ וְהַמֶּלֶךְ לֹא יְדָעָהּ: 5 וַאֲדֹנִיָּה בֶן־
חַגִּית מִתְנַשֵּׂא לֵאמֹר אֲנִי אני אֶמְלֹךְ וַיַּעַשׂ לוֹ רֶכֶב וּפָרָשִׁים
וַחֲמִשִּׁים אִישׁ ע״ה קנ״א קס״א רָצִים לְפָנָיו: 6 וְלֹא־עֲצָבוֹ אָבִיו מִיָּמָיו
לֵאמֹר מַדּוּעַ כָּכָה עָשִׂיתָ וְגַם יגל ־הוּא טוֹב והו ־תֹּאַר מְאֹד
מ״ה וְאֹתוֹ יָלְדָה אַחֲרֵי אַבְשָׁלוֹם: 7 וַיִּהְיוּ דְבָרָיו ראה עִם יוֹאָב
בֶּן־צְרוּיָה וְעִם אֶבְיָתָר הַכֹּהֵן מלה וַיַּעְזְרוּ אַחֲרֵי אֲדֹנִיָּה:
8 וְצָדוֹק הַכֹּהֵן מלה וּבְנָיָהוּ בֶן־יְהוֹיָדָע וְנָתָן הַנָּבִיא וְשִׁמְעִי
וְרֵעִי וְהַגִּבּוֹרִים אֲשֶׁר לְדָוִד לֹא הָיוּ עִם־אֲדֹנִיָּהוּ: 9 וַיִּזְבַּח
אֲדֹנִיָּהוּ צֹאן וּבָקָר וּמְרִיא עִם אֶבֶן יוד הה ואו הה הַזֹּחֶלֶת אֲשֶׁר־

who were royal officials, [10] but he did not invite Nathan the prophet or Benaiah or the special guard or his brother Solomon.

[11] Then Nathan asked Bathsheba, Solomon's mother, "Have you not heard that Adonijah, the son of Haggith, has become king without our Lord David's knowing it?

[12] Now then, let me advise you how you can save your own life and the life of your son Solomon.

[13] Go in to King David and say to him, "My Lord the king, did you not swear to me your servant: 'Surely Solomon your son shall be king after me, and he will sit on my throne?' Why then has Adonijah become king?"

[14] While you are still there talking to the king, I will come in and confirm what you have said."

[15] So Bathsheba went to see the aged king in his room, where Abishag the Shunammite was attending him.

[16] Bathsheba bowed low and knelt before the king. "What is it you want?" the king asked.

[17] She said to him, "My Lord, you yourself swore to me your servant by the Lord your God: 'Solomon your son shall be king after me, and he will sit on my throne.'

[18] But now Adonijah has become king, and you, my Lord the king, do not know about it.

[19] He has sacrificed great numbers of cattle, fattened calves, and sheep, and has invited all the king's sons, Abiathar the priest and Joab the commander of the army, but he has not invited Solomon your servant.

[20] My Lord the king, the eyes of all Israel are on you, to learn from you who will sit on the throne of my Lord the king after him.

[21] Otherwise, as soon as my Lord the king is laid to rest with his fathers, I and my son Solomon will be treated as criminals."

[22] While she was still speaking with the king, Nathan the prophet arrived.

אֵצֶל עֵין ריבוע מ"ה רֹגֵל וַיִּקְרָא עם ה' אותיות = ב"פ קס"א אֶת־כָּל ילי ־אֶחָיו
בְּנֵי הַמֶּלֶךְ וּלְכָל יה - אדני ־אַנְשֵׁי יְהוּדָה עַבְדֵי הַמֶּלֶךְ׃ 10 וְאֶת־
נָתָן הַנָּבִיא וּבְנָיָהוּ וְאֶת־הַגִּבּוֹרִים וְאֶת־שְׁלֹמֹה אָחִיו לֹא
קָרָא׃ 11 וַיֹּאמֶר נָתָן אֶל־בַּת־שֶׁבַע אלהים דיודין - ע"ב אֵם יוהך ־שְׁלֹמֹה
לֵאמֹר הֲלוֹא שָׁמַעַתְּ כִּי מָלַךְ אֲדֹנִיָּהוּ בֶן־חַגִּית וַאֲדֹנֵינוּ דָוִד
לֹא יָדָע׃ 12 וְעַתָּה לְכִי אִיעָצֵךְ נָא עֵצָה וּמַלְּטִי אֶת־נַפְשֵׁךְ
וְאֶת־נֶפֶשׁ רמ"ח - ז' הויות בְּנֵךְ שְׁלֹמֹה׃ 13 לְכִי וּבֹאִי | אֶל־הַמֶּלֶךְ
דָּוִד וְאָמַרְתְּ אֵלָיו הֲלֹא־אַתָּה אֲדֹנִי הַמֶּלֶךְ נִשְׁבַּעְתָּ לַאֲמָתְךָ
לֵאמֹר כִּי־שְׁלֹמֹה בְנֵךְ יִמְלֹךְ אַחֲרַי וְהוּא יֵשֵׁב עַל־כִּסְאִי
וּמַדּוּעַ מָלַךְ אֲדֹנִיָּהוּ׃ 14 הִנֵּה מ"ה יה עוֹדָךְ מְדַבֶּרֶת ראה שָׁם
עִם־הַמֶּלֶךְ וַאֲנִי אני אָבוֹא אַחֲרַיִךְ וּמִלֵּאתִי אֶת־דְּבָרָיִךְ ראה׃
15 וַתָּבֹא בַת־שֶׁבַע אלהים דיודין - ע"ב אֶל־הַמֶּלֶךְ הַחַדְרָה וְהַמֶּלֶךְ
זָקֵן מְאֹד מ"ה וַאֲבִישַׁג הַשּׁוּנַמִּית מְשָׁרַת אֶת־הַמֶּלֶךְ׃ 16 וַתִּקֹּד
בַּת־שֶׁבַע אלהים דיודין - ע"ב וַתִּשְׁתַּחוּ לַמֶּלֶךְ וַיֹּאמֶר הַמֶּלֶךְ מַה מ"ה
־לָּךְ׃ 17 וַתֹּאמֶר לוֹ אֲדֹנִי אַתָּה נִשְׁבַּעְתָּ בַּיהוָהיאהדונהי אֱלֹהֶיךָ
ילה לַאֲמָתֶךָ כִּי־שְׁלֹמֹה בְנֵךְ יִמְלֹךְ אַחֲרָי וְהוּא יֵשֵׁב עַל־
כִּסְאִי׃ 18 וְעַתָּה הִנֵּה אֲדֹנִיָּה מָלָךְ וְעַתָּה אֲדֹנִי הַמֶּלֶךְ לֹא
יָדָעְתָּ׃ 19 וַיִּזְבַּח שׁוֹר אבגית"ץ, ושר, אהבת חנם וּמְרִיא־וְצֹאן מלוי אהיה דיודין ע"ה
לָרֹב וַיִּקְרָא עם ה' אותיות = ב"פ קס"א לְכָל יה - אדני ־בְּנֵי הַמֶּלֶךְ וּלְאֶבְיָתָר
הַכֹּהֵן מלה וּלְיֹאָב שַׂר אלהים דיודין - רבוע אלהים הַצָּבָא וְלִשְׁלֹמֹה
עַבְדְּךָ פוי לֹא קָרָא׃ 20 וְאַתָּה אֲדֹנִי הַמֶּלֶךְ עֵינֵי ריבוע מ"ה כָּל ילי
־יִשְׂרָאֵל עָלֶיךָ לְהַגִּיד לָהֶם מִי ילי יֵשֵׁב עַל־כִּסֵּא אֲדֹנִי־הַמֶּלֶךְ

23 And they told the king, "Nathan the prophet is here." So he went before the king and bowed with his face to the ground.

24 Nathan said, "Have you, my Lord the king, declared that Adonijah shall be king after you, and that he will sit on your throne?

25 Today he has gone down and sacrificed great numbers of cattle, fattened calves, and sheep. He has invited all the king's sons, the commanders of the army and Abiathar the priest. Right now they are eating and drinking with him and saying, 'Long live King Adonijah!'

26 But me your servant, and Zadok the priest, and Benaiah son of Jehoiada, and your servant Solomon he did not invite.

27 Is this something my Lord the king has done without letting his servants know who should sit on the throne of my Lord the king after him?"

28 Then King David said, "Call in Bathsheba." So she came into the king's presence and stood before him.

29 The king then took an oath: "As surely as the Lord lives, who has delivered me out of every trouble,

30 I will surely carry out today what I swore to you by the Lord, the God of Israel: Solomon your son shall be king after me, and he will sit on my throne in my place."

31 Then Bathsheba bowed low with her face to the ground and, kneeling before the king, said, "May my Lord King David live forever."

אַחֲרָיו׃ 21 וְהָיָה יהוה, יהה כִּשְׁכַב אֲדֹנִי־הַמֶּלֶךְ עִם־אֲבֹתָיו
וְהָיִיתִי אֲנִי אני וּבְנִי שְׁלֹמֹה חַטָּאִים׃ 22 וְהִנֵּה מ״ה יה עוֹדֶנָּה
מְדַבֶּרֶת ראה עִם־הַמֶּלֶךְ וְנָתָן הַנָּבִיא בָּא׃ 23 וַיַּגִּידוּ ייי לַמֶּלֶךְ
לֵאמֹר הִנֵּה מ״ה יה נָתָן הַנָּבִיא וַיָּבֹא לִפְנֵי הַמֶּלֶךְ וַיִּשְׁתַּחוּ לַמֶּלֶךְ
עַל־אַפָּיו אָרְצָה אלהים דההין ע״ה׃ 24 וַיֹּאמֶר נָתָן אֲדֹנִי הַמֶּלֶךְ אַתָּה
אָמַרְתָּ אֲדֹנִיָּהוּ יִמְלֹךְ אַחֲרָי וְהוּא יֵשֵׁב עַל־כִּסְאִי׃ 25 כִּי |
יָרַד הַיּוֹם נגד, זן, מזבח וַיִּזְבַּח שׁוֹר אבגיתצ, ושר, אהבת חנם וּמְרִיא־וְצֹאן
מלוי אהיה דיודין ע״ה לָרֹב וַיִּקְרָא עם ה׳ אותיות = ב״פ קס״א לְכָל יה ־ אדני ־בְּנֵי
הַמֶּלֶךְ וּלְשָׂרֵי הַצָּבָא וּלְאֶבְיָתָר הַכֹּהֵן מלה וְהִנָּם אֹכְלִים
וְשֹׁתִים לְפָנָיו וַיֹּאמְרוּ יְחִי הַמֶּלֶךְ אֲדֹנִיָּהוּ׃ 26 וְלִי אֲנִי אני ־עַבְדֶּךָ
פוי וּלְצָדֹק הַכֹּהֵן מלה וְלִבְנָיָהוּ בֶן־יְהוֹיָדָע וְלִשְׁלֹמֹה עַבְדְּךָ פוי
לֹא קָרָא׃ 27 אִם יוהך מֵאֵת אֲדֹנִי הַמֶּלֶךְ נִהְיָה הַדָּבָר ראה הַזֶּה
והו וְלֹא הוֹדַעְתָּ אֶת־עַבְדְּךָ פוי (כתיב: עבדיך) מִי ילי יֵשֵׁב עַל־
כִּסֵּא אֲדֹנִי־הַמֶּלֶךְ אַחֲרָיו׃ [ס] 28 וַיַּעַן הַמֶּלֶךְ דָּוִד וַיֹּאמֶר
קִרְאוּ־לִי לְבַת־שָׁבַע אלהים דיודין ־ ע״ב וַתָּבֹא לִפְנֵי הַמֶּלֶךְ וַתַּעֲמֹד
לִפְנֵי הַמֶּלֶךְ׃ 29 וַיִּשָּׁבַע הַמֶּלֶךְ וַיֹּאמַר חַי־יְהֹוָהאדניאהדונהי אֲשֶׁר־
פָּדָה אֶת־נַפְשִׁי מִכָּל ילי ־צָרָה אלהים דההין׃ 30 כִּי כַּאֲשֶׁר נִשְׁבַּעְתִּי
לְךָ בַּיהֹוָהאדניאהדונהי אֱלֹהֵי דמב, ילה יִשְׂרָאֵל לֵאמֹר כִּי־שְׁלֹמֹה בְנֵךְ
יִמְלֹךְ אַחֲרַי וְהוּא יֵשֵׁב עַל־כִּסְאִי תַּחְתָּי כִּי כֵּן אֶעֱשֶׂה הַיּוֹם
נגד, זן, מזבח הַזֶּה והו׃ 31 וַתִּקֹּד בַּת־שֶׁבַע אלהים דיודין ־ ע״ב אַפַּיִם אֶרֶץ
אלהים דאלפין וַתִּשְׁתַּחוּ לַמֶּלֶךְ וַתֹּאמֶר יְחִי אֲדֹנִי הַמֶּלֶךְ דָּוִד
לְעֹלָם ריבוע ס״ג ־ י׳ אותיות׃ [פ]

TOLDOT

THE LESSON OF TOLDOT
(Genesis 25:19-28:9)

The Book of Genesis includes the stories of the Creation, the Flood, the Separation, the lives of the patriarchs and matriarchs, and the selling of Joseph. It narrates the history of the people of Israel until the time they went down to Egypt. The *Zohar* says that every story in the Bible is a lesson on how to get closer to the Light of the Creator. These events may seem purely historical, but when examined on a very deep level, they teach people how to tap into the Universal Laws that govern all of humanity.

The true wisdom of the Book of Genesis is not concerned with specific precepts, such as what to do and what not to do, or what to eat and what not to eat. Rather, the Book of Genesis teaches us how to live in the deepest sense, which is the basis for all the teachings and lessons that we find in the rest of the Bible. From Abraham the Patriarch, we learn how to behave toward the people around us and how to make them feel welcome and safe. From Isaac the Patriarch, we learn how to use discernment and judgment as a tool for revealing the Light in any situation. And from Jacob, we learn the power of truth, as it is written: "Perform the truth to Jacob and the mercy to Abraham." *(Micah 7:20)*

Every event in the Bible brings us a lesson we can learn and use in our daily lives. Whether we learn from the actions of our forefathers or of any other people described in the Bible, all of us can find things in our lives similar to the events described there. When we look deeply into the meaning of these stories—not just seeing them as historical events that happened more than 3000 years ago—we will be able to live our lives as the Holy Bible teaches us.

The Matter of Esau and Jacob

Jacob and Esau were born to the same mother at the same time. Even so, they were fundamentally different people from the very moment of birth. Jacob was drawn to spirituality and Bible study, as it is written: "And Jacob was a simple man who sat in his tent." (*Genesis 25:27*) Esau, on the other hand, was pulled by his desires, as we read: "And Esau was a man who knew how to hunt and was a man of the field." Here the word "field" alludes to the level of *Malchut*, our physical world.

Every person contains elements of both Jacob and Esau, and inside each of us there wages a never-ending battle between these two sets of attributes. A *Midrash* says that during Rebecca's pregnancy, whenever she would pass the entrance to a place of learning, Jacob would push within her womb. Whenever she would pass a place of impurity, Esau would push inside her.

All throughout the nine months, there was an ongoing battle between the two boys: Who would be stronger and rule the world? Would it be Jacob and the powers of holiness, or Esau and the powers of impurity?

This battle still continues, and we are all taking part in it. The first precondition for victory is the recognition that this really is a battle. Without that understanding, we have no chance of overcoming our own darker side. We must always remember that the Opponent, the Negative Side, never rests, so we must constantly be alert and ready for an attack. There is a story about a rabbi who one day was awakened for prayers by his students. Since he was very tired, he told them, "I won't go today." But after a second, he reconsidered. "No, I will go! I am tired and want to sleep, but the Other Side never sleeps. If I sleep, I will have no chance against Satan."

The readings about Jacob and Esau give us the strength and Light to connect to the side of Jacob and to win the battle against the Negative Side. We can derive inspiration for this by following the example of Rachel, of whom it is written: "And she went to demand of God." Like her, whenever we encounter any problem in our spiritual work, we should go and "demand of God." We must ask for help from the Creator or from people who are closer to the Creator than we are.

This is why many people go to righteous individuals or to the graves of the sages and ancient kabbalists to receive guidance. Consulting with spiritually advanced individuals is the only way to be safe, to be certain we are doing the right thing. The average person does not have the ability to see things as they really are; only a righteous person who is close to the Creator can do that. Until we achieve a higher level of spiritual being, there are veils that keep us separated from the Light. By helping us to see, a righteous person or spiritual teacher literally helps us to live.

From Jacob and Esau, we can also learn to use both our positive and negative sides to do the Creator's work. It is written: "And you will love the Lord your God with all your heart." (Deuteronomy 6:5) The sages explain that this means: "with both your desires."

How is it possible to worship the Creator even with traits such as pride and laziness? Do these not come from the Negative Side? They do, but everything has two sides. Ego, for example, may seem to be a very negative thing, but a person without any self-esteem has no desire for achievement and will never put any effort into spiritual work.

Ego is negative when it makes us feel superior to others or when it causes us to act only so that others will appreciate us. But within us, our ego helps us to appreciate our own strength and to know that we can do great and amazing things. By far, the most important of these tasks is revealing the Light of the Creator.

In the verse: "And Rebecca said to Isaac, 'I am weary...,'" *(Genesis 27:46)* the letter *Kof* in the word *katzti* (weary, or disgusted) is a small letter. *Kof* is the only letter that extends below the baseline, symbolizing the effect of the Light that is given to the Negative Side. The presence of free will makes negativity inevitable in the world. The effects of this negativity come from the letter *Kof* because without energy from the Creator, nothing can exist.

Our negative traits give energy to the Negative Side. But, as explained earlier, when we use these traits to serve the Creator, we are preventing the Opponent from becoming even stronger. We acquire this strength from the small letter *Kof.* This is the strength of the Messiah, who provides the power that ensures that the Light of the Creator will go, not to the Opponent but only to the Positive Side.

Regarding the subject of the ego, it is written in the book Avnei Zikaron: "Once the Seer of Lublin (Rav Ya'akov Yitzchak of Lublin, 1745–1815) said joyfully that he saw by means of the Divine Spirit that the Redemption was very near. 'There has been an awakening because this is the time from Above,' he said. A short time after this, the Seer of Lublin began to weep and said that he had just seen through the Divine Spirit a voice coming out of the sky and calling everyone back. The time of Redemption had been pushed back because the people were fighting about which of them would rule over the other."

It is also written about the Seer of Lublin: "He was once very anxious for the Redemption to come that year, yet it did not happen. He said that ordinary people had repented completely, and if it were up to them, the Redemption would have come. But it did not come because of people whose position and pride prevented them from humbling themselves. They could not really repent."

From this, we learn the importance of working on our ego, although we should not erase it completely. We should simply be aware that despite any power we have in the material world, the power of the Creator is always infinitely greater. We should use our awareness of our physical strength to humble ourselves in the spiritual realm.

Regarding the prayer of Isaac

It is written: "And Isaac prayed in front of his wife." *(Genesis 25:21).* As we know, Rebecca did not have a womb and was unable to bear children, but because of Isaac's prayers, Jacob and Esau were born to her. Therefore, in the morning prayers on Shabbat, we say, "By the mouths of the upright, You shall be exalted. And by the lips of the righteous, You shall be blessed. And by the tongues of the pious, You shall be sanctified. And among the holy ones, You shall be lauded." Together, the first letters of these Aramaic words spell out the names of Isaac and Rebecca. Thus we are reminded to pray for others just as Isaac prayed for Rebecca.

It is also written: "The Creator answered him, and his wife Rebecca became pregnant." Why were the prayers of Isaac answered, rather than those of Rebecca? The Creator is teaching us that we should pray not only for our own needs, but also for the needs of others. If we do not pray for others, there is a judgment on us, and our desires will be checked even if our actions are worthy. But when we pray for others as well as for ourselves, the Creator sometimes gives us what we ask for, even if we are unworthy of it.

SYNOPSIS OF TOLDOT

In this section, the ultimate struggle between good and evil in the physical world is depicted for the first time. Jacob represents the force of good, and Esau the force of evil. This reading enables us to connect with the forces represented by Jacob while overcoming the forces of evil.

19 *And these are the generations of Isaac, the son of Abraham. Abraham became
the father of Isaac,* 20 *and Isaac was forty years old when he married Rebecca,
daughter of Bethuel the Syrian from Padanaram, the sister of Laban the
Syrian.*

21 *And Isaac prayed to the Lord on behalf of his wife, because she was barren. The
Lord answered his prayer, and his wife Rebecca became pregnant.*

22 *The children struggled together within her, and she said, "If it be so, why am I
thus?" So she went to inquire of the Lord.*

23 *And the Lord said to her, "Two nations are in your womb, and two manner of people
will be separated from within you; and one people will be stronger than the other
people, and the older will serve the younger."* 24 *When the time came for her to give
birth, there were twins in her womb.*

FROM THE RAV

"How can I fool my father?" Jacob asked. Not why should I fool my father? His question was how could he impersonate Esau, whose skin was hairy, and whose voice was deep.

Remember, the patriarchs are not just prophets. Not only are these people completely aware of what's going on, they are also chariots: They have complete control over the physical world. They are connected to the Upper World where there is no time, space, or motion. We are talking about people of that caliber and that consciousness, so why would Jacob ask this question?

The *Zohar* begins to provide us with a clear definition and explanation of what we are to draw from Jacob's question. The point is that you have to play the game right. And it is a game. We have been given the tools to play the Game of Life. If we don't make use of the tools, if we don't make use of the technology and system of Kabbalah, we cannot remove chaos from our lives.

People think that it was deception when Jacob took the blessing from Isaac. Deception is not what the Torah is talking about. Forget what the story appears to say. It's only a clue and a hint.

The important aspect and teaching of this biblical story is that we can go back in time. We do it all the time, with the *Ana Beko'ach*, with the "*Yud, Kaf, Shin.*" That's how Jacob became the first-born.

When we dip in the Mikveh, we meditate on the *Yud, Kaf, Shin*. What does this do? In the Mikveh we are fooling Satan. Satan is eating away at the healthy cells and multiplying at the same time. We are totally indebted to the *Zohar* for giving us this. The *Yud, Kaf, Shin* takes away the cell's nourishment, the Lightforce, thus making the cell appear to die. But it doesn't really die. Satan, however, is fooled and leaves because he has no reason to stay—Satan needs nourishment and can only receive this from something that contains energy, in this case, a living cell.

And when Satan is no longer there, the cell "becomes alive" again. We are making Satan believe that the cell is dead. That is deceiving. This deception is what the Torah is talking about and what is behind the story of Jacob "deceiving" Isaac.

FIRST READING - ABRAHAM - CHESED

19 וְאֵלֶּה תּוֹלְדֹת יִצְחָק ד"פ ב"ן בֶּן־אַבְרָהָם ח"פ אל, רמ"ח אַבְרָהָם
ח"פ אל, רמ"ח הוֹלִיד אֶת־יִצְחָק ד"פ ב"ן׃ 20 וַיְהִי יִצְחָק ד"פ ב"ן בֶּן־אַרְבָּעִים
שָׁנָה בְּקַחְתּוֹ אֶת־רִבְקָה בַּת־בְּתוּאֵל הָאֲרַמִּי מִפַּדַּן אֲרָם
אֲחוֹת לָבָן הָאֲרַמִּי לוֹ לְאִשָּׁה׃ 21 וַיֶּעְתַּר יִצְחָק ד"פ ב"ן לַיהֹוָהאדניאהדונהי
לְנֹכַח ג"פ יהוה אִשְׁתּוֹ ס"ת הוה כִּי עֲקָרָה הִוא וַיֵּעָתֶר לוֹ יְהֹוָהאדניאהדונהי
וַתַּהַר רִבְקָה אִשְׁתּוֹ׃ 22 וַיִּתְרֹצְצוּ הַבָּנִים בְּקִרְבָּהּ וַתֹּאמֶר אִם
יוהך ־כֵּן לָמָּה זֶּה אָנֹכִי איע וַתֵּלֶךְ לִדְרֹשׁ אֶת־יְהֹוָהאדניאהדונהי׃
23 וַיֹּאמֶר יְהֹוָהאדניאהדונהי לָהּ שְׁנֵי גוֹיִם (כתיב: גיים) בְּבִטְנֵךְ וּשְׁנֵי
לְאֻמִּים מִמֵּעַיִךְ יִפָּרֵדוּ וּלְאֹם מִלְאֹם יֶאֱמָץ וְרַב יצחק, ד"פ ב"ן יַעֲבֹד
צָעִיר׃ 24 וַיִּמְלְאוּ יָמֶיהָ לָלֶדֶת וְהִנֵּה תוֹמִם בְּבִטְנָהּ׃ 25 וַיֵּצֵא
הָרִאשׁוֹן אַדְמוֹנִי כֻּלּוֹ כְּאַדֶּרֶת שֵׂעָר וַיִּקְרְאוּ שְׁמוֹ מהש ע"ה עֵשָׂו׃
26 וְאַחֲרֵי־כֵן יָצָא אָחִיו וְיָדוֹ אֹחֶזֶת בַּעֲקֵב ב"פ מום עֵשָׂו

וַיֶּעְתַּר

Genesis 25:21 – Rebecca was born without a uterus, so she was unable to have children, but Isaac prayed that she would be able to conceive. It is important to note that Isaac could have had children with someone else. From his act of sharing—that is, his prayers for Rebecca—we see the power of praying for others, which can create miracles on their behalf.

וַיֹּאמֶר

Genesis 25:23 – Rebecca conceived twins: Jacob, who was completely positive, and Esau, who was entirely negative. During her pregnancy, Jacob would kick when Rebecca walked past a positive place where there was Light being revealed through acts of sharing, while Esau would kick near locations where acts of negativity were being manifested.

One of Rashi's explanations for this was that the children were already struggling for possession of both worlds. This was very confusing to Rebecca and made her think she was carrying only one child, who seemed unable to distinguish between positive and negative energies.

When people lack spiritual direction, they are never completely committed to any course of action or growth. In a way, this is the worst possible state of being. If a person is completely negative, at least the situation is clear and there is a potential for change.

25 The first came out red all over like a hairy garment; so they named him Esau.

26 And after that, his brother came out, with his hand grasping Esau's heel; and he was named Jacob. And Isaac was sixty years old when Rebecca gave birth to them.

27 And the boys grew, and Esau became a skillful hunter, a man of the field, and Jacob was a quiet man, staying among the tents.

28 And Isaac loved Esau because he ate of his venison, but Rebecca loved Jacob.

29 And Jacob was cooking soup when Esau came in from the field, famished.

30 And Esau said to Jacob, "Feed me, I pray you, with that red soup for I am famished; that is why he was also called Edom.

31 And Jacob replied, "Sell me this day your birthright."

32 And Esau said, "Look, I am about to die, what good is the birthright to me?"

33 And Jacob said, "Swear to me this day." And he swore an oath to him, and he sold his birthright to Jacob.

34 Then Jacob gave Esau some bread and some lentil soup. And he ate and drank, and then got up and left. Thus Esau despised his birthright.

26 1 And there was a famine in the land, besides the first famine of Abraham's time. And Isaac went to Abimelech, king of the Philistines in Gerar.

2 And the Lord appeared to Isaac and said, "Do not go down to Egypt; live in the land
which I tell you of. 3 Stay in this land for a while, and I will be with you and will bless

---

הַלְעִיטֵנִי

Genesis 25:30 – Esau came home and found Jacob making lentil soup while in mourning for his grandfather, Abraham. Both men were very tired—Jacob from making the soup and Esau because he had just fought and killed Nimrod.

> *"And Rebecca took the best clothes of her elder son, Esau." (Genesis 27:15)*

These are the garments Esau took from Nimrod. They are the precious garments from Adam, which came to the hands of Nimrod, who used them when he hunted, as it is written: "He was a mighty hunter before God." (Genesis 10:9) And Esau went into the field, where he fought with and killed Nimrod, removing the garments from him. This is the meaning of "...and Esau came in from the field, and he was faint." (Genesis 25:29) It has already been explained why it is here written:

וַיִּקְרָא עם ה' אותיות = ב"פ קס"א שְׁמוֹ מהש ע"ה יַעֲקֹב יאהדונהי - אידהנויה וְיִצְחָק
ד"פ ב"ן בֶּן־שִׁשִּׁים שָׁנָה בְּלֶדֶת אֹתָם׃ 27 וַיִּגְדְּלוּ יזל הַנְּעָרִים וַיְהִי
עֵשָׂו אִישׁ ע"ה קנ"א קס"א יֹדֵעַ צַיִד ב"פ ב"ן אִישׁ ע"ה קנ"א קס"א שָׂדֶה וְיַעֲקֹב
יאהדונהי - אידהנויה אִישׁ ע"ה קנ"א קס"א תָּם י"פ רבוע אהיה יֹשֵׁב אֹהָלִים׃
28 וַיֶּאֱהַב יִצְחָק ד"פ ב"ן אֶת־עֵשָׂו כִּי־צַיִד ב"פ ב"ן בְּפִיו וְרִבְקָה
אֹהֶבֶת אֶת־יַעֲקֹב יאהדונהי - אידהנויה׃ 29 וַיָּזֶד יַעֲקֹב יאהדונהי - אידהנויה
נָזִיד וַיָּבֹא עֵשָׂו מִן־הַשָּׂדֶה שדי וְהוּא עָיֵף׃ 30 וַיֹּאמֶר עֵשָׂו אֶל־
יַעֲקֹב יאהדונהי - אידהנויה הַלְעִיטֵנִי נָא מִן־הָאָדֹם מ"ה הָאָדֹם מ"ה הַזֶּה
והו כִּי עָיֵף אָנֹכִי איע עַל־כֵּן קָרָא־שְׁמוֹ מהש ע"ה אֱדוֹם׃ 31 וַיֹּאמֶר
יַעֲקֹב יאהדונהי - אידהנויה מִכְרָה כַיּוֹם נגד, זן, מזבח אֶת־בְּכֹרָתְךָ לִי׃
32 וַיֹּאמֶר עֵשָׂו הִנֵּה מ"ה יה אָנֹכִי איע הוֹלֵךְ מיה לָמוּת וְלָמָּה־זֶּה לִי
בְּכֹרָה׃ 33 וַיֹּאמֶר יַעֲקֹב יאהדונהי - אידהנויה הִשָּׁבְעָה לִּי כַּיּוֹם נגד, זן, מזבח
וַיִּשָּׁבַע לוֹ וַיִּמְכֹּר אֶת־בְּכֹרָתוֹ לְיַעֲקֹב יאהדונהי - אידהנויה׃ 34 וְיַעֲקֹב
יאהדונהי - אידהנויה נָתַן לְעֵשָׂו לֶחֶם ג"פ יהוה וּנְזִיד עֲדָשִׁים וַיֹּאכַל וַיֵּשְׁתְּ
וַיָּקָם וַיֵּלַךְ כלי וַיִּבֶז עֵשָׂו אֶת־הַבְּכֹרָה׃ [פ] 26 1 וַיְהִי רָעָב
רבוע אלהים רבוע יהוה בָּאָרֶץ אלהים דאלפין מִלְּבַד הָרָעָב רבוע אלהים רבוע יהוה
הָרִאשׁוֹן אֲשֶׁר הָיָה יהה בִּימֵי אַבְרָהָם וו"פ אל, רמ"ח וַיֵּלֶךְ כלי יִצְחָק ד"פ ב"ן אֶל־

"and he was faint," and elsewhere, "for my soul faints before the slayers." (Jeremiah 4:31) THESE ARE ANALOGOUS. THERE IT IS WRITTEN "FAINT" TO REFER TO KILLING. HERE, TOO, THERE IS KILLING, BECAUSE ESAU MURDERED NIMROD.

– The Zohar, Toldot 17:13

The sages say that Esau was exhausted because he had committed five crimes that day: He had violated a betrothed maiden, killed Nimrod, denied God, denied the Resurrection of the Dead, and spurned the birthright. (*Baba Basra 16b*)

When Esau asked Jacob for some soup, Jacob replied that he wanted Esau's first-born rights in exchange. Esau agreed, and Jacob gave him the soup. Everyone makes trade-offs in life, but we must take care lest we give up something very important to get something very small. Our immediate needs can seem so overwhelming at times that we lose perspective of the big picture—our long term goals, rights, and duties.

you. For to you and your descendants I will give all these lands and will confirm the oath I swore to Abraham, your father. [4] And I will make your seed multiply as the stars in the heaven, and will give to your seed all these countries, and in your seed all nations of the earth will be blessed, [5] because Abraham obeyed My voice and kept My charge, My commandments, My statutes, and My laws."

SECOND READING - ISAAC - GEVURAH

[6] And Isaac dwelt in Gerar. [7] And the men of the place asked him about his wife, and he said, "She is my sister," because he was afraid to say, "She is my wife." He thought, "Lest the men of the place kill me for Rebecca, because she is fair to look at."

[8] And it came to pass, when he had been there a long time, Abimelech, king of the Philistines, looked out of a window and saw Isaac caressing Rebecca, his wife.

[9] And Abimelech called Isaac and said, "See, for sure she is your wife: and why did you say, 'She is my sister'?" And Isaac said to him, "Because I said, lest I die for her."

[10] And Abimelech said, "What is this you have done to us? One of the men might well have lain with your wife, and you would have brought guilt upon us."

[11] And Abimelech charged all his people, saying: "He that touches this man or his wife shall surely be put to death."

[12] Then Isaac planted crops in that land and in the same year reaped a hundredfold, because the Lord blessed him.

וַיֵּרָא

Genesis 26:2 – Even though in earlier years, God had allowed Abraham and Jacob to go to Egypt, the Creator instructed Isaac not to go. This is because Isaac represents judgment. Only the land of Israel could contain the strength and intensity of the power of this judgment, and so Isaac had to stay in Israel; if he had left Israel, judgment would have been unleashed to reign unfettered in the universe. We, too, must be aware of the need to limit our judgment.

When we encounter people who hurt or anger us, we must use the tools of Kabbalah to compose ourselves so that our emotions are not allowed to run out of control.

אֲחֹותִי

Genesis 26:7 – Having settled in Gerar, Isaac, afraid he would be killed by others who desired his wife, told the townspeople that Rebecca was his sister. When Abimelech, the Philistine king, found this was untrue, he became very angry with Isaac for lying to him. But like his father, Abraham, before him, Isaac was not lying. This is because Rebecca was his soul mate, and therefore she embodied the *Shechina*, which Kabbalah describes as our "sister."

אֲבִימֶלֶךְ מֶלֶךְ־פְּלִשְׁתִּים י״פ אלהים גְּרָרָה׃ 2 וַיֵּרָא אֵלָיו יְהֹוָהאדניאהדונהי
וַיֹּאמֶר אַל־תֵּרֵד מִצְרָיְמָה מצר שְׁכֹן בָּאָרֶץ אלהים דאלפין אֲשֶׁר אֹמַר
אֵלֶיךָ אני׃ 3 גּוּר ד״פ ב״ן ע״ה בָּאָרֶץ אלהים דאלפין הַזֹּאת וְאֶהְיֶה עִמְּךָ נמם
וַאֲבָרְכֶךָּ כִּי־לְךָ וּלְזַרְעֲךָ אֶתֵּן אֶת־כָּל ילי ־הָאֲרָצֹת הָאֵל
לאה (אלד ע״ה) וַהֲקִמֹתִי אֶת־הַשְּׁבֻעָה אֲשֶׁר נִשְׁבַּעְתִּי לְאַבְרָהָם
וו״פ אל, רמ״ח אָבִיךָ׃ 4 וְהִרְבֵּיתִי אֶת־זַרְעֲךָ כְּכוֹכְבֵי הַשָּׁמַיִם
י״פ טל, י״פ כוזו וְנָתַתִּי לְזַרְעֲךָ אֵת כָּל ילי ־הָאֲרָצֹת הָאֵל לאה (אלד ע״ה)
וְהִתְבָּרְכוּ יהוה ע״ב ריבוע מ״ה בְזַרְעֲךָ כֹּל ילי גּוֹיֵי הָאָרֶץ אלהים דההין ע״ה׃
5 עֵקֶב ב״פ מום אֲשֶׁר־שָׁמַע אַבְרָהָם וו״פ אל, רמ״ח בְּקֹלִי וַיִּשְׁמֹר
מִשְׁמַרְתִּי מִצְוֺתַי פוי חֻקּוֹתַי וְתוֹרֹתָי׃

SECOND READING - ISAAC - GEVURAH

6 וַיֵּשֶׁב יִצְחָק ד״פ ב״ן בִּגְרָר׃ 7 וַיִּשְׁאֲלוּ אַנְשֵׁי הַמָּקוֹם יהוה ברבוע, ו״פ אל
לְאִשְׁתּוֹ וַיֹּאמֶר אֲחֹתִי הִוא כִּי יָרֵא לֵאמֹר אִשְׁתִּי פֶּן־יַהַרְגֻנִי
אַנְשֵׁי הַמָּקוֹם יהוה ברבוע, ו״פ אל עַל־רִבְקָה כִּי־טֹבַת מַרְאֶה הִוא׃
8 וַיְהִי אל כִּי אָרְכוּ־לוֹ שָׁם הַיָּמִים נלך וַיַּשְׁקֵף אֲבִימֶלֶךְ מֶלֶךְ
פְּלִשְׁתִּים י״פ אלהים בְּעַד הַחַלּוֹן מנד וַיַּרְא וְהִנֵּה מ״ה יה יִצְחָק ד״פ ב״ן
מְצַחֵק אֵת רִבְקָה אִשְׁתּוֹ׃ 9 וַיִּקְרָא עם ה׳ אותיות = ב״פ קס״א אֲבִימֶלֶךְ
לְיִצְחָק ד״פ ב״ן וַיֹּאמֶר אַךְ אהיה הִנֵּה מ״ה יה אִשְׁתְּךָ הִוא וְאֵיךְ אָמַרְתָּ
אֲחֹתִי הִוא וַיֹּאמֶר אֵלָיו יִצְחָק ד״פ ב״ן כִּי אָמַרְתִּי י״פ אדני ע״ה פֶּן־אָמוּת
עָלֶיהָ פהל׃ 10 וַיֹּאמֶר אֲבִימֶלֶךְ מַה מ״ה ־זֹּאת עָשִׂיתָ לָּנוּ אלהים, מום
כִּמְעַט שָׁכַב אַחַד אהבה, דאגה הָעָם אֶת־אִשְׁתֶּךָ וְהֵבֵאתָ עָלֵינוּ רבוע ס״ג
אָשָׁם׃ 11 וַיְצַו אֲבִימֶלֶךְ אֶת־כָּל ילי ־הָעָם לֵאמֹר הַנֹּגֵעַ

THIRD READING - JACOB - TIFERET

13 And the man became great, and went forward, and grew until he became very wealthy.

14 He possessed so many flocks and possessed so many herds and a large amount of servants, and the Philistines envied him.

15 For all the wells that his father's servants had dug in the time of his father Abraham, the Philistines stopped up, and filled them with earth.

16 And Abimelech said to Isaac, "Go from us; for you are mightier than us."

17 And Isaac departed from there and pitched his tent in the Valley of Gerar and settled there.

18 And Isaac reopened the wells that had been dug in the time of Abraham his father, for the Philistines had stopped up after Abraham died, and he gave them the same names by which his father had given them.

19 And Isaac's servants dug in the valley and discovered there a well of spring water.

20 And the herdsmen of Gerar quarreled with Isaac's herdsmen, saying, "The water is ours." And he named the well Esek, because they quarreled with him.

21 And they dug another well, but they quarreled over that one also; and he named it Sitnah.

22 And he moved on from there and dug another well, and no one quarreled over it, and he named it Rehoboth, saying, "For now the Lord has made room for us and we will be fruitful in the land."

הַבְּאֵרֹת

Genesis 26:15 – By digging wells, Isaac attempted to restore the power of water that was present before the Sin of Adam and the Flood. The Negative Side had tried to take that power away, as was evidenced by the actions both of the Philistines in filling up the wells and of the herdsmen of Gerar who quarreled over every new well that Isaac dug. God appeared to Isaac in a dream, assuring him that he was protected. Almost immediately afterward, Abimelech came to him seeking peace. No matter how many obstacles stand before us, no matter how vulnerable we feel, we will be protected and will succeed in our endeavors if we are connected to the Light of the Creator.

Isaac's determination to keep digging is mirrored in the determination with which we keep "digging" into ourselves, looking for the Light that is in each one of us.

וַיַּעְתֵּק

Genesis 26:22 – Once Isaac and Abimelech had made peace, Isaac's servants came to tell him they had found water. Isaac was then able to restore the power of water that had been present before the Sin of Adam and the Flood.

בָּאִ֥ישׁ ע״ה קנ״א קס״א הַזֶּ֛ה והו וּבְאִשְׁתּ֖וֹ מ֥וֹת יוּמָֽת׃ 12 וַיִּזְרַ֤ע יִצְחָק֙ ד״פ ב״ן
בָּאָ֣רֶץ אלהים דאלפין הַהִ֔וא וַיִּמְצָ֛א בַּשָּׁנָ֥ה הַהִ֖וא מֵאָ֣ה שְׁעָרִ֑ים כתר
וַֽיְבָרְכֵ֖הוּ יְהֹוָֽה אדני יאהדונהי׃

THIRD READING - JACOB - TIFERET

13 וַיִּגְדַּ֖ל יזל הָאִ֑ישׁ ז״פ אדם וַיֵּ֤לֶךְ כלי הָלוֹךְ֙ וְגָדֵ֔ל עַ֥ד כִּֽי־גָדַ֖ל מְאֹֽד מ״ה׃
14 וַֽיְהִי־ אל ל֤וֹ מִקְנֵה־צֹאן֙ מלוי אהיה דיודין ע״ה וּמִקְנֵ֣ה בָקָ֔ר וַעֲבֻדָּ֖ה רַבָּ֑ה
וַיְקַנְא֥וּ אֹת֖וֹ פְּלִשְׁתִּֽים י״פ אלהים׃ 15 וְכָל ילי ־הַבְּאֵרֹ֗ת אֲשֶׁ֤ר חָֽפְרוּ֙
עַבְדֵ֣י אָבִ֔יו בִּימֵ֖י אַבְרָהָ֣ם ח״פ אל, רמ״ח אָבִ֑יו סִתְּמ֣וּם פְּלִשְׁתִּ֔ים י״פ אלהים
וַיְמַלְא֖וּם עָפָֽר׃ 16 וַיֹּ֥אמֶר אֲבִימֶ֖לֶךְ אֶל־יִצְחָ֑ק ד״פ ב״ן לֵ֚ךְ מֵעִמָּ֔נוּ
ריבוע ס״ג כִּֽי־עָצַֽמְתָּ מִמֶּ֖נּוּ מְאֹֽד מ״ה׃ 17 וַיֵּ֥לֶךְ כלי מִשָּׁ֖ם יִצְחָ֑ק ד״פ ב״ן וַיִּ֥חַן
בְּנַֽחַל־גְּרָ֖ר וַיֵּ֥שֶׁב שָֽׁם׃ 18 וַיָּ֣שָׁב יִצְחָ֗ק ד״פ ב״ן וַיַּחְפֹּ֣ר ׀ אֶת־בְּאֵרֹ֣ת
הַמַּ֡יִם אֲשֶׁ֤ר חָֽפְרוּ֙ בִּימֵי֙ אַבְרָהָ֣ם ח״פ אל, רמ״ח אָבִ֔יו וַיְסַתְּמ֣וּם פְּלִשְׁתִּ֔ים
י״פ אלהים אַחֲרֵ֖י מ֣וֹת אַבְרָהָ֑ם ח״פ אל, רמ״ח וַיִּקְרָ֤א עם ה׳ אותיות = ב״פ קס״א לָהֶן֙
שֵׁמ֔וֹת כַּשֵּׁמֹ֕ת אֲשֶׁר־קָרָ֥א לָהֶ֖ן אָבִֽיו׃ 19 וַיַּחְפְּר֥וּ עַבְדֵֽי־יִצְחָ֖ק ד״פ ב״ן
בַּנָּ֑חַל וַיִּ֨מְצְאוּ־שָׁ֔ם בְּאֵ֖ר קנ״א + ב״ן מַ֥יִם חַיִּֽים בינה ע״ה׃ 20 וַיָּרִ֜יבוּ רֹעֵ֣י
גְרָ֗ר עִם־רֹעֵ֥י יִצְחָ֛ק ד״פ ב״ן לֵאמֹ֖ר לָ֣נוּ אלהים, מום הַמָּ֑יִם ר״ת ללה, אדני וַיִּקְרָ֤א
עם ה׳ אותיות = ב״פ קס״א שֵֽׁם יהוה שדי ־הַבְּאֵר֙ קנ״א + ב״ן עֵ֔שֶׂק כִּ֥י הִֽתְעַשְּׂק֖וּ עִמּֽוֹ׃
21 וַֽיַּחְפְּרוּ֙ בְּאֵ֣ר קנ״א + ב״ן אַחֶ֔רֶת וַיָּרִ֖יבוּ גַּם יגל ־עָלֶ֑יהָ פהל וַיִּקְרָ֥א
עם ה׳ אותיות = ב״פ קס״א שְׁמָ֖הּ שִׂטְנָֽה ע״ה אלהים דיודין + אדני׃ 22 וַיַּעְתֵּ֣ק מִשָּׁ֗ם
וַיַּחְפֹּר֙ בְּאֵ֣ר קנ״א + ב״ן אַחֶ֔רֶת וְלֹ֥א רָב֖וּ עָלֶ֑יהָ וַיִּקְרָ֤א עם ה׳ אותיות = ב״פ קס״א
שְׁמָהּ֙ רְחֹב֔וֹת קס״א קס״א קנ״א קמ״ג וַיֹּ֗אמֶר כִּֽי־עַתָּ֞ה הִרְחִ֧יב יְהֹוָ֛ה אדני יאהדונהי
לָ֖נוּ אלהים, מום וּפָרִ֥ינוּ בָאָֽרֶץ אלהים דאלפין׃

FOURTH READING - MOSES - NETZACH

23 And he went up from there to Beersheba.

24 And the Lord appeared to him that night and said, "I am the God of Abraham, your father. Do not be afraid, for I am with you; and I will bless you and will multiply your seed for My servant Abraham's sake."

25 And he built an altar there and called upon the name of the Lord, and pitched his tent there, and there Isaac's servants dug a well.

26 Then Abimelech came to him from Gerar, with Ahuzzath, one of his friends, and Phicol, the chief captain of his army.

27 And Isaac asked them, "Why have you come to me, since you hate me and have sent me away from you?"

28 And they said, "We saw clearly that the Lord was with you; and we said, 'Let there
now be an oath between us—between us and you—and let's make a covenant with
you, 29 that you will do us no harm, as we have not harmed you and as we have done
nothing but good to you, and have sent you away in peace. You are now the blessed
of the Lord."

FIFTH READING - AARON - HOD

30 And he made them a feast, and they ate and drank.

31 And they rose up early in the morning and swore an oath one to each other, and Isaac sent them away, and they departed from him in peace.

32 And it came to pass that same day that Isaac's servants came and told him about the well they had dug. And they said to him, "We have found water!"

33 And he called it Shebah, and the name of the city is Beersheba till this day.

FOURTH READING - MOSES - NETZACH

23 וַיַּעַל מִשָּׁם בְּאֵר קנ"א - ב"ן שָׁבַע אלהים דיודין - ע"ב׃ 24 וַיֵּרָא אֵלָיו
יְהֹוָהאדניאהדונהי בַּלַּיְלָה מלה הַהוּא וַיֹּאמֶר אָנֹכִי איע אֱלֹהֵי דמב, ילה
אַבְרָהָם ח"פ אל, רמ"ח אָבִיךָ אַל־תִּירָא כִּי־אִתְּךָ אָנֹכִי איע וּבֵרַכְתִּיךָ
וְהִרְבֵּיתִי אֶת־זַרְעֲךָ בַּעֲבוּר אַבְרָהָם ח"פ אל, רמ"ח עַבְדִּי׃ 25 וַיִּבֶן
שָׁם מִזְבֵּחַ זן, נגד וַיִּקְרָא עם ה' אותיות = ב"פ קס"א בְּשֵׁם שדי יהוה יְהֹוָהאדניאהדונהי
וַיֶּט־שָׁם אָהֳלוֹ וַיִּכְרוּ־שָׁם עַבְדֵי־יִצְחָק ד"פ ב"ן בְּאֵר קנ"א - ב"ן׃
26 וַאֲבִימֶלֶךְ הָלַךְ מיה אֵלָיו מִגְּרָר וַאֲחֻזַּת מֵרֵעֵהוּ וּפִיכֹל שַׂר
אלהים דיודין ורבוע אלהים ־צְבָאוֹ׃ 27 וַיֹּאמֶר אֲלֵהֶם יִצְחָק ד"פ ב"ן מַדּוּעַ
בָּאתֶם אֵלָי וְאַתֶּם שְׂנֵאתֶם אֹתִי וַתְּשַׁלְּחוּנִי מֵאִתְּכֶם׃ 28 וַיֹּאמְרוּ
רָאוֹ רָאִינוּ כִּי־הָיָה יהה יְהֹוָהאדניאהדונהי | עִמָּךְ נמם וַנֹּאמֶר תְּהִי נָא
אָלָה בֵּינוֹתֵינוּ בֵּינֵינוּ וּבֵינֶךָ וְנִכְרְתָה בְרִית עִמָּךְ נמם׃ 29 אִם יוהך
־תַּעֲשֵׂה עִמָּנוּ ריבוע ס"ג רָעָה רהע כַּאֲשֶׁר לֹא נְגַעֲנוּךָ וְכַאֲשֶׁר
עָשִׂינוּ עִמְּךָ נמם רַק־טוֹב והו וַנְּשַׁלֵּחֲךָ בְּשָׁלוֹם אַתָּה עַתָּה בְּרוּךְ
יהוה ע"ב רבוע מ"ה יְהֹוָהאדניאהדונהי׃

FIFTH READING - AARON - HOD

30 וַיַּעַשׂ לָהֶם מִשְׁתֶּה וַיֹּאכְלוּ וַיִּשְׁתּוּ׃ 31 וַיַּשְׁכִּימוּ בַבֹּקֶר
וַיִּשָּׁבְעוּ אִישׁ ע"ה קנ"א קס"א לְאָחִיו וַיְשַׁלְּחֵם יִצְחָק ד"פ ב"ן וַיֵּלְכוּ מֵאִתּוֹ
בְּשָׁלוֹם׃ 32 וַיְהִי אל | בַּיּוֹם נגד, זן, מזבח הַהוּא וַיָּבֹאוּ עַבְדֵי יִצְחָק
ד"פ ב"ן וַיַּגִּדוּ לוֹ עַל־אֹדוֹת הַבְּאֵר קנ"א - ב"ן אֲשֶׁר חָפָרוּ וַיֹּאמְרוּ לוֹ
מָצָאנוּ מָיִם׃ 33 וַיִּקְרָא עם ה' אותיות = ב"פ קס"א אֹתָהּ שִׁבְעָה עַל־כֵּן

34 And Esau was forty years old when he took to wife Judith, the daughter of Beeri the
Hittite, and Basemath, the daughter of Elon the Hittite, 35 which were a source of grief
to Isaac and Rebecca.

27 1 And it came to pass that when Isaac was old and his eyes dim so that he could
not see, he called Esau, his older son, and said to him, "My son." And he said to him,
"Behold, here I am."

2 And he said, "See, I am now old, and don't know the day of my death.

3 Now then, get, I pray you, your weapons, your quiver and your bow, and go out to
the field and hunt me some venison; 4 and make me savory meat, just as I love; and
bring it to me so that I may eat and that my soul may bless you before I die."

5 And Rebecca heard when Isaac spoke to his son Esau. And Esau went to the field
to hunt for venison and bring it back.

6 And Rebecca said to her son Jacob, "Look, I heard your father say to Esau, your
brother, 7 'Bring me venison and make me savory meat that I may eat, and bless you
before the Lord, before my death.'

8 Now, therefore, my son, obey my voice and do what I command you: 9 Go now to
the flock and fetch me from there two choice kid goats, and I will make from them
savory meat for your father, just the way he loves it.

10 And you will take it to your father so that he may eat, and that he may bless you
before his death."

11 And Jacob said to Rebecca his mother, "But Esau, my brother is a hairy man, and
I am a man with smooth skin.

12 What if my father will touch me and I would appear to be deceiving him? I will bring

---

בֶּן־אַרְבָּעִים

Genesis 26:34 – Esau copied his father by marrying at the age of forty and by taking two wives. Indeed, Esau copied Isaac in many other respects as well. But Esau was merely mimicking Isaac without being able to achieve the same level of consciousness as his father. When we truly want to grow, we must go beyond external elements and trappings. We have to do the inner spiritual work to reach the next level.

כִּי־זָקֵן יִצְחָק

Genesis 27:1 – Isaac had a blessing to give to one of his sons, and he chose to give it to Esau. This was because Isaac embodied the energy of judgment, which he also recognized in Esau. We should not judge Isaac's choice of Esau, however, because it is human nature to share with those whose characteristics seem most like our own.

שֵׁם יהוה שדי ־הָעִיר סנדלפון, ערי, סנדלפו"ן בְּאֵר קנ"א - ב"ן שֶׁבַע אלהים דיודין - ע"ב
עַד הַיּוֹם נגד, זן, מזבח הַזֶּה והו: [ס] 34 וַיְהִי אל עֵשָׂו בֶּן־אַרְבָּעִים שָׁנָה
וַיִּקַּח ועם אִשָּׁה אֶת־יְהוּדִית בַּת־בְּאֵרִי הַחִתִּי וְאֶת־בָּשְׂמַת בַּת־
אֵילֹן הַחִתִּי: 35 וַתִּהְיֶיןָ מֹרַת רוּחַ מלוי אלהים דיודין לְיִצְחָק ד"פ ב"ן
וּלְרִבְקָה: [ס] 27 1 וַיְהִי אל כִּי־זָקֵן יִצְחָק ד"פ ב"ן וַתִּכְהֶיןָ
עֵינָיו ריבוע מ"ה מֵרְאֹת וַיִּקְרָא עם ה' אותיות = ב"פ קס"א אֶת־עֵשָׂו | בְּנוֹ
הַגָּדֹל להח, מבה, יזל, אום וַיֹּאמֶר אֵלָיו בְּנִי וַיֹּאמֶר אֵלָיו הִנֵּנִי: 2 וַיֹּאמֶר
הִנֵּה מ"ה יה ־נָא זָקַנְתִּי לֹא יָדַעְתִּי יוֹם נגד, זן, מזבח מוֹתִי: 3 וְעַתָּה
שָׂא־נָא כֵלֶיךָ כלי תֶּלְיְךָ וְקַשְׁתֶּךָ וְצֵא הַשָּׂדֶה שדי וְצוּדָה לִּי צָיִד
(כתיב: צידה): 4 וַעֲשֵׂה־לִי מַטְעַמִּים כַּאֲשֶׁר אָהַבְתִּי וְהָבִיאָה לִּי
וְאֹכֵלָה בַּעֲבוּר תְּבָרֶכְךָ נַפְשִׁי בְּטֶרֶם רמ"ח ע"ה אָמוּת:
5 וְרִבְקָה שֹׁמַעַת בְּדַבֵּר ראה יִצְחָק ד"פ ב"ן אֶל־עֵשָׂו בְּנוֹ וַיֵּלֶךְ כלי
עֵשָׂו הַשָּׂדֶה לָצוּד צַיִד ב"פ ב"ן לְהָבִיא: 6 וְרִבְקָה אָמְרָה אֶל־יַעֲקֹב
יאהדונהי - אידהנויה בְּנָהּ לֵאמֹר הִנֵּה מ"ה יה שָׁמַעְתִּי אֶת־אָבִיךָ מְדַבֵּר
ראה אֶל־עֵשָׂו אָחִיךָ לֵאמֹר: 7 הָבִיאָה לִּי צַיִד ב"פ ב"ן וַעֲשֵׂה־לִי

וְרִבְקָה שֹׁמַעַת

Genesis 27:5 – When Rebecca heard of Isaac's intention, she told Jacob to bring her some meat so that she could prepare a meal for him to give to Isaac. She was planning that Isaac give his blessing to Jacob rather than Esau, but Jacob feared that he would be cursed rather than blessed if his father were to discover the deception. Rebecca reassured Jacob by saying, "Your curse will be upon me." *(Genesis 27:13)* The meaning of this stems from the fact that Rebecca was the reincarnation of Eve. As Eve, her actions had brought a curse upon Adam and all mankind, but later, as Rebecca, she was able to complete the *tikkun* (correction) of Eve by helping Jacob to receive the blessing and to restore the Light that she (as Eve) had taken from the world. About the verse: "Let the curse fall on me, my son," the Ari wrote:

Rebecca is an incarnation of Eve, because of whom the man, who is Jacob, was cursed. Jacob's beauty was like Adam's beauty. Now they had to correct this curse by hearing Rebecca for good, somewhat like Adam had heard Eve, but at that time [of the first sin] in a bad way, as written: "Because you have hearkened to the voice of your wife." (Genesis 3:17) This is the meaning of "only obey (lit. 'hear') my voice," (Genesis 27:13) the sense of which is that now he heard for good, and so it follows that earlier it had been for evil.

– The Writings of Rav Isaac Luria

a curse upon myself and not a blessing."

13 And his mother said to him, "Let the curse fall on me, my son. Just obey my voice
and go fetch them for me."

14 And he went and fetched, and brought them to his mother, and his mother made
savory meat, just the way his father loved it.

15 And Rebecca took the best clothes of her older son, Esau, which were in her house,
and put them on Jacob, her younger son; 16 and she put the skins of kid goats over
his hands and upon the smooth part of his neck; 17 and she gave the savory meat and
bread which she had prepared into the hand of her son Jacob.

18 And he came to his father and said, "My father." And he said, "Here I am. Who are
you, my son?"

19 And Jacob said to his father, "I am Esau, your firstborn. I have done as you have
told me. I pray you, sit and eat of my venison that your soul may bless me."

20 And Isaac said to his son, "How is it that you have found it so quickly, my son?"
And he said, "The Lord your God brought it to me."

וַתִּקַּח

Genesis 27:15 – Rebecca dressed Jacob in Esau's clothing, which was also the clothing of Adam. Earlier on the same day that Esau asked Jacob for the lentil soup, Esau had killed Nimrod to obtain this clothing, which had the power to make animals bow down to anyone wearing it. This unique clothing is what made hunting so easy for Adam. Today, although we do not have the clothing that Adam wore, by hearing this reading, we can become clothed in spiritual power that can protect us and help us succeed in our endeavors.

הַקֹּל קוֹל יַעֲקֹב

Genesis 27:22 – Isaac, who was now blind, touched Jacob and said, "The voice is the voice of Jacob but the hands are the hands of Esau." At the same moment, Isaac caught the scent of the Garden of Eden on Jacob's clothes; that scent had entered the tent with Jacob because he was the reincarnation of Adam. Isaac then blessed Jacob. The *Zohar* says:

> *Esau hid these garments with Rebecca and wore them when he went hunting. On the day WHEN ISAAC SENT FOR HIM TO RECEIVE THE BLESSINGS, he did not take them to the field and was therefore late. When Esau wore them, they put forth no scent at all, but when Jacob wore them, the lost object was restored AS THEY RETURNED TO THE ASPECT OF ADAM. For the beauty of Jacob was the beauty of Adam; [the garments] therefore returned to their condition and emitted fragrance.*
>
> – *The Zohar, Toldot 17:132*

We cannot receive this blessing ourselves until our own inner transformation takes place because in our own blindness, we are incapable of seeing spiritual truth. Our blessings come as a result of actions that we have done ourselves in this lifetime or another—actions that have opened our spiritual vision.

מַטְעַמִּים וְאֹכֵלָה וַאֲבָרֶכְכָה לִפְנֵי יְהֹוָה(אדני)יאהדונהי לִפְנֵי מוֹתִי׃
8 וְעַתָּה בְנִי שְׁמַע בְּקֹלִי לַאֲשֶׁר אֲנִי אני מְצַוָּה פוי אֹתָךְ׃ 9 לֶךְ־
נָא אֶל־הַצֹּאן מלוי אהיה דיודין ע״ה וְקַח־לִי מִשָּׁם שְׁנֵי גְּדָיֵי והו עִזִּים
טֹבִים וְאֶעֱשֶׂה אֹתָם מַטְעַמִּים לְאָבִיךָ כַּאֲשֶׁר אָהֵב׃ 10 וְהֵבֵאתָ
לְאָבִיךָ וְאָכָל בַּעֲבֻר אֲשֶׁר יְבָרֶכְךָ לִפְנֵי מוֹתוֹ׃ 11 וַיֹּאמֶר יַעֲקֹב
יאהדונהי - אידהנויה אֶל־רִבְקָה אִמּוֹ הֵן עֵשָׂו אָחִי אִישׁ ע״ה קנ״א קס״א שָׂעִר
וְאָנֹכִי איע אִישׁ ע״ה קנ״א קס״א חָלָק יהוה אהיה יהוה אדני׃ 12 אוּלַי אום יְמֻשֵּׁנִי
אָבִי וְהָיִיתִי בְעֵינָיו ריבוע מ״ה כִּמְתַעְתֵּעַ וְהֵבֵאתִי עָלַי קְלָלָה וְלֹא
בְרָכָה׃ 13 וַתֹּאמֶר לוֹ אִמּוֹ עָלַי קִלְלָתְךָ בְּנִי ר״ת ב״פ אלהים אַךְ אהיה
שְׁמַע בְּקֹלִי וְלֵךְ קַח־לִי׃ 14 וַיֵּלֶךְ כלי וַיִּקַּח חעם וַיָּבֵא לְאִמּוֹ
וַתַּעַשׂ אִמּוֹ מַטְעַמִּים כַּאֲשֶׁר אָהֵב אָבִיו׃ 15 וַתִּקַּח רִבְקָה
אֶת־בִּגְדֵי עֵשָׂו בְּנָהּ הַגָּדֹל להח, מבה, יזל, אום הַחֲמֻדֹת אֲשֶׁר אִתָּהּ
בַּבָּיִת ב״פ ראה וַתַּלְבֵּשׁ אֶת־יַעֲקֹב יאהדונהי - אידהנויה בְּנָהּ הַקָּטָן׃ 16 וְאֵת
עֹרֹת גְּדָיֵי והו הָעִזִּים הִלְבִּישָׁה עַל־יָדָיו וְעַל חֶלְקַת צַוָּארָיו׃
17 וַתִּתֵּן ב״פ כהת אֶת־הַמַּטְעַמִּים וְאֶת־הַלֶּחֶם ג״פ יהוה אֲשֶׁר עָשָׂתָה
בְּיַד יַעֲקֹב יאהדונהי - אידהנויה בְּנָהּ׃ 18 וַיָּבֹא אֶל־אָבִיו וַיֹּאמֶר אָבִי
וַיֹּאמֶר הִנֶּנִּי מִי ילי אַתָּה בְּנִי׃ 19 וַיֹּאמֶר יַעֲקֹב יאהדונהי - אידהנויה
אֶל־אָבִיו אָנֹכִי איע עֵשָׂו בְּכֹרֶךָ עָשִׂיתִי כַּאֲשֶׁר דִּבַּרְתָּ ראה אֵלָי
קוּם־נָא שְׁבָה וְאָכְלָה מִצֵּידִי בַּעֲבוּר תְּבָרְכַנִּי נַפְשֶׁךָ׃
20 וַיֹּאמֶר יִצְחָק ד״פ ב״ן אֶל־בְּנוֹ מַה מ״ה ־זֶּה מִהַרְתָּ לִמְצֹא בְּנִי
וַיֹּאמֶר כִּי הִקְרָה יְהֹוָה(אדני)יאהדונהי אֱלֹהֶיךָ ילה לְפָנָי׃ 21 וַיֹּאמֶר
יִצְחָק ד״פ ב״ן אֶל־יַעֲקֹב יאהדונהי - אידהנויה גְּשָׁה־נָּא וַאֲמֻשְׁךָ בְּנִי
הַאַתָּה זֶה בְּנִי עֵשָׂו אִם יוהך ־לֹא׃ 22 וַיִּגַּשׁ יַעֲקֹב יאהדונהי - אידהנויה
אֶל־יִצְחָק ד״פ ב״ן אָבִיו וַיְמֻשֵּׁהוּ וַיֹּאמֶר הַקֹּל קוֹל ע״ב ס״ג ע״ה יַעֲקֹב

[21] *And Isaac said to Jacob, "Come near, I pray you, that I may feel you, my son, to know whether you really are my son Esau or not."*

[22] *And Jacob went near to Isaac, his father, and he felt him and said, "The voice is the voice of Jacob, but the hands are the hands of Esau."*

[23] *And he did not recognize him, because his hands were hairy like those of his brother Esau's; so he blessed him.* [24] *And he said, "Are you really my son Esau?" And he said, "I am."* [25] *And he said, "Bring it near to me and I will eat my son's venison, that my soul may bless you." And he brought it near to him and he ate; and he brought him wine and he drank.* [26] *And his father Isaac said to him, "Come near now, and kiss me, my son."* [27] *And he came near and kissed him, and he smelled the smell of his clothes, and blessed him and said, "See, the smell of my son is the smell of a field which the Lord has blessed:*

SIXTH READING - JOSEPH - YESOD

[28] *Therefore God give you of the dew of heaven, and the fatness of the earth, and plenty of grain and wine;* [29] *let people serve you and nations bow down to you. Be lord over your brethren, and let your mother's sons bow down to you: May those who curse you be cursed and those who bless you be blessed."* [30] *And it came to pass as soon as Isaac finished blessing Jacob and Jacob had scarcely left the presence of Isaac,*

Genesis 27:30 – After Jacob departed, Esau went in to see his father. The *Zohar* says that Isaac trembled when his son entered because Esau carried with him the scent of Hell.

> *"...and Isaac trembled (lit. 'trembled very great trembling')." HE ASKS, "What is the meaning of the word 'great' as used in the scripture?" AND HE ANSWERS, "It is written 'great' here and elsewhere, as in 'and this great fire.' (Deuteronomy 18:16) IN BOTH VERSES, IT REFERS TO A GREAT FIRE, MEANING that Gehenom (Hell) entered with him.*
>
> *– The Zohar, Toldot 19:175*

Isaac's high level of discernment was available to help him sense the spiritual attributes of his sons. From this, we also learn that any given situation can be Heaven for one person and Hell for another: Everything depends on our consciousness, which is more powerful than any external circumstances.

Genesis 27:33 – After he discovered how his father had been duped, Esau pleaded with Isaac to at least give him some kind of blessing. The true blessing had already been given to Jacob, but Isaac did give Esau a lesser form. This incident teaches us the danger of being content with less; in our spiritual work, we should always do the maximum we can possibly manage and push ourselves to go the extra mile.

יאהדונהי ÷ אידהנויה וְהַיָּדַיִם יְדֵי עֵשָׂו׃ 23 וְלֹא הִכִּירוֹ כִּי־הָיוּ יָדָיו
כִּידֵי עֵשָׂו אָחִיו שְׂעִרֹת וַיְבָרְכֵהוּ׃ 24 וַיֹּאמֶר אַתָּה זֶה בְּנִי
עֵשָׂו וַיֹּאמֶר אָנִי אני׃ 25 וַיֹּאמֶר הַגִּשָׁה לִּי וְאֹכְלָה מִצֵּיד ב״פ ב״ן
בְּנִי לְמַעַן תְּבָרֶכְךָ נַפְשִׁי וַיַּגֶּשׁ־לוֹ וַיֹּאכַל וַיָּבֵא לוֹ יַיִן מיכ, י״פ האא
וַיֵּשְׁתְּ׃ 26 וַיֹּאמֶר אֵלָיו יִצְחָק ד״פ ב״ן אָבִיו גְּשָׁה־נָּא וּשְׁקָה־לִּי
בְּנִי׃ 27 וַיִּגַּשׁ וַיִּשַּׁק־לוֹ וַיָּרַח אֶת־רֵיחַ בְּגָדָיו וַיְבָרְכֵהוּ וַיֹּאמֶר
רְאֵה ראה רֵיחַ בְּנִי כְּרֵיחַ שָׂדֶה אֲשֶׁר בֵּרֲכוֹ יהוה ע״ב ריבוע מ״ה
יְהֹוָהאדני יאהדונהי ר״ת אבי׃

SIXTH READING - JOSEPH - YESOD

28 וְיִתֶּן י״פ מלוי ע״ב ־לְךָ הָאֱלֹהִים ילה, מום מִטַּל כוזו הַשָּׁמַיִם י״פ טל, י״פ כוזו
וּמִשְׁמַנֵּי הָאָרֶץ אלהים דההין ע״ה וְרֹב יצחק, ד״פ ב״ן דָּגָן וְתִירֹשׁ׃ 29 יַעַבְדוּךָ
עַמִּים וְיִשְׁתַּחֲוֻ (כתיב: וישתחוו) לְךָ לְאֻמִּים הֱוֵה גְבִיר לְאַחֶיךָ
וְיִשְׁתַּחֲווּ לְךָ בְּנֵי אִמֶּךָ אֹרְרֶיךָ אָרוּר וּמְבָרְכֶיךָ בָּרוּךְ
יהוה ע״ב רבוע מ״ה׃ 30 וַיְהִי אל כַּאֲשֶׁר כִּלָּה יִצְחָק ד״פ ב״ן לְבָרֵךְ אֶת־
יַעֲקֹב יאהדונהי ÷ אידהנויה וַיְהִי אל אַךְ אהיה יָצֹא יָצָא יַעֲקֹב יאהדונהי ÷ אידהנויה
מֵאֵת פְּנֵי חכמה ÷ בינה יִצְחָק ד״פ ב״ן אָבִיו וְעֵשָׂו אָחִיו בָּא מִצֵּידוֹ׃
31 וַיַּעַשׂ גַּם יגל ־הוּא מַטְעַמִּים וַיָּבֵא לְאָבִיו וַיֹּאמֶר לְאָבִיו יָקֻם
אָבִי וְיֹאכַל מִצֵּיד ב״פ ב״ן בְּנוֹ בַּעֲבֻר תְּבָרְכַנִּי נַפְשֶׁךָ׃ 32 וַיֹּאמֶר
לוֹ יִצְחָק ד״פ ב״ן אָבִיו מִי ילי ־אָתָּה וַיֹּאמֶר אֲנִי אני בִּנְךָ בְכֹרְךָ
עֵשָׂו׃ 33 וַיֶּחֱרַד יִצְחָק ד״פ ב״ן חֲרָדָה גְּדֹלָה להח, מבה, יזל, אום עַד־מְאֹד
מ״ה וַיֹּאמֶר מִי ילי ־אֵפוֹא הוּא הַצָּד־צַיִד ב״פ ב״ן וַיָּבֵא לִי וָאֹכַל
מִכֹּל ילי בְּטֶרֶם רמ״ח תָּבוֹא וָאֲבָרְכֵהוּ גַּם יגל ־בָּרוּךְ יהוה ע״ב רבוע מ״ה

*his father, that Esau, his brother, came in from his hunting. 31 And he also had made
savory meat, and brought it to his father, and said to father, "Let my father arise and
eat of his son's venison, that your soul may bless me." 32 And Isaac, his father said to
him, "Who are you?" And he said, "I am your son, your firstborn, Esau." 33 And Isaac
trembled violently and said, "Who and where is he that took venison and brought it
to me, and I have eaten it all before you came and have blessed him? Yes, and he will
be blessed."*

*34 When Esau heard his father's words, he burst out with a loud and bitter cry and
said to his father, "Bless me also, O my father" 35 And he said, "Your brother came
deceitfully and took away your blessing."*

36 And he said, "Isn't he rightly named Jacob? He has deceived me these two times: He took away my birthright, and now he has taken away my blessing!" And he said, "Have you not reserved any blessing for me?"

37 And Isaac answered and said to Esau, "See, I have made him lord over you and have made all his brethren his servants, and I have sustained him with grain and wine. So what can I possibly do for you now, my son?"

38 And Esau said to his father, "Do you have only one blessing, my father? Bless me too, O my father." And Esau raised his voice and wept.

39 And Isaac, his father, answered him, "Behold, your dwelling will be away from the earth's richness, away from the dew of heaven above.

40 You will live by the sword and you will serve your brother. But when you grow restless, you will throw his yoke from off your neck."

41 And Esau hated Jacob because of the blessing his father had given him. And Esau said to himself, "The days of mourning for my father are near; then I will kill my brother Jacob."

42 And these words of Esau her oldest son, were told to Rebecca, and she sent for her younger son Jacob and said to him, "Behold, your brother Esau, as touching you, is consoling himself with the thought of killing you.

43 Now then, my son, obey my voice: Arise and flee to my brother Laban in Haran.

וְאַהַרְגָה אֶת־יַעֲקֹב

Genesis 27:41 – Esau wanted to kill his brother because Jacob had stolen his blessing, so Rebecca told Jacob to run away to her family.

The real spiritual reason for Jacob's departure, however, is that he was required to go through a cleansing process, a *tikkun*, to merit his eventual procreation of the Twelve Tribes. The actions he would take affected and continue to affect the future of all humanity forever.

יִהְיֶה ייי: 34 כִּשְׁמֹעַ עֵשָׂו אֶת־דִּבְרֵי ראה אָבִיו וַיִּצְעַק צְעָקָה
גְּדֹלָה להח, מבה, יזל, אום וּמָרָה עַד־מְאֹד מ"ה וַיֹּאמֶר לְאָבִיו בָּרְכֵנִי
גַם יג"ל ־אָנִי אני אָבִי: 35 וַיֹּאמֶר בָּא אָחִיךָ בְּמִרְמָה וַיִּקַּח וזעם
בִּרְכָתֶךָ: 36 וַיֹּאמֶר הֲכִי קָרָא שְׁמוֹ מהש ע"ה יַעֲקֹב יאהדונהי - אידהנויה
וַיַּעְקְבֵנִי זֶה פַעֲמַיִם אֶת־בְּכֹרָתִי לָקָח וְהִנֵּה מ"ה יה עַתָּה לָקַח
בִּרְכָתִי וַיֹּאמַר הֲלֹא־אָצַלְתָּ לִּי בְּרָכָה: 37 וַיַּעַן יִצְחָק ד"פ ב"ן
וַיֹּאמֶר לְעֵשָׂו הֵן גְּבִיר שַׂמְתִּיו לָךְ וְאֶת־כָּל יל"י ־אֶחָיו נָתַתִּי לוֹ
לַעֲבָדִים וְדָגָן וְתִירֹשׁ סְמַכְתִּיו וּלְכָה אֵפוֹא מָה מ"ה אֶעֱשֶׂה
בְּנִי: 38 וַיֹּאמֶר עֵשָׂו אֶל־אָבִיו הַבְרָכָה עסמ"ב אַחַת הִוא־לְךָ אָבִי
בָּרְכֵנִי גַם יג"ל ־אָנִי אני אָבִי וַיִּשָּׂא עֵשָׂו קֹלוֹ וַיֵּבְךְּ: 39 וַיַּעַן יִצְחָק
ד"פ ב"ן אָבִיו וַיֹּאמֶר אֵלָיו הִנֵּה מ"ה יה מִשְׁמַנֵּי הָאָרֶץ אלהים דההין ע"ה
יִהְיֶה ייי מוֹשָׁבֶךָ וּמִטַּל כוזו הַשָּׁמַיִם י"פ טל, י"פ כוזו מֵעָל עלם: 40 וְעַל־
חַרְבְּךָ תִחְיֶה וְאֶת־אָחִיךָ תַּעֲבֹד וְהָיָה יהוה, יהה כַּאֲשֶׁר תָּרִיד
וּפָרַקְתָּ עֻלּוֹ מֵעַל עלם צַוָּארֶךָ: 41 וַיִּשְׂטֹם עֵשָׂו אֶת־יַעֲקֹב
יאהדונהי - אידהנויה עַל־הַבְּרָכָה עסמ"ב אֲשֶׁר בֵּרְכוֹ יהוה ע"ב ריבוע מ"ה אָבִיו
וַיֹּאמֶר עֵשָׂו בְּלִבּוֹ יִקְרְבוּ יְמֵי אֵבֶל אָבִי וְאַהַרְגָה אֶת־יַעֲקֹב
יאהדונהי - אידהנויה אָחִי: 42 וַיֻּגַּד לְרִבְקָה אֶת־דִּבְרֵי ראה עֵשָׂו בְּנָהּ
הַגָּדֹל להח, מבה, יזל, אום וַתִּשְׁלַח וַתִּקְרָא לְיַעֲקֹב יאהדונהי - אידהנויה בְּנָהּ
הַקָּטָן וַתֹּאמֶר אֵלָיו הִנֵּה מ"ה יה עֵשָׂו אָחִיךָ מִתְנַחֵם לְךָ לְהָרְגֶךָ:
43 וְעַתָּה בְנִי שְׁמַע בְּקֹלִי וְקוּם בְּרַח־לְךָ אֶל־לָבָן אָחִי חָרָנָה:
44 וְיָשַׁבְתָּ עִמּוֹ יָמִים נלך אֲחָדִים עַד אֲשֶׁר־תָּשׁוּב חֲמַת אָחִיךָ:
45 עַד־שׁוּב אַף־אָחִיךָ מִמְּךָ וְשָׁכַח אֵת אֲשֶׁר־עָשִׂיתָ לּוֹ
וְשָׁלַחְתִּי וּלְקַחְתִּיךָ מִשָּׁם לָמָה אֶשְׁכַּל גַּם יג"ל ־שְׁנֵיכֶם
יוֹם נגד, זן, מזבח אֶחָד אהבה, דאגה: 46 וַתֹּאמֶר רִבְקָה אֶל־יִצְחָק ד"פ ב"ן

*44 Stay with him for a few days until your brother's fury turns away, 45 until your
brother's anger turns away from you and he forgets what you did to him. Then I will
send and fetch you back from there. Why should I be deprived of you both in one
day?"*

46 And Rebecca said to Isaac, "I am weary of my life because of the daughters of Heth. If Jacob takes a wife from among the daughters of Heth, these daughters of the land, what good shall my life do me?"

28 1 And Isaac called Jacob and blessed him and charged him, saying: "You shall not take a wife of the daughters of Canaan.

2 Arise, go to Paddan Aram, to the house of Bethuel, your mother's father, and there take a wife for yourself from the daughters of Laban, your mother's brother.

3 May God Almighty bless you, and make you fruitful and multiply you that you may become a multitude of people.

4 And give the blessing of Abraham to you and your seed with you, so that you may inherit the land where you are now a stranger, the land which God gave to Abraham."

SEVENTH READING - DAVID - MALCHUT

5 And Isaac sent Jacob away, and he went to Paddan Aram, to Laban, son of Bethuel the Syrian, the brother of Rebecca, Jacob and Esau's mother.

6 When Esau saw that Isaac had blessed Jacob and had sent him away to Paddan Aram to take a wife from there, and that when he blessed him he charged him saying, "You shall not take a wife of the daughters of Canaan;"

קַצְתִּי

Genesis 27:46 – The Aramaic letter *Kof* goes below the baseline. In this verse, the word *katzti* (I am weary) has a small *Kof*, so the letter does not go below the line. While the regular *Kof* gives a little taste of energy to Satan, the small *Kof* denies that taste.

Genesis 28:5 – Isaac told Jacob to marry only someone from his own family, just as Isaac

קַצְתִּי בְחַיַּי מִפְּנֵי בְּנוֹת חֵת אִם יוהך ־לֹקֵחַ יַעֲקֹב יאהדונהי + אידהנויה
אִשָּׁה מִבְּנוֹת־חֵת כָּאֵלֶּה מִבְּנוֹת הָאָרֶץ אלהים דההין ע"ה לָמָּה לִּי
חַיִּים בינה ע"ה׃ 28 1 וַיִּקְרָא עם ה' אותיות = ב"פ קס"א יִצְחָק ד"פ ב"ן אֶל־יַעֲקֹב
יאהדונהי + אידהנויה וַיְבָרֶךְ עסמ"ב אֹתוֹ וַיְצַוֵּהוּ פוי וַיֹּאמֶר לוֹ לֹא־תִקַּח
אִשָּׁה מִבְּנוֹת כְּנָעַן׃ 2 קוּם לֵךְ פַּדֶּנָה אֲרָם בֵּיתָה ב"פ ראה בְתוּאֵל
אֲבִי אִמֶּךָ וְקַח־לְךָ מִשָּׁם אִשָּׁה מִבְּנוֹת לָבָן אֲחִי אִמֶּךָ׃ 3 וְאֵל
שַׁדַּי מהש יְבָרֵךְ עסמ"ב אֹתְךָ וְיַפְרְךָ וְיַרְבֶּךָ וְהָיִיתָ לִקְהַל עַמִּים
ע"ה קס"א׃ 4 וְיִתֶּן י"פ מלוי ע"ב ־לְךָ אֶת־בִּרְכַּת אַבְרָהָם וו"פ אל, רמ"ח לְךָ
וּלְזַרְעֲךָ אִתָּךְ לְרִשְׁתְּךָ אֶת־אֶרֶץ אלהים דאלפין מְגֻרֶיךָ אֲשֶׁר־נָתַן
אֱלֹהִים ילה, מום לְאַבְרָהָם וו"פ אל, רמ"ח׃

SEVENTH READING - DAVID - MALCHUT

5 וַיִּשְׁלַח יִצְחָק ד"פ ב"ן אֶת־יַעֲקֹב יאהדונהי + אידהנויה וַיֵּלֶךְ כלי פַּדֶּנָה
אֲרָם אֶל־לָבָן בֶּן־בְּתוּאֵל הָאֲרַמִּי אֲחִי רִבְקָה אֵם יוהך יַעֲקֹב
יאהדונהי + אידהנויה וְעֵשָׂו׃ 6 וַיַּרְא עֵשָׂו כִּי־בֵרַךְ יִצְחָק ד"פ ב"ן אֶת־
יַעֲקֹב יאהדונהי + אידהנויה וְשִׁלַּח אֹתוֹ פַּדֶּנָה אֲרָם לָקַחַת־לוֹ מִשָּׁם
אִשָּׁה בְּבָרְכוֹ יהוה ע"ב ריבוע מ"ה אֹתוֹ וַיְצַו עָלָיו לֵאמֹר לֹא־תִקַּח
אִשָּׁה מִבְּנוֹת כְּנָעַן׃

---

himself had once been told to marry a woman from his father, Abraham's, family. When Esau found this out, he took another wife—the daughter of Ishmael, his uncle. His action, however, was only an imitation of the deed that would bring true spiritual growth to Jacob. Esau was not willing to do the real inner work that was required. Life is not just about performing correct actions; true spirituality is always a process of conscious transformation.

MAFTIR

7 and that Jacob obeyed his father and his mother and had gone to Paddan Aram;

8 Esau realized how displeasing the daughters of Canaan were to Isaac, his father;

9 so he went to Ishmael and married Mahalath, daughter of Ishmael Abraham's son,
the sister of Nebaioth, in addition to the wives he already had.

HAFTARAH OF TOLDOT

The prophet Malachi discusses Esau and Jacob and the differences between them. From Malachi's words, we learn to apply this analysis to see both the positive and the negative in ourselves. We must

Malachi 1:1-2:7

1 1 An oracle: The word of the Lord to Israel through Malachi.

2 "I have loved you," says the Lord. "But you ask, 'How have You loved us?' Was
not Esau Jacob's brother?" the Lord says. "Yet I have loved Jacob, 3 but Esau I have
hated, and I have turned his mountains into a wasteland and left his inheritance to
the desert jackals."

4 Edom may say, "Though we have been crushed, we will rebuild the ruins." But this
is what the Lord Almighty says: "They may build, but I will demolish. They will be
called the Wicked Land, a people always under the wrath of the Lord.

5 You will see it with your own eyes and say, 'Great is the Lord—even beyond the
borders of Israel!'

6 A son honors his father, and a servant his master. If I am a Father, where is the honor

MAFTIR

7 וַיִּשְׁמַע יַעֲקֹב יאהדונהי ‑ אידהנויה אֶל־אָבִיו וְאֶל־אִמּוֹ וַיֵּלֶךְ כלי פַּדֶּנָה
אֲרָם: 8 וַיַּרְא עֵשָׂו כִּי רָעוֹת בְּנוֹת כְּנָעַן בְּעֵינֵי ריבוע מ״ה יִצְחָק
ד״פ ב״ן אָבִיו: 9 וַיֵּלֶךְ כלי עֵשָׂו אֶל־יִשְׁמָעֵאל וַיִּקַּח חעם אֶת־מָחֲלַת |
בַּת־יִשְׁמָעֵאל בֶּן־אַבְרָהָם ח״פ אל, רמ״ח אֲחוֹת נְבָיוֹת עַל־נָשָׁיו לוֹ
לְאִשָּׁה: [ס] [ס] [ס]

HAFTARAH OF TOLDOT

understand that this dichotomy exists in each of us, and we should work spiritually to reveal the positive sharing aspect in ourselves while minimizing our negative, selfish, ego-based desires.

מלאכי פרק 1–2

1 1 מַשָּׂא דְבַר ראה ־יְהֹוָה אדני יאהדונהי אֶל־יִשְׂרָאֵל בְּיַד מַלְאָכִי:
2 אָהַבְתִּי אֶתְכֶם אָמַר יְהֹוָה אדני יאהדונהי וַאֲמַרְתֶּם בַּמָּה אֲהַבְתָּנוּ
הֲלוֹא־אָח עֵשָׂו לְיַעֲקֹב יאהדונהי ‑ אידהנויה נְאֻם־יְהֹוָה אדני יאהדונהי וָאֹהַב
אֶת־יַעֲקֹב יאהדונהי ‑ אידהנויה: 3 וְאֶת־עֵשָׂו שָׂנֵאתִי וָאָשִׂים אֶת־הָרָיו
שְׁמָמָה וְאֶת־נַחֲלָתוֹ לְתַנּוֹת מִדְבָּר: 4 כִּי־תֹאמַר אֱדוֹם רֻשַּׁשְׁנוּ
וְנָשׁוּב וְנִבְנֶה חֳרָבוֹת כֹּה היי אָמַר יְהֹוָה אדני יאהדונהי צְבָאוֹת פני שכינה
הֵמָּה יִבְנוּ וַאֲנִי ע״ה ב״פ אהיה ‑ יהוה אֶהֱרוֹס וְקָרְאוּ לָהֶם גְּבוּל רִשְׁעָה
וְהָעָם אֲשֶׁר־זָעַם יְהֹוָה אדני יאהדונהי עַד־עוֹלָם: 5 וְעֵינֵיכֶם ריבוע מ״ה
תִּרְאֶינָה וְאַתֶּם תֹּאמְרוּ יִגְדַּל יזל יְהֹוָה אדני יאהדונהי מֵעַל עלם לִגְבוּל

due Me? If I am a Master, where is the respect due Me?" says the Lord Almighty. "It is you, priests, who show contempt for My name. But you ask, 'How have we shown contempt for Your name?'

7 You place defiled food on My altar. But you ask, 'How have we defiled You?' By saying that the Lord's table is contemptible.

8 When you bring blind animals for sacrifice, is that not wrong? When you sacrifice crippled or diseased animals, is that not wrong? Try offering them to your governor! Would he be pleased with you? Would he accept you?" says the Lord Almighty.

9 "Now implore God to be gracious to us. With such offerings from your hands, will he accept you?" says the Lord Almighty.

10 "Oh, that one of you would shut the Temple doors, so that you would not light useless fires on My altar! I am not pleased with you," says the Lord Almighty, "and I will accept no offering from your hands.

11 My Name will be great among the nations, from the rising to the setting of the sun. In every place incense and pure offerings will be brought to My Name, because My Name will be great among the nations," says the Lord Almighty.

12 "But you profane it by saying of the Lord's Table, 'It is defiled,' and of its food, 'It is contemptible.'

13 And you say, 'What a burden!' and you sniff at it contemptuously," says the Lord Almighty. "When you bring injured, crippled or diseased animals and offer them as sacrifices, should I accept them from your hands?" says the Lord.

14 "Cursed is the cheat who has an acceptable male in his flock and vows to give it, but then sacrifices a blemished animal to the Lord. For I am a great King," says the Lord Almighty, "and My name is to be feared among the nations."

2 1 "And now this admonition is for you, priests.

יִשְׂרָאֵל: 6 בֵּן יְכַבֵּד אָב וְעֶבֶד אֲדֹנָיו וְאִם יוהך ־אָב אָנִי אני אַיֵּה
כְבוֹדִי וְאִם יוהך ־אֲדוֹנִים אָנִי אני אַיֵּה מוֹרָאִי אָמַר | יְהֹוָה יאהדונהי
צְבָאוֹת פני שכינה לָכֶם הַכֹּהֲנִים מלה בּוֹזֵי שְׁמִי רבוע ע״ב - רבוע ס״ג
וַאֲמַרְתֶּם בַּמֶּה בָזִינוּ אֶת־שְׁמֶךָ: 7 מַגִּישִׁים עַל־מִזְבְּחִי זן, נגד
לֶחֶם ג״פ יהוה מְגֹאָל וַאֲמַרְתֶּם בַּמֶּה גֵאַלְנוּךָ בֶּאֱמָרְכֶם שֻׁלְחַן
יְהֹוָה יאהדונהי נִבְזֶה הוּא: 8 וְכִי־תַגִּשׁוּן עִוֵּר לִזְבֹּחַ אֵין רָע וְכִי
תַגִּישׁוּ פִּסֵּחַ וְחֹלֶה להח אֵין רָע הַקְרִיבֵהוּ נָא לְפֶחָתֶךָ הֲיִרְצְךָ
אוֹ הֲיִשָּׂא פָנֶיךָ ס״ג - מ״ה - ב״ן אָמַר יְהֹוָה יאהדונהי צְבָאוֹת פני שכינה:
9 וְעַתָּה חַלּוּ־נָא פְנֵי חכמה - בינה ־אֵל ייא״י וִיחָנֵנוּ מִיֶּדְכֶם הָיְתָה
זֹּאת הֲיִשָּׂא מִכֶּם פָּנִים ע״ב ס״ג מ״ה אָמַר יְהֹוָה יאהדונהי צְבָאוֹת
פני שכינה: 10 מִי ילי גַם יגל ־בָּכֶם ב״פ אל וְיִסְגֹּר דְּלָתַיִם וְלֹא־תָאִירוּ
מִזְבְּחִי זן, נגד חִנָּם אֵין־לִי חֵפֶץ בָּכֶם אָמַר יְהֹוָה יאהדונהי צְבָאוֹת
פני שכינה וּמִנְחָה ע״ה ב״פ ב״ן לֹא־אֶרְצֶה מִיֶּדְכֶם: 11 כִּי מִמִּזְרַח־שֶׁמֶשׁ
ב״פ ש״ך וְעַד־מְבוֹאוֹ גָּדוֹל להח, מבה, יזל, אום שְׁמִי רבוע ע״ב - רבוע ס״ג בַּגּוֹיִם
וּבְכָל לכב ־מָקוֹם יהוה ברבוע מֻקְטָר מֻגָּשׁ לִשְׁמִי רבוע ע״ב - רבוע ס״ג
וּמִנְחָה ע״ה ב״פ ב״ן טְהוֹרָה י״פ אכא כִּי־גָדוֹל להח, מבה, יזל, אום שְׁמִי רבוע ע״ב - רבוע ס״ג
בַּגּוֹיִם אָמַר יְהֹוָה יאהדונהי צְבָאוֹת פני שכינה: 12 וְאַתֶּם מְחַלְּלִים
אוֹתוֹ בֶּאֱמָרְכֶם שֻׁלְחַן אֲדֹנָי ללה מְגֹאָל הוּא וְנִיבוֹ נִבְזֶה אָכְלוֹ:
13 וַאֲמַרְתֶּם הִנֵּה מ״ה יה מַתְּלָאָה וְהִפַּחְתֶּם אוֹתוֹ אָמַר
יְהֹוָה יאהדונהי צְבָאוֹת פני שכינה וַהֲבֵאתֶם גָּזוּל וְאֶת־הַפִּסֵּחַ וְאֶת־
הַחוֹלֶה להח וַהֲבֵאתֶם אֶת־הַמִּנְחָה ע״ה ב״פ ב״ן הַאֶרְצֶה אוֹתָהּ מִיֶּדְכֶם
אָמַר יְהֹוָה יאהדונהי: [ס] 14 וְאָרוּר נוֹכֵל וְיֵשׁ בְּעֶדְרוֹ זָכָר וְנֹדֵר
וְזֹבֵחַ מָשְׁחָת לַאדֹנָי ללה כִּי מֶלֶךְ גָּדוֹל להח, מבה, יזל, אום אָנִי אני אָמַר
יְהֹוָה יאהדונהי צְבָאוֹת פני שכינה וּשְׁמִי נוֹרָא ג״פ אלהים בַגּוֹיִם: 2 1 וְעַתָּה

2 If you do not listen, and if you do not set your heart to honor My name," says the Lord Almighty, "I will send a curse upon you, and I will curse your blessings. Yes, I have already cursed them, because you have not set your heart to honor Me.

3 Because of you I will rebuke your descendants; I will spread on your faces the offal from your festival sacrifices, and you will be carried off with it.

4 And you will know that I have sent you this admonition so that My Covenant with Levi may continue," says the Lord Almighty.

5 "My Covenant was with him, a Covenant of life and peace, and I gave them to him; this called for reverence, and he revered Me and stood in awe of My Name.

6 True instruction was in his mouth and nothing false was found on his lips. He walked with Me in peace and uprightness, and turned many from sin.

7 For the lips of a priest ought to preserve knowledge, and from his mouth men should seek instruction—because he is the messenger of the Lord Almighty."

אֲלֵיכֶם הַמִּצְוָה פוי הַזֹּאת הַכֹּהֲנִים מלה: 2 אִם יוהך ־לֹא תִשְׁמְעוּ
וְאִם יוהך ־לֹא תָשִׂימוּ עַל־לֵב לָתֵת כָּבוֹד ל"ב לִשְׁמִי רבוע ע"ב - רבוע ס"ג
אָמַר יְהוָהאדניאהדונהי צְבָאוֹת פני שכינה וְשִׁלַּחְתִּי בָכֶם ב"פ אל אֶת־
הַמְּאֵרָה וְאָרוֹתִי אֶת־בִּרְכוֹתֵיכֶם וְגַם יגל אָרוֹתִיהָ כִּי אֵינְכֶם
שָׂמִים עַל־לֵב: 3 הִנְנִי גֹעֵר לָכֶם אֶת־הַזֶּרַע וְזֵרִיתִי פֶרֶשׁ עַל־
פְּנֵיכֶם פֶּרֶשׁ חַגֵּיכֶם וְנָשָׂא אֶתְכֶם אֵלָיו: 4 וִידַעְתֶּם כִּי שִׁלַּחְתִּי
אֲלֵיכֶם אֵת הַמִּצְוָה פוי הַזֹּאת לִהְיוֹת בְּרִיתִי אֶת־לֵוִי דמב, מלוי ע"ב
אָמַר יְהוָהאדניאהדונהי צְבָאוֹת פני שכינה: 5 בְּרִיתִי | הָיְתָה אִתּוֹ הַחַיִּים
בינה ע"ה וְהַשָּׁלוֹם וָאֶתְּנֵם־לוֹ מוֹרָא וַיִּירָאֵנִי וּמִפְּנֵי שְׁמִי רבוע ע"ב - רבוע ס"ג
נִחַת הוּא: 6 תּוֹרַת אֱמֶת אהיה פעמים אהיה, ז"פ ס"ג הָיְתָה בְּפִיהוּ וְעַוְלָה
לֹא־נִמְצָא בִשְׂפָתָיו בְּשָׁלוֹם וּבְמִישׁוֹר הָלַךְ מיה אִתִּי וְרַבִּים
הֵשִׁיב מֵעָוֹן ג"פ מ"ב: 7 כִּי־שִׂפְתֵי כֹהֵן מלה יִשְׁמְרוּ־דַעַת וְתוֹרָה
יְבַקְשׁוּ מִפִּיהוּ כִּי מַלְאַךְ יְהוָהאדניאהדונהי־צְבָאוֹת פני שכינה הוּא:

VAYETZE

LESSON OF VAYETZE
(Genesis 28:10-32:3)

"And Jacob went out..." (Genesis 28:10)

Jacob left the land of Israel and went to Charan at the suggestion of his parents. Rebecca sent him away because the spirit of God told her that Esau wanted to kill him. Isaac sent him away because he was worried about the nationality of the woman whom Jacob would marry. Yet neither of these is the real reason that Jacob had to leave, to "go out" from his place.

Jacob had to leave for his own sake, not because of his father or his mother or his brother. In the Bible, it is simply written: "And Jacob left." No reason involving another person is given. Jacob was required to go both because of his work in this world and because of the spiritual level that he embodied. There are things in our own lives that we are required to do, even when we are unwilling. When we see this to be true in a specific situation—one where we really have no choice except to take a certain action—we can be sure that our path is being shown to us by the Creator so that we can take action. We are told that when we do take that difficult action, we can be given Divine help, in much the same way that when Jacob left Beersheba, the angels carried him. (Socher Tov 91:6)

Although it is true that leaving Israel is considered "going downward" in a spiritual sense, this is not the case when it pertains to a righteous person like Jacob, our Patriarch. He is, after all, a chariot for the *Sefira* of *Tiferet* as well as being the father of the Twelve Tribes of Israel. After Jacob struggled with the angel, the Creator gave him the name "Israel."

> *Then he said, "Your name will no longer be Jacob, but Israel, because you have struggled with God and with men and have overcome."*
>
> *– Genesis 32:29*

When Jacob left Beersheba, the holiness of Israel went with him, which is why it is not written that he "went down," but rather that he "went out." Even though Jacob was physically outside of Israel, he was still there spiritually.

Being outside of Israel, we can still make a connection to its energy as long as we have the holiness of Israel within us. This is the channel that Jacob opened for us: People who need to be away from Israel for any reason can take Israel with them, inside their heart and soul.

Why was Jacob chosen to be the channel to take the energy of Israel outside of Israel? It was because he was an incarnation of Adam. In fact, we are all part of Adam, and we were separated from Adam and from each other only after Adam sinned. Only the incarnation of Adam, however, could be a channel for the whole nation of Israel to bring its Light outside of its physical borders. Only Jacob could connect *Right* and *Left Columns,* uniting elements that by nature are opposed to one another. Mercy and judgment—that is, Abraham and Isaac—cannot be unified; we are in judgment or we are in mercy, but not both together. Only Jacob, the *Central Column*, could resolve this fundamental dichotomy. Jacob is the filament in the light bulb, the conduit between the positive and the negative energies.

> *But Jacob was strong on all sides, on the side of Isaac and the side of Abraham. SAMAEL came to the right and saw Abraham strong with the vigor of day, namely the Right Side, which is Chesed. He came to the left, and saw Isaac powerful with the strength of rigorous judgment. He came to the body, NAMELY TO THE CENTRAL COLUMN, and saw Jacob strong on both sides. ABRAHAM AND ISAAC surrounded him, one on each side. Then "when he saw that he did not prevail against Jacob, he touched the hollow of his thigh," (Genesis 32:26) a place outside the body, the one pillar of the body ON WHICH THE WHOLE BODY IS SUPPORTED, NAMELY NETZACH, THE PILLAR OF TIFERET, CALLED "BODY." Then "and the hollow of Jacob's thigh was put out of joint, as he wrestled with him…." (ibid)*
>
> *– The Zohar, Toldot 19:197*

When we embody the consciousness of the *Central Column*, we are able to unite truth and peace and loving-kindness, and we can connect to Jacob and the complete energy he possessed. We can be channels for the same balancing, resistive energy as Jacob, regardless of where we live or where we travel. People who live in Israel—and those who do not—can all connect to this power by reading this section of the Bible.

Rachel and Leah

Jacob loved Rachel, but the Creator gave Leah the merit to marry Jacob first, and later, Leah bore children when Rachel could not. On reading this simple story, one might wonder what kind of Creator could bring such chaos to a family.

Even in death, Rachel was separated from Jacob. Leah is buried with Jacob, while Rachel, who died giving birth to Benjamin, is buried alone on the road to Bethlehem. The *Zohar* explains the following:

> *Since Leah went and wept by the highway for Jacob, she merited to be buried with him. Rachel, who did not want to go out to pray for him, was therefore buried by the highway. The secret of this matter is that the one is disclosed and the other undisclosed.*
>
> *– The Zohar, Vayechi 29:273*

But there is a reason for everything that happens. How we see things is not always how they really are. The lives of Jacob, Rachel, and Leah were not like the lives of other people. They are all chariots—very high spiritual souls that as human beings release and manifest certain cosmic forces. By so doing, they reveal the way that the energetic structure of the universe operates, and this plays a major role in the destiny of humanity. Everything that Jacob, Rachel, and Leah experienced still affects every single person who has ever existed or will ever exist in the world.

"Rachel" is a code for the way we think, and "Leah" is a code for the way we should see our lives. Rachel represents *Malchut*, the physical world, or manifestation; Leah represents *Binah*, the spiritual world, or potential.

> *Come and behold: this is assuredly so. All that pertains to the Upper World, LEAH, is hidden, and all that pertains to the Lower World is revealed. Therefore, Leah was hidden and buried in the cave of the Machpelah, and Rachel was buried by the open road. The one is hidden, and the other is open. Thus, the upper world excels in secrecy,*
>
> *– The Zohar, Vayetze 24:243*

The problem is that we love Rachel, and we want so much for everything to be good for her. Leah, however, represents the real life that we are not even aware we want. We must learn to live the life of Leah, which is the level of *Binah*, as if it were the life of Rachel, which is *Malchut*. We must love Leah as if she were Rachel, and love the spiritual as if it were the physical. If we are able to transform our physical longings into spiritual longings, each of our desires and actions will lead us closer to God. There is a saying that one must learn to love the giver and not the gift; for example, if we desire beautiful flowers, we must learn to desire the Creator of the flowers instead. In that way, the physical world is transcended and we grow to love the spiritual as if it were the physical—or Leah as if she were Rachel.

The question lies in what we value most. How many people in the world really care that there is no Temple? Who weeps over its destruction? Yet if we lose money on a business transaction, we cry bitterly over the loss. We love Rachel—our physical life here in the world—so much that we experience very little spiritual growth. Only when we learn to love Leah as we do Rachel will we truly be able to reveal the Light of the Creator in this world.

SYNOPSIS OF VAYETZE

Vayetze means "he went out." The message for humanity is that it is only when we "go out" of ourselves, leaving our comfort zones and rising above our nature and our selfish desires, that we begin our true spiritual journey. In this story, Jacob had to "go out" to embark on his path toward becoming "Israel"—the conduit of energy for the nation of Israel.

By connecting with this particular reading, we can acquire the power to leave behind our own imperfect nature in order to make a dramatic change in our life and create a new destiny.

FIRST READING - ABRAHAM - CHESED

10 And Jacob left Beersheba and set out for Haran.

11 He reached a certain place, and stayed there for the night because the sun had set, and he took of the stones from there, and put them for his pillows and lay down in that place to sleep.

12 And he dreamed, and saw a ladder set up on earth, and the top of it reached to heaven, and he saw the angels of God ascending and descending on it.

13 And behold, the Lord stood above it and said: "I am the Lord, the God of Abraham,
your father, and the God of Isaac. The land on which you lie, I will give to you and to
your seed; 14 and your seed will be like the dust of the earth, and you will spread to
the west and to the east, to the north and to the south; and in your seed will all the families of the earth be blessed.

15 And, behold, I am with you and will watch over you wherever you go, and I will bring you back again to this land, for I will not leave you until I have done what I have promised you."

16 And Jacob awoke from his sleep and said, "Surely the Lord is in this place, and I
was not aware of it." 17 And he was afraid and said, "How awesome is this place! This
is none other than the house of God; and this is the gate of heaven."

FROM THE RAV

Laban agreed that Jacob could have all the livestock that was spotted, speckled, and flecked because it was very unusual for livestock to have spotted, speckled, and flecked offspring.

This story makes no sense at all if we read it on a literal level. The *Zohar* explains, however, that it is really about creating different universes. We have an opportunity here, says the *Zohar*, to go back to the moment of Creation and change things at the seed level.

Rav Ashlag explains in *Ten Luminous Emanations* (*Talmud Eser Sefirot*) that there are three origins of Creation—*nekudim* (spots), *akudim* (speckles), and *berudim* (flecks)—which contain all the secrets of the Universe. We are talking about the first moments in time before everything emerged and became manifested in a physical state—a time even before the stem cell. If we go back to the root and activate the stem cells, as we do when reciting the "*Keter*" section of the *Musaf* prayer connection, then we can start to regenerate and rejuvenate our cells—and even create new ones. We—at least for those of us who believe we can—can regenerate different parts of our body that have become weakened. We have the ability through this *Story of Vayetze* to create each day anew on the physical level. Just by reading these three words (*nekudim, akudim, berudim*), we can absorb the ability to remove chaos from our lives and can affect change in our destiny by going back to the time before physicality, a time of antimatter.

FIRST READING - ABRAHAM - CHESED

10 וַיֵּצֵא יַעֲקֹב יאהדונהי - אידהנויה מִבְּאֵר קנ"א - ב"ן שָׁבַע אלהים דיודין - ע"ב
וַיֵּלֶךְ כלי חָרָנָה׃ 11 וַיִּפְגַּע בַּמָּקוֹם יהוה ברבוע וַיָּלֶן שָׁם כִּי־בָא הַשֶּׁמֶשׁ
ב"פ ש"ך וַיִּקַּח חעם מֵאַבְנֵי הַמָּקוֹם יהוה ברבוע וַיָּשֶׂם מְרַאֲשֹׁתָיו
ריבוע אלהים - אלהים דיודין ע"ה וַיִּשְׁכַּב בַּמָּקוֹם יהוה ברבוע הַהוּא׃ 12 וַיַּחֲלֹם
וְהִנֵּה מ"ה יה סֻלָּם נמם מֻצָּב אַרְצָה אלהים דההין ע"ה וְרֹאשׁוֹ מַגִּיעַ הַשָּׁמָיְמָה
וְהִנֵּה מ"ה יה מַלְאֲכֵי אֱלֹהִים ילה, מום עֹלִים וְיֹרְדִים בּוֹ׃ 13 וְהִנֵּה מ"ה
יה יְהֹוָהאדניאהדונהי נִצָּב עָלָיו וַיֹּאמַר אֲנִי אני יְהֹוָהאדניאהדונהי אֱלֹהֵי דמב, ילה
אַבְרָהָם ח"ו"פ אל, רמ"ח אָבִיךָ וֵאלֹהֵי לכב, דמב, ילה יִצְחָק ד"פ ב"ן הָאָרֶץ
אלהים דההין ע"ה אֲשֶׁר אַתָּה שֹׁכֵב עָלֶיהָ פהל לְךָ אֶתְּנֶנָּה וּלְזַרְעֶךָ׃
14 וְהָיָה יהוה, יהה זַרְעֲךָ כַּעֲפַר הָאָרֶץ אלהים דההין ע"ה וּפָרַצְתָּ יָמָּה
וָקֵדְמָה וְצָפֹנָה וָנֶגְבָּה ע"ה עסמ"ב וְנִבְרְכוּ יהוה ע"ב ריבוע מ"ה בְךָ כָּל־ ילי
מִשְׁפְּחֹת הָאֲדָמָה וּבְזַרְעֶךָ׃ 15 וְהִנֵּה מ"ה יה אָנֹכִי איע עִמָּךְ נמם
וּשְׁמַרְתִּיךָ בְּכֹל לכב אֲשֶׁר־תֵּלֵךְ וַהֲשִׁבֹתִיךָ אֶל־הָאֲדָמָה הַזֹּאת
כִּי לֹא אֶעֱזָבְךָ עַד אֲשֶׁר אִם יוהך ־עָשִׂיתִי אֵת אֲשֶׁר־דִּבַּרְתִּי ראה
לָךְ׃ 16 וַיִּיקַץ יַעֲקֹב יאהדונהי - אידהנויה מִשְּׁנָתוֹ וַיֹּאמֶר אָכֵן יהוה מ"ה יֵשׁ
יְהֹוָהאדניאהדונהי בַּמָּקוֹם יהוה ברבוע הַזֶּה והו וְאָנֹכִי איע לֹא יָדָעְתִּי׃

וַיַּחֲלֹם

Genesis 28:12 – **Jacob's Ladder**. One night during his journey, Jacob had a dream in which he saw angels ascending and descending a ladder to Heaven.

"And he dreamed, and behold a ladder set up on the earth, and the top of it reached to Heaven." (Beresheet 28:12)

It is six grades up from the level of a dream, HOD OF THE NUKVA, to the two grades of prophecy, NETZACH AND HOD OF ZEIR ANPIN. The six grades are YESOD OF ZEIR ANPIN, CHESED, GEVURAH, TIFERET, NETZACH, AND HOD OF THE NUKVA. Therefore, a dream is one part out of sixty of prophecy, FOR EACH OF THESE SIX SEFIROT INCLUDES TEN SEFIROT, AND TEN TIMES SIX IS SIXTY. AND A DREAM, WHICH IS THE LOWEST, CONTAINS ONE OUT OF

[18] *And Jacob rose up early in the morning and took the stone he had placed as a pillow and set it up as a pillar and poured oil on top of it.*

[19] *And he called that place Bethel, but the name of that city used to be called Luz.*

[20] *And Jacob made a vow, saying, "If God will be with me and will watch over me on*
this journey I am taking, and will give me bread to eat and clothes to wear, [21] so that
I return to my father's house in peace, then the Lord will be my God: [22] and this stone
that I have set up as a pillar will be God's house, and of all that You give me I will
surely give one tenth to You."

SECOND READING - ISAAC - GEVURAH

29[1] Then Jacob went on his journey and came to the land of the people of the east.

[2] *And he looked and saw a well in the field, and there were three flocks of sheep lying near it, for out of the well they watered the flocks. And a great stone was over the mouth of the well.*

[3] *And all the flocks were gathered there, and they rolled the stone from the well's mouth and watered the sheep, and put the stone again over the well's mouth in his place.*

SIXTY. The ladder alludes to him seeing his children receive the Torah on Mount Sinai in the future, because the ladder represents Sinai, for MOUNT SINAI, AS SCRIPTURE READS, "is on the ground," "and its top," NAMELY, ITS HIGHEST POINT, reaches Heaven. And all the Chariots and troops of the High Angels descended there with the Holy One, blessed be He, when he gave them the Torah, AS IT IS WRITTEN: "THE ANGELS OF ELOHIM ASCENDING AND DESCENDING ON IT."

– The Zohar, Vayetze 11:70

Throughout the dream, Jacob's current angels were being exchanged for others. While he had been in Israel, Jacob needed angels only to support him spiritually, but once he left his country, he needed angels for physical as well as spiritual support. This reminds us that in our own lives, we must learn to use the kabbalistic tools that are appropriate to our situation. When we recite the Prayer of the Kabbalist: The 42-Letter Name of God, known as the *Ana Beko'ach* prayer, we receive the support and the protection of Monday angels on Monday, Tuesday angels on Tuesday, and so on, always calling upon and attracting the angels that are appropriate to a specific time and place.

Jacob's dream took place on what is now the Temple Mount in Jerusalem. Jacob needed a greater connection to the Creator for sustenance, so he made an agreement with God: To receive protection and blessings, food and clothing, Jacob would give one tenth of everything he had. This is the beginning of the spiritual tool of tithing. When we tithe, we form a partnership with God whereby we receive protection and blessings from the Creator in exchange for the fruits of our labor. Jacob understood the universal laws such as Bread of Shame and acted in accordance with the system of the universe.

17 וַיִּירָא וַיֹּאמַר מַה מ״ה ־נּוֹרָא ע״ה ג״פ אלהים הַמָּקוֹם יהוה ברבוע הַזֶּה והו
אֵין זֶה כִּי אִם יוהך ־בֵּית ב״פ ראה אֱלֹהִים ילה, מום וְזֶה שַׁעַר הַשָּׁמָיִם
י״פ טל, י״פ כוזו: 18 וַיַּשְׁכֵּם יַעֲקֹב יאהדונהי - אידהנויה בַּבֹּקֶר וַיִּקַּח וזעם אֶת־
הָאֶבֶן יוד הה ואו הה אֲשֶׁר־שָׂם מְרַאֲשֹׁתָיו ריבוע אלהים - אלהים דיודין ע״ה וַיָּשֶׂם
אֹתָהּ מַצֵּבָה וַיִּצֹק שֶׁמֶן י״פ טל, י״פ כוזו, ביט עַל־רֹאשָׁהּ ריבוע אלהים - אלהים דיוד־
דין ע״ה: 19 וַיִּקְרָא עם ה׳ אותיות = ב״פ קס״א אֶת־שֵׁם שדי יהוה ־הַמָּקוֹם יהוה ברבוע
הַהוּא בֵּית ב״פ ראה ־אֵל ייא״י וְאוּלָם לוּז שֵׁם שדי יהוה ־הָעִיר סוזוהר, ערי, סנדלפון
לָרִאשֹׁנָה: 20 וַיִּדַּר יַעֲקֹב יאהדונהי - אידהנויה נֶדֶר לֵאמֹר אִם יוהך ־
יִהְיֶה ייי אֱלֹהִים ילה, מום עִמָּדִי וּשְׁמָרַנִי בַּדֶּרֶךְ ב״פ יב״ק הַזֶּה והו אֲשֶׁר
אָנֹכִי איע הוֹלֵךְ מיה וְנָתַן אבגיתצ, ושר, אהבת חנם ־לִי לֶחֶם ג״פ יהוה לֶאֱכֹל
וּבֶגֶד לִלְבֹּשׁ: 21 וְשַׁבְתִּי בְשָׁלוֹם אֶל־בֵּית ב״פ ראה אָבִי וְהָיָה יהוה, יהה
יְהֹוָהאדני יאהדונהי לִי לֵאלֹהִים ילה, מום: 22 וְהָאֶבֶן יוד הה ואו הה הַזֹּאת אֲשֶׁר־
שַׂמְתִּי מַצֵּבָה יִהְיֶה ייי בֵּית ב״פ ראה אֱלֹהִים ילה, מום וְכֹל ילי אֲשֶׁר תִּתֶּן
ב״פ כהת ־לִי עַשֵּׂר אֲעַשְּׂרֶנּוּ לָךְ:

SECOND READING - ISAAC - GEVURAH

29 1 וַיִּשָּׂא יַעֲקֹב יאהדונהי - אידהנויה רַגְלָיו וַיֵּלֶךְ כלי אַרְצָה אלהים דההין ע״ה
בְּנֵי־קֶדֶם רבוע ב״ן: 2 וַיַּרְא וְהִנֵּה מ״ה יה בְאֵר קנ״א - ב״ן בַּשָּׂדֶה וְהִנֵּה מ״ה יה ־שָׁם
שְׁלֹשָׁה עֶדְרֵי־צֹאן מלוי אהיה דיודין ע״ה רֹבְצִים עָלֶיהָ פהל כִּי מִן־הַבְּאֵר
קנ״א - ב״ן הַהִוא יַשְׁקוּ הָעֲדָרִים וְהָאֶבֶן יוד הה ואו הה גְּדֹלָה להח, מבה, יזל, אום
עַל־פִּי הַבְּאֵר קנ״א - ב״ן: 3 וְנֶאֶסְפוּ־שָׁמָּה מהש כָל ילי ־הָעֲדָרִים וְגָלְלוּ
אֶת־הָאֶבֶן יוד הה ואו הה מֵעַל עלם פִּי הַבְּאֵר קנ״א - ב״ן וְהִשְׁקוּ אֶת־
הַצֹּאן וְהֵשִׁיבוּ אֶת־הָאֶבֶן יוד הה ואו הה עַל־פִּי הַבְּאֵר קנ״א - ב״ן לִמְקֹמָהּ:

[4] And Jacob said to them, "My brothers, where are you from?" And they said, "We're from Haran."

[5] And he said to them, "Do you know Laban, the son of Nahor?" and they said, "We know him." [6] And he said to them, "Is he well?" And they said, "He is well. See, here comes Rachel, his daughter with the sheep."

[7] And he said, "Look the day is still high; it is not time for the cattle to be gathered together; water the sheep and go and feed them." [8] And they said, "We cannot, until all the flocks are gathered and till they roll the stone from the well's mouth, then we water the sheep."

[9] And while he was talking with them, Rachel came with her father's sheep, for she kept them.

[10] And it came to pass, when Jacob saw Rachel, daughter of Laban, his mother's brother, and the sheep of Laban, his mother's brother, he went near and rolled the stone from the mouth of the well and watered the flock of Laban, his mother's brother.

[11] And Jacob kissed Rachel and raised his voice and wept. [12] And Jacob told Rachel that he was her father's brother and that he was Rebecca's son; and she ran and told her father. [13] And it came to pass, when Laban heard the news of Jacob, his sister's son, he ran to meet him, and embraced him and kissed him and brought him to his house, and he told Laban all these things. [14] And Laban said to him, "Surely you are my bone and my flesh." And Jacob stayed with him for a whole month.

רָחֵל

Genesis 29:6 – When he reached Charan, Jacob met Rachel at the well. Once again, we see the deep symbolism and power of water. Jacob kissed Rachel and then began to weep because he was able to see his future with her—that their relationship would be a bittersweet one, that she would die in childbirth, and that they would not be buried together.

וַתָּרָץ

Genesis 29:12 – Rachel went home and told Laban, her father, that Jacob had arrived, and Laban ran to Jacob and kissed and embraced him. However, Laban was actually more interested in finding out how much money Jacob had brought with him, recalling that when Abraham's servant had come for Rebecca, he brought with him a great herd of animals and many gifts. A commentary tells us that Laban was so sure that Jacob must have money that he tried everything to find out where it was. But there was no money.

וַיֹּאמֶר

Genesis 29:14 – Laban made a deal with Jacob whereby he would give Jacob his daughter Rachel if Jacob was willing to work for him for seven years. At the end of that time, however, Laban tricked Jacob and gave him Leah to marry instead.

Jacob's example of persistence shows us that no matter how defeated we feel, we can still overcome Satan, the Opponent, if we do enough hard work and retain our absolute certainty in the final outcome.

4 וַיֹּאמֶר לָהֶם יַעֲקֹב יאהדונהי - אידהנויה אַחַי מֵאַיִן אַתֶּם וַיֹּאמְרוּ
מֵחָרָן ג"פ אלהים אֲנָחְנוּ: 5 וַיֹּאמֶר לָהֶם הַיְדַעְתֶּם אֶת־לָבָן בֶּן־נָחוֹר
וַיֹּאמְרוּ יָדָעְנוּ: 6 וַיֹּאמֶר לָהֶם הֲשָׁלוֹם לוֹ וַיֹּאמְרוּ שָׁלוֹם וְהִנֵּה
מ"ה יה רָחֵל רבוע ס"ג - ע"ב בִּתּוֹ בָּאָה עִם־הַצֹּאן מלוי אהיה דיודין ע"ה: 7 וַיֹּאמֶר
הֵן עוֹד הַיּוֹם נגד, זן, מזבח גָּדוֹל להח, מבה, יזל, אום לֹא־עֵת י"פ אהיה - י' הויות
הֵאָסֵף הַמִּקְנֶה הַשְׁקוּ הַצֹּאן מלוי אהיה דיודין ע"ה וּלְכוּ רְעוּ: 8 וַיֹּאמְרוּ
לֹא נוּכַל עַד אֲשֶׁר יֵאָסְפוּ כָל ילי ־הָעֲדָרִים וְגָלְלוּ אֶת־הָאֶבֶן
יוד הה ואו הה מֵעַל עלם פִּי הַבְּאֵר קנ"א - ב"ן וְהִשְׁקִינוּ הַצֹּאן מלוי אהיה דיודין ע"ה:
9 עוֹדֶנּוּ מְדַבֵּר ראה עִמָּם עמם וְרָחֵל רבוע ס"ג - ע"ב | בָּאָה עִם־הַצֹּאן
מלוי אהיה דיודין ע"ה אֲשֶׁר לְאָבִיהָ כִּי רֹעָה הִוא: 10 וַיְהִי אל כַּאֲשֶׁר
רָאָה ראה יַעֲקֹב יאהדונהי - אידהנויה אֶת־רָחֵל רבוע ס"ג - ע"ב בַּת־לָבָן אֲחִי
אִמּוֹ וְאֶת־צֹאן מלוי אהיה דיודין ע"ה לָבָן אֲחִי אִמּוֹ וַיִּגַּשׁ יַעֲקֹב
יאהדונהי - אידהנויה וַיָּגֶל להח אֶת־הָאֶבֶן יוד הה ואו הה מֵעַל עלם פִּי הַבְּאֵר
קנ"א - ב"ן וַיַּשְׁקְ אֶת־צֹאן מלוי אהיה דיודין ע"ה לָבָן אֲחִי אִמּוֹ: 11 וַיִּשַּׁק
יַעֲקֹב יאהדונהי - אידהנויה לְרָחֵל רבוע ס"ג - ע"ב וַיִּשָּׂא אֶת־קֹלוֹ וַיֵּבְךְּ: 12 וַיַּגֵּד
יַעֲקֹב יאהדונהי - אידהנויה לְרָחֵל רבוע ס"ג - ע"ב כִּי אֲחִי אָבִיהָ הוּא וְכִי בֶן־
רִבְקָה הוּא וַתָּרָץ וַתַּגֵּד לְאָבִיהָ: 13 וַיְהִי כִשְׁמֹעַ לָבָן אֶת־
שֵׁמַע | יַעֲקֹב יאהדונהי - אידהנויה בֶּן־אֲחֹתוֹ וַיָּרָץ לִקְרָאתוֹ וַיְחַבֶּק־לוֹ
וַיְנַשֶּׁק־לוֹ וַיְבִיאֵהוּ אֶל־בֵּיתוֹ ב"פ ראה וַיְסַפֵּר לְלָבָן אֵת כָּל־ ילי
הַדְּבָרִים ראה הָאֵלֶּה: 14 וַיֹּאמֶר לוֹ לָבָן אַךְ אהיה עַצְמִי וּבְשָׂרִי
אָתָּה וַיֵּשֶׁב עִמּוֹ חֹדֶשׁ י"ב הוויות יָמִים נלך: 15 וַיֹּאמֶר לָבָן לְיַעֲקֹב
יאהדונהי - אידהנויה הֲכִי־אָחִי אַתָּה וַעֲבַדְתַּנִי חִנָּם הַגִּידָה לִּי מַה־ מ"ה
מַשְׂכֻּרְתֶּךָ: 16 וּלְלָבָן שְׁתֵּי בָנוֹת שֵׁם שדי יהוה הַגְּדֹלָה להח, מבה, יזל, אום

15 And Laban said to Jacob, "Because you are my brother, should you work for me for nothing? Tell me what your wages should be."

16 And Laban had two daughters; the name of the older was Leah, and the name of
the younger was Rachel. 17 Leah was tender-eyed, but Rachel was beautiful and well
favored.

THIRD READING - JACOB - TIFERET

18 And Jacob loved Rachel and said, "I'll work for you seven years in return for Rachel, your younger daughter."

19 And Laban said, "It is better that I give her to you than to some other man. Stay here with me."

20 And Jacob served seven years for Rachel, and they seemed like only a few days to him because of his love for her.

21 And Jacob said to Laban, "Give me my wife, for my days are fulfilled so that I may go in unto her."

22 And Laban gathered together all the men of the place and made a feast.

23 And it came to pass in the evening that he took Leah, his daughter, and brought her to Jacob, and he went in unto her.

24 And Laban gave to his daughter Leah, Zilpah his servant girl, as her handmaid.

וַיֶּאֱהַב

Genesis 29:18 – Although it might seem odd for Jacob to have had so many children with Leah, whom he loved less than Rachel, we should be cautious about using our limited perceptions of reality to understand this spiritual matter, as we will surely be misled. It is vital to apply a spiritual awareness to each story in the Bible and not to take literally what is actually a profound coded lesson about the true nature of reality.

תִּתִּי

Genesis 29:19 – After being deceived into marriage with Leah, Jacob still desired to marry Rachel, so Laban struck another deal with him. Laban would give Rachel to Jacob if he was willing to work another seven years. We are told that Laban was trying to prevent the creation of the Twelve Tribes of Israel by thwarting the union of Rachel with Jacob. Essentially, he was trying to prevent the Light from being revealed through Jacob, Rachel, Leah, and the Twelve Tribes. Jacob, however,

לֵאָה לאה (אלד ע"ה) וְשֵׁם שדי יהוה הַקְּטַנָּה רָחֵל רבוע ס"ג - ע"ב׃
17 וְעֵינֵי ריבוע מ"ה לֵאָה לאה (אלד ע"ה) רַכּוֹת וְרָחֵל רבוע ס"ג - ע"ב הָיְתָה יְפַת־
תֹּאַר וִיפַת מַרְאֶה ר"ת יתום׃

THIRD READING - JACOB - TIFERET

18 וַיֶּאֱהַב יַעֲקֹב יאהדונהי - אידהנויה אֶת־רָחֵל רבוע ס"ג - ע"ב וַיֹּאמֶר אֶעֱבָדְךָ
שֶׁבַע אלהים דיודין - ע"ב שָׁנִים בְּרָחֵל רבוע ס"ג - ע"ב בִּתְּךָ הַקְּטַנָּה׃
19 וַיֹּאמֶר לָבָן טוֹב והו תִּתִּי אֹתָהּ לָךְ מִתִּתִּי אֹתָהּ לְאִישׁ ע"ה קנ"א קס"א
אַחֵר שְׁבָה עִמָּדִי׃ 20 וַיַּעֲבֹד יַעֲקֹב יאהדונהי - אידהנויה בְּרָחֵל רבוע ס"ג - ע"ב
שֶׁבַע אלהים דיודין - ע"ב שָׁנִים וַיִּהְיוּ בְעֵינָיו מלוי ס"ג כְּיָמִים ריבוע מ"ה נלך
אֲחָדִים בְּאַהֲבָתוֹ אֹתָהּ׃ 21 וַיֹּאמֶר יַעֲקֹב יאהדונהי - אידהנויה אֶל־לָבָן
הָבָה אֶת־אִשְׁתִּי כִּי מָלְאוּ יָמָי וְאָבוֹאָה אֵלֶיהָ׃ 22 וַיֶּאֱסֹף לָבָן
אֶת־כָּל ילי ־אַנְשֵׁי הַמָּקוֹם יהוה ברבוע וַיַּעַשׂ מִשְׁתֶּה׃ 23 וַיְהִי בָעֶרֶב
רבוע אלהים רבוע יהוה וַיִּקַּח חעם אֶת־לֵאָה לאה (אלד ע"ה) בִּתּוֹ וַיָּבֵא אֹתָהּ אֵלָיו
וַיָּבֹא אֵלֶיהָ׃ 24 וַיִּתֵּן לָבָן לָהּ אֶת־זִלְפָּה שִׁפְחָתוֹ לְלֵאָה לאה (אלד ע"ה)

---

eventually overcame Laban's treacherous efforts to stop his marriage with Rachel.

> *Jacob inherited two worlds, the revealed world and the hidden world. Accordingly, from the hidden world, FROM LEAH, the six tribes were issued; and from the revealed world, FROM RACHEL, the other two tribes. Also, the hidden world, LEAH, THE NUKVA OF ZEIR ANPIN, put forth six ends, and the revealed world, RACHEL, issued two. And Jacob was found between the two worlds, THE REVEALED AND THE HIDDEN, in their very shape. Therefore, all that Leah said was covered, and all that Rachel said was uncovered.*
>
> *– The Zohar, Vayetze 14:105*

Our lesson here is that no matter how defeated we feel, we can, with absolute certainty and desire for the Light, overcome anything—even Satan.

The essence of certain aspects of the Creator is hidden within the astrological symbols that are alluded to in the following paragraphs. Each of these aspects varies according to the spiritual essence of each of the sons of Jacob (and therefore of each of the Tribes of Israel). When these aspects are then linked with their associated letters in the Aramaic alphabet, a subtle influence is hinted at that can be used to explore these same characteristics within ourselves. It is not necessary to examine these logically, but only to let their influence touch us at the deepest levels. Kabbalistic astrology merely reveals the assets and handicaps we possess on

*25 And it came to pass that in the morning, behold it was Leah: and he said to Laban,
"What is this you have done to me? Did I not serve you for Rachel? Why have you
deceived me?"*

*26 And Laban said, "It is not a custom in our country to give the younger before the
firstborn. 27 Fulfill her week; and we will give you this also for the service of another
seven years of work."*

*28 And Jacob did so. He fulfilled her week, and he gave him Rachel, his daughter, to
wife also. 29 And Laban gave to Rachel, his daughter, Bilhah, his handmaid, to be her
maid. 30 And he went in also unto Rachel, and he loved Rachel more than Leah, and
served with him yet another seven years. 31 And when the Lord saw that Leah was
hated, he opened her womb, but Rachel was barren. 32 And Leah conceived and gave
birth to a son. And she named him Reuben, for she said, "Surely the Lord has seen
my affliction. Now therefore my husband will love me." 33 And she conceived again,
and gave birth to a son and said, "Because the Lord heard that I am hated, he has
also given me this son." And she named him Shimon. 34 And she conceived again,*

---

entering this world before our free will adds to, enhances, or corrects these traits and before our destiny tests them in action. It is in no way to be construed as an unalienable fate. Astrology does not control us; this is why the sons of Jacob are said to control the astrological signs, rather than the other way around. Do not look to the Heavens for power; rather, send your own spiritual power to the Heavens, where it will be reflected in the Light that comes from the Creator.

רְאוּבֵן - (דה)

Genesis 29:32 – Reuben, Leah's first-born, controls the month of Aries (*Nissan*) with the letters *Dalet* and *Hei*. When Jacob had intercourse with Leah, he was mislead; in his consciousness, he thought she was Rachel, so the first drop of Jacob's semen was kept back by the Creator so that when Rachel later conceived Joseph, her son would be the real first-born son. Because of this action of the Creator, Reuben, Leah's first-born, was not truly conceived from the first drop of Jacob's semen and was therefore not Jacob's first-born.

שִׁמְעוֹן - (פו)

Genesis 29:33 – Simon controls the month of Taurus (*Iyar*) with the letters *Pei* and *Vav*. Simon represents harsh judgment, being the strongest of the brothers and the leader of the army. In fact, the sages tell us that Simon was the brother who actually threw Joseph into the pit and who ordered the others to stone him. (*Beresheet Rabba 84:16; Tanchuma, ed. Buber, Vayeshev 13*)

לֵוִי - (רז)

Genesis 29:34 – Levi controls the month of Gemini (*Sivan*) with the letters *Reish* and *Zayin*. From Levi descended Moses, Aaron, the Levites, and the Kohanim, or priests. It is said that none of the tribal ancestors lived longer than Levi, and as long as he was alive, Israel was not enslaved by Egypt. (*Seder Olam Rabba 3*)

יְהוּדָה - (חת)

Genesis 29:35 – Judah controls the month of Cancer (*Tammuz*) with the letters *Chet* and *Tav*.

בִּתּוֹ שִׁפְחָה ג' מלויי אהיה: 25 וַיְהִי אל בַבֹּקֶר וְהִנֵּה מ"ה יה ־הִוא
לֵאָה לאה (אלד ע"ה) וַיֹּאמֶר אֶל־לָבָן מַה מ"ה ־זֹּאת עָשִׂיתָ לִּי הֲלֹא
בְרָחֵל רבוע ס"ג ־ ע"ב עָבַדְתִּי עִמָּךְ נמם וְלָמָּה רִמִּיתָנִי: 26 וַיֹּאמֶר לָבָן
לֹא־יֵעָשֶׂה כֵן בִּמְקוֹמֵנוּ לָתֵת הַצְּעִירָה לִפְנֵי הַבְּכִירָה: 27 מַלֵּא
שְׁבֻעַ אלהים דיודין ־ ע"ב זֹאת וְנִתְּנָה לְךָ גַּם יג"ל ־אֶת־זֹאת בַּעֲבֹדָה
אֲשֶׁר תַּעֲבֹד עִמָּדִי עוֹד שֶׁבַע אלהים דיודין ־ ע"ב־שָׁנִים אֲחֵרוֹת:
28 וַיַּעַשׂ יַעֲקֹב יאהדונהי ־ אידהנויה כֵּן וַיְמַלֵּא שְׁבֻעַ אלהים דיודין ־ ע"ב זֹאת
וַיִּתֶּן י"פ מלוי ע"ב ־לוֹ אֶת־רָחֵל רבוע ס"ג ־ ע"ב בִּתּוֹ לוֹ לְאִשָּׁה: 29 וַיִּתֵּן לָבָן
לְרָחֵל רבוע ס"ג ־ ע"ב בִּתּוֹ אֶת־בִּלְהָה מ"ב שִׁפְחָתוֹ לָהּ לְשִׁפְחָה:
30 וַיָּבֹא גַּם יג"ל אֶל־רָחֵל רבוע ס"ג ־ ע"ב וַיֶּאֱהַב גַּם יג"ל ־אֶת־רָחֵל
רבוע ס"ג ־ ע"ב מִלֵּאָה לאה (אלד ע"ה) וַיַּעֲבֹד עִמּוֹ עוֹד שֶׁבַע אלהים דיודין ־ ע"ב־שָׁנִים
אֲחֵרוֹת: 31 וַיַּרְא יְהוָה יאהדונהי כִּי־שְׂנוּאָה לֵאָה לאה (אלד ע"ה)
וַיִּפְתַּח אֶת־רַחְמָהּ וְרָחֵל רבוע ס"ג ־ ע"ב עֲקָרָה: 32 וַתַּהַר לֵאָה
לאה (אלד ע"ה) וַתֵּלֶד בֵּן וַתִּקְרָא שְׁמוֹ מהש ע"ה רְאוּבֵן ג"פ אלהים כִּי אָמְרָה
כִּי־רָאָה ראה יְהוָה יאהדונהי בְּעָנְיִי ריבוע מ"ה כִּי עַתָּה יֶאֱהָבַנִי אִישִׁי:
33 וַתַּהַר עוֹד וַתֵּלֶד בֵּן וַתֹּאמֶר כִּי־שָׁמַע יְהוָה יאהדונהי כִּי־
שְׂנוּאָה אָנֹכִי איע וַיִּתֶּן י"פ מלוי ע"ב ־לִי גַּם יג"ל ־אֶת־זֶה וַתִּקְרָא שְׁמוֹ
מהש ע"ה שִׁמְעוֹן: 34 וַתַּהַר עוֹד וַתֵּלֶד בֵּן וַתֹּאמֶר עַתָּה הַפַּעַם יִלָּוֶה
אִישִׁי אֵלַי כִּי־יָלַדְתִּי לוֹ שְׁלֹשָׁה בָנִים עַל־כֵּן קָרָא־שְׁמוֹ מהש ע"ה
לֵוִי דמב, מלוי ע"ב: 35 וַתַּהַר עוֹד וַתֵּלֶד בֵּן וַתֹּאמֶר הַפַּעַם אוֹדֶה
אֶת־יְהוָה יאהדונהי עַל־כֵּן קָרְאָה שְׁמוֹ מהש ע"ה יְהוּדָה וַתַּעֲמֹד

Judah controls the disease of cancer. It is interesting to note that the story tells how Judah himself was "cured." We are told that Judah imposed a ban upon himself by vowing to bring Benjamin back to their father. During the years that Israel wandered in the desert, Judah's bones rolled around in his grave. Once Moses came and prayed for mercy, Judah was effectually absolved of the ban, and his limbs then reassembled themselves. (*Sotah 7b*)

*and gave birth to a son and said, "Now this time my husband will be joined to me,
because I have borne him three sons." So he was named Levi. 35 And she conceived
again, and gave birth to a son and she said, "Now I will praise the Lord." So she
named him Yehuda and left bearing. 30:1 And when Rachel saw that she was not
bearing Jacob any children, Rachel envied her sister, and said to Jacob, "Give me
children, or else I die." 2 And Jacob's anger was kindled against Rachel and he said,
"Am I in the place of God, who has kept you from the fruit of your womb?" 3 And she
said, "See my maid Bilhah, go unto her and she shall bear upon my knees that I may
also have children by her. 4 And she gave him Bilhah her handmaid as a wife, and
Jacob went in unto her. 5 And Bilhah became pregnant and bore Jacob a son. 6 And
Rachel said, "God has judged me; and he has also heard my voice and has given me
a son." Therefore, she named him Dan. 7 And Bilhah, Rachel's maid conceived again
and bore Jacob a second son. 8 And Rachel said, "I have wrestled a great struggle
with my sister, and I have won." And she named him Naphtali. 9 When Leah saw that
she had stopped having children, she took Zilpah, her maid, and gave her to Jacob
as a wife. 10 And Zilpah, Leah's maid, bore Jacob a son. 11 And Leah said, "A troop
comes." So she named him Gad. 12 And Zilpah, Leah's maid, bore Jacob a second
son. 13 And Leah said, "Happy am I, for the daughters will call me blessed." And she
named him Asher.*

וַתְּקַנֵּא

Genesis 30:1 – Rachel became jealous of Leah because she was angry that Jacob had married Leah instead of her. Without judging Rachel, we need to remember that we must not be jealous of others based solely on what we see at any present moment because we can never see the whole picture. Today's events may be the result of something that happened long ago, perhaps even in a previous lifetime.

On another note, Rachel was actually envious not so much of Leah's relationship with Jacob as of Leah's undoubtedly good deeds, which had earned her the right to bear children to him. (*Beresheet Rabba 52*)

בִּלְהָה

Genesis 30:3 – Rachel could not conceive, so she gave her handmaiden, Bilhah, to Jacob so that he could father children with her.

דָּן - (דנ)

Genesis 30:6 – Dan controls the month of Scorpio (*Mar Cheshvan*) with the letters *Dalet* and *Nun*. This is the month of the Flood. Rashi commented that Dan would avenge his people on the Philistines, and when Moses blessed the children of Israel, he said, "Dan is a lion's whelp: He shall leap from Bashan." (*Deuteronomy 33:22*)

נַפְתָּלִי - (סג)

Genesis 30:8 – Naftali controls the month of Sagittarius (*Kislev*) with the letters *Samech* and *Gimmel*. This is the month of miracles. It is said that Naftali was a herald of good tidings.

גָּד - (עב)

Genesis 30:11 – Gad controls the month of Capricorn (*Tevet*) with the letters *Ayin* and *Bet*. These two letters represent the 72 Names of God.

מִלֶּדֶת׃ 30 1 וַתֵּרֶא רָחֵל רבוע ס״ג ‑ ע״ב כִּי לֹא יָלְדָה לְיַעֲקֹב יאהדונהי ‑ אידהנויה
וַתְּקַנֵּא רָחֵל רבוע ס״ג ‑ ע״ב בַּאֲחֹתָהּ וַתֹּאמֶר אֶל־יַעֲקֹב יאהדונהי ‑ אידהנויה
הָבָה־לִּי בָנִים וְאִם יוהך ־אַיִן מֵתָה אָנֹכִי איע׃ 2 וַיִּחַר־אַף יַעֲקֹב
יאהדונהי ‑ אידהנויה בְּרָחֵל רבוע ס״ג ‑ ע״ב וַיֹּאמֶר הֲתַחַת אֱלֹהִים ילה, מום אָנֹכִי
איע אֲשֶׁר־מָנַע מִמֵּךְ פְּרִי ע״ה אלהים דאלפין ־בָטֶן׃ 3 וַתֹּאמֶר הִנֵּה
אֲמָתִי בִלְהָה מ״ב בֹּא אֵלֶיהָ וְתֵלֵד עַל־בִּרְכַּי וְאִבָּנֶה גַם יג״ל ־אָנֹכִי
איע מִמֶּנָּה׃ 4 וַתִּתֶּן ב״פ כהת ־לוֹ אֶת־בִּלְהָה מ״ב שִׁפְחָתָהּ לְאִשָּׁה
וַיָּבֹא אֵלֶיהָ יַעֲקֹב יאהדונהי ‑ אידהנויה׃ 5 וַתַּהַר בִּלְהָה מ״ב וַתֵּלֶד לְיַעֲקֹב
יאהדונהי ‑ אידהנויה בֵּן׃ 6 וַתֹּאמֶר רָחֵל רבוע ס״ג ‑ ע״ב דָּנַנִּי אֱלֹהִים ילה, מום
וְגַם יג״ל שָׁמַע בְּקֹלִי וַיִּתֶּן י״פ מלוי ע״ב ־לִי בֵּן עַל־כֵּן קָרְאָה שְׁמוֹ
מהש ע״ה דָּן׃ 7 וַתַּהַר עוֹד וַתֵּלֶד בִּלְהָה מ״ב שִׁפְחַת רָחֵל רבוע ס״ג ‑ ע״ב
בֵּן שֵׁנִי לְיַעֲקֹב יאהדונהי ‑ אידהנויה׃ 8 וַתֹּאמֶר רָחֵל רבוע ס״ג ‑ ע״ב נַפְתּוּלֵי
אֱלֹהִים ילה, מום | נִפְתַּלְתִּי עִם־אֲחֹתִי גַּם יג״ל ־יָכֹלְתִּי וַתִּקְרָא שְׁמוֹ
מהש ע״ה נַפְתָּלִי׃ 9 וַתֵּרֶא לֵאָה לאה (אלד ע״ה) כִּי עָמְדָה מִלֶּדֶת וַתִּקַּח
אֶת־זִלְפָּה שִׁפְחָתָהּ וַתִּתֵּן ב״פ כהת אֹתָהּ לְיַעֲקֹב יאהדונהי ‑ אידהנויה לְאִשָּׁה׃
10 וַתֵּלֶד זִלְפָּה שִׁפְחַת לֵאָה לאה (אלד ע״ה) לְיַעֲקֹב יאהדונהי ‑ אידהנויה בֵּן׃
11 וַתֹּאמֶר לֵאָה בָּא גָד (כתיב: בגד) וַתִּקְרָא אֶת־שְׁמוֹ מהש ע״ה גָּד׃
12 וַתֵּלֶד זִלְפָּה שִׁפְחַת לֵאָה לאה (אלד ע״ה) בֵּן שֵׁנִי לְיַעֲקֹב יאהדונהי ‑ אידהנויה׃
13 וַתֹּאמֶר לֵאָה לאה (אלד ע״ה) בְּאָשְׁרִי כִּי אִשְּׁרוּנִי בָּנוֹת וַתִּקְרָא
אֶת־שְׁמוֹ מהש ע״ה אָשֵׁר ריבוע אלהים ‑ אלהים דיודין ע״ה׃

Moses used these sequences and formulae to overcome the laws of nature and to split the Red Sea. *(Exodus 14:19-21)* The splitting of the Red Sea is an instance of control over nature. On a personal level, it denotes control over our reactive impulses. By simply scanning these configurations of letters, we gain the power to overcome our reactive nature, helping us to become more connected to the Light in every situation.

אָשֵׁר – (צב)

Genesis 30:13 – Asher controls the month of Aquarius (*Shevat*) with the letters *Tzadi* and

FOURTH READING - MOSES - NETZACH

*14 During the days of the wheat harvest, Reuben went out into the fields and found
mandrakes, and he brought them to his mother Leah. Then Rachel said to Leah,
"Give me, I pray you, of your son's mandrakes."*

*15 And she said to her, "Is it a small matter that you have taken my husband? Will you
take my son's mandrakes too?" And Rachel said, "Very well, he can lie with you
tonight in return for your son's mandrakes."*

*16 And Jacob came in from the fields that evening, and Leah went out to meet him
and said, "You must come in unto me for I have hired you with my son's mandrakes."
And he lay with her that night. 17 And God listened to Leah, and she became pregnant
and bore Jacob a fifth son. 18 And Leah said, "God has rewarded me for giving my
maidservant to my husband." And she named him Issachar. 19 And Leah conceived
again and bore Jacob a sixth son. 20 And Leah said, "God has presented me with a
precious gift. Now my husband will dwell with me, because I have borne him six
sons." And she named him Zebulun. 21 And afterward she gave birth to a daughter
and named her Dinah.*

Bet. According to the *Sefer Yetzirah* (*the Book of Formation*) written by Abraham the Patriarch, the name Asher means "pleasure," or "happiness," and Asher is the personification of the olive tree from which the oil of blessing comes. The *Zohar* says:

> *This is the secret of the verse "Out of Asher, his bread shall be fat, and he shall yield royal dainties," WHICH MEANS THAT ASHER IS THE SAID RIGHTEOUS...THAT POURS DAINTIES UPON THE NUKVA.... From the World to Come, BINAH, there issues a flow upon the righteous to pour delicacies and dainties upon the Earth, which was the bread of poverty but turned into millet bread.*
>
> *– The Zohar, Vayechi, 74:751-752*

דוּדָאִים

Genesis 30:14 – Throughout the ages, mandrake roots have been thought to cure infertility. When neither Rachel nor Leah could conceive, Reuben brought mandrake root for Leah, his mother. Rachel became jealous and demanded that Leah give her some of the mandrake.

Leah told Rachel, "You have taken everything from me: first, my husband, and now, my ability to have children." But Leah restricted her anger toward her sister by giving Rachel the mandrake, and with this unconditional act of sharing, Leah enabled both of them to bear children. Leah became pregnant with Issachar and Rachel with Joseph.

Yet we read in the *Zohar* that it was God—not the mandrake—who opened Rachel's womb. This reminds us to place the Cause of All Causes at the center of our thinking. The *Zohar* says:

> *It may be said that the mandrakes opened Rachel's womb. This is not so, as it is written: "...and the Lord hearkened to her and opened her womb." (Genesis 30:22) Thus it was God who OPENED HER WOMB, and nothing else. As for the mandrakes, although they have the power of action*

FOURTH READING - MOSES - NETZACH

14 וַיֵּלֶךְ כלי רְאוּבֵן ג״פ אלהים בִּימֵי קְצִיר־חִטִּים וַיִּמְצָא דוּדָאִים
בַּשָּׂדֶה וַיָּבֵא אֹתָם אֶל־לֵאָה לאה (אלד ע״ה) אִמּוֹ וַתֹּאמֶר רָחֵל רבוע ס״ג
- ע״ב אֶל־לֵאָה לאה (אלד ע״ה) תְּנִי־נָא לִי מִדּוּדָאֵי בְּנֵךְ׃ 15 וַתֹּאמֶר לָהּ
הַמְעַט קַחְתֵּךְ אֶת־אִישִׁי וְלָקַחַת גַּם יג״ל אֶת־דּוּדָאֵי בְּנִי וַתֹּאמֶר
רָחֵל רבוע ס״ג - ע״ב לָכֵן יִשְׁכַּב עִמָּךְ נמם הַלַּיְלָה מלה תַּחַת דּוּדָאֵי בְנֵךְ׃
16 וַיָּבֹא יַעֲקֹב יאהדונהי - אידהנויה מִן־הַשָּׂדֶה שדי בָּעֶרֶב רבוע אלהים רבוע יהוה
וַתֵּצֵא לֵאָה לאה (אלד ע״ה) לִקְרָאתוֹ וַתֹּאמֶר אֵלַי תָּבוֹא כִּי שָׂכֹר
י״פ ב״ן שְׂכַרְתִּיךָ בְּדוּדָאֵי בְּנִי וַיִּשְׁכַּב עִמָּהּ בַּלַּיְלָה מלה הוּא׃
17 וַיִּשְׁמַע אֱלֹהִים ילה, מום אֶל־לֵאָה לאה (אלד ע״ה) וַתַּהַר וַתֵּלֶד לְיַעֲקֹב
יאהדונהי - אידהנויה בֵּן חֲמִישִׁי׃ 18 וַתֹּאמֶר לֵאָה לאה (אלד ע״ה) נָתַן אֱלֹהִים
ילה, מום שְׂכָרִי אֲשֶׁר־נָתַתִּי שִׁפְחָתִי לְאִישִׁי וַתִּקְרָא שְׁמוֹ מהש ע״ה
יִשָּׂשכָר י״פ ב״ן - י״פ אל׃ 19 וַתַּהַר עוֹד לֵאָה לאה (אלד ע״ה) וַתֵּלֶד בֵּן־שִׁשִּׁי
לְיַעֲקֹב יאהדונהי - אידהנויה׃ 20 וַתֹּאמֶר לֵאָה לאה (אלד ע״ה) זְבָדַנִי אֱלֹהִים
ילה, מום | אֹתִי זֵבֶד טוֹב והו הַפַּעַם יִזְבְּלֵנִי אִישִׁי כִּי־יָלַדְתִּי לוֹ
שִׁשָּׁה בָנִים וַתִּקְרָא אֶת־שְׁמוֹ מהש ע״ה זְבֻלוּן׃ 21 וְאַחַר יָלְדָה בַּת

---

above, it is not in their power to give children, because children depend upon Mazal, and nothing else.
– The Zohar, Vayetze 23:199

יִשָּׂשכָר – (כט)

Genesis 30:18 – Issachar controls the month of Leo (*Av*) with the letters *Kaf* and *Tet*. Leo is extremely important as it is associated with the birth of the Messiah; the *Talmud* tells us that the Messiah will be born on the ninth day of *Av*.

זְבֻלוּן – (רי)

Genesis 30:20 – Zebulun controls the month of Virgo (*Elul*) with the letters *Reish* and *Yud*. Issachar and Zebulun reached an agreement that divided the physical and the spiritual

*22 And God remembered Rachel; and God hearkened to her and opened her womb.
23 And she conceived and gave birth to a son and said, "God has taken away my
reproach." 24 She named him Joseph, and said, "The Lord shall add to me another
son." 25 And it came to pass when Rachel gave birth to Joseph that Jacob said to
Laban, "Send me on my way so I can go back to my own place and to my own
country. 26 Give me my wives and children, for whom I have served you, and let me
go, for you know how much work I've done for you." 27 And Laban said to him, "I pray
you, if I have found favor in your eyes, please stay. I have learned by experience that
the Lord has blessed me because of you."*

FIFTH READING - AARON - HOD

*28 And he said, "Name your wages, and I will give it." 29 And he said to him, "You know
how I have worked for you and how your cattle were taken care of by me. 30 The little
you had before I came has increased into a multitude, and the Lord has blessed you
since my arrival; and now, when may I provide for my own household?"*

*31 And he said, "What shall I give you?" And Jacob said, "Don't give me anything, and
if you will do this for me, I will go on feeding and keeping your flock: 32 I will pass
through all your flock today and remove from them all the speckled and spotted*

---

realms between them, yet made them mutually supportive of one another. Issachar studied all day, while Zebulun was responsible for business affairs. Zebulun supported Issachar financially, and Issachar gave half of all his spiritual Light to Zebulun.

דִּינָה

Genesis 30:21 – Leah had a daughter named Dinah. Originally, the child was to have been a boy, but Leah prayed for a girl so that Rachel could be the foundation of at least two tribes.

יוֹסֵף – (קג)

Genesis 30:24 – At last, Rachel gave birth to Joseph, who controls the month of Pisces (*Adar*) with the letters *Kof* and *Gimel*. According to the *Zohar*, he was conceived from the first drop of semen of Jacob, which God had protected and intended for this purpose. The *Zohar* expains:

> *It was revealed before God that all Jacob, the perfect one, did was true, and that he harbored thoughts of Truth. The night he had intercourse with Leah, his thoughts were of Rachel. He was with Leah and thought of Rachel, and his issue came from that thought.*
>
> *– The Zohar, Vayetze 22:185*

שְׂכָרִי

Genesis 30:32 – Finally, after working 14 years for Leah and Rachel, Jacob began to work for himself and his own physical sustenance. According to the agreement he made with Laban, his father-in-law was allowed to keep all the spotted goats and sheep from the herd. Jacob could keep the solid-colored animals as well as

וַתִּקְרָא אֶת־שְׁמָהּ דִּינָה׃ 22 וַיִּזְכֹּר ע״ב - קס״א, יהי אור ע״ה אֱלֹהִים ילה, מום
אֶת־רָחֵל רבוע ס״ג - ע״ב וַיִּשְׁמַע אֵלֶיהָ אֱלֹהִים ילה, מום וַיִּפְתַּח אֶת־
רַחְמָהּ׃ 23 וַתַּהַר וַתֵּלֶד בֵּן וַתֹּאמֶר אָסַף אֱלֹהִים ילה, מום אֶת־
חֶרְפָּתִי׃ 24 וַתִּקְרָא אֶת־שְׁמוֹ מהש ע״ה יוֹסֵף ציון, קנאה, ו״פ יהוה, ה״פ אל לֵאמֹר
יֹסֵף ציון, קנאה, ו״פ יהוה, ה״פ אל יְהֹוָהאדני יאהדונהי לִי בֵּן אַחֵר׃ 25 וַיְהִי כַּאֲשֶׁר
יָלְדָה רָחֵל רבוע ס״ג - ע״ב אֶת־יוֹסֵף ציון, קנאה, ו״פ יהוה, ה״פ אל וַיֹּאמֶר יַעֲקֹב
יאהדונהי - אידהנויה אֶל־לָבָן שַׁלְּחֵנִי וְאֵלְכָה אֶל־מְקוֹמִי וּלְאַרְצִי׃
26 תְּנָה נתה, קס״א - קנ״א - קמ״ג אֶת־נָשַׁי וְאֶת־יְלָדַי אֲשֶׁר עָבַדְתִּי אֹתְךָ
בָּהֵן וְאֵלֵכָה כִּי אַתָּה יָדַעְתָּ אֶת־עֲבֹדָתִי אֲשֶׁר עֲבַדְתִּיךָ׃
27 וַיֹּאמֶר אֵלָיו לָבָן אִם יוהך ־נָא מָצָאתִי חֵן מוזי בְּעֵינֶיךָ ריבוע מ״ה
נִחַשְׁתִּי וַיְבָרְכֵנִי יְהֹוָהאדני יאהדונהי בִּגְלָלֶךָ׃

FIFTH READING - AARON - HOD

28 וַיֹּאמַר נָקְבָה שְׂכָרְךָ עָלַי וְאֶתֵּנָה נתה, קס״א - קנ״א - קמ״ג׃ 29 וַיֹּאמֶר
אֵלָיו אַתָּה יָדַעְתָּ אֵת אֲשֶׁר עֲבַדְתִּיךָ וְאֵת אֲשֶׁר־הָיָה יהה מִקְנְךָ
אִתִּי׃ 30 כִּי מְעַט אֲשֶׁר־הָיָה יהה לְךָ לְפָנַי וַיִּפְרֹץ לָרֹב וַיְבָרֶךְ
עסמ״ב יְהֹוָהאדני יאהדונהי אֹתְךָ לְרַגְלִי וְעַתָּה מָתַי אֶעֱשֶׂה גַם יג״ל ־אָנֹכִי
איע לְבֵיתִי ב״פ ראה׃ 31 וַיֹּאמֶר מָה מ״ה אֶתֶּן־לָךְ וַיֹּאמֶר יַעֲקֹב יאהדונהי - אידהנויה
לֹא־תִתֶּן ב״פ כהת ־לִי מְאוּמָה אִם יוהך ־תַּעֲשֶׂה־לִּי הַדָּבָר ראה הַזֶּה
והו אָשׁוּבָה אֶרְעֶה צֹאנְךָ אֶשְׁמֹר׃ 32 אֶעֱבֹר בְּכָל לכב ־צֹאנְךָ
הַיּוֹם נגד, זן, מזבח הָסֵר מִשָּׁם כָּל ילי ־שֶׂה | נָקֹד וְטָלוּא וְכָל ילי ־שֶׂה־
חוּם בַּכְּשָׂבִים וְטָלוּא וְנָקֹד בָּעִזִּים וְהָיָה יהוה, יהה שְׂכָרִי׃ 33 וְעָנְתָה־
בִּי צִדְקָתִי בְּיוֹם נגד, זן, מזבח מָחָר כִּי־תָבוֹא עַל־שְׂכָרִי

cattle, and all the brown stock among the sheep, and the spotted and speckled among the goats, and they will be my wages.

*33 And my honesty will testify for me in time to come, when you will come to check on
the wages you have paid me. Any goat that is not speckled and spotted, and brown
among the sheep, will be considered stolen by me." 34 And Laban said, "Behold, let
it be as you have said." 35 And he removed that day all the male goats that were ring-
streaked and spotted, and all the female goats that were speckled and spotted, and
everyone that had some white in it, and all the brown among the sheep, and he
placed them into the hands of his sons.*

*36 And he set three days journey between himself and Jacob, and Jacob fed the rest
of Laban's flocks. 37 And Jacob took him fresh-cut branches from poplar, and of the
hazel and chestnut tree, and made white streaks in them by exposing the white inner
wood of the branches. 38 And he set the peeled branches before the flocks in the
gutters in the watering troughs when the flocks came to drink, that they should
conceive when they came to drink.*

*39 And the flocks conceived before the branches, and brought forth cattle ring-
streaked, speckled, and spotted. 40 And Jacob separated the lambs and set the faces
of the blocks toward the ring-streaked, and all the brown in the flock of Laban; and
he put his own flocks by themselves and put them not with Laban's cattle.*

*41 And it came to pass that whenever the stronger females did conceive, that Jacob
would place the branches in the gutters in front of the eyes of the cattle so they might
conceive among the rods.*

*42 But when the cattle were feeble, he would not place them there. So the feebler were
Laban's and the stronger were Jacob's. 43 And the man grew exceedingly prosperous
and had much cattle, and maidservants and menservants, and camels and asses.*

---

any speckled animals born from those of solid color. After Jacob placed some peeled wooden rods in the watering tanks, the Light caused all further newborns to be born speckled so that they would all belong to Jacob. In this way, God ensured Jacob's sustenance. We learn from this that when we follow a spiritual path—when we are entirely guided by the Light—our material needs will be provided for. The *Zohar* says:

> *When all the channels are filled on all four sides of the world, then all the flocks are given water, each according to its grade, FROM THE FOUR ASPECTS OF CHOCHMAH, BINAH, TIFERET, AND MALCHUT. When Jacob came to purify this grade, THE NUKVA, he chose the right side, which was worthy of him. The Other Side, which was not worthy, was separated from him, as it is written: "... and he put his own flocks apart and put them not to Laban's cattle." He was "apart," on his own, and did not worship strange gods from the other sides. Happy is the portion of Israel, of whom it is written: "For you are a holy people to the Lord your God, and God has chosen you...." (Deuteronomy 14:2)*
>
> – *The Zohar, Vayetze 38:353*

וַיִּשְׁמַע

Genesis 31:1 – Jacob heard Laban's sons saying that Jacob had stolen from their father. God then told Jacob that his work in Laban's

לְפָנֶיךָ ס״ג - מ״ה - ב״ן כֹּל ילי אֲשֶׁר־אֵינֶנּוּ נָקֹד וְטָלוּא בָּעִזִּים וְחוּם
בַּכְּשָׂבִים גָּנוּב הוּא אִתִּי: 34 וַיֹּאמֶר לָבָן הֵן לוּ יְהִי כִדְבָרֶךָ ראה:
35 וַיָּסַר בַּיּוֹם נגד, זן, מזבח הַהוּא אֶת־הַתְּיָשִׁים הָעֲקֻדִּים וְהַטְּלֻאִים
וְאֵת כָּל ילי ־הָעִזִּים הַנְּקֻדּוֹת וְהַטְּלֻאֹת כֹּל ילי אֲשֶׁר־לָבָן בּוֹ וְכָל
ילי ־חוּם בַּכְּשָׂבִים וַיִּתֵּן בְּיַד־בָּנָיו: 36 וַיָּשֶׂם דֶּרֶךְ ב״פ יב״ק שְׁלֹשֶׁת
יָמִים נלך בֵּינוֹ וּבֵין יַעֲקֹב יאהדונהי - אידהנויה וְיַעֲקֹב יאהדונהי - אידהנויה רֹעֶה
רהע אֶת־צֹאן מלוי אהיה דיודין ע״ה לָבָן הַנּוֹתָרֹת: 37 וַיִּקַּח חעם ־לוֹ יַעֲקֹב
יאהדונהי - אידהנויה מַקַּל לִבְנֶה לַח וְלוּז וְעַרְמוֹן וַיְפַצֵּל בָּהֵן פְּצָלוֹת
לְבָנוֹת מַחְשֹׂף הַלָּבָן אֲשֶׁר עַל־הַמַּקְלוֹת: 38 וַיַּצֵּג אֶת־הַמַּקְלוֹת
אֲשֶׁר פִּצֵּל בָּרְהָטִים בְּשִׁקְתוֹת הַמָּיִם אֲשֶׁר תָּבֹאןָ הַצֹּאן
מלוי אהיה דיודין ע״ה לִשְׁתּוֹת לְנֹכַח ג״פ יהוה הַצֹּאן מלוי אהיה דיודין ע״ה וַיֵּחַמְנָה
בְּבֹאָן לִשְׁתּוֹת: 39 וַיֶּחֱמוּ הַצֹּאן מלוי אהיה דיודין ע״ה אֶל־הַמַּקְלוֹת
וַתֵּלַדְןָ הַצֹּאן מלוי אהיה דיודין ע״ה עֲקֻדִּים נְקֻדִּים וּטְלֻאִים: 40 וְהַכְּשָׂבִים
הִפְרִיד יַעֲקֹב יאהדונהי - אידהנויה וַיִּתֵּן י״פ מלוי ע״ב פְּנֵי חכמה - בינה הַצֹּאן
מלוי אהיה דיודין ע״ה אֶל־עָקֹד וְכָל ילי ־חוּם בְּצֹאן מלוי אהיה דיודין ע״ה לָבָן
וַיָּשֶׁת־לוֹ עֲדָרִים לְבַדּוֹ מ״ב וְלֹא שָׁתָם עַל־צֹאן מלוי אהיה דיודין ע״ה
לָבָן: 41 וְהָיָה יהוה, יהה בְּכָל לכב ־יַחֵם הַצֹּאן מלוי אהיה דיודין ע״ה הַמְקֻשָּׁרוֹת
וְשָׂם יַעֲקֹב יאהדונהי - אידהנויה אֶת־הַמַּקְלוֹת לְעֵינֵי ריבוע מ״ה הַצֹּאן
מלוי אהיה דיודין ע״ה בָּרְהָטִים לְיַחְמֶנָּה בַּמַּקְלוֹת: 42 וּבְהַעֲטִיף הַצֹּאן
מלוי אהיה דיודין ע״ה לֹא יָשִׂים וְהָיָה יהוה, יהה הָעֲטֻפִים לְלָבָן וְהַקְּשֻׁרִים
לְיַעֲקֹב יאהדונהי - אידהנויה: 43 וַיִּפְרֹץ הָאִישׁ ז״פ אדם מְאֹד מ״ה מְאֹד מ״ה
וַיְהִי אל ־לוֹ צֹאן מלוי אהיה דיודין ע״ה רַבּוֹת וּשְׁפָחוֹת וַעֲבָדִים וּגְמַלִּים
וַחֲמֹרִים: 31 1 וַיִּשְׁמַע אֶת־דִּבְרֵי ראה בְנֵי־לָבָן לֵאמֹר לָקַח

31[1] And he heard the words of Laban's sons saying, "Jacob has taken away all that was our fathers and of that which was our fathers has he gained all this wealth." [2] And Jacob beheld the countenance of Laban and saw that it was not what it had been before. [3] And the Lord said to Jacob, "Go back to the land of your fathers and to your kindred, and I will be with you."

[4] And Jacob sent word to Rachel and Leah to come out to the fields, to his flocks, [5] and said to them, "I see that your father's countenance toward me is not what it was before, but the God of my father has been with me, [6] and you know that I've worked for your father with all my power, [7] and your father has deceived me, and changed my wages ten times, but God has not allowed him to hurt me.

[8] If he said, 'The speckled will be your wages,' then all the cattle bore speckled; and if he said, 'The ring-streaked will be your wages,' then bore all the cattle ring-streaked.

[9] So God has taken away your father's cattle and given them to me.

[10] And it came to pass at the time that the cattle conceived, that I lifted up my eyes and saw in a dream that the rams which leaped upon the cattle were ring-streaked, speckled, and spotted. [11] And the angel of God spoke to me in the dream saying, 'Jacob.' And I said, 'Here I am.'

[12] And he said, 'Lift up your eyes and see that all the rams that leap upon the cattle are ring-streaked, speckled, and spotted, for I have seen all that Laban has been doing to you.

[13] I am the God of Bethel, where you anointed a pillar and where you made a vow to Me: now arise, leave this land at once and return to the land of your kindred.' "

[14] And Rachel and Leah answered and said to him, "Is there still any portion or inheritance for us in our father's house?

---

household was finished and it was now time for him to move on. Jacob had worked fourteen years for his two wives and an additional six years to build up his flocks. But when he heard the accusation that he was a thief, he was open to God's message that he should depart. From this lesson, we learn that once our *tikkun*, our spiritual correction, is completed, our work is done with regard to a specific area of our life. So when we are given a sign from the Creator that it is time to move on, we will be supported by the Light so that we can follow through on that decision.

וַיֹּאמֶר

Genesis 31:5 – Jacob explained to Rachel and Leah how he had acquired all his sheep and goats. He had had a dream about animals that were ringed, spotted, and flecked, and was given an explanation and instructions by an angel. The Ari wrote that Jacob's dream referred to the dimensions of the Upper Worlds; because Jacob came from the Upper Worlds, he had dominion even over the Lower Realms.

יַעֲקֹב יאהדונהי - אידהנויה אֵת כָּל ילי ־אֲשֶׁר לְאָבִינוּ וּמֵאֲשֶׁר לְאָבִינוּ
עָשָׂה אֵת כָּל ילי ־הַכָּבֹד הַזֶּה והו׃ 2 וַיַּרְא יַעֲקֹב יאהדונהי - אידהנויה
אֶת־פְּנֵי חכמה - בינה לָבָן וְהִנֵּה מ״ה יה אֵינֶנּוּ עִמּוֹ כִּתְמוֹל שִׁלְשׁוֹם׃
3 וַיֹּאמֶר יְהֹוָה(אדני) יאהדונהי אֶל־יַעֲקֹב יאהדונהי - אידהנויה שׁוּב אֶל־אֶרֶץ
אלהים דאלפין אֲבוֹתֶיךָ וּלְמוֹלַדְתֶּךָ וְאֶהְיֶה אהיה עִמָּךְ נמם׃ 4 וַיִּשְׁלַח
יַעֲקֹב יאהדונהי - אידהנויה וַיִּקְרָא עם ה׳ אותיות = ב״פ קס״א לְרָחֵל רבוע ס״ג - ע״ב
וּלְלֵאָה לאה (אלד ע״ה) הַשָּׂדֶה שדי אֶל־צֹאנוֹ׃ 5 וַיֹּאמֶר לָהֶן רֹאֶה ראה
אָנֹכִי איע אֶת־פְּנֵי חכמה - בינה אֲבִיכֶן כִּי־אֵינֶנּוּ אֵלַי כִּתְמֹל שִׁלְשֹׁם
וֵאלֹהֵי לכב, דמב, ילה אָבִי הָיָה יהה עִמָּדִי׃ 6 וְאַתֵּנָה יְדַעְתֶּן כִּי בְּכָל
לכב ־כֹּחִי עָבַדְתִּי אֶת־אֲבִיכֶן׃ 7 וַאֲבִיכֶן הֵתֶל בִּי וְהֶחֱלִף אֶת־
מַשְׂכֻּרְתִּי עֲשֶׂרֶת מֹנִים וְלֹא־נְתָנוֹ אֱלֹהִים ילה, מום לְהָרַע עִמָּדִי׃
8 אִם יוהך ־כֹּה היי יֹאמַר נְקֻדִּים יִהְיֶה ייי שְׂכָרֶךָ וְיָלְדוּ כָל־ ילי
הַצֹּאן מלוי אהיה דיודין ע״ה נְקֻדִּים וְאִם יוהך ־כֹּה היי יֹאמַר עֲקֻדִּים יִהְיֶה
ייי שְׂכָרֶךָ וְיָלְדוּ כָל ילי ־הַצֹּאן מלוי אהיה דיודין ע״ה עֲקֻדִּים׃ 9 וַיַּצֵּל
אֱלֹהִים ילה, מום אֶת־מִקְנֵה אֲבִיכֶם וַיִּתֶּן י״פ מלוי ע״ב ־לִי׃ 10 וַיְהִי בְּעֵת
י״פ אהיה - י הוויות יַחֵם הַצֹּאן מלוי אהיה דיודין ע״ה וָאֶשָּׂא עֵינַי ריבוע מ״ה וָאֵרֶא
בַּחֲלוֹם וְהִנֵּה הָעַתֻּדִים הָעֹלִים עַל־הַצֹּאן מלוי אהיה דיודין ע״ה עֲקֻדִּים
נְקֻדִּים וּבְרֻדִּים׃ 11 וַיֹּאמֶר אֵלַי מַלְאַךְ הָאֱלֹהִים ילה, מום בַּחֲלוֹם
יַעֲקֹב יאהדונהי - אידהנויה וָאֹמַר הִנֵּנִי׃ 12 וַיֹּאמֶר שָׂא־נָא עֵינֶיךָ ע״ה קס״א
וּרְאֵה ראה כָּל־ ילי הָעַתֻּדִים הָעֹלִים עַל־הַצֹּאן מלוי אהיה דיודין ע״ה
עֲקֻדִּים נְקֻדִּים וּבְרֻדִּים כִּי רָאִיתִי אֵת כָּל ילי ־אֲשֶׁר לָבָן עֹשֶׂה
לָּךְ׃ 13 אָנֹכִי איע הָאֵל לאה (אלד ע״ה) בֵּית ב״פ ראה ־אֵל ייאי אֲשֶׁר מָשַׁחְתָּ
שָּׁם מַצֵּבָה אֲשֶׁר נָדַרְתָּ לִּי שָּׁם נֶדֶר עַתָּה קוּם צֵא מִן־הָאָרֶץ
אלהים דההין ע״ה הַזֹּאת וְשׁוּב אֶל־אֶרֶץ אלהים דאלפין מוֹלַדְתֶּךָ׃

[15] Does he not regard us as strangers, because he has sold us, and has used up our money?

[16] For all the riches that God has taken from our father is ours and our children's now, so do whatever God has told you to do."

SIXTH READING - JOSEPH - YESOD

[17] Then Jacob rose up and put his sons and his wives on camels, [18] and he carried
away all his cattle and all his goods he had gotten, the cattle which he got in Paddan Aram, to go to Isaac, his father, in the land of Canaan.

[19] And Laban went to shear his sheep and Rachel stole the idols that were her father's.

[20] And Jacob stole away without telling Laban the Syrian that he was leaving.

[21] So he fled with all that he had, and he rose up and passed over the River, and he headed toward the mount Gilead.

[22] And Laban was told on the third day Laban that Jacob had fled.

[23] And he took his brethren with him, and pursued Jacob for seven days and caught up with him in the mount of Gilead.

[24] And God came to Laban the Syrian in a dream at night and said to him, "Take heed to not say anything to Jacob, either good or bad."

[25] Then Laban overtook Jacob. Now Jacob had pitched his tent in the mount, and Laban with his brethren pitched in the mount of Gilead.

[26] And Laban said to Jacob, "What have you done? You have left without me knowing, and carried away my daughters like captives taken with a sword.

וַתַּעַן

Genesis 31:14 – Rachel and Leah said that they felt like strangers in their own father's house because all the money went to Laban; their father shared nothing. Therefore, the whole family decided to run away. Rachel took her father's idols, which had the power of magic and prophecy from the Negative Side. Rashi says that Rachel took the idols to keep her father from idol-worship and that therefore she had noble intentions.

וַיֻּגַּד

Genesis 31:22 – When Laban discovered that Jacob and his family had fled along with their

14 וַתַּעַן רָחֵל רבוע ס״ג ּ ע״ב וְלֵאָה לאה (אלד ע״ה) וַתֹּאמַרְנָה לוֹ הַעוֹד לָנוּ
אלהים, מום חֵלֶק וְנַחֲלָה בְּבֵית ב״פ ראה אָבִינוּ׃ 15 הֲלוֹא נָכְרִיּוֹת נֶחְשַׁבְנוּ
לוֹ כִּי מְכָרָנוּ וַיֹּאכַל גַּם יגל -אָכוֹל אֶת-כַּסְפֵּנוּ׃ 16 כִּי כָל- ילי
הָעֹשֶׁר אֲשֶׁר הִצִּיל אֱלֹהִים ילה, מום מֵאָבִינוּ לָנוּ אלהים, מום הוּא
וּלְבָנֵינוּ וְעַתָּה כֹּל ילי אֲשֶׁר אָמַר אֱלֹהִים ילה, מום אֵלֶיךָ אני עֲשֵׂה׃

SIXTH READING - JOSEPH - YESOD

17 וַיָּקָם יַעֲקֹב יאהדונהי ּ אידהנויה וַיִּשָּׂא אֶת-בָּנָיו וְאֶת-נָשָׁיו עַל-
הַגְּמַלִּים׃ 18 וַיִּנְהַג אֶת-כָּל ילי -מִקְנֵהוּ וְאֶת-כָּל ילי -רְכֻשׁוֹ אֲשֶׁר
רָכָשׁ מִקְנֵה קִנְיָנוֹ אֲשֶׁר רָכַשׁ בְּפַדַּן אֲרָם לָבוֹא אֶל-יִצְחָק ד״פ ב״ן
אָבִיו אַרְצָה אלהים דההין ע״ה כְּנָעַן׃ 19 וְלָבָן הָלַךְ מיה לִגְזֹז אֶת-צֹאנוֹ
וַתִּגְנֹב רָחֵל רבוע ס״ג ּ ע״ב אֶת-הַתְּרָפִים אֲשֶׁר לְאָבִיהָ׃ 20 וַיִּגְנֹב
יַעֲקֹב יאהדונהי ּ אידהנויה אֶת-לֵב לָבָן הָאֲרַמִּי עַל-בְּלִי הִגִּיד לוֹ כִּי
בֹרֵחַ הוּא׃ 21 וַיִּבְרַח הוּא וְכָל ילי -אֲשֶׁר-לוֹ וַיָּקָם וַיַּעֲבֹר
אֶת-הַנָּהָר רפ״ח, ע״ב ּ רי״ו וַיָּשֶׂם אֶת-פָּנָיו הַר רבוע אלהים ּ ה׳ הַגִּלְעָד׃
22 וַיֻּגַּד לְלָבָן בַּיּוֹם נגד, זן, מזבח הַשְּׁלִישִׁי כִּי בָרַח יַעֲקֹב יאהדונהי ּ אידהנויה׃
23 וַיִּקַּח חעם אֶת-אֶחָיו עִמּוֹ וַיִּרְדֹּף אַחֲרָיו דֶּרֶךְ ב״פ יב״ק שִׁבְעַת
יָמִים נלך וַיַּדְבֵּק אֹתוֹ בְּהַר אור, רז הַגִּלְעָד׃ 24 וַיָּבֹא אֱלֹהִים ילה, מום
אֶל-לָבָן הָאֲרַמִּי בַּחֲלֹם ג׳ הויות הַלָּיְלָה מלה וַיֹּאמֶר לוֹ הִשָּׁמֶר לְךָ
פֶּן-תְּדַבֵּר ראה עִם-יַעֲקֹב יאהדונהי ּ אידהנויה מִטּוֹב והו עַד-רָע׃ 25 וַיַּשֵּׂג
לָבָן אֶת-יַעֲקֹב יאהדונהי ּ אידהנויה וְיַעֲקֹב יאהדונהי ּ אידהנויה תָּקַע ב״פ סוזוף
אֶת-אָהֳלוֹ בָּהָר אור, רז וְלָבָן תָּקַע ב״פ סוזוף אֶת-אֶחָיו בְּהַר אור, רז
הַגִּלְעָד׃ 26 וַיֹּאמֶר לָבָן לְיַעֲקֹב יאהדונהי ּ אידהנויה מֶה מ״ה עָשִׂיתָ

27 Why did you run off secretly and steal away from me, and not tell me, so that I could send you away with joy and with songs, with tambourines and with harps?

28 And not allowed me to kiss my sons and my daughters? You have done a foolish thing.

29 It is in the power of my hand to hurt you; but the God of your father said to me last night, 'Take heed not to say anything to Jacob, either good or bad.'

30 And now, though you desire to be gone because you longed to return to your
father's house, yet why did you steal my gods?"
31 Jacob answered and said to Laban,
"Because I was afraid, for I said that you might take your daughters away from me by force.

32 With whoever you find your gods, let him not live: Before our brethren, discern for yourself what is yours with me; and take it to yourself." For Jacob knew not that Rachel had stolen them.

33 And Laban went into Jacob's tent and into Leah's tent and into the tent of the two
maidservants, but he found nothing. Then he went out of Leah's tent, and entered
into Rachel's tent.
34 Now Rachel had taken the idols and put them inside her camel's
saddle and sat upon them. And Laban searched the whole tent but found no idols.

35 And she said to her father, "Let it not upset my lord, that I cannot rise before you, for the custom of women is upon me." And he searched but could not find the idols.

36 And Jacob was angry and took Laban to task, and Jacob said to Laban, "What is my crime, what is my sin, that you have pursued me so hotly?

37 Now that you have searched all my goods, what have you found of your household stuff? Put it here in front of my brethren and your brethren so that they may judge between the two of us.

38 For the twenty years I have been with you, your ewes and your she-goats have not miscarried, and I have not eaten the rams of your flock.

---

flocks and possessions—and his precious idols—he set off in pursuit. In a dream, God told Laban not to give anything to Jacob. This was because Laban was so negative that everything he touched became corrupted. For this very reason, we ourselves should be careful about accepting things from negative people, even if we are attracted to what they offer.

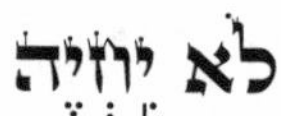

Genesis 31:32 – **The Power of Evil Speech.** Laban declared that he had nothing to say to Jacob, but he did ask, "Who took my idols?" Jacob replied, "Whoever stole your idols shall not live!" But tragically, Jacob was unaware that

וַתִּגְנֹב אֶת־לְבָבִי בוכו וַתְּנַהֵג אֶת־בְּנֹתַי כִּשְׁבֻיוֹת חָרֶב: 27 לָמָּה
נַחְבֵּאתָ לִבְרֹחַ וַתִּגְנֹב אֹתִי וְלֹא־הִגַּדְתָּ לִּי וָאֲשַׁלֵּחֲךָ בְּשִׂמְחָה
וּבְשִׁרִים בְּתֹף וּבְכִנּוֹר: 28 וְלֹא נְטַשְׁתַּנִי לְנַשֵּׁק לְבָנַי וְלִבְנֹתָי
עַתָּה הִסְכַּלְתָּ עֲשׂוֹ: 29 יֶשׁ־לְאֵל אל יָדִי לַעֲשׂוֹת עִמָּכֶם רָע
וֵאלֹהֵי לכב, דמב, ילה אֲבִיכֶם אֶמֶשׁ | אָמַר אֵלַי לֵאמֹר הִשָּׁמֶר לְךָ
מִדַּבֵּר ראה עִם־יַעֲקֹב יאהדונהי - אידהנויה מִטּוֹב והו עַד־רָע: 30 וְעַתָּה
הָלֹךְ מיה הָלַכְתָּ כִּי־נִכְסֹף נִכְסַפְתָּה לְבֵית ב"פ ראה אָבִיךָ לָמָּה
גָנַבְתָּ אֶת־אֱלֹהָי דמב, ילה: 31 וַיַּעַן יַעֲקֹב יאהדונהי - אידהנויה וַיֹּאמֶר לְלָבָן
כִּי יָרֵאתִי כִּי אָמַרְתִּי פֶּן־תִּגְזֹל אֶת־בְּנוֹתֶיךָ מֵעִמִּי: 32 עִם אֲשֶׁר
תִּמְצָא אֶת־אֱלֹהֶיךָ ילה לֹא יִחְיֶה נֶגֶד זן, מזבח אַחֵינוּ הַכֶּר־לְךָ מָה
מ"ה עִמָּדִי וְקַח־לָךְ וְלֹא־יָדַע ב"פ מ"ב יַעֲקֹב יאהדונהי - אידהנויה כִּי רָחֵל
רבוע ס"ג - ע"ב גְּנָבָתַם: 33 וַיָּבֹא לָבָן בְּאֹהֶל לאה (אלד ע"ה) יַעֲקֹב יאהדונהי - אידהנויה |
וּבְאֹהֶל לאה (אלד ע"ה) לֵאָה לאה (אלד ע"ה) וּבְאֹהֶל לאה (אלד ע"ה) שְׁתֵּי הָאֲמָהֹת
וְלֹא מָצָא ריבוע מ"ה ע"ה וַיֵּצֵא מֵאֹהֶל לאה (אלד ע"ה) לֵאָה לאה (אלד ע"ה) וַיָּבֹא
בְּאֹהֶל לאה (אלד ע"ה) רָחֵל רבוע ס"ג - ע"ב: 34 וְרָחֵל רבוע ס"ג - ע"ב לָקְחָה אֶת־
הַתְּרָפִים וַתְּשִׂמֵם בְּכַר הַגָּמָל ג' הויות וַתֵּשֶׁב עֲלֵיהֶם וַיְמַשֵּׁשׁ לָבָן
אֶת־כָּל ילי ־הָאֹהֶל לאה (אלד ע"ה) וְלֹא מָצָא ריבוע מ"ה ע"ה: 35 וַתֹּאמֶר אֶל־
אָבִיהָ אַל־יִחַר בְּעֵינֵי ריבוע מ"ה אֲדֹנִי כִּי לוֹא אוּכַל לָקוּם מִפָּנֶיךָ
ס"ג - מ"ה - ב"ן כִּי־דֶרֶךְ ב"פ יב"ק נָשִׁים לִי וַיְחַפֵּשׂ וְלֹא מָצָא ריבוע מ"ה ע"ה
אֶת־הַתְּרָפִים: 36 וַיִּחַר לְיַעֲקֹב יאהדונהי - אידהנויה וַיָּרֶב בְּלָבָן וַיַּעַן
יַעֲקֹב יאהדונהי - אידהנויה וַיֹּאמֶר לְלָבָן מַה מ"ה ־פִּשְׁעִי מַה מ"ה חַטָּאתִי
כִּי דָלַקְתָּ אַחֲרָי: 37 כִּי־מִשַּׁשְׁתָּ אֶת־כָּל ילי ־כֵּלַי כלי מַה מ"ה ־מָּצָאתָ
מִכֹּל ילי כְּלֵי כלי ־בֵיתֶךָ ב"פ ראה שִׂים כֹּה היי נֶגֶד זן, מזבח אַחַי וְאַחֶיךָ

39 I did not bring you the animals torn by wild beasts; I bore the loss myself. And you required payment from me for whatever was stolen by day or night. 40 This was my situation: in the day the drought consumed me and the frost by night, and my sleep departed from my eyes.

41 For the twenty years I was in your household I worked for you fourteen years for your two daughters and six years for your flocks, and you changed my wages ten times. 42 If the God of my father, the God of Abraham and the Fear of Isaac, had not been with me, you would surely have sent me away empty-handed. But God has seen my hardship and the toil of my hands, and rebuked you last night."

SEVENTH READING - DAVID - MALCHUT

43 And Laban answered and said to Jacob, "These daughters are my daughters, and these children are my children, and these cattle are my cattle, and all you see is mine. Yet what can I do today about these daughters of mine, or about the children they have borne?

44 Now therefore, come let us make a covenant, you and I, and let it serve as a witness between us."

45 And Jacob took a stone and set it up as a pillar. 46 And Jacob said to his brethren, "Gather stones." And they took stones and piled them in a heap, and they ate there on the heap.

47 And Laban called it Jegar Sahadutha, and Jacob called it Galeed.

48 And Laban said, "This heap is a witness between you and me this day." That is why it was called Galeed,

---

it was Rachel who had taken them. As a result of what Jacob said, Rachel had to die, and so eventually she died in childbirth. There is an overwhelmingly important lesson here: We must be very careful of what we say, always refraining from evil speech (Heb. *lashon hara*), especially when we are depressed or angry. This is because the negative angels will hold our words against us. For example, if a woman should say in anger, "I'll never have children!" she can prevent herself from becoming pregnant, even if she wants to conceive.

בְּרִית

Genesis 31:44 – Jacob made a pact of separation with Laban, such that neither of

וְיוֹכִ֖יחוּ בֵּ֥ין שְׁנֵֽינוּ׃ 38 זֶה֩ עֶשְׂרִ֨ים שָׁנָ֤ה אָנֹכִי֙ איע עִמָּ֔ךְ נמם רְחֵלֶ֥יךָ
וְעִזֶּ֖יךָ לֹ֣א שִׁכֵּ֑לוּ וְאֵילֵ֥י צֹאנְךָ֖ לֹ֥א אָכָֽלְתִּי׃ 39 טְרֵפָה֙ לֹא־הֵבֵ֣אתִי
אֵלֶ֔יךָ אני אָנֹכִ֣י איע אֲחַטֶּ֔נָּה מִיָּדִ֖י תְּבַקְשֶׁ֑נָּה גְּנֻֽבְתִ֣י י֔וֹם נגד, זן, מזבח
וּגְנֻֽבְתִ֖י לָֽיְלָה׃ מלה 40 הָיִ֧יתִי בַיּ֛וֹם נגד, זן, מזבח אֲכָלַ֥נִי חֹ֖רֶב וְקֶ֣רַח
בַּלָּ֑יְלָה מלה וַתִּדַּ֥ד שְׁנָתִ֖י מֵעֵינָֽי׃ ריבוע מ"ה 41 זֶה־לִּ֞י עֶשְׂרִ֣ים שָׁנָה֮
בְּבֵיתֶךָ֒ ב"פ ראה עֲבַדְתִּ֜יךָ אַרְבַּֽע־עֶשְׂרֵ֤ה שָׁנָה֙ בִּשְׁתֵּ֣י בְנֹתֶ֔יךָ וְשֵׁ֥שׁ
שָׁנִ֖ים בְּצֹאנֶ֑ךָ וַתַּחֲלֵ֥ף אֶת־מַשְׂכֻּרְתִּ֖י עֲשֶׂ֥רֶת מֹנִֽים׃ 42 לוּלֵ֡י
אֱלֹהֵ֣י דמב, ילה אָבִי֩ אֱלֹהֵ֨י דמב, ילה אַבְרָהָ֜ם ח"פ אל, רמ"ח וּפַ֣חַד יִצְחָק֮ ד"פ ב"ן
הָ֣יָה יהה לִ֔י כִּ֥י עַתָּ֖ה רֵיקָ֣ם שִׁלַּחְתָּ֑נִי אֶת־עָנְיִ֞י ריבוע מ"ה וְאֶת־יְגִ֧יעַ
כַּפַּ֛י רָאָ֥ה ראה אֱלֹהִ֖ים ילה, מום וַיּ֥וֹכַח אָֽמֶשׁ׃

SEVENTH READING - DAVID - MALCHUT

43 וַיַּ֨עַן לָבָ֜ן וַיֹּ֣אמֶר אֶֽל־יַעֲקֹ֗ב יאהדונהי - אידהנויה הַבָּנ֨וֹת בְּנֹתַ֜י וְהַבָּנִ֣ים
בָּנַ֗י וְהַצֹּ֣אן מלוי אהיה דיודין ע"ה צֹאנִ֔י וְכֹ֛ל ילי אֲשֶׁר־אַתָּ֥ה רֹאֶ֖ה ראה לִי־
ה֑וּא וְלִבְנֹתַ֞י מָֽה מ"ה ־אֶעֱשֶׂ֤ה לָאֵ֙לֶּה֙ הַיּ֔וֹם נגד, זן, מזבח א֥וֹ לִבְנֵיהֶ֖ן
אֲשֶׁ֥ר יָלָֽדוּ׃ 44 וְעַתָּ֗ה לְכָ֛ה נִכְרְתָ֥ה בְרִ֖ית אֲנִ֣י אני וָאָ֑תָּה וְהָיָ֥ה
יהוה, יהה לְעֵ֖ד בֵּינִ֥י וּבֵינֶֽךָ׃ 45 וַיִּקַּ֥ח חעם יַעֲקֹ֖ב יאהדונהי - אידהנויה אָ֑בֶן יוד הה ואו הה
וַיְרִימֶ֖הָ מַצֵּבָֽה׃ 46 וַיֹּ֨אמֶר יַעֲקֹ֤ב יאהדונהי - אידהנויה לְאֶחָיו֙ לִקְט֣וּ אֲבָנִ֔ים
וַיִּקְח֥וּ חעם אֲבָנִ֖ים וַיַּעֲשׂוּ־גָ֑ל וַיֹּ֥אכְלוּ שָׁ֖ם עַל־הַגָּֽל׃ 47 וַיִּקְרָא־
עם ה' אותיות = ב"פ קס"א ל֙וֹ לָבָ֔ן יְגַ֖ר קס"א ב"ן שָׂהֲדוּתָ֑א וְיַעֲקֹ֕ב יאהדונהי - אידהנויה
קָ֥רָא ל֖וֹ גַּלְעֵֽד׃ 48 וַיֹּ֣אמֶר לָבָ֔ן הַגַּ֥ל הַזֶּ֛ה והו עֵ֥ד בֵּינִ֖י וּבֵינְךָ֣

---

them would trespass on the other's territory. This represents the total separation of good and evil. Although good and evil are clearly defined, often we cannot tell one from the other. We must foster the ability within ourselves to clearly recognize good and evil as well as to make the right choice between them.

49 and Mizpah, because he said, "May the Lord keep watch between you and me when we are away from each other.

50 If you shall mistreat my daughters or if you take other wives besides my daughters, no man is with us, God is a witness between you and me."

51 And Laban said to Jacob, "Behold this heap, and see this pillar which I have cast between you and me.

52 This heap is a witness, and this pillar is a witness, that I will not go past this heap to you and that you will not go past this heap and pillar to me, to harm.

53 May the God of Abraham and the God of Nahor, the God of their father, judge between us." So Jacob swore by fear in the name of his father Isaac.

54 Then Jacob offered a sacrifice upon the mount and called his relatives to eat bread. And they did eat, and they spent the night there.

MAFTIR

55 And early in the morning Laban rose up and kissed his sons and his daughters, and blessed them; and Laban departed and returned to his place.

32:1 Jacob also went on his way, and the angels of God met him.

2 When Jacob saw them, he said, "This is the camp of God!" So he named that place Mahanaim.

וַיִּפְגְּעוּ־בוֹ

Genesis 32:2 – Jacob went on his way. Although the angels met him again, he no longer needed their spiritual protection, nor did he need their help in his cleansing process.

As the *Zohar* explains:

> *When Jacob turned to go toward Charan, he was unmarried. It is written: "And he lighted on a certain place...." (Genesis 28:11) Then he was answered only in a dream. After he was married*

הַיּ֖וֹם נגד, זן, מזבח עַל־כֵּ֥ן קָֽרָא־שְׁמ֖וֹ מהש ע״ה גַּלְעֵֽד׃ 49 וְהַמִּצְפָּה֙ אֲשֶׁ֣ר
אָמַ֔ר יִ֥צֶף יְהֹוָ֖אדניאהדונהי בֵּינִ֣י וּבֵינֶ֑ךָ כִּ֥י נִסָּתֵ֖ר ב״פ מצר אִ֥ישׁ ע״ה קנ״א קס״א
מֵרֵעֵֽהוּ׃ 50 אִם יוהך ־תְּעַנֶּ֣ה אֶת־בְּנֹתַ֗י וְאִם יוהך ־תִּקַּ֤ח נָשִׁים֙ עַל־
בְּנֹתַ֔י אֵ֥ין אִ֖ישׁ ע״ה קנ״א קס״א עִמָּ֑נוּ ריבוע ס״ג רְאֵ֕ה ראה אֱלֹהִ֥ים ילה, מום עֵ֖ד בֵּינִ֥י
וּבֵינֶֽךָ׃ 51 וַיֹּ֥אמֶר לָבָ֖ן לְיַעֲקֹ֑ב יאהדונהי - אידהנויה הִנֵּ֣ה מ״ה יה | הַגַּ֣ל הַזֶּ֗ה והו
וְהִנֵּה֙ מ״ה יה הַמַּצֵּבָ֔ה אֲשֶׁ֥ר יָרִ֖יתִי בֵּינִ֥י וּבֵינֶֽךָ׃ 52 עֵ֚ד הַגַּ֣ל הַזֶּ֔ה והו
וְעֵדָ֖ה הַמַּצֵּבָ֑ה אִם יוהך ־אָ֗נִי אני לֹֽא־אֶעֱבֹ֤ר אֵלֶ֙יךָ֙ אֶת־הַגַּ֣ל הַזֶּ֔ה
והו וְאִם יוהך ־אַ֠תָּה לֹא־תַעֲבֹ֨ר אֵלַ֜י אֶת־הַגַּ֥ל הַזֶּ֛ה והו וְאֶת־הַמַּצֵּבָ֥ה
הַזֹּ֖את לְרָעָֽה רהע׃ 53 אֱלֹהֵ֨י דמב, ילה אַבְרָהָ֜ם ח״פ אל, רמ״ח וֵֽאלֹהֵ֤י (וזול)
נָחוֹר֙ יִשְׁפְּט֣וּ בֵינֵ֔ינוּ אֱלֹהֵ֖י (וזול) אֲבִיהֶ֑ם וַיִּשָּׁבַ֣ע יַעֲקֹ֔ב יאהדונהי - אידהנויה
בְּפַ֖חַד אָבִ֥יו יִצְחָֽק ד״פ ב״ן׃ 54 וַיִּזְבַּ֨ח יַעֲקֹ֥ב יאהדונהי - אידהנויה זֶ֙בַח֙ בָּהָ֔ר
אור, רז וַיִּקְרָ֥א עם ה' אותיות = ב״פ קס״א לְאֶחָ֖יו לֶאֱכָל־לָ֑חֶם ג״פ יהוה וַיֹּ֣אכְלוּ
לֶ֔חֶם ג״פ יהוה וַיָּלִ֖ינוּ בָּהָֽר אור, רז׃

MAFTIR

55 וַיַּשְׁכֵּ֨ם לָבָ֜ן בַּבֹּ֗קֶר וַיְנַשֵּׁ֛ק לְבָנָ֥יו וְלִבְנוֹתָ֖יו וַיְבָ֣רֶךְ עסמ״ב אֶתְהֶ֑ם
וַיֵּ֛לֶךְ כלי וַיָּ֥שָׁב לָבָ֖ן לִמְקֹמֽוֹ׃ 32 1 וְיַעֲקֹ֖ב יאהדונהי - אידהנויה הָלַ֣ךְ מיה
לְדַרְכּ֑וֹ וַיִּפְגְּעוּ־ב֖וֹ מַלְאֲכֵ֥י אֱלֹהִֽים ילה, מום׃ 2 וַיֹּ֤אמֶר יַעֲקֹב֙ יאהדו
נהי - אידהנויה כַּאֲשֶׁ֣ר רָאָ֔ם מַחֲנֵ֥ה אֱלֹהִ֖ים ילה, מום זֶ֑ה וַיִּקְרָ֛א
עם ה' אותיות = ב״פ קס״א שֵֽׁם שדי יהוה ־הַמָּק֥וֹם יהוה ברבוע הַה֖וּא מַחֲנָֽיִם׃ [פ] [פ] [פ]

---

and came to all the tribes, the supernal camps met him and entreated him, as it is written: "...and angels of the Lord met (also: 'entreated') him." Now they came to meet him. First he WAS BEGGING, as it is written: "... and he lighted (Heb. vayifga) on a certain place." Now they BEGGED, AS IT IS WRITTEN: "...and angels of the Lord met (Heb. vayifge'u) him."

– The Zohar, Vayetze 43:386

HAFTARAH OF VAYETZE

Although this Haftarah discusses Jacob's flight from Laban, the important lesson here is the warning against idol worship. Ego, power, money, and a hundred other forces can be our idols in the material world. Anything is an idol if we are enslaved to it and if that slavery prevents us from connecting to the Light. We all have at least one idol, whether we know it or not. For a business executive who works 14 hours a day and is almost never home, his altar is his desk, before which

Hosea 11:7 - 12:12

11 7 "My people are determined to turn from Me. Even if they call to the Most High, He will by no means exalt them. 8 How can I give you up, Ephraim? How can I hand you over, Israel? How can I treat you like Admah? How can I make you like Zeboiim? My heart is changed within Me; all My compassion is aroused.

9 I will not carry out my fierce anger, nor will I turn and devastate Ephraim. For I am God, and not man—the Holy One among you. I will not come in wrath.

10 They will follow the Lord; He will roar like a lion. When He roars, His children will come trembling from the west.

11 They will come trembling like birds from Egypt, like doves from Assyria. I will settle them in their homes," declares the Lord.

12 1 "Ephraim has surrounded Me with lies, the house of Israel with deceit. And Judah is unruly against God, even against the faithful Holy One."

2 "Ephraim feeds on the wind; he pursues the east wind all day and multiplies lies and violence. He makes a treaty with Assyria and sends olive oil to Egypt.

3 The Lord has a charge to bring against Judah; He will punish Jacob according to his ways and repay him according to his deeds.

4 In the womb he grasped his brother's heel; as a man he struggled with God.

*5 He struggled with the angel and overcame Him; he wept and begged for His favor.
He found Him at Bethel and talked with Him there, 6 the Lord God Almighty; the Lord
is His name of renown!*

7 But you must return to your God; maintain love and justice, and wait for your God always.

HAFTARAH OF VAYETZE

he sustains himself in his endless worship of the money god. Your altar is a strong indication of what you worship, consciously or unconsciously. Altars and idols can be permanent or temporary, external or internal, but one thing is for certain: Your idol is most surely your place of focus. Meditating and participating in this reading helps us identify our personal idols, and it also gives us the strength to break away from them and reconnect ourselves with the Light of Creation.

הושע פרק 11–12

11 7 וְעַמִּי תְלוּאִים לִמְשׁוּבָתִי וְאֶל־עַל יִקְרָאֻהוּ יַחַד לֹא יְרוֹמֵם׃
8 אֵיךְ אל אֶתֶּנְךָ אֶפְרַיִם אל מצפץ אֲמַגֶּנְךָ יִשְׂרָאֵל אֵיךְ אל אֶתֶּנְךָ
כְאַדְמָה אֲשִׂימְךָ כִּצְבֹאיִם נֶהְפַּךְ עָלַי לִבִּי יַחַד נִכְמְרוּ נִחוּמָי׃
9 לֹא אֶעֱשֶׂה חֲרוֹן אַפִּי לֹא אָשׁוּב לְשַׁחֵת אֶפְרָיִם אל מצפץ כִּי אֵל
יי״א אָנֹכִי איע וְלֹא־אִישׁ ע״ה קנ״א קס״א בְּקִרְבְּךָ קָדוֹשׁ וְלֹא אָבוֹא
בְּעִיר סנדלפרך, ערי, סנדלפרין׃ 10 אַחֲרֵי יְהֹוָאדניאהדונהי יֵלְכוּ כְּאַרְיֵה רי״ו יִשְׁאָג
כִּי־הוּא יִשְׁאַג וְיֶחֶרְדוּ בָנִים מִיָּם ילי׃ 11 יֶחֶרְדוּ כְצִפּוֹר מִמִּצְרַיִם
מצר וּכְיוֹנָה יהוה מ״ה מֵאֶרֶץ אלהים דאלפין אַשּׁוּר סנדלפרך ע״ה וְהוֹשַׁבְתִּים עַל־
בָּתֵּיהֶם ב״פ ראה נְאֻם־יְהֹוָאדניאהדונהי׃ [ס] 12 1 סְבָבֻנִי בְכַחַשׁ אֶפְרַיִם
אל מצפץ וּבְמִרְמָה בֵּית ב״פ ראה יִשְׂרָאֵל וִיהוּדָה עֹד רָד עִם־אֵל יי״א
וְעִם־קְדוֹשִׁים נֶאֱמָן׃ 2 אֶפְרַיִם אל מצפץ רֹעֶה רהע רוּחַ מלוי אלהים דיודין
וְרֹדֵף קָדִים כָּל ילי ־הַיּוֹם נגד, זן, מזבח כָּזָב וָשֹׁד יַרְבֶּה וּבְרִית
עִם־אַשּׁוּר אבגיתץ ע״ה, ושר ע״ה יִכְרֹתוּ וְשֶׁמֶן י״פ טל, י״פ כוזו, ביט לְמִצְרַיִם מצר
יוּבָל׃ 3 וְרִיב לַיהֹוָאדניאהדונהי עִם־יְהוּדָה וְלִפְקֹד עַל־יַעֲקֹב יאהדוי־
נהי ־ אידהנויה כִּדְרָכָיו ב״פ יב״ק כְּמַעֲלָלָיו יָשִׁיב לוֹ׃ 4 בַּבֶּטֶן עָקַב ב״פ מום
אֶת־אָחִיו וּבְאוֹנוֹ שָׂרָה אֶת־אֱלֹהִים ילה, מום׃ 5 וַיָּשַׂר אֶל־מַלְאָךְ
וַיֻּכָל בָּכָה וַיִּתְחַנֶּן־לוֹ בֵּית ב״פ ראה ־אֵל יי״א יִמְצָאֶנּוּ וְשָׁם יְדַבֵּר

8 The merchant uses dishonest scales; he loves to defraud.

9 Ephraim boasts, 'I am very rich; I have become wealthy. With all my wealth they will not find in me any iniquity or sin.'"

10 "I am the Lord your God, who brought you out of Egypt; I will make you live in tents again, as in the days of your appointed feasts.

11 I spoke to the prophets, gave them many visions and told parables through them."

12 Is Gilead wicked? Its people are worthless! Do they sacrifice bulls in Gilgal? Their altars will be like piles of stones on a plowed field.

ראה עִמָּנוּ ריבוע ס״ג׃ 6 וַיהוָאדניאהדונהי אֱלֹהֵי דמב, ילה הַצְּבָאוֹת יְהוָאדניאהדונהי
זִכְרוֹ׃ 7 וְאַתָּה בֵּאלֹהֶיךָ ילה תָשׁוּב חֶסֶד ע״ב, ריבוע יהוה וּמִשְׁפָּט
ע״ה ה״פ אלהים שְׁמֹר וְקַוֵּה אֶל־אֱלֹהֶיךָ ילה תָּמִיד נתה, קס״א - קנ״א - קמ״ג׃
8 כְּנַעַן בְּיָדוֹ מֹאזְנֵי מִרְמָה לַעֲשֹׁק אָהֵב׃ 9 וַיֹּאמֶר אֶפְרַיִם אל
מצפץ אַךְ אהיה עָשַׁרְתִּי מָצָאתִי אוֹן לִי כָּל ילי ־יְגִיעַי לֹא יִמְצְאוּ־לִי
עָוֺן אֲשֶׁר־חֵטְא׃ 10 וְאָנֹכִי איע יְהוָאדניאהדונהי אֱלֹהֶיךָ ילה מֵאֶרֶץ
אלהים דאלפין מִצְרָיִם מצר עֹד אוֹשִׁיבְךָ בָאֳהָלִים כִּימֵי מוֹעֵד׃
11 וְדִבַּרְתִּי ראה עַל־הַנְּבִיאִים וְאָנֹכִי איע חָזוֹן הִרְבֵּיתִי וּבְיַד
הַנְּבִיאִים אֲדַמֶּה׃ 12 אִם יוהך ־גִּלְעָד אָוֶן אַךְ אהיה ־שָׁוְא הָיוּ
בַּגִּלְגָּל שְׁוָרִים זִבֵּחוּ גַּם מִזְבְּחוֹתָם כְּגַלִּים עַל תַּלְמֵי שָׂדָי׃

VAYISHLACH

LESSON OF VAYISHLACH
(Genesis 32:4-36:43)

Concerning Jacob's fear of Esau's aggression, Rashi wrote: "Rav Shimon Bar Yochai said that Esau hated Jacob, but his mercy overcame him at that moment and he kissed him with all his heart." Very simply, while this section concerns hatred, mercy, and forgiveness, most of us focus only on the hatred. Kabbalah teaches that we are responsible for the hate in our lives.

If we focus only on Esau's hatred of Jacob, we will connect with the energy of hatred. However, if we focus on the words: "...his mercy overcame him and he kissed him with all his heart," we connect with a very different energy. It is important to be able to see both aspects of this story. It all depends on us and only on us. If we can see only one side, this shows us that it is our nature to *Desire to Receive for the Self Alone*, which is the law of "Esau hates Jacob."

When we find ways to rise above our own natural tendencies, we transform our *Desire to Receive for the Self Alone* to the *Desire to Receive for the Sake of Sharing*, and thus connect to the Light. We can rise above judgment, since if we are judged it is only because we have exercised judgment against others. If we can forego judgmental thoughts, no one can condemn us, not even Satan, and we will be loved by others because we are projecting and focusing on love.

If we do not understand why we are suffering, we should examine our actions, and if we do not find a reason for the suffering, we should begin spiritual study. Only by our studying the spiritual nature of the universe will our eyes open to the truth. The *Zohar* explains:

> *In the Beginning: Beresheet. Rav Shimon opened the discussion with the verse, "And I have put My words in your mouth," (Isaiah 51:16) meaning how important it is for a person to study spirituality laboriously, day and night. This is very important, because God listens attentively to the voices of those who occupy themselves with the study of the Torah. And every word that receives a new interpretation by a person who delves into the study of the Torah creates a new Heaven.*
>
> *– The Zohar, Prologue 61*

> *"Because they accept that advice FROM THE SAGE, I forgive their iniquities and they will be received pleasantly into My presence." All this God instructs for those who strive in Torah and because of this, happy and praiseworthy are those who study Torah. Those who are occupied and study Torah are great trees in this world.*
>
> *– The Zohar, Balak 28:319*

From the above explanations, we can see that this story of the Bible in particular contains a unique energy to help us to understand the truth. If we all commit ourselves to studying a little more than usual, we will earn and gain more happiness, more understanding, and even more miracles in our lives.

SYNOPSIS OF VAYISHLACH

Vayishlach means "to send away." This word encompasses the energy and consciousness required to let go of something or someone. Often, we have difficulty detaching ourselves from negative people and situations, but this particular story of Genesis gives us the power to do so.

FIRST READING - ABRAHAM - CHESED

3 *And Jacob sent messengers ahead of him to his brother Esau in the land of
Seir, the country of Edom. 4 He instructed them: "This is what you are to say
to my master Esau: 'Your servant Jacob says, I have been staying with Laban
and have remained there till now. 5 I have cattle and donkeys, sheep and
goats, menservants and maidservants. Now I am sending this message to my lord,
that I may find favor in your eyes.' " 6 When the messengers returned to Jacob, they
said, "We went to your brother Esau, and now he is coming to meet you, and four
hundred men are with him." 7 In great fear and distress Jacob divided the people who
were with him into two groups, and the flocks and herds and camels as well. 8 He
said, "If Esau comes and attacks one group, the group that is left shall escape."*

FROM THE RAV

Esau wanted to kill his brother, but he didn't know how to do it. He felt love for Jacob in spite of himself. In Esau, we can see the story of a whole group of people who were born not just to give in to negativity, but actually to strive for it the way we are supposed to strive for righteousness. There is an element of Esau in all of us, an aspect of us that is plainly determined to go against our own best interests. When you say to yourself, "Hey, why isn't everything turning out the way I want? Why isn't my life going the way it's supposed to?" that is the Esau within you speaking. When you have feelings like that in your heart, you are one with Esau.

When Esau went to grab Jacob's neck, he never intended Jacob to walk away. But the power of Esau's negativity could not penetrate the protective shield that Jacob had acquired. Jacob had succeeded in dominating the negative angel and was now the Chariot of Israel. This was his destiny, and he was now ready to fulfill it. There is a lesson here for us, too. We also need to be tested by the Negative Side, and only by passing that test can we become the people we were meant to be. We must defeat the Esau within to protect ourselves from any external evil force, even death itself.

When Esau approached Jacob, something changed at the metaphysical level, and that change determined the physical action that Esau was able to take. The change happened when Esau felt the Light that was flowing into the physical world through Jacob. Every negative thought Esau had about how he would treat Jacob simply evaporated. He embraced Jacob and loved him—truly loved him. Hate turned into love. This is an incredible lesson that I learned from my teacher, who learned it from his teacher.

Jacob and Esau serve as metaphors for teaching us basic facts of life. As we know, Light and darkness cannot coexist in the same place on the physical realm. When we bring the Light to bear on darkness, darkness must disappear. It has no choice. Put on a light in a darkened auditorium, and no matter how small that light might be, it makes darkness disappear out of all proportion to the size of the light itself. The same principle works on every level throughout the Universe, whether it's a candle in an auditorium or the transformation of Esau from a person of hatred to a person of love.

The Light of the *Zohar* can do more than protect us from the darkness. It can literally transform the Negative Side into something positive.

FIRST READING - ABRAHAM - CHESED

3 וַיִּשְׁלַח יַעֲקֹב יאהדונהי - אידהנויה מַלְאָכִים לְפָנָיו אֶל־עֵשָׂו אָחִיו
אַרְצָה אלהים דההין ע"ה שֵׂעִיר שְׂדֵה אֱדוֹם: 4 וַיְצַו אֹתָם לֵאמֹר כֹּה
היי תֹאמְרוּן לַאדֹנִי לְעֵשָׂו כֹּה היי אָמַר עַבְדְּךָ פוי יַעֲקֹב יאהדונהי - אידהנויה
עִם־לָבָן גַּרְתִּי וָאֵחַר עַד־עָתָּה: 5 וַיְהִי־לִי שׁוֹר אבגיתצ, ושר, אהבת חנם
וַחֲמוֹר צֹאן מלוי אהיה דיודין ע"ה וְעֶבֶד וְשִׁפְחָה ג' מלויי אהיה וָאֶשְׁלְחָה לְהַגִּיד
לַאדֹנִי לִמְצֹא־חֵן מוזי בְּעֵינֶיךָ ע"ה קס"א: 6 וַיָּשֻׁבוּ הַמַּלְאָכִים אֶל־
יַעֲקֹב יאהדונהי - אידהנויה לֵאמֹר בָּאנוּ אֶל־אָחִיךָ אֶל־עֵשָׂו וְגַם יגל
הֹלֵךְ מיה לִקְרָאתְךָ וְאַרְבַּע־מֵאוֹת אִישׁ ע"ה קנ"א קס"א עִמּוֹ: 7 וַיִּירָא
יַעֲקֹב יאהדונהי - אידהנויה מְאֹד וַיֵּצֶר לוֹ וַיַּחַץ אֶת־הָעָם אֲשֶׁר־אִתּוֹ
וְאֶת־הַצֹּאן מלוי אהיה דיודין ע"ה וְאֶת־הַבָּקָר וְהַגְּמַלִּים לִשְׁנֵי מַחֲנוֹת:
8 וַיֹּאמֶר אִם יוהך ־יָבוֹא עֵשָׂו אֶל־הַמַּחֲנֶה הָאַחַת וְהִכָּהוּ וְהָיָה
יהוה, יהה הַמַּחֲנֶה הַנִּשְׁאָר לִפְלֵיטָה: 9 וַיֹּאמֶר יַעֲקֹב יאהדונהי - אידהנויה
אֱלֹהֵי דמב, ילה אָבִי אַבְרָהָם ח"פ אל, רמ"ח וֵאלֹהֵי לכב, דמב, ילה אָבִי

וַיִּשְׁלַח

Genesis 32:4 – Jacob sent angels to his brother, Esau. The angels returned to tell Jacob that Esau had 400 men—which we can understand to be evil angels—with him. Preparation was underway for the battle between good and evil.

וַיַּחַץ

Genesis 32:8 – Jacob split his camp into two. By doing this, he hoped that if one half of his people were killed, the other half might still survive. The Bible also says that Jacob was afraid and distressed, which Rashi explains by telling us that Jacob was afraid he might be killed and distressed that he might have to kill someone else. Therefore, he made sure that he was well-prepared. From this, we learn that while our first priority must always be the spiritual dimension, we must also take care of the physical realm.

וַיֹּאמֶר

Genesis 32:10 – **Jacob Prayed**. In the face of the impending conflict with his brother and the forces of evil, Jacob prayed, reminding the Creator of His promise to make Jacob's offspring as numerous as the grains of sand in the desert.

[9] Then Jacob prayed, "O God of my father Abraham, God of my father Isaac, O Lord, who said to me, 'Go back to your country and your relatives, and I will make you prosper,' [10] I am unworthy of all the kindness and faithfulness you have shown your servant. I had only my staff when I crossed this Jordan, but now I have become two groups. [11] Save me, I pray, from the hand of my brother Esau, for I am afraid he will come and attack me, and also the mothers with their children. [12] But you have said, 'I will surely make you prosper and will make your descendants like the sand of the sea, which cannot be counted.' "

SECOND READING - ISAAC - GEVURAH

[13] He spent the night there, and from what he had with him he selected a sacrifice for his brother Esau: [14] two hundred female goats and twenty male goats, two hundred ewes and twenty rams, [15] thirty female camels with their young, forty cows and ten bulls, and twenty female donkeys and ten male donkeys. [16]He put them in the care of his servants, each herd by itself, and said to his servants, "Go ahead of me, and keep some space between the herds."

[17] He instructed the one in the lead: "When my brother Esau meets you and asks, 'To whom do you belong, and where are you going, and who owns all these animals in front of you?' [18] then you are to say, 'They belong to your servant Jacob. They are a sacrifice sent to my lord Esau, and he is coming behind us.' "

[19] He also instructed the second, the third, and all the others who followed the herds: "You are to say the same thing to Esau when you meet him. [20] And be sure to say, 'Your servant Jacob is coming behind us.' " For he thought, "I will pacify him with these sacrifices I am sending on ahead; later, when I see him, perhaps he will receive

---

This reminds us that whenever we are facing something potentially negative, we can transform it through the power of prayer. The *Zohar* tells us:

> *It was Jacob's prayer that protected him from Esau, AND NOT HIS MERIT, because he wished to keep [his merit] in reserve for his descendants and not spend it to serve his own needs against Esau. He therefore prayed to God, and did not rely upon his merit for his rescue.*
>
> *– The Zohar, Vayishlach 3:58*

מִנְחָה

Genesis 32:14 – Jacob offered a tribute to Esau, sending him a huge portion of his flocks. In the same way, we should always give something to the Negative Side, just as we give a small piece of bread on Shabbat. By distracting Satan with our gifts, we can gain control over the Negative Side.

> *Similarly, on that day OF YOM KIPPUR, Satan is ready to spy out the land, and we should place something before him*

יִצְחָק ד"פ ב"ן יְהֹוָהאדניאהדונהי הָאֹמֵר אֵלַי שׁוּב לְאַרְצְךָ וּלְמוֹלַדְתְּךָ
וְאֵיטִיבָה עִמָּךְ נמם: 10 קָטֹנְתִּי מִכֹּל ילי הַחֲסָדִים ע"ב, ריבוע יהוה
וּמִכָּל ילי ־הָאֱמֶת אהיה פעמים אהיה, ז"פ ס"ג אֲשֶׁר עָשִׂיתָ אֶת־עַבְדֶּךָ פוי כִּי
בְמַקְלִי עָבַרְתִּי אֶת־הַיַּרְדֵּן י"פ יהוה וד' אותיות הַזֶּה והו וְעַתָּה הָיִיתִי
לִשְׁנֵי מַחֲנוֹת: 11 הַצִּילֵנִי נָא מִיַּד אָחִי מִיַּד עֵשָׂו כִּי־יָרֵא אָנֹכִי
איע אֹתוֹ פֶּן־יָבוֹא וְהִכַּנִי אֵם יוהך עַל־בָּנִים: 12 וְאַתָּה אָמַרְתָּ
הֵיטֵב אֵיטִיב עִמָּךְ נמם וְשַׂמְתִּי אֶת־זַרְעֲךָ כְּחוֹל רבוע אהיה הַיָּם ילי
אֲשֶׁר לֹא־יִסָּפֵר מֵרֹב:

SECOND READING - ISAAC - GEVURAH

13 וַיָּלֶן שָׁם בַּלַּיְלָה מלה הַהוּא וַיִּקַּח ועם מִן־הַבָּא בְיָדוֹ מִנְחָה
ע"ה ב"פ ב"ן לְעֵשָׂו אָחִיו: 14 עִזִּים מָאתַיִם וּתְיָשִׁים עֶשְׂרִים רְחֵלִים
מָאתַיִם וְאֵילִים עֶשְׂרִים: 15 גְּמַלִּים מֵינִיקוֹת וּבְנֵיהֶם שְׁלֹשִׁים
פָּרוֹת אַרְבָּעִים וּפָרִים עֲשָׂרָה אֲתֹנֹת עֶשְׂרִים וַעְיָרִם עֲשָׂרָה:
16 וַיִּתֵּן י"פ מלוי ע"ב בְּיַד־עֲבָדָיו עֵדֶר עֵדֶר לְבַדּוֹ מ"ב וַיֹּאמֶר אֶל־
עֲבָדָיו עִבְרוּ לְפָנַי וְרֶוַח תָּשִׂימוּ בֵּין עֵדֶר וּבֵין עֵדֶר: 17 וַיְצַו
אֶת־הָרִאשׁוֹן לֵאמֹר כִּי יִפְגָשְׁךָ עֵשָׂו אָחִי וּשְׁאֵלְךָ לֵאמֹר לְמִי
ילי ־אַתָּה וְאָנָה תֵלֵךְ וּלְמִי ילי אֵלֶּה לְפָנֶיךָ ס"ג - מ"ה - ב"ן: 18 וְאָמַרְתָּ
לְעַבְדְּךָ פוי לְיַעֲקֹב יאהדונהי - אידהנויה מִנְחָה ע"ה ב"פ ב"ן הִוא שְׁלוּחָה
לַאדֹנִי לְעֵשָׂו וְהִנֵּה גַם יג"ל ־הוּא אַחֲרֵינוּ: 19 וַיְצַו גַּם יג"ל אֶת־
הַשֵּׁנִי גַּם יג"ל אֶת־הַשְּׁלִישִׁי גַּם יג"ל אֶת־כָּל ילי ־הַהֹלְכִים מיה אַחֲרֵי
הָעֲדָרִים לֵאמֹר כַּדָּבָר ראה הַזֶּה והו תְּדַבְּרוּן ראה אֶל־עֵשָׂו בְּמֹצַאֲכֶם
אֹתוֹ: 20 וַאֲמַרְתֶּם גַּם יג"ל הִנֵּה מ"ה יה עַבְדְּךָ פוי יַעֲקֹב יאהדונהי - אידהנויה

me." [21] *So Jacob's sacrifice went on ahead of him, but he himself spent the night in the camp.* [22] *That night Jacob got up and took his two wives, his two maidservants, and his eleven sons and crossed the ford of the Yabok.* [23] *After he had sent them across the stream, he sent over all his possessions.* [24] *So Jacob was left alone, and a man wrestled with him till daybreak.* [25] *When the man saw that he could not overpower him, he touched the socket of Jacob's hip so that his hip was wrenched as he wrestled with him.* [26] *Then the man said, "Let me go, for it is daybreak." But Jacob replied, "I will not let you go unless you bless me."* [27] *He asked him, "What is your name?" "Jacob," he answered.* [28] *Then he said, "Your name will no longer be Jacob, but Israel, because you have struggled with God and with men and have overcome."* [29] *Jacob said, "Please tell me your name." But he replied, "Why do you ask my name?" And he blessed him there.*

THIRD READING - JACOB - TIFERET

[30] *So Jacob called the place Peniel, saying, "It is because I saw God face to face, and yet my life was spared."* [31] *The sun rose above him as he passed Peniel, and he was limping because of his hip.* [32] *Therefore, to this day the Israelites do not eat the sciatic*

---

with which he can keep busy. While he is occupied with it, he will leave Israel alone.

– The Zohar, Emor 34:243

וַיֵּאָבֵק

Genesis 32:25 – Jacob fought with an angel who, according to Rashi, was Esau's Guardian Angel. This represents the battle between good and evil, and we learn that what happens on the physical level is a manifestation of what is happening on the spiritual level: as Above, so Below. We are told that God reminded the angel about Jacob's five great merits, whereupon the angel saw that he could not overcome the man. (*Shir HaShirim Rabba 3:5*)

בֵּרַכְתָּנִי

Genesis 32:27 – When Jacob won the battle with the angel, he asked the angel for a blessing. Since this was Esau's Guardian Angel, the lesson here pertains to the necessity for Esau to let go. When Esau had asked his father, Isaac, for his blessing, he felt that Jacob had stolen it from him and that he—Esau—still deserved it. Through the defeat of his angel, we see that Esau was finally letting go of his desire for his father's blessing. Because he lost the battle to Jacob, Esau's angel gave up Esau's claim to the blessing.

יִשְׂרָאֵל

Genesis 32:29 – After their fight was over, the angel changed Jacob's name to Israel, signifying Jacob's ascent to a higher spiritual level. The name Yisrael (Israel) is truly all-inclusive. The *Yud* stands for Jacob and Isaac (Yaakov and Yitzchak in Aramaic); the *Shin* stands for Sarah; the *Reish* is for Rachel and Rebecca (Rivka in Aramaic); the *Alef* stands for Abraham (Avraham in Aramaic), and the *Lamed* for Leah. Furthermore, the name Israel represents the Twelve Tribes of Israel. Through this one name, therefore, we can connect with the power of the matriarchs, the patriarchs, and all Twelve Tribes.

אַחֲרֵינוּ כִּי־אָמַר אֲכַפְּרָה פָנָיו בַּמִּנְחָה ע"ה ב"פ ב"ן הַהֹלֶכֶת לְפָנָי
חכמה - בינה וְאַחֲרֵי־כֵן אֶרְאֶה פָנָיו אוּלַי אום יִשָּׂא פָנָי חכמה - בינה:
21 וַתַּעֲבֹר הַמִּנְחָה ע"ה ב"פ ב"ן עַל־פָּנָיו וְהוּא לָן בַּלַּיְלָה מלה ־הַהוּא
בַּמַּחֲנֶה: 22 וַיָּקָם | בַּלַּיְלָה מלה הוּא וַיִּקַּח ווע"ם אֶת־שְׁתֵּי נָשָׁיו
וְאֶת־שְׁתֵּי שִׁפְחֹתָיו וְאֶת־אַחַד אהבה, דאגה עָשָׂר יְלָדָיו וַיַּעֲבֹר
רפ"ח, ע"ב - רי"ו אֵת מַעֲבַר יַבֹּק יהוה - אלהים, יהוה - אהיה - אדני: 23 וַיִּקָּחֵם ווע"ם
וַיַּעֲבִרֵם אֶת־הַנָּחַל וַיַּעֲבֵר רפ"ח, ע"ב - רי"ו אֶת־אֲשֶׁר־לוֹ: 24 וַיִּוָּתֵר
יַעֲקֹב יאהדונהי - אידהנויה לְבַדּוֹ מ"ב וַיֵּאָבֵק אִישׁ ע"ה קנ"א קס"א עִמּוֹ עַד
עֲלוֹת הַשָּׁחַר: 25 וַיַּרְא כִּי לֹא יָכֹל לוֹ וַיִּגַּע בְּכַף־יְרֵכוֹ וַתֵּקַע
כַּף־יֶרֶךְ ב"פ סנדלפון - י' אותיות יַעֲקֹב יאהדונהי - אידהנויה בְּהֵאָבְקוֹ עִמּוֹ:
26 וַיֹּאמֶר שַׁלְּחֵנִי כִּי עָלָה הַשָּׁחַר וַיֹּאמֶר לֹא אֲשַׁלֵּחֲךָ כִּי אִם
יוהך ־בֵּרַכְתָּנִי: 27 וַיֹּאמֶר אֵלָיו מַה מ"ה ־שְּׁמֶךָ וַיֹּאמֶר יַעֲקֹב
יאהדונהי - אידהנויה: 28 וַיֹּאמֶר לֹא יַעֲקֹב יאהדונהי - אידהנויה יֵאָמֵר עוֹד
שִׁמְךָ כִּי אִם יוהך ־יִשְׂרָאֵל כִּי־שָׂרִיתָ עִם־אֱלֹהִים ילה, מום וְעִם־אֲנָשִׁים
וַתּוּכָל: 29 וַיִּשְׁאַל יַעֲקֹב יאהדונהי - אידהנויה וַיֹּאמֶר הַגִּידָה־נָּא שְׁמֶךָ
וַיֹּאמֶר לָמָּה זֶּה תִּשְׁאַל לִשְׁמִי וַיְבָרֶךְ עסמ"ב אֹתוֹ שָׁם:

THIRD READING - JACOB - TIFERET

30 וַיִּקְרָא עם ה' אותיות = ב"פ קס"א יַעֲקֹב יאהדונהי - אידהנויה שֵׁם שדי יהוה הַמָּקוֹם
יהוה ברבוע פְּנִיאֵל כִּי־רָאִיתִי אֱלֹהִים ילה, מום פָּנִים ע"ב ס"ג מ"ה אֶל־פָּנִים

The Ari wrote:

> *By now calling Jacob by the name Israel, God was giving him a hint that all the patriarchs and matriarchs would be included in the name Israel—the initials of Isaac, Jacob, Sarah, Rebecca, Rachel, Abraham and Leah—for he was the mainstay of all of them.*
>
> *– Writings of Rav Isaac Luria*

nerve attached to the socket of the hip, because the socket of Jacob's hip was touched near that sinew.

33 1 Jacob looked up and there was Esau, coming with his four hundred men; so he divided the children among Leah, Rachel, and the two maidservants.

2 He put the maidservants and their children in front, Leah and her children next, and Rachel and Joseph last.

3 He went on ahead and bowed down to the ground seven times as he approached his brother.

4 But Esau ran to meet Jacob and embraced him; he fell upon his neck and kissed him, and they wept.

5 Then Esau looked up and saw the women and children, and he said, "Who are these with you?" Jacob answered, "They are the children God has graciously given your servant."

FOURTH READING - MOSES - NETZACH

6 Then the maidservants and their children approached and bowed down.

7 Next, Leah and her children came and bowed down. Last came Joseph and Rachel, and they bowed down.

8 Esau asked, "What do you mean by all these droves I met?" "To find favor in your eyes, my lord," he said.

9 But Esau said, "I already have plenty, my brother. Keep what you have for yourself."

צלע

Genesis 32:32 – After the fight, Jacob was limping from sciatica because during the struggle, the angel struck Jacob on his sciatic nerve. Of the 365 sinews and nerves of the body, Satan has complete control only of the sciatic nerve, so this was the only place on Jacob's body that the negative angel could penetrate and strike.

Genesis 33:4 – There are dots over each letter of *vayishakehu* (he kissed him) in this verse. Esau ran to Jacob and kissed him. Rav Shimon bar Yochai tells us that although Esau hated Jacob, at the exact moment he ran to kiss him, he actually loved him. Even though Esau was totally negative and Jacob was completely

ע"ב ס"ג מ"ה וַתִּנָּצֵל נַפְשִׁי׃ 31 וַיִּזְרַח־לוֹ הַשֶּׁמֶשׁ ב"פ ש"ך כַּאֲשֶׁר עָבַר
אֶת־פְּנוּאֵל וְהוּא צֹלֵעַ עַל־יְרֵכוֹ׃ 32 עַל־כֵּן לֹא־יֹאכְלוּ בְנֵי־
יִשְׂרָאֵל אֶת־גִּיד הַנָּשֶׁה אֲשֶׁר עַל־כַּף הַיָּרֵךְ עַד הַיּוֹם נגד, זן, מזבח
הַזֶּה והו כִּי נָגַע בְּכַף־יֶרֶךְ יַעֲקֹב יאהדונהי - אידהנויה בְּגִיד הַנָּשֶׁה׃
33 1 וַיִּשָּׂא יַעֲקֹב יאהדונהי - אידהנויה עֵינָיו ריבוע מ"ה וַיַּרְא וְהִנֵּה עֵשָׂו בָּא
וְעִמּוֹ אַרְבַּע מֵאוֹת אִישׁ ע"ה קנ"א קס"א וַיַּחַץ אֶת־הַיְלָדִים עַל־לֵאָה
לאה (אלד ע"ה) וְעַל־רָחֵל רבוע ס"ג - ע"ב וְעַל שְׁתֵּי הַשְּׁפָחוֹת׃ 2 וַיָּשֶׂם אֶת־
הַשְּׁפָחוֹת וְאֶת־יַלְדֵיהֶן רִאשֹׁנָה וְאֶת־לֵאָה לאה (אלד ע"ה) וִילָדֶיהָ
אַחֲרֹנִים וְאֶת־רָחֵל רבוע ס"ג - ע"ב וְאֶת־יוֹסֵף ציון, קנאה, ו"פ יהוה, ה"פ אל
אַחֲרֹנִים׃ 3 וְהוּא עָבַר לִפְנֵיהֶם וַיִּשְׁתַּחוּ אַרְצָה אלהים דההין ע"ה
שֶׁבַע אלהים דיודין - ע"ב פְּעָמִים עַד־גִּשְׁתּוֹ עַד־אָחִיו׃ 4 וַיָּרָץ עֵשָׂו
לִקְרָאתוֹ וַיְחַבְּקֵהוּ וַיִּפֹּל עַל־צַוָּארָו וַיִּשָּׁקֵהוּ וַיִּבְכּוּ׃
5 וַיִּשָּׂא אֶת־עֵינָיו ריבוע מ"ה וַיַּרְא אֶת־הַנָּשִׁים וְאֶת־הַיְלָדִים וַיֹּאמֶר
מִי ילי ־אֵלֶּה לָּךְ וַיֹּאמַר הַיְלָדִים אֲשֶׁר־חָנַן אֱלֹהִים ילה, מום אֶת־
עַבְדֶּךָ פוי׃

FOURTH READING - MOSES - NETZACH

6 וַתִּגַּשְׁןָ הַשְּׁפָחוֹת הֵנָּה מ"ה יה וְיַלְדֵיהֶן וַתִּשְׁתַּחֲוֶיןָ׃ 7 וַתִּגַּשׁ גַּם־ יגל
לֵאָה לאה (אלד ע"ה) וִילָדֶיהָ וַיִּשְׁתַּחֲווּ וְאַחַר נִגַּשׁ יוֹסֵף ציון, קנאה, ו"פ יהוה, ה"פ אל

positive, love and human dignity were still possible in their relationship. We should attempt to emulate those positive feelings toward those around us, and the dots over the word *vayishakehu* give us energy and strength to do this.

Since the same root *Nun-Shin-Kuf* also means "to be lit, lighted, or ignited," we can think about the possibility that Jacob's soul enabled the Light for his brother and thus caused the love that filled Esau at that moment. Our own sensibilities can often catalyze the sensibilities of others.

[10] "No, please!" said Jacob. "If I have found favor in your eyes, accept this offering from me. For to see your face is like seeing the face of God, now that you have received me favorably.

[11] Please accept the blessing that I brought to you, for God has been gracious to me and I have all I need." And because Jacob insisted, Esau accepted it.

[12] Then Esau said, "Let us be on our way; I'll accompany you."

[13] But Jacob said to him, "My lord knows that the children are tender and that I must care for the ewes and cows that are nursing their young. If they are driven hard just one day, all the animals will die.

[14] So let my lord go on ahead of his servant, while I move along slowly at the pace of
the droves before me and that of the children, until I come to my lord in Seir." [15] Esau
said, "Then let me leave some of my men with you." "But why do that?" Jacob asked. "Just let me find favor in the eyes of my lord."

[16] So that day Esau started on his way back to Seir. [17] Jacob, however, went to
Succoth, where he built a place for himself and made shelters for his livestock. That is why the place is called Succoth.

[18] After Jacob came from Paddan Aram, he arrived safely at the city of Shechem in Canaan and camped within sight of the city.

[19] For a hundred pieces of silver, he bought from the sons of Hamor, the father of Shechem, the plot of ground where he pitched his tent.

[20] There he set up an altar and called it El Elohe Israel.

וְלָקַחְתָּ

Genesis 33:10 – Jacob wanted to give Esau everything, but Esau did not want to accept so much. Yet Jacob knew that Satan, the Negative Side, had to receive something, and that by giving to Esau, Jacob would be able to control how much Satan got. There is an old saying about "giving Satan his due." What this really means is that the Negative Side will always take some part of what we do, no matter what. If we resist this process, we make it possible for Satan to take even more and perhaps even everything.

Genesis 33:18 – Jacob came to the city of Shechem (now Nablus), where he bought a piece of land that would eventually be the burial place of Joseph. This spot is a place of high energy, but it is not the fact that Joseph is buried there that makes the place holy, since the physical can never be a cause of the spiritual. The seed level—the Cause—of anything is always spiritual. Joseph was buried in this spot because it is a place of powerful energy.

וְרָחֵל רבוע ס״ג - ע״ב וַיִּשְׁתַּחֲוּוּ׃ 8 וַיֹּאמֶר מִי ילי לְךָ כָּל ילי ־הַמַּחֲנֶה הַזֶּה
והו אֲשֶׁר פָּגָשְׁתִּי וַיֹּאמֶר לִמְצֹא־חֵן מוזי בְּעֵינֵי ריבוע מ״ה אֲדֹנִי׃
9 וַיֹּאמֶר עֵשָׂו יֶשׁ־לִי רָב אָחִי יְהִי לְךָ אֲשֶׁר־לָךְ׃ 10 וַיֹּאמֶר
יַעֲקֹב יאהדונהי - אידהנויה אַל־נָא אִם יוהך ־נָא מָצָאתִי חֵן מוזי בְּעֵינֶיךָ
ע״ה קס״א וְלָקַחְתָּ מִנְחָתִי מִיָּדִי כִּי עַל־כֵּן רָאִיתִי פָנֶיךָ ס״ג - מ״ה - ב״ן
כִּרְאֹת פְּנֵי חכמה - בינה אֱלֹהִים ילה, מום וַתִּרְצֵנִי׃ 11 קַח־נָא אֶת־בִּרְכָתִי
אֲשֶׁר הֻבָאת לָךְ כִּי־חַנַּנִי אֱלֹהִים ילה, מום וְכִי יֶשׁ־לִי־כֹל ילי וַיִּפְצַר־
בּוֹ וַיִּקָּח ווּעם׃ 12 וַיֹּאמֶר נִסְעָה וְנֵלֵכָה וְאֵלְכָה לְנֶגְדֶּךָ זן, מזבח׃
13 וַיֹּאמֶר אֵלָיו אֲדֹנִי יֹדֵעַ כִּי־הַיְלָדִים רַכִּים וְהַצֹּאן מלוי אהיה דיודין ע״ה
וְהַבָּקָר עָלוֹת עָלָי וּדְפָקוּם יוֹם נגד, זן, מזבח אֶחָד אהבה, דאגה וָמֵתוּ כָּל
ילי ־הַצֹּאן מלוי אהיה דיודין ע״ה׃ 14 יַעֲבָר־נָא אֲדֹנִי לִפְנֵי עַבְדּוֹ וַאֲנִי אני
אֶתְנָהֲלָה לְאִטִּי לְרֶגֶל עסמ״ב ע״ה הַמְּלָאכָה אֲשֶׁר־לְפָנַי וּלְרֶגֶל
עסמ״ב ע״ה הַיְלָדִים עַד אֲשֶׁר־אָבֹא אֶל־אֲדֹנִי שֵׂעִירָה׃ 15 וַיֹּאמֶר
עֵשָׂו אַצִּיגָה־נָּא עִמְּךָ נמם מִן־הָעָם אֲשֶׁר אִתִּי וַיֹּאמֶר לָמָּה זֶּה
אֶמְצָא־חֵן מוזי בְּעֵינֵי ריבוע מ״ה אֲדֹנִי׃ 16 וַיָּשָׁב בַּיּוֹם נגד, זן, מזבח הַהוּא
עֵשָׂו לְדַרְכּוֹ שֵׂעִירָה׃ 17 וְיַעֲקֹב יאהדונהי - אידהנויה נָסַע סֻכֹּתָה וַיִּבֶן
לוֹ בָּיִת ב״פ ראה וּלְמִקְנֵהוּ עָשָׂה סֻכֹּת עַל־כֵּן קָרָא שֵׁם־ שדי יהוה
הַמָּקוֹם יהוה ברבוע סֻכּוֹת׃ [ס] 18 וַיָּבֹא יַעֲקֹב יאהדונהי - אידהנויה שָׁלֵם ש״ע
עִיר בוזפך, ערי, סנדלפו״ן שְׁכֶם אֲשֶׁר בְּאֶרֶץ אלהים דאלפין כְּנַעַן בְּבֹאוֹ
מִפַּדַּן אֲרָם וַיִּחַן אֶת־פְּנֵי חכמה - בינה הָעִיר בוזפך, ערי, סנדלפו״ן׃ 19 וַיִּקֶן אֶת־
חֶלְקַת הַשָּׂדֶה אֲשֶׁר נָטָה־שָׁם אָהֳלוֹ מִיַּד בְּנֵי־חֲמוֹר אֲבִי
שְׁכֶם בְּמֵאָה מלוי ע״ב, דמב קְשִׂיטָה׃ 20 וַיַּצֶּב־שָׁם מִזְבֵּחַ זן, נגד
וַיִּקְרָא עם ה׳ אותיות = ב״פ קס״א ־לוֹ אֵל ייא״י אֱלֹהֵי דמב, ילה יִשְׂרָאֵל׃ [ס]

FIFTH READING - AARON - HOD

34[1] Now Dinah, the daughter Leah had borne to Jacob, went out to visit the women of the land. [2] When Shechem, son of Hamor the Hivite, the ruler of that area, saw her, he took her, lay with her, and violated her.

[3] His heart cleaved to Dinah, daughter of Jacob, and he loved the girl and spoke tenderly to her. [4] And Shechem said to his father Hamor, "Get me this girl as my wife."

[5] When Jacob heard that his daughter Dinah had been defiled, his sons were in the fields with his livestock; so he kept quiet about it until they came home.

[6] Then Shechem's father Hamor went out to talk with Jacob.

[7] Now Jacob's sons had come in from the fields as soon as they heard what had happened. They were filled with grief and fury, because Shechem had done a disgraceful thing in Israel by lying with Jacob's daughter—a thing that should not be done.

[8] But Hamor said to them, "My son Shechem has his heart set on your daughter. Please give her to him as his wife.

[9] Intermarry with us; give us your daughters and take our daughters for yourselves.

[10] You can settle among us; the land is open to you. Live in it, trade in it, and acquire property in it."

[11] Then Shechem said to Dinah's father and brothers, "Let me find favor in your eyes, and I will give you whatever you ask.

[12] Make the price for the bride and the gift I am to bring as great as you like, and I'll pay whatever you ask me. Only give me the girl as my wife."

[13] Because their sister Dinah had been defiled, Jacob's sons replied deceitfully as they spoke to Shechem and his father Hamor.

[14] They said to them, "We can't do such a thing; we can't give our sister to a man who is not circumcised. That would be a disgrace to us.

וּתְנוּ־לִי

Genesis 34:12 – Shechem (who has the same name as the city), son of Hamor, the prince of the region, wanted to marry Dinah, the daughter of Jacob and Leah, after raping her. Shechem was told that he could marry Dinah only if he would first circumcise all the men of his town.

FIFTH READING - AARON - HOD

34 1 וַתֵּצֵא דִינָה בַּת־לֵאָה לאה (אלד ע"ה) אֲשֶׁר יָלְדָה לְיַעֲקֹב
יאהדונהי ∸ אידהנויה לִרְאוֹת בִּבְנוֹת הָאָרֶץ אלהים דההין ע"ה: 2 וַיַּרְא אֹתָהּ
שְׁכֶם בֶּן־חֲמוֹר הַחִוִּי נְשִׂיא הָאָרֶץ אלהים דההין ע"ה וַיִּקַּח חעם אֹתָהּ
וַיִּשְׁכַּב אֹתָהּ וַיְעַנֶּהָ: 3 וַתִּדְבַּק נַפְשׁוֹ בְּדִינָה בַּת־יַעֲקֹב
יאהדונהי ∸ אידהנויה וַיֶּאֱהַב אֶת־הַנַּעֲרָ וַיְדַבֵּר ראה עַל־לֵב הַנַּעֲרָ:
4 וַיֹּאמֶר שְׁכֶם אֶל־חֲמוֹר אָבִיו לֵאמֹר קַח־לִי אֶת־הַיַּלְדָּה
הַזֹּאת לְאִשָּׁה: 5 וְיַעֲקֹב יאהדונהי ∸ אידהנויה שָׁמַע כִּי טִמֵּא אֶת־דִּינָה
בִתּוֹ וּבָנָיו הָיוּ אֶת־מִקְנֵהוּ בַּשָּׂדֶה וְהֶחֱרִשׁ יַעֲקֹב יאהדונהי ∸ אידהנויה
עַד־בֹּאָם: 6 וַיֵּצֵא חֲמוֹר אֲבִי־שְׁכֶם אֶל־יַעֲקֹב יאהדונהי ∸ אידהנויה
לְדַבֵּר ראה אִתּוֹ: 7 וּבְנֵי יַעֲקֹב יאהדונהי ∸ אידהנויה בָּאוּ מִן־הַשָּׂדֶה שדי
כְּשָׁמְעָם וַיִּתְעַצְּבוּ הָאֲנָשִׁים וַיִּחַר לָהֶם מְאֹד מ"ה כִּי־נְבָלָה עָשָׂה
בְיִשְׂרָאֵל לִשְׁכַּב אֶת־בַּת־יַעֲקֹב יאהדונהי ∸ אידהנויה וְכֵן לֹא יֵעָשֶׂה:
8 וַיְדַבֵּר ראה חֲמוֹר אִתָּם לֵאמֹר שְׁכֶם בְּנִי חָשְׁקָה נַפְשׁוֹ בְּבִתְּכֶם
תְּנוּ נָא אֹתָהּ לוֹ לְאִשָּׁה: 9 וְהִתְחַתְּנוּ אֹתָנוּ בְּנֹתֵיכֶם תִּתְּנוּ־לָנוּ
אלהים, מום וְאֶת־בְּנֹתֵינוּ תִּקְחוּ לָכֶם: 10 וְאִתָּנוּ תֵּשֵׁבוּ וְהָאָרֶץ
אלהים דההין ע"ה תִּהְיֶה לִפְנֵיכֶם שְׁבוּ וּסְחָרוּהָ וְהֵאָחֲזוּ בָּהּ: 11 וַיֹּאמֶר
שְׁכֶם אֶל־אָבִיהָ וְאֶל־אַחֶיהָ אֶמְצָא־חֵן מוחי בְּעֵינֵיכֶם ריבוע מ"ה
וַאֲשֶׁר תֹּאמְרוּ אֵלַי אֶתֵּן: 12 הַרְבּוּ עָלַי מְאֹד מ"ה מֹהַר וּמַתָּן
וְאֶתְּנָה נתה, קס"א ∸ קנ"א ∸ קמ"ג כַּאֲשֶׁר תֹּאמְרוּ אֵלָי וּתְנוּ־לִי אֶת־הַנַּעֲרָ
לְאִשָּׁה: 13 וַיַּעֲנוּ בְנֵי־יַעֲקֹב יאהדונהי ∸ אידהנויה אֶת־שְׁכֶם וְאֶת־חֲמוֹר
אָבִיו בְּמִרְמָה וַיְדַבֵּרוּ ראה אֲשֶׁר טִמֵּא אֵת דִּינָה אֲחֹתָם:
14 וַיֹּאמְרוּ אֲלֵיהֶם לֹא נוּכַל לַעֲשׂוֹת הַדָּבָר ראה הַזֶּה והו לָתֵת

15 *We will give our consent to you on one condition only: that you become like us by circumcising all your males.*

16 *Then we will give you our daughters and take your daughters for ourselves. We'll settle among you and become one people with you.*

17 *But if you will not agree to be circumcised, we'll take our sister and go."*

18 *Their proposal seemed good to Hamor and his son Shechem.*

19 *The young man, who was the most honored of his father's entire household, lost no time in doing what they said, because he was delighted with Jacob's daughter.*

20 *So Hamor and his son Shechem went to the gate of their city to speak to their fellow townsmen.*

21 *"These men are friendly toward us," they said. "Let them live in our land and trade in it; the land has plenty of room for them. We can marry their daughters and they can marry ours.*

22 *But the men will consent to live with us as one people only on the condition that our males are circumcised, as they themselves are.*

23 *Won't their livestock, their property and all their other animals become ours? So let us give our consent to them, and they will settle among us."*

24 *All the men who went out of the city gate agreed with Hamor and his son Shechem, and every male in the city was circumcised.*

25 *Three days later, while all of them were still in pain, two of Jacob's sons, Simeon and Levi, Dinah's brothers, took their swords and attacked the unsuspecting city, killing every male.*

וַיְהִי

Genesis 34:25 – On the third day after the circumcision, when the pain of the men of Shechem was at its worst, Simon and Levi, Dinah's brothers, slaughtered all the newly circumcised men.

We have already learned that Simon embodied the quality of harsh judgment and that Levi was his second in this matter. (Indeed, the word levi means "secondary" or "adjunct.") The *Zohar* says:

> *These are Simon and Levi, who were brothers in every respect, because they both came from the side of Harsh Judgment, and their anger was murderous anger, as it is written: "Cursed be their anger, for it was fierce; and their wrath, for it was cruel." (Genesis 49:7)*
>
> *– The Zohar, Vayeshev 12:109*

אֶת־אֲחֹתֵנוּ לְאִישׁ ע"ה קנ"א קס"א אֲשֶׁר־לוֹ עָרְלָה כִּי־חֶרְפָּה הִוא לָנוּ
אלהים, מום: 15 אַךְ אהיה ־בְּזֹאת נֵאוֹת לָכֶם אִם יוהך תִּהְיוּ כָמֹנוּ לְהִמֹּל
לָכֶם כָּל ילי ־זָכָר: 16 וְנָתַנּוּ אֶת־בְּנֹתֵינוּ לָכֶם וְאֶת־בְּנֹתֵיכֶם נִקַּח־
לָנוּ אלהים, מום וְיָשַׁבְנוּ אִתְּכֶם וְהָיִינוּ לְעַם עלם אֶחָד אהבה, דאגה: 17 וְאִם
יוהך ־לֹא תִשְׁמְעוּ אֵלֵינוּ לְהִמּוֹל וְלָקַחְנוּ אֶת־בִּתֵּנוּ וְהָלָכְנוּ מיה:
18 וַיִּיטְבוּ דִבְרֵיהֶם ראה בְּעֵינֵי ריבוע מ"ה חֲמוֹר וּבְעֵינֵי ריבוע מ"ה שְׁכֶם
בֶּן־חֲמוֹר: 19 וְלֹא־אֵחַר הַנַּעַר ש"ך לַעֲשׂוֹת הַדָּבָר ראה כִּי חָפֵץ
בְּבַת־יַעֲקֹב יאהדונהי - אידהנויה וְהוּא נִכְבָּד מִכֹּל ילי בֵּית ב"פ ראה אָבִיו:
20 וַיָּבֹא חֲמוֹר וּשְׁכֶם בְּנוֹ אֶל־שַׁעַר עִירָם בוזזרך, ערי, סנדלפון וַיְדַבְּרוּ
ראה אֶל־אַנְשֵׁי עִירָם בוזזרך, ערי, סנדלפון לֵאמֹר: 21 הָאֲנָשִׁים הָאֵלֶּה
שְׁלֵמִים הֵם אִתָּנוּ וְיֵשְׁבוּ בָאָרֶץ אלהים דאלפין וְיִסְחֲרוּ אֹתָהּ וְהָאָרֶץ
אלהים דההין ע"ה הִנֵּה רַחֲבַת־יָדַיִם לִפְנֵיהֶם אֶת־בְּנֹתָם נִקַּח־לָנוּ
אלהים, מום לְנָשִׁים וְאֶת־בְּנֹתֵינוּ נִתֵּן לָהֶם: 22 אַךְ אהיה ־בְּזֹאת יֵאֹתוּ
לָנוּ אלהים, מום הָאֲנָשִׁים לָשֶׁבֶת אִתָּנוּ לִהְיוֹת לְעַם עלם אֶחָד אהבה, דאגה
בְּהִמּוֹל לָנוּ אלהים, מום כָּל ילי ־זָכָר כַּאֲשֶׁר הֵם נִמֹּלִים: 23 מִקְנֵהֶם
וְקִנְיָנָם וְכָל ילי ־בְּהֶמְתָּם הֲלוֹא לָנוּ אלהים, מום הֵם אַךְ אהיה נֵאוֹתָה
לָהֶם וְיֵשְׁבוּ אִתָּנוּ: 24 וַיִּשְׁמְעוּ אֶל־חֲמוֹר וְאֶל־שְׁכֶם בְּנוֹ כָּל ילי
־יֹצְאֵי שַׁעַר עִירוֹ בוזזרך, ערי, סנדלפון וַיִּמֹּלוּ כָּל ילי ־זָכָר כָּל ילי ־יֹצְאֵי
שַׁעַר עִירוֹ בוזזרך, ערי, סנדלפון: 25 וַיְהִי אל בַיּוֹם נגד, זן, מזבח הַשְּׁלִישִׁי
בִּהְיוֹתָם כֹּאֲבִים וַיִּקְחוּ חעם שְׁנֵי־בְנֵי־יַעֲקֹב יאהדונהי - אידהנויה

Although Shechem was known as a place of negative energies and had many negative people living in it, the attack was carried out without the assistance of the other brothers. The circumcision of the men of Shechem symbolizes the need for atonement and purification before death, and the entire story shows how wicked acts will attract harsh judgment without mercy. The deaths that occurred were a cleansing of judgment for the entire city of Shechem. There are some people who are entirely negative, and although none of us can really determine who they are, Jacob and his sons were able to make this judgment.

[26] They put Hamor and his son Shechem to the sword and took Dinah from Shechem's house and left.

[27] The sons of Jacob came upon the dead bodies and looted the city where their sister had been defiled.

[28] They seized their flocks and herds and donkeys and everything else of theirs in the
city and out in the fields. [29] They carried off all their wealth and all their women and
children, taking as plunder everything in the houses.

[30] Then Jacob said to Simeon and Levi, "You have brought trouble on me by making
me a stench to the Canaanites and Perizzites, the people living in this land. We are
few in number, and if they join forces against me and attack me, I and my household
will be destroyed." [31] But they replied, "Should he have treated our sister like a
prostitute?"

35[1] Then God said to Jacob, "Go up to Bethel and settle there, and build an altar
there to God, who appeared to you when you were fleeing from your brother Esau." [2]
So Jacob said to his household and to all who were with him, "Get rid of the foreign
gods you have with you, and purify yourselves and change your clothes.

[3] Then come, let us go up to Bethel, where I will build an altar to God, who answered me in the day of my distress and who has been with me wherever I have gone."

[4] So they gave Jacob all the foreign gods they had and the rings in their ears, and
Jacob buried them under the oak at Shechem. [5] Then they set out, and the terror of
God fell upon the towns all around them so that no one pursued them.

[6] Jacob and all the people with him came to Luz (that is, Bethel) in the land of Canaan.

They knew exactly who needed to be eliminated for the cleansing to take place, and they carried out this task.

עֲלֵה

Genesis 35:1 – **Going Back to the Land of Israel**. God told Jacob to return to the place where Jacob had had the dream of the angels going up and down the ladder. This was the spot where the Temple would eventually be built. But first, Jacob had to deal with the idols that the people were worshipping.

וַיִּטְמֹן

Genesis 35:4 – Before Jacob took everyone to Israel, he instructed his whole household to get rid of their idols. In this case, he was dealing with the disposal of the physical idols that people worshipped, but the meaning of idol-worship is often over-simplified. The concept is broader than just the worship of statues or nature spirits. The more prevalent and negative forms of idol-worship include devotion to such things as ego, power, control, and wealth. Whenever there is something in our life that is more important to us than our devotion to the Light of the Creator, we are engaging in idol-worship.

שִׁמְעוֹן וְלֵוִי דמב, מלוי ע"ב אֲחֵי דִינָה אִישׁ ע"ה קנ"א קס"א חַרְבּוֹ
רי"ו, גבורה וַיָּבֹאוּ עַל־הָעִיר סוזוף, ערי, סנדלפון בֶּטַח וַיַּהַרְגוּ כָּל ילי ־זָכָר:
26 וְאֶת־חֲמוֹר וְאֶת־שְׁכֶם בְּנוֹ הָרְגוּ לְפִי־חָרֶב וַיִּקְחוּ חעם אֶת־דִּינָה
מִבֵּית ב"פ ראה שְׁכֶם וַיֵּצֵאוּ: 27 בְּנֵי יַעֲקֹב יאהדונהי - אידהנויה בָּאוּ עַל־הַחֲלָלִים
וַיָּבֹזּוּ הָעִיר סוזוף, ערי, סנדלפון אֲשֶׁר טִמְּאוּ אֲחוֹתָם: 28 אֶת־צֹאנָם
וְאֶת־בְּקָרָם וְאֶת־חֲמֹרֵיהֶם וְאֵת אֲשֶׁר־בָּעִיר סוזוף, ערי, סנדלפון וְאֶת־
אֲשֶׁר בַּשָּׂדֶה לָקָחוּ: 29 וְאֶת־כָּל ילי ־חֵילָם ומב וְאֶת־כָּל ילי ־טַפָּם
וְאֶת־נְשֵׁיהֶם שָׁבוּ וַיָּבֹזּוּ וְאֵת כָּל ילי ־אֲשֶׁר בַּבָּיִת ב"פ ראה: 30 וַיֹּאמֶר
יַעֲקֹב יאהדונהי - אידהנויה אֶל־שִׁמְעוֹן וְאֶל־לֵוִי דמב, מלוי ע"ב עֲכַרְתֶּם אֹתִי
לְהַבְאִישֵׁנִי בְּיֹשֵׁב הָאָרֶץ אלהים דההין ע"ה בַּכְּנַעֲנִי וּבַפְּרִזִּי וַאֲנִי אני, ב"פ
אהיה - יהוה מְתֵי מִסְפָּר וְנֶאֶסְפוּ עָלַי וְהִכּוּנִי וְנִשְׁמַדְתִּי אֲנִי אני וּבֵיתִי
ב"פ ראה: 31 וַיֹּאמְרוּ הַכְזוֹנָה יַעֲשֶׂה אֶת־אֲחוֹתֵנוּ: [פ] 35 1 וַיֹּאמֶר
אֱלֹהִים ילה, מום אֶל־יַעֲקֹב יאהדונהי - אידהנויה קוּם עֲלֵה בֵית ב"פ ראה ־אֵל
יי"א וְשֶׁב־שָׁם וַעֲשֵׂה־שָׁם מִזְבֵּחַ זן, נגד לָאֵל יי"א הַנִּרְאֶה אֵלֶיךָ אני
בְּבָרְחֲךָ מִפְּנֵי חכמה - בינה עֵשָׂו אָחִיךָ: 2 וַיֹּאמֶר יַעֲקֹב יאהדונהי - אידהנויה
אֶל־בֵּיתוֹ ב"פ ראה וְאֶל כָּל ילי ־אֲשֶׁר עִמּוֹ הָסִרוּ אֶת־אֱלֹהֵי דמב, ילה
הַנֵּכָר אֲשֶׁר בְּתֹכְכֶם וְהִטַּהֲרוּ י"פ אכא וְהַחֲלִיפוּ שִׂמְלֹתֵיכֶם:
3 וְנָקוּמָה וְנַעֲלֶה בֵּית ב"פ ראה ־אֵל יי"א וְאֶעֱשֶׂה־שָּׁם מִזְבֵּחַ זן, נגד
לָאֵל יי"א הָעֹנֶה אֹתִי בְּיוֹם נגד, זן, מזבח צָרָתִי וַיְהִי אל עִמָּדִי בַּדֶּרֶךְ
ב"פ יב"ק אֲשֶׁר הָלָכְתִּי מיה: 4 וַיִּתְּנוּ אֶל־יַעֲקֹב יאהדונהי - אידהנויה אֵת כָּל
ילי ־אֱלֹהֵי דמב, ילה הַנֵּכָר אֲשֶׁר בְּיָדָם וְאֶת־הַנְּזָמִים אֲשֶׁר בְּאָזְנֵיהֶם
יוד הי ואו הה וַיִּטְמֹן אֹתָם יַעֲקֹב יאהדונהי - אידהנויה תַּחַת הָאֵלָה אֲשֶׁר
עִם־שְׁכֶם: 5 וַיִּסָּעוּ וַיְהִי אל | חִתַּת אֱלֹהִים ילה, מום עַל־הֶעָרִים
אֲשֶׁר סְבִיבוֹתֵיהֶם וְלֹא רָדְפוּ אַחֲרֵי בְּנֵי יַעֲקֹב יאהדונהי - אידהנויה:

7 There he built an altar, and he called the place El Bethel, because it was there that God revealed himself to him when he was fleeing from his brother.

8 Now Deborah, Rebecca's nurse, died and was buried under the oak below Bethel. So it was named Allon Bacuth.

9 After Jacob returned from Paddan Aram, God appeared to him again and blessed
him. 10 God said to him, "Your name is Jacob, but you will no longer be called Jacob;
your name will be Israel." So, he named him Israel.

11 And God said to him, "I am God Almighty; be fruitful and increase in number. A nation and a community of nations will come from you, and kings will come from your body.

SIXTH READING - JOSEPH - YESOD

12 The land I gave to Abraham and Isaac I also give to you, and I will give this land to
your descendants after you." 13 Then God went up from him at the place where he
had talked with him.

14 Jacob set up a stone pillar at the place where God had talked with him, and he poured out a drink offering on it; he also poured oil on it.

15 Jacob called the place where God had talked with him Bethel. 16 Then they moved
on from Bethel. While they were still some distance from Ephrath, Rachel began to
give birth and had a hard labor.

וַתָּמָת

Genesis 35:8 – *Rebecca's Nurse, Deborah, Died and was Buried.* Quite abruptly, the Bible states that Rebecca's nurse died. However, our sages explain that it is really Rebecca who died, but Jacob was not present to honor her at the time of her death. He was allowed to be absent because he was engaged in the important spiritual work of struggling with Esau's angel.

There are times when we cannot fulfill certain obligations because we have other more pressing duties. Sometimes, a higher spiritual purpose takes us away from our everyday responsibilities, and it is the higher spiritual purpose that must always take precedence. There are also times when Satan causes us to miss an obligation, and once he's accomplished this, he goes on to make us feel guilty about it.

יִשְׂרָאֵל

Genesis 35:10 – Rav Bachya ben Asher (1255-1340), said that after God renamed Jacob "Israel," the name Jacob would continue to be used for matters pertaining to the physical world, while the name Israel would be used for spiritual matters, including the spiritual role of Jacob's descendants.

6 וַיָּבֹא יַעֲקֹב יאהדונהי - אידהנויה לוּזָה אֲשֶׁר בְּאֶרֶץ אלהים דאלפין כְּנַעַן
הִוא בֵּית ב"פ ראה ־אֵל ייא"י הוּא וְכָל ילי ־הָעָם אֲשֶׁר־עִמּוֹ: 7 וַיִּבֶן
שָׁם מִזְבֵּחַ נגד, זן וַיִּקְרָא עם ה' אותיות = ב"פ קס"א לַמָּקוֹם יהוה ברבוע אֵל ייא"י
בֵּית ב"פ ראה ־אֵל ייא"י כִּי שָׁם נִגְלוּ אֵלָיו הָאֱלֹהִים ילה, מום בְּבָרְחוֹ
מִפְּנֵי חכמה - בינה אָחִיו: 8 וַתָּמָת דְּבֹרָה מֵינֶקֶת רִבְקָה וַתִּקָּבֵר
מִתַּחַת לְבֵית ב"פ ראה ־אֵל ייא"י תַּחַת הָאַלּוֹן וַיִּקְרָא עם ה' אותיות = ב"פ קס"א
שְׁמוֹ מהש ע"ה אַלּוֹן בָּכוּת: [פ] 9 וַיֵּרָא אֱלֹהִים ילה, מום אֶל־יַעֲקֹב
יאהדונהי - אידהנויה עוֹד בְּבֹאוֹ מִפַּדַּן אֲרָם וַיְבָרֶךְ עסמ"ב אֹתוֹ: 10 וַיֹּאמֶר־
לוֹ אֱלֹהִים ילה, מום שִׁמְךָ יַעֲקֹב יאהדונהי - אידהנויה לֹא־יִקָּרֵא שִׁמְךָ עוֹד
יַעֲקֹב יאהדונהי - אידהנויה כִּי אִם־ יוהך יִשְׂרָאֵל יִהְיֶה ייי שְׁמֶךָ וַיִּקְרָא
עם ה' אותיות = ב"פ קס"א אֶת־שְׁמוֹ מהש ע"ה יִשְׂרָאֵל: 11 וַיֹּאמֶר לוֹ אֱלֹהִים
ילה, מום אֲנִי אני אֵל שַׁדַּי מהש פְּרֵה וּרְבֵה גּוֹי מלוי מ"ה וּקְהַל גּוֹיִם יִהְיֶה
ייי מִמֶּךָּ וּמְלָכִים מֵחֲלָצֶיךָ יֵצֵאוּ:

SIXTH READING - JOSEPH - YESOD

12 וְאֶת־הָאָרֶץ אלהים דההין ע"ה אֲשֶׁר נָתַתִּי לְאַבְרָהָם ח"פ אל, רמ"ח וּלְיִצְחָק
לְךָ ד"פ ב"ן אֶתְּנֶנָּה וּלְזַרְעֲךָ אַחֲרֶיךָ אֶתֵּן אֶת־הָאָרֶץ אלהים דההין ע"ה:
13 וַיַּעַל מֵעָלָיו אֱלֹהִים ילה, מום בַּמָּקוֹם יהוה ברבוע אֲשֶׁר־דִּבֶּר ראה
אִתּוֹ: 14 וַיַּצֵּב יַעֲקֹב יאהדונהי - אידהנויה מַצֵּבָה בַּמָּקוֹם יהוה ברבוע אֲשֶׁר־
דִּבֶּר ראה אִתּוֹ מַצֶּבֶת אָבֶן יוד הה ואו הה וַיַּסֵּךְ עָלֶיהָ פהל נֶסֶךְ וַיִּצֹק
עָלֶיהָ פהל שָׁמֶן י"פ טל, י"פ כוזו, ביט: 15 וַיִּקְרָא עם ה' אותיות = ב"פ קס"א יַעֲקֹב
יאהדונהי - אידהנויה אֶת־שֵׁם שדי יהוה הַמָּקוֹם יהוה ברבוע אֲשֶׁר דִּבֶּר ראה אִתּוֹ
שָׁם אֱלֹהִים ילה, מום בֵּית ב"פ ראה ־אֵל ייא"י: 16 וַיִּסְעוּ מִבֵּית ב"פ ראה

17 And as she was having great difficulty in childbirth, the midwife said to her, "Don't be afraid, for you have another son."

18 As her soul departed—for she was dying—she named her son Ben-Oni. But his father named him Benjamin.

19 So Rachel died and was buried on the way to Ephrath (that is, Bethlehem).

20 Over her tomb Jacob set up a pillar, and to this day that pillar marks Rachel's tomb.

21 Israel moved on again and pitched his tent beyond Migdal Eder.

22 While Israel was living in that region, Reuben went in and slept with his father's concubine Bilhah, and Israel heard of it. Jacob had twelve sons: 23 The sons of Leah: Reuben the firstborn of Jacob, Simeon, Levi, Judah, Issachar, and Zebulun.

24 The sons of Rachel: Joseph and Benjamin. 25 The sons of Rachel's maidservant Bilhah: Dan and Naphtali.

26 The sons of Leah's maidservant Zilpah: Gad and Asher. These were the sons of Jacob, who were born to him in Paddan Aram.

27 Jacob came home to his father Isaac in Mamre, near Kiriath Arba (that is, Hebron), where Abraham and Isaac had lived.

28 Isaac lived a hundred and eighty years.

בִּנְיָמִין – (פל)

Genesis 35:18 – Benjamin controls the month of Libra (*Tishrei*), symbolized by the letters *Pei* and *Lamed*. He was the twelfth of Jacob's sons and of vital importance in his connection to the work of Jacob and Joseph, as the *Zohar* explains:

> *The Shechina is LOCATED between two righteous beings—the supernal righteous, Joseph, and the righteous below, Benjamin. This JOSEPH is the husband of the Queen, and BENJAMIN is the host. Therefore it is written: "He makes the barren woman to keep house." (Psalms 113:9) This refers to the revealed world, meaning the lower Shechina who is the mainstay of the home, the mainstay of this world, Rachel. AND SHE IS between two righteous, the Upper and the Lower.*
>
> *– The Zohar, Hashmatot 32:198*

וַתָּמָת

Genesis 35:19 – Rachel died just as Benjamin was born. On the surface, it may seem that Rachel led a miserable life. She was forced to wait seven years to marry Jacob, who instead married her sister, Leah, first. When she was finally allowed to marry Jacob, she was not able to bear children. When she was finally able to bear children, she died giving birth to her second child. Her apparent misfortune continued even after her passing, when she was not buried with her husband. However, the sages tell us that Jacob buried Rachel on the road so that when the exiles would pass by in

אֵל ייא״י וַיְהִי אל ־עוֹד כִּבְרַת־הָאָרֶץ אלהים דההין ע״ה לָבוֹא אֶפְרָתָה
וַתֵּלֶד רָחֵל רבוע ס״ג ÷ ע״ב וַתְּקַשׁ בְּלִדְתָּהּ׃ 17 וַיְהִי בְהַקְשֹׁתָהּ בְּלִדְתָּהּ
וַתֹּאמֶר לָהּ הַמְיַלֶּדֶת אַל־תִּירְאִי כִּי־גַם יג״ל ־זֶה לָךְ בֵּן׃ 18 וַיְהִי
בְּצֵאת נַפְשָׁהּ ר״ת בין כִּי מֵתָה וַתִּקְרָא שְׁמוֹ מהש ע״ה בֶּן־אוֹנִי בינה
וְאָבִיו קָרָא־לוֹ בִנְיָמִין׃ 19 וַתָּמָת רָחֵל רבוע ס״ג ÷ ע״ב וַתִּקָּבֵר בְּדֶרֶךְ
ב״פ יב״ק אֶפְרָתָה הִוא בֵּית ב״פ ראה לָחֶם ג״פ יהוה׃ 20 וַיַּצֵּב יַעֲקֹב
יאהדונהי ÷ אידהנויה מַצֵּבָה עַל־קְבֻרָתָהּ הִוא מַצֶּבֶת קְבֻרַת־רָחֵל רבוע ס״ג
÷ ע״ב עַד־הַיּוֹם נגד, זן, מזבח׃ 21 וַיִּסַּע יִשְׂרָאֵל וַיֵּט אָהֳלֹה מֵהָלְאָה
לְמִגְדַּל־עֵדֶר׃ 22 וַיְהִי בִּשְׁכֹּן יִשְׂרָאֵל בָּאָרֶץ אלהים דאלפין הַהִוא
וַיֵּלֶךְ כלי רְאוּבֵן ג״פ אלהים וַיִּשְׁכַּב אֶת־בִּלְהָה מ״ב פִּילֶגֶשׁ אָבִיו
וַיִּשְׁמַע יִשְׂרָאֵל [פ] וַיִּהְיוּ אל בְנֵי־יַעֲקֹב יאהדונהי ÷ אידהנויה שְׁנֵים עָשָׂר׃

---

the future on their way to Babylon, she would sense their distress and send up prayers for them. (*Beresheet Rabba 82:10*)

From this, we see the enormous importance both of Rachel's place in the story of Israel and of the power she had to draw mercy from the Upper Worlds for her people, even after her death. She bears the pain of all humanity. The *Zohar* says that Rachel's burial place will never disappear until the day that God resurrects all the dead.

> *And these are the two Messiahs—Messiah, son of Joseph, and Messiah, son of Jacob—that will pass by Rachel's tomb, when they will come to redeem Israel.*
> *– Tikuna Kadma'a, The Sixth Tikkun 1:9*

וַיִּשְׁכַּב

Genesis 35:22 – Reuben, the son of Jacob, supposedly slept with Bilhah, his father's concubine. A break in the verse (a space between the words) narrating this event indicates that something important is to be understood. Although the commentaries teach that Reuben did not actually have intercourse with Bilhah, some transgression certainly occurred because he lost his birthright as a result.

After Rachel died, Reuben wanted his father, Jacob, to move into the tent of Leah, Reuben's mother. But Jacob had already moved his bed into the tent of Bilhah, Leah's maidservant. Reuben then showed disrespect for his father by physically moving Jacob's bed into Leah's tent. When Reuben went to move the bed, Bilhah was lying in it, and the moment Reuben saw her, he desired her. Because a person's level of spiritual consciousness truly determines the nature of his actions, and because Reuben's consciousness included lust, it was as if he had slept with Bilhah, regardless of what actually took place on the physical level. From this, we are taught that we should learn to control even our thoughts by means of our higher spiritual awareness, since every thought has an effect, even if it doesn't always manifest.

29 Then he breathed his last and died and was gathered to his people, old and full of years. And his sons Esau and Jacob buried him.

36 1 These are the generations of Esau (that is, Edom).

2 Esau took his wives from the women of Canaan: Adah, daughter of Elon the Hittite, and Oholibamah, daughter of Anah and granddaughter of Zibeon the Hivite, 3 also Basemath, daughter of Ishmael and sister of Nebaioth.

4 Adah bore Eliphaz to Esau, Basemath bore Reuel, 5 and Oholibamah bore Jeush, Jalam, and Korah. These were the sons of Esau, who were born to him in Canaan.

6 Esau took his wives and sons and daughters and all the souls of his household, as well as his livestock and all his other animals and all the goods he had acquired in Canaan, and moved to a land some distance from his brother Jacob.

7 Their possessions were too great for them to remain together; the land where they were staying could not support them both because of their livestock.

8 So Esau (that is, Edom) settled in the hill country of Seir.

9 These are the generations of Esau, the father of the Edomites in the hill country of Seir.

וַיָּמָת

Genesis 35:29 – Isaac died, having lived a long and fulfilled life. At the precise moment we leave this world, our soul is in transition. Our bodies are still here, but we are also connected to the Upper Worlds. In the case of highly spiritual people, precisely at the moment of the person's passing, their righteousness and their consciousness, as well as all the Light they revealed in this world, are available and accessible to us in their totality.

That is why it is important to make a connection with our sages on the anniversaries of their deaths—because this is the time when their great spiritual Light is most available.

Rashi says that Isaac was one of only six people over whom the Angel of Death had no power; instead, he died from a kiss from the Divine Presence. The *Zohar* states the following:

And so one whose soul departs through a kiss joins another spirit, MEANING THE SPIRIT OF GOD, a spirit never to part from him. This is what is meant by a kiss. So the Congregation of Israel said, "Let him kiss me with the kiss of his mouth" in order that one spirit cling to the other and never part.

– The Zohar, Mishpatim 27:552

תֹּלְדוֹת

Genesis 36:1 – The Descendants of Esau. The names of Esau's descendants represent different categories of negativity. This list of names provides a set of markers by which we can first learn to identify the particular negativities manifesting in our own behaviors and then learn how to overcome them. Very often, we know we have a problem, but we do not know what we need to let go of to release the problem. The key is to identify two things: what is causing the problem at the seed level and how to transform it.

23 בְּנֵי לֵאָה לאה (אלד ע"ה) בְּכוֹר יַעֲקֹב יאהדונהי - אידהנויה רְאוּבֵן ג"פ אלהים
וְשִׁמְעוֹן וְלֵוִי דמב, מלוי ע"ב וִיהוּדָה וְיִשָּׂשכָר וּזְבֻלוּן: 24 בְּנֵי רָחֵל
רבוע ס"ג - ע"ב יוֹסֵף ציון, קנאה, ו"פ יהוה, ה"פ אל וּבִנְיָמִן: 25 וּבְנֵי בִלְהָה מ"ב
שִׁפְחַת רָחֵל רבוע ס"ג - ע"ב דָּן וְנַפְתָּלִי: 26 וּבְנֵי זִלְפָּה שִׁפְחַת לֵאָה
לאה (אלד ע"ה) גָּד וְאָשֵׁר אלהים דיודין ורבוע אלהים ע"ה אֵלֶּה בְּנֵי יַעֲקֹב
יאהדונהי - אידהנויה אֲשֶׁר יֻלַּד־לוֹ בְּפַדַּן אֲרָם: 27 וַיָּבֹא יַעֲקֹב
יאהדונהי - אידהנויה אֶל־יִצְחָק ד"פ ב"ן אָבִיו מַמְרֵא סוזוף ע"ה קִרְיַת הָאַרְבַּע
הִוא חֶבְרוֹן אֲשֶׁר־גָּר־שָׁם אַבְרָהָם וז"פ אל, רמ"ח וְיִצְחָק ד"פ ב"ן: 28 וַיִּהְיוּ
אל יְמֵי יִצְחָק ד"פ ב"ן מְאַת שָׁנָה וּשְׁמֹנִים שָׁנָה: 29 וַיִּגְוַע יִצְחָק ד"פ ב"ן
וַיָּמָת וַיֵּאָסֶף אֶל־עַמָּיו זָקֵן וּשְׂבַע יָמִים נלך וַיִּקְבְּרוּ אֹתוֹ עֵשָׂו
וְיַעֲקֹב יאהדונהי - אידהנויה בָּנָיו: [פ] 36 1 וְאֵלֶּה תֹּלְדוֹת עֵשָׂו הוּא אֱדוֹם:
2 עֵשָׂו לָקַח אֶת־נָשָׁיו מִבְּנוֹת כְּנָעַן אֶת־עָדָה בַּת־אֵילוֹן הַחִתִּי
וְאֶת־אָהֳלִיבָמָה בַּת־עֲנָה בַּת־צִבְעוֹן הַחִוִּי: 3 וְאֶת־בָּשְׂמַת בַּת־
יִשְׁמָעֵאל אֲחוֹת נְבָיוֹת: 4 וַתֵּלֶד עָדָה לְעֵשָׂו אֶת־אֱלִיפָז וּבָשְׂמַת
יָלְדָה אֶת־רְעוּאֵל: 5 וְאָהֳלִיבָמָה יָלְדָה אֶת־יְעוּשׁ (כתיב: יעיש)
וְאֶת־יַעְלָם וְאֶת־קֹרַח אֵלֶּה בְּנֵי עֵשָׂו אֲשֶׁר יֻלְּדוּ־לוֹ בְּאֶרֶץ
כְּנָעַן אלהים דאלפין: 6 וַיִּקַּח וזעם עֵשָׂו אֶת־נָשָׁיו וְאֶת־בָּנָיו וְאֶת־בְּנֹתָיו
וְאֶת־כָּל ילי ־נַפְשׁוֹת בֵּיתוֹ ב"פ ראה וְאֶת־מִקְנֵהוּ וְאֶת־כָּל־ ילי
בְּהֶמְתּוֹ וְאֵת כָּל ילי ־קִנְיָנוֹ אֲשֶׁר רָכַשׁ בְּאֶרֶץ אלהים דאלפין כְּנָעַן
וַיֵּלֶךְ כלי אֶל־אֶרֶץ אלהים דאלפין מִפְּנֵי יַעֲקֹב יאהדונהי - אידהנויה אָחִיו: 7 כִּי־
הָיָה יהה רְכוּשָׁם רָב מִשֶּׁבֶת יַחְדָּו וְלֹא יָכְלָה אֶרֶץ אלהים דאלפין
מְגוּרֵיהֶם לָשֵׂאת אֹתָם מִפְּנֵי מִקְנֵיהֶם: 8 וַיֵּשֶׁב עֵשָׂו בְּהַר אור, רז
שֵׂעִיר עֵשָׂו הוּא אֱדוֹם: 9 וְאֵלֶּה תֹּלְדוֹת עֵשָׂו אֲבִי אֱדוֹם בְּהַר
אור, רז שֵׂעִיר: 10 אֵלֶּה שְׁמוֹת בְּנֵי־עֵשָׂו אֱלִיפַז בֶּן־עָדָה אֵשֶׁת

[10] These are the names of Esau's sons: Eliphaz, the son of Esau's wife Adah, and Reuel, the son of Esau's wife Basemath.

[11] The sons of Eliphaz: Teman, Omar, Zepho, Gatam, and Kenaz.

[12] Esau's son Eliphaz also had a concubine named Timna, who bore him Amalek. These were grandsons of Esau's wife Adah.

[13] The sons of Reuel: Nahath, Zerah, Shammah, and Mizzah. These were the grandsons of Esau's wife Basemath.

[14] The sons of Esau's wife Oholibamah, daughter of Anah and granddaughter of Zibeon, whom she bore to Esau: Jeush, Jalam, and Korah.

[15] These were the chiefs among Esau's descendants: The sons of Eliphaz, the firstborn of Esau: Chiefs Teman, Omar, Zepho, Kenaz, [16] Korah, Gatam, and Amalek. These were the chiefs descended from Eliphaz in Edom; they were grandsons of Adah.

[17] The sons of Esau's son Reuel: Chiefs Nahath, Zerah, Shammah, and Mizzah. These were the chiefs descended from Reuel in Edom; they were grandsons of Esau's wife Basemath.

[18] The sons of Esau's wife Oholibamah: Chiefs Jeush, Jalam, and Korah. These were the chiefs descended from Esau's wife Oholibamah, daughter of Anah.

[19] These were the sons of Esau (that is, Edom), and these were their chiefs.

SEVENTH READING - DAVID - MALCHUT

[20] These were the sons of Seir the Horite, who were living in the region: Lotan, Shobal, Zibeon, Anah, [21] Dishon, Ezer, and Dishan. These sons of Seir in Edom were Horite chiefs.

[22] The sons of Lotan: Hori and Homam. Timna was Lotan's sister. [23] The sons of Shobal: Alvan, Manahath, Ebal, Shepho, and Onam.

[24] The sons of Zibeon: Aiah and Anah. This is the Anah who discovered the hot springs in the desert while he was grazing the donkeys of his father Zibeon.

[25] The children of Anah: Dishon and Oholibamah, daughter of Anah.

[26] The sons of Dishon: Hemdan, Eshban, Ithran, and Keran. [27] The sons of Ezer: Bilhan, Zaavan, and Akan.

עֵשָׂו רְעוּאֵל בֶּן־בָּשְׂמַת אֵשֶׁת עֵשָׂו׃ 11 וַיִּהְיוּ בְּנֵי אֱלִיפָז תֵּימָן
אוֹמָר צְפוֹ וְגַעְתָּם וּקְנַז׃ 12 וְתִמְנַע ב״פ סוזחך | הָיְתָה פִילֶגֶשׁ לֶאֱלִיפַז
בֶּן־עֵשָׂו וַתֵּלֶד לֶאֱלִיפַז אֶת־עֲמָלֵק אֵלֶּה בְּנֵי עָדָה אֵשֶׁת עֵשָׂו׃
13 וְאֵלֶּה בְּנֵי רְעוּאֵל נַחַת וָזֶרַח שַׁמָּה וּמִזָּה אֵלֶּה הָיוּ בְּנֵי בָשְׂמַת
אֵשֶׁת עֵשָׂו׃ 14 וְאֵלֶּה הָיוּ בְּנֵי אָהֳלִיבָמָה בַת־עֲנָה בַּת־צִבְעוֹן
אֵשֶׁת עֵשָׂו וַתֵּלֶד לְעֵשָׂו אֶת־יְעוּשׁ (כתיב: יעיש) וְאֶת־יַעְלָם וְאֶת־
קֹרַח׃ 15 אֵלֶּה אַלּוּפֵי בְנֵי־עֵשָׂו בְּנֵי אֱלִיפַז בְּכוֹר עֵשָׂו אַלּוּף
תֵּימָן אַלּוּף אוֹמָר אַלּוּף צְפוֹ אַלּוּף קְנַז׃ 16 אַלּוּף־קֹרַח אַלּוּף
גַּעְתָּם אַלּוּף עֲמָלֵק אֵלֶּה אַלּוּפֵי אֱלִיפַז בְּאֶרֶץ אלהים דאלפין אֱדוֹם
אֵלֶּה בְּנֵי עָדָה׃ 17 וְאֵלֶּה בְּנֵי רְעוּאֵל בֶּן־עֵשָׂו אַלּוּף נַחַת אַלּוּף
זֶרַח אַלּוּף שַׁמָּה אַלּוּף מִזָּה אֵלֶּה אַלּוּפֵי רְעוּאֵל בְּאֶרֶץ אלהים דאלפין
אֱדוֹם אֵלֶּה בְּנֵי בָשְׂמַת אֵשֶׁת עֵשָׂו׃ 18 וְאֵלֶּה בְּנֵי אָהֳלִיבָמָה
אֵשֶׁת עֵשָׂו אַלּוּף יְעוּשׁ אַלּוּף יַעְלָם אַלּוּף קֹרַח אֵלֶּה אַלּוּפֵי
אָהֳלִיבָמָה בַּת־עֲנָה אֵשֶׁת עֵשָׂו׃ 19 אֵלֶּה בְנֵי־עֵשָׂו וְאֵלֶּה
אַלּוּפֵיהֶם הוּא אֱדוֹם׃ [ס]

SEVENTH READING - DAVID - MALCHUT

20 אֵלֶּה בְנֵי־שֵׂעִיר הַחֹרִי יֹשְׁבֵי הָאָרֶץ אלהים דההין ע״ה לוֹטָן וְשׁוֹבָל
וְצִבְעוֹן וַעֲנָה׃ 21 וְדִשׁוֹן וְאֵצֶר וְדִישָׁן אֵלֶּה אַלּוּפֵי הַחֹרִי בְּנֵי
שֵׂעִיר בְּאֶרֶץ אלהים דאלפין אֱדוֹם׃ 22 וַיִּהְיוּ בְנֵי־לוֹטָן חֹרִי וְהֵימָם
וַאֲחוֹת לוֹטָן תִּמְנָע ב״פ סוזחך׃ 23 וְאֵלֶּה בְּנֵי שׁוֹבָל עַלְוָן וּמָנַחַת
וְעֵיבָל שְׁפוֹ וְאוֹנָם׃ 24 וְאֵלֶּה בְנֵי־צִבְעוֹן וְאַיָּה וַעֲנָה הוּא עֲנָה
אֲשֶׁר מָצָא אֶת־הַיֵּמִם בַּמִּדְבָּר רמ״ח, אברהם בִּרְעֹתוֹ אֶת־הַחֲמֹרִים

28 The sons of Dishan: Uz and Aran.

29 These were the Horite chiefs: Lotan, Shobal, Zibeon, Anah, 30 Dishon, Ezer, and
Dishan. These were the Horite chiefs, according to their divisions, in the land of
Seir.

31 These were the kings who reigned in Edom before any Israelite king reigned: 32
Bela, son of Beor, became king of Edom. His city was named Dinhabah.

33 When Bela died, Jobab, son of Zerah from Bozrah, succeeded him as king.

34 When Jobab died, Husham from the land of the Temanites succeeded him as king.

35 When Husham died, Hadad, son of Bedad, who defeated Midian in the country of Moab, succeeded him as king. His city was named Avith.

36 When Hadad died, Samlah from Masrekah succeeded him as king.

37 When Samlah died, Shaul from Rehoboth on the river succeeded him as king.

38 When Shaul died, Baal-Hanan, son of Acbor, succeeded him as king.

39 When Baal-Hanan, son of Acbor, died, Hadad succeeded him as king. His city was named Pau, and his wife's name was Mehetabel, daughter of Matred, the daughter of Me-Zahab.

הַמְּלָכִים

Genesis 36:31 – **The Eight Kings.** The Ari writes that the story of the eight kings actually concerns the giving of the *Sefirot* to the physical dimension in which we live.

> *You will thus understand how Hadar, the eighth king, is literally Yesod, and precedes the Chesed we now call Chesed. After the seven Sefirot have emerged, the kings were corrected again and were all included in the seven Sefirot, after having filtered out their Judgment. The refuse was refined, and the rest was included and sweetened in those seven Sefirot, each according to its level, for the kings are themselves those seven Sefirot.*
>
> *– The Writings of Rav Isaac Luria Vol 5, p.189*

This section shows very clearly the importance of remembering that the Bible is a coded text that should not be read or taken literally. Rav Shimon bar Yochai said that it would be better for a person to have never been born than for him to take the Bible at face value without penetrating into its deeper meanings.

> *And thus he ALSO causes THE STUDY OF Kabbalah and wisdom to be removed from the Oral Torah and the Written Torah, with the result that people will not study them. Whoever says that the Torah and the Talmud have only a literal meaning, assuredly it is as if he*

לְצִבְע֥וֹן אָבִֽיו׃ 25 וְאֵ֥לֶּה בְנֵי־עֲנָ֖ה דִּשֹׁ֑ן וְאָהֳלִיבָמָ֖ה בַּת־עֲנָֽה׃
26 וְאֵ֖לֶּה בְּנֵ֣י דִישָׁ֑ן חֶמְדָּ֥ן וְאֶשְׁבָּ֖ן וְיִתְרָ֥ן וּכְרָֽן׃ 27 אֵ֖לֶּה בְּנֵי־
אֵ֑צֶר בִּלְהָ֥ן וְזַעֲוָ֖ן וַעֲקָֽן׃ 28 אֵ֥לֶּה בְנֵי־דִישָׁ֖ן ע֥וּץ וַאֲרָֽן׃ 29 אֵ֖לֶּה
אַלּוּפֵ֣י הַחֹרִ֑י אַלּ֤וּף לוֹטָן֙ אַלּ֣וּף שׁוֹבָ֔ל אַלּ֥וּף צִבְע֖וֹן אַלּ֥וּף עֲנָֽה׃
30 אַלּ֥וּף דִּשֹׁ֛ן אַלּ֥וּף אֵ֖צֶר אַלּ֣וּף דִּישָׁ֑ן אֵ֣לֶּה אַלּוּפֵ֧י הַחֹרִ֛י
לְאַלֻּפֵיהֶ֖ם בְּאֶ֥רֶץ אלהים דאלפין שֵׂעִֽיר׃ [פ] 31 וְאֵ֙לֶּה֙ הַמְּלָכִ֔ים אֲשֶׁ֥ר
מָלְכ֖וּ בְּאֶ֣רֶץ אלהים דאלפין אֱד֑וֹם לִפְנֵ֥י מְלָךְ־מֶ֖לֶךְ לִבְנֵ֥י יִשְׂרָאֵֽל׃
32 וַיִּמְלֹ֣ךְ בֶּאֱד֔וֹם בֶּ֖לַע בֶּן־בְּע֑וֹר וְשֵׁ֥ם שדי יהוה עִיר֖וֹ סוז"ף, ערי, סנדלפו"ן
דִּנְהָֽבָה׃ 33 וַיָּ֖מָת בָּ֑לַע וַיִּמְלֹ֣ךְ תַּחְתָּ֔יו יוֹבָ֥ב בֶּן־זֶ֖רַח מִבָּצְרָֽה׃
34 וַיָּ֖מָת יוֹבָ֑ב וַיִּמְלֹ֣ךְ תַּחְתָּ֔יו חֻשָׁ֖ם מֵאֶ֥רֶץ אלהים דאלפין הַתֵּימָנִֽי׃
35 וַיָּ֖מָת חֻשָׁ֑ם וַיִּמְלֹ֣ךְ תַּחְתָּ֗יו הֲדַ֤ד אאא"י בֶּן־בְּדַ֔ד הַמַּכֶּ֤ה אֶת־
מִדְיָן֙ בִּשְׂדֵ֣ה מוֹאָ֔ב יוד הא ואו הה וְשֵׁ֥ם עִיר֖וֹ סוז"ף, ערי, סנדלפו"ן עֲוִֽית׃
36 וַיָּ֖מָת הֲדָ֑ד אאא"י וַיִּמְלֹ֣ךְ תַּחְתָּ֔יו שַׂמְלָ֖ה מִמַּשְׂרֵקָֽה׃ 37 וַיָּ֖מָת
שַׂמְלָ֑ה וַיִּמְלֹ֣ךְ תַּחְתָּ֔יו שָׁא֖וּל מֵרְחֹב֥וֹת הַנָּהָֽר׃ 38 וַיָּ֖מָת שָׁא֑וּל
וַיִּמְלֹ֣ךְ תַּחְתָּ֔יו בַּ֥עַל חָנָ֖ן בֶּן־עַכְבּֽוֹר׃ 39 וַיָּ֜מָת בַּ֣עַל חָנָ֣ן בֶּן־
עַכְבּ֗וֹר וַיִּמְלֹ֤ךְ תַּחְתָּיו֙ הֲדַ֔ר ר"פ ב"ן ע"ה וְשֵׁ֥ם שדי יהוה עִיר֖וֹ סוז"ף, ערי, סנדלפו"ן
פָּ֑עוּ וְשֵׁ֣ם אִשְׁתּ֞וֹ מְהֵֽיטַבְאֵ֛ל בַּת־מַטְרֵ֔ד בַּ֖ת מֵ֥י ילי זָהָֽב׃

REMOVES the flow from that river, YESOD, and from that garden, MALCHUT. Woe to him, it is better for him not to have been born in the world and not teach the Written Torah and Oral Torah, for it is considered, IF HE DOES NOT STUDY KABBALAH, as if he had returned the world to formlessness and the void. FOR THE WORLD IS CORRECTED BY THE REVELATION OF SUPERNAL SECRETS AND THE MYSTERIES OF THE TORAH WHICH ARE CALLED"'LIGHT." THUS, ARE FORMLESSNESS AND THE VOID, WHICH PREVAILED BEFORE THE CORRECTION, CORRECTED. AND WHOEVER DOES NOT PAY ATTENTION TO UNDERSTAND THE SECRETS OF THE TORAH, WHICH IS THE MAIN PART OF THE CORRECTION OF THE WORLD, IS CONSIDERED TO HAVE RETURNED THE WORLD TO CHAOS. And he brings poverty and lengthy exile to the world.

– Tikuna Tresar, Tikuna Forty Three for the Twenty Second Day 1:2

MAFTIR

40 These were the chiefs descended from Esau, by name, according to their clans and regions: Timna, Alvah, Jetheth,
41 Oholibamah, Elah, Pinon,
42 Kenaz, Teman, Mibzar,
43 Magdiel, and Iram. These were the chiefs of Edom, according to their settlements in the land they occupied. This was Esau, the father of the Edomites.

HAFTARAH OF VAYISHLACH

The prophet Obadiah discusses the demise of Edom. The Second Temple was destroyed by the Romans, who were Edom (that is, Esau). The end of our current exile from the Light will be the Final Redemption, which will eliminate all chaos and negativity.

> *"And these are the kings that reigned in the land of Edom." (Genesis 36:31); "...the land..." is the side of Esau's grade, as it is written: "Esau, who is Edom." All THESE KINGS came from the side of the unclean spirit. "...before there reigned any king over the children of Israel" (ibid.) refers to these grades OF ESAU, which stand at the lower gates and are the first TO BE PERFECTED. The reason Jacob said, "Let my lord, I pray you, pass over before his servant," (Genesis 33:14) is that Esau's grades are the first to enter AND BE PERFECTED, FOR THE*

Obadiah 1:1-21

1[1] The vision of Obadiah. This is what the Sovereign Lord says about Edom—We have heard a message from the Lord: An envoy was sent to the nations to say, "Rise, and let us go against her for battle"

אַלּוּפֵי עֵשָׂו

Genesis 36:40 – The Generals of Esau's Army. Each of Esau's generals named in this section represents a different negative force. By reading these names, we can gain immunity to the damaging influences of those forces.

MAFTIR

40 וְאֵלֶּה שְׁמוֹת אַלּוּפֵי עֵשָׂו לְמִשְׁפּוֹחֹתָם לִמְקוֹמֹתָם בִּשְׁמֹתָם
אַלּוּף תִּמְנָע ב״פ סוזוהך אַלּוּף עַלְוָה אַלּוּף יְתֵת: 41 אַלּוּף אָהֳלִיבָמָה
אַלּוּף אֵלָה אַלּוּף פִּינֹן: 42 אַלּוּף קְנַז אַלּוּף תֵּימָן אַלּוּף מִבְצָר:
43 אַלּוּף מַגְדִּיאֵל אַלּוּף עִירָם אֵלֶּה | אַלּוּפֵי אֱדוֹם לְמֹשְׁבֹתָם
בְּאֶרֶץ אלהים דאלפין אֲחֻזָּתָם הוּא עֵשָׂו אֲבִי אֱדוֹם: [פ] [פ] [פ]

HAFTARAH OF VAYISHLACH

LOWER GRADES ARE CORRECTED FIRST AND THE HIGHER GRADES LATER.
– The Zohar, Vayishlach 24:242

This Haftarah pertains to the way in which supremely important things are sold for financial gain, as when Joseph was sold by his brothers. When we commit such an act, we forfeit our ultimate fulfillment merely for the sake of immediate gratification. The prophet speaks about how the hidden actions of Esau will be sought out and known, and that we ourselves must never doubt that all of our deeds—good and evil—are known Above and will have their consequences in the Final Redemption. We lose something fundamentally important whenever we sell off our precious time for meditation, our precious time with our families, our precious time to do good works—all just to satisfy the demands of our material and physical desires.

עובדיה פרק 1

1 1 חֲזוֹן עֹבַדְיָה כֹּה היי ־אָמַר אֲדֹנָי ללה יֱהֹוִהיאהדונהי לֶאֱדוֹם
שְׁמוּעָה שָׁמַעְנוּ מֵאֵת יְהֹוָהאדניאהדונהי וְצִיר בַּגּוֹיִם שֻׁלָּח קוּמוּ
וְנָקוּמָה עָלֶיהָ פהל לַמִּלְחָמָה: 2 הִנֵּה קָטֹן נְתַתִּיךָ בַּגּוֹיִם בָּזוּי
אַתָּה מְאֹד מ״ה: 3 זְדוֹן לִבְּךָ הִשִּׁיאֶךָ שֹׁכְנִי בְחַגְוֵי־סֶלַע מְרוֹם
שִׁבְתּוֹ אֹמֵר בְּלִבּוֹ מִי ילי יוֹרִדֵנִי אָרֶץ אלהים דאלפין: 4 אִם יוהך ־תַּגְבִּיהַ

2 "See, I will make you small among the nations; you will be utterly despised. 3 The pride of your heart has deceived you, you who live in the clefts of the rocks and make your home on the heights, you who say to yourself, 'Who can bring me down to the ground?' 4 Though you soar like the eagle and make your nest among the stars, from there I will bring you down," declares the Lord.

5 "If thieves came to you, if robbers in the night—Oh, what a disaster awaits you—would they not steal only as much as they wanted? If grape pickers came to you, would they not leave a few grapes?

6 But how Esau will be ransacked, his hidden treasures pillaged! 7 All your allies will force you to the border; your friends will deceive and overpower you; those who eat your bread will set a trap for you, but you will not detect it."

8 "In that day," declares the Lord, "will I not destroy the wise men of Edom, men of understanding in the mountains of Esau?

9 Your warriors, Teman, will be terrified, and everyone in Esau's mountains will be cut down in the slaughter.

10 Because of the violence against your brother Jacob, you will be covered with shame; you will be destroyed forever. 11 On the day you stood aloof while strangers carried off his wealth and foreigners entered his gates and cast lots for Jerusalem, you were like one of them.

12 You should not look down on your brother in the day of his misfortune, nor rejoice over the people of Judah in the day of their destruction, nor boast so much in the day of their trouble.

13 You should not march through the gates of My people in the day of their disaster, nor look down on them in their calamity in the day of their disaster, nor seize their wealth in the day of their disaster.

14 You should not wait at the crossroads to cut down their fugitives, nor hand over their survivors in the day of their trouble.

15 The day of the Lord is near for all nations. As you have done, it will be done to you; your deeds will return upon your own head.

16 Just as you drank on My holy hill, so all the nations will drink continually; they will drink and drink and be as if they had never been. 17 But on Mount Zion will be

כַּנֶּשֶׁר וְאִם יוהך -בֵּין כּוֹכָבִים שִׂים קִנֶּךָ מִשָּׁם אוֹרִידְךָ נְאֻם-
יְהוָֹאדניאהדונהי׃ 5 אִם יוהך -גַּנָּבִים בָּאוּ-לְךָ אִם יוהך -שׁוֹדְדֵי לַיְלָה
מלה אֵיךְ אל נִדְמֵיתָה הֲלוֹא יִגְנְבוּ דַּיָּם אִם יוהך -בֹּצְרִים בָּאוּ לָךְ
הֲלוֹא יַשְׁאִירוּ עֹלֵלוֹת׃ 6 אֵיךְ אל נֶחְפְּשׂוּ עֵשָׂו נִבְעוּ מַצְפֻּנָיו׃
7 עַד-הַגְּבוּל שִׁלְּחוּךָ כֹּל ילי אַנְשֵׁי בְרִיתֶךָ הִשִּׁיאוּךָ יָכְלוּ לְךָ
אַנְשֵׁי שְׁלֹמֶךָ לַחְמְךָ יָשִׂימוּ מָזוֹר תַּחְתֶּיךָ אֵין תְּבוּנָה בּוֹ׃ 8 הֲלוֹא
בַּיּוֹם נגד, זן, מזבח הַהוּא נְאֻם-יְהוָֹאדניאהדונהי וְהַאֲבַדְתִּי חֲכָמִים
מֵאֱדוֹם וּתְבוּנָה מֵהַר עֵשָׂו׃ 9 וְחַתּוּ גִבּוֹרֶיךָ תֵּימָן לְמַעַן יִכָּרֶת-
אִישׁ ע"ה קנ"א קס"א מֵהַר עֵשָׂו מִקָּטֶל׃ 10 מֵחֲמַס אָחִיךָ יַעֲקֹב
יאהדונהי - אידהנויה תְּכַסְּךָ בוּשָׁה וְנִכְרַתָּ לְעוֹלָם ריבוע ס"ג - י' אותיות׃ 11 בְּיוֹם
נגד, זן, מזבח עֲמָדְךָ מִנֶּגֶד בְּיוֹם נגד, זן, מזבח שְׁבוֹת זָרִים חֵילוֹ ומב
וְנָכְרִים בָּאוּ שְׁעָרָו וְעַל-יְרוּשָׁלִַם יַדּוּ גוֹרָל גַּם יגל -אַתָּה כְּאַחַד
אהבה, דאגה מֵהֶם׃ 12 וְאַל-תֵּרֶא בְיוֹם נגד, זן, מזבח -אָחִיךָ בְּיוֹם נגד, זן, מזבח
נָכְרוֹ וְאַל-תִּשְׂמַח לִבְנֵי-יְהוּדָה בְּיוֹם נגד, זן, מזבח אָבְדָם וְאַל-תַּגְדֵּל
פִּיךָ בְּיוֹם נגד, זן, מזבח צָרָה אלהים דההין׃ 13 אַל-תָּבוֹא בְשַׁעַר-עַמִּי
בְּיוֹם נגד, זן, מזבח אֵידָם אַל-תֵּרֶא גַם יגל -אַתָּה בְּרָעָתוֹ בְּיוֹם נגד, זן, מזבח
אֵידוֹ וְאַל-תִּשְׁלַחְנָה בְחֵילוֹ ומב בְּיוֹם נגד, זן, מזבח אֵידוֹ׃ 14 וְאַל-
תַּעֲמֹד עַל-הַפֶּרֶק לְהַכְרִית אֶת-פְּלִיטָיו וְאַל-תַּסְגֵּר שְׂרִידָיו
בְּיוֹם נגד, זן, מזבח צָרָה אלהים דההין׃ 15 כִּי-קָרוֹב יוֹם נגד, זן, מזבח -יְהוָֹאדניאהדונהי
עַל-כָּל ילי, עמם -הַגּוֹיִם כַּאֲשֶׁר עָשִׂיתָ יֵעָשֶׂה לָּךְ גְּמֻלְךָ יָשׁוּב
בְּרֹאשֶׁךָ ריבוע אלהים - אלהים דיודין ע"ה׃ 16 כִּי כַּאֲשֶׁר שְׁתִיתֶם עַל-הַר
קָדְשִׁי יִשְׁתּוּ כָל ילי -הַגּוֹיִם תָּמִיד וְשָׁתוּ וְלָעוּ וְהָיוּ כְּלוֹא הָיוּ׃
17 וּבְהַר צִיּוֹן יוסף, קנאה, ו"פ יהוה, ה"פ אל תִּהְיֶה פְלֵיטָה וְהָיָה יהוה, יהה קֹדֶשׁ
וְיָרְשׁוּ בֵּית ב"פ ראה יַעֲקֹב יאהדונהי - אידהנויה אֵת מוֹרָשֵׁיהֶם׃

deliverance; it will be holy, and the house of Jacob will possess its inheritance.

[18] The house of Jacob will be a fire and the house of Joseph a flame; the house of Esau will be stubble, and they will set it on fire and consume it. There will be no survivors from the house of Esau. The Lord has spoken."

[19] People from the Negev will occupy the mountains of Esau, and people from the foothills will possess the land of the Philistines. They will occupy the fields of Ephraim and Samaria, and Benjamin will possess Gilead.

[20] This company of Israelite exiles who are in Canaan will possess the land as far as Zarephath; the exiles from Jerusalem who are in Sepharad will possess the towns of the Negev.

[21] Deliverers will go up on Mount Zion to govern the mountains of Esau. And the kingdom will be the Lord's.

18 וְהָיָה יהוה, יהה בֵית ב"פ ראה יַעֲקֹב יאהדונהי - אידהנויה אֵשׁ וּבֵית ב"פ ראה
יוֹסֵף ציון, קנאה, ו"פ יהוה, ה"פ אל לֶהָבָה וּבֵית ב"פ ראה עֵשָׂו לְקַשׁ וְדָלְקוּ
בָהֶם וַאֲכָלוּם וְלֹא־יִהְיֶה ייי שָׂרִיד לְבֵית ב"פ ראה עֵשָׂו כִּי
יְהֹוָהאדניאהדונהי דִּבֵּר ראה: 19 וְיָרְשׁוּ הַנֶּגֶב אֶת־הַר רבוע אלהים - ה' עֵשָׂו
וְהַשְּׁפֵלָה אֶת־פְּלִשְׁתִּים י"פ אלהים וְיָרְשׁוּ אֶת־שְׂדֵה אֶפְרַיִם אל מצפצ
וְאֵת שְׂדֵה שֹׁמְרוֹן וּבִנְיָמִן אֶת־הַגִּלְעָד: 20 וְגָלֻת הַחֵל להח ־הַזֶּה
והו לִבְנֵי יִשְׂרָאֵל אֲשֶׁר־כְּנַעֲנִים עַד־צָרְפַת וְגָלֻת יְרוּשָׁלִַם רי"ו - ש"ע
אֲשֶׁר בִּסְפָרַד יִרְשׁוּ אֵת עָרֵי הַנֶּגֶב: 21 וְעָלוּ מוֹשִׁעִים בְּהַר
צִיּוֹן יוסף, קנאה, ו"פ יהוה, ה"פ אל לִשְׁפֹּט אֶת־הַר רבוע אלהים - ה' עֵשָׂו וְהָיְתָה
לַיהֹוָהאדניאהדונהי הַמְּלוּכָה:

VAYESHEV

THE LESSON OF VAYESHEV

(Genesis 37:1–40:23)

"The Light was there when they decided to sell Joseph."

> *The Holy One, blessed be He, consented to the act OF SELLING JOSEPH TO EGYPT so that the decree the Creator made between the pieces would be fulfilled...*
> *– The Zohar, Vayeshev 19:195*

In Genesis 37:12, we encounter something that happens only ten times in the whole Bible: We find two dots over the word *et* (the). The verse reads: "Now his brothers had gone to graze their father's flock near Shechem." Before we can explain the significance of the dots, we need to address another question about this verse. The *Zohar* says that the word *et* is extraneous; we can understand the verse perfectly well without it. In fact, although it roughly translates to "the," there really isn't an exact translation for *et* in English or any other language.

The passage from the *Zohar* reads: "The Holy One, blessed be He, consented to the act OF SELLING JOSEPH TO EGYPT...." But why are there dots over the letters *Alef* and *Tav* (et)? Elsewhere in the Bible, there are no dots when the Light is present. The Light was with Abraham and the other righteous people, but there were no dots.

Furthermore, are we to understand that the Light wanted Joseph to be sold and taken to Egypt? Ten people were reincarnated and killed because of the sin of selling Joseph. If the Light intended Joseph's brothers to undertake this action, we must wonder why there was any punishment for it.

One thing is clear: Joseph had to go to Egypt. This was necessary so that the spiritual cleansing (*tikkun*) of the people of Israel could take place; consequently, this would allow them to receive the Torah. In this sense, Joseph's trip to Egypt and his sojourn there were essential, not just for his own *tikkun*, but for the *tikkun* of the whole world. So in fact, the lesson and power indicated by the two dots is that the Light of the Creator is with us, not just in the good times but also during those times that seem so chaotic and distressing to us at the moment they are happening.

Suppose a man misses his airplane flight. He is furious because he has so many things to do at his destination and others are depending on him. Unbeknownst to him, however, there is a bomb on the plane; were he aware of this fact, he would kiss the ground he walks on. His anger and frustration are completely misplaced, yet he does not know this because he is unable to see the bigger picture. Those who are connected to the Light, however, consider that there may be a positive aspect to every event, and they trust and appreciate that the Light is working on their behalf.

The *Gemara* (that part of the *Talmud* that contains rabbinical commentaries and analysis of its predecessor, the *Mishnah*) tells of a man called Nachum, who always said, "This is also for the best," no matter what was happening. Once, the people of Israel wanted to send a present—a box full of precious gemstones—to the king, and they asked Nachum to deliver the present because he was so learned. On his travels, he slept at an inn overnight. The innkeeper opened the box, stole the precious stones, and filled the box with ashes. When Nachum arrived at the king's palace, the box was opened and the ashes were discovered.

The king thundered, "Are the people of Israel laughing at me?" He ordered Nachum to be killed, but even then Nachum said, "This is also for the best!" At that moment, his purity and certainty were such that he merited the presence of the prophet Elijah, who approached the king disguised as one of his most trusted courtiers. Elijah said, "Sire, these ashes are from their Patriarch Abraham. When Abraham used to scatter these ashes, they would turn into swords, and with the swords, he could vanquish any enemy."

Astonished by the news of his good fortune, the king filled the box with precious stones and sent Nachum home with great respect and gratitude. On the way back home, Nachum again slept in the same inn, where the innkeeper was surprised to see him still alive.

The innkeeper asked, "What did you take to the king?

Nachum answered, "Just what I took from the inn."

So the innkeeper took all the ashes from his house and brought them to the king. But Elijah, still disguised as the trusted courtier, told the king that these ashes had no magical power. The king, angry at being deceived, ordered the innkeeper to be killed.

We must remember that the Creator intends only what is best for us. By understanding the dots in this section and by connecting with their power, we will all learn and deserve to see the good in everything that happens, even the small and sometimes extraneous things like the word *et*.

"And Reuben heard and saved him from their hands." (Genesis 37:21)

There are teachings in the Bible that are hugely significant, but we can easily miss their importance because they are mentioned in just a few words. Examples of this are the events in Abraham's life from his childhood until he was 74 and the events in the life of Moses from the age 13 to 80. After all, Abraham and Moses were not just ordinary people: They were and are still, to this day, chariots of the spiritual system—carriers of the Light. Every moment of their lives was crucial and affects every moment of our own lives, even today.

In a similar way, our own actions reverberate throughout the world. We must recognize the importance of what we do because each of us contributes to the spiritual system and has a unique Light that only we can reveal.

When Reuben came to save his brother Joseph, he understood that he was doing the right thing, but he did not know how much of an effect his action would have on generations to come. If Reuben had known how much importance the Light gave his act, he certainly would have attached greater significance to his own action. This teaches us that we should consider our every deed as if it were building a whole world for all time. Every one of us must do more and push ourselves at every moment to go that extra mile to reveal the Light. We can never know if "just one more thing" will not only change our own lives, but will also transform the whole world.

SYNOPSIS OF VAYESHEV

After all his trials and tests, Jacob had become complacent. He felt that he had accomplished everything he was supposed to do. It was at this point that his son Joseph was taken from him. From this, we learn that we should never rest on our laurels, spiritually speaking. We should always be ready to grow and to undertake the spiritual work that such growth requires.

FIRST READING - ABRAHAM - CHESED

37 1 Jacob lived in the land where his father had stayed, the land of Canaan.

2 These are the generations of Jacob. Joseph, a young man of seventeen, was tending the flocks with his brothers, the sons of Bilhah and the sons of Zilpah, his father's wives, and he brought their father a bad report about them.

3 Now Israel loved Joseph more than any of his other sons, because he had been born to him in his old age; and he made a striped robe of many colors for him. 4 When his brothers saw that their father loved him more than any of them, they hated him and could not speak a kind word to him.

FROM THE RAV

The *Zohar* asks what "Jacob loved Joseph more" means? It is just too outlandish to assume that these spiritual giants enacted the same behaviors that we observe at our much lower spiritual level. What the Torah is teaching us is that Jacob is the Chariot of *Tiferet* on the Upper Triad of the Shield of David and Joseph is the Chariot of *Yesod* on the Lower Triad, also of *Central Column* energy. Their affinity was because they both represented the aspect of *Central Column.*

However, in our physical world of *Malchut,* we must overcome the characterization of the separateness of each other, and again connect on a soul level. At the soul level, there is very little difference between us. By going right back almost to the beginning to the point where we were all one soul, we can overcome the illusion of separateness we experience now. When we go back, we elevate our consciousness, where we are suddenly on a quantum level and begin to feel unity and an affinity with people who are not even related to us.

We must rise above the differentiation that exists in this lifetime, and even in prior lifetimes to achieve the unity and oneness that is the Light of the Creator. Separation is the basic reason why we have war, pain, and suffering. These are all a result of the fragmentation that exists not only in our consciousness but also in the way we behave every day. However, our primary desire is to connect with the Lightforce of God. God will never experience the chaos, pain, and suffering that we mortals do. By connecting with the Light, we immediately go beyond the limitations of time, space, and motion. We go beyond all pain, suffering, and even death.

The *Zohar* explains to us that the reason we come to hear this Bible story is because when chaos reigns in anyone's family, it is because of the existence of jealousy, which is only there to validate our hatred. We hate and we want to validate it. We hate, we envy someone who actually did much wrong to us, so why do we have to turn the other cheek? The *Zohar* says if you are really bent on removing chaos, if you do lack something, do not dwell on how someone else has something you do not have; instead, be happy for them and do something to draw the thing that you lack into your life.

This paradox is what we have here: Did Jacob give his son a coat, when he knew Joseph's brothers already hated him? The answer is no! Jacob was not interested in creating further hatred or jealousy, but he was demonstrating for us what goes on in

FIRST READING - ABRAHAM - CHESED

37 1 וַיֵּשֶׁב יַעֲקֹב יאהדונהי - אידהנויה בְּאֶרֶץ אלהים דאלפין מְגוּרֵי אָבִיו
בְּאֶרֶץ אלהים דאלפין כְּנָעַן׃ 2 אֵלֶּה | תֹּלְדוֹת יַעֲקֹב יאהדונהי - אידהנויה יוֹסֵף
ציון, קנאה, ו"פ יהוה, ה"פ אל בֶּן־שְׁבַע אלהים דיודין - ע"ב ־עֶשְׂרֵה שָׁנָה הָיָה יהה
רֹעֶה רהע אֶת־אֶחָיו בַּצֹּאן וְהוּא נַעַר ש"ך אֶת־בְּנֵי בִלְהָה וְאֶת־
בְּנֵי זִלְפָּה נְשֵׁי אָבִיו וַיָּבֵא יוֹסֵף ציון, קנאה, ו"פ יהוה, ה"פ אל אֶת־דִּבָּתָם
רָעָה רהע אֶל־אֲבִיהֶם׃ 3 וְיִשְׂרָאֵל אָהַב אֶת־יוֹסֵף ציון, קנאה, ו"פ יהוה, ה"פ אל
מִכָּל ילי ־בָּנָיו כִּי־בֶן־זְקֻנִים הוּא לוֹ וְעָשָׂה לוֹ כְּתֹנֶת פַּסִּים׃
4 וַיִּרְאוּ אֶחָיו כִּי־אֹתוֹ אָהַב אֲבִיהֶם מִכָּל ילי ־אֶחָיו וַיִּשְׂנְאוּ אֹתוֹ
וְלֹא יָכְלוּ דַּבְּרוֹ ראה לְשָׁלֹם׃ 5 וַיַּחֲלֹם יוֹסֵף ציון, קנאה, ו"פ יהוה, ה"פ אל

---

this world that we live in. The only path we can take to remove chaos from our lives is to treat everyone with human dignity. It must be understood that although someone may seem to be our "enemy," he or she, too, has that spark of God within. It is only through the absence of envy, with unity, that we will be saved.

כְּתֹנֶת פַּסִּים

Genesis 37:3 – Jacob made a multi-color coat for Joseph. The Aramaic words for the coat are *ketonet passim*, an acronym for the four special angels who would constantly protect him. Rashi says that the four letters of the word *passim* (*Pei*, *Samech*, *Yud*, *Mem*) refer to Joseph's troubles, since he was sold to Potiphar, to the merchants (*Socharim*), to the Ishmaelites, and to the Midianites.

וַיִּשְׂנְאוּ

Genesis 37:4 – The brothers were jealous of Joseph's relationship with their father, Jacob, but Jacob himself was partly responsible for this because he appeared to favor Joseph so greatly. But in fact, according to Rashi, Jacob tried to make Joseph forget his dreams so that his brothers would not hate him. However, his attempt to defuse the tension between his sons was unsuccessful. As parents, we must make an extra effort to treat our children evenhandedly. Although we may feel a greater affinity for one child than for another, we should make an effort to keep this from influencing our actions. If we do not make this effort, we are partly responsible for any jealousy that may ensue.

וַיַּחֲלֹם

Genesis 37:5 – Joseph had two dreams that revealed the ways in which his life would differ from the lives of his brothers. This section shows

[5] Joseph dreamt a dream, and when he told it to his brothers, they hated him all the more.

*[6] He said to them, "Listen to this dream I had: [7] We were binding sheaves of grain out in the
field when suddenly my sheaf rose and stood upright, while your sheaves gathered around
mine and bowed down to it." [8] His brothers said to him, "Do you intend to reign over us?
Will you actually rule us?" And they hated him all the more because of his dream and what
he had said. [9] Then he had another dream, and he told it to his brothers. "Listen," he said,
"I had another dream, and this time the sun and moon and eleven stars were bowing down
to me." [10] When he told his father as well as his brothers, his father rebuked him and said,
"What is this dream you had? Will your mother and I and your brothers actually come and
bow down to the ground before you?" [11] His brothers were jealous of him, but his father kept
the matter in mind.*

SECOND READING - ISAAC - GEVURAH

*[12] Now his brothers had gone to graze their father's flocks near Shechem. [13] And Israel said
to Joseph, "As you know, your brothers are grazing the flocks near Shechem. Come, and I
will send you to them." "Here I am," he replied.*

---

us the power of dreams. Dreams can sometimes tell the future, but there are some principles we must respect so that we can understand and use our dreams correctly. Not everything in a dream will necessarily take place in our waking lives, nor are all the events in our dreams significant. Because of this, we should carefully select those people with whom we choose to discuss our dreams. Their interpretation will have an impact on our dream's meaning for us and on the parts of the dream that seem important. We should tell our dreams to someone who loves us and whom we love in return. In the *Zohar*, we read this:

> *Rav Chiya and Rav Yosi were with Rav Shimon. Rav Chiya said, "We have learned that an uninterpreted dream resembles an unopened letter." HE ASKS, "Does this mean that the dream comes true without the dreamer being conscious of it, or that it does not come true at all?" He answers, "IT MEANS THAT the dream comes true, but the dreamer does not know it, for there is a power dwelling upon the dream THAT FORCES IT TO COME TRUE. The dreamer, however, is not aware whether the dream comes true or not, JUST AS ONE DOES NOT KNOW THE CONTENTS OF AN UNOPENED LETTER."*
>
> *– The Zohar, Vayeshev 7:93.*

Genesis 37:12 – **The Two Dots Over the Word et (the).** This is one of only ten instances in the entire Bible where two dots appear over a word. Joseph went to Egypt, and the *Zohar* reveals that God was involved in this event—although the brothers were wrong to sell Joseph, the Light was always in control. When painful things happen to us, we should always remember that the Light is still present: We are never alone.

The *Zohar* tells us that Rav Shimon asked about the dots over the particle "*et*" and was told that the dots represent the *Shechina*, who dwelt among ten of the twelve brothers, excluding Joseph and Benjamin.

> *Rav Shimon asked, "Why is the particle Et (the) added?" HE ANSWERS, "THE PREPOSITION Et has dots over it, which*

חֲלוֹם וַיַּגֵּד לְאֶחָיו וַיּוֹסִפוּ עוֹד שְׂנֹא אֹתוֹ׃ 6 וַיֹּאמֶר אֲלֵיהֶם
שִׁמְעוּ־נָא הַחֲלוֹם הַזֶּה והו אֲשֶׁר חָלָמְתִּי׃ 7 וְהִנֵּה מ"ה יה אֲנַחְנוּ
מְאַלְּמִים אֲלֻמִּים בְּתוֹךְ הַשָּׂדֶה שדי וְהִנֵּה קָמָה אֲלֻמָּתִי
וְגַם יג"ל ־נִצָּבָה וְהִנֵּה תְסֻבֶּינָה אֲלֻמֹּתֵיכֶם וַתִּשְׁתַּחֲוֶיןָ לַאֲלֻמָּתִי׃
8 וַיֹּאמְרוּ לוֹ אֶחָיו הֲמָלֹךְ תִּמְלֹךְ עָלֵינוּ אִם יוהך ־מָשׁוֹל תִּמְשֹׁל
בָּנוּ וַיּוֹסִפוּ עוֹד שְׂנֹא אֹתוֹ עַל־חֲלֹמֹתָיו וְעַל־דְּבָרָיו ראה׃ 9 וַיַּחֲלֹם
עוֹד חֲלוֹם אַחֵר וַיְסַפֵּר אֹתוֹ לְאֶחָיו וַיֹּאמֶר הִנֵּה חָלַמְתִּי חֲלוֹם
עוֹד וְהִנֵּה הַשֶּׁמֶשׁ ב"פ ש"ך וְהַיָּרֵחַ וְאַחַד אהבה, דאגה עָשָׂר כּוֹכָבִים
מִשְׁתַּחֲוִים לִי׃ 10 וַיְסַפֵּר אֶל־אָבִיו וְאֶל־אֶחָיו וַיִּגְעַר־בּוֹ אָבִיו
וַיֹּאמֶר לוֹ מָה מ"ה הַחֲלוֹם הַזֶּה והו אֲשֶׁר חָלָמְתָּ הֲבוֹא נָבוֹא אֲנִי
אני וְאִמְּךָ וְאַחֶיךָ לְהִשְׁתַּחֲוֺת לְךָ אָרְצָה אלהים דההין ע"ה׃ 11 וַיְקַנְאוּ־
בוֹ אֶחָיו וְאָבִיו שָׁמַר אֶת־הַדָּבָר ראה׃

SECOND READING - ISAAC - GEVURAH

12 וַיֵּלְכוּ אֶחָיו לִרְעוֹת אֶת־צֹאן מלוי אהיה דיודין ע"ה אֲבִיהֶם בִּשְׁכֶם׃
13 וַיֹּאמֶר יִשְׂרָאֵל אֶל־יוֹסֵף ציון, קנאה, ר"פ יהוה, ה"פ אל הֲלוֹא אַחֶיךָ רֹעִים

---

represent the Shechina, FOR THE SHECHINA, NAMED 'ET,' dwelt with them because they were a group of ten. WHEREVER THERE ARE TEN MEN, THE SHECHINA HOVERS ABOVE THEM. They were ten because Joseph was not with them and little Benjamin was at home. When they went, the Shechina was among them, signified by the dots ABOVE THE PARTICLE 'ET.'"
– The Zohar, Vayeshev 8:95

Now that we see that the ten brothers were connected with the *Shechina* when they sold Joseph shows us how the Light manages affairs for the greater good of those people who learn to follow it.

For that reason, they were in collaboration with the Shechina when they sold Joseph; they made her a partner to their oath and made her vow NOT TO REVEAL THE SALE OF JOSEPH. Thus, until it was made known, the Shechina did not rest upon Jacob.
– The Zohar, Vayeshev 8:96

14 So he said to him, "Go and see if all is well with your brothers and with the flocks, and bring word back to me." Then he sent him out of the Valley of Hebron. When Joseph arrived at Shechem, 15 a man found him wandering around in the fields and asked him, "What are you looking for?"

16 He replied, "I'm looking for my brothers. Can you tell me where they are feeding their flocks?"

17 "They have moved on from here," the man answered. "I heard them say, 'Let's go to Dothan.' " So Joseph went after his brothers and found them near Dothan.

18 But they saw him in the distance, and before he reached them, they plotted to kill him.

19 "Here comes that dreamer!" they said to each other.

20 "Come now, let's kill him and throw him into one of these cisterns and say that a ferocious animal devoured him. Then we'll see what comes of his dreams."

21 When Reuben heard this, he tried to rescue him from their hands. "Let's not take his life," he said.

22 "Don't shed any blood. Throw him into this cistern here in the desert, but don't lay a hand on him." Reuben said this to rescue him from them and take him back to his father.

אִישׁ

Genesis 37:15 – Before his brothers threw him into the pit, Joseph was looking for them, having no idea where they were. He asked someone for help, and a man, whose name is not given, told Joseph where his brothers could be found. The word used to describe this person is *ish*, which is the Aramaic word for "man." It is important to note that the word *ish* is also used with reference to Esau's Guardian Angel. We know that the man who helped Joseph was positive, while the angel of Esau was negative, yet they are both referred to by the same word. From this, we learn that actions express our spiritual nature; actions are the evidence of our level of consciousness. *Ish* shows that man can be both positive and negative.

Another explanation given by the *Zohar* says that the "man" who directed Joseph to his brothers refers to the angel Gabriel:

> *"And a certain man found him" refers to Gabriel. It has been explained here that it is written: "And a certain man found him," and elsewhere it is written: "The man Gabriel, whom I had seen in the vision at the beginning." (Daniel 9:21) BY ANALOGY, WE LEARN THAT THE MAN IN THE FIRST SENTENCE IS ALSO GABRIEL. And "Joseph was wandering" (Genesis 37:15) in every way because of trusting his brothers; he was seeking fraternity but not obtaining it, and looking for them without finding them. Therefore, "the man asked him, saying, 'What are you seeking?'"*
>
> *– The Zohar, Vayeshev 10:105*

Thus, we can see how all the supernal forces conspired to move Joseph along the path he was meant to follow. The Light of this passage opens our eyes and shows us the way to freedom by allowing us to recognize life's hardships for what

בִּשְׁכֶם לְכָה וְאֶשְׁלָחֲךָ אֲלֵיהֶם וַיֹּאמֶר לוֹ הִנֵּנִי: 14 וַיֹּאמֶר לוֹ
לֶךְ־נָא רְאֵה ראה אֶת־שְׁלוֹם אַחֶיךָ וְאֶת־שְׁלוֹם הַצֹּאן מלוי אהיה דיודין ע"ה
וַהֲשִׁבֵנִי דָּבָר ראה וַיִּשְׁלָחֵהוּ מֵעֵמֶק חֶבְרוֹן וַיָּבֹא שְׁכֶמָה:
15 וַיִּמְצָאֵהוּ אִישׁ ע"ה קנ"א קס"א וְהִנֵּה תֹעֶה בַּשָּׂדֶה וַיִּשְׁאָלֵהוּ הָאִישׁ
ז"פ אדם לֵאמֹר מַה מ"ה ־תְּבַקֵּשׁ: 16 וַיֹּאמֶר אֶת־אַחַי אָנֹכִי איע מְבַקֵּשׁ
הַגִּידָה־נָּא לִי אֵיפֹה הֵם רֹעִים: 17 וַיֹּאמֶר הָאִישׁ ז"פ אדם נָסְעוּ מִזֶּה
כִּי שָׁמַעְתִּי אֹמְרִים נֵלְכָה דֹּתָיְנָה וַיֵּלֶךְ כלי יוֹסֵף ציון, קנאה, ו"פ יהוה, ה"פ אל
אַחַר אֶחָיו וַיִּמְצָאֵם בְּדֹתָן ע"ה נתה: 18 וַיִּרְאוּ אֹתוֹ מֵרָחֹק שדי
וּבְטֶרֶם רמ"ח ע"ה יִקְרַב אֲלֵיהֶם וַיִּתְנַכְּלוּ אֹתוֹ לַהֲמִיתוֹ: 19 וַיֹּאמְרוּ
אִישׁ ע"ה קנ"א קס"א אֶל־אָחִיו הִנֵּה מ"ה יה בַּעַל הַחֲלֹמוֹת הַלָּזֶה בָּא:
20 וְעַתָּה | לְכוּ וְנַהַרְגֵהוּ וְנַשְׁלִכֵהוּ בְּאַחַד אהבה, דאגה הַבֹּרוֹת
וְאָמַרְנוּ חַיָּה רָעָה רהע אֲכָלָתְהוּ וְנִרְאֶה מַה מ"ה ־יִּהְיוּ אל חֲלֹמֹתָיו:
21 וַיִּשְׁמַע רְאוּבֵן ג"פ אלהים וַיַּצִּלֵהוּ מִיָּדָם וַיֹּאמֶר לֹא נַכֶּנּוּ נָפֶשׁ
רמ"ח + ד' הויות: 22 וַיֹּאמֶר אֲלֵהֶם | רְאוּבֵן ג"פ אלהים אַל־תִּשְׁפְּכוּ־דָם רבוע אהיה
הַשְׁלִיכוּ אֹתוֹ אֶל־הַבּוֹר יצחק, ד"פ ב"ן הַזֶּה והו אֲשֶׁר בַּמִּדְבָּר רמ"ח, אברהם
וְיָד אַל־תִּשְׁלְחוּ־בוֹ לְמַעַן הַצִּיל אֹתוֹ מִיָּדָם לַהֲשִׁיבוֹ אֶל־
אָבִיו:

---

they really are: opportunities to rise above the power of impulse and thus effect inner transformation.

וַיִּתְנַכְּלוּ

Genesis 37:18 – When Joseph met his brothers, they wanted to kill him, but Reuben convinced them to throw Joseph into a pit instead. Eventually, the brothers sold Joseph into slavery and he was taken down to Egypt.

The *Zohar* explains that the reason the brothers could do such a thing to Joseph was that they knew some Kabbalah, and with the little knowledge that they had, they concluded that it was not necessary for Joseph to live. The brothers knew just enough to be dangerous.

This is an excellent example of the principle that a little knowledge is a dangerous thing. We must never be complacent or arrogant about our knowledge. It is important to be proactive about learning more, about asking questions of our teachers, and about striving for greater wisdom and understanding.

THIRD READING - JACOB - TIFERET

*23 So when Joseph came to his brothers, they stripped him of his robe, the striped
robe he was wearing, 24 and they took him and threw him into the cistern. Now the
cistern was empty; there was no water in it. 25 As they sat down to eat their meal, they
looked up and saw a caravan of Ishmaelites coming from Gilead. Their camels were
loaded with spices, balm, and myrrh, and they were on their way to take them down
to Egypt. 26 Judah said to his brothers, "What will we gain if we kill our brother and
cover up his blood? 27 Come, let's sell him to the Ishmaelites and not lay our hands
on him; after all, he is our brother, our own flesh and blood." His brothers agreed. 28
So when the Midianite merchants came by, his brothers pulled Joseph up out of the
cistern and sold him for twenty shekels of silver to the Ishmaelites, who took him to
Egypt. 29 When Reuben returned to the cistern and saw that Joseph was not there,
he tore his clothes. 30 He went back to his brothers and said, "The boy isn't there!
Where can I turn now?" 31 Then they got Joseph's robe, slaughtered a goat, and*

בְּעֶשְׂרִים כָּסֶף

Genesis 37:28 – The amount of money for which Joseph was sold, 20 pieces of silver, is related to the Redemption of the Firstborn. When the firstborn son is redeemed in the *Pidyon HaBen* ceremony, called "The Redemption of the Firstborn," the money offered up is to complete some of the *tikkun* (correction) for the brothers' sin of selling Joseph.

וַיָּשָׁב

Genesis 37:29 – Reuben believed that the brothers had only thrown Joseph into a pit, and he returned later to rescue the boy. But he found Joseph had disappeared—the brothers had actually sold him into slavery. Jacob had entrusted one of his sons each day with responsibility for everything that took place that day. Reuben was responsible for the day that Joseph was thrown into the pit, and he tried at least to make sure that Joseph was safe in the pit and that nothing worse would happen to him while he was there.

> *Look what Reuben did. He wisely joined them and said, "Let us not kill him," (Genesis 37:21) instead of "Do not take his life," for he was not there when Joseph was sold. They each then attended their father for one day. When it was Reuben's day, he did not want Joseph to perish. It is therefore written: "And Reuben returned to the pit and, behold, Joseph was not in the pit"—NOT EVEN DEAD—"and he rent his clothes." (ibid., 29) Immediately, "he returned to his brothers, and said, 'The child is not.'" (ibid., 30)*
>
> *– The Zohar, Vayeshev, 13:137*

However, had Reuben made the extra effort, not just to protect Joseph in the pit but also to get him out once the brothers had left and to help him escape, Joseph would not have been sold into slavery. When we undertake to perform a spiritual action, we should never be satisfied with doing the minimum. We must always motivate ourselves to do our utmost, seeking out more opportunities to expand and build our Vessel to receive the Light.

וַיָּבִיאוּ

Genesis 37:32 – **The Brothers Showed Joseph's Coat to Jacob.** The brothers did not know how to tell their father what they had done to Joseph. Rather than tell the truth or even to speak a lie,

THIRD READING - JACOB - TIFERET

23 וַיְהִי אל כַּאֲשֶׁר־בָּא יוֹסֵף ציון, קנאה, ו"פ יהוה, ה"פ אל אֶל־אֶחָיו וַיַּפְשִׁיטוּ
אֶת־יוֹסֵף ציון, קנאה, ו"פ יהוה, ה"פ אל אֶת־כֻּתָּנְתּוֹ אֶת־כְּתֹנֶת הַפַּסִּים אֲשֶׁר
עָלָיו: 24 וַיִּקָּחֻהוּ חעם וַיַּשְׁלִכוּ אֹתוֹ הַבֹּרָה וְהַבּוֹר יצחק, ד"פ ב"ן רֵק אֵין
בּוֹ מָיִם: 25 וַיֵּשְׁבוּ לֶאֱכָל־לֶחֶם ג"פ יהוה וַיִּשְׂאוּ עֵינֵיהֶם ריבוע מ"ה
וַיִּרְאוּ וְהִנֵּה מ"ה יה אֹרְחַת יִשְׁמְעֵאלִים בָּאָה מִגִּלְעָד וּגְמַלֵּיהֶם
נֹשְׂאִים נְכֹאת וּצְרִי מצפצ, י"פ ייי, אלהים דיודין וָלֹט הוֹלְכִים לְהוֹרִיד
מִצְרָיְמָה מצר: 26 וַיֹּאמֶר יְהוּדָה אֶל־אֶחָיו מַה מ"ה ־בֶּצַע כִּי נַהֲרֹג
אֶת־אָחִינוּ וְכִסִּינוּ אֶת־דָּמוֹ: 27 לְכוּ וְנִמְכְּרֶנּוּ לַיִּשְׁמְעֵאלִים וְיָדֵנוּ
אַל־תְּהִי־בוֹ כִּי־אָחִינוּ בְשָׂרֵנוּ הוּא וַיִּשְׁמְעוּ אֶחָיו: 28 וַיַּעַבְרוּ
אֲנָשִׁים מִדְיָנִים סֹחֲרִים וַיִּמְשְׁכוּ וַיַּעֲלוּ אֶת־יוֹסֵף ציון, קנאה, ו"פ יהוה, ה"פ אל
מִן־הַבּוֹר יצחק, ד"פ ב"ן וַיִּמְכְּרוּ אֶת־יוֹסֵף ציון, קנאה, ו"פ יהוה, ה"פ אל
לַיִּשְׁמְעֵאלִים בְּעֶשְׂרִים כָּסֶף וַיָּבִיאוּ אֶת־יוֹסֵף ציון, קנאה, ו"פ יהוה, ה"פ אל
מִצְרָיְמָה מצר: 29 וַיָּשָׁב רְאוּבֵן ג"פ אלהים אֶל־הַבּוֹר יצחק, ד"פ ב"ן וְהִנֵּה
אֵין־יוֹסֵף ציון, קנאה, ו"פ יהוה, ה"פ אל בַּבּוֹר יצחק, ד"פ ב"ן וַיִּקְרַע אֶת־בְּגָדָיו:
30 וַיָּשָׁב אֶל־אֶחָיו וַיֹּאמַר הַיֶּלֶד אֵינֶנּוּ וַאֲנִי אני, ב"פ אהיה ÷ יהוה אָנָה
אֲנִי אני ־בָא: 31 וַיִּקְחוּ חעם אֶת־כְּתֹנֶת יוֹסֵף ציון, קנאה, ו"פ יהוה, ה"פ אל
וַיִּשְׁחֲטוּ שְׂעִיר עִזִּים וַיִּטְבְּלוּ אֶת־הַכֻּתֹּנֶת בַּדָּם רבוע אהיה:
32 וַיְשַׁלְּחוּ אֶת־כְּתֹנֶת הַפַּסִּים וַיָּבִיאוּ אֶל־אֲבִיהֶם וַיֹּאמְרוּ זֹאת
מָצָאנוּ הַכֶּר־נָא הַכְּתֹנֶת בִּנְךָ הִוא אִם יוהך ־לֹא: 33 וַיַּכִּירָהּ
וַיֹּאמֶר כְּתֹנֶת בְּנִי חַיָּה רָעָה רהע אֲכָלָתְהוּ טָרֹף רמ"ח ע"ה טֹרַף רמ"ח ע"ה
יוֹסֵף ציון, קנאה, ו"פ יהוה, ה"פ אל: 34 וַיִּקְרַע יַעֲקֹב יאהדונהי ÷ אידהנויה שִׂמְלֹתָיו
וַיָּשֶׂם שַׂק בְּמָתְנָיו וַיִּתְאַבֵּל עַל־בְּנוֹ יָמִים נלך רַבִּים: 35 וַיָּקֻמוּ

dipped the robe in the blood. [32] *They took the striped robe back to their father and said, "We found this. Examine it to see whether it is your son's robe."* [33] *He recognized it and said, "It is my son's robe! Some ferocious animal has devoured him. Joseph has surely been torn to pieces."* [34] *Then Jacob tore his clothes, put on sackcloth, and mourned for his son many days.* [35] *All his sons and daughters came to comfort him, but he refused to be comforted. "No," he said, "in mourning will I go down to the grave to my son." So his father wept for him.* [36] *Meanwhile, the Midianites sold Joseph in Egypt to Potiphar, one of Pharaoh's officials, the captain of the guard.*

FOURTH READING - MOSES - NETZACH

38 [1] *At that time, Judah left his brothers and went down to stay with a man of Adullam named Hirah.* [2] *There Judah met the daughter of a Canaanite man named Shua. He married her and lay with her;* [3] *she became pregnant and gave birth to a son, who was named Er.* [4] *She conceived again and gave birth to a son and named him Onan.* [5] *She gave birth to yet another son and named him Shelah. It was at Kezib that she gave birth to him.* [6] *Judah got a wife for Er, his firstborn, and her name was Tamar.* [7]

---

they merely took the multi-colored coat belonging to Joseph, dipped it in goat's blood, and showed it to Jacob. They did not actually lie to their father, but their actions caused Jacob to believe something that was not true.

Jacob, of course, had done something very similar to his own father. He had deceived Isaac by presenting himself in Esau's clothing, thereby causing his father to draw an untrue conclusion.

> *It is written of JACOB: "And she put the skins of the kids of the goats upon his hands, and upon the smooth of his neck." (Genesis 27:16) Therefore it is said OF HIS SONS: "And they dipped the coat in the blood." (Genesis 37:31) This was measure for measure. Since Jacob had been the cause that "Isaac trembled very much," (Genesis 27:33) HIS SONS made him tremble when they said, "Know now whether it be your son's coat or not?" (Genesis 37:32)*
>
> *– The Zohar, Vayeshev 13:142*

Lying is one of the ways that we strip ourselves of the multi-colored Light that surrounds us. To strip it from someone else by causing them pain is inexcusable, and such acts always carry consequences. One of the laws of the universe is that we pay in kind for our own acts of treachery.

Genesis 38:1 – Judah had made the suggestion to sell Joseph. Later, he was overcome with guilt, and he left the family to marry and have three children. Eventually, his oldest son took a wife whose name was Tamar. When this son died without having sired any children, his brother was supposed to marry the widow so that the line could be continued. This custom is called Levirite Marriage. But unfortunately, this brother also died, both brothers thus perishing for their negativity. The *Zohar* says:

> *When a man is unsuccessful IN BEGETTING CHILDREN in this world, God uproots him FROM THIS WORLD and replants him again and again. THAT IS, HE DIES AND IS BORN AGAIN INTO*

כָּל ילי -בָּנָיו וְכָל ילי -בְּנֹתָיו לְנַחֲמוֹ וַיְמָאֵן לְהִתְנַחֵם וַיֹּאמֶר כִּי-
אֵרֵד אֶל-בְּנִי אָבֵל שְׁאֹלָה וַיֵּבְךְּ אֹתוֹ אָבִיו: 36 וְהַמְּדָנִים מָכְרוּ
אֹתוֹ אֶל-מִצְרָיִם מצר לְפוֹטִיפַר סְרִיס פַּרְעֹה שַׂר אלהים דיודין ורבוע אלהים
הַטַּבָּחִים: [פ]

FOURTH READING - MOSES - NETZACH

38 1 וַיְהִי בָּעֵת הַהִוא וַיֵּרֶד ריי יְהוּדָה מֵאֵת אֶחָיו וַיֵּט עַד-אִישׁ
ע"ה קנ"א קס"א עֲדֻלָּמִי וּשְׁמוֹ מהש ע"ה חִירָה: 2 וַיַּרְא-שָׁם יְהוּדָה בַּת-
אִישׁ ע"ה קנ"א קס"א כְּנַעֲנִי וּשְׁמוֹ מהש ע"ה שׁוּעַ וַיִּקָּחֶהָ חעם וַיָּבֹא אֵלֶיהָ:
3 וַתַּהַר וַתֵּלֶד בֵּן וַיִּקְרָא עם ה' אותיות = ב"פ קס"א אֶת-שְׁמוֹ מהש ע"ה עֵר:
4 וַתַּהַר עוֹד וַתֵּלֶד בֵּן וַתִּקְרָא אֶת-שְׁמוֹ מהש ע"ה אוֹנָן: 5 וַתֹּסֶף
עוֹד וַתֵּלֶד בֵּן וַתִּקְרָא אֶת-שְׁמוֹ מהש ע"ה שֵׁלָה וְהָיָה יהוה, יהה בִכְזִיב
בְּלִדְתָּהּ אֹתוֹ: 6 וַיִּקַּח חעם יְהוּדָה אִשָּׁה לְעֵר בְּכוֹרוֹ וּשְׁמָהּ תָּמָר
ב"פ ש"ך: 7 וַיְהִי עֵר בְּכוֹר יְהוּדָה רַע בְּעֵינֵי ריבוע מ"ה יְהֹוָהאדניאהדונהי
וַיְמִתֵהוּ יְהֹוָהאדניאהדונהי: 8 וַיֹּאמֶר יְהוּדָה לְאוֹנָן בֹּא אֶל-אֵשֶׁת

THE WORLD UNTIL HE SUCCEEDS IN BEGETTING CHILDREN.
– The Zohar, Vayeshev 16:157

However, if the man's widow marries his brother and they succeed in having a child, the man is redeemed from his childless state. The *Zohar* says:

> *A dark room becomes progressively brighter with each new candle that is lit. Every soul that comes into this world is likened to a candle. Although True Reality, which is our ultimate destination, offers immortality and endless fulfillment, during the course of human spiritual evolution, the Light is temporarily dimmed. Immortality is relegated to the act of procreation and childbearing, which ensures the ongoing entrance of new souls into this world for the purpose of bringing about the Final Correction of humanity. In other words, the chain of humanity is immortal, while the individual body remains perishable and finite. All men live for the existence of the chain until such time as humanity completes its spiritual correction and transformation. At that juncture, the force of immortality will expand and bring endless life. This transformation, the Final Redemption, is hastened by bringing new souls into this world, whose Light, through the path of the Bible, helps diminish darkness and*

But Er, Judah's firstborn, was wicked in the Lord's sight; so the Lord put him to
death. 8 Then Judah said to Onan, "Lie with your brother's wife and fulfill your duty
to her as a brother-in-law to produce offspring for your brother." 9 But Onan knew that
the offspring would not be his; so whenever he lay with his brother's wife, he spilled
his semen on the ground to keep from producing offspring for his brother. 10 What he
did was wicked in the Lord's sight; so He put him to death also. 11 Judah then said to
his daughter-in-law Tamar, "Live as a widow in your father's house until my son
Shelah grows up." For he thought, "He may die too, just like his brothers." So Tamar
went to live in her father's house. 12 After a long time, Judah's wife, the daughter of
Shua, died. When Judah had recovered from his grief, he went up to Timnah, to the
men who were shearing his sheep, and his friend Hirah the Adullamite went with
him. 13 When Tamar was told, "Your father-in-law is on his way to Timnah to shear his
sheep," 14 she took off her widow's clothes, covered herself with a veil to disguise
herself, and then sat down at the entrance to Enaim, which is on the road to Timnah.
For she saw that though Shelah had now grown up she had not been given to him as
his wife. 15 When Judah saw her, he thought she was a prostitute, for she had covered
her face. 16 Not realizing that she was his daughter-in-law, he went over to her by the
roadside and said, "Come now, let me sleep with you." "And what will you give me to
sleep with you?" she asked. 17 "I'll send you a young goat from my flock," he said.
"Will you give me something as a pledge until you send it?" she asked. 18 He said,
"What pledge should I give you?" "Your seal and its cord, and the staff in your hand,"
she answered. So he gave them to her and slept with her, and she became pregnant
by him. 19 After she left, she took off her veil and put on her widow's clothes again.

20 Meanwhile Judah sent the young goat by his friend the Adullamite in order to get
his pledge back from the woman, but he did not find her.

> *death and accelerate the process of correction.*
> *– The Zohar, Vayeshev 16*

וַיֹּאמֶר

Genesis 38: 11 – Rather than having Tamar marry his third son (and perhaps cause his death, too), Judah sent Tamar away. We learn from the *Zohar*:

> *If the one coming FROM THE SECOND HUSBAND removes the former spirit OF THE FIRST HUSBAND, it leaves and goes away. At times, the first pushes away the second and attacks it, until it takes it out of the world. In relation to this, we learned that from two or more, THAT IS, AFTER HER TWO HUSBANDS DIED, a man should not marry this woman, because the Angel of Death is strong in her.*
> *– The Zohar, Mishpatim 3:148*

Later on, after Judah's wife had died, he decided to visit a prostitute. Tamar, his own daughter-in-law, dressed as a prostitute and seduced Judah. King David descended from this line—in spite of this act that appears so sinful. This is also the line from which the Messiah will come. The *Zohar* says:

> *...could it be that Tamar, a priest's daughter, who was always modest, would commit incest with her father-in-law? HE ANSWERS, "She was a righteous woman AND did this with wisdom. She was not lewd, but wise, and KNEW WHAT WOULD COME OF IT. She approached him to do kindness and truth by him."*
> *– The Zohar, Vayeshev 18:189*

אָחִיךָ וְיַבֵּם אֹתָהּ וְהָקֵם הקם זֶרַע לְאָחִיךָ׃ 9 וַיֵּדַע אוֹנָן כִּי לֹּא
לּוֹ יִהְיֶה ייי הַזָּרַע וְהָיָה יהוה, יהה אִם יוהך ־בָּא אֶל־אֵשֶׁת אָחִיו וְשִׁחֵת
אַרְצָה לְבִלְתִּי נְתָן־זֶרַע לְאָחִיו׃ 10 וַיֵּרַע בְּעֵינֵי ריבוע מ״ה יְהֹוָה אדני אהדונהי
אֲשֶׁר עָשָׂה וַיָּמֶת גַּם יגל ־אֹתוֹ׃ 11 וַיֹּאמֶר יְהוּדָה לְתָמָר ב״פ ש״ך
כַּלָּתוֹ שְׁבִי אַלְמָנָה כוק בֵית ב״פ ראה ־אָבִיךְ עַד־יִגְדַּל יזל שֵׁלָה בְנִי
כִּי אָמַר פֶּן־יָמוּת גַּם יגל ־הוּא כְּאֶחָיו וַתֵּלֶךְ תָּמָר ב״פ ש״ך וַתֵּשֶׁב
בֵּית ב״פ ראה אָבִיהָ׃ 12 וַיִּרְבּוּ הַיָּמִים נלך וַתָּמָת בַּת־שׁוּעַ אֵשֶׁת־
יְהוּדָה וַיִּנָּחֶם יְהוּדָה וַיַּעַל עַל־גֹּזְזֵי צֹאנוֹ הוּא וְחִירָה רֵעֵהוּ
הָעֲדֻלָּמִי תִּמְנָתָה׃ 13 וַיֻּגַּד לְתָמָר ב״פ ש״ך לֵאמֹר הִנֵּה חָמִיךְ עֹלֶה
תִמְנָתָה לָגֹז צֹאנוֹ׃ 14 וַתָּסַר בִּגְדֵי אַלְמְנוּתָהּ מֵעָלֶיהָ פהל וַתְּכַס
בַּצָּעִיף וַתִּתְעַלָּף וַתֵּשֶׁב בְּפֶתַח עֵינַיִם ריבוע מ״ה אֲשֶׁר עַל־דֶּרֶךְ
תִּמְנָתָה ב״פ יב״ק כִּי רָאֲתָה כִּי־גָדַל שֵׁלָה וְהִוא לֹא־נִתְּנָה לוֹ
לְאִשָּׁה׃ 15 וַיִּרְאֶהָ ראה יְהוּדָה וַיַּחְשְׁבֶהָ לְזוֹנָה כִּי כִסְּתָה פָּנֶיהָ׃
16 וַיֵּט אֵלֶיהָ אֶל־הַדֶּרֶךְ ב״פ יב״ק וַיֹּאמֶר הָבָה־נָּא אָבוֹא אֵלַיִךְ
אני; ר״ת ב״ן כִּי לֹא יָדַע כִּי כַלָּתוֹ הִוא וַתֹּאמֶר מַה מ״ה ־תִּתֶּן ב״פ כהת ־לִּי
ר״ת ה״פ אלהים כִּי תָבוֹא אֵלָי׃ 17 וַיֹּאמֶר אָנֹכִי איע אֲשַׁלַּח גְּדִי והו ־עִזִּים
מִן־הַצֹּאן מלוי אהיה דיודין ע״ה וַתֹּאמֶר אִם יוהך ־תִּתֵּן ב״פ כהת עֵרָבוֹן עַד
שָׁלְחֶךָ׃ 18 וַיֹּאמֶר מָה מ״ה הָעֵרָבוֹן אֲשֶׁר אֶתֶּן־לָּךְ וַתֹּאמֶר חֹתָמְךָ
וּפְתִילֶךָ י״פ ב״ן וּמַטְּךָ אֲשֶׁר בְּיָדֶךָ וַיִּתֶּן־ י״פ מלוי ע״ב לָהּ וַיָּבֹא אֵלֶיהָ
וַתַּהַר לוֹ׃ 19 וַתָּקָם וַתֵּלֶךְ וַתָּסַר צְעִיפָהּ מֵעָלֶיהָ פהל וַתִּלְבַּשׁ
בִּגְדֵי אַלְמְנוּתָהּ׃ 20 וַיִּשְׁלַח יְהוּדָה אֶת־גְּדִי והו הָעִזִּים בְּיַד רֵעֵהוּ
הָעֲדֻלָּמִי לָקַחַת הָעֵרָבוֹן מִיַּד הָאִשָּׁה וְלֹא מְצָאָהּ׃ 21 וַיִּשְׁאַל
אֶת־אַנְשֵׁי מְקֹמָהּ לֵאמֹר אַיֵּה הַקְּדֵשָׁה הִוא בָעֵינַיִם ריבוע מ״ה עַל־
הַדָּרֶךְ ב״פ יב״ק וַיֹּאמְרוּ לֹא־הָיְתָה בָזֶה קְדֵשָׁה׃ 22 וַיָּשָׁב אֶל־

21 He asked the men who lived there, "Where is the shrine prostitute who was beside the road at Enaim?" "There hasn't been any shrine prostitute here," they said.

22 So he went back to Judah and said, "I didn't find her. Besides, the men who lived there said, 'There hasn't been any shrine prostitute here.' "

23 Then Judah said, "Let her keep what she has, or we will become a laughingstock. After all, I did send her this young goat, but you didn't find her."

24 About three months later Judah was told, "Your daughter-in-law Tamar is guilty of prostitution, and as a result she is now pregnant." Judah said, "Bring her out and have her burned to death!"

25 As she was being brought out, she sent a message to her father-in-law. "I am pregnant by the man who owns these," she said. And she added, "See if you recognize whose seal and cord and staff these are."

26 Judah recognized them and said, "She is more righteous than I, since I wouldn't give her to my son Shelah." And he did not sleep with her again.

27 When the time came for her to give birth, there were twin boys in her womb. 28 As
she was giving birth, one of them put out his hand; so the midwife took a scarlet thread and tied it on his wrist and said, "This one came out first."

29 But when he drew back his hand, his brother came out, and she said, "How have you broken out?" And he was named Perez.

30 Then his brother, who had the scarlet thread on his wrist, came out and he was given the name Zerah.

FIFTH READING - AARON - HOD

39 1 Now Joseph had been taken down to Egypt. Potiphar, an Egyptian who was one of Pharaoh's officials, the captain of the guard, bought him from the Ishmaelites who
had taken him there. 2 The Lord was with Joseph and he prospered, and he lived in

---

There is also another lesson here. The *Zohar* tells us that when a righteous soul is about to come to this world, Satan tries to put obstacles in the way of this happening. In this particular case, King David came from ancestors who lived in very negative situations, and when a circumstance seems sufficiently negative, Satan does not feel that it is necessary to intervene because no Light would come from it. But the Light overcomes the negativity, and the righteous soul can then be born.

הוּרַד

Genesis 39:1 – Joseph was taken to Egypt as a slave, but he did not have to live his whole life in bondage. Since he always maintained an elevated consciousness, he never saw himself as a victim and did not take on the consciousness of a slave; wherever he was, he always became a master. The *Zohar* says:

יְהוּדָה וַיֹּאמֶר לֹא מְצָאתִיהָ וְגַם אַנְשֵׁי הַמָּקוֹם יהוה ברבוע אָמְרוּ
לֹא־הָיְתָה בָזֶה קְדֵשָׁה׃ 23 וַיֹּאמֶר יְהוּדָה תִּקַּח־לָהּ פֶּן נִהְיֶה
לָבוּז הִנֵּה שָׁלַחְתִּי הַגְּדִי יהו הַזֶּה והו וְאַתָּה לֹא מְצָאתָהּ׃ 24 וַיְהִי |
כְּמִשְׁלֹשׁ חֳדָשִׁים י״ב הוויות וַיֻּגַּד לִיהוּדָה לֵאמֹר זָנְתָה תָּמָר ב״פ ש״ך
כַּלָּתֶךָ וְגַם הִנֵּה הָרָה לִזְנוּנִים וַיֹּאמֶר יְהוּדָה הוֹצִיאוּהָ וְתִשָּׂרֵף׃
25 הִוא מוּצֵאת וְהִיא שָׁלְחָה אֶל־חָמִיהָ לֵאמֹר לְאִישׁ ע״ה קנ״א קס״א
אֲשֶׁר־אֵלֶּה לּוֹ אָנֹכִי איע הָרָה וַתֹּאמֶר הַכֶּר־נָא לְמִי ילי הַחֹתֶמֶת
וְהַפְּתִילִים י״פ ב״ן וְהַמַּטֶּה הָאֵלֶּה׃ 26 וַיַּכֵּר יְהוּדָה וַיֹּאמֶר צָדְקָה
ע״ה ריבוע אלהים מִמֶּנִּי כִּי־עַל־כֵּן לֹא־נְתַתִּיהָ לְשֵׁלָה בְנִי וְלֹא־יָסַף
עוֹד לְדַעְתָּהּ׃ 27 וַיְהִי אל בְּעֵת י״פ אהיה + י׳ הוויות לִדְתָּהּ וְהִנֵּה מ״ה יה
תְאוֹמִים בְּבִטְנָהּ׃ 28 וַיְהִי בְלִדְתָּהּ וַיִּתֶּן י״פ מלוי ע״ב יָד וַתִּקַּח
הַמְיַלֶּדֶת וַתִּקְשֹׁר עַל־יָדוֹ שָׁנִי לֵאמֹר זֶה יָצָא רִאשֹׁנָה׃
29 וַיְהִי אל | כְּמֵשִׁיב יָדוֹ וְהִנֵּה מ״ה יה יָצָא אָחִיו וַתֹּאמֶר מַה מ״ה -
פָּרַצְתָּ עָלֶיךָ פָּרֶץ וַיִּקְרָא עם ה׳ אותיות = ב״פ קס״א שְׁמוֹ מהש ע״ה פָּרֶץ׃
30 וְאַחַר יָצָא אָחִיו אֲשֶׁר עַל־יָדוֹ הַשָּׁנִי וַיִּקְרָא עם ה׳ אותיות = ב״פ קס״א
שְׁמוֹ מהש ע״ה זָרַח׃ [ס]

FIFTH READING - AARON - HOD

39 1 וְיוֹסֵף ציון, קנאה, ו״פ יהוה, ה״פ אל הוּרַד מִצְרָיְמָה מצר וַיִּקְנֵהוּ פּוֹטִיפַר
שכינה סְרִיס פַּרְעֹה שַׂר אלהים דיודין ורבוע אלהים הַטַּבָּחִים אִישׁ ע״ה קנ״א קס״א
מִצְרִי מצר מִיַּד הַיִּשְׁמְעֵאלִים אֲשֶׁר הוֹרִדֻהוּ שָׁמָּה מהש׃ 2 וַיְהִי אל
יְהֹוָהאדניאהדונהי אֶת־יוֹסֵף ציון, קנאה, ו״פ יהוה, ה״פ אל וַיְהִי אל אִישׁ ע״ה קנ״א קס״א
מַצְלִיחַ וַיְהִי אל בְּבֵית ב״פ ראה אֲדֹנָיו הַמִּצְרִי מצר׃ 3 וַיַּרְא אֲדֹנָיו כִּי
יְהֹוָהאדניאהדונהי אִתּוֹ וְכֹל ילי אֲשֶׁר־הוּא עֹשֶׂה יְהֹוָהאדניאהדונהי מַצְלִיחַ

the house of his Egyptian master. [3] *When his master saw that the Lord was with him*
and that the Lord gave him success in everything he did, [4] *Joseph found favor in his*
eyes and became his attendant. Potiphar put him in charge of his household, and he
entrusted to his care everything he owned. [5] *From the time he put him in charge of*
his household and of all that he owned, the Lord blessed the household of the Egyptian
because of Joseph. The blessing of the Lord was on everything Potiphar had, both in
the house and in the field. [6] *So he left in Joseph's care everything he had; with Joseph*
in charge, he did not concern himself with anything except the food he ate. Now
Joseph was well-built and handsome,

SIXTH READING - JOSEPH - YESOD

[7] *and after a while his master's wife took notice of Joseph and said, "Come to bed*
with me!" [8] *But he refused. "With me in charge," he told her, "my master does not*
concern himself with anything in the house; everything he owns he has entrusted to
my care. [9] *No one is greater in this house than I am. My master has withheld nothing*
from me except you, because you are his wife. How then could I do such a wicked
thing and sin against God?"

[10] *And though she spoke to Joseph day after day, he refused to go to bed with her or*
even be with her.

[11] *One day he went into the house to attend to his duties, and none of the household*
servants was inside.

Because the Shechina was with Joseph, whatever he did by his hand prospered. If he had something in his hand, but his master asked for something else, what was in his hand would turn into that which his master wanted…for God was with him.

– The Zohar, Vayeshev 20:206

וַתֹּאמֶר

Genesis 39:7 – Zelicha, the wife of Potiphar, Joseph's master, tried to seduce Joseph. Although she grabbed at his clothing, he refused to be seduced and he escaped. Out of spite, she accused Joseph of raping her, and he was thrown in jail. A commentary says this about the episode:

"A savage beast has devoured him!" (Genesis 37:33) Divine inspiration was instilled within him. [The savage beast] was Potiphar's wife.

– Beresheet Rabba 84:19

Genesis 39:12 – When Joseph resisted the sexual advances of Potiphar's wife, he achieved the spiritual level of *Yesod*, the level he was predestined to reach in his lifetime. We learn from Joseph's actions that two conditions must be met for us to reach our destined spiritual level. First, we must undergo an intense test of our resistance to temptation, and second, we must go through a process of spiritual cleansing.

בְּיָדוֹ׃ 4 וַיִּמְצָא יוֹסֵף ציון, קנאה, ו"פ יהוה, ה"פ אל חֵן מוזי בְּעֵינָיו ריבוע מ"ה
וַיְשָׁרֶת אֹתוֹ וַיַּפְקִדֵהוּ עַל־בֵּיתוֹ ב"פ ראה וְכָל־ ילי יֶשׁ־לוֹ נָתַן בְּיָדוֹ׃
5 וַיְהִי אל מֵאָז ומב הִפְקִיד אֹתוֹ בְּבֵיתוֹ ב"פ ראה וְעַל כָּל־ ילי, עמם אֲשֶׁר
יֶשׁ־לוֹ וַיְבָרֶךְ עסמ"ב יְהוָה אדני-אהדונהי אֶת־בֵּית ב"פ ראה הַמִּצְרִי מצר בִּגְלַל
יוֹסֵף ציון, קנאה, ו"פ יהוה, ה"פ אל וַיְהִי אל בִּרְכַּת יְהוָה אדני-אהדונהי בְּכָל־ לכב אֲשֶׁר
יֶשׁ־לוֹ בַּבַּיִת ב"פ ראה וּבַשָּׂדֶה׃ 6 וַיַּעֲזֹב כָּל־ ילי אֲשֶׁר־לוֹ בְּיַד־יוֹסֵף
ציון, קנאה, ו"פ יהוה, ה"פ אל וְלֹא־יָדַע אִתּוֹ מְאוּמָה כִּי אִם־ יוהך הַלֶּחֶם
ג"פ יהוה אֲשֶׁר־הוּא אוֹכֵל וַיְהִי יוֹסֵף ציון, קנאה, ו"פ יהוה, ה"פ אל יְפֵה אל אדני
־תֹאַר וִיפֵה אל אדני מַרְאֶה ר"ת יתום׃

SIXTH READING - JOSEPH - YESOD

7 וַיְהִי אל אַחַר הַדְּבָרִים ראה הָאֵלֶּה וַתִּשָּׂא אֵשֶׁת־אֲדֹנָיו אֶת־
עֵינֶיהָ ריבוע מ"ה אֶל־יוֹסֵף ציון, קנאה, ו"פ יהוה, ה"פ אל וַתֹּאמֶר שִׁכְבָה עִמִּי׃
8 וַיְמָאֵן ׀ וַיֹּאמֶר אֶל־אֵשֶׁת אֲדֹנָיו הֵן אֲדֹנִי לֹא־יָדַע אִתִּי מַה
מ"ה ־בַּבָּיִת ב"פ ראה וְכֹל ילי אֲשֶׁר־יֶשׁ־לוֹ נָתַן בְּיָדִי׃ 9 אֵינֶנּוּ
גָדוֹל להח, מבה, יזל, אום בַּבַּיִת ב"פ ראה הַזֶּה והו מִמֶּנִּי וְלֹא־חָשַׂךְ מִמֶּנִּי
מְאוּמָה כִּי אִם יוהך ־אוֹתָךְ בַּאֲשֶׁר אַתְּ־אִשְׁתּוֹ וְאֵיךְ אל אֶעֱשֶׂה
הָרָעָה רהע הַגְּדֹלָה להח, מבה, יזל, אום הַזֹּאת וְחָטָאתִי לֵאלֹהִים ילה, מום׃
10 וַיְהִי אל כְּדַבְּרָהּ ראה אֶל־יוֹסֵף ציון, קנאה, ו"פ יהוה, ה"פ אל יוֹם נגד, זן, מזבח ׀
יוֹם נגד, זן, מזבח וְלֹא־שָׁמַע אֵלֶיהָ לִשְׁכַּב אֶצְלָהּ לִהְיוֹת עִמָּהּ׃ 11 וַיְהִי
אל כְּהַיּוֹם נגד, זן, מזבח הַזֶּה והו וַיָּבֹא הַבַּיְתָה ב"פ ראה לַעֲשׂוֹת מְלַאכְתּוֹ
וְאֵין אִישׁ ע"ה קנ"א קס"א מֵאַנְשֵׁי הַבַּיִת ב"פ ראה שָׁם בַּבָּיִת ב"פ ראה׃
12 וַתִּתְפְּשֵׂהוּ בְּבִגְדוֹ לֵאמֹר שִׁכְבָה עִמִּי וַיַּעֲזֹב בִּגְדוֹ בְּיָדָהּ וַיָּנָס

[12] She caught him by his cloak and said, "Come to bed with me!" But he left his cloak in her hand and ran out of the house.

[13] When she saw that he had left his cloak in her hand and had run out of the house,
[14] she called her household servants. "Look," she said to them, "this Hebrew has been brought to us to make fun of us! He came in here to sleep with me, but I screamed out.

[15] When he heard me scream for help, he left his cloak beside me and ran out of the house."

[16] She kept his cloak beside her until his master came home. [17] Then she told him this story: "That Hebrew slave you brought us came to me to mock me.

[18] But as soon as I screamed for help, he left his cloak beside me and ran out of the house."

[19] When his master heard the story his wife told him, saying, "This is how your slave treated me," he burned with anger.

[20] Joseph's master took him and put him in prison, the place where the king's prisoners were confined. But while Joseph was there in the prison, [21] the Lord was with him; He showed him kindness and granted him favor in the eyes of the prison warden.

[22] So the warden put Joseph in charge of all those held in the prison, and he was made responsible for all that was done there.

[23] The warden paid no attention to anything under Joseph's care, because the Lord was with Joseph and gave him success in whatever he did.

When Potiphar's wife tried to seduce Joseph, he desired her—but he resisted his passion. After this act of restriction, Joseph, although innocent, was condemned to prison. It was the period of his imprisonment that accomplished his spiritual cleansing. By resisting temptation in whatever form it appears to us and through our willingness to undergo a cleansing, we can connect with our higher spiritual potential and complete our *tikkun* in this specific area. Joseph's example gives us the inspiration and the spiritual strength and support to do this.

הַסֹּהַר

Genesis 39:20 – Joseph was in jail, but he was respected by the prison warden. Because Joseph had a high spiritual consciousness, he did not see himself as a victim; as a result, he became the master of the jail. How people experience life is not determined by their physical circumstances, but rather by their spiritual level of consciousness.

וַיֵּצֵא הַחוּצָה׃ 13 וַיְהִי אל כִּרְאוֹתָהּ כִּי־עָזַב בִּגְדוֹ בְּיָדָהּ
וַיָּנָס הַחוּצָה׃ 14 וַתִּקְרָא לְאַנְשֵׁי בֵיתָהּ ב"פ ראה וַתֹּאמֶר לָהֶם
לֵאמֹר רְאוּ הֵבִיא לָנוּ אלהים, מום אִישׁ ע"ה קנ"א קס"א עִבְרִי לְצַחֶק בָּנוּ
בָּא אֵלַי לִשְׁכַּב עִמִּי וָאֶקְרָא בְּקוֹל ע"ב - ס"ג ע"ה גָּדוֹל להח, מבה, יזל, אום׃
15 וַיְהִי אל כְשָׁמְעוֹ כִּי־הֲרִימֹתִי קוֹלִי וָאֶקְרָא וַיַּעֲזֹב בִּגְדוֹ
אֶצְלִי וַיָּנָס וַיֵּצֵא הַחוּצָה׃ 16 וַתַּנַּח בִּגְדוֹ אֶצְלָהּ עַד־בּוֹא אֲדֹנָיו
אֶל־בֵּיתוֹ ב"פ ראה׃ 17 וַתְּדַבֵּר ראה אֵלָיו כַּדְּבָרִים ראה הָאֵלֶּה לֵאמֹר
בָּא־אֵלַי הָעֶבֶד הָעִבְרִי אֲשֶׁר־הֵבֵאתָ לָּנוּ אלהים, מום לְצַחֶק בִּי׃
18 וַיְהִי אל כַּהֲרִימִי קוֹלִי וָאֶקְרָא וַיַּעֲזֹב בִּגְדוֹ אֶצְלִי וַיָּנָס
הַחוּצָה׃ 19 וַיְהִי אל כִשְׁמֹעַ אֲדֹנָיו אֶת־דִּבְרֵי ראה אִשְׁתּוֹ אֲשֶׁר
דִּבְּרָה ראה אֵלָיו לֵאמֹר כַּדְּבָרִים ראה הָאֵלֶּה עָשָׂה לִי עַבְדֶּךָ פוי
וַיִּחַר אַפּוֹ׃ 20 וַיִּקַּח חעם אֲדֹנֵי יוֹסֵף ציון, קנאה, ו"פ יהוה, ה"פ אל אֹתוֹ
וַיִּתְּנֵהוּ אֶל־בֵּית ב"פ ראה הַסֹּהַר מְקוֹם אֲשֶׁר־אֲסִירֵי (כתיב: אסורי)
הַמֶּלֶךְ אֲסוּרִים וַיְהִי אל ־שָׁם בְּבֵית ב"פ ראה הַסֹּהַר׃
21 וַיְהִי אל יְהֹוָהאדניאהדונהי אֶת־יוֹסֵף ציון, קנאה, ו"פ יהוה, ה"פ אל וַיֵּט
אֵלָיו חָסֶד ע"ב, ריבוע יהוה וַיִּתֵּן י"פ מלוי ע"ב חִנּוֹ בְּעֵינֵי ריבוע מ"ה שַׂר
אלהים דיודין ורבוע אלהים בֵּית ב"פ ראה ־הַסֹּהַר׃ 22 וַיִּתֵּן י"פ מלוי ע"ב שַׂר
אלהים דיודין ורבוע אלהים בֵּית ב"פ ראה ־הַסֹּהַר בְּיַד־יוֹסֵף ציון, קנאה, ו"פ יהוה, ה"פ אל
אֵת כָּל ילי ־הָאֲסִירִם אֲשֶׁר בְּבֵית ב"פ ראה הַסֹּהַר וְאֵת כָּל ילי ־אֲשֶׁר
עֹשִׂים שָׁם הוּא הָיָה יהה עֹשֶׂה׃ 23 אֵין | שַׂר אלהים דיודין ורבוע אלהים
בֵּית ב"פ ראה ־הַסֹּהַר רֹאֶה ראה אֶת־כָּל ילי ־מְאוּמָה בְּיָדוֹ
בַּאֲשֶׁר יְהֹוָהאדניאהדונהי אִתּוֹ וַאֲשֶׁר־הוּא עֹשֶׂה יְהֹוָהאדניאהדונהי
מַצְלִיחַ׃ [פ]

SEVENTH READING - DAVID - MALCHUT

40 1 Some time later, the cupbearer and the baker of the king of Egypt offended their master, the king of Egypt. 2 Pharaoh was angry with his two officials, the chief cupbearer and the chief baker, 3 and put them in custody in the house of the captain of the guard, in the same prison where Joseph was confined. 4 The captain of the guard assigned them to Joseph, and he attended them. After they had been in custody for some time, 5 each of the two men—the cupbearer and the baker of the king of Egypt, who were being held in prison—had a dream the same night, and each dream had a meaning of its own. 6 When Joseph came to them the next morning, he saw that they were dejected.

7 So he asked Pharaoh's officials who were in custody with him in his master's house, "Why are your faces so sad today?"

8 "We both had dreams," they answered, "but there is no one to interpret them." Then Joseph said to them, "Do not interpretations belong to God? Tell me your dreams."

Genesis 40:3 – Pharaoh's wine steward and his chief baker were sent to jail. They were imprisoned with Joseph, and each of them had a dream on the same night that filled them with concern. Joseph interpreted their dreams, determining that one of the two men, the wine steward, would live, but that the chief baker would be hanged.

In the men's dreams, there were three baskets of bread and three vines with grapes on them. Joseph interpreted this as a reference to Pharaoh's birthday, which was to occur in three days time. When the three days passed, both the wine steward and the baker were released from prison. The wine steward was re-instated to his former position, while Pharaoh had the baker hanged.

The *Zohar* asks: "Why did Joseph make this interpretation? What are the differences between the dreams?" The wine steward dreamed about grapes, and grapes relate to the building of the Temple. Grapes (and wine) have the power to elevate the spirit, so this was a positive dream about creating something. But the baker had a dream about carrying baskets of bread upon his head but the bread was being eaten by birds, which Joseph understood to be a vision of the destruction of the Temple. Based on the positive and negative content of the two men's dreams, Joseph immediately knew the destiny of each dreamer.

> *There are two grades that they had seen. THE CHIEF BUTLER saw the supernal grade, ZEIR ANPIN, ascending to rule, and the moon, THE NUKVA, shining. THE CHIEF BAKER saw darkness and the evil Serpent ruling over THE NUKVA. Joseph therefore looked into the dream and gave it an evil interpretation. Thus, everything depends on the interpretation. The two of them saw the two grades RULING OVER THE NUKVA—[EITHER] ZEIR ANPIN, OR THE EVIL SERPENT. One or the other rules—either ZEIR ANPIN, or that EVIL One, THE SERPENT.*
>
> *– The Zohar, Vayeshev 24:272*

Our dreams are expressions of our consciousness, and our consciousness is what determines which forces create our particular reality.

SEVENTH READING - DAVID - MALCHUT

40 1 וַיְהִי אל אַחַר הַדְּבָרִים ראה הָאֵלֶּה חָטְאוּ מַשְׁקֵה מֶלֶךְ־
מִצְרַיִם מצר וְהָאֹפֶה לַאֲדֹנֵיהֶם לְמֶלֶךְ מִצְרָיִם מצר: 2 וַיִּקְצֹף פַּרְעֹה
עַל שְׁנֵי סָרִיסָיו עַל שַׂר אלהים דיודין ורבוע אלהים הַמַּשְׁקִים וְעַל שַׂר
אלהים דיודין ורבוע אלהים הָאוֹפִים: 3 וַיִּתֵּן י"פ מלוי ע"ב אֹתָם בְּמִשְׁמַר בֵּית
ב"פ ראה שַׂר אלהים דיודין ורבוע אלהים הַטַּבָּחִים אֶל־בֵּית ב"פ ראה הַסֹּהַר
מְקוֹם יהוה ברבוע אֲשֶׁר יוֹסֵף ציון, קנאה, ו"פ יהוה, ה"פ אל אָסוּר שָׁם: 4 וַיִּפְקֹד
שַׂר אלהים דיודין ורבוע אלהים הַטַּבָּחִים אֶת־יוֹסֵף ציון, קנאה, ו"פ יהוה, ה"פ אל אִתָּם
וַיְשָׁרֶת אֹתָם וַיִּהְיוּ אל יָמִים נלך בְּמִשְׁמָר: 5 וַיַּחַלְמוּ חֲלוֹם שְׁנֵיהֶם
אִישׁ ע"ה קנ"א קס"א חֲלֹמוֹ בְּלַיְלָה מלה אֶחָד אהבה, דאגה אִישׁ ע"ה קנ"א קס"א
כְּפִתְרוֹן חֲלֹמוֹ הַמַּשְׁקֶה וְהָאֹפֶה אֲשֶׁר לְמֶלֶךְ מִצְרַיִם מצר
אֲשֶׁר אֲסוּרִים בְּבֵית ב"פ ראה הַסֹּהַר: 6 וַיָּבֹא אֲלֵיהֶם יוֹסֵף
ציון, קנאה, ו"פ יהוה, ה"פ אל בַּבֹּקֶר וַיַּרְא אֹתָם וְהִנָּם זֹעֲפִים: 7 וַיִּשְׁאַל
אֶת־סְרִיסֵי פַרְעֹה אֲשֶׁר אִתּוֹ בְמִשְׁמַר בֵּית ב"פ ראה אֲדֹנָיו
לֵאמֹר מַדּוּעַ פְּנֵיכֶם רָעִים הַיּוֹם נגד, זן, מזבח: 8 וַיֹּאמְרוּ אֵלָיו חֲלוֹם
חָלַמְנוּ וּפֹתֵר אלהים - ב"פ אלהים דיודין אֵין אֹתוֹ וַיֹּאמֶר אֲלֵהֶם יוֹסֵף
ציון, קנאה, ו"פ יהוה, ה"פ אל הֲלוֹא לֵאלֹהִים ילה, מום פִּתְרֹנִים סַפְּרוּ־נָא לִי:
9 וַיְסַפֵּר שַׂר אלהים דיודין ורבוע אלהים הַמַּשְׁקִים אֶת־חֲלֹמוֹ לְיוֹסֵף
ציון, קנאה, ו"פ יהוה, ה"פ אל וַיֹּאמֶר לוֹ בַּחֲלוֹמִי וְהִנֵּה מ"ה יה גֶפֶן לְפָנָי:
10 וּבַגֶּפֶן שְׁלֹשָׁה שָׂרִיגִם אלהים דיודין ורבוע אלהים - ב"ן ע"ה וְהִוא כְפֹרַחַת
עָלְתָה נִצָּהּ הִבְשִׁילוּ אַשְׁכְּלֹתֶיהָ עֲנָבִים ב"פ אלהים: 11 וְכוֹס אלהים, מום
פַּרְעֹה בְּיָדִי וָאֶקַּח אֶת־הָעֲנָבִים ב"פ אלהים וָאֶשְׂחַט אֹתָם אֶל־כּוֹס
אלהים, מום פַּרְעֹה וָאֶתֵּן אֶת־הַכּוֹס אלהים, מום עַל־כַּף פַּרְעֹה: 12 וַיֹּאמֶר
לוֹ יוֹסֵף ציון, קנאה, ו"פ יהוה, ה"פ אל זֶה פִּתְרֹנוֹ שְׁלֹשֶׁת הַשָּׂרִגִים
ריבוע אלהים - אלהים דיודין - ב"ן ע"ה שְׁלֹשֶׁת יָמִים נלך הֵם: 13 בְּעוֹד | שְׁלֹשֶׁת

9 So the chief cupbearer told Joseph his dream. He said to him, "In my dream I saw a vine in front of me, 10 and on the vine were three branches. As soon as it budded, it blossomed, and its clusters ripened into grapes.

11 Pharaoh's cup was in my hand, and I took the grapes, squeezed them into Pharaoh's cup and put the cup in his hand."

12 "This is what it means," Joseph said to him. "The three branches are three days.

13 Within three days Pharaoh will lift up your head and restore you to your position and you will put Pharaoh's cup in his hand, just as you used to do when you were his cupbearer.

14 But when all goes well with you, remember me and show me kindness; mention me to Pharaoh and get me out of this prison.

15 For I was forcibly carried off from the land of the Hebrews, and even here I have done nothing to deserve being put in a dungeon."

16 When the chief baker saw that Joseph had given a favorable interpretation, he said to Joseph, "I too had a dream: On my head were three baskets of bread.

17 In the top basket were all kinds of baked goods for Pharaoh, but the birds were eating them out of the basket on my head."

18 "This is what it means," Joseph said. "The three baskets are three days.

19 Within three days Pharaoh will lift off your head and hang you on a tree. And the birds will eat away your flesh."

MAFTIR

20 Now the third day was Pharaoh's birthday, and he gave a feast for all his officials. He lifted up the heads of the chief cupbearer and the chief baker in the presence of his officials: 21 He restored the chief cupbearer to his position, so that he once again put the cup into Pharaoh's hand, 22 but he hanged the chief baker, just as Joseph had said to them in his interpretation.

23 The chief cupbearer, however, did not remember Joseph; he forgot him.

וְהִזְכַּרְתַּנִי

Genesis 40:14 – Joseph asked the wine steward to plead on his behalf to Pharaoh, but the Bible says that the steward forgot about Joseph. The *Zohar* explains that Joseph, by asking this favor of the wine steward, had put his hope in a human being rather than simply having absolute certainty in the Light of the Creator. By doing this, Joseph actually lengthened the cleansing process of his imprisonment by two years.

ימים נלך ישא פרעה את־ראשך והשיבך על־כנך ונתת כוס
אלהים, מום פרעה בידו כמשפט ע"ה ה"פ אלהים הראשון אשר היית
משקהו: 14 כי אם יהך זכרתני אתך כאשר ייטב לך ועשית־
נא עמדי חסד ע"ב, ריבוע יהוה והזכרתני אל־פרעה והוצאתני מן־
הבית ב"פ ראה הזה והו: 15 כי־גנב גנבתי מארץ אלהים דאלפין העברים
וגם יגל פה מילה, ע"ה אלהים, ע"ה מום לא־עשיתי מאומה כי־שמו אתי
בבור יצחק, ד"פ ב"ן: 16 וירא שר אלהים דיודין ורבוע אלהים האפים כי טוב
והו, אום פתר ויאמר אל־יוסף ציון, קנאה, ו"פ יהוה, ה"פ אל אף־אני אני בחלומי
והנה מ"ה יה שלשה סלי חרי על־ראשי ריבוע אלהים + אלהים דיודין ע"ה:
17 ובסל העליון מכל ילי מאכל פרעה מעשה אפה והעוף
ציון, יוסף, ו"פ יהוה, ה"פ אל אכל אתם מן־הסל מעל עלם ראשי
ריבוע אלהים + אלהים דיודין ע"ה: 18 ויען יוסף ציון, קנאה, ו"פ יהוה, ה"פ אל ויאמר זה
פתרנו שלשת הסלים שלשת ימים נלך הם: 19 בעוד | שלשת
ימים נלך ישא פרעה את־ראשך מעליך ותלה אותך על־עץ
ע"ה קס"א ואכל העוף ציון, יוסף, ו"פ יהוה, ה"פ אל את־בשרך מעליך:

MAFTIR

20 ויהי אל | ביום נגד, זן, מזבח השלישי יום נגד, זן, מזבח הלדת את־
פרעה ויעש משתה לכל יה + אדני עבדיו וישא את־ראש
ריבוע אלהים + אלהים דיודין ע"ה | שר אלהים דיודין ורבוע אלהים המשקים ואת־
ראש ריבוע אלהים + אלהים דיודין ע"ה שר אלהים דיודין ורבוע אלהים האפים בתוך
עבדיו: 21 וישב את־שר אלהים דיודין ורבוע אלהים המשקים על־משקהו
ויתן הכוס אלהים, מום על־כף פרעה: 22 ואת שר אלהים דיודין ורבוע אלהים
האפים תלה כאשר פתר להם יוסף ציון, קנאה, ו"פ יהוה, ה"פ אל:
23 ולא־זכר שר אלהים דיודין ורבוע אלהים המשקים את־יוסף
ציון, קנאה, ו"פ יהוה, ה"פ אל וישכחהו: [פ] [פ] [פ]

HAFTARAH OF VAYESHEV

This Haftarah reading clearly shares with us the truth that in life, we often give away a great deal for very little in return. We sell ourselves short. We tend to settle for immediate gratification because we do not have the trust, certainty, or patience that our fulfillment will eventually come.

There is a story about a poor, lonely man who prayed to the Creator to send him someone to share Shabbat with. Through God's great compassion, the Creator decided to send Elijah the prophet to the poor man; this would have helped the man reach great spiritual heights. As Elijah was preparing for his journey, the man became desperate and impatient. He decided to begin Shabbat by going into his barn and

Amos 2:6 -3:8

2 6 This is what the Lord says: "For three sins of Israel, even for four, I will not turn back. They sell the righteous for silver, and the needy for a pair of sandals.

7 They trample on the heads of the poor as upon the dust of the ground and deny
justice to the oppressed. Father and son use the same girl and so profane My Holy
Name. 8 They lie down beside every altar on garments taken in pledge. In the house
of their god they drink wine taken as fines.

9 I destroyed the Amorite before them, though he was tall as the cedars and strong as the oaks. I destroyed his fruit above and his roots below.

10 I brought you up out of Egypt, and I led you forty years in the desert to give you the land of the Amorites.

11 I also rose up prophets from among your sons and Nazirites from among your young men. Is this not true, people of Israel?" declares the Lord.

12 "But you made the Nazirites drink wine and commanded the prophets not to prophesy.

13 Now then, I will crush you as a cart crushes when loaded with grain.

HAFTARAH OF VAYESHEV

making a blessing on the wine and the bread, having only his donkey to accompany him. The Creator saw this and decided that the man did not need Elijah the prophet after all. The man spent the rest of Shabbat alone with his mule.

We must never substitute anything or anyone for the presence of God and the heavenly messengers. Reading this section will assist us in building our absolute certainty in the Light, and it will fortify us for the times when our patience wears thin.

עמוס פרק 2–3

2 6 כֹּה הי אָמַר יְהֹוָאדנהי יאהדונהי עַל־שְׁלֹשָׁה פִּשְׁעֵי יִשְׂרָאֵל וְעַל־
אַרְבָּעָה לֹא אֲשִׁיבֶנּוּ עַל־מִכְרָם בַּכֶּסֶף צַדִּיק וְאֶבְיוֹן בַּעֲבוּר
נַעֲלָיִם׃ 7 הַשֹּׁאֲפִים עַל־עֲפַר־אֶרֶץ אלהים דאלפין בְּרֹאשׁ
ריבוע אלהים - אלהים דיודין ע״ה דַּלִּים וְדֶרֶךְ ב״פ יב״ק עֲנָוִים ענו יַטּוּ וְאִישׁ
ע״ה קנ״א קס״א וְאָבִיו יֵלְכוּ כלי אֶל־הַנַּעֲרָה לְמַעַן חַלֵּל אֶת־שֵׁם שדי יהוה
קָדְשִׁי׃ 8 וְעַל־בְּגָדִים חֲבֻלִים יַטּוּ אֵצֶל כָּל ילי ־מִזְבֵּחַ זן, נגד וְיֵין
מיכ, י״פ האא עֲנוּשִׁים יִשְׁתּוּ בֵּית ב״פ ראה אֱלֹהֵיהֶם ילה׃ 9 וְאָנֹכִי איע
הִשְׁמַדְתִּי אֶת־הָאֱמֹרִי מִפְּנֵיהֶם אֲשֶׁר כְּגֹבַהּ אֲרָזִים גָּבְהוֹ וְחָסֹן
הוּא כָּאַלּוֹנִים וָאַשְׁמִיד פִּרְיוֹ מִמַּעַל עלם וְשָׁרָשָׁיו מִתָּחַת׃
10 וְאָנֹכִי איע הֶעֱלֵיתִי אֶתְכֶם מֵאֶרֶץ אלהים דאלפין מִצְרָיִם מצר וָאוֹלֵךְ
אֶתְכֶם בַּמִּדְבָּר רמ״ח, אברהם אַרְבָּעִים שָׁנָה לָרֶשֶׁת אֶת־אֶרֶץ
אלהים דאלפין הָאֱמֹרִי׃ 11 וָאָקִים מִבְּנֵיכֶם לִנְבִיאִים וּמִבַּחוּרֵיכֶם
לִנְזִרִים הַאַף אֵין־זֹאת בְּנֵי יִשְׂרָאֵל נְאֻם־יְהֹוָאדנהי יאהדונהי׃ 12 וַתַּשְׁקוּ
אֶת־הַנְּזִרִים יָיִן מיכ, י״פ האא וְעַל־הַנְּבִיאִים צִוִּיתֶם פוי לֵאמֹר לֹא

[14] The swift will not escape, the strong will not muster their strength, and the warrior will not save his life.

[15] The archer will not stand his ground, the fleet-footed soldier will not get away, and the horseman will not save his life.

[16] Even the bravest warriors will flee naked on that day," declares the Lord.

3 [1] Hear this word the Lord has spoken against you, people of Israel—against the whole family I brought up out of Egypt: [2] "Only you have I chosen of all the families of the Earth; therefore I will punish you for all your sins."

[3] Do two walk together unless they have agreed to do so?

[4] Does a lion roar in the thicket when he has no prey? Does he growl in his den when he has caught nothing?

[5] Does a bird fall into a trap on the ground where no snare has been set? Does a trap spring up from the earth when there is nothing to catch?

[6] When a trumpet sounds in a city, do not the people tremble? When disaster comes to a city, has not the Lord caused it?

[7] Surely the Sovereign Lord does nothing without revealing His plan to His servants the prophets.

[8] The lion has roared—who will not fear? The Sovereign Lord has spoken—who can but prophesy?

תנבאו: 13 הנה מ"ה יה אנכי איע מעיק תחתיכם כאשר תעיק
העגלה המלאה לה עמיר: 14 ואבד מנוס מקל נמם וחזק פהל
לא־יאמץ כחו וגבור לא־ימלט נפשו: 15 ותפש הקשת לא
יעמד וקל נמם ברגליו לא ימלט ורכב הסוס ריבוע אדני, כוק לא
ימלט נפשו: 16 ואמיץ לבו בגבורים ערום ינוס ביום נגד, זן, מזבח
־ההוא נאם־יהוהאדניאהדונהי: [פ] 3 1 שמעו את־הדבר ראה הזה והו
אשר דבר ראה יהוהאדניאהדונהי עליכם בני ישראל על כל ילי, עמם
־המשפחה אשר העליתי מארץ אלהים דאלפין מצרים מצר לאמר:
2 רק אתכם ידעתי מכל ילי משפחות האדמה על־כן אפקד
עליכם את כל ילי ־עונתיכם: 3 הילכו שנים יחדו בלתי אם
יוהך ־נועדו: 4 הישאג אריה רי"ו ביער סןזפחך, ערי, סנדלפון וטרף רמ"ח ע"ה
אין לו היתן כפיר קולו ממענתו בלתי אם יוהך ־לכד: 5 התפל
צפור על־פח הארץ אלהים דההין ע"ה ומוקש אין לה היעלה־פח מן־
האדמה ולכוד לא ילכוד: 6 אם יוהך ־יתקע ב"פ סןזפחך - י' אותיות
שופר בעיר סןזפחך, ערי, סנדלפון ועם לא יחרדו אם יוהך ־תהיה רעה
רהע בעיר סןזפחך, ערי, סנדלפון ויהוהאדניאהדונהי לא עשה: 7 כי לא יעשה
אדני ללה יהוהיאהדונהי דבר ראה כי אם יוהך ־גלה סודו מיכ, י"פ האא אל־
עבדיו הנביאים: 8 אריה רי"ו שאג מי ילי לא יירא אדני ללה
יהוהיאהדונהי דבר ראה מי ילי לא ינבא:

MIKETZ

LESSON OF MIKETZ (Genesis 41:1–44:17)

The Story of Miketz begins: "When two full years had passed, Pharaoh had a dream..." In his dream, there were lean cattle and fattened cattle. The real purpose of the dream was two-fold: It warned not only of the forthcoming famine but also that it would be Joseph who would uncover the meaning of the dream, thus ensuring that he would be appointed to a high position, second only to the king. Actually, the dream was supposed to have occurred two years earlier, but because Joseph had had two years added to his prison sentence, the dream was delayed for that length of time. This is clear in the way the verse is written: "When two full years had passed, Pharaoh had a dream..."

The lesson here partly pertains to the way we try to make desired events happen as quickly as possible. We should remember that everything has already been prepared for us. Our efforts and our desires are important and can have an effect, but when our efforts are on behalf of ourselves, our power is drastically limited.

The secret lies in knowing what kind of effort is important and how much of an effort is enough. When a person questions if it pays to pray in the morning even when it makes them late for work, the answer is: "Yes, of course, it pays." But there has to be an understanding and a willingness to make the extra effort. The truth is that if we had our heart and our consciousness in the right place, we would be enabled instantly to have everything we need in just one second. While it is very nice to have money (the result of our work), the effort to raise the spiritual consciousness that we are talking about here brings not just money but literally complete joy and fulfillment in all things.

Imagine two stores. In one, the employees work all day and succeed in making a certain amount of money. In the other store, the staff sells almost nothing during the whole day, but just before closing, a customer appears and spends thousands of dollars. This principle does not apply only to money. We don't have to be running ourselves ragged at every moment to get what we want and need. It is possible to gain more in a second than we have gained in a year.

The results of our work in this life are not so much about our physical effort as about our spiritual effort. It is important to truly believe that blessings do not come to us as a result of our own physical actions, but rather that they come from the Creator and that our spiritual effort to connect to the Creator draws them to us.

A person who believes only in himself and his own effort might make some money, but in the end, this will not make him happy.

There is a story about the head of a yeshiva (a Jewish seminary) who asked the Chafetz Chaim (Rav Israel Meir the Kohen), a great scholar and spiritual leader, to recommend a supervisor for his yeshiva. The Chafetz Chaim suggested a young man who had a big heart and could make a difference in the spiritual level of the yeshiva, and of course, the head of the yeshiva proceeded to take his advice.

Several days later, the Chafetz Chaim reconsidered his recommendation. When the head of the yeshiva asked the reason, the Chafetz Chaim answered that some days earlier, the young man had been complaining about his life and about not having any money. The Chafetz Chaim said that because of this, he took back his recommendation, since a person who complained about the physical conditions of his life could not be a spiritual influence in a yeshiva.

If Joseph had accepted his long imprisonment with the certainty that the Creator would release him when the time was right, he could have avoided the two additional years in prison. If he had been patient for just a few more days, his problem would have been solved.

It has been said that people get sick according to the judgment that they bring upon themselves through their actions and that they regain their health through their desire for God. Even if they are working hard toward healing themselves, it is the Creator Who makes that healing possible. Thus, it is written in the *Gemara*: "...a doctor will heal." This means that permission from the Creator is given to doctors for healing. It does not necessarily mean that the sick have permission to be healed, but rather that the doctors are allowed to heal them. The *Zohar* says:

> *Man becomes pure solely through words of spiritual study. For this reason, words of Torah never receive defilement, since THE FUNCTION OF THE TORAH is to purify the unclean. There is healing in the Torah, as it is written: "It shall be health to your navel, and marrow to your bones." (Proverbs 3:8) There is purity in the Torah, as it is written: "The fear of God is clean, enduring forever." (Psalms 19:10) What is meant by "enduring forever?" IT MEANS that it remains constantly in the state of purity, which is never removed from it.*
>
> -- *The Zohar, Kedoshim 3:11*

We are told that someone who is truly in awe of God will be released from the constraints of natural law. This is because nature was created for those people who do not make an effort in their lives to discover the truth of the Creator; nature takes its course with those people. On the other hand, when a person is above nature and knows that he can trust in God alone for his entire lifetime, God will be his security. Any and all circumstances in our lives are a direct effect of the desire of the Creator and our ability to carry out the Creator's will.

So when we feel pressure and stress, we need to stop reacting and exercise patience and certainty instead. By not reacting, we make room for the Light to be revealed within us. Ultimately, that is the only way we can really eliminate chaos from our lives.

SYNOPSIS OF MIKETZ

This story is almost always read on the Shabbat of Chanukah, the time of miracles. Most cosmic events possess a lower level of spiritual energy than Shabbat does. This is because the energy of cosmic events and supernal holidays is spread over an entire year, while the energy obtained and available on Shabbat is more potent because it controls a shorter period of time—one week. So when a cosmic event such as Chanukah, Rosh Hashana, or Yom Kippur falls on Shabbat, this event offers us a higher level of spiritual energy.

When Joseph put his faith in the wine steward instead of the Light of the Creator, two more years were added to his time in prison. This story in the Book of Genesis begins at the conclusion of those two years.

FIRST READING - ABRAHAM - CHESED

41 [1] When two full years had passed, Pharaoh had a dream: He was standing
by the Nile, [2] when out of the river there came up seven cows, sleek
and fat, and they grazed among the reeds.

*[3] After them seven other cows, ugly and gaunt, came up out of the Nile and stood
beside those on the riverbank. [4] And the cows that were ugly and gaunt ate up the
seven sleek, fat cows. Then Pharaoh woke up. [5] He fell asleep again and had a
second dream: Seven heads of grain, healthy and good, were growing on a single
stalk. [6] After them, seven other heads of grain sprouted—thin and scorched by the
east wind. [7] The thin heads of grain swallowed up the seven healthy, full heads. Then
Pharaoh woke up; it had been a dream.*

*[8] In the morning his mind was troubled, so he sent for all the magicians and wise men
of Egypt. Pharaoh told them his dreams, but no one could interpret them for him.*

FROM THE RAV

While Joseph was in the dungeon, he was in total control. The jailers gave him control. It was very uncomfortable living in the dungeon, but he never gave up; he always maintained his certainty in the Lightforce of God. He understood that his discomfort was all part of a process of cleansing, and in doing this, he defeated his Negative Side. This didn't mean that he was happy about what he was going through, but he understood what it was all about. Satan grabs us when we confuse difficulty with what is really for our good. The Torah is teaching us that we create our own freedom!

Joseph represents *Yesod*, a higher dimension far beyond our physical realm of *Malchut*. Joseph's lesson to us is about temptation and the danger of doubt, and the inclination to believe that our destiny is outside our grasp. Remember: Satan is not only trying to get us to commit crimes. What he hopes for—and what he has successfully accomplished for over 3400 years—is to make certain that human beings do not have control over their consciousness. Satan is always there to say that we are not responsible for what happens in our lives. Somebody else is bringing on all this chaos. It's so easy to fall into this trap. We all assume we are in control of our consciousness, and that assumption is Satan's major weapon. His job is to convince us to relinquish control over our minds. We need to regain control of our minds, and we need to use the tools, technology, and systems of Kabbalah to make it happen.

Thousands of thoughts come into our minds every single minute. We don't have control. This is what we learn from Joseph. We learn that there is another place—not in Heaven but in our consciousness—where we can and must maintain control.

We should never lose sight of this fact and recognize the constant battle to maintain ownership of our consciousness. Then, and only then, will we find there is nothing of a physical, material nature that we cannot overcome in this world. Even today, science says our minds are 99 percent of who we are, not the one percent physicality where we place the emphasis.

FIRST READING - ABRAHAM - CHESED

41 1 וַיְהִי אל מִקֵּץ מנק שְׁנָתַיִם יָמִים נלך וּפַרְעֹה חֹלֵם ג"פ יהוה וְהִנֵּה
מ"ה יה עֹמֵד עַל־הַיְאֹר כף ויו זין ויו: 2 וְהִנֵּה מִן־הַיְאֹר כף ויו זין ויו עֹלֹת
אבגיתצ, ושר, אהבת חנם שֶׁבַע אלהים דיודין - ע"ב פָּרוֹת יְפוֹת מַרְאֶה וּבְרִיאֹת
בָּשָׂר וַתִּרְעֶינָה בָּאָחוּ: 3 וְהִנֵּה שֶׁבַע אלהים דיודין - ע"ב פָּרוֹת אֲחֵרוֹת
עֹלוֹת אבגיתצ, ושר, אהבת חנם אַחֲרֵיהֶן מִן־הַיְאֹר כף ויו זין ויו רָעוֹת מַרְאֶה
וְדַקּוֹת בָּשָׂר וַתַּעֲמֹדְנָה אֵצֶל הַפָּרוֹת עַל־שְׂפַת הַיְאֹר כף ויו זין ויו:
4 וַתֹּאכַלְנָה הַפָּרוֹת רָעוֹת הַמַּרְאֶה וְדַקֹּת הַבָּשָׂר אֵת שֶׁבַע
אלהים דיודין - ע"ב הַפָּרוֹת יְפֹת הַמַּרְאֶה וְהַבְּרִיאֹת ר"ת היהו וַיִּיקַץ פַּרְעֹה:
5 וַיִּישָׁן ש"ע נהורין וַיַּחֲלֹם שֵׁנִית וְהִנֵּה | שֶׁבַע אלהים דיודין - ע"ב שִׁבֳּלִים
עֹלוֹת בְּקָנֶה ע"ה = ציון, קנאה, ו"פ יהוה, ה"פ אל אֶחָד אהבה, דאגה בְּרִיאוֹת וְטֹבוֹת:
6 וְהִנֵּה מ"ה יה שֶׁבַע אלהים דיודין - ע"ב שִׁבֳּלִים דַּקּוֹת וּשְׁדוּפֹת קָדִים
צֹמְחוֹת אַחֲרֵיהֶן: 7 וַתִּבְלַעְנָה הַשִּׁבֳּלִים הַדַּקּוֹת אֵת שֶׁבַע
אלהים דיודין - ע"ב הַשִּׁבֳּלִים הַבְּרִיאוֹת וְהַמְּלֵאוֹת וַיִּיקַץ פַּרְעֹה וְהִנֵּה
חֲלוֹם: 8 וַיְהִי אל בַבֹּקֶר וַתִּפָּעֶם רוּחוֹ וַיִּשְׁלַח וַיִּקְרָא עם ה' אותיות = ב"פ קס"א

חֹלֵם

Genesis 41:1 – Pharaoh dreamed two dreams, which showed him the future of Egypt. Because he was responsible for the country, Pharaoh was allowed to receive these messages despite the fact that he was not at a very high spiritual level. The same principle applies in our own lives. We are granted dreams pertaining to areas within our own domain—about the people and things we are close to—even though we may not be on a very high spiritual level. Parents, for example, often receive dreams about their children and families.

People on a high spiritual level can receive their supernal teachings through dreams. The Ari wrote:

> *"When Rav Yitzchak said, 'Is there, Heaven forbid, no more hope for us?' my teacher said to him, 'If you merit it, I shall come and teach you.' Rav Yitzchak asked, 'How can you come and teach us after you die from this world?' and he answered, 'Secret things are not your business, how I shall come to you, whether in a dream, or awake, or in a vision.'"*
>
> *—The Writings of the Ari, Gate of Reincarnation, Introduction 39:65*

[9] *Then the chief cupbearer said to Pharaoh, "Today I am reminded of my faults.*

[10] *Pharaoh was once angry with his servants, and he imprisoned me and the chief baker in the house of the captain of the guard.*

[11] *Each of us had a dream the same night, and each dream had a meaning of its own.*

[12] *Now a young Hebrew was there with us, a servant of the captain of the guard. We told him our dreams, and he interpreted them for us, giving each man the interpretation of his dream.*

[13] *And things turned out exactly as he interpreted them to us: I was restored to my position, and the other man was hanged."*

[14] *So Pharaoh sent for Joseph, and he was quickly brought from the dungeon. When he had shaved and changed his clothes, he came before Pharaoh.*

SECOND READING - ISAAC - GEVURAH

[15] *Pharaoh said to Joseph, "I had a dream, and no one can interpret it. But I have heard it said of you that when you hear a dream you can interpret it."*

[16] *"I cannot do it," Joseph replied to Pharaoh, "but God will give Pharaoh the answer he desires."*

[17] *Then Pharaoh said to Joseph, "In my dream I was standing on the bank of the Nile,*

מַזְכִּיר

Genesis 41:9 – **The Wine Steward Remembered Joseph.** Although Joseph's interpretation of the wine steward's dream had saved the man's life, he forgot Joseph once he was out of prison. Two years later, when Pharaoh had a dream that needed interpretation, the wine steward remembered Joseph. People often forget what someone has done for them in the past, thinking only, "What have you done for me lately?" But we can never tell when someone to whom we have been helpful long ago will suddenly return that goodness to us.

אֶת־כָּל ילי ־חַרְטֻמֵּי מִצְרַיִם מצר וְאֶת־כָּל ילי ־חֲכָמֶיהָ וַיְסַפֵּר פַּרְעֹה
לָהֶם אֶת־חֲלֹמוֹ וְאֵין־פּוֹתֵר אוֹתָם לְפַרְעֹה׃ 9 וַיְדַבֵּר ראה שַׂר
אלהים דיודין ורבוע אלהים הַמַּשְׁקִים אֶת־פַּרְעֹה לֵאמֹר אֶת־חֲטָאַי אֲנִי אני
מַזְכִּיר הַיּוֹם נגד, זן, מזבח׃ 10 פַּרְעֹה קָצַף עַל־עֲבָדָיו וַיִּתֵּן אֹתִי
בְּמִשְׁמַר בֵּית ב״פ ראה שַׂר אלהים דיודין ורבוע אלהים הַטַּבָּחִים אֹתִי וְאֵת
שַׂר אלהים דיודין ורבוע אלהים הָאֹפִים׃ 11 וַנַּחַלְמָה חֲלוֹם בְּלַיְלָה מלה
אֶחָד אהבה, דאגה אֲנִי אני וָהוּא אִישׁ ע״ה קנ״א קס״א כְּפִתְרוֹן חֲלֹמוֹ חָלָמְנוּ׃
12 וְשָׁם אִתָּנוּ נַעַר ש״ך עִבְרִי עֶבֶד לְשַׂר אלהים דיודין ורבוע אלהים הַטַּבָּחִים
וַנְּסַפֶּר־לוֹ וַיִּפְתָּר־לָנוּ אלהים, מום אֶת־חֲלֹמֹתֵינוּ אִישׁ ע״ה קנ״א קס״א
כַּחֲלֹמוֹ פָּתָר׃ 13 וַיְהִי אל כַּאֲשֶׁר פָּתַר־לָנוּ אלהים, מום כֵּן הָיָה יהה
אֹתִי הֵשִׁיב עַל־כַּנִּי וְאֹתוֹ תָלָה י״פ אלהים + ה׳׃ 14 וַיִּשְׁלַח פַּרְעֹה
וַיִּקְרָא עם ה׳ אותיות = ב״פ קס״א אֶת־יוֹסֵף ציון, קנאה, ו״פ יהוה, ה״פ אל וַיְרִיצֻהוּ
מִן־הַבּוֹר יצחק, ד״פ ב״ן וַיְגַלַּח וַיְחַלֵּף שִׂמְלֹתָיו וַיָּבֹא אֶל־פַּרְעֹה׃

SECOND READING - ISAAC - GEVURAH

15 וַיֹּאמֶר פַּרְעֹה אֶל־יוֹסֵף ציון, קנאה, ו״פ יהוה, ה״פ אל חֲלוֹם חָלַמְתִּי וּפֹתֵר
אֵין אֹתוֹ וַאֲנִי אני שָׁמַעְתִּי עָלֶיךָ לֵאמֹר תִּשְׁמַע חֲלוֹם לִפְתֹּר

וַיִּקְרָא

Genesis 41:14 – **Joseph was Summoned to Pharaoh.** According to the *Midrash*, to speak to Pharaoh, one had to be able to climb 70 steps, with each step requiring the knowledge of a different language. We're told that the night before Joseph was to appear before Pharaoh, the angel Gabriel visited him in prison and taught him the 70 languages. Joseph also gained protection against the negative forces and the black magic that surrounded Pharaoh. Whenever we have to defend ourselves or appear before people who may in some way be our adversaries, we must acquire the appropriate protection. The way we receive this protection is by watching how we speak and what we say. In addition, we must ask the Light to speak through us. This is the "right language" we need to call upon in uncertain situations. The 72 Names of God meditation for speaking the right words (*Yud, Yud, Zayin*) is a very powerful tool to achieve this end.

[18] when out of the river there came up seven cows, fat and sleek, and they grazed among the reeds.

[19] After them, seven other cows came up—scrawny and very ugly and lean. I had never seen such ugly cows in all the land of Egypt.

[20] The lean, ugly cows ate up the seven fat cows that came up first. [21] But even after they ate them, no one could tell that they had done so; they looked just as ugly as before. Then I woke up. [22] "In my dreams I also saw seven heads of grain, full and good, growing on a single stalk.

[23] After them, seven other heads sprouted—withered and thin and scorched by the east wind. [24] The thin heads of grain swallowed up the seven good heads. I told this to the magicians, but none could explain it to me."

[25] Then Joseph said to Pharaoh, "The dreams of Pharaoh are one and the same. God has revealed to Pharaoh what He is about to do.

בַּחֲלֹמִי

Genesis 41:17 – **Pharoah Told Joseph the Two Dreams.** When Pharaoh recounted his dreams to Joseph, he changed some details to test Joseph's understanding. Joseph not only told Pharaoh the meaning of the dreams, he was also able to correct Pharaoh's recounting of them. Joseph was in tune not only with the inner meaning of the dreams, but also with the signs that appeared in them. The Ari tells us that the interpretation of a dream is of a higher level than the dream itself because it is through the one who does the interpreting that the higher meaning is made plain.

> *This is the inner meaning of "Joseph is a fruitful bough (Heb. porat)," (Genesis 49:22) because in Yesod, Joseph, all the brains gather. He was then called "Joseph is a fruitful bough" and became the interpreter of dreams. Hence, the interpretation is of a higher level than the dream because the dream is the inner meaning of the brains apart, when they are stuck in the throat, while the interpreter is the secret of the brains when revealed Below in Yesod, when the dream is recognized that is above, hidden.*
>
> *– The Writings of Rav Isaac Luria, Vayeshev 26*

וַיֹּאמֶר

Genesis 41:25 – **Joseph Interpreted the Dreams.** Joseph foresaw seven plentiful years followed by seven years of famine. Because of Joseph's correct interpretation, Pharaoh's overseers were able to save many people from starvation by storing up grain during the good years. Joseph's ability to interpret the dream had powerful consequences in the material world, but only because the overseers took the necessary steps to avert the disaster that was being foretold and because they acted on behalf of all the people of the country, not just themselves. When information is received from the Upper Worlds, the physical work must still be done on this level to make best use of what we are being told by the Creator.

From the years of feast and famine in Egypt, we can make an analogy to our own lives, where we have a choice between feast and famine on a daily basis. When used with the correct consciousness of sharing, the tools of Kabbalah connect us to a realm of unlimited abundance and prosperity.

אֹתוֹ: 16 וַיַּעַן יוֹסֵף ציון, קנאה, ו"פ יהוה, ה"פ אל אֶת־פַּרְעֹה לֵאמֹר בִּלְעָדָי
אֱלֹהִים ילה, מום יַעֲנֶה אֶת־שְׁלוֹם פַּרְעֹה: 17 וַיְדַבֵּר ראה פַּרְעֹה אֶל־
יוֹסֵף ציון, קנאה, ו"פ יהוה, ה"פ אל בַּחֲלֹמִי הִנְנִי עֹמֵד עַל־שְׂפַת הַיְאֹר
כף ויו זין ויו: 18 וְהִנֵּה מִן־הַיְאֹר כף ויו זין ויו עֹלֹת אבגיתצ, ושר, אהבת חנם שֶׁבַע
אלהים דיודין + ע"ב פָּרוֹת בְּרִיאוֹת בָּשָׂר וִיפֹת תֹּאַר וַתִּרְעֶינָה בָּאָחוּ:
19 וְהִנֵּה שֶׁבַע־ אלהים דיודין + ע"ב פָּרוֹת אֲחֵרוֹת עֹלוֹת אבגיתצ, ושר, אהבת חנם
אַחֲרֵיהֶן דַּלּוֹת וְרָעוֹת תֹּאַר מְאֹד וְרַקּוֹת בָּשָׂר לֹא־רָאִיתִי
כָהֵנָּה בְּכָל לכב־אֶרֶץ אלהים דאלפין מִצְרַיִם מצר לָרֹעַ: 20 וַתֹּאכַלְנָה
הַפָּרוֹת הָרַקּוֹת וְהָרָעוֹת אֵת שֶׁבַע אלהים דיודין + ע"ב הַפָּרוֹת הָרִאשֹׁנוֹת
הַבְּרִיאֹת: 21 וַתָּבֹאנָה אֶל־קִרְבֶּנָה וְלֹא נוֹדַע כִּי־בָאוּ אֶל־
קִרְבֶּנָה וּמַרְאֵיהֶן רַע כַּאֲשֶׁר בַּתְּחִלָּה וָאִיקָץ: 22 וָאֵרֶא בַּחֲלֹמִי
וְהִנֵּה מ"ה יה | שֶׁבַע אלהים דיודין + ע"ב שִׁבֳּלִים עֹלֹת אבגיתצ, ושר, אהבת חנם
בְּקָנֶה ע"ה = ציון, קנאה, ו"פ יהוה, ה"פ אל אֶחָד אהבה, דאגה מְלֵאֹת וְטֹבוֹת: 23 וְהִנֵּה
מ"ה יה שֶׁבַע אלהים דיודין + ע"ב שִׁבֳּלִים צְנֻמוֹת דַּקּוֹת שְׁדֻפוֹת קָדִים
צֹמְחוֹת אַחֲרֵיהֶם: 24 וַתִּבְלַעְןָ הַשִּׁבֳּלִים הַדַּקֹּת אֵת שֶׁבַע
אלהים דיודין + ע"ב הַשִּׁבֳּלִים הַטֹּבוֹת וָאֹמַר אֶל־הַחַרְטֻמִּים וְאֵין מַגִּיד
לִי: 25 וַיֹּאמֶר יוֹסֵף ציון, קנאה, ו"פ יהוה, ה"פ אל אֶל־פַּרְעֹה חֲלוֹם פַּרְעֹה
אֶחָד אהבה, דאגה הוּא אֵת אֲשֶׁר הָאֱלֹהִים ילה, מום עֹשֶׂה הִגִּיד לְפַרְעֹה:
26 שֶׁבַע אלהים דיודין + ע"ב פָּרֹת הַטֹּבֹת שֶׁבַע אלהים דיודין + ע"ב שָׁנִים הֵנָּה
מ"ה יה וְשֶׁבַע אלהים דיודין + ע"ב הַשִּׁבֳּלִים הַטֹּבֹת שֶׁבַע אלהים דיודין + ע"ב
שָׁנִים הֵנָּה מ"ה יה חֲלוֹם אֶחָד אהבה, דאגה הוּא: 27 וְשֶׁבַע אלהים דיודין + ע"ב
הַפָּרוֹת הָרַקּוֹת וְהָרָעֹת הָעֹלֹת אבגיתצ, ושר, אהבת חנם אַחֲרֵיהֶן שֶׁבַע
אלהים דיודין + ע"ב שָׁנִים הֵנָּה מ"ה יה וְשֶׁבַע אלהים דיודין + ע"ב הַשִּׁבֳּלִים

[26] The seven good cows are seven years, and the seven good heads of grain are seven years; it is one and the same dream. [27] The seven lean, ugly cows that came up afterward are seven years, and so are the seven worthless heads of grain scorched by the east wind: They are seven years of famine. [28] "It is just as I said to Pharaoh: God has shown Pharaoh what He is about to do.

[29] Seven years of great abundance are coming throughout the land of Egypt, [30] but seven years of famine will follow them. Then all the abundance in Egypt will be forgotten, and the famine will ravage the land.

[31] The abundance in the land will not be remembered because the famine that follows it will be so severe.

[32] The reason the dream was given to Pharaoh in two forms is that the matter has been firmly decided by God, and God will do it soon.

[33] "And now let Pharaoh look for a discerning and wise man and put him in charge of the land of Egypt.

[34] Let Pharaoh appoint commissioners over the land to take a fifth of the harvest of Egypt during the seven years of abundance.

[35] They should collect all the food of these good years that are coming and store up the grain under the authority of Pharaoh, to be kept in the cities for food.

[36] This food should be held in reserve for the country, to be used during the seven years of famine that will come upon Egypt, so that the country may not be ruined by the famine."

וִישִׁיתֵהוּ

Genesis 41:33 – Joseph became Pharaoh's closest advisor, second in rank only to the ruler himself. This was the person who had been sold into slavery and who had spent years in prison, yet he became second in power only to the king of Egypt. From this episode, we learn that if we keep the right consciousness, everything will turn out well for us. The opposite is also true: If we are not thinking of our fellow man as well as ourselves, the present may seem rewarding, but eventually things will fall apart.

A commentary says that just as Joseph was small in his own eyes when he was a slave, so he was small in his own eyes after he became a viceroy as well. (*Shemot Rabba 1:7*) Such humility always goes hand-in-hand with true spiritual greatness because a person like Joseph truly believes that all his powers and sustenance come from God.

לְפִקָּדוֹן

Genesis 41:36 – Joseph had a plan to save Egypt in the years of famine, and because he had control over all the food in Egypt, he was able to carry out his plan. The *Zohar* says:

> *It is written: "And Joseph was the governor of the land." Joseph is the sun,*

הָרֵקוֹת שְׁדֻפוֹת הַקָּדִים יִהְיוּ שֶׁבַע אלהים דיודין + ע"ב שְׁנֵי רָעָב
רבוע אלהים + ע"ב: 28 הוּא הַדָּבָר ראה אֲשֶׁר דִּבַּרְתִּי ראה אֶל־פַּרְעֹה
אֲשֶׁר הָאֱלֹהִים ילה, מום עֹשֶׂה הֶרְאָה אֶת־פַּרְעֹה: 29 הִנֵּה שֶׁבַע
אלהים דיודין + ע"ב שָׁנִים בָּאוֹת שָׂבָע אלהים דיודין + ע"ב גָּדוֹל להח, מבה, יזל, אום
בְּכָל לכב ־אֶרֶץ אלהים דאלפין מִצְרָיִם מצר: 30 וְקָמוּ שֶׁבַע אלהים דיודין + ע"ב
שְׁנֵי רָעָב רבוע אלהים + ע"ב אַחֲרֵיהֶן וְנִשְׁכַּח כָּל ילי ־הַשָּׂבָע אלהים דיודין + ע"ב
בְּאֶרֶץ אלהים דאלפין מִצְרָיִם מצר וְכִלָּה הָרָעָב רבוע אלהים + ע"ב אֶת־הָאָרֶץ
אלהים דההין ע"ה: 31 וְלֹא־יִוָּדַע הַשָּׂבָע אלהים דיודין + ע"ב בָּאָרֶץ אלהים דאלפין
מִפְּנֵי הָרָעָב רבוע אלהים + ע"ב הַהוּא אַחֲרֵי־כֵן כִּי־כָבֵד הוּא
מְאֹד מ"ה: 32 וְעַל הִשָּׁנוֹת הַחֲלוֹם אֶל־פַּרְעֹה פַּעֲמָיִם כִּי־נָכוֹן
הַדָּבָר ראה מֵעִם הָאֱלֹהִים ילה, מום וּמְמַהֵר הָאֱלֹהִים ילה, מום לַעֲשֹׂתוֹ:
33 וְעַתָּה יֵרֶא פַרְעֹה אִישׁ ע"ה קנ"א קס"א נָבוֹן וְחָכָם וִישִׁיתֵהוּ עַל
־אֶרֶץ אלהים דאלפין מִצְרָיִם מצר: 34 יַעֲשֶׂה פַרְעֹה וְיַפְקֵד פְּקִדִים עַל
־הָאָרֶץ אלהים דההין ע"ה וְחִמֵּשׁ אֶת־אֶרֶץ אלהים דאלפין מִצְרַיִם מצר בְּשֶׁבַע
אלהים דיודין + ע"ב שְׁנֵי הַשָּׂבָע אלהים דיודין + ע"ב: 35 וְיִקְבְּצוּ אֶת־כָּל ילי ־אֹכֶל
הַשָּׁנִים הַטֹּבוֹת הַבָּאֹת הָאֵלֶּה וְיִצְבְּרוּ־בָר תַּחַת יַד־פַּרְעֹה אֹכֶל
בֶּעָרִים וְשָׁמָרוּ: 36 וְהָיָה יהוה, יהה הָאֹכֶל לְפִקָּדוֹן לָאָרֶץ אלהים דאלפין
לְשֶׁבַע אלהים דיודין + ע"ב שְׁנֵי הָרָעָב רבוע אלהים + ע"ב אֲשֶׁר תִּהְיֶיןָ

ZEIR ANPIN, FOR JOSEPH IS YESOD OF ZEIR ANPIN, which rules over the moon, THE NUKVA, shining upon and sustaining her. "...and he it was that sold to all the people of the land," as the river that flows and comes out FROM EDEN, YESOD CALLED JOSEPH, supplies everybody with nourishment.

– The Zohar, Miketz 7:113

For us today, there are two people with whom we must connect to ensure sustenance. One is Joseph and the other is Rav Shimon bar Yochai. The importance of Rav Shimon in the matter of sustenance was revealed to Rav Berg by his teacher, Rav Brandwein: "Rav Brandwein said that I should always realize that Rav Shimon was with me. 'Have no fear,' he said, 'and be certain that all the money of the world is there in the treasury of Rav Shimon bar Yochai.'" (*Yedid Nafshi, p.26*)

37 The plan seemed good to Pharaoh and to all his officials. 38 So Pharaoh asked them, "Can we find anyone like this man, one in whom is the spirit of God?"

THIRD READING - JACOB - TIFERET

39 Then Pharaoh said to Joseph, "Since God has made all this known to you, there is no one so discerning and wise as you.

40 You shall be in charge of my palace, and all my people are to submit to your orders. Only with respect to the throne will I be greater than you."

41 So Pharaoh said to Joseph, "I hereby put you in charge of the whole land of Egypt."

42 Then Pharaoh took his signet ring from his finger and put it on Joseph's finger. He dressed him in robes of fine linen and put a gold chain around his neck.

43 He had him ride in a chariot as his second-in-command, and men shouted before him, "Make way!" Thus he put him in charge of the whole land of Egypt.

44 Then Pharaoh said to Joseph, "I am Pharaoh, but without your word no one will lift hand or foot in all Egypt."

45 Pharaoh gave Joseph the name Zaphenath-Paneah and gave him Asenath, daughter of Potiphera, priest of On, to be his wife. And Joseph went throughout the land of Egypt.

46 Joseph was thirty years old when he entered the service of Pharaoh, king of Egypt. And Joseph went out from Pharaoh's presence and traveled throughout Egypt.

אָסְנַת

Genesis 41:45 – Joseph married Asenath, the daughter of the wife of his former master, Potiphar. Asenath's mother was the very woman who had tried to seduce Joseph. When people come into our lives, we must recognize that we have a *tikkun* with them. We do not always know how long it will take to complete our *tikkun*—it could be a minute, a few weeks, or a lifetime—so it is important to neither underestimate nor overestimate the importance to our lives of all the people we meet.

A commentary says that Asenath was actually the daughter of Dinah and that the angel Michael had brought her down to Egypt into the house of Potiphar, where Potiphar's wife raised her as a daughter. (*Yalkut Shimoni, Vayishlach 134*) All the major events of Joseph's life occurred through Divine intervention, so closely was he linked to the Divine Plan.

בְּאֶרֶץ אלהים דאלפין מִצְרָיִם מצר וְלֹא־תִכָּרֵת הָאָרֶץ אלהים דההין ע״ה בָּרָעָב
רבוע אלהים - ע״ב: 37 וַיִּיטַב הַדָּבָר ראה בְּעֵינֵי ריבוע מ״ה פַרְעֹה וּבְעֵינֵי
ריבוע מ״ה כָּל ילי ־עֲבָדָיו: 38 וַיֹּאמֶר פַּרְעֹה אֶל־עֲבָדָיו הֲנִמְצָא כָזֶה
אִישׁ ע״ה קנ״א קס״א אֲשֶׁר רוּחַ מלוי אלהים דיודין אֱלֹהִים ילה, מום בּוֹ:

THIRD READING - JACOB - TIFERET

39 וַיֹּאמֶר פַּרְעֹה אֶל־יוֹסֵף ציון, קנאה, ו״פ יהוה, ה״פ אל אַחֲרֵי הוֹדִיעַ אֱלֹהִים
ילה, מום אוֹתְךָ אֶת־כָּל ילי ־זֹאת אֵין־נָבוֹן וְחָכָם כָּמוֹךָ אלהים: 40 אַתָּה
תִּהְיֶה עַל־בֵּיתִי ב״פ ראה וְעַל־פִּיךָ יִשַּׁק כָּל ילי ־עַמִּי רַק הַכִּסֵּא אלהים
אֶגְדַּל מִמֶּךָּ: 41 וַיֹּאמֶר פַּרְעֹה אֶל־יוֹסֵף ציון, קנאה, ו״פ יהוה, ה״פ אל רְאֵה
ראה נָתַתִּי אֹתְךָ עַל כָּל ילי, עמם ־אֶרֶץ אלהים דאלפין מִצְרָיִם מצר: 42 וַיָּסַר
פַּרְעֹה אֶת־טַבַּעְתּוֹ מֵעַל עלם יָדוֹ וַיִּתֵּן אֹתָהּ עַל־יַד יוֹסֵף
ציון, קנאה, ו״פ יהוה, ה״פ אל וַיַּלְבֵּשׁ אֹתוֹ בִּגְדֵי־שֵׁשׁ וַיָּשֶׂם רְבִד הַזָּהָב וזהו
עַל־צַוָּארוֹ: 43 וַיַּרְכֵּב אֹתוֹ בְּמִרְכֶּבֶת הַמִּשְׁנֶה אֲשֶׁר־לוֹ וַיִּקְרְאוּ
לְפָנָיו אַבְרֵךְ וְנָתוֹן אֹתוֹ עַל כָּל ילי, עמם ־אֶרֶץ אלהים דאלפין מִצְרָיִם
מצר: 44 וַיֹּאמֶר פַּרְעֹה אֶל־יוֹסֵף ציון, קנאה, ו״פ יהוה, ה״פ אל אֲנִי אני פַרְעֹה
וּבִלְעָדֶיךָ לֹא־יָרִים אִישׁ ע״ה קנ״א קס״א אֶת־יָדוֹ וְאֶת־רַגְלוֹ בְּכָל לכב
־אֶרֶץ אלהים דאלפין מִצְרָיִם מצר: 45 וַיִּקְרָא עם ה׳ אותיות = ב״פ קס״א פַרְעֹה
שֵׁם שדי יהוה ־יוֹסֵף ציון, קנאה, ו״פ יהוה, ה״פ אל צָפְנַת פַּעְנֵחַ וַיִּתֶּן י״פ מלוי ע״ב ־לוֹ
אֶת־אָסְנַת יהוה מצפצ יהוה ע״ה ברבוע בַּת־פּוֹטִי פֶרַע כֹּהֵן מלה אֹן לְאִשָּׁה
וַיֵּצֵא יוֹסֵף ציון, קנאה, ו״פ יהוה, ה״פ אל עַל־אֶרֶץ אלהים דאלפין מִצְרָיִם מצר:
46 וְיוֹסֵף ציון, קנאה, ו״פ יהוה, ה״פ אל בֶּן־שְׁלֹשִׁים שָׁנָה בְּעָמְדוֹ לִפְנֵי פַּרְעֹה
מֶלֶךְ־מִצְרָיִם מצר וַיֵּצֵא יוֹסֵף ציון, קנאה, ו״פ יהוה, ה״פ אל מִלִּפְנֵי פַרְעֹה

47 During the seven years of abundance the land produced plentifully.

48 Joseph collected all the food produced in those seven years of abundance in Egypt and stored it in the cities. In each city he put the food grown in the fields surrounding it.

49 Joseph stored up huge quantities of grain, like the sand of the sea; it was so much that he stopped keeping records because it was beyond measure.

50 Before the years of famine came, two sons were born to Joseph by Asenath, daughter of Potiphera, priest of On.

51 Joseph named his firstborn Manasseh and said, "It is because God has made me forget all my trouble and all my father's household."

52 The second son he named Ephraim and said, "It is because God has made me fruitful in the land of my suffering."

FOURTH READING - MOSES - NETZACH

53 The seven years of abundance in Egypt came to an end, 54 and the seven years of famine began, just as Joseph had said. There was famine in all the other lands, but in the whole land of Egypt there was food.

55 When all Egypt began to feel the famine, the people cried to Pharaoh for food. Then Pharaoh told all the Egyptians, "Go to Joseph and do what he tells you."

56 When the famine had spread over the whole country, Joseph opened the storehouses and sold grain to the Egyptians, for the famine was severe throughout Egypt.

רָעָב

Genesis 41:54 – The famine also devastated the lands around Egypt, yet everyone was able to go to Joseph and get provisions. Just as Joseph served as a source of sustenance during the period of famine, there are certain times of the year that generate more sustenance than other times in the form of extra energy. This energy may be either positive or negative, but by connecting with the periods of positive energy, we can gain strength for difficult times. The energy of Shabbat, for example, can sustain us for the entire week.

וַיַּעֲבֹר רפ״ח, ע״ב - רי״ו בְּכָל לכב ־אֶרֶץ אלהים דאלפין מִצְרָיִם מצר׃ 47 וַתַּעַשׂ
הָאָרֶץ אלהים דההין ע״ה בְּשֶׁבַע אלהים דיודין - ע״ב שְׁנֵי הַשָּׂבָע לִקְמָצִים׃
48 וַיִּקְבֹּץ אֶת־כָּל ילי ־אֹכֶל | שֶׁבַע אלהים דיודין - ע״ב שָׁנִים אֲשֶׁר הָיוּ
בְּאֶרֶץ אלהים דאלפין מִצְרַיִם מצר וַיִּתֶּן י״פ מלוי ע״ב ־אֹכֶל בֶּעָרִים אֹכֶל
שְׂדֵה־הָעִיר סנדלפון, ערי, סנדלפון אֲשֶׁר סְבִיבֹתֶיהָ נָתַן בְּתוֹכָהּ׃ 49 וַיִּצְבֹּר
יוֹסֵף ציון, קנאה, ו״פ יהוה, ה״פ אל בַּר כְּחוֹל ריבוע אהיה הַיָּם ילי הַרְבֵּה מְאֹד מ״ה
עַד כִּי־חָדַל לִסְפֹּר כִּי־אֵין מִסְפָּר׃ 50 וּלְיוֹסֵף ציון, קנאה, ו״פ יהוה, ה״פ אל
יֻלַּד שְׁנֵי בָנִים בְּטֶרֶם תָּבוֹא שְׁנַת הָרָעָב רבוע אלהים - ע״ב אֲשֶׁר
יָלְדָה־לּוֹ אָסְנַת יהוה מצפצ יהוה ברבוע ע״ה בַּת־פּוֹטִי פֶרַע כֹּהֵן מלה אוֹן׃
51 וַיִּקְרָא עם ה׳ אותיות = ב״פ קס״א יוֹסֵף ציון, קנאה, ו״פ יהוה, ה״פ אל אֶת־שֵׁם שדי יהוה
הַבְּכוֹר מְנַשֶּׁה כִּי־נַשַּׁנִי אֱלֹהִים ילה, מום אֶת־כָּל ילי ־עֲמָלִי וְאֵת כָּל
ילי ־בֵּית ב״פ ראה אָבִי׃ 52 וְאֵת שֵׁם שדי יהוה הַשֵּׁנִי קָרָא אֶפְרָיִם
אל מצפץ כִּי־הִפְרַנִי אֱלֹהִים ילה, מום בְּאֶרֶץ אלהים דאלפין עָנְיִי ריבוע מ״ה׃

FOURTH READING - MOSES - NETZACH

53 וַתִּכְלֶינָה שֶׁבַע אלהים דיודין - ע״ב שְׁנֵי הַשָּׂבָע אלהים דיודין - ע״ב אֲשֶׁר
הָיָה יהה בְּאֶרֶץ אלהים דאלפין מִצְרָיִם מצר׃ 54 וַתְּחִלֶּינָה שֶׁבַע אלהים דיודין - ע״ב
שְׁנֵי הָרָעָב רבוע אלהים - ע״ב לָבוֹא כַּאֲשֶׁר אָמַר יוֹסֵף ציון, קנאה, ו״פ יהוה, ה״פ אל
וַיְהִי רָעָב רבוע אלהים - ע״ב בְּכָל לכב ־הָאֲרָצוֹת וּבְכָל לכב ־אֶרֶץ אלהים דאלפין
מִצְרַיִם מצר הָיָה יהה לָחֶם ג״פ יהוה׃ 55 וַתִּרְעַב כָּל ילי ־אֶרֶץ אלהים דאלפין
מִצְרַיִם מצר וַיִּצְעַק הָעָם אֶל־פַּרְעֹה לַלָּחֶם ג״פ יהוה וַיֹּאמֶר פַּרְעֹה
לְכָל יה - אדני ־מִצְרַיִם מצר לְכוּ אֶל־יוֹסֵף ציון, קנאה, ו״פ יהוה, ה״פ אל
אֲשֶׁר־יֹאמַר לָכֶם תַּעֲשׂוּ׃ 56 וְהָרָעָב רבוע אלהים - ע״ב הָיָה יהה עַל

57 And all the countries came to Egypt to buy grain from Joseph, because the famine was severe in all the world.

42:1 When Jacob learned that there was grain in Egypt, he said to his sons, "Why do you just keep looking at each other?"

2 He continued, "I have heard that there is grain in Egypt. Go down there and buy some for us, so that we may live and not die."

3 Then ten of Joseph's brothers went down to buy grain from Egypt.

4 But Jacob did not send Benjamin, Joseph's brother, with the others, because he was afraid that harm might come to him.

5 So Israel's sons were among those who went to buy grain, for the famine was in the land of Canaan also.

6 Now Joseph was the governor of the land, the one who sold grain to all its people. So when Joseph's brothers arrived, they bowed down to him with their faces to the ground.

7 As soon as Joseph saw his brothers, he recognized them, but he pretended to be a

---

רְדוּ

Genesis 42:2 – Jacob sent his sons to Egypt to get food. Rashi tells us that Jacob said, "Get you down," (Heb. *redu*) not just "Go." Since the numerical value of *redu* is 210, this is an allusion to the 210 years of physical slavery that the people of Israel would suffer in Egypt. When Joseph's brothers entered Egypt, this was the true start of the Exile in that country. Because this is the seed level of the Exile, we have the power through reading this section of the Bible to gain freedom from any spiritual "Egypt" or enslavement that we may otherwise experience in our lives.

וַיַּרְא

Genesis 42:7 – When Joseph saw his brothers coming to ask for food, he was very cruel to them and accused them of being spies. He did this because he knew that they needed to be spiritually cleansed for the sin of selling him into slavery. Joseph wanted to be an agent of their cleansing, rather than leaving it to Satan, because he could administer it in a merciful way.

If there is a cleansing that needs to take place in our life, it is first undertaken with mercy by the Light. If the person resists, however, Satan takes over, and the cleansing becomes more painful.

> *God is AWARE that Samael, who is the patron of Esau, will come to remind the Creator of the sins of Israel, and will have accumulated all THEIR INIQUITIES to have them available for the Day of Judgment. And God will give them a remedy beforehand so that for each and every iniquity, God smote and cleansed them with sufferings, little by little. That is the meaning of "cleansing" BEFOREHAND, through sufferings. As a result of this, at the true trial IN THE FUTURE, "I will not cleanse you" from the world through judgment since you have already suffered affliction AT EACH GIVEN TIME, little by little.*
>
> *– The Zohar, Balak 20:274*

כָּל יל״י, עמם ־פְּנֵי וחכמה + בינה הָאָרֶץ אלהים דההין ע״ה וַיִּפְתַּח יוֹסֵף ציון, קנאה, ר״פ יהוה, ה״פ אל
אֶת־כָּל יל״י ־אֲשֶׁר בָּהֶם וַיִּשְׁבֹּר לְמִצְרַיִם מצר וַיֶּחֱזַק פהל הָרָעָב
רבוע אלהים + ע״ב בְּאֶרֶץ אלהים דאלפין מִצְרָיִם מצר׃ 57 וְכָל יל״י ־הָאָרֶץ
אלהים דההין ע״ה בָּאוּ מִצְרַיְמָה מצר לִשְׁבֹּר אֶל־יוֹסֵף ציון, קנאה, ר״פ יהוה, ה״פ אל
כִּי־חָזַק פהל הָרָעָב רבוע אלהים + ע״ב בְּכָל לכב ־הָאָרֶץ אלהים דההין ע״ה׃
42 1 וַיַּרְא יַעֲקֹב יאהדונהי + אידהנויה כִּי יֶשׁ־שֶׁבֶר בְּמִצְרָיִם מצר וַיֹּאמֶר
יַעֲקֹב יאהדונהי + אידהנויה לְבָנָיו לָמָּה תִּתְרָאוּ׃ 2 וַיֹּאמֶר הִנֵּה מ״ה יה
שָׁמַעְתִּי כִּי יֶשׁ־שֶׁבֶר בְּמִצְרָיִם מצר רְדוּ י״פ אהיה ־שָׁמָּה מהש
וְשִׁבְרוּ־לָנוּ אלהים, מום מִשָּׁם וְנִחְיֶה וְלֹא נָמוּת׃ 3 וַיֵּרְדוּ רי״י אֲחֵי־יוֹסֵף
ציון, קנאה, ר״פ יהוה, ה״פ אל עֲשָׂרָה לִשְׁבֹּר בָּר מִמִּצְרָיִם מצר׃ 4 וְאֶת־בִּנְיָמִין
אֲחִי יוֹסֵף ציון, קנאה, ר״פ יהוה, ה״פ אל לֹא־שָׁלַח יַעֲקֹב יאהדונהי + אידהנויה אֶת־
אֶחָיו כִּי אָמַר פֶּן־יִקְרָאֶנּוּ אָסוֹן׃ 5 וַיָּבֹאוּ בְּנֵי יִשְׂרָאֵל לִשְׁבֹּר
בְּתוֹךְ הַבָּאִים כִּי־הָיָה יהה הָרָעָב רבוע אלהים + ע״ב בְּאֶרֶץ אלהים דאלפין
כְּנָעַן׃ 6 וְיוֹסֵף ציון, קנאה, ר״פ יהוה, ה״פ אל הוּא הַשַּׁלִּיט עַל־הָאָרֶץ
אלהים דההין ע״ה הוּא הַמַּשְׁבִּיר לְכָל יה + אדני ־עַם הָאָרֶץ אלהים דההין ע״ה
וַיָּבֹאוּ אֲחֵי יוֹסֵף ציון, קנאה, ר״פ יהוה, ה״פ אל וַיִּשְׁתַּחֲווּ־לוֹ אַפַּיִם אָרְצָה׃
7 וַיַּרְא יוֹסֵף ציון, קנאה, ר״פ יהוה, ה״פ אל אֶת־אֶחָיו וַיַּכִּרֵם וַיִּתְנַכֵּר
אֲלֵיהֶם וַיְדַבֵּר ראה אִתָּם קָשׁוֹת וַיֹּאמֶר אֲלֵהֶם מֵאַיִן בָּאתֶם
וַיֹּאמְרוּ מֵאֶרֶץ אלהים דאלפין כְּנַעַן לִשְׁבָּר־אֹכֶל׃ 8 וַיַּכֵּר יוֹסֵף
ציון, קנאה, ר״פ יהוה, ה״פ אל אֶת־אֶחָיו וְהֵם לֹא הִכִּרֻהוּ׃ 9 וַיִּזְכֹּר
ע״ב + קס״א, יהי אור ע״ה יוֹסֵף ציון, קנאה, ר״פ יהוה, ה״פ אל אֵת הַחֲלֹמוֹת אֲשֶׁר חָלַם
לָהֶם ג״פ יהוה וַיֹּאמֶר אֲלֵהֶם מְרַגְּלִים אַתֶּם לִרְאוֹת אֶת־עֶרְוַת
הָאָרֶץ אלהים דההין ע״ה בָּאתֶם׃ 10 וַיֹּאמְרוּ אֵלָיו לֹא אֲדֹנִי וַעֲבָדֶיךָ
בָּאוּ לִשְׁבָּר־אֹכֶל׃ 11 כֻּלָּנוּ בְּנֵי אִישׁ ע״ה קנ״א קס״א ־אֶחָד אהבה, דאגה נָחְנוּ

stranger and spoke harshly to them. "Where do you come from?" he asked. "From the land of Canaan," they replied, "to buy food."

[8] Although Joseph recognized his brothers, they did not recognize him. [9] Then he remembered his dreams about them and said to them, "You are spies! You have come to see where our land is unprotected." [10] "No, my lord," they answered. "Your servants have come to buy food. [11] We are all the sons of one man. Your servants are honest men, not spies."

[12] "No!" he said to them. "You have come to see where our land is unprotected."

[13] But they replied, "Your servants were twelve brothers, the sons of one man, who lives in the land of Canaan. The youngest is now with our father, and one is no more."

[14] Joseph said to them, "It is just as I told you: You are spies!

[15] And this is how you will be tested: As surely as Pharaoh lives you will not leave this place unless your youngest brother comes here.

[16] Send one of your number to get your brother; the rest of you will be kept in prison, so that your words may be tested to see if you are telling the truth. If you are not, then as surely as Pharaoh lives you are spies!"

[17] And he put them all in custody for three days. [18] On the third day, Joseph said to them, "Do this and you will live, for I fear God:

FIFTH READING - AARON - HOD

[19] If you are honest men, let one of your brothers stay here in prison, while the rest of you go and take grain back for your starving households.

אֲשֵׁמִים

Genesis 42:21 – Out of nowhere, one of the brothers remarked, "Maybe this is happening because we sold our brother…" We should note here that the brothers had gone through many years of spiritual processes; each night, they examined their shortcomings and they searched their souls on Yom Kippur, but they had never before truly experienced the consequences of the wrong they had done to Joseph. It was only when they experienced this physical cleansing—suffering through famine, having to answer to Joseph, and being accused of a crime they did not commit—that they became aware of their true misdeeds. Sometimes, we also need a physical manifestation of our transgressions (i.e., a cleansing by Satan) before we finally recognize our own misdeeds.

כֵּנִים אֲנַחְנוּ לֹא־הָיוּ עֲבָדֶיךָ מְרַגְּלִים: 12 וַיֹּאמֶר אֲלֵהֶם לֹא כִּי־
עֶרְוַת הָאָרֶץ אלהים דההין ע"ה בָּאתֶם לִרְאוֹת ר"ת הבל: 13 וַיֹּאמְרוּ שְׁנֵים
עָשָׂר עֲבָדֶיךָ אַחִים | אֲנַחְנוּ בְּנֵי אִישׁ ע"ה קנ"א קס"א ־אֶחָד אהבה, דאגה
בְּאֶרֶץ אלהים דאלפין כְּנָעַן וְהִנֵּה הַקָּטֹן אֶת־אָבִינוּ הַיּוֹם נגד, זן, מזבח
וְהָאֶחָד אהבה, דאגה אֵינֶנּוּ: 14 וַיֹּאמֶר אֲלֵהֶם יוֹסֵף ציון, קנאה, ו"פ יהוה, ה"פ אל
הוּא אֲשֶׁר דִּבַּרְתִּי ראה אֲלֵכֶם לֵאמֹר מְרַגְּלִים אַתֶּם: 15 בְּזֹאת
תִּבָּחֵנוּ חֵי פַרְעֹה אִם יוהך ־תֵּצְאוּ מִזֶּה כִּי אִם יוהך ־בְּבוֹא אֲחִיכֶם
הַקָּטֹן הֵנָּה מ"ה יה: 16 שִׁלְחוּ מִכֶּם אֶחָד אהבה, דאגה וְיִקַּח חעם אֶת־
אֲחִיכֶם וְאַתֶּם הֵאָסְרוּ וְיִבָּחֲנוּ דִּבְרֵיכֶם ראה הַאֱמֶת אהיה פעמים אהיה, ז"פ ס"ג
אִתְּכֶם וְאִם יוהך ־לֹא חֵי פַרְעֹה כִּי מְרַגְּלִים אַתֶּם: 17 וַיֶּאֱסֹף
אֹתָם אֶל־מִשְׁמָר שְׁלֹשֶׁת יָמִים נלך: 18 וַיֹּאמֶר אֲלֵהֶם יוֹסֵף
ציון, קנאה, ו"פ יהוה, ה"פ אל בַּיּוֹם נגד, זן, מזבח הַשְּׁלִישִׁי זֹאת עֲשׂוּ וִחְיוּ אֶת־
הָאֱלֹהִים ילה, מום אֲנִי אני יָרֵא:

FIFTH READING - AARON - HOD

19 אִם יוהך ־כֵּנִים אַתֶּם אֲחִיכֶם אֶחָד אהבה, דאגה יֵאָסֵר בְּבֵית ב"פ ראה
מִשְׁמַרְכֶם וְאַתֶּם לְכוּ הָבִיאוּ שֶׁבֶר רַעֲבוֹן בָּתֵּיכֶם ב"פ ראה:
20 וְאֶת־אֲחִיכֶם הַקָּטֹן תָּבִיאוּ אֵלַי וְיֵאָמְנוּ דִבְרֵיכֶם ראה וְלֹא
תָמוּתוּ וַיַּעֲשׂוּ־כֵן: 21 וַיֹּאמְרוּ אִישׁ ע"ה קנ"א קס"א אֶל־אָחִיו אֲבָל
אֲשֵׁמִים | אֲנַחְנוּ עַל־אָחִינוּ אֲשֶׁר רָאִינוּ צָרַת נַפְשׁוֹ בְּהִתְחַנְנוֹ
אֵלֵינוּ וְלֹא שָׁמָעְנוּ עַל־כֵּן בָּאָה אֵלֵינוּ הַצָּרָה אלהים דההין הַזֹּאת:
22 וַיַּעַן רְאוּבֵן ג"פ אלהים אֹתָם לֵאמֹר הֲלוֹא אָמַרְתִּי אֲלֵיכֶם |
לֵאמֹר אַל־תֶּחֶטְאוּ בַיֶּלֶד וְלֹא שְׁמַעְתֶּם וְגַם יגל ־דָּמוֹ הִנֵּה מ"ה יה

*[20] But you must bring your youngest brother to me, so that your words may be verified
and that you may not die." This they proceeded to do.*

*[21] They said to one another, "Surely we are being punished because of our brother.
We saw how distressed he was when he pleaded with us for his life, but we would not
listen; that's why this distress has come upon us." [22] Reuben replied, "Didn't I tell you
not to sin against the boy? But you wouldn't listen! Now we must give an accounting
for his blood." [23] They did not realize that Joseph could understand them, since he
was using an interpreter.*

*[24] He turned away from them and began to weep, but then turned back and spoke to
them again. He had Simeon taken from them and bound before their eyes. [25] Joseph
gave orders to fill their bags with grain, to put each man's silver back in his sack, and
to give them provisions for their journey. After this was done for them, [26] they loaded
their grain on their donkeys and left. [27] At the place where they stopped for the night,
one of them opened his sack to get feed for his donkey, and he saw his silver in the
mouth of his sack.*

*[28] "My silver has been returned," he said to his brothers. "Here it is in my sack." Their
hearts sank and they turned to each other trembling and said, "What is this that God
has done to us?" [29] When they came to their father Jacob in the land of Canaan, they
told him all that had happened to them. They said, [30] "The man who is lord over the
land spoke harshly to us and treated us as though we were spying on the land. [31] But
we said to him, 'We are honest men; we are not spies. [32] We were twelve brothers,
sons of one father. One is no more, and the youngest is now with our father in
Canaan.' [33] Then the man who is lord over the land said to us, 'This is how I will know
whether you are honest men: Leave one of your brothers here with me, and take food
for your starving households and go.*

*[34] But bring your youngest brother to me so I will know that you are not spies but
honest men. Then I will give your brother back to you, and you can trade in the
land.' "*

וַיְצַו

Genesis 42:25 – Joseph sent the brothers back to their father with some food, but he only let them go on one condition: They had to bring back their youngest brother, Benjamin, to him. Rashi said that Joseph took Simon hostage as surety because he remembered what had happened in Nablus, the city of Shechem, and he knew that if Simon and Levi were together, they might conspire to kill him.

וַיָּבֹאוּ

Genesis 42:29 – Returning home, the brothers told Jacob what had happened in Egypt. Reuben asked his family to send Benjamin with him to Egypt, and he swore on the heads of his own two sons that he would bring Benjamin safely back again. Jacob refused the offer because he no longer trusted Reuben; he remembered that Reuben had been in charge that day so many years earlier when Joseph had disappeared.

נִדְרָשׁ׃ 23 וְהֵם לֹא יָדְעוּ כִּי שֹׁמֵעַ יוֹסֵף ציון, קנאה, ו"פ יהוה, ה"פ אל כִּי
הַמֵּלִיץ בֵּינֹתָם׃ 24 וַיִּסֹּב מֵעֲלֵיהֶם וַיֵּבְךְּ וַיָּשָׁב אֲלֵהֶם וַיְדַבֵּר ראה
אֲלֵהֶם וַיִּקַּח וזעם מֵאִתָּם אֶת־שִׁמְעוֹן וַיֶּאֱסֹר אֹתוֹ לְעֵינֵיהֶם ריבוע מ"ה׃
25 וַיְצַו פוי יוֹסֵף ציון, קנאה, ו"פ יהוה, ה"פ אל וַיְמַלְאוּ אֶת־כְּלֵיהֶם בָּר וּלְהָשִׁיב
כַּסְפֵּיהֶם אִישׁ ע"ה קנ"א קס"א אֶל־שַׂקּוֹ וְלָתֵת לָהֶם צֵדָה לַדָּרֶךְ ב"פ יב"ק
וַיַּעַשׂ לָהֶם כֵּן׃ 26 וַיִּשְׂאוּ אֶת־שִׁבְרָם עַל־חֲמֹרֵיהֶם וַיֵּלְכוּ מִשָּׁם׃
27 וַיִּפְתַּח הָאֶחָד אהבה, דאגה אֶת־שַׂקּוֹ לָתֵת מִסְפּוֹא לַחֲמֹרוֹ בַּמָּלוֹן
וַיַּרְא אֶת־כַּסְפּוֹ וְהִנֵּה מ"ה יה ־הוּא בְּפִי אַמְתַּחְתּוֹ׃ 28 וַיֹּאמֶר אֶל־
אֶחָיו הוּשַׁב כַּסְפִּי וְגַם הִנֵּה בְאַמְתַּחְתִּי וַיֵּצֵא לִבָּם וַיֶּחֶרְדוּ אִישׁ
ע"ה קנ"א קס"א אֶל־אָחִיו לֵאמֹר מַה מ"ה ־זֹּאת עָשָׂה אֱלֹהִים ילה, מום לָנוּ
אלהים, מום׃ 29 וַיָּבֹאוּ אֶל־יַעֲקֹב יאהדונהי - אידהנויה אֲבִיהֶם אַרְצָה
אלהים דההין ע"ה כְּנָעַן וַיַּגִּידוּ ייז לוֹ אֵת כָּל ילי ־הַקֹּרֹת אֹתָם לֵאמֹר׃
30 דִּבֶּר ראה הָאִישׁ ז"פ אדם אֲדֹנֵי הָאָרֶץ אלהים דההין ע"ה אִתָּנוּ קָשׁוֹת
וַיִּתֵּן אֹתָנוּ כִּמְרַגְּלִים אֶת־הָאָרֶץ אלהים דההין ע"ה׃ 31 וַנֹּאמֶר אֵלָיו
כֵּנִים אֲנָחְנוּ לֹא הָיִינוּ מְרַגְּלִים׃ 32 שְׁנֵים־עָשָׂר אֲנַחְנוּ אַחִים
בְּנֵי אָבִינוּ הָאֶחָד אהבה, דאגה אֵינֶנּוּ וְהַקָּטֹן הַיּוֹם נגד, זן, מזבח אֶת־אָבִינוּ
בְּאֶרֶץ אלהים דאלפין כְּנָעַן׃ 33 וַיֹּאמֶר אֵלֵינוּ הָאִישׁ ז"פ אדם אֲדֹנֵי
הָאָרֶץ אלהים דההין ע"ה בְּזֹאת אֵדַע כִּי כֵנִים אַתֶּם אֲחִיכֶם הָאֶחָד
אהבה, דאגה הַנִּיחוּ אִתִּי וְאֶת־רַעֲבוֹן בָּתֵּיכֶם ב"פ ראה קְחוּ וָלֵכוּ׃
34 וְהָבִיאוּ אֶת־אֲחִיכֶם הַקָּטֹן אֵלַי וְאֵדְעָה כִּי לֹא מְרַגְּלִים
אַתֶּם כִּי כֵנִים אַתֶּם אֶת־אֲחִיכֶם אֶתֵּן לָכֶם וְאֶת־הָאָרֶץ
אלהים דההין ע"ה תִּסְחָרוּ׃ 35 וַיְהִי אל הֵם מְרִיקִים שַׂקֵּיהֶם וְהִנֵּה מ"ה יה
־אִישׁ ע"ה קנ"א קס"א צְרוֹר־כַּסְפּוֹ בְּשַׂקּוֹ וַיִּרְאוּ אֶת־צְרֹרוֹת כַּסְפֵּיהֶם
הֵמָּה וַאֲבִיהֶם וַיִּירָאוּ׃ 36 וַיֹּאמֶר אֲלֵהֶם יַעֲקֹב יאהדונהי - אידהנויה

35 As they were emptying their sacks, there in each man's sack was his pouch of silver! When they and their father saw the money pouches, they were frightened.

36 Their father Jacob said to them, "You have deprived me of my children. Joseph is no more and Simeon is no more, and now you want to take Benjamin. Everything is against me!"

37 Then Reuben said to his father, "You may put both of my sons to death if I do not
bring him back to you. Entrust him to my care, and I will bring him back." 38 But
Jacob said, "My son will not go down there with you; his brother is dead and he is the only one left. If harm comes to him on the journey you are taking, you will bring my
gray head down to the grave in sorrow." 43 1 Now the famine was still severe in the
land. 2 So when they had eaten all the grain they had brought from Egypt, their father
said to them, "Go back and buy us a little more food."

3 But Judah said to him, "The man warned us solemnly, 'You will not see my face
again unless your brother is with you.' 4 If you will send our brother along with us, we
will go down and buy food for you. 5 But if you will not send him, we will not go down,
because the man said to us, 'You will not see my face again unless your brother is
with you.' " 6 Israel asked, "Why did you bring this trouble on me by telling the man
you had another brother?" 7 They replied, "The man questioned us closely about
ourselves and our family. 'Is your father still living?' he asked us. 'Do you have another brother?' We simply answered his questions. How were we to know he would say,
'Bring your brother down here'?" 8 Then Judah said to Israel his father, "Send the boy
along with me and we will go at once, so that we and you and our children may live and not die.

9 I myself will guarantee his safety; you can hold me personally responsible for him.

שֻׁבוּ

Genesis 43:2 – The famine persisted. As the provisions ran out, Jacob told his sons to go to Egypt for more food. The sons protested that they would not be able to get more food unless they took Benjamin along with them.

וְחָטָאתִי

Genesis 43:9 – Judah begged his father to let him be the one to take Benjamin to Egypt, saying that he would bear the blame if anything should happen to his youngest brother. With this action, Judah began his *tikkun*, or process of correction. Because it was he who had actually sold Joseph into slavery, he was now willing to undergo the necessary cleansing. It was this willingness that made it possible for the brothers and Joseph to be reunited—physically, emotionally, and spiritually.

Connecting to Judah helps us to initiate the correction process in our own lives. Whenever we take an action, the energy of that action comes back to us. Judah initiated the brothers' selling of Joseph, so he in turn became the instrument of their cleansing. If we show genuine love and care for others, this love and care will come back to us. If we show jealousy or anger toward others, this negativity will eventually reappear in our own lives. This is the Universal Law of Cause and Effect.

אֲבִיהֶם אֹתִי שִׁכַּלְתֶּם יוֹסֵף ציון, קנאה, ו"פ יהוה, ה"פ אל אֵינֶנּוּ וְשִׁמְעוֹן
אֵינֶנּוּ וְאֶת־בִּנְיָמִן תִּקָּחוּ עָלַי הָיוּ כֻלָּנָה׃ 37 וַיֹּאמֶר רְאוּבֵן ג"פ אלהים
אֶל־אָבִיו לֵאמֹר אֶת־שְׁנֵי בָנַי תָּמִית אִם יוהך ־לֹא אֲבִיאֶנּוּ אֵלֶיךָ
תְּנָה נתה, קס"א - קנ"א - קמ"ג אֹתוֹ עַל־יָדִי וַאֲנִי אני אֲשִׁיבֶנּוּ אֵלֶיךָ אני׃
38 וַיֹּאמֶר לֹא־יֵרֵד בְּנִי עִמָּכֶם כִּי־אָחִיו מֵת וְהוּא לְבַדּוֹ מ"ב
נִשְׁאָר וּקְרָאָהוּ אָסוֹן בַּדֶּרֶךְ ב"פ יב"ק אֲשֶׁר תֵּלְכוּ־בָהּ וְהוֹרַדְתֶּם
אֶת־שֵׂיבָתִי בְּיָגוֹן שְׁאוֹלָה׃ 43 1 וְהָרָעָב רבוע אלהים - ע"ב כָּבֵד בָּאָרֶץ
אלהים דאלפין׃ 2 וַיְהִי אל כַּאֲשֶׁר כִּלּוּ לֶאֱכֹל אֶת־הַשֶּׁבֶר אֲשֶׁר הֵבִיאוּ
מִמִּצְרָיִם מצר וַיֹּאמֶר אֲלֵיהֶם אֲבִיהֶם שֻׁבוּ שִׁבְרוּ־לָנוּ אלהים, מום
מְעַט־אֹכֶל׃ 3 וַיֹּאמֶר אֵלָיו יְהוּדָה לֵאמֹר הָעֵד הֵעִד בָּנוּ הָאִישׁ
ז"פ אדם לֵאמֹר לֹא־תִרְאוּ פָנַי חכמה - בינה בִּלְתִּי אֲחִיכֶם אִתְּכֶם׃
4 אִם יוהך ־יֶשְׁךָ מְשַׁלֵּחַ אֶת־אָחִינוּ אִתָּנוּ נֵרְדָה וְנִשְׁבְּרָה לְךָ
אֹכֶל׃ 5 וְאִם יוהך ־אֵינְךָ מְשַׁלֵּחַ לֹא נֵרֵד כִּי־הָאִישׁ ז"פ אדם אָמַר
אֵלֵינוּ לֹא־תִרְאוּ פָנַי חכמה - בינה בִּלְתִּי אֲחִיכֶם אִתְּכֶם׃ 6 וַיֹּאמֶר
יִשְׂרָאֵל לָמָה הֲרֵעֹתֶם לִי לְהַגִּיד לָאִישׁ ע"ה קנ"א קס"א הַעוֹד לָכֶם
אָח׃ 7 וַיֹּאמְרוּ שָׁאוֹל שָׁאַל־הָאִישׁ ז"פ אדם לָנוּ אלהים, מום וּלְמוֹלַדְתֵּנוּ
לֵאמֹר הַעוֹד אֲבִיכֶם חַי הֲיֵשׁ לָכֶם אָח וַנַּגֶּד־לוֹ עַל־פִּי הַדְּבָרִים
ראה הָאֵלֶּה הֲיָדוֹעַ נֵדַע כִּי יֹאמַר הוֹרִידוּ אֶת־אֲחִיכֶם׃
8 וַיֹּאמֶר יְהוּדָה אֶל־יִשְׂרָאֵל אָבִיו שִׁלְחָה הַנַּעַר ש"ך אִתִּי
וְנָקוּמָה וְנֵלֵכָה וְנִחְיֶה וְלֹא נָמוּת גַּם יגל ־אֲנַחְנוּ גַם יגל ־אַתָּה
גַּם יגל ־טַפֵּנוּ׃ 9 אָנֹכִי איע אֶעֶרְבֶנּוּ מִיָּדִי תְּבַקְשֶׁנּוּ אִם יוהך ־לֹא
הֲבִיאֹתִיו אֵלֶיךָ וְהִצַּגְתִּיו לְפָנֶיךָ ס"ג - מ"ה - ב"ן וְחָטָאתִי לְךָ כָּל ילי
־הַיָּמִים נלך׃ 10 כִּי לוּלֵא בינה, ע"ה חיים הִתְמַהְמָהְנוּ כִּי־עַתָּה שַׁבְנוּ
זֶה פַעֲמָיִם׃ 11 וַיֹּאמֶר אֲלֵהֶם יִשְׂרָאֵל אֲבִיהֶם אִם יוהך ־כֵּן | אֵפוֹא

If I do not bring him back to you and set him here before you, I will bear the blame before you all my life. [10] As it is, if we had not delayed, we could have gone and returned twice."

[11] Then their father Israel said to them, "If it must be, then do this: Put some of the best products of the land in your bags and take them down to the man as a gift—a little balm and a little honey, some spices and myrrh, some pistachio nuts and almonds.

[12] Take double the amount of silver with you, for you must return the silver that was put back into the mouths of your sacks. Perhaps it was a mistake.

[13] Take your brother also and go back to the man at once.

[14] And may God Almighty grant you mercy before the man so that he will let your other brother and Benjamin come back with you. As for me, if I am bereaved of my children, I am bereaved."

[15] So the men took the gifts and double the amount of silver, and Benjamin also. They hurried down to Egypt and presented themselves to Joseph.

SIXTH READING - JOSEPH - YESOD

[16] When Joseph saw Benjamin with them, he said to the steward of his house, "Take these men to my house, slaughter an animal and prepare dinner; they are to eat with me at noon."

[17] The man did as Joseph told him and took the men to Joseph's house.

[18] Now the men were frightened when they were taken to his house. They thought, "We were brought here because of the silver that was put back into our sacks the first time. He wants to attack us and overpower us and seize us as slaves and take our donkeys."

בִּנְיָמִן

Genesis 43:16 – These verses tell about the brothers' final test. When they set off to go back to Egypt, Benjamin was accused of stealing. Again and again, as the brothers felt that things could not get any worse, they did. The brothers had been comfortable with their own negativity, so as a result, their situation continued to deteriorate until they were called upon to leave Benjamin in Egypt, condemned as a thief. The lesson we learn from this section is that complacency is one of our greatest enemies because our attitude can cause things to get worse and worse until we finally meet our own iniquities head-on. Our spiritual work is never done: Just because we think that we have completed one aspect of our *tikkun* process does not mean that we are now finished.

זֹאת עֲשׂוּ קְחוּ מִזִּמְרַת הָאָרֶץ אלהים דההין ע"ה בִּכְלֵיכֶם כלי וְהוֹרִידוּ
לָאִישׁ ע"ה קנ"א קס"א מִנְחָה ע"ה ב"פ ב"ן מְעַט צֳרִי מצפצ, י"פ ייי, אלהים דיודין וּמְעַט
דְּבַשׁ נְכֹאת וָלֹט בָּטְנִים וּשְׁקֵדִים צדנלבש: 12 וְכֶסֶף מִשְׁנֶה קְחוּ
בְיֶדְכֶם וְאֶת־הַכֶּסֶף הַמּוּשָׁב בְּפִי אַמְתְּחֹתֵיכֶם תָּשִׁיבוּ בְיֶדְכֶם
אוּלַי אום מִשְׁגֶּה הוּא: 13 וְאֶת־אֲחִיכֶם קָחוּ וְקוּמוּ שׁוּבוּ אֶל־
הָאִישׁ ו"פ אדם: 14 וְאֵל שַׁדַּי מהש יִתֵּן לָכֶם רַחֲמִים לִפְנֵי הָאִישׁ ו"פ אדם
וְשִׁלַּח לָכֶם אֶת־אֲחִיכֶם אַחֵר וְאֶת־בִּנְיָמִין וַאֲנִי אני, ב"פ אהיה + יהוה
כַּאֲשֶׁר שָׁכֹלְתִּי שָׁכָלְתִּי: 15 וַיִּקְחוּ וועם הָאֲנָשִׁים אֶת־הַמִּנְחָה
ע"ה ב"פ ב"ן הַזֹּאת וּמִשְׁנֶה־כֶּסֶף לָקְחוּ בְיָדָם וְאֶת־בִּנְיָמִן וַיָּקֻמוּ
וַיֵּרְדוּ רי"י מִצְרַיִם מצר וַיַּעַמְדוּ לִפְנֵי יוֹסֵף ציון, קנאה, ו"פ יהוה, ה"פ אל:

SIXTH READING - JOSEPH - YESOD

16 וַיַּרְא יוֹסֵף ציון, קנאה, ו"פ יהוה, ה"פ אל אִתָּם אֶת־בִּנְיָמִין וַיֹּאמֶר לַאֲשֶׁר
עַל־בֵּיתוֹ ב"פ ראה הָבֵא אֶת־הָאֲנָשִׁים הַבָּיְתָה ב"פ ראה וּטְבֹחַ טֶבַח
וְהָכֵן כִּי אִתִּי יֹאכְלוּ הָאֲנָשִׁים בַּצָּהֳרָיִם: 17 וַיַּעַשׂ הָאִישׁ ו"פ אדם
כַּאֲשֶׁר אָמַר יוֹסֵף ציון, קנאה, ו"פ יהוה, ה"פ אל וַיָּבֵא הָאִישׁ ו"פ אדם אֶת־
הָאֲנָשִׁים בֵּיתָה ב"פ ראה יוֹסֵף ציון, קנאה, ו"פ יהוה, ה"פ אל: 18 וַיִּירְאוּ הָאֲנָשִׁים
כִּי הוּבְאוּ בֵּית ב"פ ראה יוֹסֵף ציון, קנאה, ו"פ יהוה, ה"פ אל וַיֹּאמְרוּ עַל־דְּבַר
ראה הַכֶּסֶף הַשָּׁב בְּאַמְתְּחֹתֵינוּ בַּתְּחִלָּה אֲנַחְנוּ מוּבָאִים לְהִתְגֹּלֵל
עָלֵינוּ וּלְהִתְנַפֵּל עָלֵינוּ וְלָקַחַת אֹתָנוּ לַעֲבָדִים וְאֶת־חֲמֹרֵינוּ:
19 וַיִּגְּשׁוּ אֶל־הָאִישׁ ו"פ אדם אֲשֶׁר עַל־בֵּית ב"פ ראה יוֹסֵף ציון, קנאה, ו"פ יהוה, ה"פ אל
וַיְדַבְּרוּ ראה אֵלָיו פֶּתַח הַבָּיִת ב"פ ראה: 20 וַיֹּאמְרוּ בִּי אֲדֹנִי יָרֹד
יָרַדְנוּ בַּתְּחִלָּה לִשְׁבָּר־אֹכֶל: 21 וַיְהִי כִּי־בָאנוּ אֶל־הַמָּלוֹן
וַנִּפְתְּחָה אֶת־אַמְתְּחֹתֵינוּ וְהִנֵּה כֶסֶף־אִישׁ ע"ה קנ"א קס"א בְּפִי אַמְתַּחְתּוֹ

19 So they went up to Joseph's steward and spoke to him at the entrance to the house.

20 "Please sir," they said, "we came down here the first time to buy food.

21 But at the place where we stopped for the night we opened our sacks and each of us found his silver—the exact weight—in the mouth of his sack. So we have brought it back with us.

22 We have also brought additional silver with us to buy food. We don't know who put our silver in our sacks."

23 "It's all right," he said. "Don't be afraid. Your God, the God of your father, has given you treasure in your sacks; I received your silver." Then he brought Simeon out to them.

24 The steward took the men into Joseph's house, gave them water to wash their feet and provided fodder for their donkeys.

25 They prepared their gifts for Joseph's arrival at noon, because they had heard that they were to eat there.

26 When Joseph came home, they presented to him the gifts they had brought into the house, and they bowed down before him to the ground.

27 He asked them how they were, and then he said, "How is your aged father you told me about? Is he still living?"

28 They replied, "Your servant our father is still alive and well." And they bowed low to pay him honor.

29 As he looked about and saw his brother Benjamin, his own mother's son, he asked, "Is this your youngest brother, the one you told me about?" And he said, "God be gracious to you, my son."

SEVENTH READING - DAVID - MALCHUT

30 Deeply moved at the sight of his brother, Joseph hurried out and looked for a place to weep. He went into his private room and wept there.

31 After he had washed his face, he came out and, controlling himself, said, "Serve the food."

32 They served him by himself, the brothers by themselves, and the Egyptians who ate with him by themselves, because Egyptians could not eat with Hebrews, for that is detestable to Egyptians.

33 The men had been seated before him in the order of their ages, from the firstborn

כַּסְפֵּנוּ בְּמִשְׁקָלוֹ וַנָּשֶׁב אֹתוֹ בְּיָדֵנוּ׃ 22 וְכֶסֶף אַחֵר הוֹרַדְנוּ
בְיָדֵנוּ לִשְׁבָּר ר"ת הבל ־אֹכֶל לֹא יָדַעְנוּ מִי ילי ־שָׂם כַּסְפֵּנוּ
בְּאַמְתְּחֹתֵינוּ׃ 23 וַיֹּאמֶר שָׁלוֹם לָכֶם אַל־תִּירָאוּ אֱלֹהֵיכֶם ילה
וֵאלֹהֵי לכב, דמב, ילה אֲבִיכֶם נָתַן לָכֶם מַטְמוֹן בְּאַמְתְּחֹתֵיכֶם כַּסְפְּכֶם
בָּא אֵלָי וַיּוֹצֵא אֲלֵהֶם אֶת־שִׁמְעוֹן׃ 24 וַיָּבֵא הָאִישׁ ו"פ אדם אֶת־
הָאֲנָשִׁים בֵּיתָה ב"פ ראה יוֹסֵף ציון, קנאה, ו"פ יהוה, ה"פ אל וַיִּתֶּן י"פ מלוי ע"ב ־מַיִם
וַיִּרְחֲצוּ רַגְלֵיהֶם וַיִּתֵּן מִסְפּוֹא לַחֲמֹרֵיהֶם׃ 25 וַיָּכִינוּ אֶת־הַמִּנְחָה
ע"ה ב"פ ב"ן עַד־בּוֹא יוֹסֵף ציון, קנאה, ו"פ יהוה, ה"פ אל בַּצָּהֳרָיִם כִּי שָׁמְעוּ כִּי־
שָׁם יֹאכְלוּ לָחֶם ג"פ יהוה׃ 26 וַיָּבֹא יוֹסֵף ציון, קנאה, ו"פ יהוה, ה"פ אל הַבַּיְתָה
ב"פ ראה וַיָּבִיאוּ לוֹ אֶת־הַמִּנְחָה ע"ה ב"פ ב"ן אֲשֶׁר־בְּיָדָם הַבָּיְתָה ב"פ ראה
וַיִּשְׁתַּחֲווּ־לוֹ אָרְצָה אלהים דההין ע"ה׃ 27 וַיִּשְׁאַל לָהֶם לְשָׁלוֹם וַיֹּאמֶר
הֲשָׁלוֹם אֲבִיכֶם הַזָּקֵן אֲשֶׁר אֲמַרְתֶּם הַעוֹדֶנּוּ חָי׃ 28 וַיֹּאמְרוּ
שָׁלוֹם לְעַבְדְּךָ פוי לְאָבִינוּ עוֹדֶנּוּ חָי וַיִּקְּדוּ וַיִּשְׁתַּחֲוֻ׃ 29 וַיִּשָּׂא
עֵינָיו ריבוע מ"ה וַיַּרְא אֶת־בִּנְיָמִין אָחִיו בֶּן־אִמּוֹ וַיֹּאמֶר הֲזֶה והו
אֲחִיכֶם הַקָּטֹן אֲשֶׁר אֲמַרְתֶּם אֵלָי וַיֹּאמַר אֱלֹהִים ילה, מום
יָחְנְךָ בְּנִי׃

SEVENTH READING - DAVID - MALCHUT

30 וַיְמַהֵר יוֹסֵף ציון, קנאה, ו"פ יהוה, ה"פ אל כִּי־נִכְמְרוּ רַחֲמָיו אֶל־אָחִיו
וַיְבַקֵּשׁ לִבְכּוֹת וַיָּבֹא הַחַדְרָה וַיֵּבְךְּ שָׁמָּה מהש׃ 31 וַיִּרְחַץ פָּנָיו
וַיֵּצֵא וַיִּתְאַפַּק וַיֹּאמֶר שִׂימוּ לָחֶם ג"פ יהוה׃ 32 וַיָּשִׂימוּ לוֹ לְבַדּוֹ מ"ב
וְלָהֶם לְבַדָּם וְלַמִּצְרִים מצר הָאֹכְלִים אִתּוֹ לְבַדָּם כִּי לֹא יוּכְלוּן
הַמִּצְרִים מצר לֶאֱכֹל אֶת־הָעִבְרִים לֶחֶם ג"פ יהוה כִּי־תוֹעֵבָה הִוא
לְמִצְרָיִם מצר׃ 33 וַיֵּשְׁבוּ לְפָנָיו הַבְּכֹר כִּבְכֹרָתוֹ וְהַצָּעִיר כִּצְעִרָתוֹ

to the youngest; and they looked at each other in astonishment. 34 When portions were served to them from Joseph's table, Benjamin's portion was five times as much as anyone else's. So they feasted and drank freely with him.

44 1 Now Joseph gave these instructions to the steward of his house: "Fill the men's sacks with as much food as they can carry, and put each man's silver in the mouth of his sack.

2 Then put my cup, the silver one, in the mouth of the youngest one's sack, along with the silver for his grain." And he did as Joseph said.

3 As morning dawned, the men were sent on their way with their donkeys.

4 They had not gone far from the city when Joseph said to his steward, "Go after those men at once, and when you catch up with them, say to them, 'Why have you repaid good with evil?

5 Isn't this the cup my master drinks from and also uses for divination? This is a wicked thing you have done.' "

6 When he caught up with them, he repeated these words to them.

7 But they said to him, "Why does my lord say such things? Far be it from your servants to do anything like that!

8 We even brought back to you from the land of Canaan the silver we found inside the mouths of our sacks. So why would we steal silver or gold from your master's house?

9 If any of your servants is found to have it, he will die; and the rest of us will become my lord's slaves."

10 "Very well, then," he said, "let it be as you say. Whoever is found to have it will become my slave; the rest of you will be free from blame."

11 Each of them quickly lowered his sack to the ground and opened it.

12 Then the steward proceeded to search, beginning with the oldest and ending with the youngest. And the cup was found in Benjamin's sack.

13 At this, they tore their clothes. Then they all loaded their donkeys and returned to the city.

וַיִּתְמְהוּ הָאֲנָשִׁים אִישׁ ע"ה קנ"א קס"א אֶל־רֵעֵהוּ׃ 34 וַיִּשָּׂא מַשְׂאֹת
מֵאֵת פָּנָיו אֲלֵהֶם וַתֵּרֶב מַשְׂאַת בִּנְיָמִן מִמַּשְׂאֹת כֻּלָּם חָמֵשׁ
יָדוֹת וַיִּשְׁתּוּ וַיִּשְׁכְּרוּ עִמּוֹ׃ 44 1 וַיְצַו אֶת־אֲשֶׁר עַל־בֵּיתוֹ ב"פ ראה
לֵאמֹר מַלֵּא אֶת־אַמְתְּחֹת הָאֲנָשִׁים אֹכֶל כַּאֲשֶׁר יוּכְלוּן שְׂאֵת
וְשִׂים כֶּסֶף־אִישׁ ע"ה קנ"א קס"א בְּפִי אַמְתַּחְתּוֹ׃ 2 וְאֶת־גְּבִיעִי גְּבִיעַ
ה"פ טוב הַכֶּסֶף תָּשִׂים בְּפִי אַמְתַּחַת הַקָּטֹן וְאֵת כֶּסֶף שִׁבְרוֹ וַיַּעַשׂ
כִּדְבַר ראה יוֹסֵף ציון, קנאה, ו"פ יהוה, ה"פ אל אֲשֶׁר דִּבֵּר ראה׃ 3 הַבֹּקֶר אוֹר
רז, אין־סוף וְהָאֲנָשִׁים שֻׁלְּחוּ הֵמָּה וַחֲמֹרֵיהֶם׃ 4 הֵם יָצְאוּ אֶת־הָעִיר
סוזפר, ערי, סנדלפון לֹא הִרְחִיקוּ וְיוֹסֵף ציון, קנאה, ו"פ יהוה, ה"פ אל אָמַר לַאֲשֶׁר
עַל־בֵּיתוֹ ב"פ ראה קוּם רְדֹף אַחֲרֵי הָאֲנָשִׁים וְהִשַּׂגְתָּם וְאָמַרְתָּ
אֲלֵהֶם לָמָּה שִׁלַּמְתֶּם רָעָה רהע תַּחַת טוֹבָה אכא׃ 5 הֲלוֹא זֶה
אֲשֶׁר יִשְׁתֶּה אֲדֹנִי בּוֹ וְהוּא נַחֵשׁ יְנַחֵשׁ בּוֹ הֲרֵעֹתֶם אֲשֶׁר
עֲשִׂיתֶם׃ 6 וַיַּשִּׂגֵם וַיְדַבֵּר ראה אֲלֵהֶם אֶת־הַדְּבָרִים ראה הָאֵלֶּה׃
7 וַיֹּאמְרוּ אֵלָיו לָמָּה יְדַבֵּר ראה אֲדֹנִי כַּדְּבָרִים ראה הָאֵלֶּה חָלִילָה
לַעֲבָדֶיךָ מֵעֲשׂוֹת כַּדָּבָר ראה הַזֶּה והו׃ 8 הֵן כֶּסֶף אֲשֶׁר מָצָאנוּ
בְּפִי אַמְתְּחֹתֵינוּ הֱשִׁיבֹנוּ אֵלֶיךָ מֵאֶרֶץ אלהים דאלפין כְּנָעַן וְאֵיךְ אל
נִגְנֹב מִבֵּית ב"פ ראה אֲדֹנֶיךָ כֶּסֶף אוֹ זָהָב׃ 9 אֲשֶׁר יִמָּצֵא אִתּוֹ
מֵעֲבָדֶיךָ וָמֵת וְגַם יגל־אֲנַחְנוּ נִהְיֶה לַאדֹנִי לַעֲבָדִים׃ 10 וַיֹּאמֶר
גַּם יגל־עַתָּה כְדִבְרֵיכֶם ראה כֶּן־הוּא אֲשֶׁר יִמָּצֵא אִתּוֹ יִהְיֶה ייי
־לִּי עָבֶד וְאַתֶּם תִּהְיוּ נְקִיִּם ע"ה קס"א׃ 11 וַיְמַהֲרוּ וַיּוֹרִדוּ אִישׁ ע"ה קנ"א קס"א
אֶת־אַמְתַּחְתּוֹ אָרְצָה אלהים דההין ע"ה וַיִּפְתְּחוּ אִישׁ ע"ה קנ"א קס"א
אַמְתַּחְתּוֹ׃ 12 וַיְחַפֵּשׂ בַּגָּדוֹל להח, מבה, יזל, אום הֵחֵל להח וּבַקָּטֹן כִּלָּה
וַיִּמָּצֵא הַגָּבִיעַ ה"פ טוב בְּאַמְתַּחַת בִּנְיָמִן׃ 13 וַיִּקְרְעוּ שִׂמְלֹתָם
וַיַּעֲמֹס אִישׁ ע"ה קנ"א קס"א עַל־חֲמֹרוֹ וַיָּשֻׁבוּ הָעִירָה סוזפר, ערי, סנדלפון׃

MAFTIR

14 Joseph was still in the house when Judah and his brothers came in and they threw themselves to the ground before him.

15 Joseph said to them, "What is this you have done? Don't you know that a man like me can find things out by divination?"

16 "What can we say to my lord?" Judah replied. "What can we say? How can we prove our innocence? God has uncovered your servants' guilt. We are now my lord's slaves—we ourselves and the one who was found to have the cup."

17 But Joseph said, "Far be it from me to do such a thing! Only the man who was found to have the cup will become my slave. The rest of you, go back to your father in peace."

HAFTARAH OF MIKETZ

This Haftarah speaks of the famous tale of the judgment of King Solomon, in which the king mediated between two women who claimed motherhood of a single baby. The wonder of this tale is that a mother existed who would rather have seen a baby sliced in half than surrender the child to another woman. Too many people can feel justified—even in taking someone's life—because of their own anger and the turmoil of their emotions.

The link between the story of Joseph and his brothers in Egypt and the wisdom of King Solomon has to do with the nature of kingship and judgment. When Joseph was elevated to his high position, he had to exercise judgment in both senses of the word—to use sensitivity, discrimination, and good

I Kings 3:15 - 4:1

3 15 Then Solomon awoke—and he realized it had been a dream. He returned to Jerusalem, stood before the ark of the Lord's covenant and sacrificed burnt offerings and fellowship offerings. Then he gave a feast for all his court.

MAFTIR

14 וַיָּבֹא יְהוּדָה וְאֶחָיו בֵּיתָה ב"פ ראה יוֹסֵף ציון, קנאה, ו"פ יהוה, ה"פ אל וְהוּא
עוֹדֶנּוּ שָׁם וַיִּפְּלוּ לְפָנָיו אָרְצָה אלהים דההין ע"ה: 15 וַיֹּאמֶר לָהֶם יוֹסֵף
ציון, קנאה, ו"פ יהוה, ה"פ אל מָה מ"ה הַמַּעֲשֶׂה הַזֶּה והו אֲשֶׁר עֲשִׂיתֶם הֲלוֹא
יְדַעְתֶּם כִּי־נַחֵשׁ יְנַחֵשׁ אִישׁ ע"ה קנ"א קס"א אֲשֶׁר כָּמֹנִי: 16 וַיֹּאמֶר
יְהוּדָה מַה מ"ה נֹּאמַר לַאדֹנִי מַה מ"ה נְּדַבֵּר ראה וּמַה מ"ה נִּצְטַדָּק
הָאֱלֹהִים ילה, מום מָצָא ריבוע מ"ה ע"ה אֶת־עֲוֺן ג"פ מ"ב עֲבָדֶיךָ הִנֶּנּוּ עֲבָדִים
לַאדֹנִי גַּם יגל אֲנַחְנוּ גַּם יגל אֲשֶׁר־נִמְצָא הַגָּבִיעַ בְּיָדוֹ:
17 וַיֹּאמֶר חָלִילָה לִּי מֵעֲשׂוֹת זֹאת הָאִישׁ ז"פ אדם אֲשֶׁר נִמְצָא
הַגָּבִיעַ ה"פ טוב בְּיָדוֹ הוּא יִהְיֶה ייי לִּי עָבֶד וְאַתֶּם עֲלוּ לְשָׁלוֹם
אֶל־אֲבִיכֶם: [ס] [ס] [ס]

HAFTARAH OF MIKETZ

judgment in his assessment of people's characters and needs, and to judge others for the purposes of punishment and mercy. These functions required both strength of character and adherence to a set of moral guidelines that both Joseph and Solomon derived from their dedication to the Creator.

In both readings—Genesis and Kings—a child is held hostage. This can be a metaphor for the "children" of our own deeds, which are the results of our own actions. The Universal Law of Cause and Effect kicks in, and it is our own actions and the strength of our desire to connect to the Light of the Creator that determine how much or how little mercy we receive in turn.

מלכים 1 פרק 3–4

3 15 וַיִּקַץ שְׁלֹמֹה וְהִנֵּה חֲלוֹם וַיָּבוֹא יְרוּשָׁלַםִ ר"ו ש"ע וַיַּעֲמֹד ׀
לִפְנֵי ׀ אֲרוֹן ג"פ אלהים בְּרִית־אֲדֹנָי ללה וַיַּעַל עֹלוֹת וַיַּעַשׂ שְׁלָמִים
וַיַּעַשׂ מִשְׁתֶּה לְכָל יה - אדני עֲבָדָיו: [פ] 16 אָז תָּבֹאנָה שְׁתַּיִם

16 *Now two prostitutes came to the king and stood before him.*

17 *One of them said, "My Lord, this woman and I live in the same house. I had a baby while she was there with me.*

18 *The third day after my child was born, this woman also had a baby. We were alone; there was no one in the house but the two of us.*

19 *During the night this woman's son died because she lay on him.*

20 *So she got up in the middle of the night and took my son from my side while I, your servant was asleep. She put him by her breast and put her dead son by my breast.*

21 *The next morning, I got up to nurse my son—and he was dead! But when I looked at him closely in the morning light, I saw that it wasn't the son I had borne."*

22 *The other woman said, "No! The living one is my son; the dead one is yours." But the first one insisted, "No! The dead one is yours; the living one is mine." And so they argued before the king.*

23 *The king said, "This one says, 'My son is alive and your son is dead,' while that one says, 'No! Your son is dead and mine is alive.' "*

24 *Then the king said, "Bring me a sword." So they brought a sword for the king.*

25 *He then gave an order: "Cut the living child in two and give half to one and half to the other."*

26 *The woman whose son was alive was filled with compassion for her son and said to the king, "Please, my Lord, give her the living baby! Don't kill him!" But the other said, "Neither I nor you shall have him. Cut him in two!"*

27 *Then the king gave his ruling: "Give the living baby to the first woman. Do not kill him; she is his mother."*

28 *When all Israel heard the verdict the king had given, they held the king in awe, because they saw that he had wisdom from God to administer justice.*

4:1 *So King Solomon ruled over all Israel.*

נָשִׁים זֹנוֹת אֶל־הַמֶּלֶךְ וַתַּעֲמֹדְנָה לְפָנָיו׃ 17 וַתֹּאמֶר הָאִשָּׁה
הָאַחַת בִּי אֲדֹנִי אֲנִי אני וְהָאִשָּׁה הַזֹּאת יֹשְׁבֹת בְּבַיִת ב״פ ראה אֶחָד
אהבה, דאגה וָאֵלֵד אלד עִמָּהּ בַּבָּיִת ב״פ ראה׃ 18 וַיְהִי אל בַּיּוֹם נגד, זן, מזבח
הַשְּׁלִישִׁי לְלִדְתִּי וַתֵּלֶד גַּם יג״ל ־הָאִשָּׁה הַזֹּאת וַאֲנַחְנוּ יַחְדָּו אֵין־
זָר אִתָּנוּ בַּבַּיִת ב״פ ראה זוּלָתִי שְׁתַּיִם־אֲנַחְנוּ בַּבָּיִת ב״פ ראה׃ 19 וַיָּמָת
בֶּן־הָאִשָּׁה הַזֹּאת לָיְלָה מלה אֲשֶׁר שָׁכְבָה עָלָיו׃ 20 וַתָּקָם בְּתוֹךְ
הַלַּיְלָה מלה וַתִּקַּח אֶת־בְּנִי מֵאֶצְלִי וַאֲמָתְךָ יְשֵׁנָה וַתַּשְׁכִּיבֵהוּ
בְּחֵיקָהּ וְאֶת־בְּנָהּ הַמֵּת הִשְׁכִּיבָה בְחֵיקִי׃ 21 וָאָקֻם בַּבֹּקֶר
לְהֵינִיק אֶת־בְּנִי וְהִנֵּה מ״ה יה ־מֵת י״פ רבוע אהיה וָאֶתְבּוֹנֵן אֵלָיו בַּבֹּקֶר
וְהִנֵּה לֹא־הָיָה יהה בְּנִי אֲשֶׁר יָלָדְתִּי׃ 22 וַתֹּאמֶר הָאִשָּׁה הָאַחֶרֶת
לֹא כִי בְּנִי הַחַי וּבְנֵךְ הַמֵּת י״פ רבוע אהיה וְזֹאת אֹמֶרֶת לֹא כִי בְּנֵךְ
הַמֵּת י״פ רבוע אהיה וּבְנִי הֶחָי וַתְּדַבֵּרְנָה ראה לִפְנֵי הַמֶּלֶךְ׃ 23 וַיֹּאמֶר
הַמֶּלֶךְ זֹאת אֹמֶרֶת זֶה־בְּנִי הַחַי וּבְנֵךְ הַמֵּת י״פ רבוע אהיה וְזֹאת
אֹמֶרֶת לֹא כִי בְּנֵךְ הַמֵּת י״פ רבוע אהיה וּבְנִי הֶחָי׃ [פ] 24 וַיֹּאמֶר
הַמֶּלֶךְ קְחוּ לִי־חָרֶב וַיָּבִאוּ הַחֶרֶב לִפְנֵי הַמֶּלֶךְ׃ 25 וַיֹּאמֶר
הַמֶּלֶךְ גִּזְרוּ אֶת־הַיֶּלֶד הַחַי לִשְׁנָיִם וּתְנוּ אֶת־הַחֲצִי לְאַחַת
וְאֶת־הַחֲצִי לְאֶחָת׃ 26 וַתֹּאמֶר הָאִשָּׁה אֲשֶׁר־בְּנָהּ הַחַי
אֶל־הַמֶּלֶךְ כִּי־נִכְמְרוּ רַחֲמֶיהָ עַל־בְּנָהּ וַתֹּאמֶר | בִּי אֲדֹנִי תְּנוּ־
לָהּ אֶת־הַיָּלוּד הַחַי וְהָמֵת אַל־תְּמִיתֻהוּ וְזֹאת אֹמֶרֶת גַּם יג״ל
־לִי גַּם יג״ל ־לָךְ לֹא יִהְיֶה ייי גְּזֹרוּ׃ 27 וַיַּעַן הַמֶּלֶךְ וַיֹּאמֶר תְּנוּ־לָהּ
אֶת־הַיָּלוּד הַחַי וְהָמֵת לֹא תְמִיתֻהוּ הִיא אִמּוֹ׃ [ס] 28 וַיִּשְׁמְעוּ
כָל ילי ־יִשְׂרָאֵל אֶת־הַמִּשְׁפָּט ע״ה ה״פ אלהים אֲשֶׁר שָׁפַט הַמֶּלֶךְ
וַיִּרְאוּ מִפְּנֵי הַמֶּלֶךְ כִּי רָאוּ כִּי־חָכְמַת אֱלֹהִים ילה, מום בְּקִרְבּוֹ
לַעֲשׂוֹת מִשְׁפָּט ע״ה ה״פ אלהים׃ [ס] 4 1 וַיְהִי הַמֶּלֶךְ שְׁלֹמֹה מֶלֶךְ
עַל־כָּל ילי, עמם ־יִשְׂרָאֵל׃ [ס]

VAYIGASH

LESSON OF VAYIGASH
(Genesis 44:18-47:27)

"And Joseph said to his brothers, 'I am Joseph.'" (Genesis 45:4)

In this biblical story Joseph finally reveals himself to his brothers. When Joseph's brothers first came to buy food in Egypt, Joseph had treated them coldly from the very start. Questions had arisen in their minds about why this was happening. They blamed each other and struggled to understand what was being done to them and why. But this ended as soon as they heard the words, "I am Joseph." At that moment, all their questions were answered. They stopped blaming each other—and they stopped doubting their connection with the Creator.

Rashi said that they were terrified, all the same, because of the shame that they felt. In the presence of the one they had wronged and who now had so much power over their lives, they were filled with fear. Most of us look to blame someone else for what is happening to us in our lives. Before we can realize that the Creator is present in every moment of our day, we must first stop blaming and being angry at others; only then can we see the big picture. Where the small picture is about what is happening right now, the big picture is like the total understanding that came to the brothers when they heard, "I am Joseph." In our own lives, this understanding arrives when we hear "I am God; I am the One Who did this for you." When we strive to remind ourselves that everything—both the good and the bad—comes from the Creator, we become blessed with Divine inspiration and guidance.

"All those who went to Egypt with Jacob..." (Genesis 46:26)

When Jacob, his sons, and their families all went down to Egypt, it is written: "All the souls of the house of Jacob that came to Egypt were 70." The word "souls" in the phrase "all the souls" is written in the singular form in Aramaic and describes everyone and everything that was in Jacob's household, even though "souls" should be written in the plural form. So why in the previous section that describes Esau's family is it written in the plural form: "Esau, Jacob's brother, took his wives, and his sons, and his daughters and all the souls of his house...?" (Genesis 36:6)

The answer to this question is that the righteous can be physically apart and living in many different places in the world, but they are always connected as one. When we say in our prayers: "One soul together," we are really together all over the world.

"Love your neighbor as yourself" is next to impossible to achieve if we think that "you are you and I am me." Only through a consciousness of unity can we love our neighbor as ourselves. If someone is in pain or going through a difficult time, we should go to help, not because we are "good people" but because we feel their pain as our own. If there is a pain in your right hand, your left hand does not say, "Well, that's not my problem." When Jacob and his family went "as one," it was because Jacob knew that this was the only way they could leave Egypt. In every generation, we have our own "Egypt," our place of spiritual exile, and only through unity will we be able to leave this exile and do our spiritual work.

Benjamin's gifts

It is written that Joseph gave more to Benjamin than to his other brothers—not just a little more but five times as much. (Genesis 45:22) Why did Joseph act in a way that might awaken jealousy among the brothers, especially since it was jealousy that had led Joseph's brothers into selling him in the first place?

To understand this, we must know that all the actions of our patriarchs were not only for themselves or for their time, but for the whole world and for all generations. If Joseph had not given Benjamin the clothes that he gave him, Mordecai would not have had the strength to fight against the wicked Haman. Only through the merit of Joseph's strength as the leader of Egypt was Mordecai able to defeat Haman. Joseph was aware of the long-term effects of his actions. The Ari wrote:

> *Since Jacob bowed to Esau and made him master over himself by his bowing, he damaged Netzach greatly, until Benjamin (Eng. "son of right") appeared, who was not yet born when Jacob bowed to Esau. Therefore, Mordecai, who did not want to bow to Haman, who is Esau, descended from Benjamin.*
>
> *– The Writings of the Ari, I Samuel 9*

We should learn from this that all the actions of all the previous generations have prepared our way. Everything is ready. God is not asking us to overcome Satan, our Opponent, all by ourselves. We are not on the level of Rav Shimon or Rav Isaac Luria (the Ari). We don't need to be because they have prepared everything for us, such as the *Zohar* and the *Writings of the Ari.* We have these books of Light and wisdom to assist us.

"My years have been few and difficult." (Genesis 47:9)

A commentary tells us that when Jacob said, "Few and evil," God said to him, "I saved you from Esau; I brought Dinah and Joseph back to you. Why are you complaining?" Because of his complaint, 33 years were taken off Jacob's life span.

We are not judging Jacob, but here we can learn a beautiful lesson. Because of his complaints, Jacob both looked much older and died much sooner than he should have. If Jacob, at his level of consciousness, would have accepted with love everything that happened to him, his physical appearance would have changed to that of somebody younger and happier. His hair would not have been white, and he would have looked younger than his age. People grow older because they do not appreciate what the Light does for them. When they are feeling good, they take things for granted. But when they are going through hard times, they cry out to the Creator, "What are You doing to me?"

It is not enough, however, that we appreciate or even know the Light. The Light has to become part of us. Our connection to the Light has to be with every muscle, every nerve, every hair on our body, until there is no room left for grief, suffering, old age, or even death.

SYNOPSIS OF VAYIGASH

Vayigash means "to come close," to draw near to the Light of the Creator. There are certain things we can do to help us move closer to the Light, while other things cause us to become more distant. Sharing brings us closer, for instance, while doubt and anger push us away. This reading gives us the power to come closer to the Light of the Creator.

FIRST READING - ABRAHAM - CHESED

18 Then Judah went up to him and said: "Please, my lord, let your servant speak a word to my lord. Do not be angry with your servant, though you are equal to Pharaoh himself. 19 My lord asked his servants, 'Do you have a father or a brother?'

20 And we answered, 'We have an aged father, and there is a young son born to him

---

FROM THE RAV

This story is about members of a family "coming close" to one another after a long separation. They had been separated in space and in time, as well as emotionally and even spiritually.

The spiritual separation, according to the *Zohar*, is also explained in the first words of the reading: "*Vayigash elav Yehuda*" (Judah came close to him). These three words are what this whole biblical story is about on a spiritual level. "Judah came close to him" means that the gap was closed between the physical world (*Malchut*) and the Flawless Universe of *Zeir Anpin*—the Tree of Life Reality at the level of *Yesod*.

To tap into and draw the sustenance that *Zeir Anpin* and everything in it contains requires a level of spiritual growth. And that is why Judah repeated the whole story. The repetition was to remove the chaos caused by separation. It was only then that Joseph revealed himself.

When one undergoes chaos, certainly today the chaos of financial instability or ill health, Satan has his ways of helping us to forget the pain once things improve. This chaos seems to disappear, but it hasn't really gone; it just comes back in different forms. What is chaos? It is the absence of Light. Removing chaos means not having its influence in our lives. This is a concept that mankind has to grasp. We need to understand that it's not enough that one form of chaos be removed from one area of our life. We are talking about turning on the Light and making the darkness disappear from all areas of our life for good. The *Zohar* explains that the reason the Torah says "and he drew close to him" is because there is only one way to remove chaos—when *Malchut* becomes one with *Yesod*.

Instead of blaming and justifying, we must take responsibility. There is a *tikkun* process. There is no such thing as a person suffering forever. There is an end to the suffering; there is a process by which *tikkun* takes place. When *Zeir Anpin* takes over, there is *rachamim* (mercy). As when the brothers recognized that maybe this chaos was happening because they had sold their brother Joseph. This recognition is what caused Joseph to reveal himself.

Do we look back and think about our own negativity, and in the moment that we experience chaos, do we ask ourselves what we did to create this situation? Most of us still want to blame others for whatever chaos we are going through. Maybe things don't always go perfectly smoothly. Chaos beset Joseph's brothers over and over for 22 years until they finally realized that this was happening to them because they had sold their brother.

We can shorten our *tikkun* process. That's what this technology of Kabbalah is all about. To shorten the *tikkun* process, we must take advantage of every moment when we can get extra Light, by accepting responsibility for our past actions and closing that chapter of our life.

This is such a powerful lesson for us, and all we have to do is open a gate in

FIRST READING - ABRAHAM - CHESED

18 וַיִּגַּשׁ אֵלָיו יְהוּדָה וַיֹּאמֶר בִּי אֲדֹנִי יְדַבֶּר ראה ־נָא עַבְדְּךָ פוי
דָבָר ראה בְּאָזְנֵי יוד הי ואו הה אֲדֹנִי וְאַל־יִחַר אַפְּךָ בְּעַבְדֶּךָ פוי כִּי
כָמוֹךָ אלהים כְּפַרְעֹה׃ 19 אֲדֹנִי שָׁאַל אֶת־עֲבָדָיו לֵאמֹר הֲיֵשׁ־
לָכֶם אָב אוֹ־אָח׃ 20 וַנֹּאמֶר אֶל־אֲדֹנִי יֶשׁ־לָנוּ אלהים, מום אָב זָקֵן
קס"א ע"ה וְיֶלֶד מ"ה ע"ה זְקֻנִים קָטָן וְאָחִיו מֵת י"פ רבוע אהיה וַיִּוָּתֵר הוּא
לְבַדּוֹ מ"ב לְאִמּוֹ וְאָבִיו אֲהֵבוֹ׃ 21 וַתֹּאמֶר אֶל־עֲבָדֶיךָ הוֹרִדֻהוּ
אֵלָי וְאָשִׂימָה עֵינִי ריבוע מ"ה עָלָיו׃ 22 וַנֹּאמֶר אֶל־אֲדֹנִי לֹא־יוּכַל
הַנַּעַר ש"ך לַעֲזֹב אֶת־אָבִיו וְעָזַב אֶת־אָבִיו וָמֵת י"פ רבוע אהיה׃

---

ourselves. But it's difficult to rid ourselves of the nonsense of "I'm still a little right about what happened." Why can't we just say in an argument, "You're right and I'm wrong?" What would happen? We need to take responsibility for our actions and all that comes to us as a consequence of them. Sometimes the chaos arises from actions in a past life. But whether this time or the previous time you have to ask yourself what you did to bring this situation about...even if it is a good thing.

We need to repeat to ourselves: "Every negative aspect in my life is only because of me." If we can do that just for an hour or two, we can access the gates that are literally opened up during the reading of this story on Shabbat. And if we still cannot let go of the idea of whose fault it is, we have wasted this opportunity.

I appeal to you: We need all the Light that can come from this story. If we can just take responsibility for all our actions, then we will have opened up the gates of abundance that have never been opened before.

וַיִּגַּשׁ

Genesis 44:18 – When Judah returned to Joseph after the family had run out of the food Joseph had given them earlier, he completed his correction by saving Benjamin and by bringing Joseph back into the family. Judah's example reminds us that long periods of time often may intervene between the beginning and end of our correction. A Cause is nearly always separated from its Effect by the passage of time. By connecting with Judah, we can gain control of time, bringing the Cause and the Effect of our actions closer together. The *Zohar* states:

> *Rav Yehuda said, "Happy are the righteous, whose coming together brings peace into the world, for they know how to bring unison and approach each other to increase peace in the world. For until Joseph and Judah came near each other, there was no peace. Once they came near each other, peace increased in the world. Joy abounded Above and Below when Joseph and Judah approached each other and all the tribes joined Joseph."*
>
> — *The Zohar, Vayigash 6:61*

in his old age. His brother is dead, and he is the only one of his mother's sons left,
and his father loves him.' [21] "Then you said to your servants, 'Bring him down to me
so I can see him for myself.' [22] And we said to my lord, 'The boy cannot leave his
father; if he leaves him, his father will die.'

[23] But you told your servants, 'Unless your youngest brother comes down with you,
you will not see my face again.' [24] When we went back to your servant my father, we
told him what my lord had said. [25] "Then our father said, 'Go back and buy a little
more food.'

[26] But we said, 'We cannot go down. Only if our youngest brother is with us will we go.
We cannot see the man's face unless our youngest brother is with us.'

[27] Your servant my father said to us, 'You know that my wife bore me two sons. [28] One
of them went away from me, and I said,"He has surely been torn to pieces. And I have
not seen him since.

[29] If you take this one from me too and harm comes to him, you will bring my gray
head down to the grave in misery." [30] So now, if the boy is not with us when I go back
to your servant my father and if my father, whose life is closely bound up with the
boy's life,

SECOND READING - ISAAC - GEVURAH

[31] sees that the boy isn't there, he will die. Your servants will bring the gray head of our father down to the grave in sorrow.

[32] Your servant guaranteed the boy's safety to my father. I said, 'If I do not bring him back to you, I will bear the blame before you, my father, all my life!'

[33] "Now then, please let your servant remain here as my lord's slave in place of the boy, and let the boy return with his brothers.

[34] How can I go back to my father if the boy is not with me? No! Do not let me see the misery that would come upon my father."

45 [1] Then Joseph could no longer control himself before all his attendants, and he cried out, "Have everyone leave my presence!" So, there was no one with Joseph when he made himself known to his brothers.

[2] And he wept so loudly that the Egyptians heard him, and Pharaoh's household heard about it.

23 וַתֹּאמֶר אֶל־עֲבָדֶיךָ אִם יוהך ־לֹא יֵרֵד אֲחִיכֶם הַקָּטֹן אִתְּכֶם
לֹא תֹסִפוּן לִרְאוֹת פָּנָי חכמה + בינה: 24 וַיְהִי אל כִּי עָלִינוּ אֶל־עַבְדְּךָ
פוי אָבִי וַנַּגֶּד־לוֹ אֵת דִּבְרֵי ראה אֲדֹנִי: 25 וַיֹּאמֶר אָבִינוּ שֻׁבוּ
שִׁבְרוּ־לָנוּ אלהים, מום מְעַט־אֹכֶל: 26 וַנֹּאמֶר לֹא נוּכַל לָרֶדֶת אִם
יוהך ־יֵשׁ אָחִינוּ הַקָּטֹן אִתָּנוּ וְיָרַדְנוּ כִּי־לֹא נוּכַל לִרְאוֹת פְּנֵי
חכמה + בינה הָאִישׁ ז"פ אדם וְאָחִינוּ הַקָּטֹן אֵינֶנּוּ אִתָּנוּ: 27 וַיֹּאמֶר עַבְדְּךָ
פוי אָבִי אֵלֵינוּ אַתֶּם יְדַעְתֶּם כִּי שְׁנַיִם יָלְדָה־לִּי אִשְׁתִּי: 28 וַיֵּצֵא
הָאֶחָד אהבה, דאגה מֵאִתִּי וָאֹמַר אַךְ אהיה טָרֹף רפ"ח ע"ה טֹרָף רפ"ח ע"ה וְלֹא
רְאִיתִיו עַד־הֵנָּה מ"ה יה: 29 וּלְקַחְתֶּם גַּם יגל ־אֶת־זֶה מֵעִם עמם פָּנַי
חכמה + בינה וְקָרָהוּ אָסוֹן וְהוֹרַדְתֶּם אֶת־שֵׂיבָתִי בְּרָעָה רהע שְׁאֹלָה:
30 וְעַתָּה כְּבֹאִי אֶל־עַבְדְּךָ פוי אָבִי וְהַנַּעַר ש"ך אֵינֶנּוּ אִתָּנוּ וְנַפְשׁוֹ
קְשׁוּרָה בְנַפְשׁוֹ:

SECOND READING - ISAAC - GEVURAH

31 וְהָיָה יהוה, יהה כִּרְאוֹתוֹ כִּי־אֵין הַנַּעַר ש"ך וָמֵת י"פ רבוע אהיה וְהוֹרִידוּ
עֲבָדֶיךָ אֶת־שֵׂיבַת עַבְדְּךָ פוי אָבִינוּ בְּיָגוֹן שְׁאֹלָה: 32 כִּי עַבְדְּךָ
פוי עָרַב רבוע אלהים + ע"ב אֶת־הַנַּעַר ש"ך מֵעִם אָבִי לֵאמֹר אִם יוהך
־לֹא אֲבִיאֶנּוּ אֵלֶיךָ וְחָטָאתִי לְאָבִי כָּל ילי ־הַיָּמִים נלך: 33 וְעַתָּה
יֵשֶׁב־נָא עַבְדְּךָ פוי תַּחַת הַנַּעַר ש"ך עֶבֶד לַאדֹנִי וְהַנַּעַר ש"ך יַעַל
עִם־אֶחָיו: 34 כִּי־אֵיךְ אל אֶעֱלֶה אֶל־אָבִי וְהַנַּעַר ש"ך אֵינֶנּוּ אִתִּי
פֶּן אֶרְאֶה בָרָע אֲשֶׁר יִמְצָא אֶת־אָבִי: 45 1 וְלֹא־יָכֹל
יוֹסֵף ציון, ו"פ יהוה, ה"פ אל לְהִתְאַפֵּק לְכֹל יה + אדני הַנִּצָּבִים עָלָיו וַיִּקְרָא
עם ה' אותיות = ב"פ קס"א הוֹצִיאוּ כָל ילי ־אִישׁ ע"ה קנ"א קס"א מֵעָלָי וְלֹא־עָמַד

3 Joseph said to his brothers, "I am Joseph! Is my father still living?" But his brothers were not able to answer him, because they were terrified at his presence.

4 Then Joseph said to his brothers, "Come close to me." When they had done so, he said, "I am your brother Joseph, the one you sold into Egypt! 5 And now, do not be distressed and do not be angry with yourselves for selling me here, because it was to save lives that God sent me ahead of you.

6 For two years now there has been famine in the land and for the next five years there will not be plowing and reaping. 7 But God sent me ahead of you to preserve for you a remnant on earth and to save your lives by a great deliverance.

THIRD READING - JACOB - TIFERET

8 So then, it was not you who sent me here, but God. He made me father to Pharaoh, lord of his entire household and ruler of all Egypt.

Genesis 45:3 – Judah made his case to Joseph, saying that he must take Benjamin back to his father, Jacob. The *Zohar* says:

> *These are Judah and Joseph, who were both kings. The two of them came together to dispute because Judah became surety for Benjamin and pledged himself before his father in this world and in the World to Come. He, therefore, came to argue with Joseph on account of Benjamin, so he would not be banned from this world and the World to Come.*
> *–The Zohar, Vayigash 3:23*

After that, Joseph said, "I am Joseph. Is my father still alive?" Although Joseph had heard Judah speak about his father, Joseph still needed more confirmation that Jacob was still living. We find from this reading that Judah showed more care for his father, Jacob, than he had years earlier for his brother. When Judah had sold Joseph into slavery, he didn't care about the harm he had done. But once Judah was personally responsible to Jacob for returning Benjamin, he had more invested and his own fate was in the balance.

We often behave in the same way. We are lax about spiritual work until it affects us personally and our own agenda is at stake. Then suddenly, we are more careful about how we think, feel, and behave.

Genesis 45:5 – Joseph told his brothers not to reproach themselves because it was God who had sent him to Egypt to be a provider. Joseph was trying to console his brothers by letting them know that the Light had always been in control.

No matter what situation we may be in, we should remember that we must trust the Light. We should not be looking for either blame or credit—whether for ourselves or for anyone else—because everything comes from the Light.

אִישׁ ע״ה קנ״א קס״א אִתּוֹ בְּהִתְוַדַּע יוֹסֵף ציון, ו״פ יהוה, ה״פ אל אֶל־אֶחָיו׃
2 וַיִּתֵּן אֶת־קֹלוֹ בִּבְכִי וַיִּשְׁמְעוּ מִצְרַיִם מצר וַיִּשְׁמַע בֵּית ב״פ ראה
פַּרְעֹה׃ 3 וַיֹּאמֶר יוֹסֵף ציון, ו״פ יהוה, ה״פ אל אֶל־אֶחָיו אֲנִי אני יוֹסֵף
ציון, ו״פ יהוה, ה״פ אל הַעוֹד אָבִי חָי וְלֹא־יָכְלוּ אֶחָיו לַעֲנוֹת אֹתוֹ כִּי
נִבְהֲלוּ מִפָּנָיו׃ 4 וַיֹּאמֶר יוֹסֵף ציון, ו״פ יהוה, ה״פ אל אֶל־אֶחָיו גְּשׁוּ־נָא
אֵלַי וַיִּגָּשׁוּ וַיֹּאמֶר אֲנִי אני יוֹסֵף ציון, ו״פ יהוה, ה״פ אל אֲחִיכֶם אֲשֶׁר־
מְכַרְתֶּם אֹתִי מִצְרָיְמָה מצר׃ 5 וְעַתָּה | אַל־תֵּעָצְבוּ וְאַל־יִחַר
בְּעֵינֵיכֶם ריבוע מ״ה כִּי־מְכַרְתֶּם אֹתִי הֵנָּה מ״ה יה כִּי לְמִחְיָה שְׁלָחַנִי
אֱלֹהִים ילה, מום לִפְנֵיכֶם׃ 6 כִּי־זֶה שְׁנָתַיִם הָרָעָב רבוע אלהים - ע״ב
בְּקֶרֶב הָאָרֶץ אלהים דההין ע״ה וְעוֹד חָמֵשׁ שָׁנִים אֲשֶׁר אֵין־חָרִישׁ
וְקָצִיר׃ 7 וַיִּשְׁלָחֵנִי אֱלֹהִים ילה, מום לִפְנֵיכֶם לָשׂוּם לָכֶם שְׁאֵרִית
בָּאָרֶץ אלהים דאלפין וּלְהַחֲיוֹת לָכֶם לִפְלֵיטָה גְּדֹלָה להח, מבה, יזל, אום׃

THIRD READING - JACOB - TIFERET

8 וְעַתָּה לֹא־אַתֶּם שְׁלַחְתֶּם אֹתִי הֵנָּה מ״ה יה כִּי הָאֱלֹהִים ילה, מום
וַיְשִׂימֵנִי לְאָב לְפַרְעֹה וּלְאָדוֹן אני לְכָל יה - אדני ־בֵּיתוֹ ב״פ ראה וּמֹשֵׁל
בְּכָל לכב ־אֶרֶץ אלהים דאלפין מִצְרָיִם מצר׃ 9 מַהֲרוּ וַעֲלוּ אֶל־אָבִי
וַאֲמַרְתֶּם אֵלָיו כֹּה היי אָמַר בִּנְךָ יוֹסֵף ציון, ו״פ יהוה, ה״פ אל שָׂמַנִי אֱלֹהִים
ילה, מום לְאָדוֹן אני לְכָל יה - אדני ־מִצְרָיִם מצר רְדָה אֵלַי אַל־תַּעֲמֹד׃

וַעֲלוּ

Genesis 45:9 – Joseph tested his brothers by sending them back to Israel and to their father, Jacob, once again. He gave each of the brothers a certain amount of food, but he gave Benjamin five times what he gave to the others. Joseph did this to see if the brothers would be jealous of Benjamin and if they would harm him in any way. It was a test of how much spiritual growth they had experienced since they had sold Joseph into slavery.

[9] Now hurry back to my father and say to him, 'This is what your son Joseph says: God has made me lord of all Egypt. Come down to me; don't delay.

[10] You shall live in the region of Goshen and be near me—you, your children and grandchildren, your flocks and herds, and all you have.

[11] I will provide for you there, because five years of famine are still to come. Otherwise you and your household and all who belong to you will become destitute.'

[12] You can see for yourselves, and so can my brother Benjamin, that it is really I who am speaking to you.

[13] Tell my father about all the honor accorded me in Egypt and about everything you have seen. And bring my father down here quickly."

[14] Then he threw his arms around his brother Benjamin and wept, and Benjamin embraced him, weeping.

[15] And he kissed all his brothers and wept over them. Afterward his brothers talked with him.

[16] When the news reached Pharaoh's palace that Joseph's brothers had come, Pharaoh and all his officials were pleased.

[17] Pharaoh said to Joseph, "Tell your brothers, 'do this: Load your animals and return
to the land of Canaan, [18] and bring your father and your households back to me. I will
give you the best of the land of Egypt and you can enjoy the fat of the land.'

FOURTH READING - MOSES - NETZACH

[19] You are also directed to tell them, 'Do this: Take some carts from Egypt for your children and your wives, and get your father and come.

[20] Never mind about your belongings, because the best of all Egypt will be yours.' "

[21] So the sons of Israel did this. Joseph gave them carts, as Pharaoh had commanded, and he also gave them provisions for their journey.

[22] To each of them he gave new clothing, but to Benjamin he gave three hundred shekels of silver and five sets of clothes.

10 וְיָשַׁבְתָּ בְאֶרֶץ אלהים דאלפין ־גֹּשֶׁן וְהָיִיתָ קָרוֹב אֵלַי אַתָּה וּבָנֶיךָ
וּבְנֵי בָנֶיךָ וְצֹאנְךָ וּבְקָרְךָ וְכָל ילי ־אֲשֶׁר־לָךְ׃ 11 וְכִלְכַּלְתִּי אֹתְךָ
שָׁם כִּי־עוֹד חָמֵשׁ שָׁנִים רָעָב רבוע אלהים - ע"ב פֶּן־תִּוָּרֵשׁ אַתָּה
וּבֵיתְךָ ב"פ ראה וְכָל ילי ־אֲשֶׁר־לָךְ׃ 12 וְהִנֵּה עֵינֵיכֶם ריבוע מ"ה רֹאוֹת
וְעֵינֵי ריבוע מ"ה אָחִי בִנְיָמִין כִּי־פִי הַמְדַבֵּר ראה אֲלֵיכֶם׃ 13 וְהִגַּדְתֶּם
לְאָבִי אֶת־כָּל ילי ־כְּבוֹדִי בְּמִצְרַיִם מצר וְאֵת כָּל ילי ־אֲשֶׁר רְאִיתֶם
וּמִהַרְתֶּם וְהוֹרַדְתֶּם אֶת־אָבִי הֵנָּה מ"ה יה׃ 14 וַיִּפֹּל עַל־צַוְּארֵי
בִנְיָמִן־אָחִיו וַיֵּבְךְּ וּבִנְיָמִן בָּכָה עַל־צַוָּארָיו׃ 15 וַיְנַשֵּׁק לְכָל
יה - אדני ־אֶחָיו וַיֵּבְךְּ עֲלֵהֶם וְאַחֲרֵי כֵן דִּבְּרוּ ראה אֶחָיו אִתּוֹ׃
16 וְהַקֹּל נִשְׁמַע בֵּית ב"פ ראה פַּרְעֹה לֵאמֹר בָּאוּ אֲחֵי יוֹסֵף
ציון, ו"פ יהוה, ה"פ אל וַיִּיטַב בְּעֵינֵי ריבוע מ"ה פַרְעֹה וּבְעֵינֵי ריבוע מ"ה עֲבָדָיו׃
17 וַיֹּאמֶר פַּרְעֹה אֶל־יוֹסֵף ציון, ו"פ יהוה, ה"פ אל אֱמֹר אֶל־אַחֶיךָ זֹאת
עֲשׂוּ טַעֲנוּ אֶת־בְּעִירְכֶם וּלְכוּ־בֹאוּ אַרְצָה אלהים דההין ע"ה כְּנָעַן׃
18 וּקְחוּ אֶת־אֲבִיכֶם וְאֶת־בָּתֵּיכֶם ב"פ ראה וּבֹאוּ אֵלָי וְאֶתְּנָה לָכֶם אֶת־
טוּב והו אֶרֶץ אלהים דאלפין מִצְרַיִם מצר וְאִכְלוּ אֶת־חֵלֶב הָאָרֶץ אלהים דההין ע"ה׃

FOURTH READING - MOSES - NETZACH

19 וְאַתָּה צֻוֵּיתָה פוי זֹאת עֲשׂוּ קְחוּ־לָכֶם מֵאֶרֶץ אלהים דאלפין מִצְרַיִם
מצר עֲגָלוֹת לְטַפְּכֶם וְלִנְשֵׁיכֶם וּנְשָׂאתֶם אֶת־אֲבִיכֶם וּבָאתֶם׃
20 וְעֵינְכֶם ריבוע מ"ה אַל־תָּחֹס עַל־כְּלֵיכֶם כלי כִּי־טוּב והו, אום כָּל ילי
־אֶרֶץ אלהים דאלפין מִצְרַיִם מצר לָכֶם הוּא׃ 21 וַיַּעֲשׂוּ־כֵן בְּנֵי יִשְׂרָאֵל
וַיִּתֵּן לָהֶם יוֹסֵף ציון, ו"פ יהוה, ה"פ אל עֲגָלוֹת עַל־פִּי פַרְעֹה וַיִּתֵּן לָהֶם
צֵדָה לַדָּרֶךְ ב"פ יב"ק׃ 22 לְכֻלָּם נָתַן לָאִישׁ ע"ה קנ"א קס"א חֲלִפוֹת שְׂמָלֹת

23 And this is what he sent to his father: ten donkeys loaded with the best things of Egypt, and ten female donkeys loaded with grain and bread and other provisions for his journey.

24 Then he sent his brothers away, and as they were leaving he said to them, "Don't quarrel on the way!"

25 So they went up out of Egypt and came to their father Jacob in the land of Canaan.

26 They told him, "Joseph is still alive! In fact, he is ruler of all Egypt." Jacob was stunned; he did not believe them.

27 But when they told him everything Joseph had said to them, and when he saw the carts Joseph had sent to carry him back, the spirit of their father Jacob revived.

FIFTH READING - AARON - HOD

28 And Israel said, "I'm convinced! My son Joseph is still alive. I will go and see him before I die."

46[1] So Israel set out with all that was his, and when he reached Beersheba, he offered

---

וַיָּפָג

Genesis 45:26 – The brothers told Jacob that Joseph was still alive, yet Jacob did not believe them. Since Jacob was such a high soul and a prophet, we must ask why he was not able to see that his son Joseph was still alive. It was because from the moment Jacob saw Joseph's bloodied clothing, he had become depressed and had thus lost his ability to be a prophet. This is a very important lesson for us today: The moment we become depressed, we lose the power of prophecy, denying ourselves the opportunity to receive messages from the angels and signs from the Light of the Creator.

Rashi tells us that Jacob's spirit revived when the brothers relayed to him the sign that Joseph had given them as proof that it was indeed he who had sent the wagons and the food and treasures. Rashi says: "This means that the *Shechina* (Divine Presence) rested on him [Jacob] again after having left him while he brooded all these past years over the loss of Joseph."

The signs from the Creator are all around us, and when we open ourselves to them, we will find our spirits revived.

וַיִּסַּע

Genesis 46:1 – Jacob went down to Egypt. God appeared to Jacob and told him not to fear, that he would be safe on his journey. So Jacob went down into Egypt, secure in the promise that he had been given. The *Zohar* says that

וּלְבִנְיָמִן נָתַן שְׁלֹשׁ מֵאוֹת כֶּסֶף וְחָמֵשׁ חֲלִפֹת שְׂמָלֹת׃ 23 וּלְאָבִיו
שָׁלַח כְּזֹאת עֲשָׂרָה חֲמֹרִים נֹשְׂאִים מִטּוּב והו מִצְרָיִם מצר וְעֶשֶׂר
אֲתֹנֹת נֹשְׂאֹת בָּר וָלֶחֶם וּמָזוֹן ג"פ יהוה לְאָבִיו לַדָּרֶךְ ב"פ יב"ק׃ 24 וַיְשַׁלַּח
אֶת־אֶחָיו וַיֵּלֵכוּ וַיֹּאמֶר כלי אֲלֵהֶם אַל־תִּרְגְּזוּ בַּדָּרֶךְ ב"פ יב"ק׃
25 וַיַּעֲלוּ מִמִּצְרָיִם מצר וַיָּבֹאוּ אֶרֶץ אלהים דאלפין כְּנַעַן אֶל־יַעֲקֹב
יאהדונהי - אידהנויה אֲבִיהֶם׃ 26 וַיַּגִּדוּ לוֹ לֵאמֹר עוֹד יוֹסֵף ציון, ו"פ יהוה, ה"פ אל
חַי וְכִי־הוּא מֹשֵׁל בְּכָל לכב ־אֶרֶץ אלהים דאלפין מִצְרָיִם מצר וַיָּפָג לִבּוֹ
כִּי לֹא־הֶאֱמִין לָהֶם׃ 27 וַיְדַבְּרוּ ראה אֵלָיו אֵת כָּל ילי ־דִּבְרֵי ראה
יוֹסֵף ציון, ו"פ יהוה, ה"פ אל אֲשֶׁר דִּבֶּר ראה אֲלֵהֶם וַיַּרְא אֶת־הָעֲגָלוֹת
אֲשֶׁר־שָׁלַח יוֹסֵף לָשֵׂאת אֹתוֹ וַתְּחִי רוּחַ מלוי אלהים דיודין
יַעֲקֹב יאהדונהי - אידהנויה אֲבִיהֶם׃

FIFTH READING - AARON - HOD

28 וַיֹּאמֶר יִשְׂרָאֵל רַב עוֹד־יוֹסֵף ציון, ו"פ יהוה, ה"פ אל בְּנִי חָי אֵלְכָה
וְאֶרְאֶנּוּ בְּטֶרֶם רמ"ח ע"ה אָמוּת׃ 46 1 וַיִּסַּע יִשְׂרָאֵל וְכָל ילי ־אֲשֶׁר־לוֹ
וַיָּבֹא בְּאֵרָה קנ"א - ב"ן שָׁבַע אלהים דיודין - ע"ב וַיִּזְבַּח זְבָחִים לֵאלֹהֵי דמב, ילה
אָבִיו יִצְחָק ד"פ ב"ן׃ 2 וַיֹּאמֶר אֱלֹהִים ילה, מום | לְיִשְׂרָאֵל בְּמַרְאֹת
הַלַּיְלָה מלה וַיֹּאמֶר יַעֲקֹב יאהדונהי - אידהנויה | יַעֲקֹב יאהדונהי - אידהנויה וַיֹּאמֶר

600,000 angels went with him. When he went to Egypt, he took everything he had and everyone who was dear to him and started out on a completely new life. He left behind all the places that were familiar and comfortable for something completely unknown, with only the certainty of the presence of the Creator in his life.

In the same way, when each of us goes down into our own personal Egypt (meaning, to finish a *tikkun* process), leaving the familiar and comfortable behind and entering into a situation where we may encounter unknown difficulties, we need to arm ourselves by using Kabbalah tools and technology like scanning the *Zohar*, meditating on the *Ana Beko'ach* and using the 72 Names of God.

sacrifices to the God of his father Isaac.

2 And God spoke to Israel in a vision at night and said, "Jacob! Jacob!" "Here I am," he replied.

3 "I am God, the God of your father," he said. "Do not be afraid to go down to Egypt, for I will make you into a great nation there.

4 I will go down to Egypt with you, and I will surely bring you back again. And Joseph's own hand will close your eyes."

5 Then Jacob left Beersheba, and Israel's sons took their father Jacob and their children and their wives in the carts that Pharaoh had sent to transport him.

6 They also took with them their livestock and the possessions they had acquired in Canaan, and Jacob and all his offspring went to Egypt.

7 He took with him to Egypt his sons and grandsons and his daughters and granddaughters—all his offspring.

8 These are the names of the sons of Israel who went to Egypt: Reuben, the firstborn of Jacob.

9 The sons of Reuben: Hanoch, Pallu, Hezron, and Carmi.

10 The sons of Simeon: Jemuel, Jamin, Ohad, Jakin, Zohar, and Shaul, the son of a Canaanite woman.

11 The sons of Levi: Gershon, Kohath, and Merari.

12 The sons of Judah: Er, Onan, Shelah, Perez, and Zerah (but Er and Onan had died in the land of Canaan). The sons of Perez: Hezron and Hamul.

13 The sons of Issachar: Tola, Puah, Jashub, and Shimron.

14 The sons of Zebulun: Sered, Elon, and Jahleel.

15 These were the sons Leah bore to Jacob in Paddan Aram, besides his daughter Dinah. These sons and daughters of his were thirty-three in all.

16 The sons of Gad: Zephon, Haggi, Shuni, Ezbon, Eri, Arodi, and Areli.

17 The sons of Asher: Imnah, Ishvah, Ishvi, and Beriah. Their sister was Serah. The sons of Beriah: Heber and Malkiel.

18 These were the children born to Jacob by Zilpah, whom Laban had given to his daughter Leah—sixteen in all.

הִנֵּנִי: 3 וַיֹּאמֶר אָנֹכִי איע הָאֵל לאה (אלד ע״ה) אֱלֹהֵי דמב, ילה אָבִיךָ אַל־
תִּירָא מֵרְדָה מִצְרַיְמָה מצר כִּי־לְגוֹי מלוי מ״ה גָּדוֹל להח, מבה, יזל, אום
אֲשִׂימְךָ שָׁם: 4 אָנֹכִי איע אֵרֵד עִמְּךָ נמם מִצְרַיְמָה מצר וְאָנֹכִי איע אַעַלְךָ
גַם יגל ־עָלֹה וְיוֹסֵף ציון, ו״פ יהוה, ה״פ אל יָשִׁית יָדוֹ עַל־עֵינֶיךָ ע״ה קס״א:
5 וַיָּקָם יַעֲקֹב יאהדונהי - אידהנויה מִבְּאֵר קנ״א - ב״ן שָׁבַע אלהים דיודין - ע״ב
וַיִּשְׂאוּ בְנֵי־יִשְׂרָאֵל אֶת־יַעֲקֹב יאהדונהי - אידהנויה אֲבִיהֶם וְאֶת־טַפָּם
וְאֶת־נְשֵׁיהֶם בָּעֲגָלוֹת אֲשֶׁר־שָׁלַח פַּרְעֹה לָשֵׂאת אֹתוֹ: 6 וַיִּקְחוּ
וזעם אֶת־מִקְנֵיהֶם וְאֶת־רְכוּשָׁם אֲשֶׁר רָכְשׁוּ בְּאֶרֶץ אלהים דאלפין
כְּנַעַן וַיָּבֹאוּ מִצְרָיְמָה מצר יַעֲקֹב יאהדונהי - אידהנויה וְכָל ילי ־זַרְעוֹ אִתּוֹ:
7 בָּנָיו וּבְנֵי בָנָיו אִתּוֹ בְּנֹתָיו וּבְנוֹת בָּנָיו וְכָל ילי ־זַרְעוֹ הֵבִיא
אִתּוֹ מִצְרָיְמָה מצר: [ס] 8 וְאֵלֶּה שְׁמוֹת בְּנֵי־יִשְׂרָאֵל הַבָּאִים
מִצְרַיְמָה מצר יַעֲקֹב יאהדונהי - אידהנויה וּבָנָיו בְּכֹר יַעֲקֹב יאהדונהי - אידהנויה
רְאוּבֵן ג״פ אלהים: 9 וּבְנֵי רְאוּבֵן ג״פ אלהים חֲנוֹךְ וּפַלּוּא וְחֶצְרֹן וְכַרְמִי:
10 וּבְנֵי שִׁמְעוֹן יְמוּאֵל וְיָמִין וְאֹהַד וְיָכִין וְצֹחַר וְשָׁאוּל בֶּן־
הַכְּנַעֲנִית: 11 וּבְנֵי לֵוִי מלוי ע״ב, דמב גֵּרְשׁוֹן ע״ה ב״פ מנצפ״ך קְהָת וּמְרָרִי:
12 וּבְנֵי יְהוּדָה עֵר י״פ ז״ך וְאוֹנָן וְשֵׁלָה וָפֶרֶץ וָזָרַח רי״ו ע״ה וַיָּמָת עֵר
וְאוֹנָן בְּאֶרֶץ אלהים דאלפין כְּנַעַן וַיִּהְיוּ מלוי ס״ג בְנֵי־פֶרֶץ חֶצְרֹן וְחָמוּל:
13 וּבְנֵי יִשָּׂשכָר תּוֹלָע אבגיתץ, ושר וּפֻוָה וְיוֹב וְשִׁמְרֹן: 14 וּבְנֵי זְבֻלוּן
סֶרֶד וְאֵלוֹן וְיַחְלְאֵל: 15 אֵלֶּה | בְּנֵי לֵאָה לאה (אלד ע״ה) אֲשֶׁר יָלְדָה
לְיַעֲקֹב יאהדונהי - אידהנויה בְּפַדַּן אֲרָם וְאֵת דִּינָה בִתּוֹ כָּל ילי ־נֶפֶשׁ
רמ״ח - ז׳ הויות בָּנָיו וּבְנוֹתָיו שְׁלֹשִׁים וְשָׁלֹשׁ: 16 וּבְנֵי גָד צִפְיוֹן וְחַגִּי
שׁוּנִי וְאֶצְבֹּן עֵרִי וַאֲרוֹדִי וְאַרְאֵלִי: 17 וּבְנֵי אָשֵׁר ריבוע אלהים - אלהים דיודין ע״ה
יִמְנָה וְיִשְׁוָה וְיִשְׁוִי וּבְרִיעָה וְשֶׂרַח אֲחֹתָם וּבְנֵי בְרִיעָה חֶבֶר
וּמַלְכִּיאֵל: 18 אֵלֶּה בְּנֵי זִלְפָּה אֲשֶׁר־נָתַן לָבָן לְלֵאָה לאה (אלד ע״ה)

[19] *The sons of Jacob's wife Rachel: Joseph and Benjamin.* [20] *In Egypt, Manasseh and Ephraim were born to Joseph by Asenath, daughter of Potiphera, priest of On.*

[21] *The sons of Benjamin: Bela, Beker, Ashbel, Gera, Naaman, Ehi, Rosh, Muppim, Huppim, and Ard.*

[22] *These were the sons of Rachel who were born to Jacob—fourteen in all.*

[23] *The son of Dan: Hushim.* [24] *The sons of Naphtali: Jahziel, Guni, Jezer, and Shillem.*

[25] *These were the sons born to Jacob by Bilhah whom Laban had given to his daughter Rachel—seven in all.*

[26] *All those who went to Egypt with Jacob—those who were his direct descendants, not counting his sons' wives—numbered sixty-six persons.*

[27] *With the two sons who had been born to Joseph in Egypt, the members of Jacob's family, which went to Egypt, were seventy in all.*

SIXTH READING - JOSEPH - YESOD

[28] *Now Jacob sent Judah ahead of him to Joseph to get directions to Goshen. When they arrived in the region of Goshen,* [29] *Joseph had his chariot made ready and went to Goshen to meet his father Israel. As soon as Joseph appeared before him, he threw his arms around his father and wept for a long time.*

[30] *Israel said to Joseph, "Now I am ready to die, since I have seen for myself that you are still alive."*

שִׁבְעִים

Genesis 46:27 – Seventy people—comprising Jacob's entire family—went into Egypt. Each of those people represented a nation. The *Zohar* says:

> *Rav Chiya was sitting before Rav Shimon. He said to him, "Why did the Bible count in the beginning that the sons of Jacob were 12, but afterwards that they were 70, as is written: 'All the souls of the house of Jacob who came into Egypt were 70.' (Genesis 46:27) And what is the reason that they were 70 and not more?" RAV SHIMON said to him, "It corresponds to the 70 nations in the world. They were one nation, equal to them all."*
>
> *– The Zohar, Shemot 11:65*

בִּתּוֹ וַתֵּלֶד אֶת־אֵלֶּה לְיַעֲקֹב יאהדונהי - אידהנויה שֵׁשׁ עֶשְׂרֵה נָפֶשׁ
רמ"ח - ז' הויות: 19 בְּנֵי רָחֵל רבוע ס"ג - ע"ב אֵשֶׁת יַעֲקֹב יאהדונהי - אידהנויה יוֹסֵף
וּבִנְיָמִן: 20 וַיִּוָּלֵד לְיוֹסֵף ציון, ר"פ יהוה, ה"פ אל בְּאֶרֶץ אלהים דאלפין ציון, ר"פ יהוה, ה"פ אל
מִצְרַיִם מצר אֲשֶׁר יָלְדָה־לּוֹ אָסְנַת יהוה מצפצ יהוה ברבוע בַּת־פּוֹטִי פֶרַע
כֹּהֵן מלה אֹן אֶת־מְנַשֶּׁה וְאֶת־אֶפְרָיִם אל מצפץ: 21 וּבְנֵי בִנְיָמִן בֶּלַע
וָבֶכֶר וְאַשְׁבֵּל גֵּרָא וְנַעֲמָן אֵחִי וָרֹאשׁ ריבוע אלהים - אלהים דיודין ע"ה מֻפִּים
וְחֻפִּים וָאָרְדְּ: 22 אֵלֶּה בְּנֵי רָחֵל רבוע ס"ג - ע"ב אֲשֶׁר יֻלַּד לְיַעֲקֹב
יאהדונהי - אידהנויה כָּל ילי ־נֶפֶשׁ רמ"ח - ז' הויות אַרְבָּעָה עָשָׂר: 23 וּבְנֵי־דָן
חֻשִׁים: 24 וּבְנֵי נַפְתָּלִי יַחְצְאֵל וְגוּנִי וְיֵצֶר וְשִׁלֵּם: 25 אֵלֶּה בְּנֵי
בִלְהָה מ"ב אֲשֶׁר־נָתַן לָבָן לְרָחֵל רבוע ס"ג - ע"ב בִּתּוֹ וַתֵּלֶד אֶת־אֵלֶּה
לְיַעֲקֹב יאהדונהי - אידהנויה כָּל ילי ־נֶפֶשׁ רמ"ח - ז' הויות שִׁבְעָה: 26 כָּל ילי
־הַנֶּפֶשׁ רמ"ח - ז' הויות הַבָּאָה לְיַעֲקֹב יאהדונהי - אידהנויה מִצְרַיְמָה מצר יֹצְאֵי
יְרֵכוֹ מִלְּבַד נְשֵׁי בְנֵי־יַעֲקֹב יאהדונהי - אידהנויה כָּל ילי ־נֶפֶשׁ רמ"ח - ז' הויות
שִׁשִּׁים וָשֵׁשׁ: 27 וּבְנֵי יוֹסֵף ציון, ר"פ יהוה, ה"פ אל אֲשֶׁר־יֻלַּד־לוֹ בְמִצְרַיִם
מצר נֶפֶשׁ רמ"ח - ז' הויות שְׁנָיִם כָּל ילי ־הַנֶּפֶשׁ רמ"ח - ז' הויות לְבֵית ב"פ ראה ־יַעֲקֹב
יאהדונהי - אידהנויה הַבָּאָה מִצְרַיְמָה מצר שִׁבְעִים: [ס]

SIXTH READING - JOSEPH - YESOD

28 וְאֶת־יְהוּדָה שָׁלַח לְפָנָיו אֶל־יוֹסֵף ציון, ר"פ יהוה, ה"פ אל לְהוֹרֹת לְפָנָיו
גֹּשְׁנָה וַיָּבֹאוּ אַרְצָה אלהים דההין ע"ה גֹּשֶׁן: 29 וַיֶּאְסֹר יוֹסֵף ציון, ר"פ יהוה, ה"פ אל

Although there are more than 200 nations in the world today, each of them originated from one of these 70. Each person who went down into Egypt was given Light representing one nation. Whenever we receive Light from the Creator, we must be aware that it is to be shared with others—even whole nations—as well as being for ourselves. We are responsible for sharing our Light with the entire world.

31 Then Joseph said to his brothers and to his father's household, "I will go up and speak to Pharaoh and will say to him, 'My brothers and my father's household, who were living in the land of Canaan, have come to me.

32 The men are shepherds; they tend livestock, and they have brought along their flocks and herds and everything they own.'

33 When Pharaoh calls you in and asks, 'What is your occupation?'

34 you should answer, 'Your servants have tended livestock from our boyhood on, just as our fathers did.' Then you will be allowed to settle in the region of Goshen, for all shepherds are detestable to the Egyptians."

47 1 Joseph went and told Pharaoh, "My father and brothers, with their flocks and herds and everything they own, have come from the land of Canaan and are now in Goshen."

2 He chose five of his brothers and presented them before Pharaoh.

3 Pharaoh asked the brothers, "What is your occupation?" "Your servants are shepherds," they replied to Pharaoh, "just as our fathers were."

4 They also said to him, "We have come to live here awhile, because the famine is severe in Canaan and your servants' flocks have no pasture. So now, please let your servants settle in Goshen."

תִּשְׁבוּ

Genesis 46:34 – Jacob Entered Egypt. Although the famine was supposed to last for seven years, it ended the moment Jacob entered Egypt. This was because righteous people have the ability to use mind over matter. In this way, they are able to change destiny and create miracles.

Instead of keeping his family in Egypt, Joseph ensured that they settled in the land of Goshen, which was a special area within Egypt where there was no negativity. Joseph did not want his family to be surrounded by the negative forces embodied by the Egyptians.

Joseph told his brothers that when Pharaoh called for them and asked them about their occupations, they should tell him, "'Your servants have tended livestock from our boyhood on, just as our fathers did.' Then you will be allowed to settle in the region of Goshen, for all shepherds are detestable to the Egyptians." (Genesis 46:34)

From this, we learn that it is very important to choose our environment. Even the most powerfully positive person living in a negative environment becomes influenced by his or her surroundings.

מֶרְכַּבְתּוֹ וַיַּעַל לִקְרַאת־יִשְׂרָאֵל אָבִיו גֹּשְׁנָה וַיֵּרָא אֵלָיו וַיִּפֹּל
עַל־צַוָּארָיו וַיֵּבְךְּ עַל־צַוָּארָיו עוֹד׃ 30 וַיֹּאמֶר יִשְׂרָאֵל אֶל־יוֹסֵף
ציון, ר״פ יהוה, ה״פ אל אָמוּתָה הַפָּעַם אַחֲרֵי רְאוֹתִי אֶת־פָּנֶיךָ ס״ג - מ״ה - ב״ן כִּי
עוֹדְךָ חָי׃ 31 וַיֹּאמֶר יוֹסֵף ציון, ר״פ יהוה, ה״פ אל אֶל־אֶחָיו וְאֶל־בֵּית ב״פ ראה
אָבִיו אֶעֱלֶה וְאַגִּידָה לְפַרְעֹה וְאֹמְרָה אֵלָיו אַחַי וּבֵית ב״פ ראה ־אָבִי
אֲשֶׁר בְּאֶרֶץ אלהים דאלפין ־כְּנַעַן בָּאוּ אֵלָי׃ 32 וְהָאֲנָשִׁים רֹעֵי צֹאן
מלוי אהיה דיודין ע״ה כִּי־אַנְשֵׁי מִקְנֶה הָיוּ וְצֹאנָם וּבְקָרָם וְכָל יל״י ־אֲשֶׁר
לָהֶם הֵבִיאוּ׃ 33 וְהָיָה יהוה, יהה כִּי־יִקְרָא לָכֶם פַּרְעֹה וְאָמַר מַה מ״ה
־מַּעֲשֵׂיכֶם׃ 34 וַאֲמַרְתֶּם אַנְשֵׁי מִקְנֶה הָיוּ עֲבָדֶיךָ מִנְּעוּרֵינוּ
וְעַד־עַתָּה גַּם יג״ל ־אֲנַחְנוּ גַּם יג״ל ־אֲבֹתֵינוּ בַּעֲבוּר תֵּשְׁבוּ בְּאֶרֶץ
אלהים דאלפין גֹּשֶׁן כִּי־תוֹעֲבַת מִצְרַיִם מצר כָּל יל״י ־רֹעֵה רהע צֹאן מלוי אהיה דיודין ע״ה׃
47 1 וַיָּבֹא יוֹסֵף ציון, ר״פ יהוה, ה״פ אל וַיַּגֵּד לְפַרְעֹה וַיֹּאמֶר אָבִי וְאַחַי
וְצֹאנָם וּבְקָרָם וְכָל יל״י ־אֲשֶׁר לָהֶם בָּאוּ מֵאֶרֶץ אלהים דאלפין כְּנָעַן
וְהִנָּם בְּאֶרֶץ אלהים דאלפין גֹּשֶׁן׃ 2 וּמִקְצֵה אֶחָיו לָקַח חֲמִשָּׁה אֲנָשִׁים
וַיַּצִּגֵם לִפְנֵי פַרְעֹה׃ 3 וַיֹּאמֶר פַּרְעֹה אֶל־אֶחָיו מַה מ״ה ־מַּעֲשֵׂיכֶם
וַיֹּאמְרוּ אֶל־פַּרְעֹה רֹעֵה רהע צֹאן מלוי אהיה דיודין ע״ה עֲבָדֶיךָ גַּם־ יג״ל
אֲנַחְנוּ גַּם יג״ל ־אֲבוֹתֵינוּ׃ 4 וַיֹּאמְרוּ אֶל־פַּרְעֹה לָגוּר בָּאָרֶץ
אלהים דאלפין בָּאנוּ כִּי־אֵין מִרְעֶה לַצֹּאן מלוי אהיה דיודין ע״ה אֲשֶׁר לַעֲבָדֶיךָ
כִּי־כָבֵד הָרָעָב רבוע אלהים - ע״ב בְּאֶרֶץ אלהים דאלפין כְּנָעַן וְעַתָּה יֵשְׁבוּ־
נָא עֲבָדֶיךָ בְּאֶרֶץ אלהים דאלפין גֹּשֶׁן׃ 5 וַיֹּאמֶר פַּרְעֹה אֶל־יוֹסֵף
ציון, ר״פ יהוה, ה״פ אל לֵאמֹר אָבִיךָ וְאַחֶיךָ בָּאוּ אֵלֶיךָ אני׃ 6 אֶרֶץ
אלהים דאלפין מִצְרַיִם מצר לְפָנֶיךָ ס״ג - מ״ה - ב״ן הִוא בְּמֵיטַב הָאָרֶץ
אלהים דההין ע״ה הוֹשֵׁב אֶת־אָבִיךָ וְאֶת־אַחֶיךָ יֵשְׁבוּ בְּאֶרֶץ אלהים דאלפין

5 Pharaoh said to Joseph, "Your father and your brothers have come to you, 6 and the land of Egypt is before you; settle your father and your brothers in the best part of the land. Let them live in Goshen. And if you know of any among them with special ability, put them in charge of my own livestock."

7 Then Joseph brought his father Jacob in and presented him before Pharaoh. After Jacob blessed Pharaoh,

8 Pharaoh asked him, "How old are you?"

9 And Jacob said to Pharaoh, "The years of my pilgrimage are a hundred and thirty. My years have been few and difficult, and they do not equal the years of the pilgrimage of my fathers."

10 Then Jacob blessed Pharaoh and went out from his presence.

SEVENTH READING - DAVID - MALCHUT

11 So Joseph settled his father and his brothers in Egypt and gave them property in the best part of the land, the district of Rameses, as Pharaoh directed.

Genesis 47:7 – Jacob and Pharaoh finally met. When Pharaoh asked Jacob his age, Jacob replied that he was 130 years old and that he had faced many difficulties in his life. A commentary tells us that Jacob looked so much like Abraham that Pharaoh asked his age to be sure he was not actually Abraham. (*Midrash HaGadol, Beresheet 47:8*)

Kabbalah teaches that the human aging process did not exist before Jacob; people simply died. Aging is actually a blessing, however, reminding us that time is passing and that we still have spiritual work that needs to be done. We can learn from Jacob not to complain about our lives or about where we are on our spiritual path. Everything comes from the Light, and every obstacle is an opportunity to work on our spiritual growth.

Genesis 47:14 – All the money of Egypt flowed through Joseph. Joseph is the chariot, the channel for the *Sefira* of *Yesod*. To reach the level of *Malchut*, all Light has to flow through the *Sefira* of *Yesod*. Because Joseph was the channel of *Yesod*, the Light flowed through him, and thus all the money flowed through him, too. This is connected to the concept "as Above, so Below." Often, we pursue only physical sustenance, but if we pursue the spiritual first, we will receive on the physical level as well. If we pursue the Light with absolute certainty, all else will be provided for us.

גֹּשֶׁן וְאִם יוהך יָדַעְתָּ וְיֶשׁ־בָּם מ"ב אַנְשֵׁי־חַיִל ומב וְשַׂמְתָּם שָׂרֵי
מִקְנֶה עַל־אֲשֶׁר־לִי: 7 וַיָּבֵא יוֹסֵף ציון, ו"פ יהוה, ה"פ אל אֶת־יַעֲקֹב
יאהדונהי - אידהנויה אָבִיו וַיַּעֲמִדֵהוּ לִפְנֵי פַרְעֹה וַיְבָרֶךְ עסמ"ב יַעֲקֹב
יאהדונהי - אידהנויה אֶת־פַּרְעֹה: 8 וַיֹּאמֶר פַּרְעֹה אֶל־יַעֲקֹב יאהדונהי - אידהנויה
כַּמָּה יְמֵי שְׁנֵי חַיֶּיךָ: 9 וַיֹּאמֶר יַעֲקֹב יאהדונהי - אידהנויה אֶל־פַּרְעֹה
יְמֵי שְׁנֵי מְגוּרַי שְׁלֹשִׁים וּמְאַת שָׁנָה מְעַט וְרָעִים הָיוּ יְמֵי שְׁנֵי
חַיַּי וְלֹא הִשִּׂיגוּ אֶת־יְמֵי שְׁנֵי חַיֵּי אֲבֹתַי בִּימֵי מְגוּרֵיהֶם: 10 וַיְבָרֶךְ
עסמ"ב יַעֲקֹב יאהדונהי - אידהנויה אֶת־פַּרְעֹה וַיֵּצֵא מִלִּפְנֵי פַרְעֹה:

SEVENTH READING - DAVID - MALCHUT

11 וַיּוֹשֵׁב יוֹסֵף ציון, ו"פ יהוה, ה"פ אל אֶת־אָבִיו וְאֶת־אֶחָיו וַיִּתֵּן לָהֶם
אֲחֻזָּה בְּאֶרֶץ אלהים דאלפין מִצְרַיִם מצר בְּמֵיטַב הָאָרֶץ אלהים דההין ע"ה
בְּאֶרֶץ אלהים דאלפין רַעְמְסֵס כַּאֲשֶׁר צִוָּה פוי פַרְעֹה: 12 וַיְכַלְכֵּל יוֹסֵף
ציון, ו"פ יהוה, ה"פ אל אֶת־אָבִיו וְאֶת־אֶחָיו וְאֵת כָּל ילי בֵּית אָבִיו לֶחֶם
ג"פ יהוה לְפִי הַטָּף: 13 וְלֶחֶם ג"פ יהוה אֵין בְּכָל לכב הָאָרֶץ אלהים דההין ע"ה
כִּי־כָבֵד הָרָעָב רבוע אלהים - ע"ב מְאֹד וַתֵּלַהּ י"פ אלהים - ה' אֶרֶץ אלהים דאלפין
מִצְרַיִם מצר וְאֶרֶץ אלהים דאלפין כְּנַעַן מִפְּנֵי הָרָעָב רבוע אלהים - ע"ב: 14 וַיְלַקֵּט
יוֹסֵף ציון, ו"פ יהוה, ה"פ אל אֶת־כָּל ילי הַכֶּסֶף הַנִּמְצָא בְאֶרֶץ אלהים דאלפין מִצְרַיִם
מצר וּבְאֶרֶץ אלהים דאלפין כְּנַעַן בַּשֶּׁבֶר אֲשֶׁר־הֵם שֹׁבְרִים וַיָּבֵא יוֹסֵף
ציון, ו"פ יהוה, ה"פ אל אֶת־הַכֶּסֶף בֵּיתָה ב"פ ראה פַּרְעֹה: 15 וַיִּתֹּם הַכֶּסֶף מֵאֶרֶץ
אלהים דאלפין מִצְרַיִם מצר וּמֵאֶרֶץ אלהים דאלפין כְּנַעַן וַיָּבֹאוּ כָל ילי מִצְרַיִם

*12 Joseph also provided his father and his brothers and all his father's household with
food, according to the number of their children.*

*13 There was no food, however, in the whole region because the famine was severe;
both Egypt and Canaan wasted away because of the famine.*

*14 Joseph collected all the money that was to be found in Egypt and Canaan in
payment for the grain they were buying, and he brought it to Pharaoh's palace.*

*15 When the money of the people of Egypt and Canaan was gone, all Egypt came to
Joseph and said, "Give us food. Why should we die before your eyes? Our money is
used up."16 "Then bring your livestock," said Joseph. "I will sell you food in exchange
for your livestock, since your money is gone." 17 So they brought their livestock to
Joseph, and he gave them food in exchange for their horses, their sheep and goats,
their cattle and donkeys. And he brought them through that year with food in exchange
for all their livestock.*

*18 When that year was over, they came to him the following year and said, "We cannot
hide from our lord the fact that since our money is gone and our livestock belongs to
you, there is nothing left for our lord except our bodies and our land.*

*19 Why should we perish before your eyes—we and our land as well? Buy us and our
land in exchange for food, and we with our land will be in bondage to Pharaoh. Give
us seed so that we may live and not die, and that the land may not become
desolate."*

*20 So Joseph bought all the land in Egypt for Pharaoh. The Egyptians, one and all, sold
their fields, because the famine was too severe for them. The land became Pharaoh's,
21 and Joseph reduced the people to servitude, from one end of Egypt to the other.*

*22 However, he did not buy the land of the priests, because they received a regular
allotment from Pharaoh and had food enough from the allotment Pharaoh gave them.
That is why they did not sell their land.*

*23 Joseph said to the people, "Now that I have bought you and your land today for
Pharaoh, here is seed for you so you can plant the ground.*

*24 But when the crop comes in, give a fifth of it to Pharaoh. The other four-fifths you
may keep as seed for the fields and as food for yourselves and your households and
your children."*

מצר אֶל־יוֹסֵף ציון, ר"פ יהוה, ה"פ אל לֵאמֹר הָבָה־לָּנוּ אלהים, מום לֶחֶם ג"פ יהוה וְלָמָּה
נָמוּת נֶגְדֶּךָ זן, מזבח כִּי אָפֵס כָּסֶף: 16 וַיֹּאמֶר יוֹסֵף ציון, ר"פ יהוה, ה"פ אל
הָבוּ אחד, אהבה, דאגה מִקְנֵיכֶם וְאֶתְּנָה נתה, קס"א - קנ"א - קמ"ג לָכֶם בְּמִקְנֵיכֶם
אִם יוהך ־אָפֵס כָּסֶף: 17 וַיָּבִיאוּ אֶת־מִקְנֵיהֶם אֶל־יוֹסֵף ציון, ר"פ יהוה, ה"פ אל
וַיִּתֵּן לָהֶם יוֹסֵף ציון, ר"פ יהוה, ה"פ אל לֶחֶם ג"פ יהוה בַּסּוּסִים ריבוע אדני, כוק
וּבְמִקְנֵה הַצֹּאן מלוי אהיה דיודין ע"ה וּבְמִקְנֵה הַבָּקָר וּבַחֲמֹרִים וַיְנַהֲלֵם
בַּלֶּחֶם ג"פ יהוה בְּכָל לכב ־מִקְנֵהֶם בַּשָּׁנָה הַהִוא: 18 וַתִּתֹּם הַשָּׁנָה
הַהִוא וַיָּבֹאוּ אֵלָיו בַּשָּׁנָה הַשֵּׁנִית וַיֹּאמְרוּ לוֹ לֹא־נְכַחֵד מֵאֲדֹנִי
כִּי אִם יוהך ־תַּם הַכֶּסֶף וּמִקְנֵה הַבְּהֵמָה ב"ן, לכב אֶל־אֲדֹנִי לֹא
נִשְׁאַר לִפְנֵי אֲדֹנִי בִּלְתִּי אִם יוהך ־גְּוִיָּתֵנוּ וְאַדְמָתֵנוּ: 19 לָמָּה נָמוּת
לְעֵינֶיךָ ע"ה קס"א גַּם יגל ־אֲנַחְנוּ גַּם אַדְמָתֵנוּ קְנֵה־אֹתָנוּ וְאֶת־אַדְמָתֵנוּ
בַּלָּחֶם ג"פ יהוה וְנִהְיֶה אֲנַחְנוּ וְאַדְמָתֵנוּ עֲבָדִים לְפַרְעֹה וְתֶן־זֶרַע
וְנִחְיֶה וְלֹא נָמוּת וְהָאֲדָמָה לֹא תֵשָׁם: 20 וַיִּקֶן יוֹסֵף ציון, ר"פ יהוה, ה"פ אל
אֶת־כָּל ילי ־אַדְמַת מִצְרַיִם מצר לְפַרְעֹה כִּי־מָכְרוּ מִצְרַיִם מצר אִישׁ
ע"ה קנ"א קס"א שָׂדֵהוּ כִּי־חָזַק פהל עֲלֵהֶם הָרָעָב רבוע אלהים - ע"ב וַתְּהִי הָאָרֶץ
אלהים דההין ע"ה לְפַרְעֹה: 21 וְאֶת־הָעָם הֶעֱבִיר אֹתוֹ לֶעָרִים מִקְצֵה
גְבוּל־מִצְרַיִם מצר וְעַד־קָצֵהוּ: 22 רַק אַדְמַת הַכֹּהֲנִים לֹא קָנָה
כִּי חֹק לַכֹּהֲנִים מֵאֵת פַּרְעֹה וְאָכְלוּ אֶת־חֻקָּם אֲשֶׁר נָתַן לָהֶם
פַּרְעֹה עַל־כֵּן לֹא מָכְרוּ אֶת־אַדְמָתָם: 23 וַיֹּאמֶר יוֹסֵף ציון, ר"פ יהוה, ה"פ אל
אֶל־הָעָם הֵן קָנִיתִי אֶתְכֶם הַיּוֹם נגד, זן, מזבח וְאֶת־אַדְמַתְכֶם לְפַרְעֹה
הֵא־לָכֶם זֶרַע וּזְרַעְתֶּם אֶת־הָאֲדָמָה: 24 וְהָיָה יהוה, יהה בַּתְּבוּאֹת
וּנְתַתֶּם חֲמִישִׁית לְפַרְעֹה וְאַרְבַּע הַיָּדֹת יִהְיֶה ייי לָכֶם לְזֶרַע
הַשָּׂדֶה שדי וּלְאָכְלְכֶם וְלַאֲשֶׁר בְּבָתֵּיכֶם וְלֶאֱכֹל לְטַפְּכֶם:

MAFTIR

25 "You have saved our lives," they said. "May we find favor in the eyes of our lord; we will be in bondage to Pharaoh."

26 So Joseph established it as a law concerning land in Egypt—still in force today—that a fifth of the produce belongs to Pharaoh. It was only the land of the priests that did not become Pharaoh's.

27 Now the Israelites settled in Egypt in the region of Goshen. They acquired property there and were fruitful and increased greatly in number.

HAFTARAH OF VAYIGASH

The Resurrection of the Dead is discussed through Ezekiel's prophecy of the "dry bones," the continuation of which pertains to this Haftarah reading. Often, the names "Joseph" and "Judah" are given to male children at their circumcision because these two names are specifically mentioned

Ezekiel 37:15-28

37 15 The word of the Lord came to me:

16 "Son of man, take a stick of wood and write on it, 'Belonging to Judah and the Israelites associated with him.' Then take another stick of wood, and write on it, 'Ephraim's stick, belonging to Joseph and all the house of Israel associated with him.'

17 Join them together into one stick so that they will become one in your hand. 18
When your countrymen ask you, 'Won't you tell us what you mean by this?'

19 say to them, 'This is what the Sovereign Lord says: "I am going to take the stick of Joseph—which is in Ephraim's hand—and of the Israelite tribes associated with him, and join it to Judah's stick, making them a single stick of wood, and they will become one in my hand."'

MAFTIR

25 ויאמרו החיתנו נמצא־חן מוזי בעיני ריבוע מ"ה אדני והיינו
עבדים לפרעה: 26 וישם אתה יוסף ציון, ו"פ יהוה, ה"פ אל לחק עד־
היום נגד, זן, מזבח הזה והו על־אדמת מצרים מצר לפרעה לחמש רק
אדמת הכהנים לבדם לא היתה לפרעה: 27 וישב ישראל
בארץ אלהים דאלפין מצרים מצר בארץ אלהים דאלפין גשן ויאחזו בה
ויפרו וירבו מאד מ"ה:

HAFTARAH OF VAYIGASH

in this prophecy. The prevalence of these names, when held by righteous people, hastens the Final Redemption, the Resurrection of the Dead, and the establishment of immortality.

יחזקאל פרק 37

37 15 ויהי אל דבר ראה ־יהוָהאדניאהדונהי אלי לאמר: 16 ואתה בן־
אדם מ"ה קח־לך עץ ע"ה קס"א אחד אהבה, דאגה וכתב עליו ליהודה
ולבני ישראל חברו ולקח עץ ע"ה קס"א אחד אהבה, דאגה וכתוב עליו
ליוסף ציון, ו"פ יהוה, ה"פ אל עץ ע"ה קס"א אפרים אל מצפץ וכל ילי ־בית ב"פ ראה ישראל
חברו: 17 וקרב אתם אחד אהבה, דאגה אל־אחד אהבה, דאגה לך לעץ
ע"ה קס"א אחד אהבה, דאגה והיו לאחדים אהבה, דאגה בידך: 18 וכאשר
יאמרו אליך בני עמך נמם לאמר הלוא־תגיד לנו אלהים, מום מה מ"ה
־אלה לך: 19 דבר ראה אלהם כה היי ־אמר אדני ללה יהוהאהדונהי
הנה מ"ה יה אני אני לקח את־עץ ע"ה קס"א יוסף ציון, ו"פ יהוה, ה"פ אל אשר
ביד־אפרים אל מצפץ ושבטי ש"ך ע"ה ישראל חבריו ונתתי אותם

[20] Hold before their eyes the sticks you have written on [21] and say to them, 'This is what the Sovereign Lord says: "I will take the Israelites out of the nations where they have gone. I will gather them from all around and bring them back into their own land.

[22] I will make them one nation in the land, on the mountains of Israel. There will be one king over all of them and they will never again be two nations or be divided into two kingdoms.

[23] They will no longer defile themselves with their idols and vile images or with any of their offenses, for I will save them from all their sinful backsliding, and I will cleanse them. They will be My People, and I will be their God.

[24] My Servant David will be king over them, and they will all have one shepherd. They will follow My Laws and be careful to keep My Decrees.

[25] They will live in the land I gave to My Servant Jacob, the land where your fathers lived. They and their children and their children's children will live there forever, and David My Servant will be their prince forever.

[26] I will make a covenant of peace with them; it will be an everlasting covenant. I will establish them and increase their numbers, and I will put My Sanctuary among them forever.

[27] My Dwelling Place will be with them; I will be their God, and they will be My People.

[28] Then the nations will know that I the Lord make Israel holy, when My Sanctuary is among them forever.' "

עָלָיו אֶת־עֵץ ע״ה קס״א יְהוּדָה וַעֲשִׂיתִם לְעֵץ ע״ה קס״א אֶחָד אהבה, דאגה
וְהָיוּ אֶחָד אהבה, דאגה בְּיָדִי׃ 20 וְהָיוּ הָעֵצִים אֲשֶׁר־תִּכְתֹּב עֲלֵיהֶם
בְּיָדְךָ בוכו לְעֵינֵיהֶם ריבוע מ״ה׃ 21 וְדַבֵּר ראה אֲלֵיהֶם כֹּה הי׳ ־אָמַר
אֲדֹנָי ללה יֱהֹוִה יאהדונהי הִנֵּה מ״ה יה אֲנִי אני לֹקֵחַ אֶת־בְּנֵי יִשְׂרָאֵל מִבֵּין
הַגּוֹיִם אֲשֶׁר הָלְכוּ מיה ־שָׁם וְקִבַּצְתִּי אֹתָם מִסָּבִיב וְהֵבֵאתִי
אוֹתָם אֶל־אַדְמָתָם׃ 22 וְעָשִׂיתִי אֹתָם לְגוֹי מלוי מ״ה אֶחָד אהבה, דאגה
בָּאָרֶץ אלהים דאלפין בְּהָרֵי יִשְׂרָאֵל וּמֶלֶךְ אֶחָד אהבה, דאגה יִהְיֶה ייי
לְכֻלָּם לְמֶלֶךְ וְלֹא יִהְיוּ אל (כתיב: יהיה) ־עוֹד לִשְׁנֵי גוֹיִם וְלֹא יֵחָצוּ
עוֹד לִשְׁתֵּי מַמְלָכוֹת עוֹד׃ 23 וְלֹא יִטַּמְּאוּ עוֹד בְּגִלּוּלֵיהֶם
וּבְשִׁקּוּצֵיהֶם וּבְכֹל לכב פִּשְׁעֵיהֶם וְהוֹשַׁעְתִּי אֹתָם מִכֹּל ילי
מוֹשְׁבֹתֵיהֶם אֲשֶׁר חָטְאוּ בָהֶם וְטִהַרְתִּי י״פ אכא אוֹתָם וְהָיוּ־לִי
לְעָם עלם וַאֲנִי אני, ב״פ אהיה + יהוה אֶהְיֶה אהיה לָהֶם לֵאלֹהִים ילה, מום׃
24 וְעַבְדִּי דָוִד מֶלֶךְ עֲלֵיהֶם וְרוֹעֶה אֶחָד אהבה, דאגה יִהְיֶה ייי לְכֻלָּם
וּבְמִשְׁפָּטַי יֵלֵכוּ כלי וְחֻקֹּתַי יִשְׁמְרוּ וְעָשׂוּ אוֹתָם׃ 25 וְיָשְׁבוּ עַל־
הָאָרֶץ אלהים דההין ע״ה אֲשֶׁר נָתַתִּי לְעַבְדִּי לְיַעֲקֹב יאהדונהי + אידהנויה אֲשֶׁר
יָשְׁבוּ־בָהּ אֲבוֹתֵיכֶם וְיָשְׁבוּ עָלֶיהָ פהל הֵמָּה וּבְנֵיהֶם וּבְנֵי בְנֵיהֶם
עַד־עוֹלָם וְדָוִד עַבְדִּי נָשִׂיא לָהֶם לְעוֹלָם ריבוע ס״ג + י׳ אותיות׃ 26 וְכָרַתִּי
לָהֶם בְּרִית שָׁלוֹם בְּרִית עוֹלָם יִהְיֶה ייי אוֹתָם וּנְתַתִּים וְהִרְבֵּיתִי
אוֹתָם וְנָתַתִּי אֶת־מִקְדָּשִׁי בְּתוֹכָם לְעוֹלָם ריבוע ס״ג + י׳ אותיות׃ 27 וְהָיָה
יהוה, יהה מִשְׁכָּנִי עֲלֵיהֶם וְהָיִיתִי לָהֶם לֵאלֹהִים ילה, מום וְהֵמָּה יִהְיוּ אל
־לִי לְעָם עלם׃ 28 וְיָדְעוּ הַגּוֹיִם כִּי אֲנִי אני יְהֹוָהאדניאהדונהי מְקַדֵּשׁ
אֶת־יִשְׂרָאֵל בִּהְיוֹת מִקְדָּשִׁי בְּתוֹכָם לְעוֹלָם ריבוע ס״ג + י׳ אותיות׃ [פ]

VAYECHI

LESSON OF VAYECHI
(Genesis 47:28–50:26)

"'Swear to me,' he said. Then Joseph swore to him..." (Genesis 47:31)

As the Ramban (Rav Moshe ben Nachman, also known as Nachmanides, 1194–1270) explains, one of the reasons that Jacob made Joseph swear to bury him in Israel in the Cave of Machpelah in Hebron—the cave where Adam, Eve, Abraham, Sarah, Isaac, Rebecca, and Leah were buried—was so that he would act with more dispatch. If Jacob had not forced Joseph to swear, there was a possibility that Joseph would not have made the extra effort and perhaps would have failed to bury his father in Israel.

Still, we know that Joseph's love for his father was something no words can begin to describe. So what did Jacob want to teach us by making Joseph swear? We know that Joseph was in danger during Jacob's funeral. Without the oath, Joseph's fear might have made him feel it was impossible to work through all the problems of taking his father to the Cave of Machpelah. When Jacob made him swear, Joseph received new strength, knowing he had the power to overcome any obstacles that might be in his way.

If we tell ourselves that it seems impossible to restrict our desires, we must awaken ourselves to realize how much we owe the Creator. God gives us air to breathe, food to eat, and a house to live in. And even more than we want to receive from the Creator, the Creator wants to give Light to us. As the *Talmud* says: "The desire of the cow to feed its calf is greater than the desire for the calf to eat."

We must remember that there is no limit to how much Light we can receive—if only we have the desire. Therefore, nothing is impossible. As the kabbalists say, "There is no such thing as can't; there is only won't."

"God who has been my shepherd all my life long..." (Genesis 48:15)

In the writings of the Elder of Kelm, it says: "I have never heard a middle class or a rich person say, 'Bless God that I had something to eat this year or that I was not sick.'" But sometimes, a righteous person will bless God, saying that everything is good, even if the situation is not so good. "The Lord is my shepherd" means "The Lord sustains me."

We constantly think and feel that we deserve good things, and we wonder why we do not have them. But it is written in the *Gemara*: "A person can be poor only in consciousness." A poor person is anyone who feels some kind of lack or emptiness, even if he has all the material things he needs. The truth is that we do not actually deserve anything. This world does not belong to us; we are just Vessels to receive and reveal the Light of the Creator. Whatever we get is not the result of our own work; it is through the mercy and justice of God. This is a very important lesson. Anyone who feels that he deserves something will, in the end, have nothing.

But anyone who believes that he does not deserve anything will, in the end, receive everything.

"Israel took his right hand and laid it upon Ephraim, the younger son's head... guiding his hands wittingly..." (Genesis 48:14)

A person who studies the Bible becomes connected to the Holy Book. Whatever he does, he does it with the Light. His hands become like the hands of the Creator. God enters every single part of his body so that his hands automatically know to do the will of God. Jacob our Patriarch was a pristine example of this: He was literally part of the Creator. We must reach the level where every part of us, including our physical body, is a channel for the Light so that we can ignite the Godly part from Above in every atom of our body.

There is a story of a righteous man who wanted to see the Garden of Eden. He had a dream in which he was shown the way to the Garden. As he followed the directions, he was expecting to see beautiful lakes, waterfalls, trees, and all the other trappings of paradise. Suddenly, he came upon two people who were sitting at a broken table eating dry bread and drinking water from broken cups. They were studying the Bible. "Where is the Garden of Eden?" he asked them. They answered that the Garden of Eden is not a place that you go to or that you can enter. The Garden of Eden is part of you.

Spirituality is not something that we "do" or "go to" for a few hours a day. It is something that becomes part of us. It is always there inside us, wherever we are.

The Meaning of Rest

To receive the Light of the Creator that is present in the Bible, we must achieve a great inner peace—rest. But what is real peace? It is something much more than just physical rest and comfort. A person who desires to rest only in the physical sense is like a man who tries to put out a fire by pouring gasoline onto it. For an instant, it looks as if he has put out the fire, but then we see that he has only made the fire flame up more furiously.

The real rest that we need in order to receive the Bible will only be achieved by overcoming our body's desire to avoid discomfort. Issachar was given responsibility for the tribes that studied the Bible. He knew the level of rest that one needs to be connected to the Light. Because of this, he became accustomed to suffering, and as a result, he attained real peace. The *Zohar* says:

> *"Issachar is a rawboned donkey lying down between two saddlebags." (Genesis 49:14) Rav Elazar said, "Why is Issachar called an ass? If it is because he studied the Torah, he should be called a horse, a lion, or a leopard. Why an ass? Because it is known that an ass will bear any burden without kicking his master the way other living creatures do. It is not fastidious and will lie down anywhere. Issachar, too, is occupied with the Torah, accepts the burden of the Torah and does not kick out at God. He is not haughty and, like the ass, does not care*

> *for his honor, but only for the honor of his Master. He is 'lying down between two saddlebags,' as we said, that one should lie on the ground, live a life of privation and labor for the Torah.*
>
> – *The Zohar, Vayechi 69:681*

A man once came to Rav Elimelech and asked, "How is it possible to work for God when there are so many problems?" Rav Elimelech told the man to go to the holy Rav Zusha, Rav Elimelech's brother, because everyone knew that Rav Zusha was beset by all the problems that could ever exist in the world. But when the man asked Rav Zusha the same question, Rav Zusha answered, "I do not have any problems!" For Rav Zusha, his certainty in the Light was so potent that it was all he really saw. The only way to reach real peace is to seek out the uncomfortable until such discomfort becomes restful in itself.

SYNOPSIS OF VAYECHI

Usually, there is some physical space between the sections in the Torah Scroll. Sometimes, it is a whole line; sometimes, it is nine characters. But here, between the beginning of this section (Vayechi) and the end of the preceding section (Vayigash), we have only one letter's width of space. The *Zohar* says:

> *"And Jacob lived in the land of Egypt…" (Genesis 47:28). HE ASKS, "Why is this portion closed, THERE BEING NO SPACE AT ALL IN THE TORAH BETWEEN THE END OF VAYIGASH AND THE BEGINNING OF THE PORTION OF VAYECHI?" Rav Yaakov said, "When Jacob died, Israel's eyes were closed." Rav Yehuda said, "Then, AFTER THE DEATH OF JACOB, they descended into exile, and THE EGYPTIANS enslaved ISRAEL."*
>
> *Here in Egypt, it is considered that "And Jacob lived" FOR IT WAS CONSIDERED LIFE FOR HIM. It was not said of him: "And lived" all his life, for his life was that of sorrow. Of him, it is written: "I had no repose" IN LABAN'S HOUSE, "nor had I rest" FROM ESAU, "nor was I quiet" BECAUSE OF DINAH AND SHECHEM; "yet trouble came" OF SELLING JOSEPH (Job 3:26). But after he went down to Egypt, it is said of him: "and lived." He saw his son a king, he saw all his sons pure and righteous, living in pleasure and luxury, and he dwelling in their midst as good wine resting on its lees. Then it is said: "and Jacob lived." THEREFORE, there is no separation, NO SPACE, between "and grew and multiplies exceedingly" and "and Jacob lived," and so it should be, THE ONE BEING THE CONTINUANCE OF THE OTHER.*
>
> – *The Zohar, Vayechi 15:110, 112*

A commentary says that this closed space alludes to the fact that Jacob had wanted to tell his children about the End of Days, meaning the time when the Messiah would come and initiate the Final Redemption. However, he could not do so because his prophetic vision was stopped, or closed; the information about the End of Days was concealed from him.

> *When Jacob opened the discussion, saying, "Gather yourselves together, that I may tell you that which shall befall you in the latter End of Days," the latter end being the Shechina, THE LAST OF THE SEFIROT. BY MENTIONING "THAT WHICH SHALL BEFALL YOU IN THE LATTER END OF DAYS," HE MENTIONED THE EXILE. The Shechina was saddened and departed. Later, his sons brought her back by the unison created by the words they uttered, "Hear, O Israel…." (Deuteronomy 6:4) Then Jacob stayed her and said: "Blessed be the Name of the glory of His sovereignty for evermore." The Shechina then settled into her place.*
>
> – *The Zohar, Vayechi 53:518*

From this very important section, we are reminded about how easy it is to create openings for Satan to enter our lives. Just a small reaction of jealousy, anger, or any other form of negative reactive behavior allows Satan to get his foot in the door.

FIRST READING - ABRAHAM - CHESED

28 And Jacob lived in Egypt seventeen years, and the years of his life were a hundred and forty-seven.

29 When the time drew near for Israel to die, he called for his son Joseph and said to him, "If I have found favor in your eyes, put your hand under my thigh and promise that you will show me kindness and faithfulness. Do not bury me in Egypt,
30 but when I rest with my fathers, carry me out of Egypt and bury me where they are buried." "I will do as you say," he said.

31 "Swear to me," he said. Then Joseph swore to him, and Israel worshipped as he leaned on the top of his staff.

48[1] Some time later Joseph was told, "Your father is ill." So he took his two sons Manasseh and Ephraim along with him.

FROM THE RAV

"And Jacob lived in Egypt for 17 years" means that the total completeness of life was revealed to Jacob in that country. But why did this take place in Egypt? The *Zohar* explains that this was because Egypt was the most negative of all the nations. What is the origin of negative energy? The *Zohar* says that it is the human body itself, whose essence is the *Desire to Receive for the Self Alone.* The negative power of the Egyptians was derived completely from their deep connection to the physical body. This is why they became such masters of the art of mummification.

With this in mind, we can begin to understand why such great revelations took place for Jacob in the land of Egypt. Egypt was the essence of physicality. It was like an infinitely deep crater of thick, adhesive mud. When a person is stuck in mud of this kind, he has to work as hard as he can to get out of it. He has to exert all his strength. He has to find more strength than he ever knew he had.

Only here, in a place like Egypt, could a person truly earn the highest level of consciousness. This elevated consciousness wasn't just given to the patriarchs and sages such as Joseph and Jacob, and Moses. They earned this consciousness in Egypt because Egypt was a place in which it was almost impossible to behave in a positive way.

It was in Egypt that Jacob achieved the level of consciousness known as nevu'a or "prophecy." Not only did he see the future of his own children in the world, but he also foresaw the many periods of exile the nation of Israel would have to endure and how this Diaspora would end with the coming of the Messiah (Mashiach).

Prophecy is not just wisdom. It is the power to see the full-grown tree in the seed, and even to see the seed that will later come forth from that full-grown tree. This is the level of prophecy that Jacob achieved in Egypt.

FIRST READING - ABRAHAM - CHESED

28 וַיְחִי יַעֲקֹב יאהדונהי + אידהנויה בְּאֶרֶץ אלהים דאלפין מִצְרַיִם מצר שְׁבַע
עֶשְׂרֵה שָׁנָה וַיְהִי אל יְמֵי־יַעֲקֹב יאהדונהי + אידהנויה שְׁנֵי חַיָּיו שֶׁבַע אלהים
דיודין + ע״ב שָׁנִים וְאַרְבָּעִים וּמְאַת שָׁנָה׃ 29 וַיִּקְרְבוּ יְמֵי־יִשְׂרָאֵל
לָמוּת וַיִּקְרָא עם ה׳ אותיות = ב״פ קס״א | לִבְנוֹ לְיוֹסֵף ציון, קנאה, ה״פ אל, ו״פ יהוה
וַיֹּאמֶר לוֹ אִם יוהך ־נָא מָצָאתִי חֵן מוזי בְּעֵינֶיךָ ע״ה קס״א שִׂים־נָא
יָדְךָ בוכו תַּחַת יְרֵכִי וְעָשִׂיתָ עִמָּדִי חֶסֶד ע״ב, ריבוע יהוה וֶאֱמֶת
אהיה פעמים אהיה, ז״פ ס״ג אַל־נָא תִקְבְּרֵנִי בְּמִצְרָיִם מצר׃ 30 וְשָׁכַבְתִּי עִם־

וַיְחִי

Genesis 47:28 – **"And Jacob lived in Egypt for seventeen years..."** After all the suffering he had endured, Jacob experienced 17 years of happiness in his life. **Vayechi** means "and he lived." The *Zohar* says:

> *"Seventeen years": HE ASKS, "Why seventeen years?" HE ANSWERS, "Rav Shimon said, 'Jacob was sorrowful all his life, and his days passed in sorrow in the beginning. When he saw Joseph standing before him, Jacob looked at Joseph and his soul was made whole as if he saw Joseph's mother. For the beauty of Joseph resembled that of Rachel and it seemed to him as if he had never known sorrow.'"*
>
> *– The Zohar, Vayechi 15:113*

We sometimes fall into the trap of existing without really living. For example, a father who works 20 hours a day "for his children" cannot really be working for them. He is working and living for himself or even for his Opponent, Satan. By the time he can appreciate his children, it is too late for him to know them at all.

וַיֹּאמֶר

Genesis 47:29 – **Jacob made Joseph Swear to Bury him in Israel.**

> *We learned that the body of Jacob had its beauty from Adam, and the image of Jacob was of the Supernal Holy form, the form of the Holy Throne. Thus he did not want to be buried among the wicked. The secret of this matter is that there is no separating the patriarchs, AND THEY ARE ALWAYS TOGETHER. It is therefore written, "I will lie with my fathers." (Beresheet 47:30)*
>
> *—The Zohar, Vayechi 29:259*

Jacob feared that Pharaoh would not allow Joseph to bury him in Israel. If Jacob had not made Joseph swear to do so—if he had simply requested it—Joseph might have given up in the face of any obstacles Pharaoh might have put in his way. By forcing Joseph to swear, Jacob reminded him that nothing is impossible.

[2] When Jacob was told, "Your son Joseph has come to you," Israel rallied his strength and sat up on the bed.

[3] Jacob said to Joseph, "God Almighty appeared to me at Luz in the land of Canaan, and there He blessed me, [4] and said to me, 'I am going to make you fruitful and will increase your numbers. I will make you a community of peoples, and I will give this land as an everlasting possession to your descendants after you.'

[5] Now then, your two sons born to you in Egypt before I came to you here will be reckoned as mine; Ephraim and Manasseh will be mine, just as Reuben and Simeon are mine.

[6] Any children born to you after them will be yours; in the territory they inherit they will be reckoned under the names of their brothers.

[7] As I was returning from Paddan, to my sorrow Rachel died in the land of Canaan while we were still on the way, a little distance from Ephrath. So I buried her there beside the road to Ephrath" (that is, Bethlehem)".

[8] When Israel saw the sons of Joseph, he asked, "Who are these?"

[9] "They are the sons God has given me here," Joseph said to his father. Then Israel said, "Bring them to me so I may bless them."

Genesis 48:1 – **Jacob Became ill.** Jacob was the first person in history to become sick. Prior to that time, people would decide when to leave the physical plane, sneeze, and immediately pass away. From this reading, we can receive the energy of protection from any illness as well as the power to heal.

> *He opened the discussion, saying, "We have learned that in the early days, before Jacob came, a person was peacefully in his home, WITHOUT ANY SICKNESS. When his time came TO DIE, he simply died without any illness. When Jacob came, he asked of the Holy One, blessed be He, 'Master of the Universe, if it is favorable before You, let a person fall into illness for two or three days. Then he should be gathered unto his people, SO THAT HE WOULD BE ABLE to arrange for his family and repent of his sins.' God told him, 'Fine, you will be an example for the world,' MEANING THAT IT WOULD START WITH JACOB. Come and see what is written concerning him: 'And it came to pass after these things, that someone told Joseph, Behold your father is sick (Heb. choleh).' (Genesis 48:1) The word 'choleh' is spelled WITHOUT A VAV, WHICH SHOWS THAT IT WAS NEW, and that no person had experienced this before."*
>
> *– The Zohar, Terumah 92:898*

אֲבֹתַי וּנְשָׂאתַנִי מִמִּצְרַיִם מצר וּקְבַרְתַּנִי בִּקְבֻרָתָם וַיֹּאמַר אָנֹכִי
איע אֶעֱשֶׂה כִדְבָרֶךָ ראה: 31 וַיֹּאמֶר הִשָּׁבְעָה לִי וַיִּשָּׁבַע לוֹ וַיִּשְׁתַּחוּ
יִשְׂרָאֵל עַל־רֹאשׁ ריבוע אלהים - אלהים דיודין ע״ה הַמִּטָּה: [פ] 48 1 וַיְהִי אל
אַחֲרֵי הַדְּבָרִים ראה הָאֵלֶּה וַיֹּאמֶר לְיוֹסֵף ציון, קנאה, ה״פ אל, ו״פ יהוה
הִנֵּה אָבִיךָ חֹלֶה להח וַיִּקַּח חעם אֶת־שְׁנֵי בָנָיו עִמּוֹ אֶת־מְנַשֶּׁה
וְאֶת־אֶפְרָיִם אל מצפץ: 2 וַיַּגֵּד לְיַעֲקֹב יאהדונהי - אידהנויה וַיֹּאמֶר הִנֵּה
בִּנְךָ יוֹסֵף ציון, קנאה, ה״פ אל, ו״פ יהוה בָּא אֵלֶיךָ אני וַיִּתְחַזֵּק פהל יִשְׂרָאֵל
וַיֵּשֶׁב עַל־הַמִּטָּה: 3 וַיֹּאמֶר יַעֲקֹב יאהדונהי - אידהנויה אֶל־יוֹסֵף
ציון, קנאה, ה״פ אל, ו״פ יהוה אֵל שַׁדַּי מהש (משה) נִרְאָה (אהרן) -אֵלַי בְּלוּז
בְּאֶרֶץ אלהים דאלפין כְּנָעַן וַיְבָרֶךְ עסמ״ב אֹתִי: 4 וַיֹּאמֶר אֵלַי הִנְנִי
מַפְרְךָ וְהִרְבִּיתִךָ וּנְתַתִּיךָ לִקְהַל עַמִּים ע״ה קס״א וְנָתַתִּי אֶת־הָאָרֶץ
אלהים דההין ע״ה הַזֹּאת לְזַרְעֲךָ אַחֲרֶיךָ אֲחֻזַּת עוֹלָם: 5 וְעַתָּה
שְׁנֵי־בָנֶיךָ הַנּוֹלָדִים לְךָ בְּאֶרֶץ אלהים דאלפין מִצְרַיִם מצר עַד־בֹּאִי
אֵלֶיךָ אני מִצְרַיְמָה מצר לִי־הֵם אֶפְרַיִם אל מצפץ וּמְנַשֶּׁה
כִּרְאוּבֵן ג״פ אלהים וְשִׁמְעוֹן יִהְיוּ אל -לִי: 6 וּמוֹלַדְתְּךָ אֲשֶׁר־הוֹלַדְתָּ
אַחֲרֵיהֶם לְךָ יִהְיוּ אל עַל שֵׁם שדי יהוה אֲחֵיהֶם יִקָּרְאוּ בְּנַחֲלָתָם:
7 וַאֲנִי אני | בְּבֹאִי מִפַּדָּן מֵתָה עָלַי רָחֵל רבוע ס״ג - ע״ב בְּאֶרֶץ
אלהים דאלפין כְּנַעַן בַּדֶּרֶךְ ב״פ יב״ק בְּעוֹד כִּבְרַת־אֶרֶץ אלהים דאלפין לָבֹא
אֶפְרָתָה וָאֶקְבְּרֶהָ שָּׁם בְּדֶרֶךְ ב״פ יב״ק אֶפְרָת הִוא בֵּית ב״פ ראה לָחֶם
ג״פ יהוה: 8 וַיַּרְא יִשְׂרָאֵל אֶת־בְּנֵי יוֹסֵף ציון, קנאה, ה״פ אל, ו״פ יהוה וַיֹּאמֶר
מִי יכי -אֵלֶּה: 9 וַיֹּאמֶר יוֹסֵף ציון, קנאה, ה״פ אל, ו״פ יהוה אֶל־אָבִיו בָּנַי הֵם
אֲשֶׁר־נָתַן־לִי אֱלֹהִים ילה, מום בָּזֶה וַיֹּאמַר קָחֶם־נָא אֵלַי
וַאֲבָרְכֵם:

SECOND READING - ISAAC - GEVURAH

10 Now Israel's eyes were failing because of old age, and he could hardly see. So Joseph brought his sons close to him, and his father kissed them and embraced them.

11 Israel said to Joseph, "I never expected to see your face again, and now God has allowed me to see your children too."

12 Then Joseph removed them from Israel's knees and bowed down with his face to
the ground. 13 And Joseph took both of them, Ephraim on his right toward Israel's left
hand and Manasseh on his left toward Israel's right hand, and brought them close to him.

14 But Israel reached out his right hand and put it on Ephraim's head, though he was the younger, and crossing his arms, he put his left hand on Manasseh's head, even though Manasseh was the firstborn.

15 Then he blessed Joseph and said, "May the God before whom my fathers Abraham
and Isaac walked, the God who has been my shepherd all my life to this day, 16 the
Angel who has delivered me from all harm—may he bless these boys. May they be called by my name and the names of my fathers Abraham and Isaac, and may they increase greatly upon the earth."

THIRD READING - JACOB - TIFERET

17 When Joseph saw his father placing his right hand on Ephraim's head he was displeased; so he took hold of his father's hand to move it from Ephraim's head to

---

Genesis 48:17 – **Jacob Blessed his Grandsons, the Sons of Joseph.** Instead of putting his right hand, which has spiritual primacy, on Joseph's older son and his left hand on the younger, Jacob crossed his hands. When Joseph questioned this, Jacob replied that the younger son had greater need for the blessing because the children who would come from the younger son would be on a higher spiritual level. Rashi said that Ephraim, the younger son, would be the ancestor of Joshua, who would give the land to the people of Israel and teach them the Bible.

From this, we can draw two lessons. First, we should never judge events by their appearances: Things are almost never what they seem. Second, there is no such thing as protocol in spiritual matters. We must do what is necessary and whatever the situation demands. Spiritual work is not rote behavior. Our actions should be in accord with our circumstances.

SECOND READING - ISAAC - GEVURAH

10 וְעֵינֵי ריבוע מ״ה יִשְׂרָאֵל כָּבְדוּ מִזֹּקֶן לֹא יוּכַל לִרְאוֹת וַיַּגֵּשׁ אֹתָם
אֵלָיו וַיִּשַּׁק לָהֶם וַיְחַבֵּק לָהֶם׃ 11 וַיֹּאמֶר יִשְׂרָאֵל אֶל־יוֹסֵף
ציון, קנאה, ה״פ אל, ו״פ יהוה רְאֹה ראה פָנֶיךָ ס״ג + מ״ה + ב״ן לֹא פִלָּלְתִּי וְהִנֵּה
הֶרְאָה אֹתִי אֱלֹהִים ילה, מום גַּם אֶת־זַרְעֶךָ׃ 12 וַיּוֹצֵא יוֹסֵף
ציון, ו״פ יהוה, ה״פ אל אֹתָם מֵעִם עמם בִּרְכָּיו וַיִּשְׁתַּחוּ לְאַפָּיו אָרְצָה
אלהים דההין ע״ה׃ 13 וַיִּקַּח וזעם יוֹסֵף ציון, קנאה, ה״פ אל, ו״פ יהוה אֶת־שְׁנֵיהֶם אֶת־
אֶפְרַיִם אל מצפץ בִּימִינוֹ מִשְּׂמֹאל יִשְׂרָאֵל וְאֶת־מְנַשֶּׁה בִשְׂמֹאלוֹ
מִימִין יִשְׂרָאֵל וַיַּגֵּשׁ אֵלָיו׃ 14 וַיִּשְׁלַח יִשְׂרָאֵל אֶת־יְמִינוֹ וַיָּשֶׁת
עַל־רֹאשׁ ריבוע אלהים + אלהים דיודין ע״ה אֶפְרַיִם אל מצפץ וְהוּא הַצָּעִיר וְאֶת־
שְׂמֹאלוֹ עַל־רֹאשׁ ריבוע אלהים + אלהים דיודין ע״ה מְנַשֶּׁה שִׂכֵּל אֶת־יָדָיו כִּי
מְנַשֶּׁה הַבְּכוֹר׃ 15 וַיְבָרֶךְ עסמ״ב אֶת־יוֹסֵף ציון, קנאה, ה״פ אל, ו״פ יהוה וַיֹּאמַר
הָאֱלֹהִים ילה, מום אֲשֶׁר הִתְהַלְּכוּ מיה אֲבֹתַי לְפָנָיו אַבְרָהָם ח״פ אל, רמ״ח
וְיִצְחָק ד״פ ב״ן הָאֱלֹהִים ילה, מום הָרֹעֶה רעה אֹתִי מֵעוֹדִי עַד־הַיּוֹם
נגד, זן, מזבח הַזֶּה והו׃ 16 הַמַּלְאָךְ פוי הַגֹּאֵל אֹתִי מִכָּל ילי ־רָע יְבָרֵךְ
עסמ״ב אֶת־הַנְּעָרִים וְיִקָּרֵא עם ה׳ אותיות = ב״פ קס״א בָהֶם שְׁמִי וְשֵׁם שדי יהוה
אֲבֹתַי אַבְרָהָם ח״פ אל, רמ״ח וְיִצְחָק ד״פ ב״ן וְיִדְגּוּ לָרֹב בְּקֶרֶב
הָאָרֶץ אלהים דההין ע״ה׃

THIRD READING - JACOB - TIFERET

17 וַיַּרְא יוֹסֵף ציון, קנאה, ה״פ אל, ו״פ יהוה כִּי־יָשִׁית אָבִיו יַד־יְמִינוֹ עַל־
רֹאשׁ ריבוע אלהים + אלהים דיודין ע״ה אֶפְרַיִם אל מצפץ וַיֵּרַע בְּעֵינָיו ריבוע מ״ה

Manasseh's head. 18 Joseph said to him, "No, my father, this one is the firstborn; put
your right hand on his head." 19 But his father refused and said, "I know, my son, I
know. He too will become a people, and he too will become great. Nevertheless, his
younger brother will be greater than he, and his descendants will become a group of
nations."

20 He blessed them that day and said, "In your name will Israel pronounce this
blessing: 'May God make you like Ephraim and Manasseh.' " So he put Ephraim
ahead of Manasseh. 21 Then Israel said to Joseph, "I am about to die, but God will be
with you and take you back to the land of your fathers. 22 And to you, as one who is
over your brothers, I give the ridge of land I took from the Amorites with my sword and
my bow."

FOURTH READING - MOSES - NETZACH

49 1 Then Jacob called for his sons and said: "Gather around so I can tell you what
will happen to you in days to come. 2 "Assemble and listen, sons of Jacob; listen to
your father Israel. 3 "Reuben, you are my firstborn, my might, the first sign of my
strength, excelling in honor, excelling in power. 4 Turbulent as the waters, you will no
longer excel, for you went up onto your father's bed, onto my couch and defiled it. 5
Simeon and Levi are brothers—their swords are weapons of violence. 6 Let me not
enter their council, let me not join their assembly, for they have killed men in their
anger and hamstrung oxen as they pleased.

וַיִּקְרָא

Genesis 49:1 – Jacob gathered his own sons to bless them before he died, blessing them individually and as a group. From this, we learn that unity is an important component of a true blessing. A consciousness of "every man for himself" cancels the energy and the purpose of blessing. The *Zohar* says:

> *There was never a more complete bed since the Universe had been created. At the time when Jacob wanted to depart from the world, Abraham was on his right, and Isaac on his left; Jacob was lying between them with the Shechina in front of him. When Jacob saw this, he called his sons and placed them around the Shechina with perfect order.*
> *– The Zohar, Vayechi 54:539*

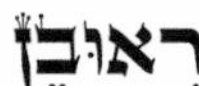

Genesis 49:3 – **Blessing of Reuben.** The *Zohar* tells us that Jacob's first three sons did not really receive his blessing. In Reuben's case, this was because of his failure to be proactive in moving his father's bed after the death of Rachel. Also, Reuben's place in the family was somewhat unclear: God had intervened at the time of his conception, withholding the first drop of Jacob's semen to save it for the conception of Joseph.

וַיִּתְמֹךְ יַד־אָבִיו לְהָסִיר אֹתָהּ מֵעַל עלם רֹאשׁ ריבוע אלהים - אלהים דיודין ע״ה
־אֶפְרַיִם אל מצפץ עַל־רֹאשׁ ריבוע אלהים - אלהים דיודין ע״ה מְנַשֶּׁה׃ 18 וַיֹּאמֶר
יוֹסֵף ציון, קנאה, ה״פ אל, ו״פ יהוה אֶל־אָבִיו לֹא־כֵן אָבִי כִּי־זֶה הַבְּכֹר שִׂים
יְמִינְךָ עַל־רֹאשׁוֹ ריבוע אלהים - אלהים דיודין ע״ה׃ 19 וַיְמָאֵן אָבִיו וַיֹּאמֶר
יָדַעְתִּי בְנִי יָדַעְתִּי גַּם יגל ־הוּא יִהְיֶה ייי ־לְּעָם עלם וְגַם יגל ־הוּא
יִגְדָּל יזל וְאוּלָם אָחִיו הַקָּטֹן יִגְדַּל יזל מִמֶּנּוּ וְזַרְעוֹ יִהְיֶה ייי
מְלֹא־הַגּוֹיִם׃ 20 וַיְבָרְכֵם בַּיּוֹם נגד, זן, מזבח הַהוּא לֵאמוֹר ר״ת הבל
בְּךָ יְבָרֵךְ עסמ״ב יִשְׂרָאֵל לֵאמֹר יְשִׂמְךָ אֱלֹהִים ילה, מום כְּאֶפְרַיִם
אל מצפץ וְכִמְנַשֶּׁה וַיָּשֶׂם אֶת־אֶפְרַיִם אל מצפץ לִפְנֵי מְנַשֶּׁה׃ 21 וַיֹּאמֶר
יִשְׂרָאֵל אֶל־יוֹסֵף ציון, קנאה, ה״פ אל, ו״פ יהוה הִנֵּה אָנֹכִי איע מֵת י״פ רבוע אהיה
וְהָיָה יהוה, יהה אֱלֹהִים ילה, מום עִמָּכֶם וְהֵשִׁיב אֶתְכֶם אֶל־אֶרֶץ
אלהים דאלפין אֲבֹתֵיכֶם׃ 22 וַאֲנִי אני, ב״פ אהיה - יהוה נָתַתִּי לְךָ שְׁכֶם אַחַד
אהבה, דאגה עַל־אַחֶיךָ אֲשֶׁר לָקַחְתִּי מִיַּד הָאֱמֹרִי בְּחַרְבִּי רי״י
וּבְקַשְׁתִּי׃ [פ]

FOURTH READING - MOSES - NETZACH

49 1 וַיִּקְרָא עם ה' אותיות = ב״פ קס״א יַעֲקֹב יאהדונהי - אידהנויה אֶל־בָּנָיו
וַיֹּאמֶר הֵאָסְפוּ וְאַגִּידָה לָכֶם אֵת אֲשֶׁר־יִקְרָא אֶתְכֶם
בְּאַחֲרִית הַיָּמִים נלך׃ 2 הִקָּבְצוּ וְשִׁמְעוּ בְּנֵי יַעֲקֹב יאהדונהי - אידהנויה
וְשִׁמְעוּ אֶל־יִשְׂרָאֵל אֲבִיכֶם׃ 3 רְאוּבֵן ג״פ אלהים בְּכֹרִי אַתָּה
כֹּחִי וְרֵאשִׁית אוֹנִי יֶתֶר שְׂאֵת וְיֶתֶר עָז׃ 4 פַּחַז כַּמַּיִם
אַל־תּוֹתַר כִּי עָלִיתָ מִשְׁכְּבֵי אָבִיךָ אָז חִלַּלְתָּ יְצוּעִי עָלָה׃ [פ]

[7] Cursed be their anger, so fierce, and their fury, so cruel! I will scatter them in Jacob and disperse them in Israel.

[8] Judah, your brothers will praise you; your hand will be on the neck of your enemies; your father's sons will bow down to you.

[9] You are a lion's cub, O Judah; you return from the prey, my son. Like a lion he crouches and lies down, like a lioness—who dares to rouse him?

[10] The scepter will not depart from Judah; nor the ruler's staff from between his feet, until he comes to whom it belongs and the obedience of the nations is his.

[11] He will tether his donkey to a vine, his colt to the choicest branch; he will wash his garments in wine, his robes in the blood of grapes.

[12] His eyes will be darker than wine, his teeth whiter than milk.

[13] Zebulun will live by the seashore and become a haven for ships; his border will extend toward Sidon.

שִׁמְעוֹן וְלֵוִי

Genesis 49:5 – **Blessing of Simon and Levi.** Because of their association with the energy of judgment, Simon and Levi were also denied a blessing. The *Zohar* says:

> *Come and see: Jacob had four wives. He begot children by them all, and was perfected through his wives. When Jacob wished to depart FROM THE WORLD, the Shechinah stood over him. He wanted to bless SHIMON AND LEVI but could not, since he feared the Shechinah. He said to himself, "How can I do this, seeing that both of them come from the side of strict judgment, AND TO BLESS THEM WILL RENDER THE SHECHINAH DEFECTIVE. I cannot force the Shechinah, since I had four wives WHO WERE DRAWN FROM THE FOUR ASPECTS, CHESED, GVURAH, TIFERET, AND MALCHUT OF THE SHECHINAH, AND I WAS PERFECTED THROUGH THEM, SINCE THEY BORE ME TWELVE TRIBES, THE SECRET OF ALL PERFECTION. SINCE I RECEIVED MY PERFECTION FROM THE SHECHINAH, HOW CAN I BLESS SHIMON AND LEVI AGAINST HER WISH? I shall deliver them to the landlord of the house, MOSES, THE HUSBAND OF THE MATRON, who is the owner, and he shall do as he pleases."*
> *– The Zohar, Vayechi 57:557*

If Jacob had blessed them, the judgment in the world would have become overwhelming.

יְהוּדָה

Genesis 49:8 – **Blessing of Judah.** Commentary says that Jacob's blessing of Judah produced 30 kings through Judah's line. (*Otzar HaMidrashim 229*) Through the blessing of Judah, we can connect to the coming of the Messianic era and gain a glimpse of what that era will be like. Chaos will be resolved into harmony, and the Tree of Life Reality will be restored.

זְבוּלֻן

Genesis 49:13 – **Blessing of Zebulun.** Zebulun had a business-oriented personality. Jacob gave him a blessing for physical sustenance because this was Zebulun's area of power and

5 שמעון ולוי מלוי ע"ב, דמב אחים כלי חמס מכרתיהם: 6 בסדם
אל-תבא נפשי בקהלם אל-תחד כבדי כי באפם הרגו איש
ע"ה קנ"א קס"א וברצנם עקרו-שור אבגיתץ, ושר, אהבת חנם: 7 ארור אפם כי
עז ועברתם כי קשתה אחלקם ביעקב יאהדונהי - אידהנויה ואפיצם
בישראל: [פ] 8 יהודה אתה יודוך אחיך ידך בוכו בערף איביך
ישתחוו לך בני אביך: 9 גור ד"פ בן ע"ה אריה רי"ו יהודה מטרף
רפ"ח ע"ה בני עלית כרע רבץ כאריה רי"ו וכלביא מי ילי יקימנו:
10 לא-יסור שבט מיהודה ומחקק מבין רגליו עד כי-
יבא שילה מהש ולו יקהת עמים ע"ה קס"א: 11 אסרי לגפן עירה
ולשרקה בני אתנו כבס ביין מיכ, י"פ האא לבשו ובדם- ריבוע אהיה
ענבים סותה: 12 חכלילי עינים ריבוע מ"ה מיין מיכ, י"פ האא ולבן-
שנים מחלב: [פ] 13 זבולן לחוף ימים נלך ישכן והוא לחוף
אנית וירכתו על-צידן: [פ] 14 יששכר י"פ אל י"פ בן חמר גרם

---

responsibility. Zebulun got his blessing before Issachar, who was more spiritual, thus demonstrating the importance of those individuals who do well in the material world providing sustenance through their work or their financial contributions, thereby enabling others to study spiritual matters.

יששכר

Genesis 49:14 – **Blessing of Issachar.** The Bible calls Issachar a donkey. This might seem to be an insult, especially since Issachar had spent his entire life studying the Bible's secrets. The *Zohar* explains:

> *"Issachar is a rawboned donkey lying down between two saddlebags." (Genesis 49:14) Rav Elazar said, "Why is Issachar called an ass? If it is because he studied the Torah, he should be called a horse, a lion, or a leopard. Why an ass? Because it is known that an ass will bear any burden without kicking his master the way other living creatures do. It is not fastidious and will lie down anywhere. Issachar, too, is occupied with the Torah, accepts the burden of the Torah and does not kick out at God. He is not haughty and, like the ass, does not care for his honor, but only for the honor of his Master. He is 'lying down between two saddlebags,' as we said, that one should lie on the ground, live a life of privation and labor for the Torah.*
> – *The Zohar, Vayechi 69:681*

By referring to him as a donkey, however, the Bible was speaking of his power to bear a heavy load and to perform work without complaint. We need this quality to pursue our own spiritual work.

14 Issachar is a rawboned donkey lying down between two saddlebags.

15 When he sees how good is his resting place and how pleasant is his land, he will bend his shoulder to the burden and submit to forced labor.

16 Dan will provide justice for his people as one of the tribes of Israel. 17 Dan will be a serpent by the roadside, a viper along the path that bites the horse's heels so that its rider tumbles backward. 18 I look for your deliverance, O Lord.

FIFTH READING - AARON - HOD

19 Gad will be attacked by a band of raiders, but he will attack them at their heels. 20 Asher's food will be rich; he will provide delicacies fit for a king. 21 Naphtali is a doe set free that bears beautiful fawns.

22 Joseph is a fruitful vine, a fruitful vine near a spring, whose branches climb over a wall. 23 With bitterness, archers attacked him; they shot at him with hostility, 24 but his

---

דָּן

Genesis 49:16 – **Blessing of Dan.** After blessing Dan, Jacob actually prayed for the first and only time. He added a special verse of prayer for Dan because Dan's purpose was judgment. In fact, the name "Dan" and the word "judgment" have the same root in both Aramaic and Hebrew.

> *For this reason, Jacob prayed, saying, "I wait for your salvation, O God." HE ASKS, "Why does he not ask for salvation in regard to the other tribes, only to this one" HE REPLIES, "This is because he has seen the force and strength of the serpent, when judgment is aroused to overpower holiness. HE THEREFORE PRAYED FOR SALVATION."*
> *– The Zohar, Vayechi 70:712*

When judgment comes upon someone, it is because that person has directed judgment toward others. Even if we deserve a certain judgment, we will not receive it unless we have activated its manifestation by our own judgmental thoughts and feelings.

גָּד

Genesis 49:19 – **Blessing of Gad.** Gad and his descendants were a warlike nation. Jacob's blessing for Gad ensured that he would not be defeated by his enemies and that Gad's people would be powerful in times of war. Our battle with our Satan within—our ego—is like a war: If we let our guard down, we are defeated. This struggle requires at least as much preparation as a war in the physical world. Hearing this blessing arms us for the constant battle with our ego.

מֵאָשֵׁר

Genesis 49:20 – **Blessing of Asher.** When Jacob blessed Asher, he said, "Asher's food will be rich; he will provide delicacies fit for a king." Asher controls the month of Aquarius. The end of chaos on the personal level comes through Asher, as does the Final Redemption when chaos will be banished forever from all Creation. In our relationships, our business, our health, and all other areas of life, Asher allows us to rise

רֹבֵץ בֵּין הַמִּשְׁפְּתָיִם׃ 15 וַיַּרְא מְנֻחָה ע״ה ב״פ ב״ן כִּי טוֹב והו, אום וְאֶת־
הָאָרֶץ אלהים דההין ע״ה כִּי נָעֵמָה ע״ה רבוע ס״ג וַיֵּט שִׁכְמוֹ לִסְבֹּל וַיְהִי
לְמַס־עֹבֵד׃ [ס] 16 דָּן יָדִין עַמּוֹ כְּאַחַד אהבה, דאגה שִׁבְטֵי ש״ך ע״ה
יִשְׂרָאֵל׃ 17 יְהִי־דָן נָחָשׁ עֲלֵי־דֶרֶךְ ב״פ יב״ק שְׁפִיפֹן מלוי נחש עֲלֵי־אֹרַח
הַנֹּשֵׁךְ עִקְּבֵי ב״פ מום ־סוּס ריבוע אדני, כוק וַיִּפֹּל רֹכְבוֹ אָחוֹר׃ 18 לִישׁוּעָתְךָ
קִוִּיתִי יְהֹוָהאדנייאהדונהי׃ [ס]

FIFTH READING - AARON - HOD

19 גָּד גְּדוּד יְגוּדֶנּוּ וְהוּא יָגֻד עָקֵב ב״פ מום׃ [ס] 20 מֵאָשֵׁר
ריבוע אלהים - אלהים דיודין ע״ה שְׁמֵנָה לַחְמוֹ וְהוּא יִתֵּן מַעֲדַנֵּי־מֶלֶךְ׃ [ס]
21 נַפְתָּלִי אַיָּלָה שְׁלֻחָה הַנֹּתֵן אבגיתץ, ושר, אהבת חנם אִמְרֵי־שָׁפֶר׃ [ס]
22 בֵּן פֹּרָת יוֹסֵף ציון, קנאה, ה״פ אל, ו״פ יהוה בֵּן פֹּרָת עֲלֵי־עָיִן ריבוע מ״ה בָּנוֹת

---

above negativity. A commentary says that Jacob told the secret of the Redemption from Egypt to Joseph, who told it to his brothers; Asher then told the secret to his daughter Serah. He said to her, "Any redeemer who will come and say, '[God] said to me, I have surely remembered you,' (Exodus 3:16) is the true redeemer." (*Shemot Rabba 5:13*)

נַפְתָּלִי

Genesis 49:21 – **Blessing of Naftali.** Naftali was blessed with physical speed. He was always a bearer of good tidings and went swiftly about his father's tasks. Often when there is something that we should not do, we are quick to do it. However, when there is a task that is spiritually worthwhile, we are often lazy and slow to begin working on it. Through the blessing of Naftali, we are given the potential to be slow in things we should avoid and to move quickly in our spiritual tasks.

בֵּן פֹּרָת יוֹסֵף

Genesis 49:22 – **Blessing of Joseph.** The blessing of Joseph is to remove the Evil Eye. Joseph controls the month of Pisces, whose symbol is the fish. Fish do not have the Evil Eye because they are always surrounded by water, which embodies the power of mercy. We can also be protected against the Evil Eye through the power of the *Zohar* and by doing acts of sharing and mercy. Even if a person deliberately intends to do someone harm, the *Zohar* is a shield that the Evil Eye cannot penetrate. Rachel is also a protector against the Evil Eye, which explains the red yarn that is placed around her tomb in Bethlehem and is imbued with her energy of protection.

bow remained steady, his strong arms stayed limber, because of the hand of the Mighty One of Jacob, because of the Shepherd, the Rock of Israel, [25] *because of your father's God, who helps you, because of the Almighty, who blesses you with blessings of the heavens above, blessings of the deep that lies below, blessings of the breast and womb.*

[26] *Your father's blessings are greater than the blessings of the ancient mountains, than the bounty of the age-old hills. Let all these rest on the head of Joseph, on the brow of the prince among his brothers.*

SIXTH READING - JOSEPH - YESOD

[27] *Benjamin is a ravenous wolf; in the morning he devours the prey, in the evening he divides the plunder."*

[28] *All these are the twelve tribes of Israel, and this is what their father said to them when he blessed them, giving each the blessing appropriate to him.* [2]

[9] *Then he gave them these instructions: "I am about to be gathered to my people. Bury me with my fathers in the cave in the field of Ephron the Hittite,* [30] *the cave in the field of Machpelah, near Mamre in Canaan, which Abraham bought as a burial place from Ephron the Hittite, along with the field.*

[31] *There Abraham and his wife Sarah were buried, there Isaac and his wife Rebecca were buried, and there I buried Leah.*

[32] *The field and the cave in it were bought from the Hittites."*

Genesis 49:27 – **Blessing of Benjamin.** "Benjamin is a ravenous wolf." The *Zohar* says that the first explanation of why Benjamin is called a wolf tells us that this was engraved upon the Throne; the second explanation interprets it as a reference to the altar upon which Benjamin offered the flesh of the daily sacrifice; and the third explanation indicated that, through sacrifices, Benjamin appeased the accusers called "wolf" so that they would not accuse Israel. The *Zohar* says:

Another explanation for "a ravenous wolf" is that the altar was in Benjamin's portion, and the altar is a wolf. If you say that Benjamin is a wolf, it is not so—the altar on his territory was the wolf, since it consumed flesh every day, NAMELY THE SACRIFICES OFFERED UPON IT. Benjamin used to feed it WITH SACRIFICES because it was in his territory. It was as if he nourished and fed that wolf. "Ravenous" MEANS FEEDING; THE VERSE MAY READ: "BENJAMIN SHALL FEED THE WOLF," THE ALTAR. Another explanation for "a ravenous wolf" is that "he shall feed the

צעדה עלי-שור אבגיתצ, ושר, אהבת חנם: 23 וימררהו ורבו וישטמהו
בעלי חצים: 24 ותשב באיתן קשתו ויפזו זרעי ידיו מידי
אביר הרח יעקב יאהדונהי - אידהנויה משם רעה רהע אבן יוד הה ואו הה
ישראל: 25 מאל אביך ויעזרך ואת שדי ויברכך ברכת
שמים י"פ טל, י"פ כוזו מעל עלם ברכת תהום י"פ מ"ה ע"ה רבצת תחת
ברכת שדים ורחם אברהם, ח"פ אל, רמ"ח: 26 ברכת אביך גברו על-
ברכת הורי עד-תאות גבעת עולם תהיין לראש
ריבוע אלהים - אלהים דיודין ע"ה יוסף ציון, קנאה, ה"פ אל, ו"פ יהוה ולקדקד נזיר
אחיו: [פ]

SIXTH READING - JOSEPH - YESOD

27 בנימין זאב יטרף בבקר יאכל עד ולערב רבוע אלהים רבוע יהוה
יחלק שלל ב"פ עס"מ: 28 כל ילי -אלה שבטי ש"ך ע"ה ישראל שנים
עשר וזאת אשר-דבר ראה להם אביהם ויברך עסמ"ב אותם איש
ע"ה קנ"א קס"א אשר כברכתו ברך אתם: 29 ויצו אותם ויאמר
אלהם אני אני נאסף אל-עמי קברו אתי אל-אבתי אל-המערה
ש"ך אשר בשדה עפרון החתי: 30 במערה אשר בשדה
המכפלה אשר על-פני חכמה - בינה ממרא סוזוך ע"ה בארץ אלהים דאלפין

---

wolf." Who is the wolf? ANGELS who are sworn to enmity, ready to accuse Israel from Above. They are all appeased by the sacrifices, aroused with the arousal above. THUS BENJAMIN, IN WHOSE TERRITORY THE ALTAR LIES, FEEDS THE ACCUSERS CALLED WOLF, SO THAT THEY WILL NOT BRING ACCUSATION UPON ISRAEL.

– The Zohar, Vayechi 78:588

Although there were separate blessings for each son (tribe), we learn that Jacob also blessed them together as a group. Even though people all have different gifts and abilities, we must always remember that we are all in this world together. Everything we do has an impact on the lives of other people. Therefore, we cannot think of "me first." Through sharing, we will reveal our awareness that we are all blessed together.

33 When Jacob had finished giving instructions to his sons, he drew his feet up into the bed, breathed his last, and was gathered to his people.

50[1] Joseph threw himself upon his father and wept over him and kissed him.

2 Then Joseph directed the physicians in his service to embalm his father Israel. So the physicians embalmed him, 3 taking a full forty days, for that was the time required for embalming. And the Egyptians mourned for him seventy days.

4 When the days of mourning had passed, Joseph said to Pharaoh's court, "If I have found favor in your eyes, speak to Pharaoh for me. Tell him 5 my father made me swear an oath and said, 'I am about to die; bury me in the tomb I dug for myself in the land of Canaan.' Now let me go up and bury my father; then I will return."

6 Pharaoh said, "Go up and bury your father, as he made you swear to do."

7 So Joseph went up to bury his father. All Pharaoh's officials accompanied him—the dignitaries of his court and all the dignitaries of Egypt, 8 besides all the members of Joseph's household and his brothers and those belonging to his father's household. Only their children and their flocks and herds were left in Goshen.

9 Chariots and horseman also went up with him. It was a very large company.

10 When they reached the threshing floor of Atad, near the Jordan, they lamented loudly and bitterly; and there Joseph observed a seven-day period of mourning for his father.

וַיֵּאָסֶף

Genesis 49:33 – The *Zohar* and the *Talmud* say that Jacob did not actually die, only that there is a grave for him and that someone is buried there. The *Zohar* says:

> *Jacob is attached to the Tree of Life, which never has any death in it, for all the living are established and perfected in this Tree that gives life to all that hold on to it. Therefore, Jacob did not die. And when did he die? It occurred when it was written: "He drew his feet into the bed." (Genesis 49:33) "The bed" is as you say, "Behold it is his litter, that of Solomon," (Song of Songs 3:7) WHICH IS MALCHUT. About this bed, it is written: "Her feet go down to death." (Proverbs 5:5) Therefore, it is written: "He gathered up his feet into the bed," and then, "and he expired and was gathered unto his people." BUT AS LONG AS HE HELD ON TO THE TREE OF LIFE, WHICH IS ZEIR ANPIN, HE DID NOT DIE BECAUSE DEATH IS ONLY FROM THE ASPECT OF MALCHUT.*
>
> – *The Zohar, Beshalach 10:97*

Death can be overcome—even physical death—and so can other endings that are like little deaths. These are the kinds of deaths that are experienced as failed relationships, unfulfilling work, and a lowered level of consciousness. To overcome these at every moment of our lives is our goal.

כְּנַעַן אֲשֶׁר קָנָה אַבְרָהָם ח״פ אל, רמ״ח אֶת־הַשָּׂדֶה שדי מֵאֵת עֶפְרֹן
הַחִתִּי לַאֲחֻזַּת־קָבֶר׃ 31 שָׁמָּה מהש קָבְרוּ אֶת־אַבְרָהָם ח״פ אל, רמ״ח
וְאֵת שָׂרָה אלהים דיודין רבוע אלהים - ה׳ אִשְׁתּוֹ שָׁמָּה מהש קָבְרוּ אֶת־יִצְחָק
ד״פ ב״ן וְאֵת רִבְקָה אִשְׁתּוֹ וְשָׁמָּה מהש קָבַרְתִּי אֶת־לֵאָה לאה (אלד ע״ה)׃
32 מִקְנֵה הַשָּׂדֶה שדי וְהַמְּעָרָה ש״ך אֲשֶׁר־בּוֹ מֵאֵת בְּנֵי־חֵת׃
33 וַיְכַל יַעֲקֹב יאהדונהי - אידהנויה לְצַוֺּת פוי אֶת־בָּנָיו וַיֶּאֱסֹף רַגְלָיו אֶל־הַמִּטָּה
וַיִּגְוַע וַיֵּאָסֶף אֶל־עַמָּיו׃ 50 1 וַיִּפֹּל יוֹסֵף ציון, קנאה, ה״פ אל, ו״פ יהוה עַל־פְּנֵי
חכמה - בינה אָבִיו וַיֵּבְךְּ עָלָיו וַיִּשַּׁק־לוֹ׃ 2 וַיְצַו פוי יוֹסֵף ציון, קנאה, ה״פ אל, ו״פ יהוה
אֶת־עֲבָדָיו אֶת־הָרֹפְאִים לַחֲנֹט אֶת־אָבִיו וַיַּחַנְטוּ הָרֹפְאִים אֶת־
יִשְׂרָאֵל׃ 3 וַיִּמְלְאוּ־לוֹ אַרְבָּעִים יוֹם נגד, זן, מזבח כִּי כֵּן יִמְלְאוּ יְמֵי
הַחֲנֻטִים וַיִּבְכּוּ אֹתוֹ מִצְרַיִם מצר שִׁבְעִים יוֹם נגד, זן, מזבח׃ 4 וַיַּעַבְרוּ
יְמֵי בְכִיתוֹ וַיְדַבֵּר ראה יוֹסֵף ציון, קנאה, ה״פ אל, ו״פ יהוה אֶל־בֵּית ב״פ ראה
פַּרְעֹה לֵאמֹר אִם יוהך ־נָא מָצָאתִי חֵן מוחי בְּעֵינֵיכֶם ריבוע מ״ה דַּבְּרוּ ראה
־נָא בְּאָזְנֵי יוד הי ואו הה פַרְעֹה לֵאמֹר׃ 5 אָבִי הִשְׁבִּיעַנִי לֵאמֹר הִנֵּה
אָנֹכִי איע מֵת י״פ רבוע אהיה בְּקִבְרִי אֲשֶׁר כָּרִיתִי לִי בְּאֶרֶץ אלהים דאלפין
כְּנַעַן שָׁמָּה מהש תִּקְבְּרֵנִי וְעַתָּה אֶעֱלֶה־נָּא וְאֶקְבְּרָה אֶת־אָבִי
וְאָשׁוּבָה׃ 6 וַיֹּאמֶר פַּרְעֹה עֲלֵה וּקְבֹר אֶת־אָבִיךָ כַּאֲשֶׁר הִשְׁבִּיעֶךָ׃
7 וַיַּעַל יוֹסֵף ציון, קנאה, ה״פ אל, ו״פ יהוה לִקְבֹּר אֶת־אָבִיו וַיַּעֲלוּ אִתּוֹ כָּל־ ילי
עַבְדֵי פַרְעֹה זִקְנֵי בֵיתוֹ ב״פ ראה וְכֹל ילי זִקְנֵי אֶרֶץ אלהים דאלפין ־מִצְרָיִם מצר׃
8 וְכֹל ילי בֵּית ב״פ ראה יוֹסֵף ציון, קנאה, ה״פ אל, ו״פ יהוה וְאֶחָיו וּבֵית ב״פ ראה
אָבִיו רַק טַפָּם וְצֹאנָם וּבְקָרָם עָזְבוּ בְּאֶרֶץ אלהים דאלפין גֹּשֶׁן׃
9 וַיַּעַל עִמּוֹ גַּם ־רֶכֶב גַּם יגל ־פָּרָשִׁים וַיְהִי אל הַמַּחֲנֶה כָּבֵד
מְאֹד מ״ה׃ 10 וַיָּבֹאוּ עַד־גֹּרֶן הָאָטָד אֲשֶׁר בְּעֵבֶר הַיַּרְדֵּן י״פ יהוה וד׳ אותיות
וַיִּסְפְּדוּ־שָׁם מִסְפֵּד ריבוע ע״ב גָּדוֹל להח, מבה, יזל, אום וְכָבֵד מְאֹד מ״ה

11 When the Canaanites who lived there saw the mourning at the threshing floor of Atad, they said, "The Egyptians are holding a solemn ceremony of mourning." That is why that place near the Jordan is called Abel Mizra'im. 12 So Jacob's sons did as he had commanded them:

13 They carried him to the land of Canaan and buried him in the cave in the field of Machpelah, near Mamre, which Abraham had bought as a burial place from Ephron the Hittite, along with the field.

14 After burying his father, Joseph returned to Egypt, together with his brothers and all the others who had gone with him to bury his father.

15 When Joseph's brothers saw that their father was dead, they said, "What if Joseph holds a grudge against us and pays us back for all the wrongs we did to him?"

16 So they sent word to Joseph, saying, "Your father left these instructions before he died, 17 'This is what you are to say to Joseph: I ask you to forgive your brothers the sins and the wrongs they committed in treating you so badly. Now please forgive the sins of the servants of the God of your father." When their message came to him, Joseph wept.

18 His brothers then came and threw themselves down before him. "We are your slaves," they said.

19 But Joseph said to them, "Do not be afraid. Am I in the place of God?

20 You intended to harm me, but God intended it for good to accomplish what is now being done, the saving of many lives.

וַיִּקְבְּרוּ

Genesis 50:13 – Jacob was buried by his sons. When we attend someone's funeral, we are performing an action for which we expect nothing in return. There are many areas of life where we should have this same consciousness, and this is particularly true of our relationships. We must try to detach ourselves from the compensations that we think we deserve whenever we perform any service for others.

יִשְׂטְמֵנוּ

Genesis 50:15 – After Jacob's death, the brothers were fearful because of all they had done to Joseph, especially since Joseph was now their ruler. They made up a story, saying that Jacob told them to tell Joseph not to harm or persecute them. However, Jacob had not said any such thing, nor had he ever thought that Joseph would persecute his brothers.

וַיַּעַשׂ לְאָבִיו אֵבֶל שִׁבְעַת יָמִים נלך׃ 11 וַיַּרְא יוֹשֵׁב הָאָרֶץ
הַכְּנַעֲנִי אלהים דההין ע"ה אֶת־הָאֵבֶל בְּגֹרֶן הָאָטָד וַיֹּאמְרוּ אֵבֶל־כָּבֵד
זֶה לְמִצְרָיִם מצר עַל־כֵּן קָרָא שְׁמָהּ אָבֵל מִצְרַיִם מצר אֲשֶׁר בְּעֵבֶר
הַיַּרְדֵּן י"פ יהוה וד' אותיות׃ 12 וַיַּעֲשׂוּ בָנָיו לוֹ כֵּן כַּאֲשֶׁר צִוָּם פוי׃ 13 וַיִּשְׂאוּ
אֹתוֹ בָנָיו אַרְצָה אלהים דההין ע"ה כְּנַעַן וַיִּקְבְּרוּ אֹתוֹ בִּמְעָרַת שְׂדֵה
הַמַּכְפֵּלָה אֲשֶׁר קָנָה אַבְרָהָם ח"פ אל, רמ"ח אֶת־הַשָּׂדֶה שדי לַאֲחֻזַּת־
קֶבֶר מֵאֵת עֶפְרֹן הַחִתִּי עַל־פְּנֵי חכמה - בינה מַמְרֵא סחזך ע"ה׃ 14 וַיָּשָׁב
יוֹסֵף ציון, קנאה, ה"פ אל, ו"פ יהוה מִצְרַיְמָה מצר הוּא וְאֶחָיו וְכָל ילי ־הָעֹלִים
אִתּוֹ לִקְבֹּר אֶת־אָבִיו אַחֲרֵי קָבְרוֹ אֶת־אָבִיו׃ 15 וַיִּרְאוּ אֲחֵי־
יוֹסֵף ציון, קנאה, ה"פ אל, ו"פ יהוה כִּי־מֵת י"פ רבוע אהיה אֲבִיהֶם וַיֹּאמְרוּ לוּ
יִשְׂטְמֵנוּ יוֹסֵף ציון, קנאה, ה"פ אל, ו"פ יהוה וְהָשֵׁב יָשִׁיב לָנוּ אלהים, מום אֵת כָּל ילי
־הָרָעָה רהע אֲשֶׁר גָּמַלְנוּ אֹתוֹ׃ 16 וַיְצַוּוּ פוי אֶל־יוֹסֵף ציון, קנאה, ה"פ אל, ו"פ יהוה
לֵאמֹר אָבִיךָ צִוָּה פוי לִפְנֵי מוֹתוֹ לֵאמֹר׃ 17 כֹּה היי ־תֹאמְרוּ
לְיוֹסֵף ציון, קנאה, ה"פ אל, ו"פ יהוה אָנָּא ב"ן, לכב שָׂא נָא פֶּשַׁע אַחֶיךָ וְחַטָּאתָם
כִּי־רָעָה רהע גְמָלוּךָ וְעַתָּה שָׂא נָא לְפֶשַׁע עַבְדֵי אֱלֹהֵי דמב, ילה
אָבִיךָ וַיֵּבְךְּ יוֹסֵף ציון, קנאה, ה"פ אל, ו"פ יהוה בְּדַבְּרָם ראה אֵלָיו׃ 18 וַיֵּלְכוּ
כלי גַּם יגל ־אֶחָיו וַיִּפְּלוּ לְפָנָיו וַיֹּאמְרוּ הִנֶּנּוּ לְךָ לַעֲבָדִים׃
19 וַיֹּאמֶר אֲלֵהֶם יוֹסֵף ציון, קנאה, ה"פ אל, ו"פ יהוה אַל־תִּירָאוּ כִּי הֲתַחַת
אֱלֹהִים ילה, מום אָנִי אני׃ 20 וְאַתֶּם חֲשַׁבְתֶּם עָלַי רָעָה רהע אֱלֹהִים
ילה, מום חֲשָׁבָהּ לְטֹבָה אכא לְמַעַן עֲשֹׂה כַּיּוֹם נגד, זן, מזבח הַזֶּה והו
לְהַחֲיֹת עַם־רָב׃

A truly spiritual person does not constantly look for the negative in other people. For example, if a spiritual person is harmed in some way, he or she focuses less on the harm and more on what can be learned from the experience. A spiritual person understands that the person who caused the harm is undergoing a process of correction, or *tikkun*, and that there is something to be learned from every event, be it good or bad.

SEVENTH READING - DAVID - MALCHUT

21 So then, don't be afraid. I will provide for you and your children." And he reassured
them and spoke kindly to them. 22 Joseph stayed in Egypt, along with all his father's
family. He lived a hundred and ten years,

MAFTIR

23 and saw the third generation of Ephraim's children. Also the children of Makir, son
of Manasseh, were placed at birth on Joseph's knees.

24 Then Joseph said to his brothers, "I am about to die. But God will surely come to
your aid and take you up out of this land to the land he promised on oath to Abraham,
Isaac, and Jacob."

25 And Joseph made the sons of Israel swear an oath and said, "God will surely come
to your aid, and then you must carry my bones up from this place." 26 So Joseph died
at the age of a hundred and ten. And after they embalmed him, he was placed in a
coffin in Egypt.

וַיָּמָת

Genesis 50:26 – Joseph died when he was 110 years old. The *Zohar* tells us that Joseph was supposed to live to 147 years of age, but he gave 37 years of his life for King David. We have learned that many of King David's ancestors gave David some of their years because he had actually been destined to die at birth. David was aware of the years that had been given to him, and he knew that each moment of his life was a gift. From David, we can learn that our own lives are precious borrowed time, so we must make the most of every moment through our spiritual work.

> *Abraham surely gave King David 5 of his years, for he lived only 175 of his 180 years, 5 years less than his due, LIKE ISAAC. Jacob could have lived as long as Abraham, 175 YEARS, but he lived only 147, which was 28 years less than his due. Thus, Abraham and Jacob gave King David 33 years of life. Joseph lived only 110 years, instead of 147, which is 37 years less than Jacob. TOGETHEßR WITH THE 33 YEARS FROM ABRAHAM AND JACOB, King David received a total of 70 years to add to his existence, and he lived all these years which the patriarchs left him.*
>
> *– The Zohar, Vayishlach 3:55*

חזק

The End of the Book of Genesis. When we finish reading a book of the Bible, we repeat the word *chazak* three times. This word means "strength," and it has the same numerical value as *Pei, Hei, Lamed* and *Mem, Hei, Shin*, which are the codes of the 72 Names of God that connect us to strength and to healing.

SEVENTH READING - DAVID - MALCHUT

21 וְעַתָּה אַל־תִּירָאוּ אָנֹכִי איע אֲכַלְכֵּל אֶתְכֶם וְאֶת־טַפְּכֶם וַיְנַחֵם
אוֹתָם וַיְדַבֵּר ראה עַל־לִבָּם׃ 22 וַיֵּשֶׁב יוֹסֵף ציון, קנאה, ה״פ אל, ו״פ יהוה
בְּמִצְרַיִם מצר הוּא וּבֵית ב״פ ראה אָבִיו וַיְחִי יוֹסֵף ציון, קנאה, ה״פ אל, ו״פ יהוה
מֵאָה מלוי ע״ב, דמב וָעֶשֶׂר שָׁנִים׃

MAFTIR

23 וַיַּרְא יוֹסֵף ציון, קנאה, ה״פ אל, ו״פ יהוה לְאֶפְרַיִם אל מצפץ בְּנֵי שִׁלֵּשִׁים גַּם
בְּנֵי מָכִיר בֶּן־מְנַשֶּׁה יֻלְּדוּ עַל־בִּרְכֵּי יוֹסֵף ציון, קנאה, ה״פ אל, ו״פ יהוה׃
24 וַיֹּאמֶר יוֹסֵף ציון, קנאה, ה״פ אל, ו״פ יהוה אֶל־אֶחָיו אָנֹכִי איע מֵת י״פ רבוע אהיה
וֵאלֹהִים ילה, מום פָּקֹד יִפְקֹד אֶתְכֶם וְהֶעֱלָה אֶתְכֶם מִן־הָאָרֶץ
אלהים דההין ע״ה הַזֹּאת אֶל־הָאָרֶץ אלהים דההין ע״ה אֲשֶׁר נִשְׁבַּע לְאַבְרָהָם
ח״פ אל, רמ״ח לְיִצְחָק ד״פ ב״ן וּלְיַעֲקֹב יאהדונהי - אידהנויה׃ 25 וַיַּשְׁבַּע יוֹסֵף
ציון, קנאה, ה״פ אל, ו״פ יהוה אֶת־בְּנֵי יִשְׂרָאֵל לֵאמֹר פָּקֹד רבוע ע״ב יִפְקֹד
אֱלֹהִים ילה, מום אֶתְכֶם וְהַעֲלִתֶם אֶת־עַצְמֹתַי מִזֶּה׃ 26 וַיָּמָת יוֹסֵף
ציון, קנאה, ה״פ אל, ו״פ יהוה בֶּן־מֵאָה מלוי ע״ב, דמב וָעֶשֶׂר שָׁנִים וַיַּחַנְטוּ אֹתוֹ
וַיִּישֶׂם בָּאָרוֹן ג״פ אלהים בְּמִצְרָיִם מצר׃ [ש]

(חסד-ימין) חֲזַק פהל (גבורה-שמאל) חֲזַק פהל (תפארת-אמצע) חֲזַק פהל, מהש

(מלכות) וְנִתְחַזֵּק

HAFTARAH OF VAYECHI

King David's last days are discussed here. During the last moments of a person's life, the soul is partly in the Upper Worlds, even though the body still exists in the physical world. For this reason, the Light from the dying person's whole life is manifested during these moments. Through our connection to King David in this Haftarah, we learn that we can be a channel between the Upper and Lower Worlds throughout our entire lives and that we should not wait until our final moments to become that channel.

"And God shall guide you continually." (Isaiah 58:11)

In relation to the sacrifices, it has been explained that all the worlds were restored through them. "And God shall guide you continually (Heb. *tamid*)" means that through the daily offering (*tamid*), all the worlds are restored, and then bounty descends from Above.

I Kings 2:1-12

2 1 When the time drew near for David to die, he gave a charge to Solomon his son.

2 "I am about to go the way of all the earth," he said. "So be strong, show yourself a
man, 3 and observe what the Lord your God requires: Walk in His ways, and keep His
decrees and commands, His laws and requirements, as written in the Law of Moses,
so that you may prosper in all you do and wherever you go, 4 and that the Lord may
keep his promise to me: 'If your descendants watch how they live, and if they walk
faithfully before Me with all their heart and soul, you will never fail to have a man on
the throne of Israel.'

5 Now you, yourself know what Joab son of Zeruiah did to me—what he did to the two commanders of Israel's armies, Abner son of Ner and Amasa son of Jether. He killed them, shedding their blood in peacetime as if in battle, and with that blood stained the belt around his waist and the sandals on his feet.

6 Deal with him according to your wisdom, but do not let his gray head go down to the grave in peace.

HAFTARAH OF VAYECHI

The Ari wrote:

> *We shall explain the high position of the first man before he sinned. It was said in the Faithful Shepherd, section Kedoshim, that the first man had nothing of this world, that he was a righteous man mating with his wife, and so on. The secret of this is: You should know that the first man comprises all souls. Before he sinned he used to be taller than what he is now in Yetzirah. And if you say that he was created from the dust of the Temple, which is from the world of Asiyah, the answer is that the worlds were not as they are now because through his sin, the first man, so to speak, caused a blemish in all the worlds, from Atzilut to Asiyah. The sense is that surely they were like the worlds—Atzilut, Briah, Yetzirah and Asiyah—but they were of a higher level than what they are now. We have already explained how, through our prayer on Shabbat day, we raise the worlds to their place and grades. Thus, the levels that only exist in our times as a result of Shabbat prayers were once in place every day of the week, even without the special prayers.*
>
> *– Writings of Rav Isaac Luria 8*

מלכים 1 פרק 2

2 1 ויקרבו ימי־דוד למות ויצו פוי את־שלמה בנו לאמר:
2 אנכי איע הלך מיה בדרך ב"פ יב"ק כל ילי ־הארץ אלהים דההין ע"ה וחזקת
פהל והיית לאיש ע"ה קנ"א קס"א: 3 ושמרת את־משמרת | יהוהאדניאהדונהי
אלהיך ילה ללכת בדרכיו ב"פ יב"ק לשמר חקתיו מצותיו פוי
ומשפטיו ועדותיו ככתוב בתורת משה מהש למען תשכיל את
כל ילי ־אשר תעשה ואת כל ילי ־אשר תפנה שם: 4 למען יקים
יהוהאדניאהדונהי את־דברו אשר דבר ראה עלי לאמר אם יוהך
־ישמרו בניך את־דרכם ב"פ יב"ק ללכת לפני באמת
אהיה פעמים אהיה, ז"פ ס"ג בכל לכב ־לבבם בוכו ובכל לכב ־נפשם לאמר
לא־יכרת לך איש ע"ה קנ"א קס"א מעל עלם כסא ישראל: 5 וגם
אתה ידעת את אשר־עשה לי יואב בן־צרויה אשר עשה
לשני־שרי צבאות ישראל לאבנר בן־נר ולעמשא בן־יתר

7 But show kindness to the sons of Barzillai of Gilead and let them be among those who eat at your table. They stood by me when I fled from your brother Absalom.

8 And remember, you have with you Shimei son of Gera, the Benjamite from Bahurim,
who called down bitter curses on me the day I went to Mahanaim. When he came
down to meet me at the Jordan, I swore to him by the Lord: 'I will not put you to death
by the sword.' 9 But now, do not consider him innocent. You are a man of wisdom;
you will know what to do to him. Bring his gray head down to the grave in blood."

10 Then David rested with his fathers and was buried in the City of David.

11 He had reigned forty years over Israel—seven years in Hebron and thirty-three in Jerusalem.

12 So Solomon sat on the throne of his father David, and his rule was firmly established.

וַיַּהַרְגֵם וַיָּשֶׂם דְּמֵי־מִלְחָמָה בְּשָׁלֹם וַיִּתֵּן דְּמֵי מִלְחָמָה בַּחֲגֹרָתוֹ
אֲשֶׁר בְּמָתְנָיו וּבְנַעֲלוֹ אֲשֶׁר בְּרַגְלָיו׃ 6 וְעָשִׂיתָ כְּחָכְמָתֶךָ וְלֹא־
תוֹרֵד שֵׂיבָתוֹ בְּשָׁלֹם שְׁאֹל׃ 7 וְלִבְנֵי בַרְזִלַּי הַגִּלְעָדִי תַּעֲשֶׂה־
חֶסֶד ע"ב, ריבוע יהוה וְהָיוּ בְּאֹכְלֵי שֻׁלְחָנֶךָ כִּי־כֵן קָרְבוּ אֵלַי בְּבָרְחִי
מִפְּנֵי אַבְשָׁלוֹם אָחִיךָ׃ 8 וְהִנֵּה מ"ה יה עִמְּךָ נמם שִׁמְעִי בֶן־גֵּרָא בֶן־
הַיְמִינִי מִבַּחֻרִים וְהוּא קִלְלַנִי קְלָלָה נִמְרֶצֶת בְּיוֹם נגד, זן, מזבח לֶכְתִּי
מַחֲנָיִם וְהוּא־יָרַד לִקְרָאתִי הַיַּרְדֵּן י"פ יהוה וד' אותיות וָאֶשָּׁבַע לוֹ
בַיהוָהאדני אהדונהי לֵאמֹר אִם יוהך ־אֲמִיתְךָ בֶּחָרֶב׃ 9 וְעַתָּה אַל־
תְּנַקֵּהוּ כִּי אִישׁ ע"ה קנ"א קס"א חָכָם אָתָּה וְיָדַעְתָּ אֵת אֲשֶׁר תַּעֲשֶׂה־
לּוֹ וְהוֹרַדְתָּ אֶת־שֵׂיבָתוֹ בְּדָם רבוע אהיה שְׁאוֹל׃ 10 וַיִּשְׁכַּב דָּוִד
עִם־אֲבֹתָיו וַיִּקָּבֵר בְּעִיר מוזחף, ערי, סנדלפו"ן דָּוִד׃ [פ] 11 וְהַיָּמִים נלך
אֲשֶׁר מָלַךְ דָּוִד עַל־יִשְׂרָאֵל אַרְבָּעִים שָׁנָה בְּחֶבְרוֹן מָלַךְ שֶׁבַע
שָׁנִים אלהים דיודין - ע"ב וּבִירוּשָׁלִַם אלהים דיודין פשוט ורבוע מָלַךְ שְׁלֹשִׁים
וְשָׁלֹשׁ שָׁנִים׃ 12 וּשְׁלֹמֹה יָשַׁב עַל־כִּסֵּא דָּוִד אָבִיו וַתִּכֹּן מַלְכֻתוֹ
מְאֹד מ"ה׃ [ס]

SPECIAL READINGS

MAFTIR SHABBAT CHANUKAH

The Torah readings for the seven days of Chanukah, and the Maftir of the Shabbat of Chanukah are all tools to download as much of that miraculous Light as possible.

Numbers 7:1-8:4

7 [1] When Moses finished setting up the Tabernacle, he anointed it and consecrated it and all its furnishings. He also anointed and consecrated the altar and all its utensils.

[2] Then the leaders of Israel, the heads of families who were the tribal leaders in charge of those who were counted, made offerings.

[3] They brought as their gifts before the Lord six covered carts and twelve oxen—an ox from each leader and a cart from every two. These they presented before the Tabernacle.

[4] The Lord said to Moses, [5] "Accept these from them, that they may be used in the work at the Tent of Meeting. Give them to the Levites as each man's work requires."

[6] So Moses took the carts and oxen and gave them to the Levites.

[7] He gave two carts and four oxen to the Gershonites, as their work required, [8] and he gave four carts and eight oxen to the Merarites, as their work required. They were all under the direction of Ithamar son of Aaron, the priest.

[9] But Moses did not give any to the Kohathites, because they were to carry on their shoulders the holy things, for which they were responsible.

[10] When the altar was anointed, the leaders brought their offerings for its dedication and presented them before the altar.

[11] For the Lord had said to Moses, "Each day one leader is to bring his offering for the dedication of the altar."

MAFTIR SHABBAT CHANUKAH

במדבר 7 פרק 1

7 1 וַיְהִי אל בְּיוֹם נגד, זן, מזבח כַּלּוֹת מֹשֶׁה מהש לְהָקִים אֶת־הַמִּשְׁכָּן ב״פ
(רבוע אלהים ‑ ה׳) וַיִּמְשַׁח אֹתוֹ וַיְקַדֵּשׁ אֹתוֹ וְאֶת־כָּל ילי ־כֵּלָיו כלי וְאֶת־
הַמִּזְבֵּחַ זן, נגד וְאֶת־כָּל ילי ־כֵּלָיו כלי וַיִּמְשָׁחֵם וַיְקַדֵּשׁ אֹתָם׃
2 וַיַּקְרִיבוּ נְשִׂיאֵי יִשְׂרָאֵל רָאשֵׁי ריבוע אלהים ‑ אלהים דיודין ע״ה בֵּית ב״פ ראה
אֲבֹתָם הֵם נְשִׂיאֵי הַמַּטֹּת הֵם הָעֹמְדִים עַל־הַפְּקֻדִים׃ 3 וַיָּבִיאוּ
אֶת־קָרְבָּנָם לִפְנֵי יְהֹוָאדהנויאהדונהי שֵׁשׁ־עֶגְלֹת צָב וּשְׁנֵי עָשָׂר בָּקָר
עֲגָלָה עַל־שְׁנֵי הַנְּשִׂאִים וְשׁוֹר אבגיתץ, ושר, אהבת חנם לְאֶחָד אהבה, דאגה
וַיַּקְרִיבוּ אוֹתָם לִפְנֵי הַמִּשְׁכָּן ב״פ (רבוע אלהים ‑ ה׳)׃ 4 וַיֹּאמֶר יְהֹוָאדהנויאהדונהי
אֶל־מֹשֶׁה מהש לֵּאמֹר׃ 5 קַח מֵאִתָּם וְהָיוּ לַעֲבֹד אֶת־עֲבֹדַת אֹהֶל
לאה, אלד ע״ה) מוֹעֵד וְנָתַתָּה אוֹתָם אֶל־הַלְוִיִּם ע״ה יהוה ‑ אהיה אִישׁ ע״ה קנ״א
קס״א כְּפִי עֲבֹדָתוֹ׃ 6 וַיִּקַּח חעם מֹשֶׁה מהש אֶת־הָעֲגָלֹת וְאֶת־הַבָּקָר
וַיִּתֵּן אוֹתָם אֶל־הַלְוִיִּם ע״ה יהוה ‑ אהיה׃ 7 אֵת | שְׁתֵּי הָעֲגָלוֹת וְאֵת
אַרְבַּעַת הַבָּקָר נָתַן לִבְנֵי גֵרְשׁוֹן ע״ה ב״פ מנצפ״ך כְּפִי עֲבֹדָתָם׃ 8 וְאֵת |
אַרְבַּע הָעֲגָלֹת וְאֵת שְׁמֹנַת הַבָּקָר נָתַן לִבְנֵי מְרָרִי כְּפִי עֲבֹדָתָם
בְּיַד אִיתָמָר בֶּן־אַהֲרֹן ע״ב ורבוע ע״ב הַכֹּהֵן מלה׃ 9 וְלִבְנֵי קְהָת לֹא נָתָן
כִּי־עֲבֹדַת הַקֹּדֶשׁ עֲלֵהֶם בַּכָּתֵף יִשָּׂאוּ׃ 10 וַיַּקְרִיבוּ הַנְּשִׂאִים אֵת
חֲנֻכַּת הַמִּזְבֵּחַ זן, נגד בְּיוֹם נגד, זן, מזבח הִמָּשַׁח אֹתוֹ וַיַּקְרִיבוּ הַנְּשִׂיאִם
אֶת־קָרְבָּנָם לִפְנֵי הַמִּזְבֵּחַ זן, נגד׃ 11 וַיֹּאמֶר יְהֹוָאדהנויאהדונהי אֶל־מֹשֶׁה
מהש נָשִׂיא אֶחָד אהבה, דאגה לַיּוֹם נגד, זן, מזבח נָשִׂיא אֶחָד אהבה, דאגה לַיּוֹם
נגד, זן, מזבח יַקְרִיבוּ אֶת־קָרְבָּנָם לַחֲנֻכַּת הַמִּזְבֵּחַ זן, נגד׃ [ס]

READING FOR FIRST DAY

Controlling the Month of Nissan/Aries

Aries – ה Mars – ד

12 The one who brought his offering on the first day was Nahshon son of Amminadab of the tribe of Judah.

13 His offering was one silver plate weighing a hundred and thirty shekels, and one silver sprinkling bowl weighing seventy shekels, both according to the sanctuary shekel, each filled with fine flour mixed with oil as a grain offering;

14 one gold dish weighing ten shekels, filled with incense; 15 one young bull, one ram and one male lamb a year old, for a burnt offering;

16 one male goat for a sin offering;

17 and two oxen, five rams, five male goats and five male lambs a year old, to be sacrificed as a fellowship offering. This was the offering of Nahshon son of Amminadab.

READING FOR THE SECOND DAY

Controlling the Month of Iyar/Taurus

Taurus – ו Venus - פ

18 On the second day Nethanel son of Zuar, the leader of Issachar, brought his offering.

19 The offering he brought was one silver plate weighing a hundred and thirty shekels, and one silver sprinkling bowl weighing seventy shekels, both according to the sanctuary shekel, each filled with fine flour mixed with oil as a grain offering;

20 one gold dish weighing ten shekels, filled with incense;

21 one young bull, one ram and one male lamb a year old, for a burnt offering;

READING FOR FIRST DAY

CONTROLLING THE MONTH OF NISSAN/ARIES

Aries – ה Mars – ד

12 וַיְהִי אל הַמַּקְרִיב בַּיּוֹם נגד, זן, מזבח הָרִאשׁוֹן אֶת־קָרְבָּנוֹ נַחְשׁוֹן
בֶּן־עַמִּינָדָב לְמַטֵּה יְהוּדָה׃ 13 וְקָרְבָּנוֹ קַעֲרַת־כֶּסֶף אַחַת
שְׁלֹשִׁים וּמֵאָה דמב, מלוי ע"ב מִשְׁקָלָהּ מִזְרָק אֶחָד אהבה, דאגה כֶּסֶף
שִׁבְעִים שֶׁקֶל בְּשֶׁקֶל הַקֹּדֶשׁ שְׁנֵיהֶם ׀ מְלֵאִים סֹלֶת בְּלוּלָה
בַשֶּׁמֶן י"פ טל, י"פ כוזו, ביט לְמִנְחָה ע"ה ב"פ ב"ן׃ 14 כַּף אַחַת עֲשָׂרָה זָהָב
מְלֵאָה קְטֹרֶת י"א אדני׃ 15 פַּר מוזוחך, ערי, סנדלפון אֶחָד אהבה, דאגה בֶּן־בָּקָר
אַיִל אֶחָד אהבה, דאגה כֶּבֶשׂ ב"פ קס"א ־אֶחָד אהבה, דאגה בֶּן־שְׁנָתוֹ לְעֹלָה׃
16 שְׂעִיר־עִזִּים אֶחָד אהבה, דאגה לְחַטָּאת׃ 17 וּלְזֶבַח הַשְּׁלָמִים בָּקָר
שְׁנַיִם אֵילִם חֲמִשָּׁה עַתּוּדִים חֲמִשָּׁה כְּבָשִׂים בְּנֵי־שָׁנָה חֲמִשָּׁה
זֶה קָרְבַּן נַחְשׁוֹן בֶּן־עַמִּינָדָב׃ [פ]

READING FOR THE SECOND DAY

CONTROLLING THE MONTH OF IYAR/TAURUS

Taurus – ו Venus - פ

18 בַּיּוֹם נגד, זן, מזבח הַשֵּׁנִי הִקְרִיב נְתַנְאֵל בֶּן־צוּעָר נְשִׂיא יִשָּׂשכָר י"פ אל י"פ
ב"ן׃ 19 הִקְרִב אֶת־קָרְבָּנוֹ קַעֲרַת־כֶּסֶף אַחַת שְׁלֹשִׁים וּמֵאָה דמב, מלוי ע"ב
מִשְׁקָלָהּ מִזְרָק אֶחָד אהבה, דאגה כֶּסֶף שִׁבְעִים שֶׁקֶל בְּשֶׁקֶל הַקֹּדֶשׁ
שְׁנֵיהֶם ׀ מְלֵאִים סֹלֶת בְּלוּלָה בַשֶּׁמֶן י"פ טל, י"פ כוזו, ביט לְמִנְחָה ע"ה ב"פ ב"ן׃
20 כַּף אַחַת עֲשָׂרָה זָהָב מְלֵאָה קְטֹרֶת י"א אדני׃ 21 פַּר מוזוחך, ערי, סנדלפון
אֶחָד אהבה, דאגה בֶּן־בָּקָר אַיִל אֶחָד אהבה, דאגה כֶּבֶשׂ ב"פ קס"א ־אֶחָד

22 *one male goat for a sin offering;*

23 *and two oxen, five rams, five male goats and five male lambs a year old, to be sacrificed as a fellowship offering. This was the offering of Nethanel son of Zuar.*

READING FOR THE THIRD DAY

CONTROLLING THE MONTH OF SIVAN/GEMINI

Mercury — ר Gemini - ז

24 *On the third day, Eliab son of Helon, the leader of the people of Zebulun, brought his offering.*

25 *His offering was one silver plate weighing a hundred and thirty shekels, and one silver sprinkling bowl weighing seventy shekels, both according to the sanctuary shekel, each filled with fine flour mixed with oil as a grain offering;*

26 *one gold dish weighing ten shekels, filled with incense;*

27 *one young bull, one ram and one male lamb a year old, for a burnt offering;*

28 *one male goat for a sin offering;*

29 *and two oxen, five rams, five male goats and five male lambs a year old, to be sacrificed as a fellowship offering. This was the offering of Eliab son of Helon.*

READING FOR THE FOURTH DAY

CONTROLLING THE MONTH OF TAMMUZ/CANCER

Moon - ת Cancer - ח

30 *On the fourth day Elizur son of Shedeur, the leader of the people of Reuben, brought his offering.*

31 *His offering was one silver plate weighing a hundred and thirty shekels, and one silver sprinkling bowl weighing seventy shekels, both according to the sanctuary shekel, each filled with fine flour mixed with oil as a grain offering;*

אהבה, דאגה בֶּן-שְׁנָתוֹ לְעֹלָה: 22 שְׂעִיר-עִזִּים אֶחָד אהבה, דאגה לְחַטָּאת:
23 וּלְזֶבַח הַשְּׁלָמִים בָּקָר שְׁנַיִם אֵילִם חֲמִשָּׁה עַתֻּדִים חֲמִשָּׁה
כְּבָשִׂים בְּנֵי-שָׁנָה חֲמִשָּׁה זֶה קָרְבַּן נְתַנְאֵל בֶּן-צוּעָר: [פ]

READING FOR THE THIRD DAY

Controlling the Month of Sivan/Gemini

Mercury – ר Gemini - ז

24 בַּיּוֹם נגד, זן, מזבח הַשְּׁלִישִׁי נָשִׂיא לִבְנֵי זְבוּלֻן אֱלִיאָב בֶּן-חֵלֹן:
25 קָרְבָּנוֹ קַעֲרַת-כֶּסֶף אַחַת שְׁלֹשִׁים וּמֵאָה דמב, מלוי ע"ב מִשְׁקָלָהּ
מִזְרָק אֶחָד אהבה, דאגה כֶּסֶף שִׁבְעִים שֶׁקֶל בְּשֶׁקֶל הַקֹּדֶשׁ שְׁנֵיהֶם |
מְלֵאִים סֹלֶת בְּלוּלָה בַשֶּׁמֶן י"פ טל, י"פ כוזו, ביט לְמִנְחָה ע"ה ב"פ בין: 26 כַּף
אַחַת עֲשָׂרָה זָהָב מְלֵאָה קְטֹרֶת י"א אדני: 27 פַּר סנדלפון, ערי, סנדלפון אֶחָד
אהבה, דאגה בֶּן-בָּקָר אַיִל אֶחָד אהבה, דאגה כֶּבֶשׂ ב"פ קס"א -אֶחָד בֶּן-
שְׁנָתוֹ לְעֹלָה: 28 שְׂעִיר-עִזִּים אֶחָד אהבה, דאגה לְחַטָּאת: 29 וּלְזֶבַח
הַשְּׁלָמִים בָּקָר שְׁנַיִם אֵילִם חֲמִשָּׁה עַתֻּדִים חֲמִשָּׁה כְּבָשִׂים
בְּנֵי-שָׁנָה חֲמִשָּׁה זֶה קָרְבַּן אֱלִיאָב בֶּן-חֵלֹן: [פ]

READING FOR THE FOURTH DAY

Controlling the Month of Tammuz/Cancer

Moon - ת Cancer - ח

30 בַּיּוֹם נגד, זן, מזבח הָרְבִיעִי נָשִׂיא לִבְנֵי רְאוּבֵן ג"פ אלהים אֱלִיצוּר בֶּן-
שְׁדֵיאוּר: 31 קָרְבָּנוֹ קַעֲרַת-כֶּסֶף אַחַת שְׁלֹשִׁים וּמֵאָה דמב, מלוי ע"ב
מִשְׁקָלָהּ מִזְרָק אֶחָד אהבה, דאגה כֶּסֶף שִׁבְעִים שֶׁקֶל בְּשֶׁקֶל הַקֹּדֶשׁ

32 one gold dish weighing ten shekels, filled with incense;

33 one young bull, one ram and one male lamb a year old, for a burnt offering;

34 one male goat for a sin offering;

35 and two oxen, five rams, five male goats and five male lambs a year old, to be sacrificed as a fellowship offering. This was the offering of Elizur son of Shedeur.

READING FOR THE FIFTH DAY

CONTROLLING THE MONTH OF MENACHEM AV/LEO

Leo – ט Sun - כ

36 On the fifth day Shelumiel son of Zurishaddai, the leader of the people of Simeon, brought his offering.

37 His offering was one silver plate weighing a hundred and thirty shekels, and one silver sprinkling bowl weighing seventy shekels, both according to the sanctuary shekel, each filled with fine flour mixed with oil as a grain offering;

38 one gold dish weighing ten shekels, filled with incense;

39 one young bull, one ram and one male lamb a year old, for a burnt offering;

40 one male goat for a sin offering;

41 and two oxen, five rams, five male goats and five male lambs a year old, to be sacrificed as a fellowship offering. This was the offering of Shelumiel son of Zurishaddai.

שְׁנֵיהֶם | מְלֵאִים סֹלֶת בְּלוּלָה בַשֶּׁמֶן י"פ טל, י"פ כוזו, ביט לְמִנְחָה ע"ה ב"פ ב"ן:
32 כַּף אַחַת עֲשָׂרָה זָהָב מְלֵאָה קְטֹרֶת י"א אדני: 33 פַּר סוזוחך, ערי, סנדלפו"ן
אֶחָד אהבה, דאגה בֶּן־בָּקָר אַיִל אֶחָד אהבה, דאגה כֶּבֶשׂ ב"פ קס"א ־אֶחָד
אהבה, דאגה בֶּן־שְׁנָתוֹ לְעֹלָה: 34 שְׂעִיר־עִזִּים אֶחָד אהבה, דאגה לְחַטָּאת:
35 וּלְזֶבַח הַשְּׁלָמִים בָּקָר שְׁנַיִם אֵילִם חֲמִשָּׁה עַתֻּדִים חֲמִשָּׁה
כְּבָשִׂים בְּנֵי־שָׁנָה חֲמִשָּׁה זֶה קָרְבַּן אֱלִיצוּר בֶּן־שְׁדֵיאוּר: [פ]

READING FOR THE FIFTH DAY

CONTROLLING THE MONTH OF MENACHEM AV/LEO

Leo – ט Sun - כ

36 בַּיּוֹם נגד, זן, מזבח הַחֲמִישִׁי נָשִׂיא לִבְנֵי שִׁמְעוֹן שְׁלֻמִיאֵל בֶּן־
צוּרִישַׁדָּי: 37 קָרְבָּנוֹ קַעֲרַת־כֶּסֶף אַחַת שְׁלֹשִׁים וּמֵאָה דמב, מלוי
ע"ב מִשְׁקָלָהּ מִזְרָק אֶחָד אהבה, דאגה כֶּסֶף שִׁבְעִים שֶׁקֶל בְּשֶׁקֶל
הַקֹּדֶשׁ שְׁנֵיהֶם | מְלֵאִים סֹלֶת בְּלוּלָה בַשֶּׁמֶן י"פ טל, י"פ כוזו, ביט לְמִנְחָה
ע"ה ב"פ ב"ן: 38 כַּף אַחַת עֲשָׂרָה זָהָב מְלֵאָה קְטֹרֶת י"א אדני: 39 פַּר
סוזוחך, ערי, סנדלפו"ן אֶחָד אהבה, דאגה בֶּן־בָּקָר אַיִל אֶחָד אהבה, דאגה כֶּבֶשׂ־ ב"פ קס"א
אֶחָד אהבה, דאגה בֶּן־שְׁנָתוֹ לְעֹלָה: 40 שְׂעִיר־עִזִּים אֶחָד אהבה, דאגה לְחַטָּאת:
41 וּלְזֶבַח הַשְּׁלָמִים בָּקָר שְׁנַיִם אֵילִם חֲמִשָּׁה עַתֻּדִים חֲמִשָּׁה כְּבָשִׂים
בְּנֵי־שָׁנָה חֲמִשָּׁה זֶה קָרְבַּן שְׁלֻמִיאֵל בֶּן־צוּרִישַׁדָּי: [פ]

READING FOR THE SIXTH DAY

CONTROLLING THE MONTH OF ELUL/VIRGO

Virgo – י Mercury – ר

42 On the sixth day Eliasaph son of Deuel, the leader of the people of Gad, brought his offering.

43 His offering was one silver plate weighing a hundred and thirty shekels, and one silver sprinkling bowl weighing seventy shekels, both according to the sanctuary shekel, each filled with fine flour mixed with oil as a grain offering;

44 one gold dish weighing ten shekels, filled with incense;

45 one young bull, one ram and one male lamb a year old, for a burnt offering;

46 one male goat for a sin offering;

47 and two oxen, five rams, five male goats and five male lambs a year old, to be sacrificed as a fellowship offering. This was the offering of Eliasaph son of Deuel.

READING FOR THE SEVENTH DAY

CONTROLLING THE MONTH OF TISHREI/LIBRA

Libra – ל Venus – פ

48 On the seventh day Elishama son of Ammihud, the leader of the people of Ephraim, brought his offering.

49 His offering was one silver plate weighing a hundred and thirty shekels, and one silver sprinkling bowl weighing seventy shekels, both according to the sanctuary shekel, each filled with fine flour mixed with oil as a grain offering;

50 one gold dish weighing ten shekels, filled with incense;

51 one young bull, one ram and one male lamb a year old, for a burnt offering;

52 one male goat for a sin offering;

READING FOR THE SIXTH DAY

CONTROLLING THE MONTH OF ELUL/VIRGO

Virgo – י Mercury – ר

42 בַּיּוֹם נגד, זן, מזבח הַשִּׁשִּׁי נָשִׂיא לִבְנֵי גָד אֶלְיָסָף בֶּן־דְּעוּאֵל׃
43 קָרְבָּנוֹ קַעֲרַת־כֶּסֶף אַחַת שְׁלֹשִׁים וּמֵאָה דמב, מלוי ע"ב מִשְׁקָלָהּ
מִזְרָק אֶחָד אהבה, דאגה כֶּסֶף שִׁבְעִים שֶׁקֶל בְּשֶׁקֶל הַקֹּדֶשׁ שְׁנֵיהֶם ׀
מְלֵאִים סֹלֶת בְּלוּלָה בַשֶּׁמֶן י"פ טל, י"פ כוזו, ביט לְמִנְחָה ע"ה ב"פ ב"ן׃ 44 כַּף
אַחַת עֲשָׂרָה זָהָב מְלֵאָה קְטֹרֶת י"א אדני׃ 45 פַּר סוזוף, ערי, סנדלפון אֶחָד
אהבה, דאגה בֶּן־בָּקָר אַיִל אֶחָד אהבה, דאגה כֶּבֶשׂ ב"פ קס"א ־אֶחָד אהבה, דאגה
בֶּן־שְׁנָתוֹ לְעֹלָה׃ 46 שְׂעִיר־עִזִּים אֶחָד אהבה, דאגה לְחַטָּאת׃ 47 וּלְזֶבַח
הַשְּׁלָמִים בָּקָר שְׁנַיִם אֵילִם חֲמִשָּׁה עַתֻּדִים חֲמִשָּׁה כְּבָשִׂים
בְּנֵי־שָׁנָה חֲמִשָּׁה זֶה קָרְבַּן אֶלְיָסָף בֶּן־דְּעוּאֵל׃ [פ]

READING FOR THE SEVENTH DAY

CONTROLLING THE MONTH OF TISHREI/LIBRA

Libra – ל Venus – פ

48 בַּיּוֹם נגד, זן, מזבח הַשְּׁבִיעִי נָשִׂיא לִבְנֵי אֶפְרָיִם אל מצפץ אֱלִישָׁמָע
בֶּן־עַמִּיהוּד׃ 49 קָרְבָּנוֹ קַעֲרַת־כֶּסֶף אַחַת שְׁלֹשִׁים וּמֵאָה דמב, מלוי
ע"ב מִשְׁקָלָהּ מִזְרָק אֶחָד אהבה, דאגה כֶּסֶף שִׁבְעִים שֶׁקֶל בְּשֶׁקֶל
הַקֹּדֶשׁ שְׁנֵיהֶם ׀ מְלֵאִים סֹלֶת בְּלוּלָה בַשֶּׁמֶן י"פ טל, י"פ כוזו, ביט לְמִנְחָה
ע"ה ב"פ ב"ן׃ 50 כַּף אַחַת עֲשָׂרָה זָהָב מְלֵאָה קְטֹרֶת י"א אדני׃ 51 פַּר
סוזוף, ערי, סנדלפון אֶחָד אהבה, דאגה בֶּן־בָּקָר אַיִל אֶחָד אהבה, דאגה כֶּבֶשׂ ב"פ
קס"א ־אֶחָד אהבה, דאגה בֶּן־שְׁנָתוֹ לְעֹלָה׃ 52 שְׂעִיר־עִזִּים אֶחָד אהבה, דאגה

53 *and two oxen, five rams, five male goats and five male lambs a year old, to be sacrificed as a fellowship offering. This was the offering of Elishama son of Ammihud.*

READING FOR THE EIGHTH DAY

Controlling the month of Mar Cheshvan/Scorpio

Scorpio – נ Mars – ד

54 *On the eighth day Gamaliel the son of Pedahzur, prince of the children of Manasseh:*

55 *The offering he brought was one silver plate weighing a hundred and thirty shekels, and one silver sprinkling bowl weighing seventy shekels, both according to the sanctuary shekel, each filled with fine flour mixed with oil as a grain offering;*

56 *one gold dish weighing ten shekels, filled with incense;*

57 *one young bull, one ram and one male lamb a year old, for a burnt offering;*

58 *one male goat for a sin offering;*

59 *and two oxen, five rams, five male goats and five male lambs a year old, to be sacrificed as a fellowship offering. This was the offering of Gamaliel the son of Pedahzur.*

Controlling the month of Kislev/Sagittarius

Jupiter – ג Sagittarius – ס

60 *On the ninth day Abidan the son of Gideoni, prince of the children of Benjamin:*

61 *The offering he brought was one silver plate weighing a hundred and thirty shekels, and one silver sprinkling bowl weighing seventy shekels, both according to the sanctuary shekel, each filled with fine flour mixed with oil as a grain offering;*

62 *one gold dish weighing ten shekels, filled with incense;*

לְחַטָּאת׃ 53 וּלְזֶבַח הַשְּׁלָמִים בָּקָר שְׁנַיִם אֵילִם חֲמִשָּׁה עַתֻּדִים
חֲמִשָּׁה כְּבָשִׂים בְּנֵי־שָׁנָה חֲמִשָּׁה זֶה קָרְבַּן אֱלִישָׁמָע בֶּן־
עַמִּיהוּד׃ [פ]

READING FOR THE EIGHTH DAY

Controlling the month of Mar Cheshvan/scorpio

Scorpio – נ Mars – ד

54 בַּיּוֹם נגד, זן, מזבח הַשְּׁמִינִי נָשִׂיא לִבְנֵי מְנַשֶּׁה גַּמְלִיאֵל בֶּן־פְּדָהצוּר׃
55 קָרְבָּנוֹ קַעֲרַת־כֶּסֶף אַחַת שְׁלֹשִׁים וּמֵאָה דמב, מלוי ע״ב מִשְׁקָלָהּ
מִזְרָק אֶחָד אהבה, דאגה כֶּסֶף שִׁבְעִים שֶׁקֶל בְּשֶׁקֶל הַקֹּדֶשׁ שְׁנֵיהֶם |
מְלֵאִים סֹלֶת בְּלוּלָה בַשֶּׁמֶן י״פ טל, י״פ כוזו, ביט לְמִנְחָה ע״ה ב״פ ב״ן׃ 56 כַּף
אַחַת עֲשָׂרָה זָהָב מְלֵאָה קְטֹרֶת י״א אדני׃ 57 פַּר סנדלפון, ערי, סנדלפו״ן אֶחָד
אהבה, דאגה בֶּן־בָּקָר אַיִל אֶחָד אהבה, דאגה כֶּבֶשׂ ב״פ קס״א ־אֶחָד אהבה, דאגה
בֶּן־שְׁנָתוֹ לְעֹלָה׃ 58 שְׂעִיר־עִזִּים אֶחָד אהבה, דאגה לְחַטָּאת׃ 59 וּלְזֶבַח
הַשְּׁלָמִים בָּקָר שְׁנַיִם אֵילִם חֲמִשָּׁה עַתֻּדִים חֲמִשָּׁה כְּבָשִׂים
בְּנֵי־שָׁנָה חֲמִשָּׁה זֶה קָרְבַּן גַּמְלִיאֵל בֶּן־פְּדָהצוּר׃ [פ]

Controlling the month of Kislev/sagittarius

Jupiter – ג Sagittarius – ס

60 בַּיּוֹם נגד, זן, מזבח הַתְּשִׁיעִי נָשִׂיא לִבְנֵי בִנְיָמִן אֲבִידָן בֶּן־גִּדְעֹנִי׃
61 קָרְבָּנוֹ קַעֲרַת־כֶּסֶף אַחַת שְׁלֹשִׁים וּמֵאָה דמב, מלוי ע״ב מִשְׁקָלָהּ
מִזְרָק אֶחָד אהבה, דאגה כֶּסֶף שִׁבְעִים שֶׁקֶל בְּשֶׁקֶל הַקֹּדֶשׁ שְׁנֵיהֶם |
מְלֵאִים סֹלֶת בְּלוּלָה בַשֶּׁמֶן י״פ טל, י״פ כוזו, ביט לְמִנְחָה ע״ה ב״פ ב״ן׃ 62 כַּף

63 one young bull, one ram and one male lamb a year old, for a burnt offering;

64 one male goat for a sin offering;

65 and two oxen, five rams, five male goats and five male lambs a year old, to be sacrificed as a fellowship offering. This was the offering of Abidan the son of Gideoni.

Controlling the month of Tevet/Capricorn

Saturn – ב Capricorn – ע

66 On the tenth day Ahiezer the son of Ammishaddai, prince of the children of Dan:

67 The offering he brought was one silver plate weighing a hundred and thirty shekels, and one silver sprinkling bowl weighing seventy shekels, both according to the sanctuary shekel, each filled with fine flour mixed with oil as a grain offering;

68 one gold dish weighing ten shekels, filled with incense;

69 one young bull, one ram and one male lamb a year old, for a burnt offering;

70 one male goat for a sin offering;

71 and two oxen, five rams, five male goats and five male lambs a year old, to be sacrificed as a fellowship offering. This was the offering of Ahiezer the son of Ammishaddai.

Controlling the month of Shevat/Aquarius

Saturn – ב Aquarius – צ

72 On the eleventh day Pagiel the son of Ochran, prince of the children of Asher:

73 The offering he brought was one silver plate weighing a hundred and thirty shekels, and one silver sprinkling bowl weighing seventy shekels, both according to the sanctuary shekel, each filled with fine flour mixed with oil as a grain offering;

אֲחַת עֲשָׂרָה זָהָב מְלֵאָה קְטֹרֶת י״א אדני: 63 פַּר סוזוך, ערי, סנדלפון אֶחָד
אהבה, דאגה בֶּן־בָּקָר אַיִל אֶחָד אהבה, דאגה כֶּבֶשׂ ב״פ קס״א ־אֶחָד אהבה, דאגה
בֶּן־שְׁנָתוֹ לְעֹלָה: 64 שְׂעִיר־עִזִּים אֶחָד אהבה, דאגה לְחַטָּאת: 65 וּלְזֶבַח
הַשְּׁלָמִים בָּקָר שְׁנַיִם אֵילִם חֲמִשָּׁה עַתֻּדִים חֲמִשָּׁה כְּבָשִׂים
בְּנֵי־שָׁנָה חֲמִשָּׁה זֶה קָרְבַּן אֲבִידָן בֶּן־גִּדְעֹנִי: [פ]

Controlling the month of Tevet/Capricorn

Saturn – ב Capricorn – ע

66 בַּיּוֹם נגד, זן, מזבח הָעֲשִׂירִי נָשִׂיא לִבְנֵי דָן אֲחִיעֶזֶר בֶּן־עַמִּישַׁדָּי:
67 קָרְבָּנוֹ קַעֲרַת־כֶּסֶף אַחַת שְׁלֹשִׁים וּמֵאָה דמב, מלוי ע״ב מִשְׁקָלָהּ
מִזְרָק אֶחָד אהבה, דאגה כֶּסֶף שִׁבְעִים שֶׁקֶל בְּשֶׁקֶל הַקֹּדֶשׁ שְׁנֵיהֶם |
מְלֵאִים סֹלֶת בְּלוּלָה בַשֶּׁמֶן י״פ טל, י״פ כוזו, ביט לְמִנְחָה ע״ה ב״פ ב״ן: 68 כַּף
אֲחַת עֲשָׂרָה זָהָב מְלֵאָה קְטֹרֶת י״א אדני: 69 פַּר סוזוך, ערי, סנדלפון אֶחָד
אהבה, דאגה בֶּן־בָּקָר אַיִל אֶחָד אהבה, דאגה כֶּבֶשׂ ב״פ קס״א ־אֶחָד אהבה, דאגה
בֶּן־שְׁנָתוֹ לְעֹלָה: 70 שְׂעִיר־עִזִּים אֶחָד אהבה, דאגה לְחַטָּאת: 71 וּלְזֶבַח
הַשְּׁלָמִים בָּקָר שְׁנַיִם אֵילִם חֲמִשָּׁה עַתֻּדִים חֲמִשָּׁה כְּבָשִׂים
בְּנֵי־שָׁנָה חֲמִשָּׁה זֶה קָרְבַּן אֲחִיעֶזֶר בֶּן־עַמִּישַׁדָּי: [פ]

Controlling the month of Shevat/Aquarius

Saturn – ב Aquarius – צ

72 בְּיוֹם נגד, זן, מזבח עַשְׁתֵּי עָשָׂר יוֹם נגד, זן, מזבח נָשִׂיא לִבְנֵי אָשֵׁר
ריבוע אלהים ÷ אלהים דיודין ע״ה פַּגְעִיאֵל בֶּן־עָכְרָן: 73 קָרְבָּנוֹ קַעֲרַת־כֶּסֶף
אַחַת שְׁלֹשִׁים וּמֵאָה דמב, מלוי ע״ב מִשְׁקָלָהּ מִזְרָק אֶחָד אהבה, דאגה

74 one gold dish weighing ten shekels, filled with incense;

75 one young bull, one ram and one male lamb a year old, for a burnt offering;

*76 one male goat for a sin offering; 77 and two oxen, five rams, five male goats and five
male lambs a year old, to be sacrificed as a fellowship offering. This was the offering
of Pagiel the son of Ochran.*

Controlling the month of Adar/Pisces

Jupiter – ג Pisces – ק

78 On the twelfth day Ahira the son of Enan, prince of the children of Naphtali:

79 The offering he brought was one silver plate weighing a hundred and thirty shekels, and one silver sprinkling bowl weighing seventy shekels, both according to the sanctuary shekel, each filled with fine flour mixed with oil as a grain offering;

80 one gold dish weighing ten shekels, filled with incense;

81 one young bull, one ram and one male lamb a year old, for a burnt offering;

82 one male goat for a sin offering;

83 and two oxen, five rams, five male goats and five male lambs a year old, to be sacrificed as a fellowship offering. This was the offering of Ahira the son of Enan.

84 These were the offerings of the Israelite leaders for the dedication of the altar when it was anointed: twelve silver plates, twelve silver sprinkling bowls and twelve gold dishes.

85 Each silver plate weighing a hundred and thirty shekels, and each sprinkling bowl seventy shekels. Altogether, the silver dishes weighed two thousand four hundred shekels, according to the sanctuary shekel.

כֶּסֶף שִׁבְעִים שֶׁקֶל בְּשֶׁקֶל הַקֹּדֶשׁ שְׁנֵיהֶם | מְלֵאִים סֹלֶת בְּלוּלָה
בַשֶּׁמֶן י״פ טל, י״פ כוזו, ביט לְמִנְחָה ע״ה ב״פ ב״ן: 74 כַּף אַחַת עֲשָׂרָה זָהָב
מְלֵאָה קְטֹרֶת י״א אדני: 75 פַּר סנזופר, ערי, סנדלפו״ן אֶחָד אהבה, דאגה בֶּן־בָּקָר
אַיִל אֶחָד אהבה, דאגה כֶּבֶשׂ ב״פ קס״א ־אֶחָד אהבה, דאגה בֶּן־שְׁנָתוֹ לְעֹלָה:
76 שְׂעִיר־עִזִּים אֶחָד אהבה, דאגה לְחַטָּאת: 77 וּלְזֶבַח הַשְּׁלָמִים בָּקָר
שְׁנַיִם אֵילִם חֲמִשָּׁה עַתֻּדִים חֲמִשָּׁה כְּבָשִׂים בְּנֵי־שָׁנָה חֲמִשָּׁה
זֶה קָרְבַּן פַּגְעִיאֵל בֶּן־עָכְרָן: [פ]

CONTROLLING THE MONTH OF ADAR/PISCES

Jupiter – ג Pisces – ק

78 בַּיּוֹם נגד, זן, מזבח שְׁנֵים עָשָׂר יוֹם נגד, זן, מזבח נָשִׂיא לִבְנֵי נַפְתָּלִי
אֲחִירַע בֶּן־עֵינָן: 79 קָרְבָּנוֹ קַעֲרַת־כֶּסֶף אַחַת שְׁלֹשִׁים וּמֵאָה
דמב, מלוי ע״ב מִשְׁקָלָהּ מִזְרָק אֶחָד אהבה, דאגה כֶּסֶף שִׁבְעִים שֶׁקֶל
בְּשֶׁקֶל הַקֹּדֶשׁ שְׁנֵיהֶם | מְלֵאִים סֹלֶת בְּלוּלָה בַשֶּׁמֶן י״פ טל, י״פ כוזו,
ביט לְמִנְחָה ע״ה ב״פ ב״ן: 80 כַּף אַחַת עֲשָׂרָה זָהָב מְלֵאָה קְטֹרֶת י״א אדני:
81 פַּר סנזופר, ערי, סנדלפו״ן אֶחָד אהבה, דאגה בֶּן־בָּקָר אַיִל אֶחָד אהבה, דאגה
כֶּבֶשׂ ב״פ קס״א ־אֶחָד אהבה, דאגה בֶּן־שְׁנָתוֹ לְעֹלָה: 82 שְׂעִיר־עִזִּים
אֶחָד אהבה, דאגה לְחַטָּאת: 83 וּלְזֶבַח הַשְּׁלָמִים בָּקָר שְׁנַיִם אֵילִם
חֲמִשָּׁה עַתֻּדִים חֲמִשָּׁה כְּבָשִׂים בְּנֵי־שָׁנָה חֲמִשָּׁה זֶה קָרְבַּן
אֲחִירַע בֶּן־עֵינָן: [פ] 84 זֹאת | חֲנֻכַּת הַמִּזְבֵּחַ בְּיוֹם נגד, זן, מזבח הִמָּשַׁח
אֹתוֹ מֵאֵת נְשִׂיאֵי יִשְׂרָאֵל קַעֲרֹת כֶּסֶף שְׁתֵּים עֶשְׂרֵה מִזְרְקֵי־
כֶסֶף שְׁנֵים עָשָׂר כַּפּוֹת זָהָב שְׁתֵּים עֶשְׂרֵה: 85 שְׁלֹשִׁים וּמֵאָה
דמב, מלוי ע״ב הַקְּעָרָה הָאַחַת כֶּסֶף וְשִׁבְעִים הַמִּזְרָק הָאֶחָד אהבה, דאגה

[86] The twelve gold dishes filled with incense weighing ten shekels each, according to the sanctuary shekel. Altogether, the gold dishes weighed a hundred and twenty shekels.

[87] The total number of animals for the burnt offering came to twelve young bulls, twelve rams and twelve male lambs a year old, together with their grain offering. Twelve male goats were used for the sin offering.

[88] The total number of animals for the sacrifice of the fellowship offering came to twenty-four oxen, sixty rams, sixty male goats and sixty male lambs a year old. These were the offerings for the dedication of the altar after it was anointed.

[89] When Moses entered the Tent of Meeting to speak with the LORD, he heard the voice speaking to him from between the two cherubim above the cover on the Ark of the Covenant. And He spoke to him.

8 [1] The LORD said to Moses, [2] "Speak to Aaron and say to him, 'When you set up the seven lamps, they are to light the area in front of the Menorah.' "

[3] Aaron did so; he set up the lamps so that they faced forward on the Menorah, just as the LORD commanded Moses.

[4] This is how the Menorah was made: It was made of hammered gold-from its base to its blossoms. The menorah was made exactly like the pattern the LORD had shown Moses.

כָּל יל׳ כֶּסֶף הַכֵּלִים כלי אַלְפַּיִם וְאַרְבַּע־מֵאוֹת בְּשֶׁקֶל הַקֹּדֶשׁ׃
86 כַּפּוֹת זָהָב שְׁתֵּים־עֶשְׂרֵה מְלֵאֹת קְטֹרֶת עֲשָׂרָה עֲשָׂרָה הַכַּף
בְּשֶׁקֶל הַקֹּדֶשׁ כָּל יל׳ זְהַב הַכַּפּוֹת עֶשְׂרִים וּמֵאָה דמב, מלוי ע״ב׃
87 כָּל יל׳ הַבָּקָר לָעֹלָה שְׁנֵים עָשָׂר פָּרִים אֵילִם שְׁנֵים־עָשָׂר
כְּבָשִׂים בְּנֵי־שָׁנָה שְׁנֵים עָשָׂר וּמִנְחָתָם וּשְׂעִירֵי עִזִּים שְׁנֵים
עָשָׂר לְחַטָּאת׃ 88 וְכֹל יל׳ בְּקַר | זֶבַח הַשְּׁלָמִים עֶשְׂרִים וְאַרְבָּעָה
פָּרִים אֵילִם שִׁשִּׁים עַתֻּדִים שִׁשִּׁים כְּבָשִׂים בְּנֵי־שָׁנָה שִׁשִּׁים
זֹאת חֲנֻכַּת הַמִּזְבֵּחַ זן, נגד אַחֲרֵי הִמָּשַׁח אֹתוֹ׃ 89 וּבְבֹא מֹשֶׁה מהש
אֶל־אֹהֶל לאה, אלד ע״ה מוֹעֵד לְדַבֵּר ראה אִתּוֹ וַיִּשְׁמַע אֶת־הַקּוֹל ע״ב ס״ג
ע״ה מִדַּבֵּר ראה אֵלָיו מֵעַל עלם הַכַּפֹּרֶת אֲשֶׁר עַל־אֲרֹן הָעֵדֻת מִבֵּין
שְׁנֵי הַכְּרֻבִים וַיְדַבֵּר ראה אֵלָיו׃ [פ] 8 1 וַיְדַבֵּר ראה יְהֹוָהאדניאהדונהי
אֶל־מֹשֶׁה מהש לֵּאמֹר׃ 2 דַּבֵּר ראה אֶל־אַהֲרֹן ע״ב - רבוע ע״ב וְאָמַרְתָּ
אֵלָיו בְּהַעֲלֹתְךָ אֶת־הַנֵּרֹת יהוה אהיה - יהוה אלהים - יהוה אדני אֶל־מוּל פְּנֵי
וחכמה - בינה הַמְּנוֹרָה יָאִירוּ שִׁבְעַת הַנֵּרוֹת יהוה אהיה - יהוה אלהים - יהוה אדני׃
3 וַיַּעַשׂ כֵּן אַהֲרֹן ע״ב - רבוע ע״ב אֶל־מוּל פְּנֵי וחכמה - בינה הַמְּנוֹרָה הֶעֱלָה
נֵרֹתֶיהָ יהוה אהיה - יהוה אלהים - יהוה אדני כַּאֲשֶׁר צִוָּה פוי יְהֹוָהאדניאהדונהי אֶת־
מֹשֶׁה מהש׃ 4 וְזֶה מַעֲשֵׂה הַמְּנֹרָה מִקְשָׁה זָהָב עַד־יְרֵכָהּ עַד־
פִּרְחָהּ מִקְשָׁה הִוא כַּמַּרְאֶה אֲשֶׁר הֶרְאָה יְהֹוָהאדניאהדונהי אֶת־
מֹשֶׁה מהש כֵּן עָשָׂה אֶת־הַמְּנֹרָה׃ [פ]

HAFTARAH OF FIRST SHABBAT OF CHANUKAH

In a vision, the prophet Zechariah sees Satan standing to the right of the High Priest. The Satan is very cunning and appears when we least expect him. He usually comes from the left side, pushing us to do negative things, but occasionally he'll come from the right, pushing us to overload ourselves with positive tasks. Satan may confront us from any direction.

Zechariah 2:10-4:7

2 [14] "Sing and rejoice, daughter of Zion; for, lo, I come, and I will dwell in the midst of you," says the Lord.

[15] "And many nations shall join themselves to the Lord in that day, and shall be My people, and I will dwell in the midst of you; and you shall know that the Lord of hosts sent Me to you.

[16] And the Lord shall inherit Judah as His portion in the Holy Land, and shall choose Jerusalem again."

[17] Be silent, all flesh, before the Lord; for He is aroused out of His holy habitation.

3 [1] Then he showed me Joshua the high priest standing before the angel of the Lord, and Satan standing at his right side to accuse him.

[2] The Lord said to Satan, "The Lord rebuke you, Satan! The Lord, who has chosen Jerusalem, rebuke you! Is not this man a burning stick snatched from the fire?"

[3] Now Joshua was dressed in filthy clothes as he stood before the angel.

[4] The angel said to those who were standing before him, "Take off his filthy clothes." Then he said to Joshua, "See, I have taken away your sin, and I will put rich garments on you."

[5] Then I said, "Put a clean turban on his head." So they put a clean turban on his head and clothed him, while the angel of the Lord stood by.

[6] The angel of the Lord gave this charge to Joshua: [7] "This is what the Lord Almighty says: 'If you will walk in My ways and keep My requirements, then you will govern

HAFTARAH OF FIRST SHABBAT OF CHANUKAH

זכריה פרק 2–4

2 14 רָנִּי ע״פ יהוה וְשִׂמְחִי בַּת־צִיּוֹן יוסף, ו׳ הויות, ה״פ אל כִּי הִנְנִי־בָא וְשָׁכַנְתִּי
בְתוֹכֵךְ נְאֻם־יְהֹוָהאדניאהדונהי: 15 וְנִלְווּ גוֹיִם רַבִּים אֶל־יְהֹוָהאדניאהדונהי
בַּיּוֹם נגד, זן, מזבח הַהוּא וְהָיוּ לִי לְעָם עלם וְשָׁכַנְתִּי בְתוֹכֵךְ וְיָדַעַתְּ
כִּי־יְהֹוָהאדניאהדונהי צְבָאוֹת פני שכינה שְׁלָחַנִי אֵלָיִךְ אני: 16 וְנָחַל
יְהֹוָהאדניאהדונהי אֶת־יְהוּדָה חֶלְקוֹ עַל אַדְמַת הַקֹּדֶשׁ וּבָחַר עוֹד
בִּירוּשָׁלִָם רי״ו ש״ע: 17 הַס אדני, ללה כָּל ילי ־בָּשָׂר מִפְּנֵי יְהֹוָהאדניאהדונהי
כִּי נֵעוֹר מִמְּעוֹן קָדְשׁוֹ: [ס] 3 1 וַיַּרְאֵנִי אֶת־יְהוֹשֻׁעַ הַכֹּהֵן מלה
הַגָּדוֹל להח, מבה, יזל, אום עֹמֵד לִפְנֵי מַלְאַךְ יְהֹוָהאדניאהדונהי וְהַשָּׂטָן עֹמֵד
עַל־יְמִינוֹ לְשִׂטְנוֹ: 2 וַיֹּאמֶר יְהֹוָהאדניאהדונהי אֶל־הַשָּׂטָן יִגְעַר
יְהֹוָהאדניאהדונהי בְּךָ הַשָּׂטָן וְיִגְעַר יְהֹוָהאדניאהדונהי בְּךָ הַבֹּחֵר בִּירוּשָׁלִָם
רי״ו ש״ע הֲלוֹא זֶה אוּד מֻצָּל מֵאֵשׁ: 3 וִיהוֹשֻׁעַ הָיָה יהה לָבֻשׁ בְּגָדִים
צוֹאִים וְעֹמֵד לִפְנֵי הַמַּלְאָךְ פוי: 4 וַיַּעַן וַיֹּאמֶר אֶל־הָעֹמְדִים
לְפָנָיו לֵאמֹר הָסִירוּ הַבְּגָדִים הַצֹּאִים מֵעָלָיו וַיֹּאמֶר אֵלָיו רְאֵה
ראה הֶעֱבַרְתִּי מֵעָלֶיךָ עֲוֹנֶךָ וְהַלְבֵּשׁ אֹתְךָ מַחֲלָצוֹת: 5 וָאֹמַר
יָשִׂימוּ צָנִיף טָהוֹר י״פ אכא עַל־רֹאשׁוֹ ריבוע אלהים ‑ אלהים דיודין ע״ה וַיָּשִׂימוּ
הַצָּנִיף הַטָּהוֹר י״פ אכא עַל־רֹאשׁוֹ ריבוע אלהים ‑ אלהים דיודין ע״ה וַיַּלְבִּשֻׁהוּ
בְּגָדִים וּמַלְאַךְ יְהֹוָהאדניאהדונהי עֹמֵד: 6 וַיָּעַד מַלְאַךְ יְהֹוָהאדניאהדונהי
בִּיהוֹשֻׁעַ לֵאמֹר: 7 כֹּה הי׳ ־אָמַר יְהֹוָהאדניאהדונהי צְבָאוֹת פני שכינה אִם
יוהך ־בִּדְרָכַי ב״פ יב״ק תֵּלֵךְ וְאִם יוהך אֶת־מִשְׁמַרְתִּי תִשְׁמֹר וְגַם־ יגל
אַתָּה תָּדִין אֶת־בֵּיתִי ב״פ ראה וְגַם יגל תִּשְׁמֹר אֶת־חֲצֵרָי וְנָתַתִּי לְךָ

My house and have charge of My courts, and I will give you a place among these standing here.

8 Listen, High Priest Joshua and your associates seated before you, who are men symbolic of things to come: I am going to bring My servant, the Branch.
9 See, the stone I have set in front of Joshua! There are seven eyes on that one stone, and I will engrave an inscription on it,' says the Lord Almighty, 'and I will remove the sin of this land in a single day.

10 In that day each of you will invite his neighbor to sit under his vine and fig tree,' declares the Lord Almighty.

4 1 Then the angel who talked with me returned and wakened me, as a man is wakened from his sleep.

2 He asked me, "What do you see?" I answered, "I see a solid gold lampstand with a bowl at the top and seven lights on it, with seven channels to the lights.

3 Also there are two olive trees by it, one on the right of the bowl and the other on its left."

4 I asked the angel who talked with me, "What are these, my Lord?"
5 He answered, "Do you not know what these are?" "No, my Lord," I replied.

6 So he said to me, "This is the word of the Lord to Zerubbabel: 'Not by might nor by power, but by My Spirit,' says the Lord Almighty.

7 What are you, O mighty mountain? Before Zerubbabel you will become level ground. Then he will bring out the capstone to shouts of 'God bless it! God bless it!' "

מַהְלְכִים מיה בֵּין הָעֹמְדִים הָאֵלֶּה: 8 שְׁמַע־נָא יְהוֹשֻׁעַ | הַכֹּהֵן מלה
הַגָּדוֹל להח, מבה, יזל, אום אַתָּה וְרֵעֶיךָ הַיֹּשְׁבִים לְפָנֶיךָ ס"ג + מ"ה + ב"ן כִּי־
אַנְשֵׁי מוֹפֵת הֵמָּה כִּי־הִנְנִי מֵבִיא אֶת־עַבְדִּי צֶמַח
יהוה + אהיה + יהוה + אדני: 9 כִּי | הִנֵּה מ"ה יה הָאֶבֶן יוד הה ואו הה אֲשֶׁר נָתַתִּי
לִפְנֵי יְהוֹשֻׁעַ עַל־אֶבֶן יוד הה ואו הה אַחַת שִׁבְעָה עֵינָיִם ריבוע מ"ה הִנְנִי
מְפַתֵּחַ פִּתֻּחָהּ נְאֻם יְהֹוָהאדני אהדונהי צְבָאוֹת פני שכינה וּמַשְׁתִּי אֶת־עֲוֺן
ג"פ מ"ב הָאָרֶץ אלהים דההין ע"ה הַהִיא בְּיוֹם נגד, זן, מזבח אֶחָד אהבה, דאגה:
10 בַּיּוֹם נגד, זן, מזבח הַהוּא נְאֻם יְהֹוָהאדני אהדונהי צְבָאוֹת פני שכינה תִּקְרְאוּ
אִישׁ ע"ה קנ"א קס"א לְרֵעֵהוּ אֶל־תַּחַת גֶּפֶן וְאֶל־תַּחַת תְּאֵנָה נתה ע"ה:
4 1 וַיָּשָׁב הַמַּלְאָךְ פוי הַדֹּבֵר ראה בִּי וַיְעִירֵנִי כְּאִישׁ ע"ה קנ"א קס"א
אֲשֶׁר־יֵעוֹר מִשְּׁנָתוֹ: 2 וַיֹּאמֶר אֵלַי מָה מ"ה אַתָּה רֹאֶה ראה וָאֹמַר
(כתיב: ויאמר) רָאִיתִי | וְהִנֵּה מ"ה יה מְנוֹרַת זָהָב כֻּלָּהּ וְגֻלָּהּ עַל־
רֹאשָׁהּ ריבוע אלהים + אלהים דיודין ע"ה וְשִׁבְעָה נֵרֹתֶיהָ יהוה אהיה + יהוה אלהים + יהוה אדני
עָלֶיהָ פהל שִׁבְעָה וְשִׁבְעָה מוּצָקוֹת לַנֵּרוֹת יהוה אהיה + יהוה אלהים + יהוה אדני
אֲשֶׁר עַל־רֹאשָׁהּ ריבוע אלהים + אלהים דיודין ע"ה: 3 וּשְׁנַיִם זֵיתִים עָלֶיהָ פהל
אֶחָד אהבה, דאגה מִימִין הַגֻּלָּה וְאֶחָד אהבה, דאגה עַל־שְׂמֹאלָהּ: 4 וָאַעַן
וָאֹמַר אֶל־הַמַּלְאָךְ פוי הַדֹּבֵר ראה בִּי לֵאמֹר מָה מ"ה ־אֵלֶּה אֲדֹנִי:
5 וַיַּעַן הַמַּלְאָךְ פוי הַדֹּבֵר ראה בִּי וַיֹּאמֶר אֵלַי הֲלוֹא יָדַעְתָּ מָה מ"ה
־הֵמָּה אֵלֶּה וָאֹמַר לֹא אֲדֹנִי: 6 וַיַּעַן וַיֹּאמֶר אֵלַי לֵאמֹר זֶה
דְּבַר ראה ־יְהֹוָהאדני אהדונהי אֶל־זְרֻבָּבֶל לֵאמֹר לֹא בְחַיִל ומב וְלֹא בְכֹחַ
כִּי אִם יוהך ־בְּרוּחִי אָמַר יְהֹוָהאדני אהדונהי צְבָאוֹת פני שכינה: 7 מִי־ ילי
אַתָּה הַר רבוע אלהים + ה' ־הַגָּדוֹל להח, מבה, יזל, אום לִפְנֵי זְרֻבָּבֶל לְמִישֹׁר
וְהוֹצִיא אֶת־הָאֶבֶן יוד הה ואו הה הָרֹאשָׁה ריבוע אלהים + אלהים דיודין ע"ה
תְּשֻׁאוֹת חֵן מוחי חֵן מוחי לָהּ: [פ]

HAFTARAH OF SECOND SHABBAT OF CHANUKAH

I Kings 7:40-50

7 40 And Hirom also made the basins and shovels and sprinkling bowls. So Hiram finished all the work he had undertaken for King Solomon in the Temple of the Lord:

41 the two pillars; the two bowl-shaped capitals on top of the pillars; the two sets of network decorating the two bowl-shaped capitals on top of the pillars;

42 the four hundred pomegranates for the two sets of network - two rows of pomegranates for each network, decorating the bowl-shaped capitals on top of the pillars

43 the ten stands with their ten basins;

44 the one sea and the twelve oxen under it;

45 the pots, shovels and sprinkling bowls. All these objects that Hiram made for King Solomon for the Temple of the Lord were of burnished bronze.

46 The king had them cast in clay molds in the plain of the Jordan between Succoth and Zarethan.

47 And Solomon left all these things unweighed, because there were so many; the weight of the bronze was not determined.

48 Solomon also made all the furnishings that were in the Lord's Temple: the golden altar; the golden table on which was the showbread;

49 the menorahs of pure gold (five on the right and five on the left, in front of the inner sanctuary the gold floral work and lamps and tongs;

50 the pure gold basins, wick trimmers, sprinkling bowls, dishes and censers; and the gold sockets for the doors of the innermost room, the Holy of Holies, and also for the doors of the main golden hall of the Temple

HAFTARAH OF SECOND SHABBAT OF CHANUKAH

מלכים 1 פרק 7

7 40 וַיַּעַשׂ חִירוֹם אֶת־הַכִּיֹּרוֹת וְאֶת־הַיָּעִים וְאֶת־הַמִּזְרָקוֹת
וַיְכַל חִירָם לַעֲשׂוֹת אֶת־כָּל יל״י ־הַמְּלָאכָה אֲשֶׁר עָשָׂה לַמֶּלֶךְ
שְׁלֹמֹה בֵּית ב״פ ראה יְהֹוָאדני יאהדונהי: 41 עַמֻּדִים שְׁנַיִם וְגֻלֹּת הַכֹּתָרֹת
אֲשֶׁר־עַל־רֹאשׁ ריבוע אלהים + אלהים דיודין ע״ה הָעַמֻּדִים שְׁתָּיִם וְהַשְּׂבָכוֹת
שְׁתַּיִם לְכַסּוֹת אֶת־שְׁתֵּי גֻּלּוֹת הַכֹּתָרֹת אֲשֶׁר עַל־רֹאשׁ
ריבוע אלהים + אלהים דיודין ע״ה הָעַמּוּדִים: 42 וְאֶת־הָרִמֹּנִים אַרְבַּע מֵאוֹת
לִשְׁתֵּי הַשְּׂבָכוֹת שְׁנֵי־טוּרִים רִמֹּנִים לַשְּׂבָכָה הָאֶחָת לְכַסּוֹת
אֶת־שְׁתֵּי גֻּלּוֹת הַכֹּתָרֹת אֲשֶׁר עַל־פְּנֵי חכמה + בינה הָעַמּוּדִים:
43 וְאֶת־הַמְּכֹנוֹת עֶשֶׂר וְאֶת־הַכִּיֹּרֹת עֲשָׂרָה עַל־הַמְּכֹנוֹת:
44 וְאֶת־הַיָּם יל״י הָאֶחָד אהבה, דאגה וְאֶת־הַבָּקָר שְׁנֵים־עָשָׂר תַּחַת
הַיָּם יל״י: 45 וְאֶת־הַסִּירוֹת וְאֶת־הַיָּעִים וְאֶת־הַמִּזְרָקוֹת וְאֵת כָּל יל״י
־הַכֵּלִים כל״י הָאֵלֶּה (כתיב: האהל) אֲשֶׁר עָשָׂה חִירָם לַמֶּלֶךְ שְׁלֹמֹה
בֵּית ב״פ ראה יְהֹוָאדני יאהדונהי נְחֹשֶׁת מְמֹרָט: 46 בְּכִכַּר הַיַּרְדֵּן
י״פ יהוה וד׳ אותיות יְצָקָם הַמֶּלֶךְ בְּמַעֲבֵה הָאֲדָמָה בֵּין סֻכּוֹת וּבֵין
צָרְתָן: 47 וַיַּנַּח שְׁלֹמֹה אֶת־כָּל יל״י ־הַכֵּלִים כל״י מֵרֹב מְאֹד מ״ה
מְאֹד מ״ה לֹא נֶחְקַר מִשְׁקַל הַנְּחֹשֶׁת: 48 וַיַּעַשׂ שְׁלֹמֹה אֵת כָּל יל״י
־הַכֵּלִים כל״י אֲשֶׁר בֵּית ב״פ ראה יְהֹוָאדני יאהדונהי אֵת מִזְבַּח זן, נגד הַזָּהָב
והו וְאֶת־הַשֻּׁלְחָן אֲשֶׁר עָלָיו לֶחֶם ג״פ יהוה הַפָּנִים ע״ב ס״ג מ״ה זָהָב:
49 וְאֶת־הַמְּנֹרוֹת חָמֵשׁ מִיָּמִין וְחָמֵשׁ מִשְּׂמֹאל לִפְנֵי הַדְּבִיר
ר״ו, גבורה זָהָב סָגוּר וְהַפֶּרַח וְהַנֵּרֹת יהוה + אהיה + יהוה + אלהים + יהוה + אדני
וְהַמֶּלְקָחַיִם זָהָב: 50 וְהַסִּפּוֹת וְהַמְזַמְּרוֹת וְהַמִּזְרָקוֹת וְהַכַּפּוֹת
וְהַמַּחְתּוֹת זָהָב סָגוּר וְהַפֹּתוֹת לְדַלְתוֹת הַבַּיִת ב״פ ראה הַפְּנִימִי
לְקֹדֶשׁ הַקֳּדָשִׁים לְדַלְתֵי הַבַּיִת ב״פ ראה לַהֵיכָל אדני, ללה זָהָב: {פ}

HAFTARAH FOR THE EVE OF ROSH CHODESH

On one level, this Haftarah concerns the eve of Rosh Chodesh. In a deeper sense, this Haftarah speaks of love between David and Jonathan. Although he himself was heir to the throne, Jonathan knew that David might become king. Yet Jonathan loved David and felt no jealousy. To truly feel love for another person, we must give up our own selfish desires. To have a successful relationship of any kind, we must be willing to sacrifice.

I Samuel 20:18-42

20 18 Then Jonathan said to David: "Tomorrow is the New Moon festival. You will be missed, because your seat will be empty.

19 The day after tomorrow, toward evening, go to the place where you hid when this trouble began, and wait by the stone Ezel.

20 I will shoot three arrows to the side of it, as though I were shooting at a target.

21 Then I will send a boy and say, 'Go, find the arrows.' If I say to him, 'Look, the arrows are on this side of you; bring them here,' then come, because, as surely as the Lord lives, you are safe; there is no danger.

22 But if I say to the boy, 'Look, the arrows are beyond you,' then you must go, because the Lord has sent you away.

23 And about the matter you and I discussed—remember, the Lord is witness between you and me forever."

24 So David hid in the field, and when the New Moon festival came, the king sat down to eat.

25 He sat in his customary place by the wall, opposite Jonathan, and Abner sat next to Saul, but David's place was empty.

26 Saul said nothing that day, for he thought, "Something must have happened to David to make him ceremonially unclean—surely he is unclean."

27 But the next day, the second day of the month, David's place was empty again.
Then Saul said to his son Jonathan, "Why hasn't the son of Jesse come to the meal,
either yesterday or today?" 28 Jonathan answered, "David earnestly asked me for
permission to go to Bethlehem.

HAFTARAH FOR THE EVE OF ROSH CHODESH

שְׁמוּאֵל 1 פֶּרֶק 20

20 18 וַיֹּאמֶר־לוֹ יְהוֹנָתָן מָחָר רמ"ח חֹדֶשׁ י"ב הוויות וְנִפְקַדְתָּ כִּי יִפָּקֵד
מוֹשָׁבֶךָ׃ 19 וְשִׁלַּשְׁתָּ תֵּרֵד מְאֹד מ"ה וּבָאתָ אֶל־הַמָּקוֹם יהוה ברבוע
אֲשֶׁר־נִסְתַּרְתָּ שָּׁם בְּיוֹם נגד, זן, מזבח הַמַּעֲשֶׂה וְיָשַׁבְתָּ אֵצֶל הָאֶבֶן
הָאָזֶל׃ יוד הה ואו הה 20 וַאֲנִי אני ב"פ אהיה יהוה שְׁלֹשֶׁת הַחִצִּים צִדָּה אוֹרֶה
לְשַׁלַּח־לִי לְמַטָּרָה׃ 21 וְהִנֵּה מ"ה יה אֶשְׁלַח אֶת־הַנַּעַר ש"ך לֵךְ מְצָא
אֶת־הַחִצִּים אִם יוהך ־אָמֹר אֹמַר לַנַּעַר ש"ך הִנֵּה מ"ה יה הַחִצִּים |
מִמְּךָ וָהֵנָּה מ"ה יה קָחֶנּוּ | וָבֹאָה כִּי־שָׁלוֹם לְךָ וְאֵין דָּבָר ראה חַי־
יְהֹוָה יאהדונהי׃ 22 וְאִם יוהך ־כֹּה היי אֹמַר לָעֶלֶם הִנֵּה מ"ה יה הַחִצִּים
מִמְּךָ וָהָלְאָה לֵךְ כִּי שִׁלַּחֲךָ יְהֹוָה יאהדונהי׃ 23 וְהַדָּבָר ראה אֲשֶׁר
דִּבַּרְנוּ ראה אֲנִי אני וָאָתָּה הִנֵּה מ"ה יה יְהֹוָה יאהדונהי בֵּינִי וּבֵינְךָ עַד־
עוֹלָם׃ [ס] 24 וַיִּסָּתֵר דָּוִד ב"פ מצר בַּשָּׂדֶה וַיְהִי הַחֹדֶשׁ י"ב הוויות וַיֵּשֶׁב
הַמֶּלֶךְ אֶל־ (כתיב: עַל־) הַלֶּחֶם ג"פ יהוה לֶאֱכוֹל׃ 25 וַיֵּשֶׁב הַמֶּלֶךְ עַל־
מוֹשָׁבוֹ כְּפַעַם | בְּפַעַם אֶל־מוֹשַׁב הַקִּיר וַיָּקָם יְהוֹנָתָן וַיֵּשֶׁב
אַבְנֵר מִצַּד שָׁאוּל וַיִּפָּקֵד מְקוֹם יהוה ברבוע דָּוִד׃ 26 וְלֹא־דִבֶּר ראה
שָׁאוּל מְאוּמָה בַּיּוֹם נגד, זן, מזבח הַהוּא כִּי אָמַר מִקְרֶה הוּא בִּלְתִּי
טָהוֹר י"פ אכא הוּא כִּי־לֹא טָהוֹר י"פ אכא׃ [ס] 27 וַיְהִי אל מִמָּחֳרַת
הַחֹדֶשׁ י"ב הוויות הַשֵּׁנִי וַיִּפָּקֵד מְקוֹם יהוה ברבוע דָּוִד [פ] וַיֹּאמֶר שָׁאוּל
אֶל־יְהוֹנָתָן בְּנוֹ מַדּוּעַ לֹא־בָא בֶן־יִשַׁי גַּם יגל ־תְּמוֹל גַּם יגל ־הַיּוֹם
נגד, זן, מזבח אֶל־הַלָּחֶם ג"פ יהוה׃ 28 וַיַּעַן יְהוֹנָתָן אֶת־שָׁאוּל נִשְׁאֹל נִשְׁאַל
דָּוִד מֵעִמָּדִי עַד־בֵּית ב"פ ראה לָחֶם׃ 29 וַיֹּאמֶר שַׁלְּחֵנִי נָא כִּי זֶבַח
מִשְׁפָּחָה לָנוּ אלהים, מום בָּעִיר סנזפר, ערי, סנדלפון וְהוּא צִוָּה פוי ־לִי אָחִי
וְעַתָּה אִם יוהך ־מָצָאתִי חֵן מוחי בְּעֵינֶיךָ ע"ה קס"א אִמָּלְטָה נָּא וְאֶרְאֶה

29 He said, 'Let me go, because our family is observing a sacrifice in the town and my brother has ordered me to be there. If I have found favor in your eyes, let me get away to see my brothers.' That is why he has not come to the king's table."

30 Saul's anger flared up at Jonathan and he said to him, "You son of a perverse and rebellious woman! Don't I know that you have sided with the son of Jesse to your own shame and to the shame of the mother who bore you?

31 As long as the son of Jesse lives on this Earth, neither you nor your kingdom will be established. Now send and bring him to me, for he must die!"

32 "Why should he be put to death? What has he done?" Jonathan asked his father.

33 But Saul hurled his spear at him to kill him. Then Jonathan knew that his father intended to kill David.

34 Jonathan got up from the table in fierce anger; on that second day of the month he did not eat, because he was grieved at his father's shameful treatment of David.

35 In the morning Jonathan went out to the field for his meeting with David. He had a small boy with him,

36 and he said to the boy, "Run and find the arrows I shoot." As the boy ran, he shot an arrow beyond him.

37 When the boy came to the place where Jonathan's arrow had fallen, Jonathan called out after him, "Isn't the arrow beyond you?"

38 Then he shouted, "Hurry! Go quickly! Don't stop!" The boy picked up the arrow and
returned to his master. 39 (The boy knew nothing of all this; only Jonathan and David
knew.)

40 Then Jonathan gave his weapons to the boy and said, "Go, carry them back to town."

41 After the boy had gone, David got up from the south side of the stone and bowed down before Jonathan three times, with his face to the ground. Then they kissed each other and wept together—but David wept the most.

42 Jonathan said to David, "Go in peace, for we have sworn friendship with each other in the name of the Lord, saying, 'The Lord is witness between you and me, and between your descendants and my descendants forever.' " Then David left, and Jonathan went back to the town.

אֶת־אֶחָי עַל־כֵּן לֹא־בָא אֶל־שֻׁלְחַן הַמֶּלֶךְ׃ [ס] 30 וַיִּחַר־אַף
שָׁאוּל בִּיהוֹנָתָן וַיֹּאמֶר לוֹ בֶּן־נַעֲוַת הַמַּרְדּוּת הֲלוֹא יָדַעְתִּי כִּי־
בֹחֵר אַתָּה לְבֶן־יִשַׁי לְבָשְׁתְּךָ וּלְבֹשֶׁת עֶרְוַת אִמֶּךָ׃ 31 כִּי כָל כלי
־הַיָּמִים נלך אֲשֶׁר בֶּן־יִשַׁי חַי עַל־הָאֲדָמָה לֹא תִכּוֹן אַתָּה
וּמַלְכוּתֶךָ וְעַתָּה שְׁלַח וְקַח אֹתוֹ אֵלַי כִּי בֶן־מָוֶת הוּא׃ [ס] 32 וַיַּעַן
יְהוֹנָתָן אֶת־שָׁאוּל אָבִיו וַיֹּאמֶר אֵלָיו לָמָּה יוּמַת מֶה מ"ה עָשָׂה׃
33 וַיָּטֶל שָׁאוּל אֶת־הַחֲנִית עָלָיו לְהַכֹּתוֹ וַיֵּדַע יְהוֹנָתָן כִּי־כָלָה
הִיא מֵעִם עמם אָבִיו לְהָמִית אֶת־דָּוִד׃ [ס] 34 וַיָּקָם יְהוֹנָתָן מֵעִם
עמם הַשֻּׁלְחָן בָּחֳרִי־אָף וְלֹא־אָכַל בְּיוֹם נגד, זן, מזבח ־הַחֹדֶשׁ י"ב הוויות
הַשֵּׁנִי לֶחֶם ג"פ יהוה כִּי נֶעְצַב אֶל־דָּוִד כִּי הִכְלִמוֹ אָבִיו׃ [ס] 35 וַיְהִי
אל בַבֹּקֶר וַיֵּצֵא יְהוֹנָתָן הַשָּׂדֶה שדי לְמוֹעֵד דָּוִד וְנַעַר ש"ך קָטֹן
עִמּוֹ׃ 36 וַיֹּאמֶר לְנַעֲרוֹ רֻץ מְצָא נָא אֶת־הַחִצִּים אֲשֶׁר אָנֹכִי אי"ע
מוֹרֶה הַנַּעַר ש"ך רָץ וְהוּא־יָרָה הַחֵצִי לְהַעֲבִרוֹ׃ 37 וַיָּבֹא הַנַּעַר
ש"ך עַד־מְקוֹם יהוה ברבוע הַחֵצִי אֲשֶׁר יָרָה יְהוֹנָתָן וַיִּקְרָא
עם ה' אותיות = ב"פ קס"א יְהוֹנָתָן אַחֲרֵי הַנַּעַר ש"ך וַיֹּאמֶר הֲלוֹא הַחֵצִי
מִמְּךָ וָהָלְאָה׃ 38 וַיִּקְרָא עם ה' אותיות = ב"פ קס"א יְהוֹנָתָן אַחֲרֵי הַנַּעַר ש"ך
מְהֵרָה חוּשָׁה אַל־תַּעֲמֹד וַיְלַקֵּט נַעַר ש"ך יְהוֹנָתָן אֶת־הַחִצִּים
(כתיב: החצי) וַיָּבֹא אֶל־אֲדֹנָיו׃ 39 וְהַנַּעַר ש"ך לֹא־יָדַע מְאוּמָה אַךְ
אהיה יְהוֹנָתָן וְדָוִד יָדְעוּ אֶת־הַדָּבָר ראה׃ [ס] 40 וַיִּתֵּן י"פ מלוי ע"ב יְהוֹנָתָן
אֶת־כֵּלָיו כלי אֶל־הַנַּעַר ש"ך אֲשֶׁר־לוֹ וַיֹּאמֶר לוֹ לֵךְ הָבֵיא הָעִיר
סוזפך, ערי, סנדלפון׃ 41 הַנַּעַר ש"ך בָּא וְדָוִד קָם מֵאֵצֶל הַנֶּגֶב וַיִּפֹּל
לְאַפָּיו אַרְצָה וַיִּשְׁתַּחוּ אלהים דההין ע"ה שָׁלֹשׁ פְּעָמִים וַיִּשְּׁקוּ ׀ אִישׁ
ע"ה קנ"א קס"א אֶת־רֵעֵהוּ וַיִּבְכּוּ אִישׁ ע"ה קנ"א קס"א אֶת־רֵעֵהוּ עַד־דָּוִד
הִגְדִּיל׃ 42 וַיֹּאמֶר יְהוֹנָתָן לְדָוִד לֵךְ לְשָׁלוֹם אֲשֶׁר נִשְׁבַּעְנוּ שְׁנֵינוּ
אֲנַחְנוּ בְּשֵׁם שדי יהוה יְהֹוָאדהנויאהדונהי לֵאמֹר יְהֹוָאדהנויאהדונהי יִהְיֶה ייי ׀
בֵּינִי וּבֵינֶךָ וּבֵין זַרְעִי וּבֵין זַרְעֲךָ עַד־עוֹלָם׃ [פ]

MAFTIR OF SHABBAT ROSH CHODESH

Numbers 28:9-15

28 9 "On the Sabbath day, make an offering of two lambs a year old without defect, together with its drink offering and a grain offering of two-tenths of an ephah of fine flour mixed with oil.

10 This is the burnt offering for every Sabbath, in addition to the regular burnt offering and its drink offering.

11 On the first of every month, present to the Lord a burnt offering of two young bulls, one ram and seven male lambs a year old, all without defect.

12 With each bull there is to be a grain offering of three-tenths of an ephah of fine flour mixed with oil; with the ram, a grain offering of two-tenths of an ephah of fine flour mixed with oil;

13 and with each lamb, a grain offering of a tenth of an ephah of fine flour mixed with oil. This is for a burnt offering, a pleasing aroma, an offering made to the Lord by fire.

14 With each bull there is to be a drink offering of half a hin of wine; with the ram, a third of a hin; and with each lamb, a quarter of a hin. This is the monthly burnt offering to be made at each new moon during the year.

15 Besides the regular burnt offering with its drink offering, one male goat is to be presented to the Lord as a sin offering."

MAFTIR OF SHABBAT ROSH CHODESH

במדבר פרק 28

28 9 וּבְיוֹם נגד, זן, מזבח הַשַּׁבָּת שְׁנֵי־כְבָשִׂים בְּנֵי־שָׁנָה תְּמִימִם וּשְׁנֵי
עֶשְׂרֹנִים סֹלֶת מִנְחָה ע"ה ב"פ ב"ן בְּלוּלָה בַשֶּׁמֶן י"פ טל, י"פ כוזו, ביט וְנִסְכּוֹ: 10 עֹלַת
שַׁבַּת בְּשַׁבַּתּוֹ עַל־עֹלַת אבגיתצ, ושר, אהבת חנם הַתָּמִיד נתה, קס"א - קנ"א - קמ"ג
וְנִסְכָּהּ: [פ] 11 וּבְרָאשֵׁי ריבוע אלהים - אלהים דיודין ע"ה חָדְשֵׁיכֶם י"ב הוויות תַּקְרִיבוּ
עֹלָה לַיהוָהאדניאהדונהי פָּרִים בְּנֵי־בָקָר שְׁנַיִם וְאַיִל אֶחָד אהבה, דאגה כְּבָשִׂים
בְּנֵי־שָׁנָה שִׁבְעָה תְּמִימִם: 12 וּשְׁלֹשָׁה עֶשְׂרֹנִים סֹלֶת מִנְחָה ע"ה ב"פ ב"ן
בְּלוּלָה בַשֶּׁמֶן י"פ טל, י"פ כוזו, ביט לַפָּר סוזוף, ערי הָאֶחָד אהבה, דאגה וּשְׁנֵי עֶשְׂרֹנִים
סֹלֶת מִנְחָה ע"ה ב"פ ב"ן בְּלוּלָה בַשֶּׁמֶן י"פ טל, י"פ כוזו, ביט לָאַיִל הָאֶחָד אהבה, דאגה:
13 וְעִשָּׂרֹן עִשָּׂרוֹן סֹלֶת מִנְחָה ע"ה ב"פ ב"ן בְּלוּלָה בַשֶּׁמֶן י"פ טל, י"פ כוזו, ביט
לַכֶּבֶשׂ ב"פ קס"א הָאֶחָד אהבה, דאגה עֹלָה רֵיחַ נִיחֹחַ אִשֶּׁה לַיהוָהאדניאהדונהי:
14 וְנִסְכֵּיהֶם חֲצִי הַהִין יִהְיֶה ייי לַפָּר סוזוף, ערי וּשְׁלִישִׁת הַהִין לָאַיִל
וּרְבִיעִת הַהִין לַכֶּבֶשׂ ב"פ קס"א יָיִן מיכ, י"פ האא זֹאת עֹלַת אבגיתצ, ושר, אהבת חנם
חֹדֶשׁ י"ב הוויות בְּחָדְשׁוֹ לְחָדְשֵׁי י"ב הוויות הַשָּׁנָה: 15 וּשְׂעִיר עִזִּים אֶחָד
אהבה, דאגה לְחַטָּאת לַיהוָהאדניאהדונהי עַל־עֹלַת אבגיתצ, ושר, אהבת חנם הַתָּמִיד
נתה, קס"א - קנ"א - קמ"ג יֵעָשֶׂה וְנִסְכּוֹ: [ס]

HAFTARAH OF SHABBAT ROSH CHODESH

Just as Shabbat cools the fires of Hell, these same fires are shut down on Rosh Chodesh, giving us the power to deflect and avoid judgment.

Isaiah 66:1-24

66 [1] This is what the Lord says: "Heaven is My Throne, and the Earth is My Footstool. Where is the House you will build for Me? Where will My Resting Place be?

[2] Has not My hand made all these things, and so they came into being?" declares the Lord. "This is the one I esteem: he who is humble and contrite in spirit, and trembles at My Word.

[3] But whoever sacrifices a bull is like one who kills a man, and whoever offers a lamb, like one who breaks a dog's neck; whoever makes a grain offering is like one who presents pig's blood, and whoever burns memorial incense, like one who worships an idol. They have chosen their own ways, and their souls delight in their abominations;

[4] so I also will choose harsh treatment for them and will bring upon them what they dread. For when I called, no one answered, when I spoke, no one listened. They did evil in My sight and chose what displeases Me."

[5] Hear the Word of the Lord, you who tremble at His Word: "Your brothers who hate you, and exclude you because of My Name, have said, 'Let the Lord be glorified, that we may see your joy!' Yet they will be put to shame.

[6] Hear that uproar from the city, hear that noise from the temple! It is the sound of the Lord repaying His enemies all they deserve.

[7] Before she goes into labor, she gives birth; before the pains come upon her, she delivers a son.

HAFTARAH OF SHABBAT ROSH CHODESH

ישעיהו פרק 66

66 1 כֹּה הי אָמַר יְהֹוָה אדני יאהדונהי הַשָּׁמַיִם י״פ טל, י״פ כוזו כִּסְאִי וְהָאָרֶץ
אלהים דההין ע״ה הֲדֹם רַגְלָי אֵי־זֶה בַיִת ב״פ ראה אֲשֶׁר תִּבְנוּ־לִי וְאֵי־זֶה
מָקוֹם יהוה ברבוע מְנוּחָתִי׃ 2 וְאֶת־כָּל ילי ־אֵלֶּה יָדִי עָשָׂתָה וַיִּהְיוּ מלוי
ס״ג כָל ילי ־אֵלֶּה נְאֻם־יְהֹוָה אדני יאהדונהי וְאֶל־זֶה אַבִּיט אֶל־עָנִי ריבוע מ״ה
וּנְכֵה־רוּחַ מלוי אלהים דיודין וְחָרֵד עַל־דְּבָרִי ראה׃ 3 שׁוֹחֵט הַשּׁוֹר
אבג״יתץ, ושר, אהבת חנם מַכֵּה־אִישׁ ע״ה קנ״א קס״א זוֹבֵחַ הַשֶּׂה עֹרֵף כֶּלֶב
מַעֲלֵה מִנְחָה ע״ה ב״פ ב״ן דַם רבוע אהיה ־חֲזִיר מַזְכִּיר לְבֹנָה מְבָרֵךְ אָוֶן
גַּם יג״ל ־הֵמָּה בָּחֲרוּ בְּדַרְכֵיהֶם ב״פ יב״ק וּבְשִׁקּוּצֵיהֶם נַפְשָׁם חָפֵצָה׃
4 גַּם יג״ל ־אֲנִי אני אֶבְחַר בְּתַעֲלֻלֵיהֶם וּמְגוּרֹתָם אָבִיא לָהֶם יַעַן
קָרָאתִי וְאֵין עוֹנֶה דִּבַּרְתִּי ראה וְלֹא שָׁמֵעוּ וַיַּעֲשׂוּ הָרַע רהע בְּעֵינַי
ריבוע מ״ה וּבַאֲשֶׁר לֹא־חָפַצְתִּי בָּחָרוּ׃ [ס] 5 שִׁמְעוּ דְּבַר ראה ־
יְהֹוָה אדני יאהדונהי הַחֲרֵדִים אֶל־דְּבָרוֹ ראה אָמְרוּ אֲחֵיכֶם שֹׂנְאֵיכֶם
מְנַדֵּיכֶם לְמַעַן שְׁמִי ריבוע ע״ב ורבוע ס״ג יִכְבַּד יְהֹוָה אדני יאהדונהי וְנִרְאֶה
בְשִׂמְחַתְכֶם וְהֵם יֵבֹשׁוּ׃ 6 קוֹל ע״ב ס״ג ע״ה שָׁאוֹן מֵעִיר סוחף, ערי, סנדלפו״ן
קוֹל ע״ב ס״ג ע״ה מֵהֵיכָל אדני, ללה קוֹל ע״ב ס״ג ע״ה יְהֹוָה אדני יאהדונהי מְשַׁלֵּם
גְּמוּל לְאֹיְבָיו׃ 7 בְּטֶרֶם רפ״ח ע״ה תָּחִיל יָלָדָה בְּטֶרֶם רפ״ח ע״ה יָבוֹא
חֵבֶל לָהּ וְהִמְלִיטָה זָכָר׃ 8 מִי ילי ־שָׁמַע כָּזֹאת מִי ילי רָאָה ראה
כָּאֵלֶּה הֲיוּחַל אֶרֶץ אלהים דאלפין בְּיוֹם נגד, זן, מזבח אֶחָד אהבה, דאגה אִם יוהך
־יִוָּלֵד גּוֹי פַּעַם אֶחָת כִּי־חָלָה להח גַּם יג״ל ־יָלְדָה צִיּוֹן יוסף, ו״פ יהוה

[8] Who has ever heard of such a thing? Who has ever seen such things? Can a country be born in a day or a nation be brought forth in a moment? Yet no sooner is Zion in labor than she gives birth to her children.

[9] Do I bring to the moment of birth and not give delivery?" says the Lord. "Do I close up the womb when I bring to delivery?" says your God.

[10] "Rejoice with Jerusalem and be glad for her, all you who love her; rejoice greatly with her, all you who mourn over her.

[11] For you will nurse and be satisfied at her comforting breasts; you will drink deeply and delight in her overflowing abundance."

[12] For this is what the Lord says: "I will extend peace to her like a river, and the wealth of nations like a flooding stream; you will nurse and be carried on her arm and dandled on her knees.

[13] As a mother comforts her child, so will I comfort you; and you will be comforted over Jerusalem."

[14] When you see this, your heart will rejoice and you will flourish like grass; the hand of the Lord will be made known to His servants, but his fury will be shown to His foes.

[15] See, the Lord is coming with fire, and His chariots are like a whirlwind; He will bring down His anger with fury, and His rebuke with flames of fire.

[16] For with fire and with his sword the Lord will execute judgment upon all men, and many will be those slain by the Lord.

[17] "Those who consecrate and purify themselves to go into the gardens, following the one in the midst of those who eat the flesh of pigs and rats and other abominable things—they will meet their end together," declares the Lord.

[18] "And I, because of their actions and their imaginations, am about to come and gather all nations and tongues, and they will come and see My glory.

אֶת־בָּנֶיהָ׃ 9 הַאֲנִי אני אַשְׁבִּיר וְלֹא אוֹלִיד יֹאמַר יְהוָה אדני יאהדונהי
אִם יוהך ־אֲנִי אני הַמּוֹלִיד וְעָצַרְתִּי אָמַר אֱלֹהָיִךְ ילה׃ [ס] 10 שִׂמְחוּ
אֶת־יְרוּשָׁלַ͏ִם רי"ו ש"ע וְגִילוּ בָהּ כָּל ילי ־אֹהֲבֶיהָ שִׂישׂוּ אִתָּהּ מָשׂוֹשׂ
כָּל ילי ־הַמִּתְאַבְּלִים עָלֶיהָ פהל׃ 11 לְמַעַן תִּינְקוּ וּשְׂבַעְתֶּם מִשֹּׁד
תַּנְחֻמֶיהָ לְמַעַן תָּמֹצּוּ וְהִתְעַנַּגְתֶּם מִזִּיז כְּבוֹדָהּ׃ [ס] 12 כִּי־כֹה הי"י |
אָמַר יְהוָה אדני יאהדונהי הִנְנִי נֹטֶה־אֵלֶיהָ כְּנָהָר שָׁלוֹם וּכְנַחַל שׁוֹטֵף
כְּבוֹד ל"ב גּוֹיִם וִינַקְתֶּם עַל־צַד תִּנָּשֵׂאוּ וְעַל־בִּרְכַּיִם תְּשָׁעֳשָׁעוּ׃
13 כְּאִישׁ ע"ה קנ"א קס"א אֲשֶׁר אִמּוֹ תְּנַחֲמֶנּוּ כֵּן אָנֹכִי איע אֲנַחֶמְכֶם
וּבִירוּשָׁלַ͏ִם רי"ו ש"ע תְּנֻחָמוּ׃ 14 וּרְאִיתֶם וְשָׂשׂ לִבְּכֶם וְעַצְמוֹתֵיכֶם
כַּדֶּשֶׁא תִפְרַחְנָה וְנוֹדְעָה יַד־יְהוָה אדני יאהדונהי אֶת־עֲבָדָיו וְזָעַם אֶת־
אֹיְבָיו׃ [ס] 15 כִּי־הִנֵּה מ"ה יה יְהוָה אדני יאהדונהי בָּאֵשׁ אלהים דיודין ע"ה יָבוֹא
וְכַסּוּפָה מַרְכְּבֹתָיו לְהָשִׁיב בְּחֵמָה אַפּוֹ וְגַעֲרָתוֹ בְּלַהֲבֵי־אֵשׁ
אלהים דיודין ע"ה ׃ 16 כִּי בָאֵשׁ אלהים דיודין ע"ה יְהוָה אדני יאהדונהי נִשְׁפָּט וּבְחַרְבּוֹ
רי"ו, גבורה אֶת־כָּל ילי ־בָּשָׂר וְרַבּוּ חַלְלֵי יְהוָה אדני יאהדונהי׃ 17 הַמִּתְקַדְּשִׁים
וְהַמִּטַּהֲרִים אֶל־הַגַּנּוֹת אַחַר אַחַת (כתיב: אחד) בַּתָּוֶךְ אֹכְלֵי בְּשַׂר
הַחֲזִיר וְהַשֶּׁקֶץ וְהָעַכְבָּר יַחְדָּו יָסֻפוּ נְאֻם־יְהוָה אדני יאהדונהי׃ 18 וְאָנֹכִי
איע מַעֲשֵׂיהֶם וּמַחְשְׁבֹתֵיהֶם בָּאָה לְקַבֵּץ אֶת־כָּל ילי ־הַגּוֹיִם
וְהַלְּשֹׁנוֹת וּבָאוּ וְרָאוּ אֶת־כְּבוֹדִי׃ 19 וְשַׂמְתִּי בָהֶם אוֹת וְשִׁלַּחְתִּי
מֵהֶם | פְּלֵיטִים אֶל־הַגּוֹיִם תַּרְשִׁישׁ פּוּל וְלוּד מֹשְׁכֵי קֶשֶׁת תֻּבַל
ב"פ רי"ו, ב"פ גבורה וְיָוָן הָאִיִּים הָרְחֹקִים אֲשֶׁר לֹא־שָׁמְעוּ אֶת־שִׁמְעִי
וְלֹא־רָאוּ אֶת־כְּבוֹדִי וְהִגִּידוּ אֶת־כְּבוֹדִי בַּגּוֹיִם׃ 20 וְהֵבִיאוּ
אֶת־כָּל ילי ־אֲחֵיכֶם מִכָּל ילי ־הַגּוֹיִם | מִנְחָה ע"ה ב"פ ב"ן | לַיהוָה אדני יאהדונהי

[19] I will set a sign among them, and I will send some of those who survive to the nations—to Tarshish, to the Libyans and Lydians (famous as archers), to Tubal and Greece, and to the distant islands that have not heard of My fame or seen My glory. They will proclaim My glory among the nations.

[20] And they will bring all your brothers, from all the nations, to My Holy Mountain in Jerusalem as an offering to the Lord—on horses, in chariots and wagons, and on mules and camels," says the Lord. "They will bring them, as the Israelites bring their grain offerings, to the Temple of the Lord in ceremonially clean vessels.

[21] And I will select some of them also to be priests and Levites," says the Lord.

[22] "As the New Heavens and the New Earth that I make will endure before Me," declares the Lord, "so will your name and descendants endure.

[23] From one New Moon to another and from one Sabbath to another, all mankind will come and bow down before Me," says the Lord.

[24] "And they will go out and look upon the dead bodies of those who rebelled against Me; their worm will not die, nor will their fire be quenched, and they will be loathsome to all mankind."

בַּסּוּסִים ריבוע אדני, כוק וּבָרֶכֶב וּבַצַּבִּים וּבַפְּרָדִים וּבַכִּרְכָּרוֹת עַל
הַר רבוע אלהים - ה' קָדְשִׁי יְרוּשָׁלִַם רי"י ש"ע אָמַר יְהֹוָה יאהדונהי כַּאֲשֶׁר
יָבִיאוּ בְנֵי יִשְׂרָאֵל אֶת־הַמִּנְחָה ע"ה ב"פ ב"ן בִּכְלִי כלי טָהוֹר י"פ אכא
בֵּית ב"פ ראה יְהֹוָה יאהדונהי: 21 וְגַם יגל ־מֵהֶם אֶקַּח לַכֹּהֲנִים מלה
לַלְוִיִּם ע"ה יהוה - אהיה אָמַר יְהֹוָה יאהדונהי: 22 כִּי כַאֲשֶׁר הַשָּׁמַיִם
י"פ טל, י"פ כוזו הַחֲדָשִׁים וְהָאָרֶץ אלהים דאלפין הַחֲדָשָׁה אֲשֶׁר אֲנִי אני עֹשֶׂה
עֹמְדִים לְפָנַי נְאֻם־יְהֹוָה יאהדונהי כֵּן יַעֲמֹד זַרְעֲכֶם וְשִׁמְכֶם:
23 וְהָיָה מִדֵּי־חֹדֶשׁ י"ב הוויות בְּחָדְשׁוֹ י"ב הוויות וּמִדֵּי שַׁבָּת בְּשַׁבַּתּוֹ
יָבוֹא כָל ילי ־בָּשָׂר לְהִשְׁתַּחֲוֺת לְפָנַי אָמַר יְהֹוָה יאהדונהי: 24 וְיָצְאוּ
וְרָאוּ בְּפִגְרֵי הָאֲנָשִׁים הַפֹּשְׁעִים בִּי כִּי תוֹלַעְתָּם לֹא תָמוּת
וְאִשָּׁם לֹא תִכְבֶּה וְהָיוּ דֵרָאוֹן לְכָל יה - אדני ־בָּשָׂר: וְהָיָה מִדֵּי־
חֹדֶשׁ י"ב הוויות בְּחָדְשׁוֹ י"ב הוויות וּמִדֵּי שַׁבָּת בְּשַׁבַּתּוֹ יָבוֹא כָל ילי ־
בָּשָׂר לְהִשְׁתַּחֲוֺת לְפָנַי אָמַר יְהֹוָה יאהדונהי:

Love and appreciation always to the Rav and Karen, Michael and Yehuda, their families, and the chevre.

Blessings of health, happiness and prosperity to our children Laura Jayne and Stephanie Jane, their husbands Billy and Matt; and our grandchildren Liam James, Ella Jane, Reilly Jayne and all future grandchildren.

May each spiritual journey reveal much light and help to bring the redemption in our times.